Vietnam and the Cold War 1945-1954

Vietnam and the Cold War 1945-1954

French Imperial Decline and Defeat at Dien Bien Phu

John Pike

Pen & Sword
MILITARY

First published in Great Britain in 2024 by
Pen & Sword Military
An imprint of
Pen & Sword Books Ltd
Yorkshire – Philadelphia

ISBN 978 1 52678 929 7

A CIP catalogue record for this book is available from the British Library.

Typeset by Mac Style
Printed in the UK by CPI Group (UK) Ltd, Croydon, CR0 4YY.

MIX
Paper | Supporting responsible forestry
FSC® C013604

Pen & Sword Books Limited incorporates the imprints of Atlas, Archaeology, Aviation, Discovery, Family History, Fiction, History, Maritime, Military, Military Classics, Politics, Select, Transport, True Crime, Air World, Frontline Publishing, Leo Cooper, Remember When, Seaforth Publishing, The Praetorian Press, Wharncliffe Local History, Wharncliffe Transport, Wharncliffe True Crime, White Owl and After the Battle.

For a complete list of Pen & Sword titles please contact

PEN & SWORD BOOKS LIMITED
47 Church Street, Barnsley, South Yorkshire, S70 2AS, England
E-mail: enquiries@pen-and-sword.co.uk
Website: www.pen-and-sword.co.uk

Or

PEN AND SWORD BOOKS
1950 Lawrence Rd, Havertown, PA 19083, USA
E-mail: Uspen-and-sword@casematepublishers.com
Website: www.penandswordbooks.com

Contents

FRENCH INDOCHINA

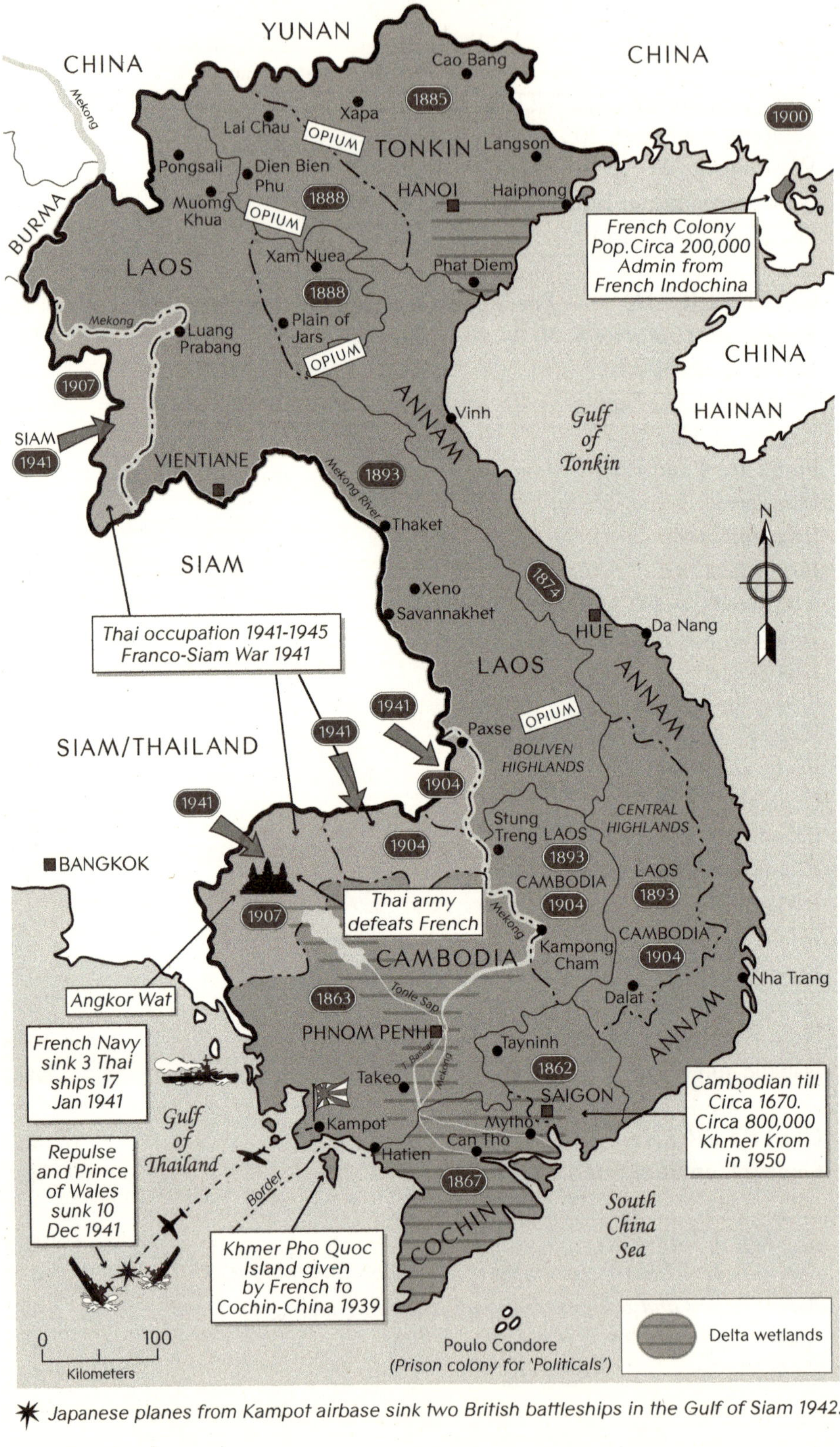

✷ *Japanese planes from Kampot airbase sink two British battleships in the Gulf of Siam 1942.*

RECONQUEST OF THE MEKONG DELTA OCT 1945 - FEB 1946

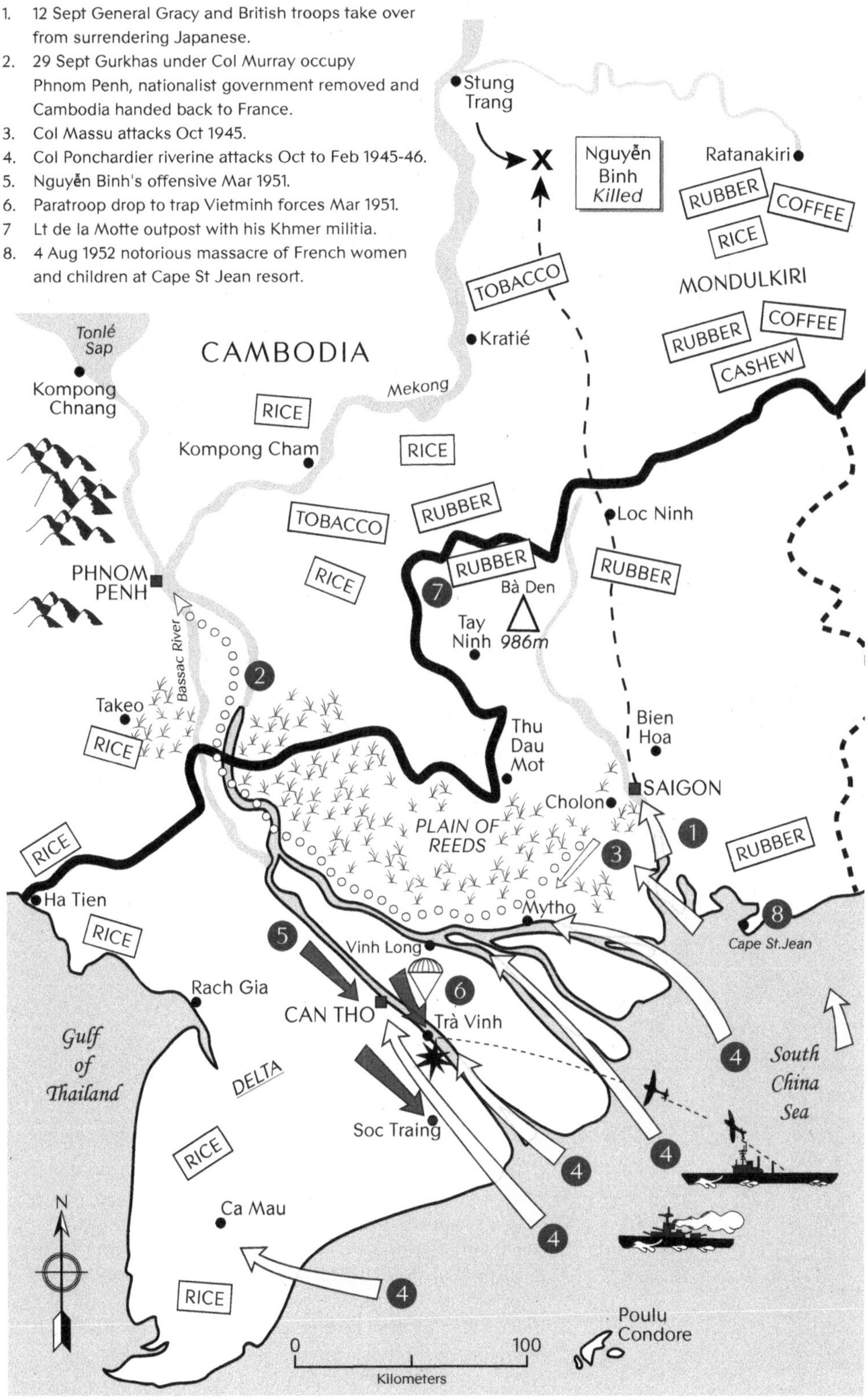

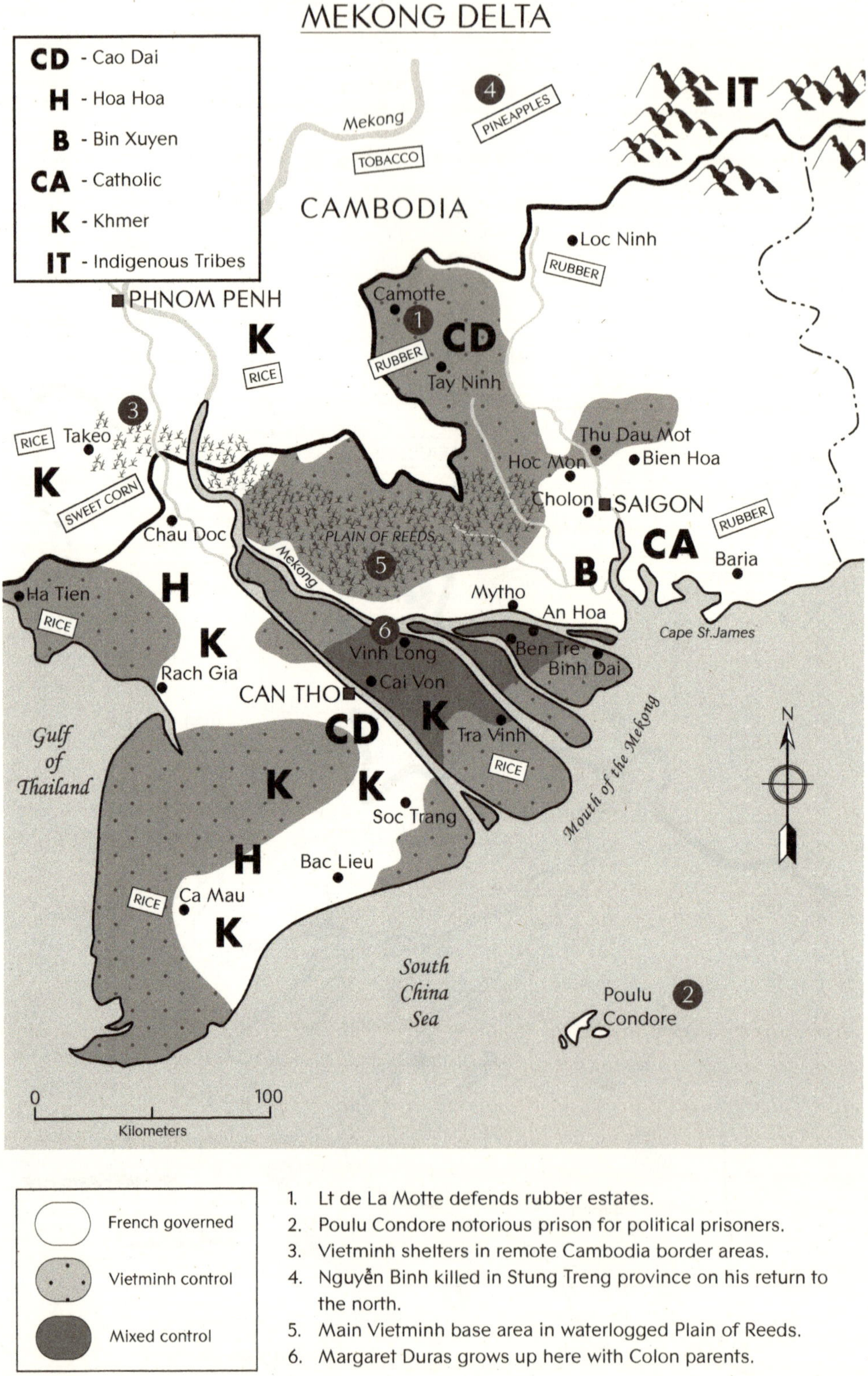

1. Lt de La Motte defends rubber estates.
2. Poulu Condore notorious prison for political prisoners.
3. Vietminh shelters in remote Cambodia border areas.
4. Nguyễn Binh killed in Stung Treng province on his return to the north.
5. Main Vietminh base area in waterlogged Plain of Reeds.
6. Margaret Duras grows up here with Colon parents.

INDOCHINA IN 1949

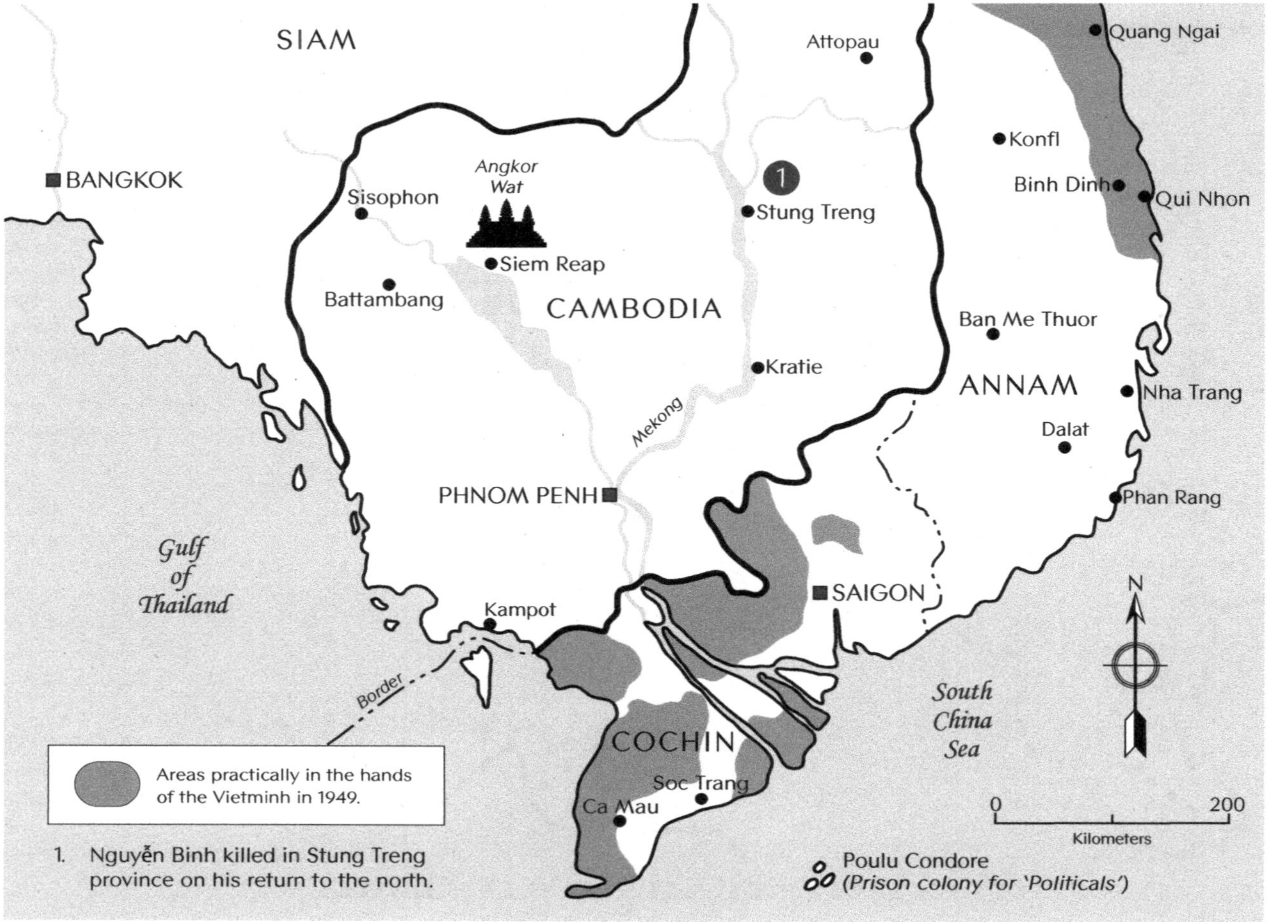

STRATEGIC MAP OF TONKIN 1945-54

1. Major VPA offensive to capture the T'ai Highlands.
2. Salan's counter-attack - Operation Lorraine to attempt to out flank Giáp.
3. 26-day siege and battle at Nà San.

A. Col Bigeard dropped with 6th BPC at Tu Lé.
B. Parachute drops to support Operation Lorraine.

✶ *Main battles in order:*

- Haiphong Nov 1946
- Hanoi Dec 1947
- Bac Kan Oct-Nov 1947
- R.C.4/Cox Ha gorge Oct 1950
- Vinh Yên Jan 1951
- Mao Khe Mar 1951
- Day river May-Jun 1951
- Nghia Lo Oct 1951 & 1952
- Lorraine Oct 1952
- Na San Nov-Dec 1952
- Xam Nuea Apr 1953
- Xieng Khouang May 1953
- Dien Bien Phu Mar-May 1954

Bigeard escapes and becomes a legend

Supply lines from Chinese border

Arromanche

Major para-drops

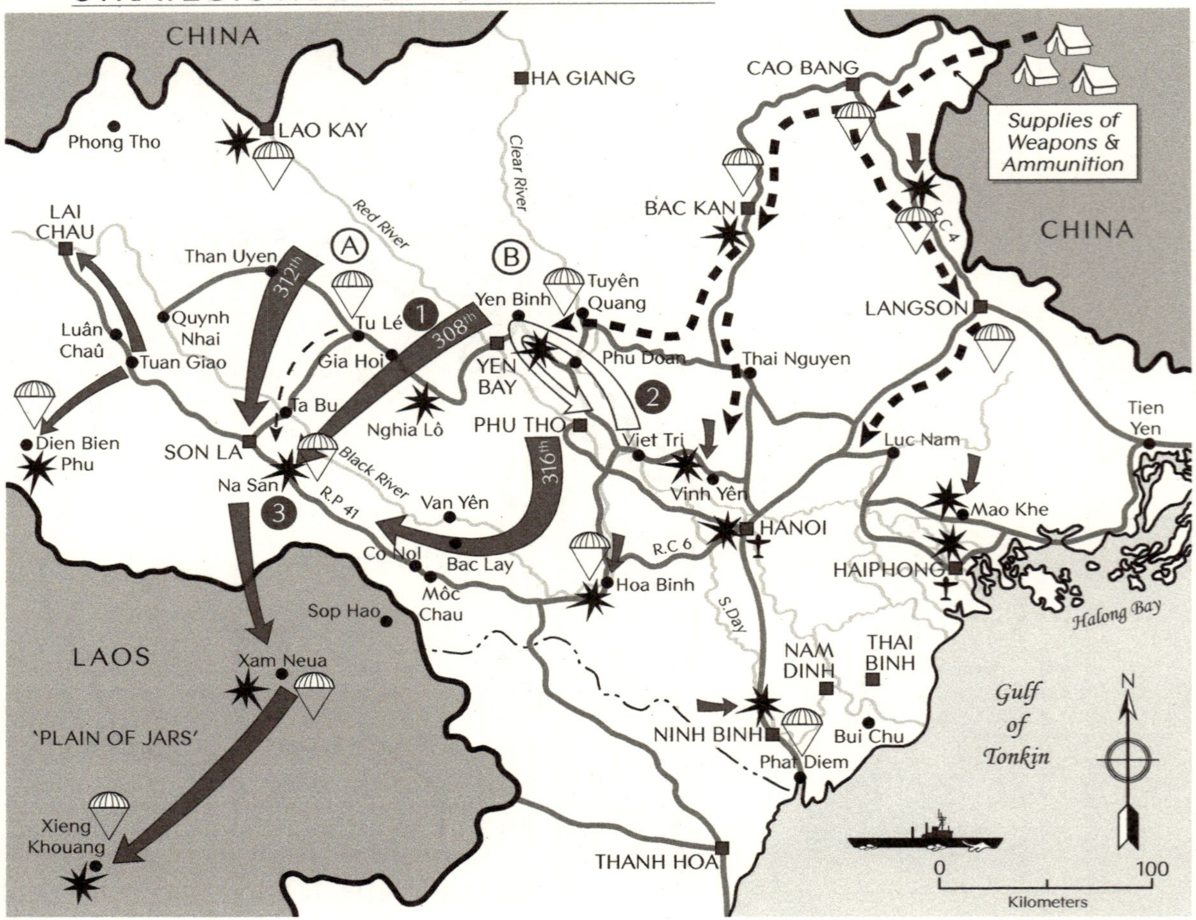

OPERATION LEA OCT 1947

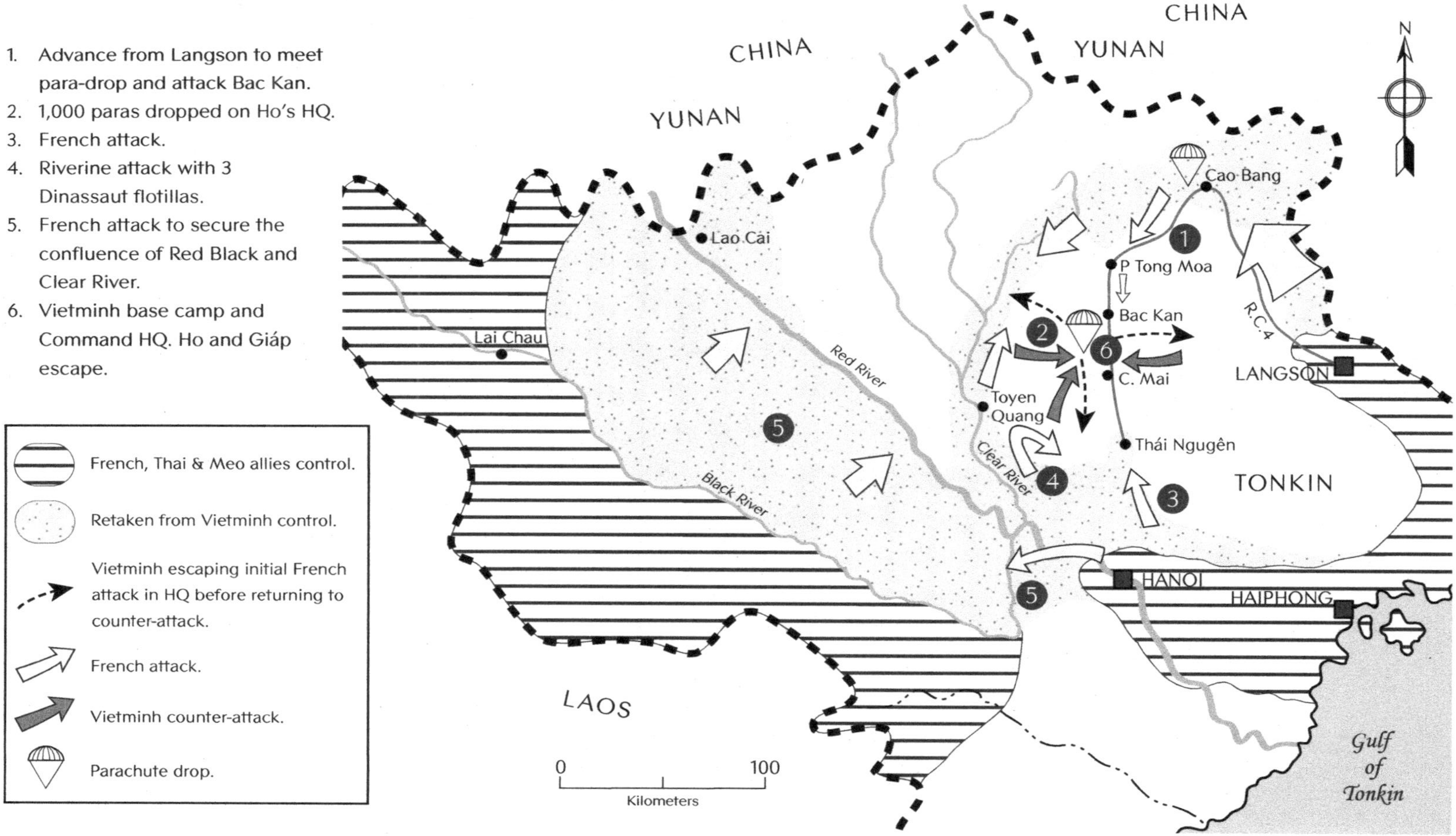

GIÁP'S R.C.4 OFFENSIVE AND FRENCH DEFEAT OCT 1950

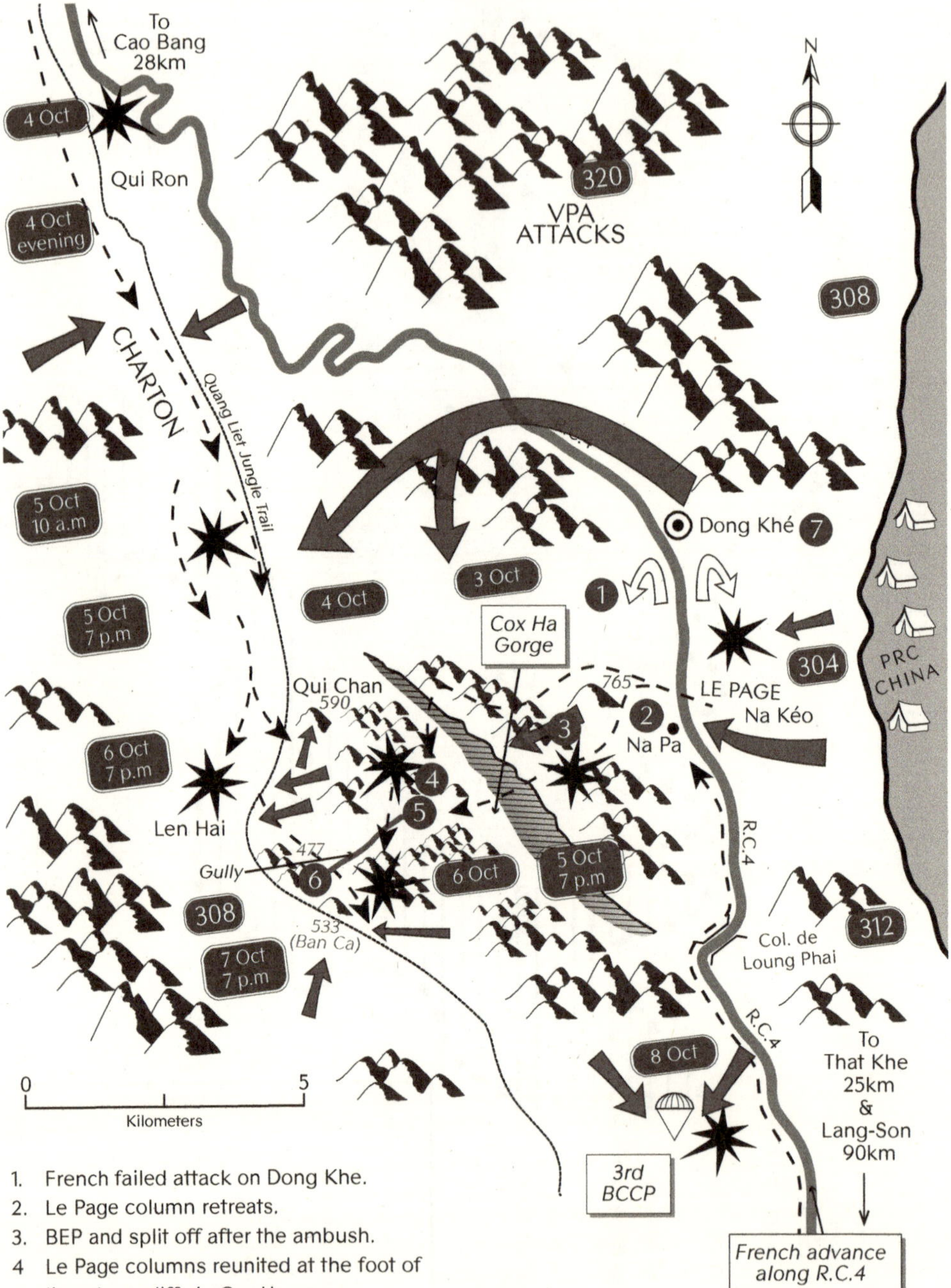

1. French failed attack on Dong Khe.
2. Le Page column retreats.
3. BEP and split off after the ambush.
4. Le Page columns reunited at the foot of limestone cliffs in Cox Ha gorge.
5. Paras and Moroccans storm the exit to access the gully to rendezvous with Charton.
6. Charton and le Page columns join but are immediately swamped by the enemy.
7. Ho at Giáp's HQ.

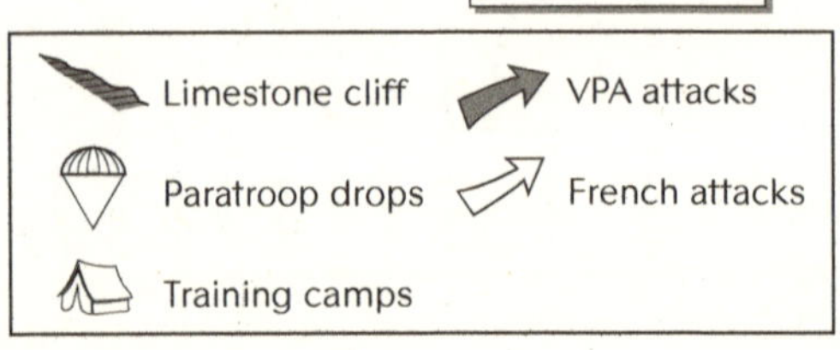

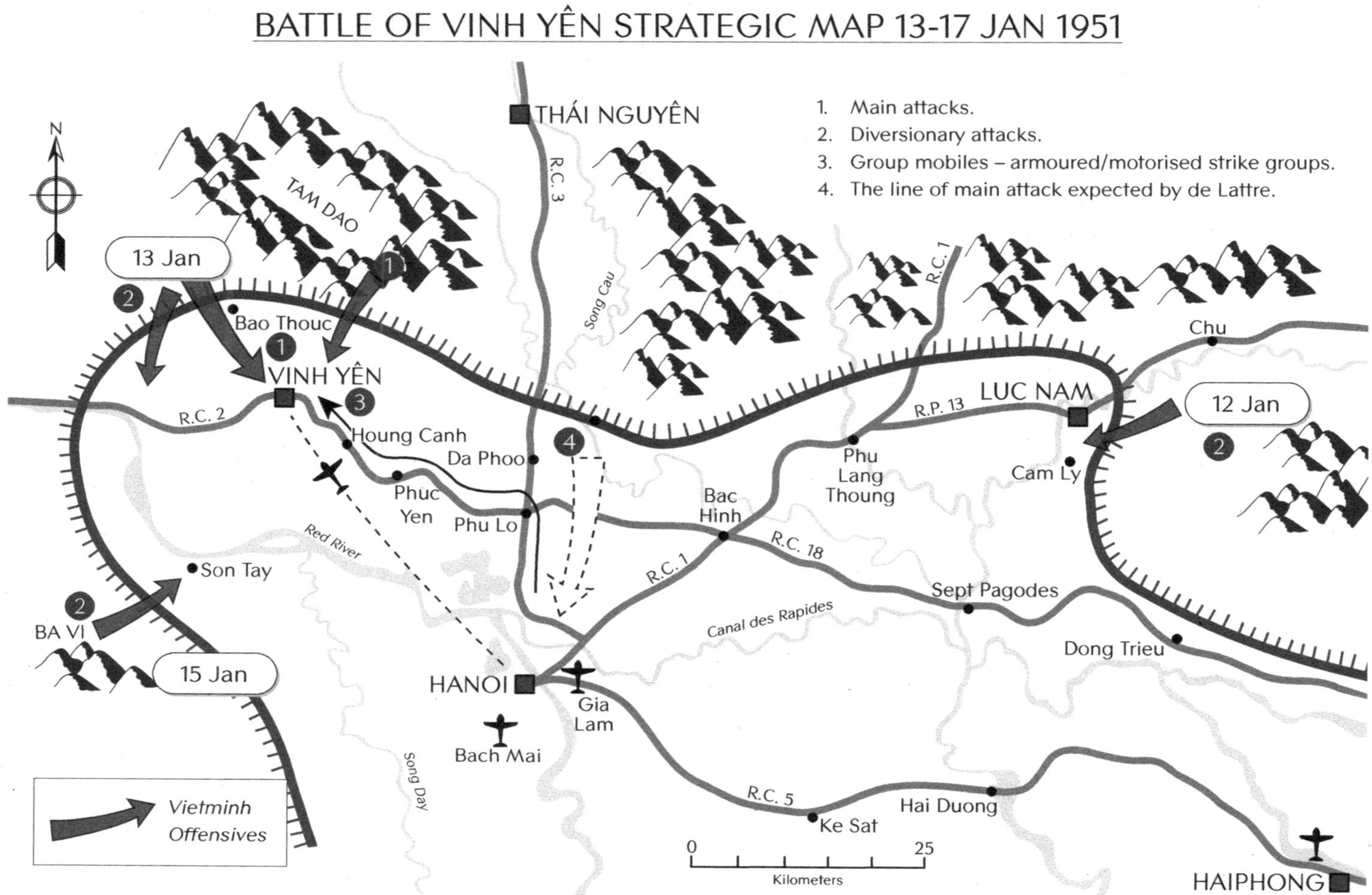
BATTLE OF VINH YÊN STRATEGIC MAP 13-17 JAN 1951
1. Main attacks.
2. Diversionary attacks.
3. Group mobiles – armoured/motorised strike groups.
4. The line of main attack expected by de Lattre.
N
TAM DAO
13 Jan
12 Jan
15 Jan
THÁI NGUYÊN
R.C. 3
Song Cau
R.C. 1
Bao Thouc
VINH YÊN
R.C. 2
Houng Canh
Da Phoo
Phuc Yen
Phu Lo
Bac Hinh
Phu Lang Thoung
R.P. 13
LUC NAM
Chu
Cam Ly
R.C. 18
Sept Pagodes
Dong Trieu
Canal des Rapides
Red River
Son Tay
BA VI
HANOI
Gia Lam
Bach Mai
Song Day
R.C. 5
Ke Sat
Hai Duong
HAIPHONG
0
25
Kilometers
Vietminh Offensives

BATTLE OF VINH YÊN 13 JAN 1951

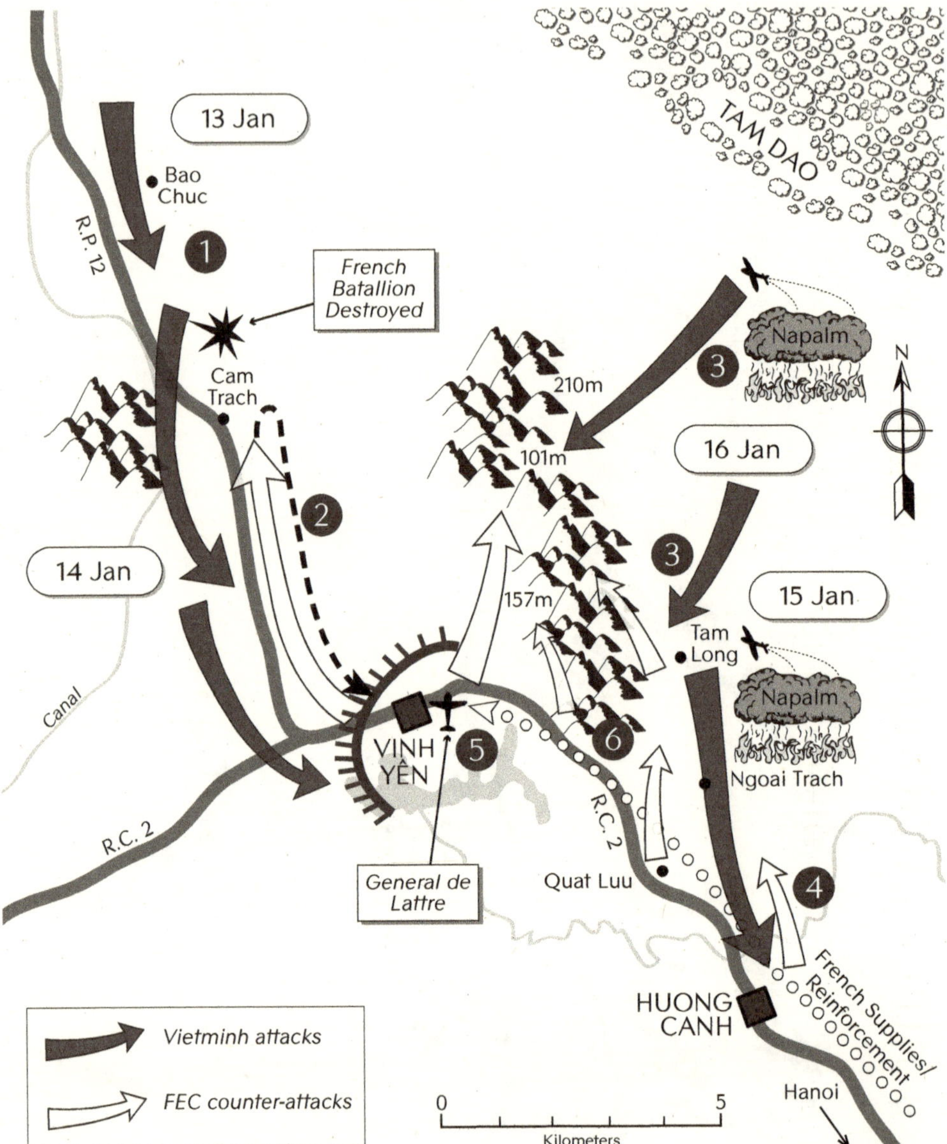

1. Divisionary attacks down R.P 12 towards Vinh Yên.
2. FEC GM of Col Vanuxem counterattacks but outflanked.
3. Vietminh launch new attacks on 15-16 Jan to take the hills in an advance on Huong Canh.
4. French counter-attacks to retake the hills.
5. De Lattre flies in on a Morane light plane to charge at the front.
6. Group mobiles arrive to support counter-attack the Vietminh.

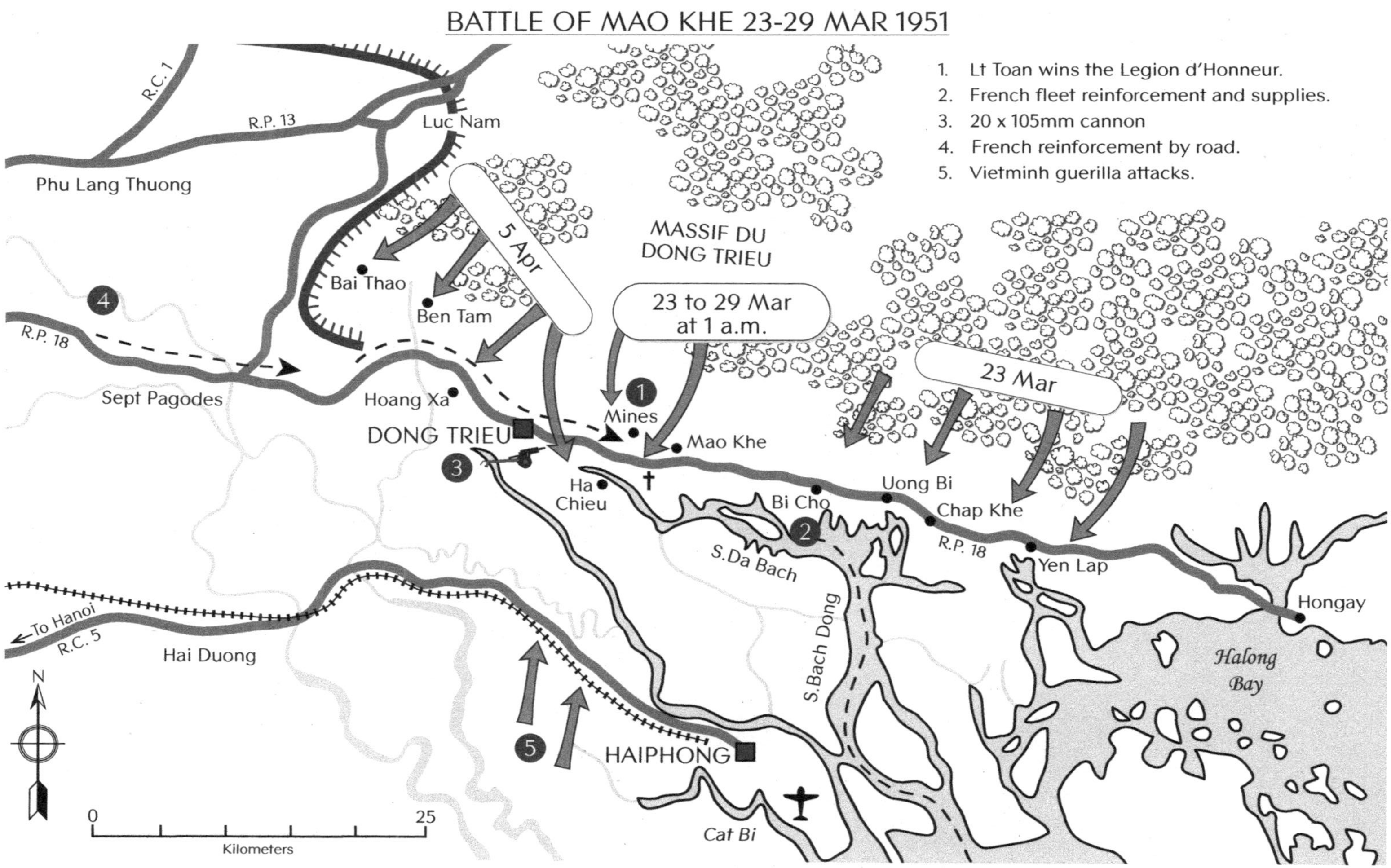
BATTLE OF MAO KHE 23-29 MAR 1951
1. Lt Toan wins the Legion d'Honneur.
2. French fleet reinforcement and supplies.
3. 20 x 105mm cannon
4. French reinforcement by road.
5. Vietminh guerilla attacks.
R.C. 1
R.P. 13
Luc Nam
Phu Lang Thuong
5 Apr
MASSIF DU
DONG TRIEU
23 to 29 Mar
at 1 a.m.
23 Mar
Bai Thao
Ben Tam
R.P. 18
Sept Pagodes
Hoang Xa
DONG TRIEU
Mines
Mao Khe
Ha
Chieu
Bi Cho
Uong Bi
Chap Khe
R.P. 18
Yen Lap
S.Da Bach
S.Bach Dong
Hongay
Halong
Bay
To Hanoi
R.C. 5
Hai Duong
HAIPHONG
Cat Bi
N
0
25
Kilometers

THE BATTLE OF THE DAY RIVER

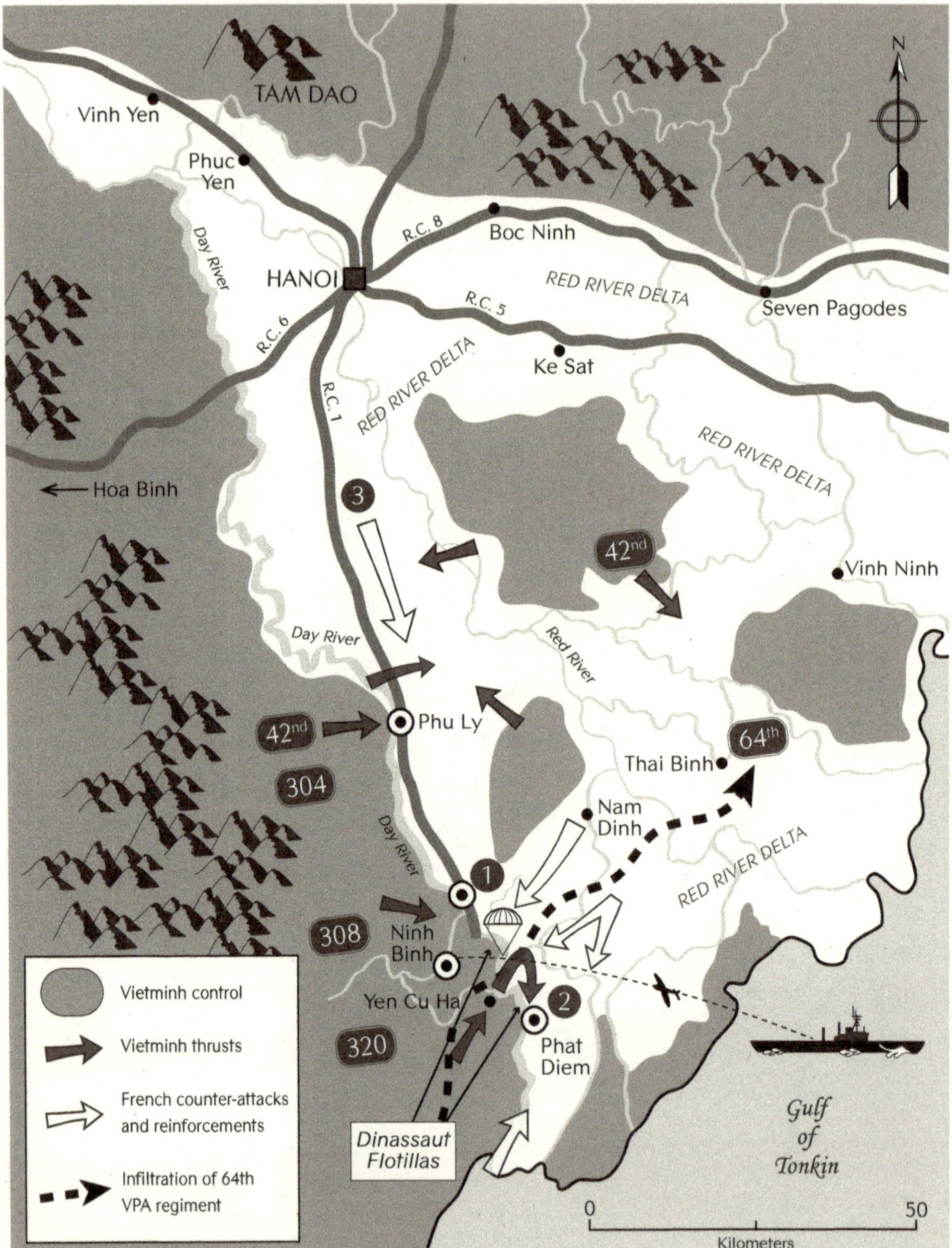

1. Death of Lt Bernard de Lattre, 1st Chasseurs 30 May 1951.
2. Catholic militia under control of the Bishop of Phat Diem, Le Huu Tu 6000 milita.
3. Groupes mobiles from Hanoi.

BATTLE OF HOA BINH OCT-FEB 1951-52

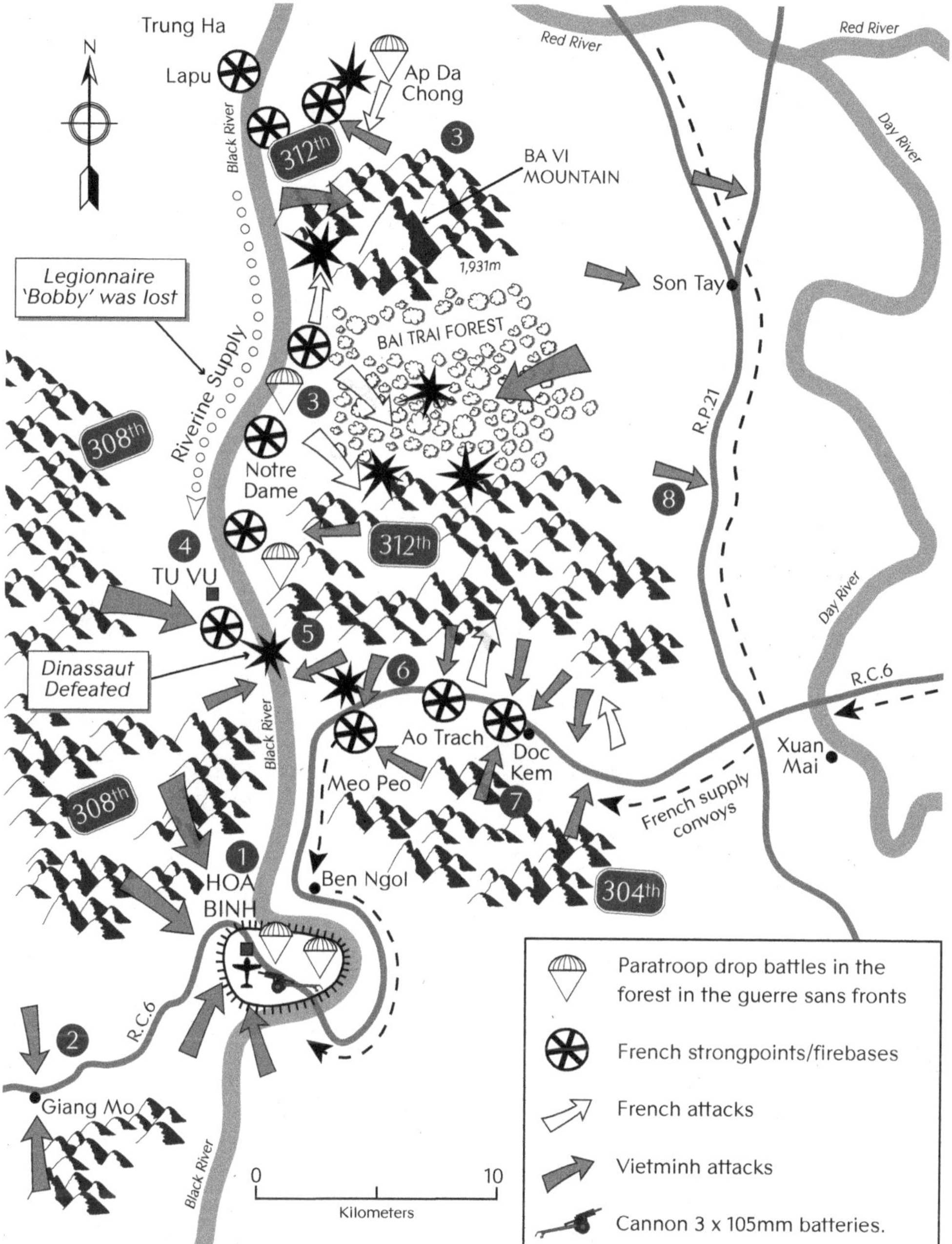

1. Paratroop drops 4-6 Oct 1951 at Hoa Binh.
2. French armoured column destroyed.
3. Series of battles for the control of the east bank of the Da River (Black River) on the slopes of Ba Vi Mountain range and Bai Tai forest.
4. Tu Vu base overrun.
5. Dinassaut flotilla and supply convoy defeated and turned back.
6. Major VPA regiment attack on Meo Peo stronghold.
7. Attacks by the VPA along the Route Colonial 26.
8. Vietminh attacks on R.P.21

VPA OFFENSIVES AFTER HOA BINH 1952-54

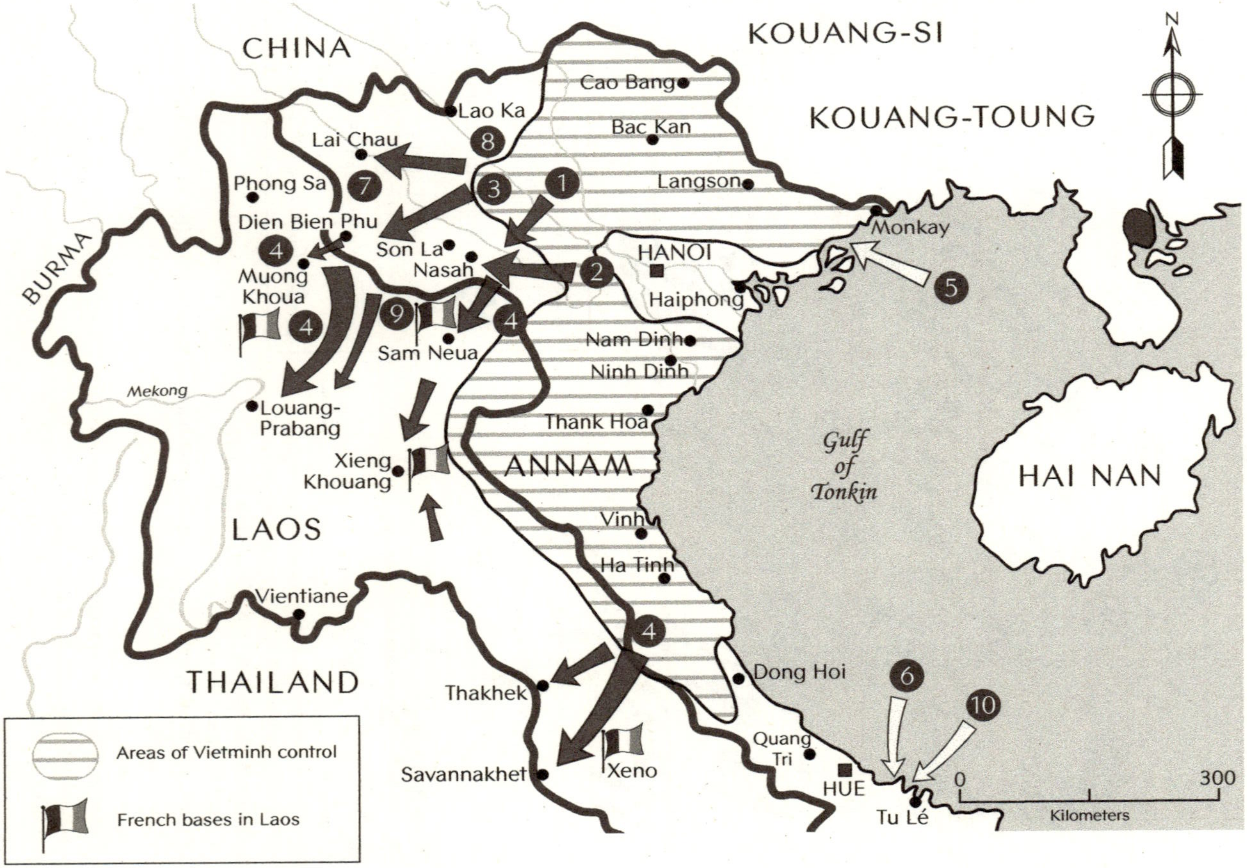

1. VPA offensive on the Black River mid Oct 1952.
2. VPA offensive against Na San 20 Nov 1952.
3. VPA advance on Dien Bien Phu Dec 1952.
4. VPA offensive against Luang Prabang, Muong Khoua and Xam Neua Apr 1953 as well as major towns on the Lao panhandle.
5. French Operation Hirondelle Jul 1953 against Langson supply base.
6. French Operation Carmague 28 Jul to 10 Aug 1953.
7. French Operation Castor Dien Bien Phu 20 Nov 1953.
8. VPA attack on Lai Chau late Nov 1953.
9. VPA Jan 1954 diversionary offensive.
10. French Operation Atlante 20 Jan 1954 to Jun 1954.

T'AI HIGHLANDS

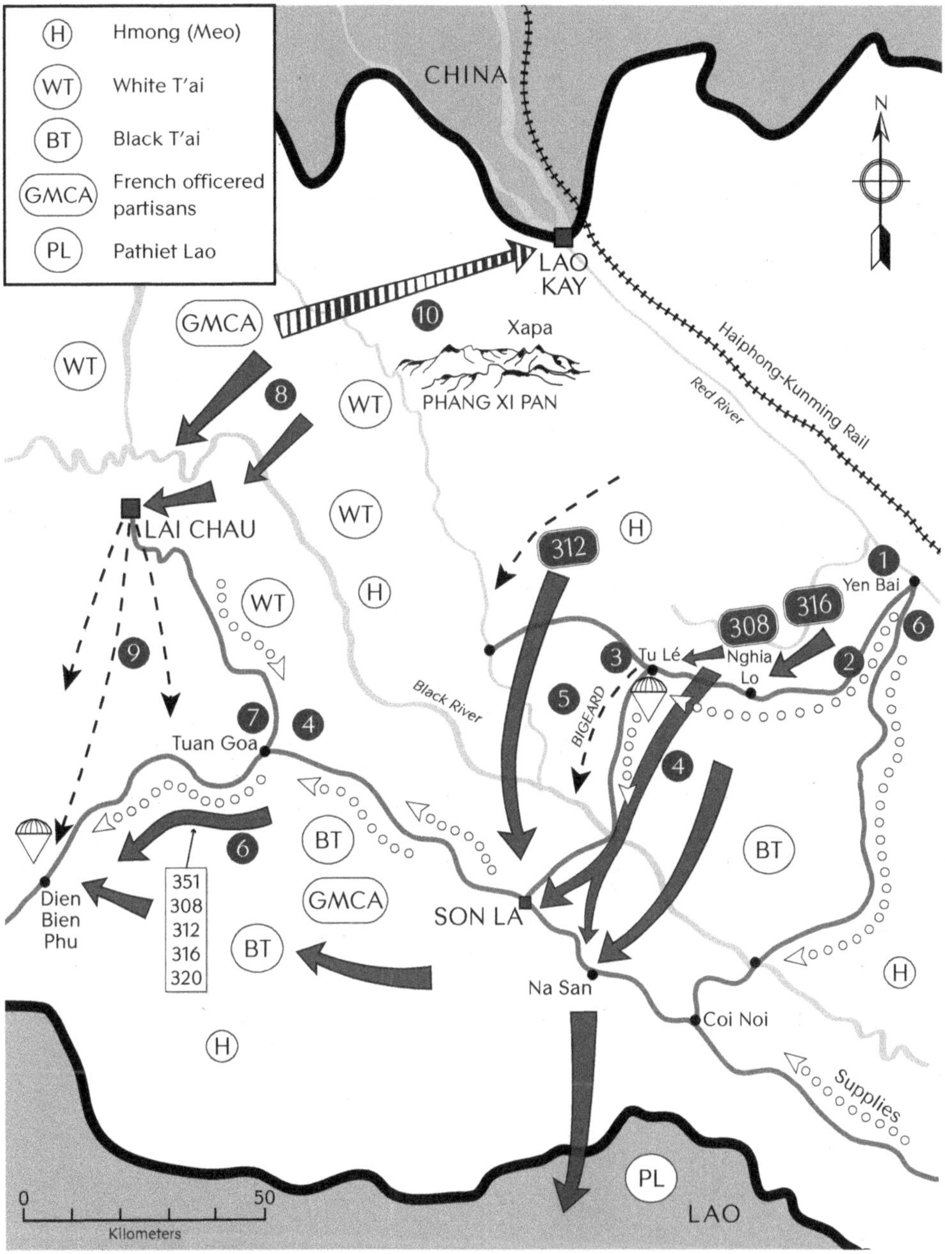

1. Yen Bai developed into a major logistics hub by Giáp 1951.
2. 2nd offensive against Nghia Lo and the T'ai Hills 16-17 Oct 1952.
3. Bigeard 6 BCP parachuted in at Tu Lé, the 308th attacks at Tu Lé 16 Oct, and the 308th attack 19 Oct.
4. VPA advance to Nà San and 26-day siege Oct-Nov 1952.
5. Bigeard's escape with 6 BPC and other remnants of hill garrisons reaching safety 22 Oct.
6. VPA advance to Dien Bien Phu after the French attack Nov-Dec 1952.
7. Giáp sets up Tuan Goa as logistics hub for Dien Bien Phu campaign Dec 1952.
8. VPA advance on White T'ai territories of La Chau 3 Dec 1953.
9. FEC indigenous T'ai battalions attempt escape but are destroyed 3-13 Dec 1953.
10. GMCA officered indigenous auxiliaries attack and capture Lao Kay in Apr 1954.

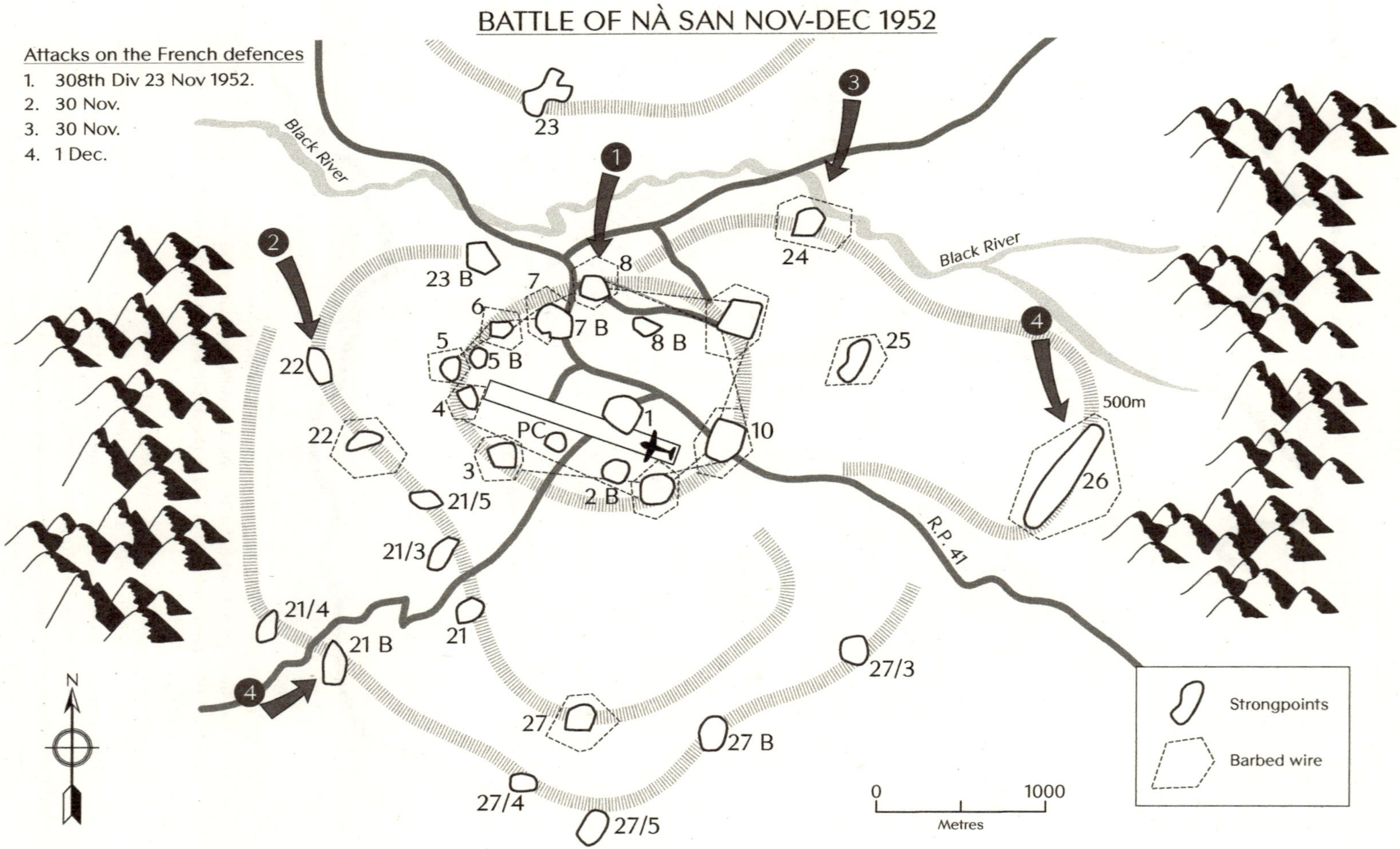
BATTLE OF NÀ SAN NOV-DEC 1952
Attacks on the French defences
1. 308th Div 23 Nov 1952.
2. 30 Nov.
3. 30 Nov.
4. 1 Dec.
Black River
Black River
R.P. 41
500m
PC
1
2 B
3
4
5
5 B
6
7
7 B
8
8 B
10
21
21 B
21/3
21/4
21/5
22
22
23
23 B
24
25
26
27
27 B
27/3
27/4
27/5
Strongpoints
Barbed wire
0
1000
Metres
N

NORTHERN LAOS, 1953-54

1. Reconnaissance in force defeated.
2. 2nd Reconnaissance in force defeated as French check escape route.
3. Attack on Hill 781 failed to find Vietminh artillery.
4. Supply line to the logistics hub at Tuan Giao 50km.
5. Vietminh 308th Division advances against Luang Prabang Apr 1953.
6. Advance south arrow direction Xam Nuea and Plain of Jars Apr 1953.
7. Alongside the 5 Jan 1953 advance on Luang Prabang.

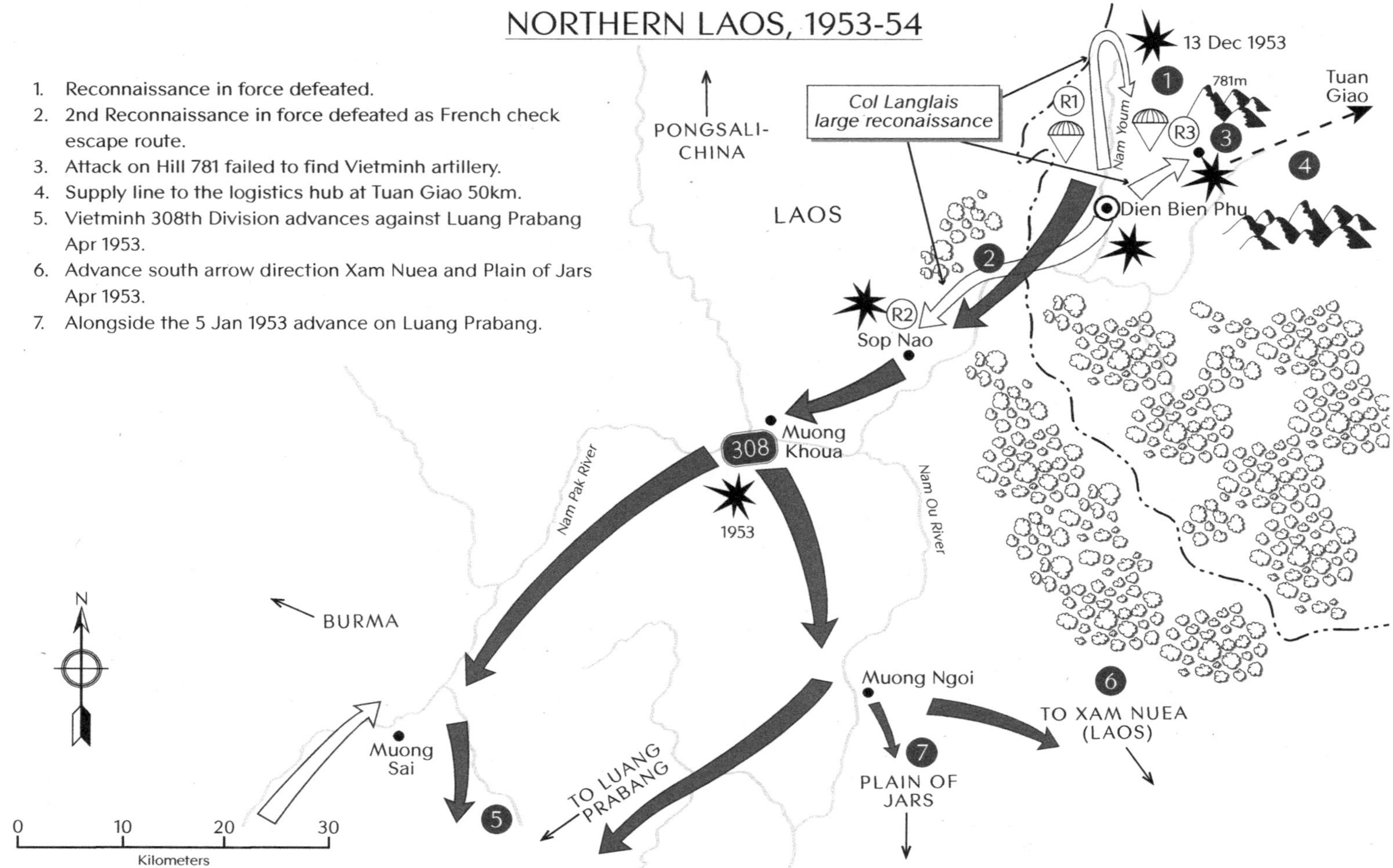

OPERATION HIRONDELLE 17 JUL 1953

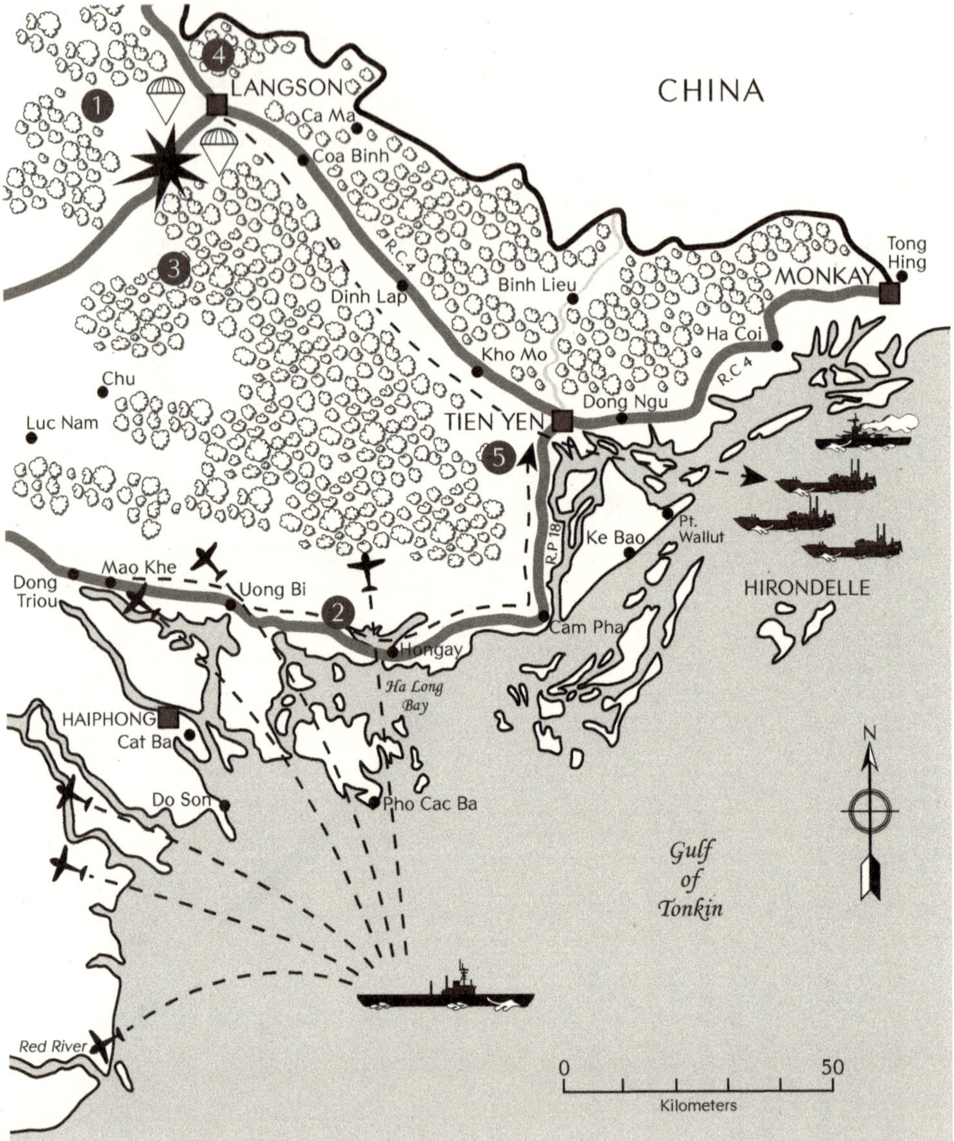

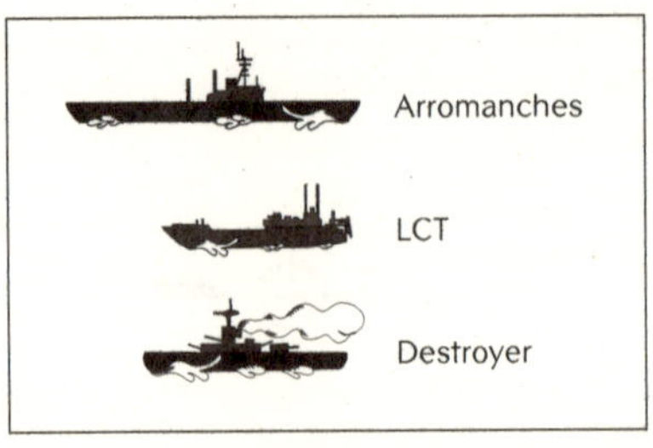

1. Parachute drops.
2. 2,500 ground troops in convoy on the R.P. 18.
3. Huge dump for amunitions, weapons, food and supplies.
4. Main provincial city Langson.
5. Retreat to the coast and fleet evacuation.

TYPICAL AMBUSH TACTICS IN TONKIN & CENTRAL HIGHLANDS

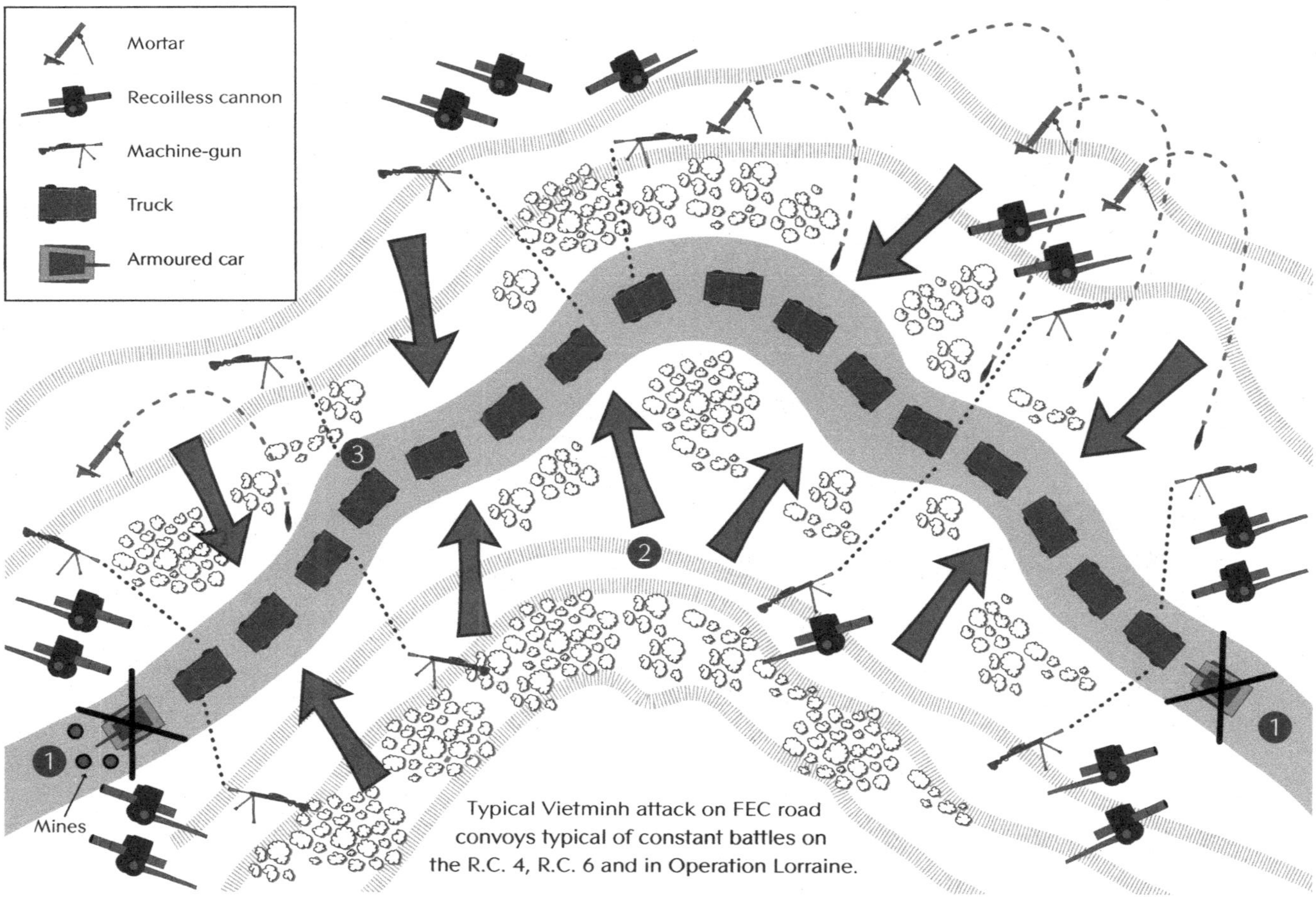

1. Lead and rear tank taken out to block road of each end of convoy. Vietminh attacks with mortars, recoilless cannons and machine-guns (on tripod).
2. Vietminh attacks to break up column.
3. Trucks and armoured cars.

DIEN BIEN PHU THE FALL OF BEATRICE AND GABRIELLE 13-14 MAR 1954

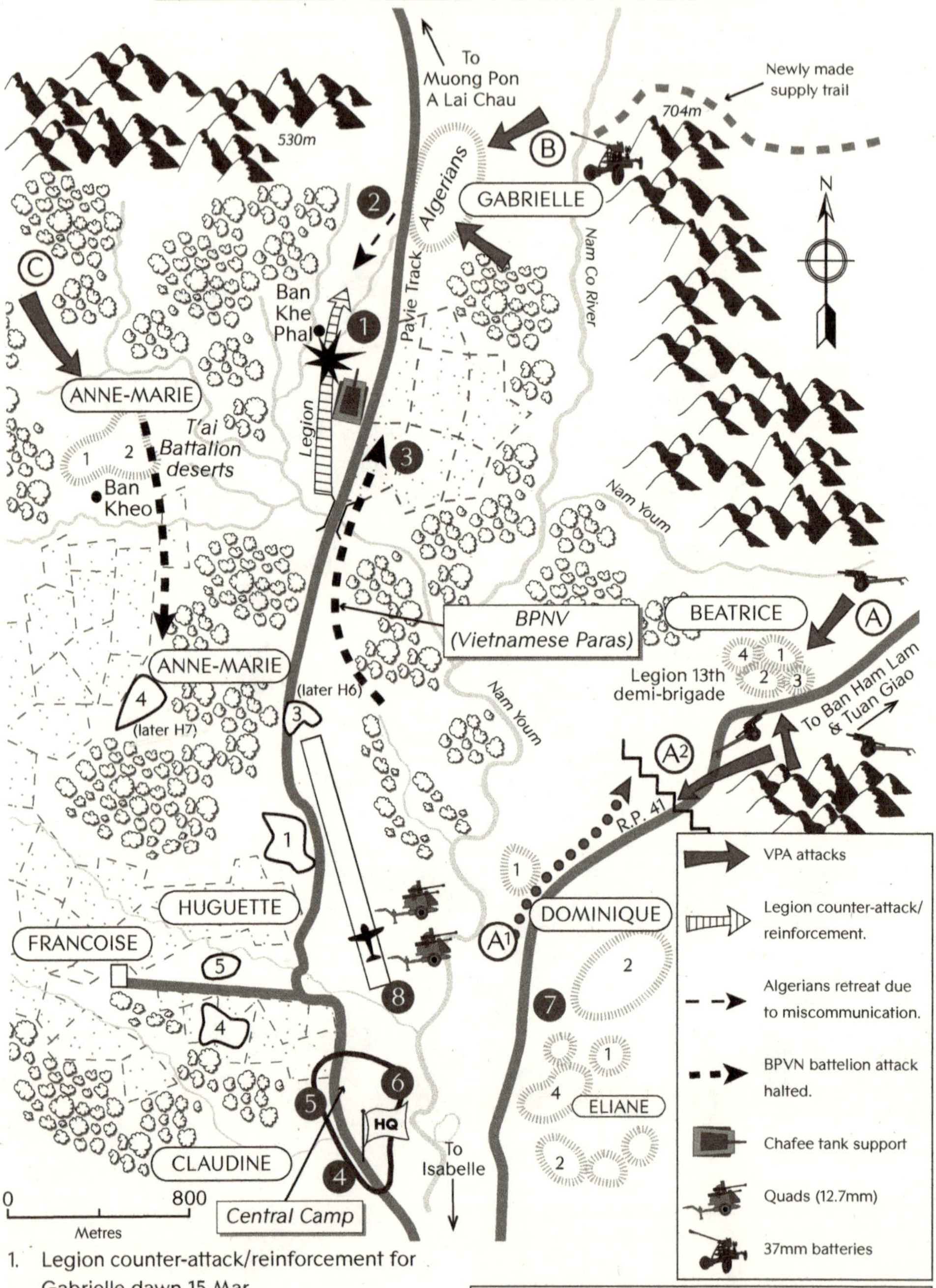

1. Legion counter-attack/reinforcement for Gabrielle dawn 15 Mar.
2. Algerians premature retreat 15 Mar.
3. BPVN paras attack falters 15 Mar.
4. De Castries HQ.
5. 155mm cannon.
6. 105mm cannon.
7. 120mm legion mortars.
8. 2 x 4 browning MG Quads.

A. The Vietminh attack on Beatrice evening of 13 Mar.
A1. The planned counter-attack.
A2. Vietminh infiltration blocks to the counter-attack early morning 14 Mar.
B. The attack on Gabrielle 15 Mar.
C. Attack on Anne-Marie 15 Mar.

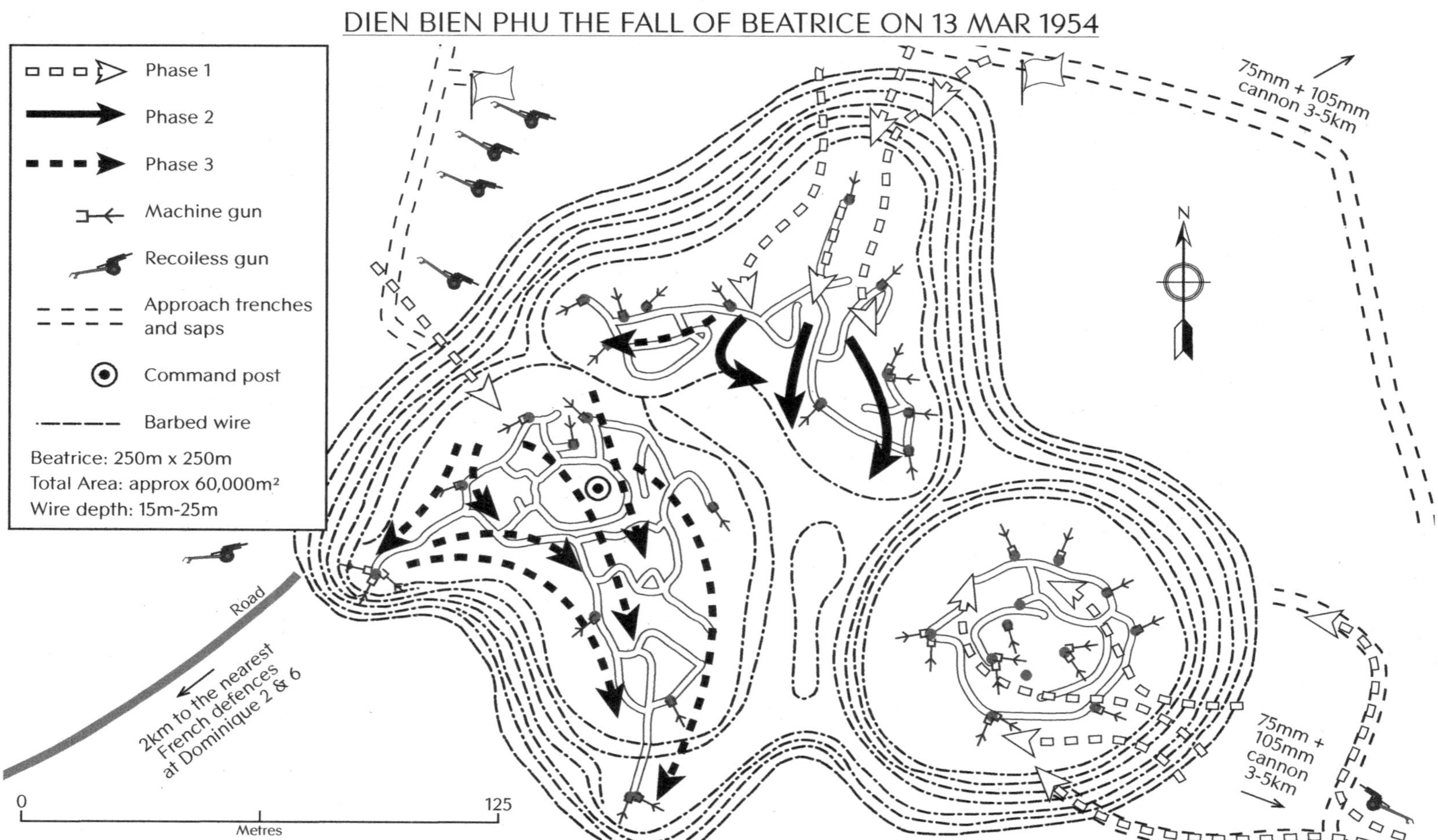

Dien Bien Phu: Giáp's description of the French defences at Beatrice.

DIEN BIEN PHU 'FIVE HILLS' DEFENCES

FIVE HILLS = D1, D2, E1, E4 & E2

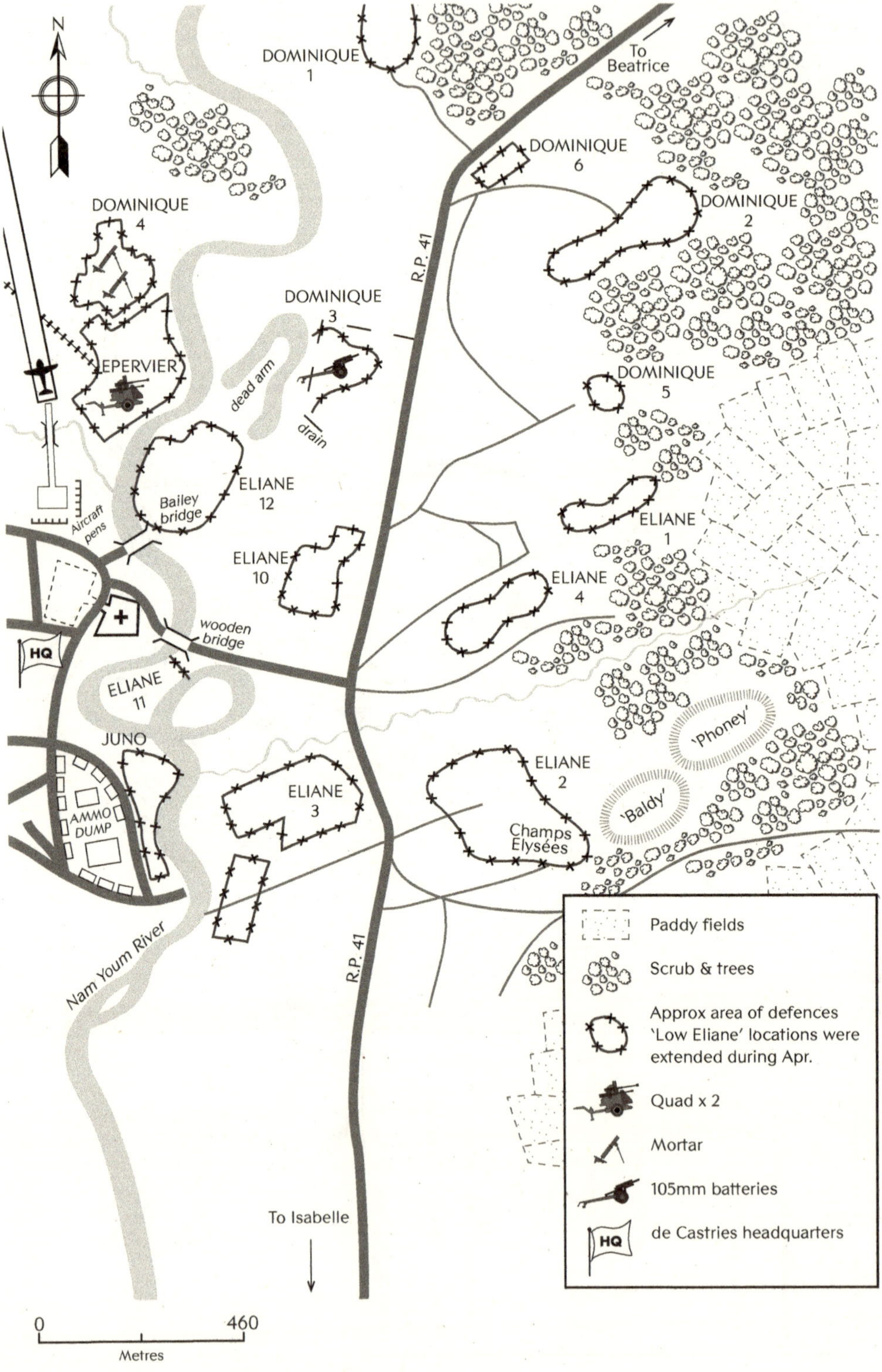

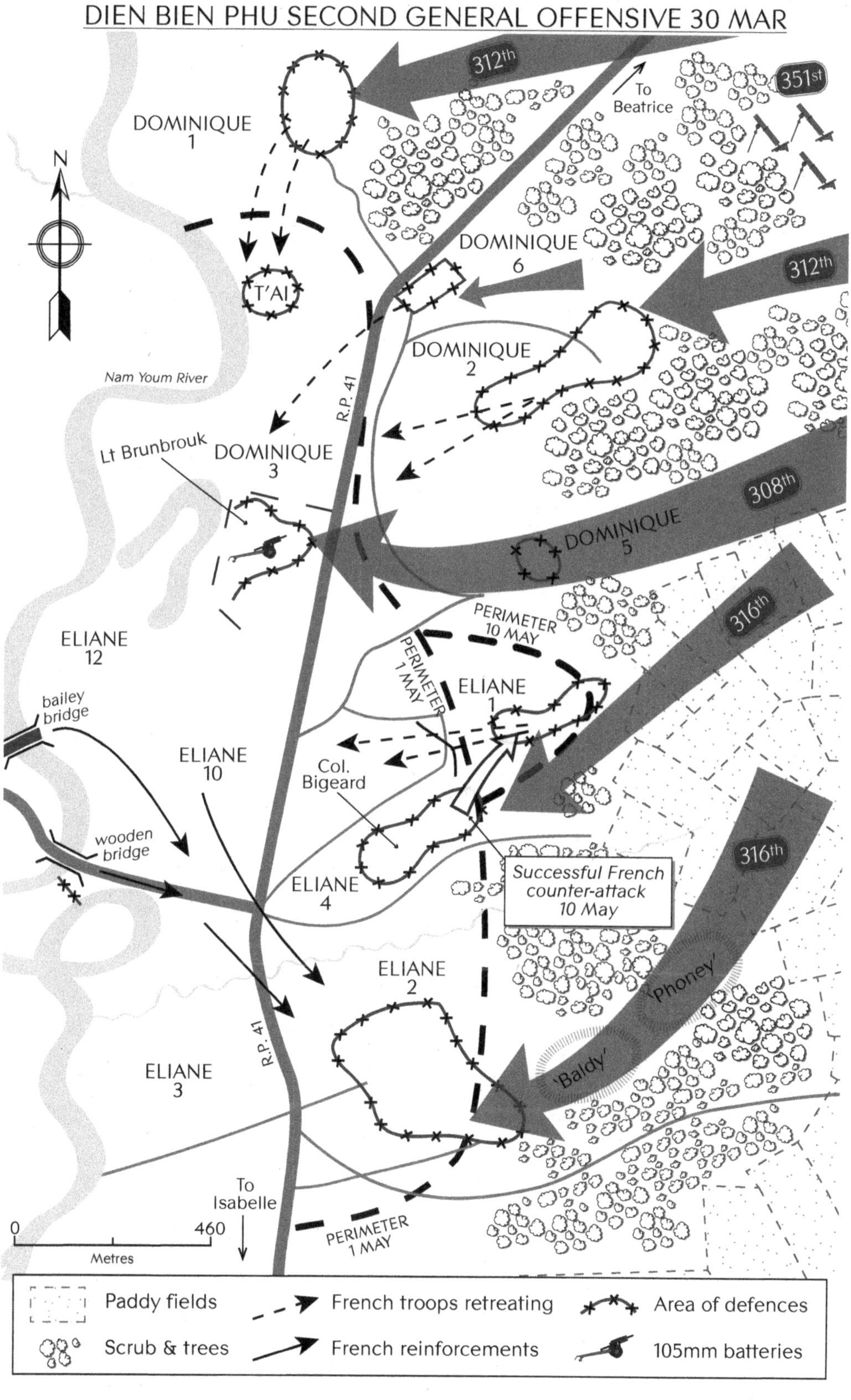
DIEN BIEN PHU SECOND GENERAL OFFENSIVE 30 MAR
312th
351st
To Beatrice
DOMINIQUE 1
T'AI
DOMINIQUE 6
312th
DOMINIQUE 2
Nam Youm River
R.P. 41
Lt Brunbrouk
DOMINIQUE 3
DOMINIQUE 5
308th
PERIMETER 10 MAY
316th
ELIANE 12
PERIMETER 1 MAY
ELIANE 1
bailey bridge
ELIANE 10
Col. Bigeard
wooden bridge
ELIANE 4
Successful French counter-attack 10 May
316th
ELIANE 2
'Phoney'
'Baldy'
ELIANE 3
R.P. 41
To Isabelle
0
460
Metres
PERIMETER 1 MAY
Paddy fields
Scrub & trees
French troops retreating
French reinforcements
Area of defences
105mm batteries

THE HUGUETTE OFFENSIVE 2-24 APR

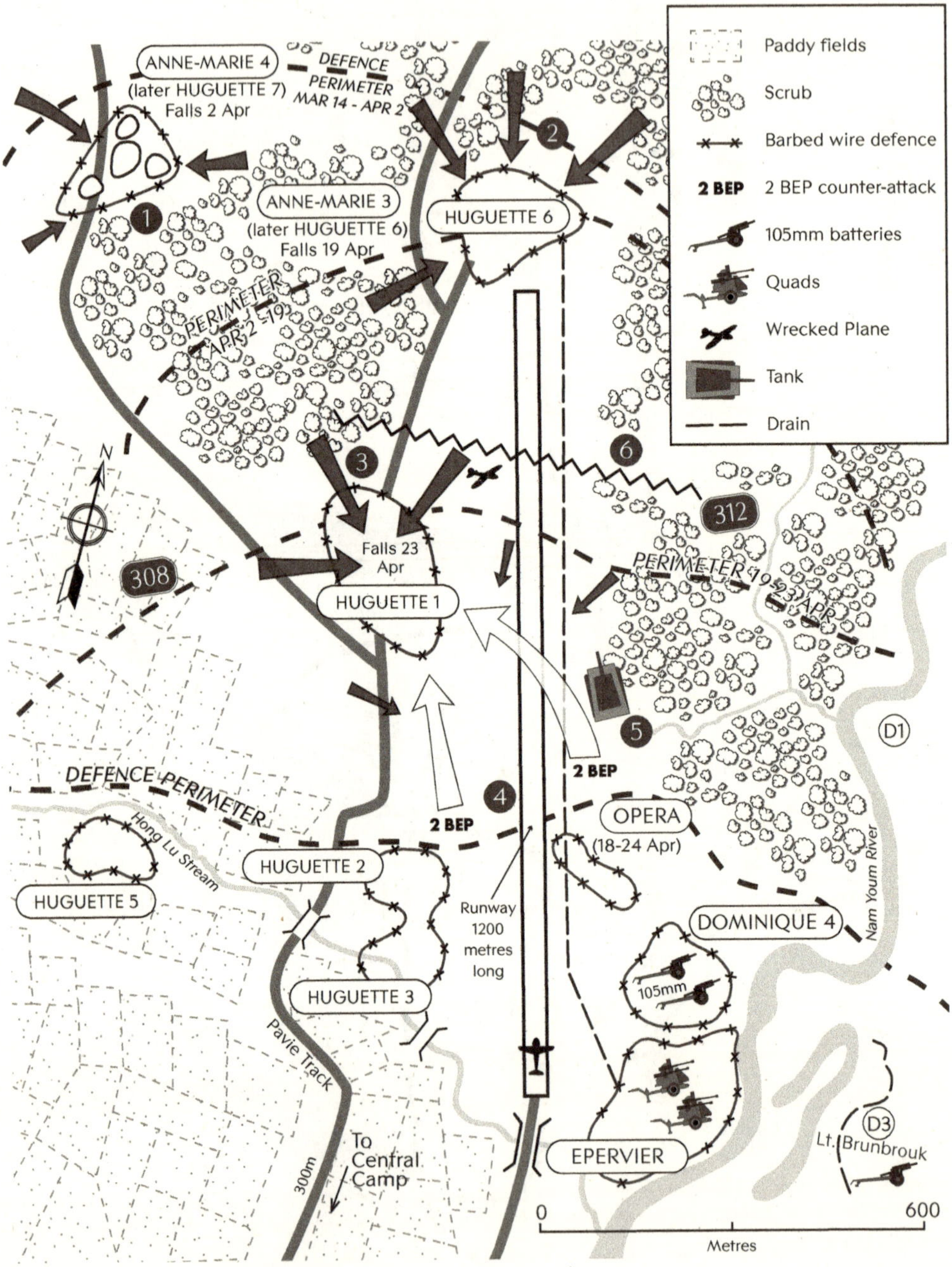

1. Anne-Marie - Huguette 7 falls.
2. Huguette 6 falls 19 Apr.
3. Huguette 1 falls 23 Apr.
4. Failed counter-attack 23 Apr.
5. Tank support.
6. VPA trench dug across runway allowed mutual reinforcement by the 308th and 312th.

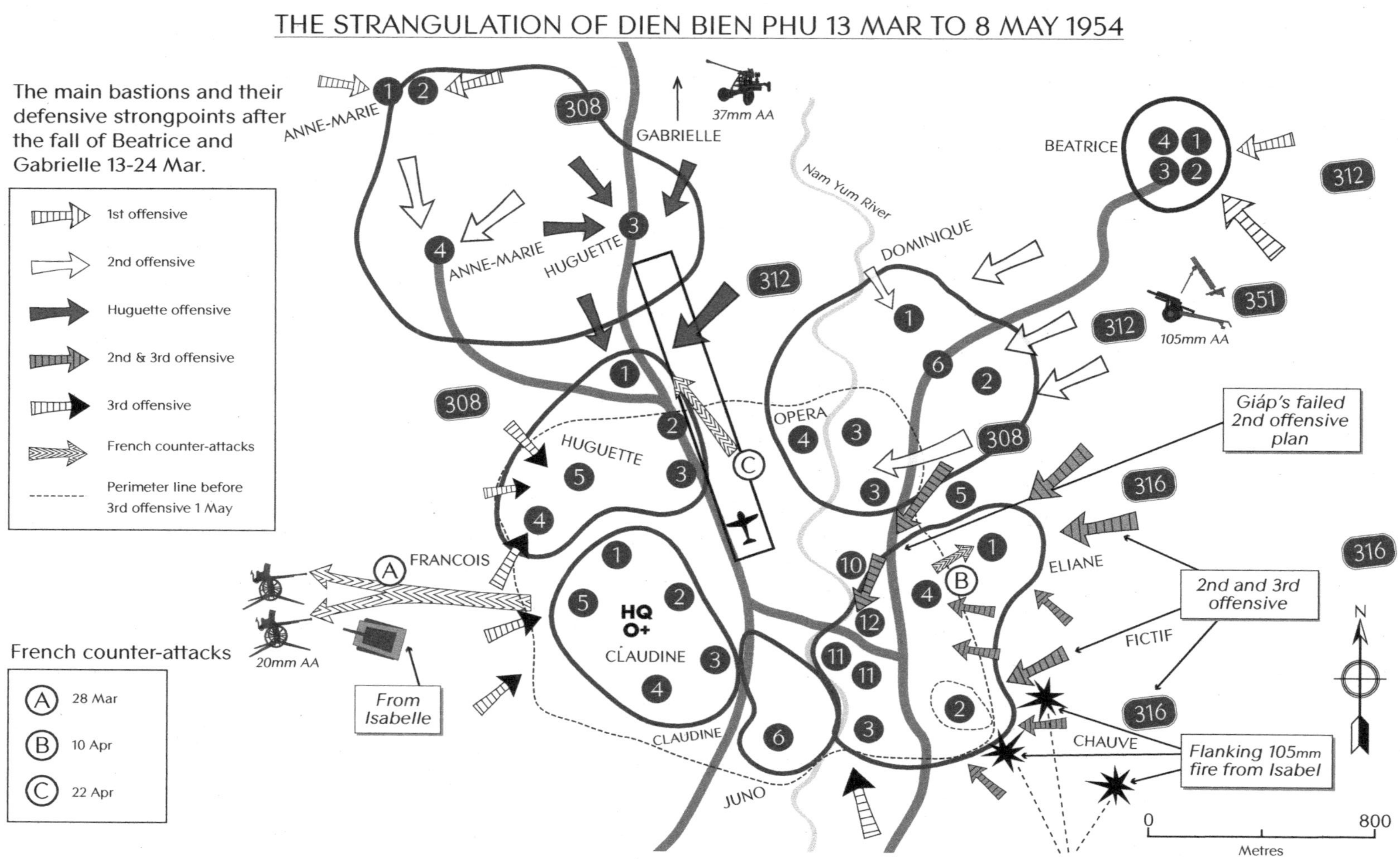
THE STRANGULATION OF DIEN BIEN PHU 13 MAR TO 8 MAY 1954
The main bastions and their defensive strongpoints after the fall of Beatrice and Gabrielle 13-24 Mar.
1st offensive
2nd offensive
Huguette offensive
2nd & 3rd offensive
3rd offensive
French counter-attacks
Perimeter line before 3rd offensive 1 May
French counter-attacks
A 28 Mar
B 10 Apr
C 22 Apr
ANNE-MARIE
GABRIELLE
37mm AA
BEATRICE
Nam Yum River
DOMINIQUE
HUGUETTE
OPERA
105mm AA
Giáp's failed 2nd offensive plan
ELIANE
2nd and 3rd offensive
FICTIF
CHAUVE
Flanking 105mm fire from Isabel
FRANCOIS
20mm AA
From Isabelle
HQ
CLAUDINE
JUNO
308
312
351
316
N
0
800
Metres

CHAPTER I

Parachutes Blooming, and the Origins of French Indochina

Introduction

The sky blooms parachutes

Three hundred kilometres to the west of Hanoi and Tonkin's Red River delta, separated by a tangle of mountains, gorges and rivers, there is a narrow verdant valley of paddy just a few kilometres from the Laos border. About 20km long and 5km wide, it is the traditional land of the black T'ai tribe. In 1953 there was a small village of stilted houses with bamboo-mat walls and grass roofs. Its name was Dien Bien Phu which, despite its exotic sound and fame, means simply 'small border post'. Apart from rice, its main economic function was to host a market for raw opium grown in the surrounding mountains by the T'ai and Meo tribes. Standing in the bottom of the valley looking west, you see the nearby Lao mountain. Looking east, a visitor sees jungle-covered low hills in several successive waves. The green of the foliage on the first hills gives way to purple shades as a barrier of much higher peaks rises up above and behind them. The optics of the view glimmers slightly in the heat, although November offers much greater clarity than in the shimmering dusty furnace at the height of the dry season.

On 20 November 1953, at about 7 a.m., Tran Can, commander of 634 Company of the 910 Battalion, Regiment 148, was preparing to march north to Muong Pon. From his encampment in the Dien Bien Phu Valley, Tran Can was conducting training exercises when a large fleet of enemy transport aircraft appeared overhead.[1] Peasants were ploughing their fields ahead of a new rice crop. It was a pastoral scene: small boys tending their bullocks and water buffalo; black-clad turban-wearing tribeswomen carrying loads on their heads or balancing pitchers of laden baskets on poles slung across their shoulders going about the regular chores of village life in Indochina. They would hardly bother to look up at first, but the sheer number of aircraft eventually intruded on their consciousness.

When it was obvious that a paratrooper drop was underway, the villagers scattered hurriedly to gather up their belongings, children and cattle, and escape to the forest while Tran Can and his men were smartly redeployed towards the drop-zone with their machine-guns and mortars. The sky was blossoming with many hundreds of red or white silk parachutes, like floating flowers. Hoang Le, political commissar of the same regiment, noted:

> *There were three types of parachute, white, cream and red. As the red ones were much less numerous, I presumed that they represented officers...we had several kilometres to cover in order to approach the enemy.*[2]

The drop was finished by 2 p.m. and fierce close-quarter fighting with grenades and machine-guns opened up immediately, sometimes when troops were still in the air, and it continued till 4 p.m.

Fighting took place in areas of long grass and paddy and there was intense street fighting in the village of Dien Bien Phu as the headquarters of 128th Regiment was forced to evacuate. Fighting was confused as Bigeard's 6th BPC had to organise themselves on landing. General Bigeard remembered:

> *Bréchignac's men and mine, we are jumping. It is not easy, it is windy. We were mixed up with the Viets. There was shooting everywhere.*

Tall grass made fighting difficult but it also shielded them from direct Vietminh fire. Newsreels show paratroopers shooting into the long, thick elephant grass, which reached well over head-height. Bigeard's troops met strong resistance from embedded machine-guns in the village and an attempted flanking by Colonel Bréchignac's 1st BPC was bogged down in an area of open paddy, which could easily be swept by machine-guns. Eventually airstrikes on the village destroyed the wood and bamboo dwellings that burnt down. Vietminh casualties were enhanced by the hail of mortar fire that targeted their path of retreat.

Deployed as mobile 'shock troops', paratroopers were used extensively in the First Vietnam War, more than in the Second World War or since, as an element that could be dropped into trouble spots at short notice. Paratroopers had a reputation for brutality and would often be shot if captured, something that they expected at Dien Bien Phu where many paratroopers buried their red berets before the surrender, except Colonel Bigeard who had a reputation to maintain.

When their ammunition was nearly exhausted, Vietminh units retreated away from the valley, where they would be vulnerable to air attack, to the neighbouring forests.[3] Tran Can's battalion withdrew after suffering heavy casualties with sixty killed and wounded, whereas the French suffered fifteen dead. However, six Vietminh soldiers were ordered to remain and merge into the local T'ai populace to gather information, including topographical details and to gain the populace's support as informants.[4]

'The enemy' was the French Fourth Republic and their colonial troops, some drawn from France but mostly from north, central and west Africa and

Indochina itself, some 228,000 in 1952. With local recruitment of units by the associated states, the total forces available to French commanders was 497,000 by 1954. Of the approximately 20,000–30,000 Foreign Legion troops engaged in Indochina where, depending on the unit, thirty to eighty percent were Germans, some were formerly members of the Wehrmacht or SS, though by 1953 this was decreasing.[5] However, most of the 'French' troops would be from Indochina: Vietnamese, Cambodians (Khmer), T'ai, Meo and Laotians. Vietnamese accounted for sixty to eighty percent of the composition of many units. The 6th BPC, the Bigeard Battalion, consisted of an effective force of 666 officers, non-commissioned officers and soldiers. Of this total, 376 soldiers were Vietnamese.[6] In the 3rd REI (Foreign Legion) thirty-three percent were German. There were many Eastern Europeans, easily lured out from the atrocious French internment camps. About five percent were Poles and three to four percent were Hungarian.[7] Eventually indigenous troops, Vietnamese, hill tribes, Laos and Khmer formed the majority of French and Vietnam government units in Indochina. Not just an imperialist war, the Indochina War 1945–54 was a war of independence, a civil war, a revolutionary war, a class war and the front line of the Cold War.

This valley during the first six months of 1954 framed one of the most momentous events of twentieth-century history, a crucible of conflict at the height of the Cold War. Dien Bien Phu became a talisman for de-colonisation and liberation struggles worldwide. The battle forged the future of Vietnam and it marked the beginning of the end for the French Fourth Republic. Ironically, the battle would help turn away France from empire and global affairs towards a new future in the Franco-German axis that would lead and shape the future of Europe. The 'European project' was an idea created and executed by the very same French political party (the Centrist Catholic party the MRP) that was simultaneously the flag-bearer for the brutal 'revanchist' colonial war in French Indochina with such belief in the imperial mission. It was led by George Bidault and the iconic founding father of the European Union, Robert Schuman.

Why did this war happen? Time was being called on the era of European empires, so why did this colonial war develop when other major colonial powers were going rapidly in the other direction? And what was the role of the US in this process? Finally, how did the French Indochina War fit into the Cold War and the geo-political and ideological ambitions of the USSR and the People's Republic of China (PRC), and Stalin and Mao respectively?

The geography of Indochina

The great majority of the territory of Tonkin was mountainous jungle with few roads. In any case, seventy percent of the roads were impassable in the monsoon season from April to September. The Central Highlands of Annam were mainly mountainous and hilly jungle with a narrow coast strip and a few patches of paddy in the interior. From a population perspective, Vietnam is a dumbbell with a thinly populated coastal bar connecting the population masses clustered in the Red River delta of the north and the Mekong delta of the south. The two densely populated centres of Indochina (Vietnam) are about 1,200km apart. They contained seventy percent of the population in their respective deltas. The length of the country is approximately 2,000km and its elongated S-shaped coastline 3,000km. In the south, Cochinchina was much forested and covered in rubber estates or paddy, mangroves or reed wetlands – such as the Plain of Reeds (*Plain des Joncs)*. There were few good places for armour to operate and plenty of areas for guerrilla armies to hide from aeroplanes or artillery. In mountainous jungle, French advantages in modern warfare, air power and firepower were mostly negated, but much less so in the heavily populated areas of Tonkin's Red River delta and at least some parts of the less sodden Mekong delta, around their respective capitals Hanoi and Saigon.

Dinassaut veteran and chronicler E. le Breton noted:

> *Progress across rice paddies and mangrove thickets forced us most of the time to wade through water and mud…traversing river channels was exhausting. Actually, due to the lack of roads, we had to carry not just our regular kit but also supplementary ammunition and support weapons, such as heavy machine guns and mortars…and these drenched men became veritable clumps of ambulating mud under a leaden sky, which added to their torment.*[8]

Riverine or 'brown water' warfare played a major role in French tactical deployment with eighty percent of marine deployment being involved with the Dinassaut flotillas, either as sailors or marines. They provided tactical flexibility in what quickly turned into a *guerre sans frontes*, where control and rapid deployment of heavily armed riverine flotillas on 2,750 miles of waterways in the Mekong delta (26,000 square miles plus 300 square miles of the Plain of Reeds) and 3,000 in the Tonkin delta basin (1,800 square miles) proved to be a useful asset in breaking up Vietminh supply lines and for launching counter-offensives against Vietminh communications.[9]

Underpopulated, mostly roadless and lacking in food resources, the Annamite mountains were populated by a multitude of tribes. Split by geography, historical development, economy, religion, racial mix and culture, the two halves of Vietnam were quite different. The main connector was the mutually understandable Vietnamese language, though the dialects and words can be very different. There are six tonal pitches in the north and five in the south, with the northern pitch being high while the south is more monotonal. Except for Vietnam, the rest of Indochina with its small populations was very backward, culturally, socially and economically. Eighty-six percent of Indochina is covered with very dense natural vegetation, and jungle extended over forty-six percent of the land mass where seventy percent is mountainous or hilly.

Lao was an afterthought in the colonisation of Indochina. It is a tiny country of one million people, half of whom were mountainous tribal people, including the Meo (Hmong), the Leu and many others. The other half were lowland Lao Thai. Lao existed as a Buddhist Ruritania, acting as a buffer state to Thailand and the British empire (Burma's Shan states). Apart from a few coal mines, the main cash crop in the highlands was opium, a trade encouraged by France. Its main purpose for France had been a chimera as the Mekong conduit to southern China.

Lao, bordered by Vietnam to the east, is a landlocked country about 2,000km long, including a panhandle along the Mekong of about 700km. It borders China for about 423km in the north and Cambodia for 541km in the south, with Thailand and Burma 1,754 and 253km to the west, with the Mekong acting as a border for much of the way. Mostly mountainous and jungle-covered, only about four percent of the land is arable.

Cambodia is similar. Its existence had been 'saved' by French imperialism in 1863 when it would have otherwise been absorbed by Siam (Thailand). With significant wetlands from an extended Mekong delta, Cambodia had a population of 3–4 million with mountainous regions around the borders with Annam, Lao, Thailand, and in the south-west. All three nations of French Indochina were festooned with puppet monarchies. Apart from being a buffer state, perhaps the most important reason for holding Cambodia was Ankor Wat, the astounding collection of temples where one million people lived in the twelfth century. Unlike Lao, Cambodia (or Cambodge as it is known in France) plays a minor role in the story.

Road systems in Indochina, in the remoter parts, are still as sparse and very poor as they were in 1946, with seventy percent being impassable in the monsoon season and drenched in a thick mist of orange dust in the dry season, which makes driving in convoy a slow and gloomy choking sort of hell.[10] Paucity in the Indochina road network provided major logistical and military challenges to fighting against the Vietminh with their adaptability to mountain and jungle tracks as well as logistical support from local porters. Lack of maintenance in the Second World War led to various main routes being overrun by nature's voracious green tentacles. How to pin down the Vietminh enemy in this fluid 'war without fronts' where the highly organised enemy alternated between terror tactics, guerrilla war and elements of classical war was the key tactical and strategic problem for French commanders who by training and experience were tied to roads and concomitant road-bound logistical systems in order to exploit their advantages in firepower as well as to compensate for smaller numbers.

Climate and environment

Climate ranges widely from north to south. The north has extremes of cold and heat as well a debilitating humidity in the wet season and only a short dry season, which is excruciatingly hot but still somewhat humid. The south is constantly hot with a moderately cool window around January. Essentially, westerners living in these regions are permanently damp: damp socks, damp underclothes, damp shirts and shorts. General Salan, who had spent much of his soldiering life in Lao and Vietnam pre- and post-Second World War, noted:

> *In the rainy season it was oppressively humid, rivers overflowed, visibility was much reduced, the earth became soft and spongy. Rain stopped all movement and leeches became a dangerous and tenacious menace.*[11]

The rainy season lasted from May to November, the dry season from December to April.

For the French and lowland Vietnamese alike, the jungle was also an alien and horrible place to fight. Lieutenant La Motte recorded his experiences of jungle fighting, including the enemy, the climate and the creatures:

> *...extraordinarily aggressive mosquitos...the repellent burns the skins but only lasts a few hours...I could hardly recognise my* nha ques *(rankers) with their faces swollen to resemble a pumpkin...if stung by a scorpion it's not deadly but you don't forget it for at least 15 days...leaches* [sic] *leave a wound which does not heal...There are two solutions;* [burning] *them off with a cigarette usually becomes infected; put your nail under the mouth of the leach and lift it off without harm.*[12]

In a rain forest where rain comes down in rods, the leeches come out in their millions, cartwheeling towards the warm-blooded heat signatures, or springing off boughs. They jump through any piece of clothing on any part of the body, then become fat and black as they fill up with blood. They were even more relentless than the Vietminh.

For the lowland Vietnamese, the majority of the Vietminh Army, jungle life and warfare was equally horrible and unfamiliar as it was for westerners. They caught malaria just the same. Forests were the dwelling places for the primitive indigenous people for whom the Vietnamese had so much disdain. So the Vietnamese were only marginally better adapted to jungle warfare. Idealistic city dwellers who followed Ho into the jungle after the Vietminh expulsion from Hanoi in 1946-47 soon returned after their miserable experience of the Arcadian hell.

A captain in the French Expeditionary Corps (FEC) remarked on the worst effect of the conditions on Indochina: 'It was fatigue due to the inextricable entanglement of a vegetation apparently allied with the enemy, the depressing climate and the thousands of hostile insects.'[13]

Legionnaire Adrian Liddell-Hart, operating in the vast Plain of Reeds, which runs north of Saigon and over the Cambodian border, lamented: 'It was an exhausting job searching a swamp under a sky which poured with torrential rain or blazed with tropical heat.'

The matrix of climate and terrain is so appalling that even the Vietminh, who might theoretically be more attuned to the conditions, launched nineteen of twenty-six offensives between September 1952 and July 1954 in the dry season. Four others were continuations of dry season offensives. Seasons in Indochina are (with minor variances between regions and due to natural fluctuation): dry October to mid-April and the monsoon season from May to the end of September. Winters in Vietnam are cold in the north but remain hot in the south.

Luo Guibo, Chinese political advisor to Ho Chi Minh's Vietminh, described his experiences of jungle life on a two-week visit in 1949:

> *The tropical miasma was overwhelming...the rats came out to enjoy themselves, the centipedes danced, poisonous snakes had fun with us squeezing into my boxes of documents and my cotton quilt, whist enormous moths circled the mosquito nets at night, the latter taking large bites out of me whenever they go the chance.*[14]

Jungle paths were draped with huge spiders' webs attended by large multicoloured and poisonous arachnids. Tigers were numerous and a real danger. When the first batch of US aid arrived for the French in 1950, it included 530 snakebite recovery kits.

On a field trip with Jean Letourneau in Indochina from 13 October 1952 for one month, secretary of state for war de Chavigne, an old soldier, experienced the following on patrol near Nam Dinh, where de Lattre had defeated Giáp's fourth major offensive on the Day River:

> *We walked for two hours in a rice field with water above the thighs, on the dykes, and in the mud, using small inflatable craft, side by side with the riflemen. We passed through huge bodies of water; sometimes getting back on our feet to climb up some of the many rocky limestone outcrops along the Day River...the minister well understood the problems of operating in inundated rice fields.*

Back in Hanoi that evening for a state banquet he remarked on the surreal contrast to the water, mud and slush.

A fearful place to have to fight in, French Indochina was an area of exceptional beauty, ancient cultures, and myriad tribes. It was controlled by a Mandarin land-owning class overlaid by a tax-collecting French bureaucracy. It was populated mainly by a very poor peasantry.

Statesmen and Indochina

The post-war story of Indochina 1945–54 drew in and actively involved most of the notable statesmen and figures of the twentieth century: Presidents Roosevelt, Truman, Eisenhower, Nixon (as vice-president), Kennedy (Jack and Bobby), Johnson, John Foster Dulles, Dean Acheson, Prime Minister Churchill, Lord Mountbatten, Sir Anthony Eden, Stalin, Georgy Molotov, Nikita Khrushchev, Mikhael Suslov, General de Gaulle, Georges Bidault, Robert Schuman, Leon Blum, Pierre Mendes-France, Francois Mitterrand, Mao Tse Tung, Chou en Lai, Li Shaoqui, Deng Xiao Ping, Ho Chi Minh, Kim Il Sung, General Giáp, Le Duan, Le Duc Tho, Truong Chin, Ngo Diem, Emperor Bao Dai, King Sihanouke, Prince Souvannathong, Generals Leclerc, Juin and Tassigny de Lattre.

Roosevelt set the tone for US attitudes. He was a passionate critic of French imperialism in particular and was well aware of pre-war atrocities and oppression. But this anti-colonial ideological idea, borne of the American Revolution, would come into conflict with the fact that the liberators were America's sworn ideological rival, the communists. How would this be resolved? An important issue for Roosevelt, it was more important seemingly than Jim Crow laws, segregation, civil rights abuse and economic oppression in the deep south.

Indochina became an issue at the Tehran conference of the 'Big Three' and was discussed at a secret meeting on 28 November 1943. However, Churchill was not present because he had been side-lined by Roosevelt who chose to accept Stalin's invitation to stay in his villa. With the imperialist-in-chief absent, Roosevelt was critical of France and questioned their honesty. Stalin agreed that 'he did not propose to have the allies shed blood to restore Indochina…to… French colonial rule.' Roosevelt was 'one hundred percent in agreement with Marshal Stalin…after 100 years of French rule the inhabitants were worse off than they had been before.' (ed. Michael Hunt, *A Vietnam War Reader*, transcript of Stalin-Roosevelt conference, 2010, p.22) Roosevelt had discussed trusteeship with Chiang Kai Shek. It became the progenitor of the split north-south post-war occupation by Kuomintang China and the British empire.

If nothing else, all of this indicates that the French Indochina War was pivotal to understanding twentieth-century history and the Cold War in particular.

Asymmetric warfare

For military historians, the varying and developing shape of revolutionary war is described in detail through different stages, from guerrilla war to hybrid guerrilla-conventional war to more classic phases of open warfare. Much of the war is characterised by the French as *la guerre sans front*. The last phase of the war was an epic siege that turned into a battle of attrition between trench systems with analogies to the First World War. The combatants' extremely contrasting styles of warfare give the conflict a sense of being an asymmetric gladiatorial contest akin to the retiarius fighting the secutor (or contra-retiarius): the one lightly armed and dancing around with a weighted entrapment net, the other heavily armoured but much less manoeuvrable.

The war in Indochina was the first great asymmetric war of the twentieth century where the asymmetry was not just in military matters but in political tactics as the Vietminh burrowed into France's soft tissue: political weakness and divisions in France's new Fourth Republic. In the November 1946 elections, the Communist Party, heroes of the resistance, commanded nearly thirty percent of the popular vote. The political front became as important as the military one, as it would in the Second Vietnam War.

At the strategic level the geography of Indochina presented extremely complex issues of logistics and movement. Moreover, the strategic links to international geo-strategic political issues, as well as the internal politics of all the members of the Security Council and China, became ever more complex as the war progressed.

CHAPTER II

The Origins and Beginnings of French Imperialism in Indochina

Origins of France's Asian empire 1615–1860

How did France come to pick on Indochina? French policy was driven by religion, trade and power politics. Jesuits came to the southern Vietnam coastal areas in 1615. Portuguese at first, they were followed by French Jesuits. France was slow to get going with colonialism and trade, but in the 1660s famous minister Colbert decided in the French manner that *dirigisme* should be applied to colonial policy. France aimed to compete with the Dutch and the English, who had started out in Asia as private enterprise ventures by risk-takers and adventurers some eighty years previously and who were subsequently organised into quasi state-backed companies, the Dutch East India Company and the (English) East India Company.

On the coast of Annam the Portuguese and then the Dutch had been trading since the early seventeenth century. Especially favoured was the port of Faifo, today the quaint tourist town of Hoi An, which sits on the coastal centre of Vietnam to the east of the old imperial capital of Hue. In 1640 the country was split between the mutually antagonistic dynasties of the Nguyễn in the south and the Trinh Trang in the north, with the divide being drawn at almost the same point on the 17th Parallel as the division between North and South Vietnam at the Geneva Conference in 1954. Having once been partners in ejecting the Chinese, the two dynasties had turned on each other over the issue of seniority. The Nguyễn controlled the southern regions of Annam and Cochin, including the detritus of the seafaring Moslem Cham empire and important elements of the Khmer empire (Cambodia), the Saigon region, which had been formally taken over in 1698. Dutch interests lay with the rival Trinh Trang regime in Tonkin. The Dutch East India Company (VOC) had a trading post and factory in Tonkin. When the Nguyễn regime took prisoner fifty shipwrecked Dutch seamen, tensions and demands mounted.

Signals of de-escalation by the Nguyễn were misinterpreted. Van Diemen, the new VOC governor general, decided to attack the Nguyễn fortress near Quinan in alliance with the Trinh Trang Army, to pressure the Nguyễn to release the seamen. Success would enhance Dutch reputation and increase their access to trade. However, in two separate engagements in 1642 and 1643, a Dutch squadron was twice attacked and defeated by about sixty Nguyễn Annamite galleys, who sank a powerful Dutch warship on each occasion then drove off the rest. These were the only occasions when the Dutch were defeated at sea by native powers in Asia in this epoque. Neither Cochinchina nor Tonkin would be occupied or even host Dutch or Portuguese fortresses. This brief story indicates two salient facts in the Vietnam story. Firstly, it points up the division between the north and south of the Annamite (or Dai Viet) territories, which was enhanced by the split geography of the Annamite coast. It also denotes the exceptional fighting spirit and proud independence of its peoples.

Despite this violent brush with westerners, the traditional enemy of Vietnam always remained and remains the Chinese. It is seared into Vietnamese cultural and political DNA, despite the role China played in their national liberation.

France's first port of call in the colonial competition was the Coromandel coast of India, which was the traditional place to start, so as to capture the textile trade. Textile products would be swapped into spices from South-East Asia and fine goods from China. Pondicherry became their base. With Colbert's encouragement, France followed up its missionary interests by trade. Soon a tradition was established of missionary-traders in the seventeenth and eighteenth centuries. Due to Dutch, Portuguese and British predominance, the only place in South-East Asia that offered real potential for a more exclusive relationship with France was coastal Annam. Particular focus was on the port of Faifo (Hoi An) and later on Cochin in the south. Over the years cordial relations were established. Of particular note was missionary Bishop Beryte, who befriended the King of Annam and secured special privileges for France.

After the severe losses of the Seven Year War, French imperial ambitions in India and Canada were severely diminished in the face of English power. Therefore, France's special focus for colonial growth and preferential rights descended on the coasts of what became 'Indochina'.

French priest Father Chevreul, of the Society of Foreign Missions, arrived in Annam in 1664 and after twelve years secured freedom of religion in the kingdom of Annam. The first ship from France arrived on 30 August 1669, with three more priests including Bishop Beryte. Beryte would leave and return again with a letter and gifts from Louis XIV. By 1722 there were four French priests in Tonkin and four in Cochinchina. As ever it was nationalist competition that drove on the European powers. A memorandum submitted to the Ministry of Marine and Foreign Affairs advised:

> *The conquests the English are making in India give them a great advantage over the French in the financial and political affairs of Europe…some means must be found to procure for France ports in Asia, which will counterbalance*

> *these English advantages...It appears that nothing remains but Cochinchina which has escaped the eyes of the English. But can we delude ourselves that they will delay in penetrating here?*[1]

Imperial competition would be a continuing and iterative theme in Indochina's development.

French interest in Cochin was stimulated by the towering charisma and enthusiasm of Pondicherry-based missionary Bishop Pigneau de Behaine. Interests of trade and religion coalesced with state policy, which increasingly viewed colonies as an accretion to status, power and trading wealth. In essence, the reasons for France's colonial project in Annam and their determination to hold on to it never changed from the logic expressed in the 1722 memorandum right up to 1954.

Despite anti-Christian pogroms at the end of the eighteenth and beginning of the nineteenth centuries, which coincided with the French Revolution and the Napoleonic wars, there was enough of a toehold of memory and missionaries to give encouragement for imperialist intervention. By such toeholds are empires created, especially when backed by modern weapons and high explosive. Nor would future generations of French rulers be discouraged by the remarkable victory of the slave population of Haiti, firstly over Revolutionary Directorate armies and latterly over those of Napoleon, under the leadership of former slave Toussaint Louverture in 1804. The lessons of imperialism were there to be taken but they were ignored. Fraternité, Egalité and Liberté were, it seems, ideals just reserved for the French.

Louis XVIII sent an expedition to Annam in 1816. However, Napoleonic-scale megalomania would return. French interest in the region had taken off when a gunboat was sent in 1845 to rescue five priests imprisoned at Hue. Napoleon III, like his forebear, had great and vainglorious ambitions. Turning France into a leading imperialist power in emulation of the British was one of his aims. An exploratory mission was sent in 1855 from Peking to report on the situation of missions and to negotiate free trade. Demands made for free trade were rebuffed. In 1858, Napoleon dispatched an expedition to Indochina, as the French now dubbed the region. The aim was to open up ports that had been closed and negotiate trade access agreements. The expedition was preceded by a threatening announcement:

> *France has attempted since the beginning of the century to have contacts with Cochinchina. The ruthless persecution of missionaries has brought our warships on more than one occasion to the coast of the Annamite kingdom but their efforts to enter into relations with the government have been futile. The government cannot allow its overtures to be scorned, therefore an expedition is planned.*[2]

Fourteen ships were sent. Tourane (Da Nang) was captured, so opening up the way to nearby Hue, the Annamite imperial capital. An army of 10,000 Annamites was defeated. In February 1859, the Saigon River was similarly opened and the city captured after hard fighting.

Imperialist competition 1860–1906

Speaking in 1890 once Indochina had been better established, former prime minister Jules Ferry explained the rationale for French imperialism in terms that were at least honest:

> *The colonial policy is the daughter of the industrial policy...The European powers of consumption are saturated. New masses of consumers must be made to arise in other parts of the world, lest bankruptcy faces modern society and the time will approach for a cataclysmic social liquidation of which we cannot calculate the consequences.*[3]

This would become crony capitalistic exploitation in a closed-end autarkic system.

As ever, the *raison d'être* for this desperate lunge for Indochina was for reasons of trade and prestige. Britain was fast establishing itself as the premier trading power in the vast Chinese market. Not least in terms of profitability was the opium trade from India followed by manufactured goods and highly prized exports such as tea, silk and Chinese porcelain through the Pearl River trade and the Yangtse trade. France wanted their own exclusive entre to China. Indochina's Mekong River and the railway from Haiphong to the Yunnan along the Red River basin seemed to provide the answer.

Imperfect understanding of geography meant that the Mekong route through Cambodia and Lao would turn out to be an impractical failure, and not only because of the dramatic Khone Falls on the Cambodia-Lao border. One of the world's most remarkable natural phenomena, they destroyed the economics of using the river. A rusting steam engine and a few rails are all that remain of this imperial folly in this remote corner.

Nor were the Khone Falls the only problem, because there are extensive rapids in central Cambodia above Kratji. The railway route from Haiphong, the main port in Tonkin, was not a success either. Constructed between 1904–1910, it cost as many as 20,000 lives to build. Running through Loy-kay into the Southern Yunnan to Kunming, it was also a relative failure because the Yunnan was a backward and poor province.

The one thing that did work was the trade in opium, exporting it from the growing areas in the T'ai Hills (not to be confused with Thailand) of western Tonkin and trading into southern China along the coast between Mong Cai and Hainan Island. It proved to be a huge money-maker for the colony, as did a detached part of Indochinese administration at Ford Bayard opposite Hainan Island with its population of 200,000 Chinese. The satellite colony acted as an opium market and distribution hub for China as well as exports to San Francisco.

Power, economic strength and prestige were increasingly seen in terms of the size of empire. European nations and even the smaller ones were outdoing each other to colour in blocks of the world map. Competition for culture was also a major issue. The British had control of the Taj Mahal and the Pyramids. The Elgin Marbles resided in the British Museum and in Berlin the Babylon Gates were housed at the Pergamon Museum. France also had to have its share of the world's archaeological treasure trove. Basking in the reflected glory of great empires past became the sport of the new European empires and emperors. 'Discovery' of Ankor Wat on the borders of Cambodge (Cambodia), in no little part, was a significant reason to propel France to imperial exertion in that place. This despite the fact that the great temple complex was not even in Cambodia but neighbouring Siam. France simply sidled over their border and co-opted Ankor Wat. It was ceded by the 1907 border treaty, which also secured the teak-forested left bank of the Mekong in Lao as it intersects with Cambodia at the Khone Falls.

Ankor Wat lent associated glory to the French state. It also gave amusement to the elites of Paris, especially during the Great Exhibition of 1889 when a recreated Ankorian temple became one of the popular centrepieces. An enormous hit, the exhibition instantly put Cambodia on the 'map'. It would start a mini boom in exotic tourism to Ankor's spectacular ruins which had, in the fourteenth and fifteenth centuries, housed an estimated one million people.

Colonial life

Café life

Moustachioed men sit about in cane chairs on the shaded terrace of a street café. They are wearing white linen suits and club ties. Cigars or cigarettes are smoked. On one table there is a bottle of Johnny Walker. At other tables the drinks are pastis or wine. There is laughter and chatter, a great sense of ease. The customers of the establishment are all men. In the background we see a tree-lined boulevard. There are a few passing cars and rickshaws. European men saunter. Women wearing the latest flapper style walk purposefully while chatting busily. A few natives of Indochina decorate the scene to remind us that we are in Indochina.

In the street passers-by are also dressed in white. They sport white topees. Others arrive at the café in rickshaws. Native drivers in sarongs and short jackets. They wear conical straw hats and stand around waiting for customers. One rickshaw pulls up and there ensues an argument between native and white man over payment. In a fit of pride, the native disdainfully refuses to take the proffered sum. The white man in white is disdainful too. It's a standoff of disdain. The rickshaw driver is probably feeling the pangs of withdrawal. It may soon be time for his opium fix, the only thing that kept most drivers going. Opium suppressed the pangs of hunger. It is estimated that twenty percent of their income was spent on low grade opium. Taxed heavily through the government permit system, the drivers lived squalid lives in slum tenements where as many as seventy percent would die of tuberculosis.[4]

The *maître'd* emerges to try to settle the matter. The other guests on the terrace are being inconvenienced by the fracas. The silent film cuts. We do not know the outcome.

Meanwhile, in another film, in the Chinese quarter of low-rise shophouses, the typical Asian bustle is apparent in streets that are humming beehives of activity. Man-drawn carts of all shapes and sizes, hawkers, stall-holders, food stalls, bobbing conical hats, women in sarongs, or *au dai*, Chinese and Vietnamese. Customers slurp noodles and pho on the trottoir, hawkers shave ice into glasses of cold water, and a little boy holds a bucket of skewered water chestnuts. The locals wear conical straw hats or fedora. An occasional one, perhaps a minor official, apes the manners of the French by dressing in white and wearing a panama or a cheap topee.

Anyone for tennis?

Bernhard Fall describes the expatriate military life at the outpost of Siem Reap in Cambodia far from the war-torn heart of the conflict. Already an important destination for well-heeled tourists visiting the ruins of Ankor Wat, all the typical colonial comforts were on offer, including luxury hotels built in the colonial style. A military posting there was a dream of a backwater. It was typical of scenes that might be found in the clubs around the posh suburbs of Hanoi and Saigon or in the expatriate resorts:

> *The officers' mess was a pleasant and well-kept place; with its wide Cambodian-style verandahs, its parasol shaded tables and well manicured lawns and beautiful red sand tennis court, I found the two officers at the tennis court in gleaming white French square bottomed shorts...matching Lacoste tennis shirts and knee length socks; their wives seated at a neighbouring table, were beautifully groomed and wore deceptively simple but oh so expensive cotton summer dresses*

clearly showing the hand of a Paris designer...three Cambodian servants, clad impeccably in white slacks and shirt, stood respectfully in the shadows of the veranda, awaiting the call of one of the officers or women for a new cool drink.[5]

At the beach resort at Kep-sur-Mer

Kep (-sur-Mer), an overgrown crab-fishing village on the Cambodian coast, which nestles beneath several jungle-covered hills, sprouted modernist French villas along a few beaches. The villas are still there, desolate and overgrown, faded, moss-covered white, springing weeds. But as the soft breeze wafts through the town on a balmy evening one can almost hear the French chatter, the clinking of champagne or cocktail glasses, the sounds of jazz or soft lapping of waves from the shallow sea, as chiffon curtains flutter and dark-skinned Khmer servants in white sarongs and tunics serve *canapés*.[6] High up on the jungle-clad promontory, King Sihanouke built a luxury villa hideaway, in the modernist style, which can still be visited in its abandoned and overgrown state, home now to poor peasant squatters, descendants of the former serving staff.

There are similar offerings at the hill station of Darlat, or at the beach resort of Cap St Jean, the 'South of France' transported to the Cochin coast or the island resort of Phyu Quoc with its exquisite beaches. Lying a few kilometres from the Cambodian coast, directly opposite Kep, Phu Quoc was a Cambodian island. But in 1939, France's governor general unilaterally decided to transfer it to Cochin control. This suited the interests of Saigon's business magnates, who were marketing shares in the newly established Phu Quoc Island Hotel Company. The Cambodian king was not consulted. (It remains a disputed territory.)

Executive life in Haiphong

In his Indochina narration, Lieutenant de Beaucorps gives a description of a typical detested colon corporate executive (detested, that is, by aristocratic army officers). He is director general of the Hong Gai coal mines:

...he was big, big in name and by his titles, polytechnician et Directeur Generale of the most important mines in Indochina. He was extremely self-conscious and radiated arrogance. His office fitted his character. An immense room, a very large empty desk, large bow windows looked out of course over Ha Long Bay.[7] (Ha Long Bay, UN World Heritage Site)

Famed paratrooper Colonel Bigeard was typical in his thoughts of the plethora of well-paid colonial administrators and businessmen:

I'm sickened by their behaviour. No sense of duty and one worry only, to enrich themselves to the maximum thanks to the opium and piastre traffic. I don't support that my men die as veritable heroes while others fill their pockets.

Colonial women

Film footage and photos show well-dressed colonial women gossiping in the street, sitting in cafés with their husbands or lovers, or shopping in fashionable Rue Catinat. Novelist Marguerite Duras, who was raised in a delta town, talks of female colons and:

> *...the marvellous domestic service provided by the houseboys, the vegetation, the dances, the villas, big enough to get lost in, occupied by officials in distant outposts. They wait, these women. They dress just for the sake of dressing. They look at themselves in the shade of their villas...they dream of romance, they already have a huge wardrobe full of more dresses than they know what to do with, added together one by one like time, like long days of waiting. Some go mad.*[8]

Her widowed mother, a school headmistress near Van Long, had bought a sad rice concession as an investment on the Cambodian coast that was disastrously inundated by salt water. Duras's schoolteacher parents had left for Indochina, having been impressed by French government-sponsored advertisements encouraging emigration for a colonial life in Indochina after the First World War.

Planters' life

In 1950, de La Motte was posted as a young lieutenant to command a company of troops mostly of Cambodian origin in a lonely posting up on a rubber plantation in the Tay Ninh region:

> *...the fellow who owned the plantation lived on the Cote d'Azur. They reinvested nothing and the plant was decrepit. He had succeeded people say in listing his company on the bourse de Paris, dished out amazing dividends... enjoying a comfortable fortune even if it was not totally legal.*[9]

The planters who lived in the country lived dangerously: 'These planters were slightly mad not least because half of them were being liquidated by the Viets.' The manager on his plantation 'lived sumptuously...on the table of the dining room there was a bowl full of Russian caviar accompanied by a magnum of champagne...so...a hectic life and steeped in the luxuries of a nabob.'[10]

Returning from a dangerous patrol in the jungle, for de La Motte this was certainly a contrast to be savoured.

Norman Lewis travelled in the Central Highlands and witnessed Indochina's heart of darkness. Michelin was not the only company that treated its employees virtually as slaves of French colonialism:

> *...the native guards brought in a half crazed creature who had escaped from one of the plantations. After having been severely beaten by one of the overseers he had run away and had made a journey through the jungle of three days and three nights to get here. The French (soldiers) treated the man kindly and told them to give him food and shelter. I gathered that it was part of their duty to see that he was sent back but they said they had no intention of doing so.*[11]

The military attitude towards colonialist planters and businessmen (*les colons*) was generally contemptuous, aristocratic officers still infested with a deep antisemitic 'Dreyfus' complex. They held opinions that were especially shaped by their aristocratic disdain of trade, which was beneath them and often Jewish. Labourers were tricked by unscrupulous agents into signing contracts that they did not understand. Many workers were shipped to plantations on south sea islands. They were in effect indentured, which is a nice word for slavery.

Colonialism, xenophobia, racism and resistance

There had been extraordinary hostility to the French from the start of their invasion of Indochina. Nationalist movements became increasingly well organised and their propaganda and leaflets attested to an extreme hatred and violent attitude to the invaders. Annamite xenophobia matched the racism and violence exhibited by many of the French settlers, whose racism was spiced and spurred by fear and the guilty knowledge of the theft they were perpetrating on their subject peoples. An example of the vitriol was a pamphlet issued by nationalist propagandist Phan Boi Chau in 1907:

> *Compared to other powers in the five continents, our country is inferior only to a few, why then do we suffer French 'Protection'...The life of thousands of Vietnamese people is not worth that of a French dog...How can they squat here defecating on our heads?*[12]

Such hatred would boil over into many bloody massacres of French civilians in the First Vietnam War.

By the 1880s, a well organised national insurgency called the C'an Vuong movement was underway. 'Hunt the westerners, kill the Catholics' was their battle cry. They would organise the printing of manifestos and calls to arms and insurrection.[13] In 1884 the Foreign Legion suffered over 600 dead in the campaign to suppress the revolt at Tuyen Quang. From 1893–96, French troops suffered over 700 casualties in guerrilla fighting and several thousand indigenous troops were killed and wounded. In 1896, Paul Bert wrote of '*Annam en au feu avec anarchie absolute et inombrable petites bandes tenant le pays, brulant et pillant.*'[14] (Annam was on fire with total anarchy with guerrilla bands in control, burning and pillaging.) Guerrilla fighting was widespread. There were atrocities on both sides and the French military, which included significant contingents of the Foreign Legion, struggled against rebels who, in a bitter analogy to Custer's massacre at the Big Horn, were often better armed with Winchester repeaters against standard issue single-shot 'chassepots' rifles of the army.

A side-effect of Napoleon III's Mexican imbroglio was the development of the legend of the Foreign Legion, whose stand at la Bataille de Camerone (April 1863) became the bedrock of myth, tradition and soldierly heroism. Celebrated annually, it is a legend that would echo down to the embattled garrison at Dien Bien Phu a hundred years later. (For modern legionnaires, Dien Bien Phu has taken an equal place in the roll call of legionnaire legend.)

Guerrilla war soon became an everyday fact of life. A typical diary entry for a military column read:

> *19/9: a flying column of 70 Legionnaires search a village; a large number of pirates [local people] leave at full speed and run away northwards, led by two men on horseback. These groups fall under fire...A good number of them are left in the field. At 6.15 the village is invaded...A group of twenty-five pirates escaped...half of them are executed...*[15]

In an echo from the future, over 200 'sweeps' were made by French columns 1885–1891, and 259 guard posts were established with local militia. The exact same strategies would be employed by the French and Americans just sixty to eighty years further on. This did not prevent the massacre of 40,000 Christians in 1885, about one third of the total. The problem for the French was that they had conquered an Annamite society that was culturally advanced, with a strong sense of racial identity forged with pride in expunging Chinese imperial dominion. How could the Annamites feel any less strongly about killing the French?

While this social mayhem was going on, high-minded sentiments were being expressed and applauded by the elite local businessmen and functionaries. Harmonious co-development and bestowing the benefits of civilisation was the future. Paul Bert, a former education minister and the resident general in Annam-Tonkin, spoke to a well-disposed local audience in 1886: 'Our two peoples are not made to fight one another but to work together and to complete the one by the other.'[16] Limited representation rights were granted. As part of his plan, education of the local elite became an important part of this mantra. They were needed as civil servants and technicians for the empire. Governor General Beau in 1906 declared that 'these people should recognise the fact that our government offers them a superior education.' He went on to waft grandly and patronisingly about:

> *...the spontaneous homage and deference which exists in the countries of the Far East. It is imposed as a social obligation – the feeling of student for teacher who instructs him.*[17]

It was a patronising romantic subjectivity that had a long life and was flagrantly racist.

At the same time as such high sentiments were being made, soldiers massacred peasants and rebels murdered collaborators: the standard menu of violence in a guerrilla war. Underlying the high-minded French sentiments was racism and a feeling of superiority. In 1861, the deputy commander in Indochina wrote bluntly: 'The government we want to establish in lower Cochinchina will be based on racial superiority.'[18] Jules Harmand in 1892 put it more elegantly but not less brutally:

> *...government and administration of this possession...must be on a paternal form...we must never allow anyone to question our right and our firm intention not to share the roles of leadership and actions that are necessarily the privilege of the conqueror.*[19]

In response to the insurgency, Premier Jules Ferry characterised resistance as mere banditry. 'The Annamese has almost no national spirit,' declared Ferry loftily and speciously. However, in an early sign that colonialism in Indochina would become a left-right domestic political issue, a radical deputy, de Lanessan, concluded differently after a visit to Indochina. 'It is in the name of patriotism that Annam rose after July 15, in the same way that Tonkin had already revolted.'

The background of revolt in Indochina left a trail of bitterness and lives damaged by oppression, which was passed down from one generation to another. Ho Chi Minh's father was a lower Mandarin official caught up in the backdraft of revolt and repression. Likewise, General Giáp was the son of a minor Mandarin and landowner who was a member of the nationalist Ca'n Vuong movement. Social control was enforced by an efficient police force, the Sûreté, established in 1919, and a vast number of informants. The national budget for the police varied from eleven percent in Cochin to nineteen percent in Tonkin.[20]

Economy and society: exploitation and development from 1880–1945

Economic geography of Indochina

Vietnam is a land of two parts from an economic, cultural and social perspective. North (Tonkin) and South (Cochin) are radically different. The large central area is poor, forested and little populated. Its narrow coast supported poor fishing villages. The Central Highlands were occupied by myriad tribes. The mountains of the north-east were mainly Hmong (Meo), White Tai or Black Tai, the latter living on the tops of mountains and highly involved with the opium trade. The Red River delta in the north and the Mekong delta in the south surrounding Hanoi and Saigon respectively held the great majority of the population, seventy-two percent of whom were Annamites (Vietnamese) in 1937. They lived on just ten percent of the land mass.[21]

Total population in 1940 was 22 million, with about fifty-five percent living in the south. Distribution was the shape of a north-south dumbbell. They were ruled and controlled by about 34,000 French, split between Cochinchina and Tonkin fifty-five/forty-five percent.[22] Saigon was the biggest French population centre with three times more colons than Hanoi. Cambodia had a population of about 4 million and Lao 1.5 million. A Khmer minority (known as Khmer Krom) of about half a million to 1 million lived in Cochinchina, an area including Saigon, which had until the end of the seventeenth century been Cambodian. There was also a small Cham Moslem minority from an ancient seafaring civilisation whose cultural detritus of temple complexes can still be seen in the region of Hoi An. Total population of Indochina in 1954 was about 32 million, of whom 14.2 million lived in North Vietnam. Rice cultivation remained the staple agricultural activity for a large part of the population – the delta wetlands of the Red River and the Mekong in the south were the main rice-producing areas. But rice had to be imported to the overcrowded north.

An economic and political vision of French Vietnamese co-development in Indochina

One strand of thought, as promoted by the French, was that France and Annam were entering into a partnership to rule and develop Indochina, large parts of which were highly underdeveloped, notably Lao, Cambodia and the Vietnamese highland. Writing in July 1939, Tien Vien noted: 'the Indochinese Nation will be the logical outcome, the last word in our evolution'.[23] Underlying this idea was the Darwinian concept, very prevalent since the late nineteenth century that the Lao and Khmer were a decadent and dying race, ripe for displacement and exploitation by the Annamites. Given the objective condition of those places, their sparse population and the cultural-political decline in evidence over seven centuries, it is not hard to see why opportunity for economic expansion by the Vietnamese allied with the idea of natural selection.

A contrary concept for the future of Indochina envisioned a federation of five states with traditional division in Annam being run as separate historic entities: Cochin (Saigon), Tonkin (Hanoi) and Annam (Hue). This opposite view was encapsulated in Pham Quynh's commentary published in 1930. 'Both ethnically and logistically Indochina never existed and will never exist...'[24] Pham became education minister and would be executed by the Vietminh along with many thousands of less well-known officials.

Tonkin

Excess population in Tonkin that could not be absorbed in industry meant that wage levels there were one third less than in Cochin. Many migrant workers went south to work on the plantation estates in Annam and Cochin.

Capable administrators such as Governor General Paul Doumer developed Vietnam, or rather its constituent parts Tonkin, Annam and Cochin, separately. In Tonkin in the north there was more focus on heavy industry and mining, including coal and iron ore. Over two million tons of anthracite per annum were produced by 1939. There were pewter, tin and zinc mines. Concrete was a major industry. In Haiphong there was shipbuilding, ship repair, the port and railway yards. However, the heavy industry sector did not require large amounts of labour. With a poor agricultural community producing only small cash surpluses, the knock-on to consumer goods production was weak. Population growth rates were very high especially in the overcrowded Red River delta where peasant farm sizes were about 1 hectare, compared to over 2 in the Mekong delta.[25] As a region Tonkin was always just one natural disaster away from famine, and when this disaster coincided with war the result was catastrophic famine. Saigon, a centre for rice milling with twenty-seven mills,[26] became the hub for processing and international distribution. They economically colonised Cambodia by taking in all their agricultural product for processing. Even today the curved Chinese dows load up rice sack by sack, back by back in the inland Cambodian port of Takeo for onwards transportation through the marshes and reed beds of the *Plain des Joncs* wetlands.

They built railways, roads and hydraulic works to serve major enterprises, but projects that would have served Vietnamese farmers were ignored. Vietnam was a predominately peasant society, and Vietnam's peasants continued to suffer from the usual droughts and floods. Per capita rice consumption declined.

Cochin economy

In Cochinchina, agriculture and plantations were the emphasis with rubber gaining increasing importance as the twentieth century progressed. Tea, coffee, sugar and cashew nuts were also developed. The fertile delta became a major rice exporter. Most of the peasantry in the south, including a large Cambodian minority, were landless estate or farm workers. In a region where nearly fifty percent of the land was controlled by absentee Chinese or French corporate owners, poverty and oppressive work conditions were rife. Not surprisingly this rural Cochin population became fertile soil for communist activity.

Annam and the highlands were also given over to plantations, while coastal regions depended on rice and fishing although the majority of the territory was untamed rainforest and mountains occupied by a small population of indigenous tribes.

In the tribal areas to the north-east and in neighbouring Lao, opium was the major crop and taxes on opium were a major element in colony financing. The main foundations of the economy were rice exports and rubber production. The entirety of the eastern side of Cambodia on the east bank of the Mekong became an economic colony of Cochinchina, with rice, rubber, coffee, tobacco and cashew nut production being absorbed into the Cochin processing system. It still is. Rice barges from the inland Cambodian provincial town of Takeo still run down through tangled waterways, the swaying reed wetlands, and the *Plain des Joncs* to the rice mills near Saigon. Rice production and milled rice increased by about 500 percent between 1880 and 1939.[27] Exports from Cochin accounted for over ninety percent of the country's exports. Rice and rubber alone accounted for fifty-six percent of Indochina exports. Business with metropolitan France accounting for fifty-three to fifty-six percent of exports and imports respectively.[28] Economic activity was maintained at a reasonable level through the war years. An agreement was made with the Japanese to supply them with products, though targets were never achieved. Admiral Decoux's Vichy government's intention was to keep French Indochina in 'being', '*on lutte pour fut maintenue une Indochine francaise.*' [29] (One fights to maintain French Indochina.)

Industry in the south was mainly light industry, and food processing for the internal market, e.g. beer, tobacco products, sugar refining, rice milling, hydraulics, rice wine, consumer products. The entrepreneurs were mainly Chinese, some of whom developed extraordinary wealth. Chinese formed a significant minority in the south of Indochina, about thirty percent of the populations of Saigon and Phnom Penh, where long-established Chinese clan associations' temples, schools and clubs can still be visited.[30]

The French in Vietnam established a monopoly in the production of salt, alcoholic beverages and opium. They taxed consumption of these. They encouraged Vietnamese to buy their opium, and money gained from the opium trade was an important part of the colonial administration's income. A French company, Société Française des Distilleries de l'Indochine (SFDIC), owned by Auguste Raphaël Fontaine, was promoted by then Governor General Paul Doumer and given a monopoly in making and selling alcoholic beverages in Vietnam, all other distilling was banned and severely punished with imprisonment and confiscation of property. From 1902, villagers were even forced to buy fixed per capita quotas of alcohol to try to forestall moonshine operations. It was deeply resented. Corruption was, of course, rife.

Transport

Captain Lucien de Reinach in his posthumously published grand survey of the Lao economy in 1911[31] provided microscopic detail and statistics on the Lao economy, but he also painted, albeit from the viewpoint of Indochina's most decrepit element in Lao, the underlying transport problems of internal communications in the region:

> *...plainly speaking, the roads across marshes, and mountains, along ridges, traversing lines of great slopes and the sides of steep hillsides. In principle they should be repaired each year and graded. The administration is gradually modifying the roads, making them more robust and permanent, and giving them more space on the ravines and watercourses. But it takes time to change the culture of the people to procure a working method that is methodical.*[32]

Similarly in Burma, in British Indochina, the transport network arranged by another exploitative imperialist power was sparse except for the mighty Irrawaddy River, and Somerset Maugham describes pre-war travel in *The Gentleman in the Parlour: A Record of a Journey From Rangoon to Haiphong*, his arduous traverse of the region along mule tracks, including the Shan states, with donkey and packhorse and by foot. The Irrawaddy Flotilla Company might have had over 600 river vessels, but its purpose and that of the colonial administration was the extraction of the teak wealth of Burma, not its economic development for the benefit of the Burmese people.

The topography of Indochina is exceptionally difficult and even the rivers are not especially useful, except in Vietnam where the Mekong delta in particular has been exploited to create the most successful agro-powerhouse in the world. But roads are a means of creating and increasing commerce, providing a road to market, which creates a cash surplus for peasant agricultural products that increases the spending power for farmers and leads to a virtuous circle of trade.

Paucity of good road transport is still a major block to wealth generation in the remoter and poorer parts of South-East Asia.

Governor General Doumer, 1897–1902, planned a national rail network in 1898. By 1936 the north-south coastal rail link was completed but it was never profitable as shipping was far more efficient and the rich simply flew to and from Saigon and Hanoi, the country's two main hubs. The most important transport project was the Hanoi-Kunming rail link to aid commercial flows into Yunnan besides the Black River which, like the Mekong, was not reliably navigable. So there never developed a lucrative trade nexus, unlike Britain's enormously successful Canton-Pearl River-Hong Kong trade. A major feat of engineering, it cost the lives of 60,000 coolies along the 290-mile route, encompassing 172 tunnels, and 107 bridges. The route was completed in 1910,[33] but it underperformed economically because the Yunan was poor. Railway construction in French Indochina up to 1939 outperformed British Burma.[34]

All together there were 2,095 miles of railroad in 1939 and 16,930 miles of road. However, there were no rail links between the component parts of Indochina. The Mekong and the fictitious hopes of a secret way into Chinese trade were the mainsprings of French interest in the Lao state. From a geographic and political point of view the Mekong was the binding *raison d'être* for the contrived geopolitical concept of Indochina, but as a major commercial conduit it was a disappointment, and still is. Saigon was already France's sixth largest port by 1937 and Haiphong was second to Saigon.

Road-building was limited to the service of the main hubs Saigon and Hanoi. The country was so long that north-south communication was served by air for passengers – only the elites – and by ship for commerce or less efficiently by rail. A few poor roads trailed into the highlands, with the title 'Route Coloniale' usually being more impressive than the rough track that the name represented. Communications to Lao and Cambodia were poor. Phnom Penh was mostly served by steam ferry from Saigon via the border town of Chau Doc, and Lao was not properly connected by road until Admiral Decoux's Vichy administration constructed roads to Lao's Mekong panhandle.

Education, culture and identity

Doumer set up a huge array of research institutes, scientific and agricultural, so aping French civil society. He encouraged education for a native elite and Paul Beau and Albert Sarraut continued the policy. However, the number processed through primary and secondary schools was still a tiny fraction of the population, ten percent at primary level and only four percent going beyond. However, under Vichy during the Second World War, the numbers passing through primary education nearly tripled to 287,000 in 1939. In secondary schools, only 465 passed through in 1939, though this increased to 6,550 in 1943. A university was established in Hanoi in 1907 with student numbers increasing from 457 to 1,575 in 1939–44.[35] Admiral Decoux, the wartime Vichy governor general, certainly pushed on the development of Indochina despite the war but the overall achievement of colonialism was poor.

Such cultural institution building did not stop there. An outstanding example of French cultural colonialism was the funding of archaeological work at Ankor Wat and other important sites. A particularly impressive French colonial achievement from 1925 was the appointment of Pondicherry-born Suzanne Kapelles as curator of the Royal Library in Phnom Penh and similarly in Luang Prabang, the Lao capital. These institutions were charged with finding, curating, translating and preserving important Buddhist texts. An outstanding linguist in the ancient Sanskrit language on which Khmer and Lao script is based, she initiated then became first secretary general of the Buddhist Institute of Cambodia, founded with French funding. She later became the chief publications officer for the École Supérieure de Pāli. This educational input even continued under Decoux's Vichy regime with impressive developments in education. However, these were all small bubbles in the sea of culture and education given the size of Indochina and its 22 million inhabitants. Thirst for education from the masses would only start to be quenched by the Vietminh.

France, through its extensive work around Ankor Wat and Buddhist academia in the first half of the twentieth century managed to do in Cambodge what it utterly failed to in the other two states of Indochina: that was to create a strong sense of national identity where none had previously existed in what had been a shabby, failed and cannibalistic monarchy in the mid-nineteenth century that was a satrapy of Siam and on the verge of cultural extinction. By the time King Norodom Sihanouke was appointed to the throne in 1941, Cambodge had a powerful national identity built around the story of Ankor Wat and its iconic building, a building that has adorned all three national flags since independence including that of the infamous Kymer Rouge regime 1975–79. The effect of this was important for the war in Indochina because strong Buddhist belief and national identity forged through the resurrected tradition and the image of King Sihanouke meant that communism had very little traction in the Kingdom. This resulted in protection for Cochin's flank against revolutionary contagion and denying easy refuge for the Vietminh. Another significance was that the potential pool of soldiery, including the large Khmer Krom minority inside Cochin who might otherwise have been available to reinforce the communists in the south, was largely denied to the Vietminh. Khmer and Khmer Krom communities mainly fed recruits into the French Expeditionary Force (FEC) or various militias, such as the one commanded by Lieutenant de La Motte in the rubber estates north of Tay ninh.

When in 1951 Nguyen Binh died outside of the river town Stung Treng in Cambodia, his long manuscript setting out plans for a logistical highway from the north to the south was found on his body. It was the genesis of the Ho Chi Minh trail.

Plantations

Introduced in 1897, rubber rapidly became one of the mainstays of the Cochin exporting economy, rising from 138 tons in 1913 to 9,627 tons in 1927 and 62,000 tons in 1939, making Indochina the third largest producer behind British Malaya and the Dutch East Indies, each of whose production was five times higher. Three large groups including Michelin and the Banque Indochine Group (eleven percent and thirty percent respectively) controlled sixty-five percent of production in 1944. Hectares of rubber production, which was 15,000 in 1919, grew to 133,000 in 1942.[36] By 1930 there were 400 plantations with 80,000 tappers.

The plantations had a particularly poor reputation for slave conditions where, for example, in 1926 seventeen percent of workers died.[37] At Suzannah Plantation, of an establishment of 450, twenty-seven percent per annum died.[38] Companies overlooked sharp and unscrupulous practice by their recruitment agencies, who foisted incomprehensible and onerous contracts on impoverished and uneducated labourers. Michelin employed 6,000 tappers, one of whom, Pham Van Phu, remembered that the overseers would:

> *...humiliate a worker then thrash him on his buttocks or whip him on the soles of the feet until he was in tatters, after which he is chained up and left without food for two or three days.*[39]

They were paid but were forced to pay high prices for food and necessities at company shops. Pham led the first tappers' strike. He was subsequently arrested for sedition and sentenced to Poulu Condore. Taking the *nom de guerre* Tran Tu Binh, he would become a senior officer in the VPA.

Tourism

Tourism started to develop. The Grand Hotel opened at Ankor Wat in 1932. A resort area was developed by the sea at Cap St Jean within easy reach of Saigon. Phu Quoc island began to be developed for hotel business, and shares in Phu Quoc Hotels would be marketed in Saigon. Kep started to become a playground for French expats with modernist villas and hotels clustered around a modest beach and with a Riviera-style strip of coastal road beneath a string of jungle-clad hills and idyllic palm-fringed Rabbit Island just a few kilometres off the shore. Most of the coast was covered with mangrove swamps.

Taxes

French taxing of local populations was extremely harsh and predatory. There was not much given back to the populace in return for the taxes. For example, Cambodia had the grand sum of thirteen colonial administrators in 1900. In 1926, there was a tax revolt in Kampong Channang in which the chief tax collector was hacked to death. To this day there are tribes buried deep in the Cambodian jungle of Banteay Sre province who fled there to escape French taxes. Tax policy was oppressive in Indochina, yet another reason why the French were roundly hated by the majority of the population. Taxes represented the high cost of French administration, which was about sixty percent of the local government budget. This was mainly for the salaries of officials. As the richest part of the Indochina Union, this figure improved for Cochin from 55.9% of the government budget in 1913 to 38.3% in 1939. But it was nonetheless a high cost, especially in comparison to the British and the Dutch colonies. One French official for every 7,900 locals considerably outdistanced Dutch Java by a factor of 1,000 percent.[40] Taxes through monopolies on alcohol, tobacco and opium as well as indirect taxes on basic producers plus direct taxes meant that rates were oppressive on poorer people, ranging from sixteen percent in Annam to seventeen percent in Tonkin and thirty-five percent in Cochin. Corvée labour, a hangover from the pre-colonial period, was gradually monetised. From 1913 to 1939, taxes doubled. Apart from taxes, Corvée labour was a major propellant for revolutionary activity in pre-war Indochina, especially in Lao where it was bitterly resented by the hill tribes.

To support the large number of expensive expatriate officials, France imposed a heavy tax burden, representing 12.4% of GDP in 1925, significantly larger than other French colonies but also much larger than comparable developing economies. It provided a strong background to general discontent since French colonisation of the country, though in truth the practice was long established in feudal Indochina. Nevertheless, it provided ample opportunity for political propaganda. One of the headline pages of *La Paria* – newspaper organ of the oppressed peoples of Indochina published by Nguyễn Ái Quốc (Ho Chi Minh) in Paris in 1922 – headlined:

> *Forced labour of indigenous people*
>
> *Civilian expenditures to GDP were close: 6.7% in France against 7.6% in the empire; as France is nine times richer than its empire, when measured in per capita terms the size of the metropolitan state is eleven times larger. If military*

expenditures are added this ratio gets even higher, as those directly allocated to the colonies, in particular through conscription, represent only a tiny share of the money spent by France for the defence of the metropolitan territory and for its imperial projection.[41]

It would not be wrong to describe French colonialism in Indochina as exploitative and parasitic to a much greater extent even than other colonial regimes.

In Vietnam, and elsewhere in Indochina, Frenchmen grabbed lands and they built plantations that produced rubber and other forest products. In the first decades of the twentieth century, France's colonial administration in Vietnam encouraged French commercial enterprises. The 1920s saw an investment boom, with a huge issuance of company stock 1915–29, for many types of enterprise for cement companies, hotel companies etc., 640 million francs (inflation adjusted) compared to 212 million 1880–1914. However, the main gainers in the capitalist boom were the Chinese. By 1920, Chinese business Banque de l'Indochine was the largest, especially for exchange operations, deposits and trade transactions.[42] Share transactions also increased.

'Our Indochina will be the first among the industrial economies of Asia,'[43] boasted the governor general in 1921. He was right, but the depression, the war and communism delayed the blossoming until the twenty-first century. There would be no sunny upland under communist oppression.

The Accumulation of Capital, written by Rosa Luxemburg and published in 1913, advanced the theory that capitalist expansion takes place in foreign markets or less developed parts of the same country, with capitalists needing to destroy these underdeveloped places as independent entities to rake in surplus profit. This frenzied fight for markets leads to war and is ultimately self-defeating:

Militarism fulfils a quite definite function in the history of capital, accompanying as it does every historical phase of accumulation. It plays a decisive part in the first stages of european capitalism, in the period of the so called 'primitive accumulation' as a means of conquering the new world.[44]

Rosa Luxemburg may sometimes have overstated her case, but when she accused the early imperialists of a desire 'to destroy the social organisations of primitive societies so that the means of production may be appropriated…' In the case of Indochina she was not wrong.

Chancers, gangs and crooks

Indochina attracted its fair share of scallywags and chancers, and those down on their luck in France. They did not all join the Foreign Legion. Some posed as respectable travellers. One such comedian was Andre Malraux, a pen-pusher of middling French novels who, having spent or speculated away his wife's money, needed to find some more to maintain his airs and graces. He would later plagiarise Conrad's seminal work, *The Heart of Darkness*, with his pathetic rendering in his book *Three Kings*. Ironically in view of his later career, in 1925 Malraux helped to organise the Young Annam League and founded a newspaper, *L'Indochine*, to champion Vietnamese independence. It was one of a growing number of newspapers and journals.

Travelling out to Indochina, Malraux posed as a tourist on his way to Ankor Wat, where he surreptitiously hired a gang to carve off and load onto transport priceless archaeological artifacts from Ankor Wat. His intention was to sell the objects on the booming market in Paris. His criminal machinations and art theft did not go unnoticed by the authorities. Arrested, Malraux was sent to trial in Hanoi and received a prison sentence for theft. Malraux would re-emerge as a resistance hero towards the end of the war in 1945, becoming one of de Gaulle's creatures. He attached himself like a limpet to the rising star of the general, becoming in the 1951 election his verbose and florid warm-up act at de Gaulle's crypto-fascist rallies. Having been a progressive in the 1920s, this unctuous chancer became, like his patron, an ultra-nationalist and imperialist. After the general had re-emerged again as first president of the Fifth Republic, Malraux the 'charlatan', 'convicted thief' and cultural larcenist would become minister for culture in the Fifth Republic, a post he held for a remarkable thirteen years. The post came with a sumptuous grace and favour apartment in Palais Royal. He was not the only comedian in de Gaulle's entourage.

After the Second World War in particular, the 'entertainment' business and the black market in Saigon became particularly important, much less so than Hanoi, which had a significantly smaller Chinese population. Prostitution, nightclubs and gambling centred on Chinese Cholon. Nevertheless, it was controlled in large part by the home-grown Binh Xuyen criminal society, which also controlled a large territory to the south of Saigon. The excesses of corruption and decadence were symbolised by gambling at the infamous Grand Monde casino. The major criminal activity involved bribery and corruption around import-export permits and the fixed piastre-France exchange rate:

> *Under-invoicing was a common practice. French investigators found examples of a shipment of watches, worth 21 million francs, that was valued at 149 million; bolts of cloth worth 10 million francs that were valued at 28 million;*

> *and worthless old boat motors valued at nearly 39 million francs. In some cases parties made requests for piastre transfers for entirely fictitious imports.*[45]

Bank profits soared. Jacques Despuech's 1953 blockbuster *Trafic de Piastres* exposed what one French newspaper called 'the scandal of the century'.

Predominantly an agricultural society in 1945

A predominantly agricultural society geared to the rhythms of monsoon and the cycle of rice-growing, the staple diet. Modernity and manufactured products intruded from time to time, but this description of rural life was as true in 1945 as it is of much of Indochina today. This passage below from Mae Elliott's book describes rural Tonkin in the early 1950s but it could be a contemporary depiction of many places in Vietnam, Cambodia, Lao or Burma:

> *The village presented an idyllic tableaux. Men walked along the narrow pathways between the rice fields, on their way to tend their crops, their spades and hoes propped on their shoulders. Women dressed in brown clothes, their heads wrapped in black turbans or hidden behind large conical hats, bent over vegetables or walked to and from, rhythmically swinging the bamboo baskets suspended at each end of their shoulder poles. Little boys herded water buffaloes, riding on the backs of the animals, or lay in the grass, while their charges munched peacefully nearby. A lone heron pecked in the fields and then took off, spreading its large wings in the sunlight. Smoke rose lazily from hundreds of cooking fires into the afternoon sky, as the villagers settled in and waited for their meal. I remember the village so different from the noises of Hanoi: the occasional barking of dogs, the crowing of roosters, the floating notes of flutes attached to kites, clinking of bowls in baskets – like tinkling music – as women walked to and from the river where they washed their dishes after meals.*[46]

CHAPTER III

Statesmen

Ho Chi Minh

Born in around 1890 in a small town near Hue, Nguyễn Ái Quốc became known to history as Ho Chi Minh, probably the most enigmatic and quixotic figure in communist revolutionary history. His life transcended the entire era of modern Vietnam in the twentieth century, but it represented much more besides. Famously to become 'Uncle Ho', Ho was indeed an avuncular figure. A convinced nationalist, ideas inherited from his father, he became an itinerant worker and ship's galley boy, sailing around the world from about 1911 to 1917. With five different birthdates and over 200 pseudonyms, plus the dubious burnishing of his biography for 'revolutionary purposes', the history of his life is quite vague and somewhat mysterious. Even the leading biographer of his early years, Sophie Quinn-Judge, finds it difficult to pin down many hard facts.[1] The fact that he was a Comintern undercover agent or a wanted revolutionary on the run for much of his life only accentuates the elusive nature of the man's life. Secrecy was seared into his DNA from the moment he took the ship to the USSR in 1923.

Apart from being a galley boy and cooking assistant on ships, he claimed to have been variously employed as a baker in New York, a chef at the Parker House in Boston and a manager for General Motors. He also lived in Brooklyn. Moving to London, he is famously believed to have worked as a pastry chef for the renowned Escoffier at the Savoy Hotel. In Paris he was able to use his knowledge to recommend the best croissant shop to croissant-lover Deng Xiao Ping, a fellow revolutionary exile. But again, no proof. A picture of him in 1912 has him wearing a bowler hat, heavy overcoat and scarf. His right hand holds a cigarette. He was a chain-smoker throughout his life and was often photographed with a cigarette in his hand. In 1917 Ho moved to France and engaged in a life of writing and political activism for nationalist causes. Other early pictures show him in dapper three-piece suits attending the Socialist International at Tours in December 1920, when the French Communist Party (PCF) was formed after a split in the socialist movement. Ho became a founding member. At this time, he also came to know Zhou Enlai and other future Chinese communist leaders. Pictures of him show a handsome young man with a thick flop of black hair wearing a high stiff Edwardian collar and a black morning coat. His expression is slightly manic. He had the eyes and demeanour of a fanatic, although in company he was not devoid of humour. In fact, his charm and wit were renowned. He enjoyed the common touch.

Despite these somewhat lowly meanderings, Ho had grown up in fairly comfortable bourgeois and intellectual circumstances around Hue, where his father was variously a Confucian scholar and imperial magistrate until fired for refusing to serve the French. Ho would later reminisce on how his father would often wonder 'who would help them to remove the yoke of French control?'[2]

His devotion to the struggles of the toiling masses was quite genuine and based on the fact that he had toiled amongst them all over the world. He developed as an excellent communicator and propagandist. With over 100,000 Vietnamese workers and soldiers shipped in to France during the First World War, there was plenty of opportunity to radicalise these vulnerable and exploited workers, some 250 of whom acquired police files.[3] However, Ho's only concrete revolutionary achievement was to use his experience and connections in political gastronomy, hitting the French elite where it hurt most, by organising a strike of 150 Vietnamese chefs.

During the Versailles Treaty negotiations, his presentation on the wrongs of colonialism to President Wilson was ignored. But his brilliance in polemic was illustrated by the way that he picked up Wilson's mantra of 'self-determination', which would result in plebiscites in Silesia and other parts of Eastern Europe, as a way of spotlighting the plight of colonial peoples in Indochina, i.e why does self-determination only apply in Europe? The notoriety he gained from his public polemic brought him to the attention of Comintern agents and Manuilsky, its head. It also brought him to the attention of the Sûréte (secret police) and the colonies minister Albert Sarraut. Cast as Public Enemy No. 1, France's secret police, their agents and informers would hound him across the globe for the next twenty-five years. Sarraut was soon reporting to Hanoi that Ai Quoc (Ho) had been tracked boarding a steamer bound for Russia, posing as a Chinese businessman. It was the start of the cloak and dagger, picaresque life of an itinerant revolutionary, a life of aliases. In Paris he left behind a desolated young seamstress. There would be others left behind on the revolutionary road. Invited to Moscow by the Soviets, by dint of hard work and excellent skills as a polemicist he rapidly came to the attention of the high echelons of the Socialist International, which had been renamed the Comintern, an organisation for the international communist brotherhood. It became the tool of the USSR for propagating communism around the world, although the truth is that after 1924 the Comintern was mainly a front for the realpolitik interests of Stalin's Russian foreign policy. However, despite meeting Zinoviev, Voroshilov and Trotsky, Ho was never granted his request to meet his hero Lenin.

By November 1924, Ho was in Canton and Shanghai as the leading organiser of the Comintern in Asia. From 1926, he resided with Borodin, Soviet head of mission to Chiang Kai Shek in Canton. Ho was in Thailand between 1927–32, where he founded the Thai Communist Party. He built strong relationships with the Chinese communist leadership at this time and was lucky to escape Shanghai in 1933 with the Sûreté on his tail when the Chinese party's leadership fled the city. When returning from Moscow in 1938, he visited Mao in the Yenan where Ho declared that the CCP was 'the elder brother of the Vietnamese people.'[4] Ho would oscillate between Moscow and China throughout his political life, always trying to keep on good terms with both.

Ho was arrested in Hong Kong and subsequently released with the aid of liberal English human rights lawyers in Hong Kong and London, including Sir Stafford Cripps who took pity on the gentleman. Hong Kong lawyer Frank Loseby would later be honoured by Ho as a national saviour. The rescue was a double-edged blessing because it would later raise suspicions in Moscow during the purge leading to him being investigated. Had he been handed over to the Sûreté following their extradition request, he would probably have been guillotined.

His escape coincided with the failed communist rebellion in Cochin and the near destruction of nearly all leading ICP cadres. However, it was too convenient and in the paranoid world of Moscow politics in the 1930s, he was suspected as a double agent. His former associations and meetings with Zinoviev and Trotsky, with whom he was photographed, might well have been fatal. A Vietnamese political rival who was on the three-man commission of inquiry in Moscow tried to condemn him. He escaped. So having survived liquidation by both the Sûreté and Lavrenti Beria's NKVD, he must have reflected on the precarious life of a revolutionary where you were as much threatened by your own side as by the enemy. After a six-year sojourn in Moscow from 1933–8 teaching, writing and studying, Ho was transferred for duties in Indochina. He was lucky to escape Stalin's 'purges', which wiped out so many 'Old Bolsheviks', but the experience trained him in keeping his real opinions to himself. Ho's elusive character and thoughts were rooted in the need to survive the Stalinist terror of the 1930s. That the party came first was stamped into his DNA, as senior defector Nguyễn Duy Thanh noted:

> *...we thought they would put first and foremost the cause of their country over party interests...our expectations were sadly belied...the communist showed up their fascist tendency...*[5]

Perhaps Ho was lucky or just skilful in finding a way out of what must have been a most ghastly and stressful era in Moscow. Perhaps his former association with Stalin's drinking crony and ally Voroshilov saved him, or possibly someone remembered his eulogy of Lenin published in Pravda in 1924. In 1936 Zinoviev was executed on trumped-up charges as a traitor and Trotsky would be assassinated in Mexico City by Stalin's agent with an ice axe hacked into his brain. It was with some relief and after much pleading for a useful task that he left for Asia in 1938, perhaps in the nick of time. It was the harshest of schools to learn about political infighting and survival. The terror and the purges would not diminish his admiration for Stalin.

The other main purpose of the Comintern in respect of Vietnam was to unify a troubled and factionalised communist movement at the first congress in Hong Kong, which was split between the Revolutionary Youth League founded by Ho Chi Minh in 1928, that became the Vietnamese Communist Party in 1929, and the breakaway Annam Communist Party. Another splinter. the League of Indochinese Communists, was separately established. The splits were linked to north-south rivalry and regional tensions between Tonkin-, Saigon- and Annam-based organisations.

Amidst the revolutionary hubbub, Ho found time to get married to a much younger Chinese woman, defending himself to his Vietnamese colleagues by citing his need of a cook and housekeeper. His personal life was functional. During his time in the Viet Bac in the guerrilla war phase, he fathered a child. Later the party procured another young woman to serve his needs, but she left him when he refused to marry her. Ho was married to the revolution.

Under instruction from the Comintern in Moscow, all the warring factions were told to come together at the first congress on 3–7 February 1930. A resolution prepared by Ho for the Vietnamese Communist Party prior to the congress in Hong Kong declared:

> *Excluding these countries is a wrong thing because Annam, Cambodia and Laos should closely contact each other in terms of politics and economics even though they do not share a language, custom, and ethic.*

The party resolved to give up the name 'Vietnamese Communist Party' and to take the new name 'Indochinese Communist Party'.

Some years later the Second Party Congress would be less subtle in their approach, declaring, 'Vietnamese party reserves the right to supervise the activities of its brother parties in Cambodia and Laos.'

Ironically, the Vietnamese communists were as imperialist and racist as the French when it came to relations with Lao and Cambodian 'sister' parties and the indigenous tribes.

Quite naturally, the Vietnamese who historically had coveted suzerainty over 'Cambodia' and 'Lao' in competition with Thailand, saw the opportunity to take these dysfunctional and weak entities under their wing, just as the Chinese sought to do the same with them.

As if readying to defend himself, Ho wrote a critique of ICP failings during its premature revolutionary upsurge in 1930–31: 'The majority of the comrades – even those in charge – do not understand the meaning of "the bourgeois democratic revolution".' He also criticised mechanistic decisions on strikes and action without consideration of the objective facts. Ho was suspicious of 'self-indulgent ideology' and complained that 'they allowed themselves to be influenced by intellectual elements.'[6] This showed his practical and non-doctrinaire attitudes to revolution. It was a stance that would get him into trouble with ideological hard-liners throughout his political career. The old and experienced cadres had been imprisoned or killed. His standing waned, which is indicated by the fact that he was only listed thirteenth in the Central Committee list that was voted at the Macao Congress in 1935. In Indochina the party was badly damaged by effective Sûreté operations. Many of the leadership were imprisoned including future leaders Pham Van Dong, Le Duan, Le Duc Tho. Party leader Van Hong, died in prison.

Communist cadres may have only numbered 4,000 at the end of the Second World War, but they were the best organised political party in a country that was in a state of chaos. By the time the fighting started in early 1947, this number had increased to 15,000, of whom just eight percent were women in 1948.[7] Nationalist groupings were bigger but less organised or centrally directed. This is the environment in which communism with its centralised and power-focused energy thrives. Ho's master trick would be to link and embed communism into a broad front political movement called the 'Vietminh', which emphasised nationalism. By degrees he would look to marginalise then liquidate rival nationalist groups.

An avuncular, charming and humorous man, Ho could be very disarming. He was funny and liked to tease his young *protégés* or flirt with them if they were women. De Gaulle's man in Asia, Major Sainteny, a committed imperialist and his counterpart in negotiation from October to March 1945–1946, recognised in him an 'indomitable will that flashed in his eyes illuminating his features and made one understand that he would not hesitate to do anything to achieve his goals.' Journalist Lacouture, in 1946, was press officer for Leclerc's high command. In a later interview he noted:

> *I have never hidden the very favourable impression that they* [the Vietminh leadership] *made on me…The 'charm' under whose spell I was,* [also touched] *Of course, we knew that they weren't lambs, that they had blood on their hands.*[8]

In the crowded field of Vietnamese nationalism, Ho used assassination to clear his path to power. Ho is suspected to have handed over nationalist rival Boi Chau to the deadly custody of the Sûreté. Another nationalist, Bui Quang Chieu, was assassinated together with his teenage daughter. Many thousands of others were murdered, especially members of VQNDD, the most effective nationalist party. Interviewed by French journalist Daniel Guerin, Ho Chi Minh more or less admitted to the assassination of his erstwhile brother revolutionary Tạ Thu Thâu, leader of the very effective Vietnamese Trotskyists who were especially powerful in Saigon. He was gunned down on the beach after a mock trial. In an unusually candid response, Ho remarked that 'people who do not follow the line which I have set out will be crushed.' Apparently emotional he commented that 'Thâu was a great patriot and we mourn him.'[9] It is the communist way of politics: power at any cost even if you had to assassinate an admired friend, because communist monopoly of power is the essential and non-negotiable mantra of Marxist-Leninism.

Uniquely, Ho's revolutionary life straddled the top leadership over both the first and second generations of both the Soviet and the Chinese communist parties. Ho kept neutral or simply avoided the ideological disputes that emerged as Mao tried to put himself on a god-like par with Marx, Lenin and Stalin. Polemics, propaganda, organisation and revolutionary strategy were his skills, not ideology.

Perhaps his time in the Comintern and his witnessing of the Moscow purges had inured him to dabbling in that 'pseudo-religious' Marxist ideology. When asked once, he replied that he left that sort of thing to Mao.[10] Ho was not a fan of complexity. He would have found the idea of ideological theorising akin to dancing on a pin-head. It required a more luxuriant intellectual pomposity that was better suited to others, such as leftist pro-Chinese ideologue Truong Chin. The Communist Party became Ho's vehicle for national liberation but the ideology suited him well enough. He felt no need to add to the lexicon of communist thought. Apologists for Ho might like to describe him as a Menshevik trapped in a Bolshevik body. Ultimately though, for Ho, the end justified the means.

'Nothing is more precious than independence and freedom' was a favourite maxim.[11] In fact, he tied Indochina to foreign and alien dogmas. These dogmas would be imposed arbitrarily, with cruel policies directed by China and the Soviet Union from the playbook of European originated totalitarian communism.

When Bernard Fall, the famed Vietnam commentator and historian, quizzed Ho about his mysterious life, Ho played with him mischievously using his delicate sense of irony and self-deprecation: 'An old man likes to have a little air of mystery about himself. I'm sure you will understand that.'

His humble disposition was most disarming. Charmed members of the American OSS thought of him as 'a sweet guy'.[12] Major Patti, who was also suffering from a mild dose of Stockholm syndrome, said of him on 1 September in an official report, 'sensible and well balanced…I am afraid the French will have to deal with him.'[13] The US state department had a more realistic view informed through their Hanoi consulate as to the bloody purge that was underway. Despite the humility, a personality cult quickly arose around his name, especially when it was realised that the shabby old man in a faded blue tunic, who sat on the second row of the 16 August party congress, was none other than a living fusion of Ho Chi Minh and the famous revolutionary leader and polemicist Nguyễn Ái Quốc.[14] Already by August 1945:

> *...printed portraits...were sold everywhere. Each of us schoolboys tried to buy one... if the adults had not already done so. We were hungry to have a national hero to worship.*[15]

Someone to lead them out of the wilderness into the promised land of freedom, independence and communism. There can be little doubt that Ho did not especially enjoy the personality cult or need it as a psychological prop, but as the ultimate pragmatist he believed that the building of his brand name would enhance the chances of national independence and revolution, by establishing the political legitimacy of the regime in the minds of the people. The political religion of 'Ho' underpinned Vietnam's political legitimacy and still does. Political expediency was always the ultimate *raison d'être* of a communist leader for a personality cult, whether it was Mao, Stalin or Kim il Sung, but some needed the adulation. A confident man, comfortable in his own skin, Ho did not need the cult as a prop for a warped ego.

General Gallagher met Ho in Hanoi but, while having respect for him, defined him as a 'product of Moscow', and he understood that Ho 'represented the real aspirations of the Vietnamese people for independence.'[16] However Ho tried, he could not escape the 'revolutionary tag' nor the obvious truth as to his background. The Americans hated the French colonial system but were heavily conflicted because of their detestation of communism. After victory over Nazi Germany, the warm glow of allied victory soon wore off as Soviet actions in Eastern Europe raised doubts as to Stalin's good faith. US attitude to Soviet clients changed. By early October 1945, Ho's flirtation with the US had cooled as Ho realised that they would eventually come down on the French side.[17]

Unlike other communist leaders, Ho was not an obvious autocrat, senselessly cruel, corrupted by power and luxury. He ruled the party by persuasion and the power of argument. He enjoyed the Asian advantage of respect for age, the veneration for a charismatic and wise old man. Giáp noted: 'He set great store by collective work.'[18] In consequence of his frugal lifestyle and demeanour, he became a sort of sage or saint to communism; a prophet to lead his people, easily displacing the notoriously decadent and absentee Emperor Bao Dai. France's ultimate political problem was the lack of a legitimate and popular alternative to Ho Chi Minh. Ho's apparent 'purity' and aestheticism appealed to the Buddhist peasantry.

Moreover, in Vietnam he stood more or less alone in his generation of revolutionaries. In Asia, with age came veneration:

> *...a frail looking older man...unlike the others who were dressed in western style clothes, Ho wore a frayed, high collared Chinese jacket. On his feet he had rubber sandals...he gave off an air of fragility, almost sickliness.*[19]

What cannot be doubted is his mental toughness, work ethic and perseverance.

A great controversy of history, was Ho a Titoist-type communist-patriot or a real international communist ultimately loyal to Moscow? It was a question much discussed in the US state department. We need look no further than Giáp who knew him best. Ho:

> *...found in Lenin's doctrines 'the symbol of faith and torch of hope'. Thus fifty years ago the great Vietnamese patriot had found in Marxism-Leninism the only way to liberation, the 'revolutionary way' for our people...the people oppressed by imperialism.*[20]

Tito would, in contrast to Ho, refuse to take orders from Moscow and insisted on equality of relations with Stalin's USSR.

Ho's reputation has been given a huge number of puffs over the years by useful idiots and fellow traveller Marxists such as Eric Hobsbawm, who describes him in saintly and nauseatingly hagiographical terms as 'the liberator of Vietnam, *the noble* Ho Chi Minh.'[21] (Author's emphasis.) However, some compliments are due, because it would be true to say that Ho Chi Minh was perhaps the nicest and wittiest mass murderer in history.

Soviet policy for Asia: Revolution, nationalism and anti-colonialism

Ho proclaimed at a communist congress in Halle 1920 that 'the struggles for national independence of the colonies must be linked with the class movement of the proletariat of the motherland.'[22]

That Ho was called to Moscow in 1923 was not simply fortuitous. After the failures of Kurt Eisner's Bavarian Revolution were Bela Kun's communist uprisings in Budapest and Spartacist, led by Karl Liebknecht and Rosa Luxemburg, all in 1919. Following these failures, Karl Radek was given responsibility for German policy but, realising that the KPD was not ready, he caused the abortion of the planned German uprising in 1923. With Germany stabilising, fantasies of a revolutionary sweep across western Europe faded. Blocked in the west the Soviet leadership needed to focus on the revolutionary possibilities in the east. Radek would be-reassigned to develop Far Eastern policy.

They were concerned to foster worldwide revolution as a matter of protection and survival. Lenin noted in Sochineniya that 'Russia, India, China, etc., constitute a gigantic majority of the population of the world.'[23] In April 1923, Stalin wrote that they could 'shake to its foundations the deep rearguard of imperialism – the eastern colonial and semi colonial countries – revolutionize them, and thus hasten revolution (in the west),'[24] even in places which, under Marxist dogma, were not ripe for revolution.

Some communists from these underdeveloped colonial societies, such as Roy and Ho, were impatient for national liberation using communism as a vehicle of national revolution. Communist parties also started to re-adjust their policies under pressure from within such as that given in an article in *l'Humanite* that was critical of PCF: 'What our parties have done in this respect is equal to nothing.'[25]

The tendency of Ho and Roy to prioritise the nationalistic aspects was deviationist heresy according to Lenin, but he was soon dead and Stalin's 'socialism in one country' became the dogma of the day.

An Indian communist from Bengal, Nahindra Roy, claimed that 'the rising in the colonies will perhaps play a dominant role in the problem of world revolution'. Impassioned anti-colonialism struck a chord in Indochina and around the world. Ho's declaration of independence on 2 December 1945 may have quoted the American constitution but it also launched this bitter cry: 'They have weakened our race with opium and alcohol…they have sucked us dry…'

The USSR's strategy was to support progressive nationalist parties such as Chiang Kai Shek's KMT, believing that such an alliance was a preparatory stage to full revolution. Such common front policies would inform Ho's founding of the broad Vietminh movement.

The head of the Comintern, Manuilsky, noted the 'obligation to support bourgeois national movements in colonial countries.'[26] However, such orthodox thinking would be turned on its head by Mao's successful revolution based on the peasant masses in China 1929–50. It was highly significant too for Ho and the Vietminh, because it offered them an ideological and practical pathway to victory in a similar agricultural society.

Progress was soon being made. At the IKKI congress February–March 1926, it was noted in the opening session that there were 'numerous delegations from the east.'[27]

The Comintern was increasingly used as a front for Stalin's Russian foreign policy under the socialism in one country mantra and became a front for Russian imperialism. Politically useful for the Soviets, in 1933 Soviet head of communications Lozovosky would talk of: 'The awakening of the national liberation movement in the east...represent a new fact of first rate importance.'[28]

Ho became a valuable asset to the Comintern so his time in Moscow was fairly brief, just enough to inculcate him into Marxist Leninist thinking and train him as a revolutionary field agent, before his posting to aid Borodin in China.

Due to the deadlock in Western Europe, suddenly revolution in Asia became a priority, with exceptional focus put on China and the anti-colonialist and revolutionary Kuomintang, which as a bourgeois party fitted Marx's idea as to the stages of revolutionary development. Soviet moves to focus on the east represented a strategic turn aimed at both undermining the economic and political structures of their sworn enemies amongst the colonialist powers, aligning the communist brand with oppressed colonial peoples while simultaneously ending the USSR's political isolation.

The Vietminh

Who were the Vietminh? When war with Japan broke out between the US and the other imperialist powers, Ho immediately realised that it presented a golden opportunity for revolution and independence in Indochina. As early as February 1943 after the Battle of the Midway had decisively tipped the scales in the Pacific, the standing committee of the party central committee had called for 'urgent preparation for insurrection', so that 'when the opportunity arises, the masses can be mobilised for the fight.'[29] As a veteran from the heady days of the First World War when the worldwide revolution had started and four empires came crashing down, Ho was well attuned to the possibilities. With France surrendering after the Nazi blitzkrieg in Europe, Ho arranged for the proclamation on 6 June 1941 calling 'fellow countrymen' to arms, 'now the opportunity has come for our liberation.'[30] Ho immediately established the 'Vietminh', a cross-party nationalist coalition, a movement rather than a party as such that subsumed the Communist Party, which pulled the strings even so. Their rival, the VNQDD, was a radical xenophobic nationalist group. The VNQDD was ideologically aligned with the Kuomintang in China and was pitched against Japanese imperialism just as much as French imperialism and the Vietminh communists.

From Jingxi, some 65km inside the Chinese border, Ho plotted the establishment of bases in border areas and the recruitment of troops for the nascent Vietminh People's Army (VPA). Such a manoeuvre was necessary for Ho because his ICP was only growing slowly due to a very efficient and brutal Sûreté. After the premature revolutions in 1930–31 and 1940, there were only 5,000 members and by August 1945, that number had not changed. However, about one third were in prison.[31] Apart from that the communists needed to present themselves in a more acceptable light to the allies and Indochinese peasantry, as nationalists rather than purveyors of an alien theology. Common ownership was, of course, anathema to the Indochinese peasanty.

The culmination of failed and premature uprisings, factionalism and efficiently ruthless work by the Sûreté meant that the communist movement in Indochina was very weak by the time opportunity beckoned in 1945. Thinly spread and suddenly overwhelmed by untrained volunteers, as Goscha points out, Ho struggled to impose the will of the Communist Party on the Vietminh movement.[32] It was a far cry from Lenin's ideal of a tightly disciplined elite who would be capable of operating the dictatorship of the proletariat. There was particular weakness in the south where in Saigon it was the Trotskyists who were making the revolutionary running. Luckily for Ho, in the hiatus following the Japanese surrender and then the Chinese occupation he would have some time to build up the institution, the ICP, at the heart of his power-grab. A year after the creation of the DRV there were 15,000 party members. In parallel to that he needed to construct an economic basis for his new regime, which needed money for armaments and munitions, a theme brilliantly researched and developed in Goscha's seminal new study. Ho's early seizure of the initiative gave him considerable advantages. With the Decoux officialdom still in prison, upon surrender the Japanese handed him the keys to the kingdom, which allowed Ho time to develop the new state and use his international links to develop cash-earning trade relations.

In his book *The Jaws of War*, Bui Diem, from an elite family, describes how 'we felt that our country was on the verge of striking out for its freedom, and there wasn't a soul who didn't want to be a part of that.'[33]

He joined the Dai Viet nationalist party. He noted: 'It was not generally known for example, that the Vietminh was communist-controlled.'[34] The common front policy was a success. A typical and clever tactic of experienced communist organisers such as Ho. Communist cadres could rely on naïve and youthful enthusiasm. 'Its *raison d'être* was national freedom,' recalled Diem. 'It was a moment of innocence.'[35]

In May 1941, the 8th Plenum of the Communist Party Central Committee took place in north-eastern Vietnam. The party decided to build a broad-based national front together with other nationalist parties and non-communist nationalists. 'World War II had broken out…great changes favourable to the revolution would certainly be produced.'[36] Called the Vietminh, it would be a communist front organisation, open to all nationalists who would be flattered with executive committee appointments. But the ICP's party machinery and military wing always came under communist control. Eight thousand kilometres away in London, General de Gaulle as head of the Free French Government in exile was mapping out a very different way forward.

General Charles de Gaulle and the road from Brazzaville

General de Gaulle did not have greatness thrust upon him, he thrust himself on greatness.

Influenced by his school teacher father, who was a follower of French authoritarian anti-democratic and extreme right ideologist Charles Maurras, creator of Action Française, de Gaulle would retain the same mystical and romantic proto fascist or falangist belief in France as a gloriously united nation under a single leader, where party politics had no place. Crucially, however, unlike others, he did not envisage France as a junior partner to Hitler's Germany or indeed anyone else.

De Gaulle had a vision of France and a charisma that rallied the nation as no one else could. His self-belief became France's self-belief. And he could also on occasions be very politically astute. He was a symbol that embodied the resurrection of French honour and hope after the Second World War. De Gaulle was intrepid in standing alone against the tide of German fascism, which so many of the French elite accepted either by easy going necessity or in many cases with wholehearted collaboration.[37]

Leader of a tank regiment, in 1940 he launched one of the few serious attempts to halt the German Panzer onslaught in northern France. While his beacon of freedom was dim at first the fire shone ever brighter with allied victories. By 1944, victory was clearly in sight and de Gaulle needed a vison of recovery to give to his people; not so much physical or material recovery but recovery of national honour and morale. De Gaulle delivered for his people a confident vision of France's place in the world. Imperialism and its restoration were integral to his vision of the future.

As allied victory came into view both in the Atlantic region and the Pacific in 1943, de Gaulle, who had maintained backchannel links to elements within the French Indochina administration, believed that he would in future be able to call upon the French Army in Indochina to rise up and massacre the Japanese garrison there.[38] De Gaulle in full Walter Mitty mode was the great ruler of a large-scale map of the world – pushing around phantom markers in an empire that existed mainly on paper and at the courtesy of the allies if there was any substance. British officials thought he was utterly deluded, as indeed he was. On 15 March 1945, de Gaulle in his finest falangist-speak rhetoric declared that 'by the trials of all the blood of the soldiers at this moment a solemn pact is sealed between France and the peoples of the Indochinese Union.' That he would eventually succeed shows the extent to which single-minded delusional behaviour can succeed in politics.

De Gaulle and France did not question the need to re-establish empire. 'I was able to lead the country to salvation' he wrote:

> *She was seen to have re-emerged from the abyss as an independent and victorious state;* in possession of her empire*; receiving the surrender of the Reich alongside Russia, America and England; formally accepting, on an equal footing with them, the capitulation of Japan: acceding as one of the big five to the rank of founder member of the United Nations Organisation and member of the Security Council with the right of veto.* (Author's emphasis.)

Only by Churchill's insistence against Roosevelt and Truman's objections was France allowed these sops to its former glory. De Gaulle's references to 'equal footing' were obviously ludicrous and delusional, but perhaps a necessary balm for the bruised egos and self-identity of France's elites.

De Gaulle regarded the sheer size of France's imperial mission as a marker of its national greatness and claims to world power. At Brazzaville in 1944, de Gaulle in his opening speech declared that France would lead its empire of 110 million people:

> …because it is France, that is to say the nation whose immortal genius *is designated for the initiatives which, by degrees, raise men to the heights of dignity and fraternity where, someday, all will be able to unite. There is henceforth, as a result, between the Metropolis and the empire, a definitive link.* (Author's emphasis.)

This speech reveals the typical conceits that its empire was an integral part of metropolitan France, that the empire's citizens were somehow French citizens and the ludicrous claim that there was unaltered loyalty following France's defeat. Some of his colonial audience might have been wondering why such 'immortal genius' had been so easily defeated by Germany. De Gaulle made the address in the open air. What is remarkable about the picture of the general before the throng is that all the faces are white, although there were black leaders in attendance, presumably at the back.

De Gaulle added:

> *The progress of 110 million men and women who live under our flag shall be in a federative form, which time will make more precise little by little, but which shall be indicated in our constitution right at the start, to allow for this development.*

From the French chateaux at Rambouillet, as he followed behind the allied front, de Gaulle issued a bulletin on 24 August 1944 on behalf of *la seule France, de la vrai France, de la France eternelle.* (The only France, the true France of the eternal France.) Looking through the patriotic drivel, he was understandably seeking the monopoly of legitimacy and sole sovereign right for his Free French government, in the rejection of any assertions by the Vichy government, or by the communist-backed Resistance who, having done nearly all the resistance, should tamely hand over their weapons, which they did.

As part of de Gaulle's gambit to assume the mantle of political legitimacy, the Free French administration followed the allied invasion in June 1944 by immediately putting out propaganda to the French people as to the recovery of empire with Indochina as a priority. Efforts were made to insert a French corps into the reconquest forces in Asia, but the allies and the US in particular were not supportive and had enough problems without French posturing. Economically important, the propaganda also pressed on the sentiments and the glory of empire. Imperial trumpeting in Free French publications of such lachrymose sentiments as these from Comandante Bonnet, who aped Gaullist drivel with purple prose about 'jewels in the crown' and 'Indochina' as a mistress 'with honeyed lips and warm embraces'. An army magazine carried a picture of a Sherman tank in front of the face of Jayaraman VII in front of the Bayon Temple at Ankor Wat.[39] There was also the usual patronising and racist claptrap. Alongside this there was a major recruitment campaign for the French Expeditionary Force (FEC). All this vainglory from a defeated nation that had made only a minor contribution to the war effort was patently ridiculous. De Gaulle failed to realise that France had lost its prestige in Indochina. By contrast, experienced colon administrator Paul Mus, who had escaped by foot to China when the Japanese took over, commented realistically, 'In even the most remote villages, the peasants knew that the positions of power in Indochina were now reversed.'[40]

On 24 March 1945, de Gaulle approved the release of an official government document announcing the following: '...the *five* countries which comprise the Indochinese Federation, which are distinctive by civilisation, race and traditions, shall keep their discrete characteristics within the federation.'[41] (Author's emphasis.) Promises included the following freedom under Union Francais: press freedom, freedom of belief, freedom of association, meetings, and free elections. A happy time for de Gaulle basking in the adulation of the crowds. Writing in the third person in his memoirs, he writes further, 'de Gaulle was acclaimed everywhere.'

De Gaulle was determined in his insistence on France's imperial mission, even in the darkest and most dependent hours. At Bayeux on 16 June 1946, he made a speech boasting:

> *...it was here that those who never ceded even in the circumstances the rallying instinct of the nation and the return of French power so giving these events* [the D-day landings by French soldiers] *their decisive justification.*

These words were spoken just as Admiral d'Argenlieu, his associate and appointee as the high commissioner in Indochina, was launching an unauthorised attack on the nascent independent state of Vietnam and the Anglo-American alliance. De Gaulle went on in his Bayeux speech:

> *...the state has safeguarded its rights, its dignity, its authority even in the midst of the vicissitudes and* actions of some and their intrigues... *the state is now capable of re-establishing its authority in regard to national unity and* imperial unity, to assemble all forms of la patrie and of the French Union, to be carried to victory. (Author's emphasis.)

High-flown as ever, but the key point was the absolute integration of imperial unity into the French union and patrie. As ludicrous as it might seem in the twenty-first century, this imperialist sense of mission was a deeply felt emotion and mindset of the French ruling elites, and not just in the army. He added, 'The state is now capable of re-establishing its authority in regards to national unity and *imperial unity*.' (Author's emphasis.)

Such sentiments were extremely well established and would remain so even with the increasing ebb of imperialist sentiment in the general populace through the course of the 1940s and early 1950s. This imprecision about the form of a union was deliberate. It was the most deliberate attempt to cover up what was always intended as a system of de facto 'colony-protectorate' in all but name. This issue of exact legal definition would be at the heart of endless negotiation and word-play with both Ho Chi Minh and Emperor Bao Dai over the exact meaning of their relationship with the French Union. The issue of course was, where is ultimate power held?

De Gaulle's position on Indochina was made abundantly clear by his appointee, acolyte and man on the spot, Admiral d'Argenlieu, who was quoted by *France-Soir* on 2 January 1947. 'Negotiations with Ho Chi Minh are no longer on the agenda.' In truth they had always been ruled out except under terms of submission.

The Soviets, whom de Gaulle had courted so assiduously during the war, also supported him, supposing rightly that he would be a thorn in the side of the Anglo-American alliance. In his dalliance with the USSR, de Gaulle was already playing with the idea of building a French neutralist power standing independently between the Russians and the 'Anglo-Saxon' block. Detested by Roosevelt but supported by Churchill, France and de Gaulle would be elevated and gifted, quite against any merit or due or earned rights, to the first rank of world nations by being given a seat at the United Nations and a share in the occupation of Germany. De Gaulle, whose country had been liberated at considerable Anglo-Saxon human cost and treasure, became an object example of the unrelenting and bottomless bitterness of the ingrate. A difficult and quarrelsome ally, Churchill said of his relationship with de Gaulle's French government in exile, 'Of all the crosses I have borne in my life, the heaviest was the Cross of Lorraine.'

France had deep-vested interests in its colonies, not just the emotional ones alluded to by de Gaulle, but economic interests in trade, plantations and other French company investments, as well as lucrative employment in colonial officialdom, civil and military, which would be jeopardised by ushering in genuine democracy. Naturally, these interests would always seek to stop independence and representative government. Except for Algeria, by far the most important economic assets in the French empire resided in French Indochina. Moreover, thanks to the accommodation of Admiral Decoux's Vichy regime with Japan, those interests had largely been preserved and even expanded during the war.

Ho and Indochina

The decision to combine Lao and Cambodia with Vietnam under the ICP umbrella was taken in Moscow. Ho was more focused on developing a Vietnamese consciousness and understood rightly that it would have better resonance especially when faced with competition with the Vietnam National Party VNQDD. Although Ho would have preferred a focus on Vietnam, it would open him up again to attacks from the ideological purists. They would seek to tag him with nationalist *petit bourgeois* slanders. Whatever Ho's views on party names, he and the party held a thoroughly imperialist attitude to the smaller nations of Indochina. In 1951, Dang Lao Dong of the Vietnamese Workers Party may have declared at the 1 February congress, 'the people of Vietnam are willing to enter long-term co-operation with Laos and Cambodia,'[42] but the truth of the relationship, which was quite different, was revealed in a Top Secret Vietminh document (1 November 1951) captured by the French. It explained that 'the Vietnamese Party reserves the right to supervise the activities of its brother parties in Cambodia and Laos.'[43] Strangely symmetrical, the Vietminh imperialist attitude to Indochina exactly mirrored the French one.

At the same congress, just one year after the Chinese Red Army arrived at the border, the subterfuge of the Vietminh was finally abandoned, but the wolf did not fully discard its sheep's clothing. The launch of the communists under the new name The Vietnam Worker's Party still kept the word 'communist' out of the limelight but openly broadcast the Marxist-Leninist agenda. Party secretary Troung Chinh noted: 'If we keep the name of "Communist Party", a certain number of landowners, progressive intellectuals and members of religious sects would not want to follow us.'[44]

In 1952, the Vietminh Information Centre put out this official statement from the VWP party, which envisaged federation of the three Indochina countries:

> *In the common interests of the three peoples, the people of Vietnam are willing to enter into long-term co-operation with the peoples of Laos and Cambodia with a view to bringing about an independent, free, strong and prosperous federation of the states of Vietnam, Laos, and Cambodia* if the three peoples so desire. (Author's emphasis. It should be added that communists never make allowances for free will.)[45]

The only difference to the French proposals was that it would be communist- and Vietnamese-dominated. Prince Souphanouvong's boast about 'forming an independent and united Pathet Lao'[46] were simply untrue, because the Pathet Lao were a front for the Vietminh and The Red Prince was a front for the Pathet Lao, and none of them was the least bit representative of Lao.

The USSR provided a model for Indochinese internal relationships. While the Soviet Union had many republics, it retained a centralised Communist Party structure subject to the rules of 'democratic centralism'. Stalin's ideological study produced at Lenin's request on the nationalities question in Russia served as the basis of the USSR's constitutional structure. (*Marxism and the National Question*, by Joseph Stalin 1913 – widely republished in the USSR in 1935.) It seemed only natural that Vietnam would rule Indochina as Russia did the USSR. The cure for nationalistic fracturing was, Stalin wrote:

> *To unite locally the workers of all nationalities of Russia into single, integral collective bodies, to unite these collective bodies into a single party...a party structure of this kind...presumes wide autonomy for the regions within the single integral party.*[47]

Despite lofty ideals of 'wide autonomy for the region', the concept could neither escape Russian xenophobia nor Communist Party control. In the USSR, Stalin's attitudes to Jews and other nationalities was certainly racist. When they met, Stalin, according to Khruschev's account, viewed Ho with condescending racist disdain. 'Dictatorship of the Proletariat' leant itself easily to the idea of 'dictatorship of primitive tribes or minorities'. Ho and his fellow communists' concept of relations with the 'sister parties' would be Stalinist. He would have been familiar with Stalin's work, his hero's work, especially as he was living in Moscow when it was re-published with much fanfare in 1935.

Apart from natural dispositions of the Vietnamese towards racism, xenophobia or superiority in regard to Khmer, hill tribes or Lao, such views were historically ingrained and predated the French, though the French certainly added to the stereotype. There is no doubt that Khmer, Lao and tribal Indochina were culturally and educationally more backward. Such difference fuelled natural xenophobia and arrogant behaviour. Laos would become of serious interest for the Viet communists, but mainly for strategic and military reasons. Cambodia was of little interest so long as Vietminh soldiers could range freely along its eastern border. Moreover, reasons of 'face' would mean that 'liberation' and revolution in neighbouring countries would not be prioritised or even allowed before Vietnam's revolution was complete. The left and internationalist wing of the Communist Party was loath to give up the idea of communist Indochina. Troung Chinh told Colonel Patti in 1945 that (based on Stalin's works), they 'held that the terms were compatible' i.e. Indochina and Vietnam.[48] It was analogous to the relationship of the USSR to Russia. Ho, in a secret document written in November 1951, envisaged a future re-unification 'with a great union of Vietnam-Laos and Cambodia'. He maintained this view until the end of his life, writing in his testament of 1965 that Vietnam should have dominant relations with the Lao and Cambodia. As with Stalin and Mao, the uncomfortable truth for 'useful idiots' and 'fellow travellers' is that kindly Uncle Ho was as much an imperialist as the French, perhaps more so. The splitting of the ICP into three different national parties was just a cynical political tactic, much as the Union of Soviet Socialist Republics (USSR) was a cover for Russian imperialism. The minnow parties were controlled by the DRV. I am firmly confident that the fraternal parties and countries will have to unite again. In fact, the original testament was more explicit in referencing control of Lao and Cambodia. But the document has been doctored by the communist regime.

General Giáp

Unlike Ho Chi Minh, Giáp could not cook. In his younger days he was once sacked from his cooking rota by his fellow residents in a communal living arrangement and made the permanent dish-washer. Born in 1902, like Ho, Giáp had had a middle-class upbringing in the region round Hue, the imperial capital. Smaller even than Ho, Giáp was truly bantam-sized. He was fiercely nationalistic and, apart from his genuine revolutionary fervour, he had more than a grudge to settle with the French. A landowner and rentier, his nationalistic and rebellious father, sometimes a minor imperial official, was jailed by the French. He died in prison in 1919. Giáp's wife, also a communist believer, was incarcerated in a French prison. His infant daughter died in prison too and his sister was guillotined. France could count on a reckoning.

Giáp described how his wife died in atrocious circumstances. Quang Thai (Giáp's wife) was a secret liaison agent of the party, who was, according to Giáp, 'tortured just to the limits of life, incapable of supporting the suffering any longer, she committed suicide in her cell…the French should be suspended by their thumbs and beaten to death.'[49]

He became a driven man.

Giáp studied variously in Hue and Hanoi. However, his studies were always interrupted by political activity. Falling foul of the police, even at the age of 14, by 1924 he had been recruited into radical leftist circles. He obtained a degree in law and political science in Hanoi but failed his qualification exams to become a lawyer due to his inattention to studies. Most of his time was spent writing journalistic articles for various revolutionary and nationalist publications. This did not pay enough for him to earn a living so, having failed to become a lawyer in Hanoi, he taught history in a private school. A favourite subject was the French Revolution and the life of Napoleon. A student who later joined a nationalist group and still later became the South Vietnamese ambassador to Washington, Bui Diem recalled the enthusiastic young teacher who taught them about the French Revolution and Napoleon's military campaigns. The young Giáp 'taught me the difference between being a slave and being a free man.'[50]

Strong music was also a passion and he especially liked listening to Beethoven. Just as significant was his study of the legendary guerrilla fighter Lawrence of Arabia, whose autobiographical adventure *Seven Pillars of Wisdom* was a favourite.

He met Ho in Canton and was immediately taken up by the veteran revolutionary who recognised his intelligence, commitment and energy. Giáp soon became Ho's *protégé* and a leading member of the party. When there was dirty work to be done, and there was plenty, Giáp was delegated to do it. Other less than attractive sides to Giáp were his bombast, pride and arrogance, his lack of self-honesty, and his stilted ideological excess.

Giáp was a romantic. He envisioned himself as a heroic revolutionary and military leader. He also had a romantic's appreciation of nature. Describing the conference in Darlat in April 1946, Giáp writes of a walk he took from his hotel:

> *…the path was covered in needles. Wild flowers grown on the banks of the stream. The town was quiet, the air was cool and the scenery beautiful…The cool pines and murmuring pines drew me on.*[51]

The other side of his romanticism was a callousness about death. He would openly declare that the number of deaths on the revolutionary road was quite immaterial in the context of the final result.

Typical of his melodramatic and pompous revolutionary-style bombast was his reflective description of the founding of the army in 1944:

> *We forgot that we were only 34 human beings equipped with rudimentary weapons. We imagined ourselves to be an army of steel, not to be defeated by any force, ready to destroy the enemy.*

Therefore, Giáp suffered jealousy and fear from party colleagues, similarly to Trotsky in the USSR, with the happy exception for him that he was an insider and pure Vietnamese, whereas Trotsky had joined the party late and was Jewish.

Giáp's career came under a shadow in 1945 when he took over the reigns as stand-in for Ho, who made an extended trip to France to try and work out a compromise with the post-war French government over the political shape of Vietnam. Giáp showed ruthless competence in Ho's absence, liquidating an estimated 6,000 political opponents. For a communist, the revolutionary end justified the means. However, power and opportunity seemed to go to his head. He took to wearing the white suit and club ties of the French elite, and worse, much worse, he pursued an open dalliance for some months with Hanoi's most famous dancer. Giáp was seen with her in public, frequenting the bars, cafés and restaurants of Hanoi's French quarter.

When Ho returned he ended the affair, then introduced Giáp to a more suitable ideological match, which led to marriage and four children. Nevertheless, the damage was done. Giáp had handed his rivals a stick with which to beat him and he would forever live in the shadow of revolutionary moral shame. Communists have a controlling puritanism in matters of sex, although private reality for those at the top of communist systems is often quite different. (Note the lives of Mao, Trotsky, Tito, Castro, Beria and many others. Ho Chi Minh was serviced with young women cadres ready to 'sacrifice themselves for the revolution'.)

There is a comic picture of the young Giáp incongruously dressed in his elegant white suit and tie standing beside a taller dishevelled Ho in shorts, revealing his spindly legs. Ho wears a ragged shirt, his wispy beard giving him the air of an eccentric Confucian scholar. In the picture Giáp looks a little sheepish and distinctly uncomfortable.

Too famous and heroic to be side-lined completely, and too talented not be used to the end of the second Indochina War in 1976, Giáp would never get the top job in Vietnam. Without Ho (and Ho's longevity as a protector) Giáp, whose star shone very brightly, may well have been removed or liquidated by more dour and mediocre 'political' rivals; people of lesser talent, apparatchiks like Le Duan, who lurked and schemed quietly in the shadows.

General Westmoreland criticised his nemesis as being wasteful of soldiers and decried his martial fame on the basis that he could have won the war had he been free to sacrifice as many men as Giáp. Former secretary of defence McNamara told Giáp in person that Vietnam had lost 3.2 million while the US had lost 58,000. However, in the history books, Giáp is the renowned and revered marshal while Westmoreland and McNamara have been tossed into the dustbin of military history.

Attuned to Marxist-Leninist focus on power, Ho and Giáp well understood that it was only winning that counted.

CHAPTER IV

French Terror

French terror and the justice system

Nguyễn Ái Quốc (Ho) writing about the rape and murder of villagers by soldiers in 1925:

> *Sadistic acts of colonialism are innumerable and incredibly cruel.*

A report in *Le Petit Parisien* in May 1930 described how:

> *In one and the same day, I saw the tribunal of Hanoi condemn a young Vietnamese student, who had committed the crime of writing a patriotic song, to three years in confinement...and a French fireman, who has killed for a trifle a worker, by kicking him with his boots, with a suspended sentence of three months in prison.*

According to Andree Viollis:

> *...the methods* [of the Sûreté] *also included deprivation of food, bastinado* [caning on the soles of the feet], *pins hammered under the nails, half hanging, deprivation of water, pincers on the temples* [to force the eyes outward] *and a number of others that are not printable.*

The level of violence used by France was revealed in trial reporting of legionnaires accused of murder, as reported by *La Franche-Indochine*, Hanoi, 12 June 1933:

> ***Lieutenant Lemoanne:*** *I received the orders of Commandant Lambert to kill all prisoners. On occasion, I captured communists in* flagrante delicto *and executed them forthwith.*
>
> ***The president:*** *You had prisoners tortured.*
>
> ***Lamoanne:*** *That was to influence the population.*
>
> *They were only following orders. The accused were acquitted.*

Poulu Condore (Con Son Island Prison), and political resistance in Indochina

Founded 1 February 1862, the official report of the prison's opening said:

> *...from today, the archipelago of Con Son* [Poulu Condore] *with its magisterial mountains, sea and blue sky pure and clean, will be transformed into a hell on earth.*[1]

Admiral Bonard, commander of the French expeditionary forces, said it was for 'dangerous men, prisoners and bad elements.' The latter soon came to be understood to be nationalist and revolutionary, although common criminals formed the majority at first. The island soon gained an ugly reputation: poor food, brutal treatment and rampant disease with little medical attention meant that few prisoners ever returned. In 1898 there were 404 deaths from 767 inmates due to beriberi. The prison soon became the favoured destination for many political prisoners from amongst the nationalist societies, such as KDDH 'new learning group' and later the VNQDD, groups who continued to resist French rule.

Cayenne, French Guiana, was the recipient of most of the 8,000 prisoners exported from Indochina between 1862–1937:

> *Prisoners from Indochina almost always occupied one of three roles: domestic servant, agricultural worker, or fisherman. Indeed, the stereotype that Indochinese (especially Vietnamese) were diligent workers sometimes assisted them in getting lighter, less guarded, tasks. For example, Cambodians were often put into domestic agricultural work, including attempts at rice cultivation* [they] *had a virtual monopoly over fishing.*[2]

The death rate in transit was usually high. Of 600 shipped on *La Martiniere* to Cayenne, only 200 survived 1906–10. Vietnamese poet Dieu, a prisoner who had escaped the prison in Guiana, wrote: 'How much misery shall my own stock endure? Extinction is mirrored glaringly before my eyes.' He would write a book in Chinese called *Vietnamese Revolutionaries in Exile.* Deaths were, according to the inspecting Dr Fernet, 'due to the exclusive diet of rice...hardly anything but rice and rotten fish. Scurvy also increased.'

There were 22,989 prisoners in 1932, of which 7,942, thirty-six percent, were political prisoners. In 1933, *L'Humanite* denounced treatment reserved for party members:

> *...comrade Doan van Hieu detainee at Poulou Condore accused of taking part in the demonstration against murderous Corvée labour was decapitated on the 10th June. Sending prisoners to Poulou Condore is a suspended death sentence. It just requires one provocation for them to be found guilty of rebellion and executed.*[3]

Future prime minister Pham van Dong, who was imprisoned from 1929, taught political economics at the prison in Block 2, specially designated for political prisoners, from 1930–31. After the failed uprisings in these years, the prison system was crammed with communists, Trotskyists and nationalists: 'Block 2 was a great school of anti-French teaching between 1934–45; the crucible of revolt against our flag.'[4] They were housed in three immense halls in Block 2. Other inmates included Le Duc Tho and future leader and party general secretary Le Duan, Vietminh commander in Cochin, Nguyễn Binh, southern Vietminh military leader, and Trotskyist leader Tạ Thu Thâu.

Poulu Condore came to represent the entire system of oppression and cruelty of French rule in Indochina. French rule became so globally notorious that even the future president of the United States, Franklin Roosevelt, became impassioned as to the cause of freedom. In Indochina, political prisoners became martyrs. 'Living in a two-meter cage…a metal bed with ropes. They tie you to it and turn on the electricity. They call our screams "prison music",' wrote Nguyễn Thi Ngia, the ICP leader who was executed in 1933.

When writer and poet Nguyễn An Ninh died in detention, his poem *vivre et mourir…c'est laissez mourir seulement son corps mourir pour la patrie*[5] (to live and die) became a symbol for nationalism, and he was eulogised by future nationalist leader President Ngo Dinh Diem.

The future Ho Chi Minh, Nguyễn Ái Quốc, wrote an article in Paris about the 1918 prison revolt and massacre: 'It was exactly that, the justice of the French in Indochina.' Such stories of the island became the folk law of the revolution. Trinh Cuc, a Chinese man originally from Hainan, became a communist activist working in a restaurant in Cholon. The effectiveness of such propaganda influenced him to record that:

> *The Vietnamese people were arrested and imprisoned, some in Con Son* [Poulu Condore]. *The stories that came back from the prisoners about torture and starvation were hair-raising.*[6]

In other symbolism, the prison also became a battleground for the communists and nationalist groupings, sometimes leading to massed fights with improvised bladed weapons. In one of these fights, future Vietminh military commander in Cochin, Nguyễn Binh, who had been sentenced to five years in Poulu Condore 1929–34, lost an eye as he defended a communist friend.

On 11 August 1936, France's new popular front government (socialists and communists) released 1,532 prisoners, including about 500 from Poulu Condore.[7] The prison would become full again under Admiral Decoux's Vichy regime. When the Japanese took over in March 1945, they released 1,500 political prisoners. After General Leclerc restored French rule, the island would fill up yet again between 1946–54.

CHAPTER V

War and Revolution 1940–45

French surrender, and revolutionary opportunity

Vichy, the Japanese and Admiral Decoux 1940–45

Admiral Decoux was offered and accepted the position of governor general on 27 June 1940. It was hardly a position he could refuse, not least because he was given the nomination by his superior, Admiral Darlan.

Despite British attempts at an accommodation, Decoux noted that he 'ordered the British offers to be rejected, due to the event at Mers-El-Kabir, it was impossible to negotiate.' [1]

After the French defeat in June 1940, diplomatic niceties were cast aside. The Japanese sent Colonel Sato to visit Decoux. 'A typical brutal Japanese soldier, ambitious and violent,'[2] he demanded rights of passage again and the use of air fields and ports, facilities for storage of munitions and food, and the cessation of Yunnan railway operations, which had been busy supplying Chinese forces through Haiphong. Finally signed on 30 August, the treaty was hardly a drawn-out negotiation between equals. Decoux described the main points:

> *Japan recognised Vichy sovereignty, France admitted the pre-eminent power of Japan in the Far East and accorded certain military facilities to Japan so that they could terminate the problems in the 'Japanese incident', and a military convention between the two sides would be drawn up to regulate the processes of the political accord.*

The products needed most in Japan were cotton, rice, castor oil and coal. Huge acreages of land were turned over to cotton and castor oil production at the expense of rice. When there were not enough ships to move rice from the Mekong delta to Tonkin, an estimated 1–2 million people starved to death 1944–45. There was plenty of rice stored in Saigon but no ships. By 1945, the nation was desperate for hope, change and revolution. For many, starvation was a spur to radicalisation and communism. Mai Elliott's sister Thang joined the communists because:

> *In Thang's case the decision was emotional. Among my siblings, Thang is perhaps the most morally pure person, someone with a strong sense of right and wrong and an unshakeable sense of duty ... the famine had horrified her.*

To this day, Vietnamese school children are taught that French imperialists caused the great famine 1944–45. It is a great communist lie. Starvation was caused by terrible flooding, the shortage or withholding of Japanese ships to move rice from the south, the hoarding of grain by the Japanese, and the exigencies of war.

Japan surrenders, and the Vietminh takeover in Tonkin

The collapse of Vichy and then Nazi Germany gave an enormous spur to Ho Chi Minh's Vietminh, and armed resistance to the Japanese occupiers became more pronounced. Japanese patience with Vichy was wearing thin. When Paris fell to the allies, the Japanese issued an ultimatum; effectively it was a demand for military surrender. Not waiting for an answer, they took over anyway on 9 March 1945. In the north, the French garrison at Lang Son fought then fell back in a long march to China. Colonel Alessandri arrived there with several thousand troops after an epic march, but other garrisons simply surrendered and were then locked up in their own prisons. The coup against French power was a shock, a serious blow and major complication affecting de Gaulle's hopes of a smooth recovery of their colony.[3]

In Lao, the French garrison under General Sabattier also beat a retreat into China, having given up on the idea of developing a base for resistance following some OSS arranged flights of American aircraft to a remote and little known airstrip just over the Lao border at a little border town, Dien Bien Phu. Despite de Gaulle's orders to Sabattier to stay in Indochina to act as a focal point for the French recovery of empire, there was no chance of realising his dreams because these second class colonial troops, operating without logistical support, could not hold out against tough Japanese professionals, let alone begin a reconquest.

Ninety-six US combat missions helped slow down the pursuing Japanese army.[4] Blinded by his frantic efforts to recover France's glory, map-bound de Gaulle had not the slightest practical understanding of topographical, logistical or military realities in Indochina.

Ho remarked on the Japanese takeover when reporting to his OSS friends. 'The French imperialist wolf was consumed by the fascist Japanese hyena.'[5] Ho could only have been delighted to see the enemies of independence at each other's throats, and he would have known well that Japan's days were also numbered. Churchill had no intention of allowing the French to play any role in Asia. There were too many complications wherever de Gaulle became involved. According to Admiral Decoux, the Japanese takeover was marked by a rapid 'transformation in radio broadcast propaganda from Radio Saigon. However, despite the precautions they could not entirely cover up the odour of defeat.'[6]

The OSS, who had sent in advisers to try to improve the effectiveness of the resistance, became close to Ho, who made great efforts to accommodate them. They also wanted to collect escapees and downed bomber pilots, for which reason a young lieutenant codenamed 'John' was parachuted into the Vietminh jungle area at Bac Kan. John reported that Ho was 'a very sweet guy' whose essential characteristic was 'gentleness'. When separated for a while, Ho sent John a letter:

> *I feel weaker since you left. Maybe I'll have to follow your advice – move to some place where food is easy to get, to improve health...I'm sending you a bottle of wine I hope you like it.*

Ho was solicitous of all Americans who came into his purview. He was politically focused, and at first this paid off in terms of an excellent relationship with OSS officers in Indochina and in China. This played well with senior officers, such as OSS's General Wedemeyer, who hated the British and French. He reported to ambassador Hurley who:

> *...had increasing evidence that the British, French, and Dutch are working... for the attainment of imperialistic policies and he felt we should do nothing to assist them in their endeavours which run counter to US policy.*[7]

The purpose of the OSS was to encourage the Vietminh to attack and kill Japanese. Ho and Giáp made a show of doing this with a few highly staged attacks on lonely outposts. Historian David Marr, the authority on Vietnam in 1945, estimates that their pinprick attacks on Japanese outposts killed about fifty of the enemy. However, the main point of friendliness with the Americans was from Ho's point of view to secure arms and money as well as to emasculate US will to intervene and close down the communist-led Vietminh. Hidden from view, the Vietminh took the arms but put their energies to using them to assassinate and wipe out their nationalist rivals, such as the Dai Viet, or seek revenge on agents of the Sûreté.[8] Like their Red Army brothers in China, Ho's strategy was to avoid wasting his armed assets on the Japanese but to prepare to wipe out the nationalist rivals who had foolishly spent their strength on the fag-end of Japanese imperialism.

By July there were perhaps 80,000 Vietminh adherent Tonkin, Amman and Cochin, 50,000, 20,000 and 10,000 respectively.[9]

Ho was so well attuned to international politics, and so well informed through the Comintern, that he understood immediately the significance of the atomic bomb drop on Hiroshima on 7 August 1945. Even before Japan surrendered on 12 August, Ho Chi Minh was mobilising for an uprising. He moved fast to exploit the situation and achieve a *fait accompli* before the French came back. There was therefore a classic vacuum of power and Marxist-Leninists, who sniff power like a shark does blood, moved in very quickly. Ho rallied a people's congress of various nationalist groups who endorsed what the Central Committee of the Indochina Communist Party had already decided on at their meeting three days prior on 13 August. On 14 August, Ho launched his bid for power. With razor-sharp instincts for power, Ho was a worthy *protégé* of Lenin, whose masterful *coup d'état* in St Petersburg (Petrograd) in October 1917 set a standard for what a focused and highly disciplined revolutionary minority could do in a time of upheaval and chaos. 'The decisive hour has struck for the destiny of our people,' proclaimed Ho. 'Forward! Forward! Under the banner of the Vietminh, let us valiantly march forward!'

Upon the Japanese surrender, Giáp notes: 'The Revolution broke out like a whirlwind within only a few days.'[10] The outbreak of euphoria was entirely spontaneous. Ho knew that the job of a Leninist revolutionary was to take control of the mob in order to control the passion and energy, to guide it in the direction of socialist revolution. Ho needed to grab the moment because 'most people did not know who the representatives of the new power were.' However, the years of hard work and ground organisation since 1941 paid dividends now. Giáp describes some details of how the organisation kicked into action: 'A cyclist would stop at a street corner and shout through his megaphone "Fellow citizens, please assemble at X for a rally".'[11]

De Gaulle was also alive to the possibilities and opportunities and reacted immediately to try to exploit what little leverage he had through his representative in Kunming, Sainteny, a talented and experienced Indochina administrator. Just after the Japanese surrender, Lieutenant de Beaucorps, who was leading a marine partisan unit in Halong Bay, received an urgent message from de Gaulle's representative in Kunming. 'You will shortly be assigned to a new post: Sainteny.'[12] Sainteny, head of M5, based in Kunming and representing France's interests in Asia, led a team of special marine commandoes, supported by OSS logistics, *Operation Normandie*, with Beaucorps in command, consisting of camouflaged armed junks with French marines in the Gulf of Tonkin on spying and raiding missions amongst the islands and in the delta.

It was suggested that de Beaucorps, a young lieutenant, should be parachuted in to Tonkin to take over the administration of Indochina. The plan was obviously fanciful and demonstrates the extent to which de Gaulle was completely uninformed and deluded about the actual situation. De Gaulle was so bitter that he cut his nose off to spite his face. On de Gaulle's orders, Admiral Decoux remained under Japanese detention, even after the surrender.

His Vichy troops remained in internment while the Vietminh took over the country. De Gaulle's plan to sprinkle a few junior officers over the country was clearly ridiculous.

De Beaucorps was relieved of his *Operation Normandie* command to focus on the new task, but the fantasy operation was soon brought down to earth. After discussions with Sainteny and his staff, de Beaucorps notes: 'Like me they were convinced that all French who parachuted into Tonkin would rapidly be arrested and imprisoned.[13] De Gaulle's hairbrained scheme was referred to contemptuously by Giáp:[14] 'They [the French] were unaware of the deep changes and most of them were caught by our men…[or] by the Japanese.' And the Japanese were not unhelpful to the Vietminh. They made a deliberate policy decision to set up independent puppet governments as a 'poison pill' to bequeath to the hated European colonialists who were on the way back. Having no illusions at this stage that they could avoid losing the war, it was a political scorched-earth policy. Like the French, Japan too had had illusions as to their great mission in the 'co-prosperity sphere'.

The five-month gap in which French officialdom was removed was critical in helping Ho Chi Minh into power. When the Japanese surrendered, Ho was in pole-position to launch his bid for power. There were no French officials or troops in a position to stop him.

Within two weeks of Hirohito's announcement of the Japanese surrender, Ho was on his way to Hanoi. In those two weeks the Communist Party had paved the way for his arrival and taken control of the main levers of power in Hanoi while the Japanese Army simply stood aside and let it happen. Japanese commanders even helped by maintaining the imprisonment of French soldiers and administrators, including the increasingly frustrated Vichy viceroy Admiral Decoux. The disarming of Japanese troops would take time. In the north this would be done by the Kuomintang Army above the 16th Parallel in a decision taken at Yalta in February 1945 without French representation. We can see Roosevelt's anti-French hand in this. Below the 16th, the British Army would have the task of occupation. In huge areas of the country there would be a vacuum of power in towns and villages because neither the British or even the Chinese with their 200,000-man army had resources in place to cover anything but Hanoi, Haiphong and Saigon.

The Vietminh moved into this vacuum. Insurrection committees were set up in towns and villages nationwide. In Hue they put 15,000 people into the streets on 23 August. A letter from Hue's insurrection committee 'sent King Bao Dai a letter demanding his abdication.'[15] On 30 August, Bao Dai duly obliged. Having been so recently installed by the Japanese as emperor, he was gone, with 10,000 Japanese troops standing aside to let it happen. Soon the whole country was bedecked with banners and agitprop slogans, which played heavily on nationalism and independence rather than social revolution, which was the eventual objective of the communist-dominated Vietminh. Slogans such as 'Vietnam for the Vietnamese', 'Down with French colonialism', 'Independence or death', and 'Support President Ho Chi Minh' were especially popular.[16]

Locked up at Loc Ninh, Decoux's unhappiness increased as orders failed to come through for his release and resumption of power. Although he heard about the Hiroshima atom bomb on 9 August, it was not until the 21st that Decoux received 'sufficiently authentic information about the proclamation of the Mikado on the 12th August, announcing the capitulation to the Japanese people.'[17] By this time it was already too late to prevent the installation of the Vietminh government, even if the Japanese had not been willing accomplices to that seminal political act. While waiting for official confirmation, Admiral Decoux pleaded in vain:

> *I addressed myself to General Tsushihashi, commander of Japanese troops in Indochina,* [demanding] *immediate release of my compatriots, the maintenance of public order, the prevention of traffic in arms, and the safeguarding of public funds.*

Decoux's proposals were referred by the Japanese to Paris who replied on the 23rd that Decoux should be left where he was, and that the new administration would take charge in due course.[18] Neither did d'Argenlieu (de Gaulle's plenipotentiary in Asia) in Calcutta nor de Gaulle in Paris wish for the release of the detested Vichy military and civilians but instead they pressed for the immediate transfer of the admiral from Calcutta to Saigon. With time passing, Ho and the Vietminh could entrench their power. The Vietminh collected arms and enjoyed collaborative and friendly relations with many Japanese soldiers of all ranks, some of whom, particularly those who had married local women, deserted to help train and arm the Vietminh military.

Independence Day

Vietminh troops, having been driven to the wildernesses of Tonkin, swarmed out of the jungles and mountains down the elegant tree-lined avenues of Hanoi past the Metropol Hotel and the Opera House. Giáp was soon on hand to take command of the city and set up Vietminh units at all the key centres of municipal power and communications, including the Port of Haiphong 80km to the east. Arriving in Hanoi in late August, on Ho's first visit for forty years, he carried an old typewriter up to his room in China Town and locked himself away for several days.

Emerging a few days later on 2 September, he was 'wearing an old hat, a high collared khaki jacket and white rubber sandals.'[19] Ho went out to face the massed and festive crowds to declare independence. A slight figure, he had an old, worn look but he surprised people by his 'lively gait'. In Hanoi, wearing a faded old khaki tunic, he proceeded to Ba Dinh Square. Following a warm-up act from Giáp, Ho was sworn in as president of Vietnam in front of Hanoi's town hall and vast crowds of up to 500,000 on 2 September 1945. By his side was Major Archimedes Pritti of the OSS. One OSS observer commented, 'From what I have seen these people mean business and I am afraid the French will have to deal with them.'[20]

Speaking with a country accent from Nghe An (near Hue), Ho opened his speech to the astonishment of the Americans there by quoting Abraham Lincoln's Gettysburg address: 'All men are created equal…endowed with inalienable right; among these are life, liberty and the pursuit of happiness.' A master propagandist, his aim, in which he invested assiduously, was to persuade the US that he was really one of them…just a patriot as they had once been patriots against the British redcoats. Well informed by western media information and perhaps by Soviet intelligence, Ho was well aware of the fissures in the Transatlantic Alliance. Knowing that the US was cool on imperialism, his was a deliberate aim to drive a wedge between the western allies. Ho spoke to an ecstatic crowd estimated by Giáp at one million: 'One million took the oath [of independence] with one voice.'

Ho concluded by declaring: 'The entire Vietnamese people are determined to mobilise all their physical and mental strength, to sacrifice their lives and property in order to safeguard their freedom and independence.'[21]

That the communists would force one and all to make these sacrifices was beyond doubt. But that was the future. For now, here was a genuine enthusiasm that greeted the birth of a new nation and independence. Ho and the Vietminh had tapped into the euphoria of hope, renewal and xenophobia. Mai Elliot, whose brothers were in the crowd, records:

> *When Ho appeared he was greeted with the thunderous chant of doc lap, doc lap – independence…to signal that a new era was dawning, the Vietminh embarked on an ambitious program of social reform, banning many vices such as prostitution and opium smoking. In addition, they launched a campaign to teach people to read and write.*[22]

Those who did not support the Vietminh or knew they were communists kept their heads down or played along with the crowd. Excited mobs roamed the streets attacking French civilians who ventured out. A Catholic priest was murdered.

Revolution spread from Hanoi to all the regional towns and cities; Mae Eliott recounts:

> *In Nam Din on the day of August 19th when the Vietminh took over Hanoi, we heard a few scattered gunshots...They drove straight to governor's residence and demanded a transfer of power...a sea of people...with fluttering red flags and unfurled banners that the Vietminh agents had handed out.*

Bored youths were energised by the exciting times and the heady cocktail of promised action, high ideals and hope for the future. They took 'part in marches, writing slogans on banners they hung from our balcony like the one about "exterminating the fascists and their running dogs".' 'Down with the governor.'[23] Soon scores and rivalries were settled, French citizens murdered and nationalists assassinated.

The following passage is typical of the wave of euphoric enthusiasm for revolution, for nationalist feeling. It was, of course, tinged with xenophobia and the bloody surge of the mob:

> *My village and all the other villages were controlled by the Vietminh...We had been slaves of the Chinese for a thousand years, slaves of the French for a hundred. Now we were going to be free. The feeling was everywhere...It was unstoppable.*[24]

At this time Wedemeyer, the head of US forces in Asia, and the OSS were indeed convinced that Ho was mainly a nationalist and gave him tacit support, anything to go against the 'Limey' colonialist policies of Mountbatten, who Wedemeyer hated. Understanding that the colonialists would soon be on the way back, and that his forces would not be strong enough to resist them, Ho attempted to negotiate a settlement. He was in a difficult position because orders from Stalin were telling him not to rock the boat for the French communists and for Stalin's tricky negotiations about the future of Germany. On the other hand, his party cadres were impatient for violent action. If he was not radical enough, he would lose support to rival parties.

Ho's other consideration was that China, to the north, was controlled by Chiang Kai Shek's nationalist government. Although precarious and topsy-turvy relations had been maintained throughout the war, the Japanese surrender meant the showdown between nationalists and communists in China was bound to come to a head. Ho, from his Moscow and Chinese communist communications would have been aware of what was coming.

Mao's Red Army moved out of its Hunan base to the northern border with Russia to be near to Russian supplies and munitions. Having done so they enjoyed the exact reverse of the strategic and logistical position in which Ho was placed. With full civil war about to break out in China, no help could be expected from the Kuomintang government on the Indochina border. Quite the contrary, his nationalist rivals could be supplied with weapons and

Kuomintang troops were due to invade down to the 16th Parallel to disarm the Japanese under the agreement with the allies. The communists might control the Vietminh from behind the scenes, but Ho had to be careful from a strategic viewpoint because he could quickly be isolated and destroyed by the Kuomintang Army, as in Shanghai in 1933. The young hotheads in the party had to be held in check.

French politics and imperial policy

On 4 June 1944, in Algiers, de Gaulle claimed: 'Indochina will fall into anarchy. We will not need to seize power then, since there will be no more power. We will form a government.' However, his ambitions looked set to be thwarted by the American government. Incensed by French colonial treatment of Indochina, Roosevelt had written, on 22 January 1944, to the British government: 'Indochina must not return to France but should be administered by a governing council under the direction of the future United Nations organisation.' After Truman took over, Roosevelt's ideological imperative was quietly side-lined.

De Gaulle's policy, which was instilled in his high commission appointee Admiral d'Argenlieu, envisaged the triple division of the Vietnamese entities of Annam, Tonkin and Cochin in stark contrast to the nationalist and communist vision of a unified Vietnamese state, based on race and language. Clearly a divide-and-rule policy, de Gaulle's vision nevertheless had some considerable basis in reality because the culture, economy and history of Cochin was significantly different to Tonkin. Annam was home to a large number of fairly primitive and largely animist highland tribes who were completely removed from Annamite culture, but its thin coastal strip was inhabited by Vietnamese farmers and fishermen. A nostalgic story of France's mission to 'protect' the tribal minorities from the Vietnamese would grow up to bolster colonial justification for continued French supervision of the federation.

However d'Argenlieu, with personal instructions from de Gaulle, was charged with establishing the sovereignty of France in Indochinese territory and Leclerc was to take military measures in support. De Gaulle had already informed Leclerc: 'We have nothing to say to the locals as long as we have no strength.'[25]

On 24 August 1945, the high commissioner issued the statement: 'France intends to recover its sovereignty in Indochina.' On 5 September, just before D'Argenlieu's departure, de Gaulle sent the admiral a message: 'Dear Admiral. There is a big piece left for us to take back, a great game to play. It's up to you.'[26] Having been briefed by the general, d'Argenlieu, even as he travelled to Indochina, sent Leclerc a message encouraging him 'to show the greatest possible force.'[27]

Revolution in the countryside and small towns

Meanwhile, the communist-led Vietminh continued to bring revolution to the countryside:

> *The Vietminh was supported by a host of popular associations for national salvation, each one covering one social group, such as women, teachers, peasants, youths, and old people. These associations helped...also allowed the Communists to sink their roots in Vietnamese society.*

From the start, the communists set up the apparatus of control and oppression. The party was assuming total control and, in some cases, arbitrary justice started to be exacted on class enemies. 'The Vietminh had unlimited power and could arrest and kill anyone they wanted.' There were also stories of mandarins being killed in other provinces.

The Vietminh was the leading national organisation. As such it benefited from being the prime mover after the Japanese surrender. However, in many villages, communes and small towns there was control by other nationalist groups, or by a powerful local landlord or Mandarin, or by non-political leaders. In such cases the communists developed their discrete strategy for winning control. Intelligence as to the village, its key influences and identification of supporters was the first task of the party cadres. The French were aware of the tactic, which is why Vietminh cadres were always sought out and shot. However, a detailed study of methodology came later under more scientific American studies. Sociological studies conducted by the Rand Corporation in 1964–5 identified the methods of takeover that were based initially on intelligence and identification of supporters and enemies, following which the Maoist procedure was to:

> *...disorganise the local administration by assassination and other forms of terror and they do not use terror indiscriminately. Officials and government sympathisers who are killed are likely to have been either intensely unpopular on the one hand, or able and well-liked and therefore particularly dangerous on the other...organisers do not rely on terror alone, They can be friendly and helpful.*[28]

The number of assassinations in the First Indochina War is estimated by some to have run into six figures. It was all part of Mao's playbook of revolution and war in the countryside.

Admiral Decoux goes home

Upon the Japanese surrender, Admiral Decoux was not treated as he expected to be. It was indeed a *point doulourex*, as he acidly described it. Rather than being restored to his former office he suffered the humiliation of being kept in confinement by the very same Japanese Army that had just admitted defeat. Still locked up at Loc Ninh, on 30 September, twenty-five days after the surrender, he was informed by a Japanese officer that: 'We had to leave Loc Ninh in military trucks at four o'clock in the morning, to catch an airplane for Saigon, and to leave directly for France.'

Admiral Decoux's request to have an interview with the general government in Saigon was brusquely set aside by the Japanese officer: 'He had no orders concerning that matter.'[29] It must have been obvious to the admiral that he was in effect a prisoner under close arrest. With utter disgust he recalled how at the very same airport, 'where I was on many occasions received with military honours, to the tune of the Marseillaise, there now fluttered the Union Jack.'

Leaving on 1 October, he was flown to Bangkok, then Calcutta on 2 October, where an order was relayed to him emanating from Thierry D'Argenlieu, de Gaulle's chosen governor general, stating: 'It is ordered that upon arrival in Calcutta Admiral Decoux should be taken to his designated hotel. He shall not be allowed to leave it under any pretext whatsoever up to his departure tomorrow morning by plane for France.'

Decoux was becoming ever more aware of the taint of Vichy, which was condemning tens of thousands of former officials to varying degrees of retribution in metropolitan France, as a nation vented self-righteous revengeful anger on *collaborateurs*. It was a significant and bitter political mood that would split the French political right for some time. Treatment given to Decoux and others was a way of trying to wash off the taint of national guilt and humiliation, the same emotional dynamic that led France to try so aggressively to recover status and honour by reoccupying its empire.

While de Gaulle's humiliation of Vichyite Decoux was going on, back in Indochina French men, women and children were being massacred and tortured by various communist and violent nationalist elements of the Vietnamese population as a collective revenge for the depredations and humiliations of colonialism. It was a portent of the horrors and counter-horrors that were to come. Arriving in Paris on 7 October, on the 8th Decoux was sent for house arrest at the hospital in Val de Grace, where he was informed that he was under investigation by the high court. He would be left kicking his heels there for twenty months, enjoying basic conditions in the company of the venerable Marshal Weygand.

There followed an interview and debrief with the ruler of France, General de Gaulle, which came on 14 October six days after his arrival. Shown into the ante room of a villa in Paris's haute bourgeois suburb of Neuilly, it was decorated with tapestries and grand epoque furniture. He was shown into de Gaulle's office. They had exchanged handshakes in 1931 at a disarmament conference, but not now. Decoux requested permission to explain his mission in Indochina, to which de Gaulle replied in a laconic fashion: 'Would you like to sit down? I will listen to you. Do you smoke?' Decoux explained the reasoning for his actions under the orders of Vichy. Essentially, he had agreed to an accommodation and stayed with Vichy because it was the only way to maintain order, the tricolour and French interests in Indochina. As he had explained to de Gaulle's agents during the war, had he not done so the Japanese would have invaded and interned all French soldiers and civilians.

De Gaulle rose and said:

> *I have listened carefully to your explanation...you committed several errors which I will indicate to you.... Firstly, you should not have accepted the position of governor general after the armistice...secondly you should not have waited till the liberation of France before coming over to me... and you should have prepared for resistance...I repeat, your fault.*[30]

It was de Gaulle at his worst: malicious, mendacious and vindictive. He was ignorant of Indochinese matters. Admiral Decoux defended himself, arguing that in the circumstances, playing for time and taking the opportunity to rule Indochina was the only way to avoid takeover and keep the French government in operational control: 'The Japanese were only waiting for an excuse to takeover completely.' Decoux was correct. There was no room for manoeuvre. Had Decoux gone over to de Gaulle and offered resistance, colonists would have been interned and likely many murdered or killed from neglect. When the French military in Indochina could not even defeat Thailand and there was no possibility of logistical supply, the idea that the colonial army could take on the Japanese in formal battle array or even as a guerrilla force was fanciful.

British troops occupy Saigon and Phnom Penh

On 12 September, immediately upon the Japanese surrender in Singapore, Major-General Gracey of the British Army landed in Saigon with a battalion of Gurkhas from the 20th Indian Division. They were welcomed by Vietnamese government officials from the committee who had taken over the city with laudatory banners: 'Welcome British and Americans, but we have no room for the French.'[31] A British Army officer recalled: 'The local French...who have been terrorised for some months by the Annamites…regard us as liberators.'[32] The relationship with both elements would soon sour.

An early problem was the way that liberated colons treated the Indian soldiers as an underclass. Their insolent racism was manifest even against their liberators, Indian officers and troops who had fought magnificently in the battles around Kohima and in Burma, while they were still 'lording it' in imperialist Vichy comfort. The celebrated feminist photographer Germaine Krull noted a class 'that was utterly cut off and out of tune with the times and the mood of the people.'[33] French prestige had been irredeemably shattered by their defeat and surrender at the start of the Second World War. So insulting and racist was their behaviour towards British Gurkha and Indian troops[34] that General Gracey had put out stern warnings on the matter to the colon community and French soldiers, informing them about equal relations and mutual respect in the British Army. Captain Cross of the 1st Gurkha Rifles spoke on behalf of his men when he noted that they were dismayed by French behaviour and unimpressed by their military showing. Why did they comport themselves with such arrogance and contempt for others?[35] Relations with Japanese surrendered enemy personnel was much better with some amount of comradeship developing despite strict orders to the contrary that stipulated: 'there will be no fraternising whatsoever…you will not shake hands…[or] feed in the same room…and not allowed to sit at the same table.'[36]

There was an uneasy relationship between the various components in the city. British high command had to deal with the French, and resistance from communist, Trotskyist and various nationalist groups, including the Hoa Hao sect and the eccentric but powerful Cao Di. The latter had a powerbase north of the city and worshipped a sort of ecumenical and eclectic mixture of gods and religions, including French novelist Victor Hugo. There were brief talks with the Vietminh-dominated committee of the south (Nam Bo committee), but these broke down. Gracey, under orders to re-establish the French as soon as possible, quickly decided to hand over control to the old colonial power on 22 September in what was effectively a coup against the Vietminh and nationalists. French soldiers had been re-armed surreptitiously by French representative Claude Cedil on the orders of the paranoid de Gaulle, who feared another British perfidy after the Syrian debacle. On 19 September, they went on a violent and vengeful tear around the city. French troops had stormed into the treasury, post office and city hall, and killed whoever stood in their way. Germaine Krull described how in the rue Catinat she saw French 'soldiers driving before them a group of Annamites bound, slave-fashion to a long rope. French women spat in their faces. They were on the verge of being lynched.'[37]

Ignoring imploring pleas from de Gaulle's representative, who had created the problem, they and parties of vigilante French citizens proceeded to exact cruel retribution on the despised inhabitants of Saigon at whose hands they had suffered oppression, humiliation and murder. Pent-up anger fuelled a crazed rampage. There was a killing spree of 'wild shootings' and random beatings administered to Vietnamese found on the streets, many of whom were thrown into prisons the French had recently vacated.

An enraged Gracey had to disarm the colons and return the French soldiery to guarded barracks. This lawlessness was to kick-off another spiral of hatred and revenge. Vietminh recruiters could hardly have asked for more. Retaliation was fast, as the Vietminh attacked the power station and set off a campaign of terror on French soldiers and citizens, which was to continue for some years.

Despite an early welcome for the liberators from the city government, Gracey's coup against the city council on 24 September changed all that, even though it was as much a counter-coup against the lawless French soldiery. Vietminh agents also started to launch anti-colonialist propaganda on Indian troops, trying to co-opt them to the common struggle, and this was backed up by Ho's radio broadcasts from Hanoi.[38]

Within the nationalist committee (the Nam Bo committee) there were scores to settle, and in a city barely under control there were many murders and shootouts as the Vietminh and other groups started to fight back. The Vietminh used the state of anarchy to liquidate their nationalist and Trotskyite rivals, whose party had become the most successful revolutionary group in the city with an electoral popularity well in advance of the communists. The Vietminh also assassinated the founder of the Hao Hoa, an act that further added to the slaughter. Killings abounded. In one incident on 24 September, Vietminh or other groups ambushed and killed Major Dewey. The senior American OSS representative in Saigon, he had been ordered out of Saigon by British General Gracey, on account of his pro-Vietminh sentiments and 'troublemaking'. His last report to his superiors stated: 'Cochinchina is burning…The French and the British are finished here and we ought to clear out of South East Asia.' Dewey represented the views of a powerful 'anti-colonial' faction within the OSS. At a checkpoint, he was mistaken for being French by Vietminh militia and shot down. His body was not recovered despite the ghoulish efforts of Captain Cross of the Gurkhas who was ordered to find it.

While Ho Chi Minh was preparing for power, on 24 August 1945 de Gaulle was addressing a press conference in Washington DC. He ignored an appeal sent to him days earlier from Ho's mouthpiece, ex-Emperor Bao Dai, to abandon his French Indochinese ambitions. In a call from 'the Mother Country *addressed to her children*' (author's emphasis), de Gaulle announced: 'France means to recover its sovereignty over Indochina.' In an official instruction to d'Argenlieu 16 August, de Gaulle had already ordered that 'the first mission is to re-establish sovereignty in over the Union of Indochina'.[39]

Despite the Brazzaville declaration, the reality was that France would not give up real sovereignty. To the intense frustration of the United States, this remained substantially the same position for the next nine years. France required control of the economy, the armed forces and foreign policy in some sort of collective association or protectorate arrangement. This policy would be rejected by the Vietminh, by Bao Dai, and by King Sihanouke of Cambodia.

Suddenly, the hatred and bitterness of the Vietnamese population against their former French masters spilled out in multiple incidents. Collaborators, including girlfriends, were targeted and servants even attacked their masters, reported Germaine Krull in her Saigon diaries.[40] In Saigon a few days later, between thirty and ninety French civilians, mainly women and children, were horribly massacred and mutilated in a leafy French suburb, probably by elements of the Binh Xuyen criminal gang who steamed through the unprotected suburb. It was a response to a mob of former French prisoner-of-war soldiers and civilians who had rampaged through the city the day before.

With Saigon descending into chaos, on 26 September Gracey, who only had 7,000 British troops on hand, was driven to re-arm Japanese troops to maintain order and show strength against the burgeoning Vietminh insurgency. As Major Philip Malin noted in a memoir:

> *At the end of September 1945 we still had very few of our own infantry on the ground. The weather was bad and the fly-in of our own troops much slower than expected. In the absence of our own troops on several occasions I commanded Japanese under Japanese officers in protecting the civil population or protecting or recapturing key installations. Casualties were nil or minimal, non-fatal. The Annamites were then easily intimidated by a show of force and never took us on in a pitched battle.*[41]

This policy was only partially successful, because a significant number of Japanese troops, including some senior officers, deserted and defected to the Vietminh or other nationalist groups taking arms and skills with them. Giáp recruited 1,500 Japanese troops, including 230 NCOs and forty-seven officers of the Kempetai (military police), many of whom were on the run from war crimes indictments.[42] Some were ideologically committed 'anti-westerner' Japanese officers who had local wives, and there were those Japanese who stood to be convicted of war crimes on the infamous Burma railway, etc. Although relatively small in number, their defection helped the Vietminh become more prepared and better trained for the struggle ahead against imperialist revanchists. The bulk of the 69,000 surrendered Japanese were returned to Japan by March 1946.

Lacking in troops, Gracey's self-determined writ was for Saigon alone and he saw himself acting in a very limited role. As an allied power, France had to be respected, and Gracey was under orders to return the 'colony' to France, even though he personally believed that the way to keep peace was to establish an orderly path to independence. He wanted his troops out as soon as possible with as few casualties as possible. However, hatred for the French spilled over into attacks on the British, Gurkhas and their Japanese auxiliaries, especially when it became clear that the British were intent on handing back Cochin to the hated French. A typical terrorist incident came when 'On the way back a grenade was thrown from the roadside into the truck in front of me,' recounted Captain Cross. 'I saw it hit a soldier on the head and roll on the floor. He picked it up and threw it away, superbly unruffled.'[43] *Sang froid*, it seems, was not just a French quality.

The countryside in the heavily populated delta was excluded, so this gave the Vietminh and others time to prepare and extend their revolution across the delta and into the Central Highlands. They took control of villages and towns by murdering leading nationalists, collaborators, Sûreté agents and non-communists. The networks established at this time, in the Mekong delta especially, would be a constant thorn in the side of the French in years to come. The extent of violence and fighting in Saigon and its environs is shown by the level of Japanese casualties in this short period. By the time they were repatriated, 700 Japanese had been killed fighting for the British against the Vietminh.

Ho Chi Min appointed Nguyễn Binh as the new Vietminh leader in the south to sharpen the armed conflict against the French as well as counter-revolutionary enemies, both pro-French collaborationist elements and nationalist rivals. In November 1945 alone, forty-one class enemies were liquidated, including local Vietnamese officials, businessmen, landowners and intellectuals. Assassination, class war, nationalism and aggressive propaganda as to the barbarity of the hated French were the tools of communist proselytisation, which turned the Mekong delta into a bastion of revolution.

By the end of September, British Major Malin noted that the mood of the people and the Vietminh began to change:

> *Although initially we had been made welcome by the Annamites, as we called them, Vietminh as they were later called, they quickly realised correctly that we were there only pending the return of the French...At first they dug up the roads and felled trees across the road at night...The Annamites set fire to buildings, sometimes using bows and arrows with cloth soaked in petrol ...By the end of September 1945 they were blockading Saigon and the main cities of French Indo China south of latitude 16 degrees north.*[44]

At the start of the re-occupation, the Vietminh held off from attacking British troops but as the occupation went on this changed. Major Malin, who was head of logistics for the British Army, recorded how he led a convoy of Gurkhas and Japanese troops to fetch supplies from a large Japanese base 11km north of Saigon: 'We were heavily attacked on our return journey the following day, losing five Gurkhas and six Dutch ex-prisoners-of-war killed and many wounded.'[45] (27 September 1945)

There were firefights every night and constant roadblocks and ambushes. Captain Cross also came under fire when on a search for Vietminh irregulars outside Saigon with his Ghurkha and Japanese troops. As the bullets fizzed by, the inexperienced Cross was approached by the Japanese interpreter: 'Respected sir, Captain Yamaguchi sends his respects and respectfully requests you to adopt the lying position.'[46] Upon repatriation to Japan in December, the captain presented Cross with a 300-year-old heir-loom, a sword made by famous swordsmith Fujiware Yositoke, addressing his captor with gratitude as a 'true gentleman and cavalier'.[47]

Bitterness and atrocity spiralled exponentially, setting the scene for the appalling horrors of the war to come. An Indian cook tempted into coitus was knifed to death while *inflagrante delicto.* Three Indian soldiers were inveigled into a local house, captured and horribly stabbed to death with skewers rammed through their eyes. Some French soldiers continued in the tradition of their colonisation. Having captured a suspected female spy they 'bastinadoed her' and she was then 'raped by all of the ten-man garrison. When she recovered consciousness, she was dragged to the market place and publicly shot.'[48] Random violence and terror against local civilians became commonplace. Disturbed by screams one night, Captain Cross witnessed a grotesque attack by French soldiers: 'In the dimly lit corridor I saw a small, stark naked Annamite boy being chased by a group of nude French soldiers, members erect…I was joined by another officer (French) whose one remark was "*Vive le sport*".'[49]

Only the Kingdom of Lao would accept the union idea. Weak and small, squeezed between covetous neighbours Vietnam, China and Thailand, the idea of French protection was appealing. Soon, however, the royal family would be split as Prince Souphanouvong, a relative of the king, transferred his allegiances to the Vietminh. He returned to start the Laotian revolution on 7 October 1945 with a squad of sixty-five Vietminh troops, so putting flesh on the bones of Ho Chi Minh's idea of a Vietnam-dominated union led by the ICP (Indochina Communist Party). As they were about to cross into Lao near to Ke Sanh, the 'prince ordered us to remove our Viet Liberation badges and replace them with Laotian badges…The Laotian leaders…manifested great distrust of us.'

The prince pushed his way into the new Issara nationalist government under a constitutional monarchy in a process originally supported by the Chinese Kuomintang Army against the French and the Vietminh. While the prince was hailed by the Vietnamese settler population, the Laotians were less appreciative of this Vietnamese invasion.[50] However, Suophanouvong's entry into government as defence minister meant that Vietminh infiltration and regional imperialism had begun. For Ho, taking the revolution to Lao was not just part of his revolutionary creed, but also a strategic and political issue so as to secure the flank of the fledgling independent state of Vietnam (DRV) and communications to comrades in the Mekong in Cochin and Cambodia.

Whereas Lao had been assigned to Chinese occupation following the Japanese surrender, responsibility for Cambodia was given to the British. Phnom Penh was only a day by river steamer from Saigon. Given the paucity of troops, General Gey sent just a platoon of Gurkhas together with two French companies under Lieutenant-Colonel E.D. Murray, to re-occupy Cambodia on behalf of France. In isolated Phnom Penh, the nationalist government of So Ngoc Thanh had been operating for three months following the Japanese surrender. When the British arrived, the Cambodian leader worked with Murray in the popular policy of clearing out ethnic Vietnamese from government posts and the railways,[51] but Thanh was arrested within ten days of General Leclerc arriving in Saigon on 9 October. Thanh was deported to prison in Saigon then taken to France. Acting as proxy for the French, Britain had restored Cambodia to French imperial rule. King Sihanouke stayed and would make an accommodation with the French, but he would prove to be a recalcitrant and wily element in French plans as this mercurial and God-like figure came to represent the national aspirations of the Cambodian people. This was in stark contrast to Emperor Bao Dai, whose claims to national leadership were entirely displaced by the charismatic persona of Ho Chi Minh.

Ho had been hoping to engage with the Americans to secure their help in the fight against colonialism, something that accounted for his very warm fostering of US relations over the previous year. However, the mood changed when Ho realised that America would not prevent French recolonisation. American General Gallagher in Hanoi reported:

> *...a noticeable change of the Annamites towards the Americans here...since they became aware of the fact that we were not going to interfere and would probably help the French...they became more antagonistic.*[52]

The 'defrocked' priest Admiral d'Argenlieu, and Leclerc arrive, 9 October 1945

General Leclerc, aristocrat and famed liberator of Paris, arrived to take over from Major-General Gracey's command on 9 October 1945. His troops, the 1st Colonial Infantry, took somewhat longer.

Another of his collection of eccentric misfits, de Gaulle's appointee and fervent apostle Admiral Thierry d'Argenlieu arrived on 31 October, just as French troops disembarked. His job was to re-establish French power in Indochina. D'Argenlieu was born into a devoutly Catholic naval family, both of which themes would dominate his life by turns. Closely associated with famed imperialist and homosexual Hugo Lyautey, after serving in the navy in the First World War, he became a priest and a Carmelite prior to 1935, but was kept on the naval reserve. Having re-joined the active list of the navy, he was captured in Cherbourg but escaped and joined the Free French in London. As de Gaulle's emissary in Africa, he was an impossibly pompous character who carried *hauteur* to excess. Having found God, he then discovered de Gaulle. Giáp exhibited his polemical viciousness by inaccurately referring to the admiral as the 'defrocked monk'.

A picture of d'Argenlieu sitting back in an easy chair in a colonial setting with his head thrown back gives exactly the picture of one who pontificates magisterially and is enamoured with his own importance and place, as if mimicking de Gaulle. His mission was de Gaulle's mission. Allied to French and local industrialists, senior Catholic clergy, planters, landowners and bankers, he saw the world through an elitist colonial prism. He would prove to be a great cabalist and a thorn in the side of any peace process. On 28 January 1946, the French took over from the British by assuming all military responsibility for Cochinchina and Annam below the 16th Parallel. France, at least in the south, was back in nominal control of its jewel in the crown.

De Gaulle resigned as provisional president on 20 January 1946. The timing was not coincidental. He could claim to have recovered France's rightful place in the world order and her colonies. His next adventure was political, to catapult himself into absolute power on the back of his record as the 'Saviour of France' and bearing the Cross of Lorraine before him.

Reconquest phase in the south, October 1945

Leclerc's forces numbered just 13,000, which was a tiny fraction of what was needed to suppress a rebellion across the huge expanse of Cochin. Nevertheless, the force was composed of toughened Second World War veterans. They were led by two redoubtable colonels, bull-necked Colonel Massu, later to achieve fame and infamy in the Kasbah at Algiers, and Colonel Ponchardier. Both aggressive and competitive, they shocked the still amateur Vietminh by their speed and ruthlessness. The first of their objectives was the provincial capital My Tho. A joint army/navy task force operating from Saigon would seize this city, situated along the northern branch of the Mekong as it runs down to the sea.

Massu arranged his formation in a self-contained mobile group with lorry-mounted troops, tanks, engineers and medical elements. He careered through the inevitable light ambushes as he took route RC16 going west to secure the vital towns of My Tho on the edge of the Plain of Reeds, just 30km from Saigon. After My Tho, he advanced on Can Tho further west, the hub of economic activity in the delta. Almost immediately following their departure along the old colonial track, the troops found this cross-country route tough-going, as:

> *...units moving overland from Saigon via Route 4 had initially been detailed to seize My Tho from the Vietminh. However, the French column found the road sabotaged, and their vehicles repeatedly bogged down in the sponge-like earth.*[53]

The city was taken instead by Ponchardier's riverine assault in the last week of October. Ponchardier, having studied the campaigns of 1862, hijacked any available small craft and made surprise amphibious landings at both delta cities. Vietminh forces suffered heavily in trying to repel them. When Groupement Massu arrived at My Tho, they were met by the sight of a dead Vietminh soldier sitting in a deckchair. From the French point of view, this would be the 'happy war' phase and gallows humour was in order. It would fade before long.

The naval brigade subsequently seized the cities of Vinh Long (29 October), nearby Sadec and Can Tho (mid-November), in an area known as the Plain of Birds, 'in the great plain of mud and rice' carrying out the second and third phases of *Operation MOUSSAC*, respectively. Margaret Duras describes the scenery:

> *...in the surrounding flatness stretching as far as the eye can see, the rivers flow as fast as if the earth sloped downwards...* [the Mekong] *picked up all it had met with since the Tonle Sap and the Cambodian forest. It carries everything along, straw huts, forests, burned out fires, dead birds, dead dogs, drowned tigers and buffaloes, drowned men, bait, islands of hyacinths all stuck together.*[54]

These last two phases were also conceived of as joint army/navy ventures. The naval force speedily navigated the delta waterways, often under cover of darkness, offering tactical surprise and mobility outside the reach of their road-bound brethren. One observer described how:

> *Progress across rice paddies and mangrove thickets forced the* [army infantry] *most of the time to struggle through water and mud...*[crossing] *river channels became exhausting; in fact, owing to the absence of roads, it was necessary to carry on one's back not only regular kit but also all the ammunition and weapons, such as machineguns and mortar...And finally, for these drenched men, veritable hunks of ambulating mud, the leaden sun added to their torment.*[55]

Triumphs were celebrated across the delta as key district towns such as Tra Vinh, Bien Hoa and Rach Gia, fell in January, and Ca Mau in the far west of the delta in early February.

Capturing the main towns and cities was one thing, but the countryside still belonged to the Vietminh. Xuan Vu reminisced of his youth in the resistance:

> *...I was fifteen when the war broke out...by the time the school year started in 1945 My Tho was blockaded...Inside the city were the French soldiers, outside the Vietminh guerrillas. My village and all the other villages were controlled by the Vietminh...We had been slaves of the Chinese for a thousand years, slaves of the French for a hundred. now we were going to be free...It was unstoppable.*[56]

It was a standoff. The Vietminh, incapable of penetration against the artillery-backed firepower and experience of the French and the French forces were likewise stymied by an enemy who disappeared with ease and became adapt at hiding. Even though Japanese soldiers had deserted to the Vietminh and perhaps made up as many as ten to fifteen percent of some units, they could not quickly turn uneducated peasants and rickshaw drivers into professional soldiers.

This period in the south was known as the 'happy war', but it was not without dangers. Soldiers died but the Vietminh were not experienced or well-armed enough to cause heavy losses on the French. For the young French officers of the FEC, war even took on a comic aspect. They were dismissive of the enemy who tirelessly made pinprick attacks, especially at night. Journalist Lucien Bodard stayed at one villa in Can Tho, the capital of the delta region, which sits on a confluence of many delta rivers and channels. He was advised:

> *...the Viets usually machine-gun us at two in the morning and we answer them. It's a sort of ceremony...if you're disturbed by a sound of footsteps, take a grenade...we have left a little pile of them, right by your bed. Just pull the pin and put your hand out between the window bars, and let it drop. Then go back to sleep, and look at your bag in the morning.*[57]

General Leclerc was impressed enough with the success of the Brigade Marine d'Extreme-Orient (BMEO) to approve the formation of the Naval Infantry River Flotilla (named Dinassaut). This riverine force of five boats and smaller craft, a subset of the BMEO, vigilantly patrolled the river network of the Mekong and the Bassac to maintain open lines of communication.

In the delta, foreign legionnaires knew they were in hostile country because in the villages all the walls were covered in propaganda such as 'long live Ho Chi Minh and socialism'. Legionnaire Karl-Heinrich Krause noted: 'We were constantly greeted with this message "don't fight for imperialism, come to us in freedom".'[58] A not inconsiderable number of his German compatriots did just that.

Hanoi: Kuomintang occupation

As agreed at Yalta, Chiang Kai Shek's Republic of China took responsibility for Tonkin down to the 16th Parallel. Commanded by General Lu Han, 180,000 'nationalist' troops descended from China. As a proto-warlord, his primary concerns were loot, opium and currency manipulation:

> *In the fall of 1945, he issued a decree increasing the exchange value of the Customs Gold Unit (a currency issued by the Central Bank of China) by 50 percent, from one to 1.5 piastres...The new rate allowed Chinese occupiers to buy up food, real estate and entire businesses at bargain basement prices, squeezing out resentful native buyers.*[59]

Meanwhile, 5,000 French troops continued to be incarcerated in the citadel where Japanese soldiers had put them after the Japanese takeover. Chinese troops did not march into the city, they ambled in as a confused mass of soldiers mixed with camp followers pulling clanking carts loaded with household goods, cooking utensils, woks and pans, and booty. There was the endless clattering sound of cheap metal on metal and the squeak of the carts. The soldiers marched any how, their uniforms were unorthodox or non-existent, weapons protruded from piles of clothes and baskets of food. 'The troops wore shoes of woven straw, cloth, or rubber cut from tires or even went barefoot. They had tattered uniforms and looked tired and thin.'[60] The Chinese Army immediately set up house wherever there was spare land in the city, in parks, streets, boulevards and private gardens.

The Chinese, advised by US Major Gallagher, accepted the Japanese surrender. Lu Hun's first act was to kick Sainteny's French delegation out of the national palace. The Americans were also displaced. Le Hun very quickly came to an accommodation with Ho Chi Minh and allowed the Vietminh to continue to rule the city, while giving him a free hand in other matters. Le Hun's main activity was enrichment, an interest he pursued aggressively by any means, including the exactions of monies for his army's supply needs. Another important interest was opium, which was liberally supplied by Ho Chi Minh, who is reported to have presented Lu with a golden opium pipe. In the T'ai Highlands and Lao, the principal activity of the Chinese Army was the expropriation of the opium harvest. Against a backdrop of horrific starvation in Tonkin, where as many as one million died, Le Hu's Chinese Nationalist Army were even shipping rice back to China or selling it on the black market.

In the meantime, no doubt in compact with Ho Chi Minh, the French continued to be humiliated at every turn. At the official Japanese surrender ceremony on 28 September in Tonkin, the Tricolour was not flown alongside the allied flags of China, the US and Britain. The French representative was

155th on the guest list. However, in return for Lu Hun's recognition, support and favours, Ho was put under increasing pressure because, as the Chinese occupation progressed, increasing support was given to the nationalist parties, especially the Việt Nam Quốc Dân Đảng (VNQDD). Operating under Lu Hu's protection, they ran several newspapers and a radio station. Against a background of armed conflict in a proto-civil war between the nationalist and Vietminh militias during November 1945, an accord was reached on 19 December 1945. Ho agreed to elections in January 1946 for a new government. The VNQDD would be guaranteed seventy seats in the national assembly.

The Americans were especially favoured by Ho. He also professed his desire for good relations with France, candidly admitting that given the Chinese occupation, support was needed to get rid of them and their influence. Ho made it clear: 'We have no hatred for the French. We want to re-establish contact with her, all the more so as others [meaning China] are interfering in our affairs.'[61]

The elections would be systematically rigged by the communists. A typical polling booth was described by voter N. Khac Huyen in Quang Binh province: 'A hall where here was a big table over which a big portrait of Chairman Ho looked down and around which sat two solemn faced officials who were also Vietminh agents.'[62] Villagers were told who to vote for or to simply leave their ballot papers on the table so that the presiding election official could fill them in on their behalf. Well organised and backed by superior military forces, Vietminh candidates scooped all the seats (about 300) except those designated for the seventy nationalists.

French representative Sainteny's request to the Vietminh for preliminary talks had occurred soon after his arrival in late August. At Vietminh insistence, pro-Vietminh American Major Patti accompanied the Frenchman in informal meetings, not with Ho Chi Minh, but with Giáp. It was an extraordinary personal confrontation between an arch imperialist-revanchist faced by his would-be hate-filled revolutionary nemesis. Patti's accounts of the meeting have been contradictory, on the one hand reporting that Giáp was cowed by the Frenchman, and on the other that, as Patti remarked: 'For the first time in his life Sainteny was meeting face to face a Vietnamese who dared stand up to a Frenchman.' Talks recommenced on substantive matters in October 1945, this time with chain-smoking Ho Chi Minh in person. (He smoked any American brand or Galois indiscriminately.) The Vietminh were under pressure due to the imminent arrival of Leclerc with the French Expeditionary Force aboard French aircraft carrier *Arromanches*. There were also French landings in Annam. Issues at stake, including the right of self-rule, were encapsulated in the word 'independence' set against the French desire for the right of French troops to take over security in Tonkin.

After months of negotiations over the meaning of 'independence' and use of the word, Ho settled for the best available deal on 6 March 1946, whereby he traded recognition for the Republic of Vietnam 'within the Indochinese Federation and French Union', but conceded that Annam and Cochin were not part of the transaction and that referenda would settle their future. French troops would be allowed into Haiphong. The main reason for agreement on these accords that were unsatisfactory to both sides is explained by de Beaucorps: 'One thing above all for the Viets and the French was to get the Chinese out.'[63]

Not only were the Chinese bad guests, consuming much rice, which added to the problems of starvation, there was a real danger that they would stay. Moreover, as they were aligned to the Dai Vet, the communists feared that a coup would be launched against them, especially with tension mounting as civil war threatened in China. Ho would have remembered only too well Chang Kai Shek's massacre of communists in Shanghai in April 1927. According to Giáp, 'local officials were worried by the disruptive activities by Chiang's troops and their agents in Hanoi and about possible dangers for Uncle Ho.'[64] With no idea of what the result in the Chinese Civil War would be, the Vietminh agreed to:

> *...let 15,000 French troops into north Vietnam for a specified time in order to drive out of the country 180,000 Chiang troops who would otherwise stay on indefinitely as they had declared.*[65]

For France there was the fear that China would annex their prized imperial possession. As part of the bargain for the Chinese Nationalist Army to leave, France signed over their territory at Fort Bayard opposite to Hainan, an enclave with some 200,000 Chinese. France also gave up its concession rights and privileges in Shanghai, Tianjin and Xiamen, and the ownership of the Hanoi to Kunming railroad.

De Beaucorps noted:

> *...the accord of the 6th March was badly received by the French in Indochina society, but also a large section of the political class who were probably more important, including de Gaulle himself.*[66]

The agreement flew in the face of de Gaulle's declarations on 25 March the previous year. He was duly furious with his former acolytes Leclerc and Sainteny. However, with de Gaulle's crony d'Argenlieu and de Gaulle loyalists General Valluy and Colonel Debes still in situ, the game was not over as they were on the spot and would aggressively follow a Gaullist policy. Even though he no longer held any official post in France, de Gaulle told General Valluy to take a hard line.

Valluy informed General Salan that he had received a letter from General de Gaulle, who expressed the view that the sending of 80,000 troops was necessary. 'There is an imperative,' wrote de Gaulle, 'to build up the Indochinese Federation and to bring it into the Francophone Union. Without wavering.'[67] The wording in Salan's memoirs suggests that Valluy showed him the letter. De Gaulle was in close contact with d'Argenlieu. It would be surprising if he was not issuing 'advice'. Despite being out of office, de Gaulle was covertly using his influence to run a parallel policy to the government. Encouraging and suggesting actions that were not sanctioned by the government, de Gaulle was undermining the French government's democratic control and fostering a culture of insubordination. This accounts for the deliberate provocations and insubordinate actions by Admiral d'Agenlieu, General Valluy and Colonel Debes.

Meanwhile, in the south, guerrilla actions round Saigon continued. In one incident on 16 April, a whole section of French troops was wiped out.

Chiang also had ulterior motives for agreeing to the withdrawal. He was suspicious of the potential warlord power of Lu Hun. Agreement to withdraw would deny Lu Hun an independent power base in Tonkin. Additionally, he needed Le Hun's troops for his civil war where he had just launched 1.8 million men against the Red Army.

The agreement was a holding action preliminary to more substantive talks to be carried out in France by a Vietminh delegation led by Ho's key subordinate Pham Van Dong, which would set off on 31 May. Ho would accompany the delegation but not be part of it. This would give him space for independent media/propaganda activity and consultations with Soviet agents. Giáp, the consummate military man of action and party organiser, was delegated to mind the shop in Hanoi while Dong and Ho were away.

In Hanoi, mass consternation had greeted the news of the agreement of 6 March, especially when the government announced the arrival of French troops and asked the populace to welcome them. 'I woke up and found Mai in a panic,' recalled one resident:

> *I ran through the city and saw emotions were running high. People were arguing fighting and yelling insults. What had caused this discord? One simple poster signed by two names, General Leclerc and Ho Chi Minh.*[68]

The VNQDD and Dai Viet jumped on this propaganda gift and were soon criticising Ho and the communists for selling out to the French. Nationalist parties had a reason to be angry because their protectors, the Kuomintang, were leaving.

Faced with internal party dissent over the deal with the French, Ho mocked his party colleagues in an aside redolent of deep-rooted anti-Chinese sentiment: 'Better to smell French shit for five years than eat Chinese shit for the rest of your lives.'[69] A massed rally was organised by the Vietminh to communicate the agreement to the citizens of Hanoi, many of whom were in shock at the apparent capitulation and reversal of fortunes. Giáp gave the warm-up speech. In his history professor mode, he lectured incomprehensibly and verbosely over the heads of his audience, comparing the 6 March agreement to the tactical retreat made by Lenin at Brest-Litovsk in 1918, when the young Soviet regime had ceded huge swathes of Russia to Germany. Recovering the situation, Ho won over the crowd to his unpopular deal with the French by using his soothing charm and charisma. He simply concentrated on the fact that France had recognised the independence of Vietnam:

> *I Ho Chi Minh have always led you on the path to freedom. I have fought my whole life for the independence of the nation...I swear to you that I did not sell you out.* (7 March)

Ho turned a crisis into a triumph. However it played out in the future, Ho would be able to exploit the fact that the Vietminh were the legitimate progenitors of an independent Vietnamese state. The crowd responded with cries of 'long live President Ho Chi Minh'. He would go to France with the mandate both from the 'elections' and from the recognition accorded by France's representative:

> *The Vietminh were now mobilising everyone to do his or her share for a country in shambles, but also to become indoctrinated into their movement.*

Mai Elliott also notes how the Vietminh were taking a grip on society: 'The head of the Vietminh on each block made sure everyone joined...and checking passers-by for identification papers.'[70]

Ever subtle, Ho had already decided to take a twin track to the upcoming talks in France. On 27 February 1946, Ho handed two letters to the respective representatives, addressed to the presidents of the US, China, Russia and Britain. He made a 'request to four powers (1) to intervene and stop the war in Indochina in order to mediate fair settlement and (2) to bring the Indochinese issue before the United Nations...' (Pentagon Papers) No replies were received. Washington had withdrawn and washed their hands of the ugly matter. Britain backed France, and China was about to sell out their nationalist cousins in Vietnam. France was now in control and Ho would have to deal with them.

A few days later, Leclerc's ships steamed into the gulf of Tonkin and the Chinese began to withdraw after a few sharp artillery exchanges. After claiming he had not been informed of the Chiang agreement, Lu Hun's Chinese troops eventually withdrew, the last to leave being those in the Northern Highlands around Lau Cai who gathered in the highlands opium crop before they left.

Why had Ho been so moderate and considered in his negotiations with the French? It was for the same reason that he wanted to present a nice face to the US, with whom he continued to engage in a friendly fashion, while preventing any criticism of America and their capitalist system, and hinting that he was really a nationalist not a communist. An interesting passage of conversation with Lieutenant Fenn of the US Army in 1945 went like this:

> *Ho said, 'You must understand that gaining independence from a great power like France is a formidable task that cannot be achieved without outside help… one must gain it* [independence] *through organisation, propaganda, training and discipline. One also needs a set of beliefs, a gospel, a practical analysis, you might even say a bible. Marxist-Leninism gave me that framework.'*

Some historians claim that this passage shows that he was a nationalist more than a communist. On the contrary, he is admitting to being a communist, which could hardly be denied, but suggesting that he is just using communism as a 'framework' for his nationalist ambitions. He was planting an interpretation in the minds of some US officials and his words cannot be taken at face value.

Ho had to try to disarm both the French and the Americans to play for time because the Chinese Communist Army had retreated to the Manchurian border regions with the USSR, and its survival was not certain let alone the prospect of victory. There was no help at hand and Indochina was way down the pecking order in terms of Soviet priorities, as Ho would discover nine years later. With no help, with no arms supplies or money, the communist movement could be throttled at birth by the major powers. Ho's humility and accommodating stance in negotiations was purely tactical. He was trading appearances for time.

While the politicians haggled and manoeuvred, ordinary families were being rent asunder by choices of politics, by emotions and incidents that stirred them, or by choices of survival. Mai Elliot tells the story of her family:

> *In my own family while Giu and Xuong went along with the Vietminh because it was popular, my sister Thang and her husband Hau supported the movement out of personal conviction. Hau was irritated by the arrogance and racism of many of the colons. They would call the Vietnamese names, dismiss them as a 'dirty race' and attack them without being prosecuted. One day, he had an argument with a French policeman. The Frenchman who was just passing by in the street, stopped to intervene and slapped Hau in the face. Hau fell in love with the ideals of socialism…The famine had horrified him.*[71]

George Wickes, an American official in Saigon, wrote in November 1945:

> *…the French are not quite so confident as they were at the start that this will be cleared up in a few weeks. I believe that unless they always keep large garrisons and patrols everywhere they will not be able to keep the country submissive.*[72]

Leclerc had started off full of optimism for the re-occupation of Indochina, announcing on arrival, in full de Gaullian hyperbole, that 'we are fighting to re-establish French greatness.'[73] However, by the end of his tour six months later in March 1946, he had become thoroughly disillusioned. Shying away from the de Gaullian mantra of empire, Leclerc believed privately that the war was not winnable and required political accommodation. Soon after the outbreak of fighting, on 5 January Leclerc wrote a report for the president of the National Defence Council. He defined the strategic and tactical morass into which France would blunder about for the next nine years:

> *In Tonkin it is now open war, the enemy has the freedom in a vast rear area to manoeuvre or retreat. We have lost the initiative. This sort of combat degenerates into guerilla war, where our ability to achieve decisive success or to inflict serious checks to gain the ascendancy, is over.*[74]

When he returned to France he met with de Gaulle at Hotel Lapérouse, where de Gaulle challenged him, saying: 'You have sold out Indochina cheaply.' Leclerc replied brutally, 'Who sold out Syria and Lebanon?'[75] Having experienced the reality of Indochina Leclerc had broken from his former boss, the cantankerous armchair imperialist.

However, de Gaulle approved of d'Agenlieu's aggressive and duplicitous policies. According to the general's letter to Valluy, d'Agenlieu's 'policy is correct, you do not compromise with this government (the Vietminh).'[76] De Gaulle was not necessarily wrong, because the communists wanted total power, using violence if necessary, to impose their totalitarian political concepts. But Leclerc realised the impossibility of winning a military victory on France's limited resources.

CHAPTER VI

War and Peace

Ho in Paris, Giáp in Hanoi

Leclerc departed for France on 23 March 1946. His last official function was to meet with Ho in Halong Bay. D'Argenlieu was there as official host. By this time their relationship had hit rock bottom as d'Argenlieu struggled to establish precedence in an environment that was bound to attach more importance to military power than political office.

Giáp met Leclerc for the first time. Upon meeting, they shook hands. Leclerc said to him gruffly, 'I love France and I want France's honour to be respected everywhere.'[1] It was clearly something of a warning to Giáp, soldier to soldier. Despite this introduction, Leclerc was very eager for a compact with Ho's communists. From his experiences in the south, he had fundamentally broken with the view of de Gaulle and Admiral d'Argenlieu, believing that a political settlement was the only way forward. Leclerc estimated that 350,000 French troops were needed to deal with the communist insurgency. He also recognised that the cost and use of French conscripts was something politically impossible for impoverished France.

General Leclerc was replaced by the tall and elegant General Valluy. With Leclerc gone, Valluy soon showed his hawkish intentions by occupying Hanoi's Finance Ministry on 27 March. There was other tension in Hanoi as the Chinese under Le Hun looked for pretexts to provoke violence as a tactical means to staying. There were numerous firefights with French soldiers, but they eventually left in September having stolen as much as possible before departure. A disaster for the VNQDD, they would soon start to feel the loss of their protectors as VNQDD and Dai Viet cadres were rounded up, shot or bound up and dropped in the river by Giáp's troops. Others were buried alive, including Dai Viet leader Ngo Diem's older brother, not just a nationalist but a Catholic. (Diem would later become president of South Vietnam and would exact a terrible revenge.) Another victim was the leading pacifist nationalist Bui Quang Chieu.[2] With French assistance the purge proceeded within weeks of the 6 March agreement. The VNQDD headquarters were attacked and overrun in July. An estimated 15,000 nationalist and others, including Trotskyists, were assassinated.

Ho Chi Minh left for Paris by ship on 31 May. On the way he met with Admiral d'Argenlieu on board a French cruiser. The meeting lasted for two hours and though details are not available we can be sure that there was not a meeting of minds and there would have been no sincerity on either side, just two enemies sizing each other up. D'Argenlieu showed off French naval power, intending to impress on Ho that to fight France was futile. It was a bizarre scene as the communist leaders and the French delegation hosted by d'Argenlieu set off for a sunset cruise of remarkable Halong Bay (now a UN World Heritage Site) aboard the cruiser *Emile Bertin*. Cocktails were served and meaningless toasts made. Ho knew exactly what was going on and remarked to an aide that 'those ships cannot sail up our rivers.'[3] He was mostly right but several important land battles would be lost by the Vietminh in 1952, for the very reason that large naval vessels could go some way upriver and/or because of Dinassaut flotillas.

Giáp's first meeting with d'Argenlieu was at Darlat on 18 April. The history of the admiral was a matter for disdain by the revolutionary communist. D'Argenlieu:

> *...had small wily eyes under a wrinkled forehead and thin lips. My impression after spending a moment with him was that he was an experienced, cunning, arrogant, mean man.*

Giáp was not inaccurate in his summary of de Gaulle's strange creature.[4] His anger was enhanced by the admiral's successful tricks and deceptions. D'Argenlieu played the communists at their own game.

D'Argenlieu, who had returned to France in February to try to reverse the drift towards recognition, shortly afterward revealed his 'de Gaulle-directed' duplicity. As Giáp noted, d'Argenlieu had decided that 'now was a good chance to implement de Gaulle's policy towards the colonies.' After Ho's departure, the admiral organised a conference at Darlat, the purpose of which was to forge a separate Cochinchina and effectively sabotage Ho's visit to Paris, where the main point on the agenda would be the unification of the whole of Vietnam. Ho had agreed that the Vietminh would participate from April to May 1946 at Darlat, where Giáp would argue that the division along the 16th Parallel was just a temporary measure due to the exigencies of war and the practical necessity of taking the surrender of Japanese troops. However, Giáp and Ho were outfoxed. At Darlat, d'Argenlieu launched a political coup behind the backs of the government in Paris by pushing through de Gaulle's policy of detaching Cochin as a separate entity and dividing Vietnam. Ho would be meeting the French government for negotiations in the face of an outrageous breach of faith.

Out of the Darlat conference, a separate Cochin government was presented as a *fait accompli* to the fury of both the communists and nationalists. As the French government was in the middle of pre-election pre-occupations, there was no censure from Paris. The admiral's views were as trenchant as ever:

> *The French government ought to gather together all pro French Annamite patriots around itself...we have committed ourselves to* protecting certain ethnic minorities *and we must uphold our role as vigilant guardians. Circumstances are now favourable to us and if we do not seize this opportunity, we will destroy what generations of colonials and Annamite patriots have built together.*[5] (Author's emphasis.)

D'Argenlieu and the French Army were out of control.

Ignoring Paris but heeding de Gaulle, the admiral ordered the army to attack and occupy Pleiku and Ton Kum in the Central Highlands, whereupon the guerrilla war in the region and in Cochin started up again. On 31 March 1946, the French Army showed their clear intention with regard to Indochina, when armoured cars, artillery and aircraft attacked the nationalist forces in Lao. Prince Souphanouvong's Issarak Lao/Vietminh forces at Thakhaek on the Mekong were overrun. Numerous but lightly armed, they were crushed within two hours.[6] Laos was re-taken. They suffered about 1,000 casualties. Badly injured when strafed by a Spitfire as he crossed the Mekong, the wounded prince found refuge in Thailand. His compatriot, Phay Dang of the Mao Resistance League, was encouraged by Red Prince Souphanouvong to continue back to the mountains: 'Arouse the people. Create a strong organisation. Later we will fight together.'[7]

King Sisavong Vong was crowned on 23 April 1946 under the nationalist banner, but after a French battalion-strength parachute-drop at Luang Prabang and Vientianne, he shifted immediately to a pro-French stance. There was no fighting in these places. Supporting the French enabled the king to encompass previously autonomous princedoms at Champassak in the south and Kouang Xian in the Plain of Jars. Prince Boun Oum of Champassak, a conservative, was awarded by France a permanent role in government and would also become prime minister 1949–51. Additionally, the Thais were forced to hand back the two substantial provinces on the left bank of the Mekong, which had been snapped off in 1941 in a Japanese-brokered settlement.[8]

Giáp had no illusions as to the purpose and inspiration behind French policy. As he wrote later: 'The Gaullists in Indochina headed by d'Argenlieu adopted a policy of *faits accompli* to further their aggressive policies.' Giáp, Ho and the Vietminh were always extremely well informed on French politics and sought to influence and play the French system. Giáp's accusation was:

> *D'Argenlieu had grossly violated the clauses of the Agreement but* never suffered any reprimands from the French government even after de Gaulle had left the political arena... *he had received support from the Inter-ministerial council on Indochina presided over by Bidault.*[9] (Author's emphasis.)

The government had backed d'Argenlieu after the event, but he had exceeded his powers at the very least. Bidault, the leader of the centrist and Catholic Movement Républicain Populaire (MRP), showed his hand from the first as a determined imperialist. Sources of information on French political division and developments were readily available to the Vietminh, not least from the French press as well as secret information from fellow travellers and communists within the French government. Ironically, most of the Cochinchina clique's sympathies had been with Petain and Vichy, so d'Argenlieu and de Gaulle's policies began the political sashay towards reconciliation with Vichy supporters on the right.

The reaction of Nguyễn Binh, the head of the defence committee of the 7th zone in Saigon, to d'Argenlieu's trick was furious and vitriolic. As the Vietminh had for once been outmanoeuvred, the tone of the loser was particularly insulting:

> *Thierry d'Argenlieu and his colonialist are raping Cochinchina...they perfidiously buy traitors who they protect with armed men while organising a separatist meeting (this ridiculous collection of dilettante, pirates, chancers, secret policemen and other wretched types)...and while they talk at Darlat French troops continue to terrorise the population and attack Vietnamese troops.* Chief of defence, 7th Zone, 19 April 1946.

Not surprisingly the guerrillas' war flared up with greater intensity.

The main agenda item in Paris would be the exact interpretation of the powers to be exercised by the Democratic Republic of Vietnam within the union. The French insisted that foreign affairs, armed forces, transport, immigration and hygiene would remain preserves of French power. It hardly seemed like independence to the Vietminh or the nationalists. Leclerc wrote to Robert Schumann 8 June 1946:

> *...it's important not to forget that he* [Ho] *is the great enemy of France' reminding him 'that he is the murderer of many pro French Annamites and proof is self-evident. We have all the documents and telegrams to prove it.*[10]

Ho arrived in France amidst yet another government crisis. The chaos resulted from the national elections in France on 2 June. It meant that Ho had to be parked in Biarritz while the French political parties bickered their way into another coalition government. Formal negotiations only began on 6 July at

Fontainebleau. Pham van Dong protested that if the French government supported the admiral's moves, then 'our conference has no further reason to meet', and referred back to the 6 March agreement. It was in essence an ultimatum: 'Agree the 6 March agreement as the basis for talks or we go to war.' But the talks went on.

The new French government was in a quandary. Quite unable to restrain the admiral or the soldiers under his command, they came up with a solution. They eventually offered a referendum but with no specific timetable. Nor would the government agree to an explicit declaration on the independence of Vietnam as a whole. Not even the communists in the new French government would offer a helping hand. French Communist Party leader Thorez, a notorious sycophant to Stalin, was playing the nationalist card, indicating that if the Vietminh did not like the terms, 'let the guns speak for us if need be.' No doubt he was instructed by Moscow where Stalin was eager not to provoke the west while he took Eastern Europe slice by slice. Stalin stuck strictly to the concept of zones of influence. For example, regarding the Balkans, he respected the Churchill-Stalin agreement at Yalta on percentages of influence. Stalin ceded Greece to one hundred percent British influence, following which the powerful Greek Communist Party was stood down and denied Soviet support. Stalin even broke with Tito's Yugoslavia on the issue.

No one in the communist movement, including Ho, should ruffle any international feathers until Stalin's primary goals in Europe had been achieved. Cowed by the US's asymmetric possession of the A-bomb, Stalin was treading carefully. Rocking the boat and conflict with the west in non-essential regions of the world might result in trouble for core strategic interests in Eastern Europe, as the Red Army-backed communist governments closed down civil society, democracy and other centres of opposition.[11] Stalin had bigger fish to fry. Moreover, with more than thirty percent of the vote in France, the PCF were sniffing at power. Hence the French communists, having led the resistance to the Nazis, had meekly handed back their weapons when this was demanded by de Gaulle. Stalin's strategy in this period 1945–47 was to insinuate the French Communist Party into respectability within the French political system then take over the country in due course by 'common front tactics', the same tactic used by the Vietminh.

Only after definitively securing Czechoslovakia in 1948 and the atom bomb in 1949 along with Mao's victory in the Chinese Civil War would Stalin release the brake on outright support for the Vietminh, including diplomatic recognition. Democratic centralism still applied in Paris as well as the jungles of the Viet Bac. On his return, Ho eulogised:

> *Comrade Stalin listened to me and said our policy was correct. When comrade Stalin says something is correct it must be correct. Comrade Maurice Thorez says that Stalin is never wrong.*[12]

In 1946, Ho must have been well aware of Moscow's cautious view. He was under direct orders, which is why he avoided bellicosity, unlike his impatient colleagues, including Nguyễn Binh in the south, who was pushing for all-out war. Binh was not a communist but a nationalist coalition partner. Pham van Dong, the head of delegation, was also bellicose and aggressive, but it is doubtful whether this was anything more than Ho and him playing 'good cop, bad cop'. While his delegates negotiated, Ho charmed Parisian intellectuals and politicians and gave interviews to the international press and local journalists, telling them for the benefit of useful idiots of the world that the Democratic Republic of Vietnam (DRV) was neutral, 'like Switzerland' (Michael Kort, *The Vietnam War Reexamined*, Cambridge, 2018, p.87) (presumably without the chocolate, cuckoo clocks or ski instructors). Behind the scenes Ho, who had remained in Paris, secured confirmation of the 6 March agreement from the minister for colonies and agreed a ceasefire in the south for 30 October. Ho was playing for time, time to prepare for battle and time for Mao's communists to make progress in the civil war, which had been raging since July 1945.

Ho nonetheless wished to delay an outbreak of fighting and head-off pre-emptive French actions by the army. So he signed one limited agreement on 14 September on financial, economic and cultural questions, and both sides dubbed it the *modus vivendi*. There was also an agreement to resume talks by January 1947. French journalist Philippe Devillers noted: 'The Hanoi government seemed, under Ho's influence, to be avoiding any policy of violence.'[13] Ho was playing for time. He must surely have reckoned that war was inevitable. De Gaulle was determined on war. He sent a message to d'Argenlieu on 5 September: 'Dear Admiral, there is a big piece left for us to take back, a great game. Its up to you.'[14]

Ho returned to Vietnam. It had not been a wasted trip because it bought some time and showed a convincing image to intellectual circles and opinion-formers in Paris, some of the 'useful idiots' who would be of service to him for the next thirty years. Meanwhile the *modus vivendi* was coming under strain. It was only meant by both sides to be a stop gap before war broke out in full, allowing both sides to arm and prepare. Ho was clear that:

> *...the* modus vivendi *can in no way have a binding effect on future negotiations. Whether future negotiations lead to a fruitful result depends on the implementation of the* modus vivendi.[15]

Already by mid-November, General Valluy was sending secret directives: 'Decent attempts at a compromise are no longer appropriate and a severe lesson is now needed.'[16] D'Argenlieu prepared the ground for Valluy by pointing out various breaches of the *modus vivendi*. By 4 December, Valluy was sending a telegram saying 'this time the chances of localisation [of the conflict] are minimal'.[17] Four days later, on 28 November, Nguyễn Bình was advising Giáp, in an intercepted message, on how to attack and delay the expected French advance from Haiphong. Near Saigon, Commissaire Le Duan was preparing as well for a general conflict by issuing guidance on 8 December that in the coming battle the role of forces in the south was to attack in Cochin and Annam, to distract French forces and prevent reinforcement in Tonkin.[18]

These directives were immediately intercepted by the Vietminh, as were most policy documents. The instructions issued by Valluy were outside of his remit and discretion, but increasingly responded to the lead given by d'Argenlieu and de Gaulle behind the scenes. The military were acting independently. Secret policies for a French *coup d'état* in Haiphong had already been in place since April 1946, according to documents intercepted by Giáp. Politicians in Paris in the Socialist Party in particular continued under the illusion that there was a pathway to peaceful negotiation. When Leon Blum, old socialist war horse of the left and premier in the pre-war common front, won the elections and formed a cabinet in December 1946, there 'seemed' to be hope for a peaceful settlement.

Across the Atlantic, Dean Acheson was receiving a report from the American consul in Haiphong, who reported on the mendacity and aggression of French commanders. 'Colonel Debes who is notorious for graft and brutality…has admitted that he cannot control his own troops.' (17 December 1946)[19]

Debes was preparing the groundwork for attacks on Vietminh positions under the direct instructions from hawkish General Valluy, who bypassed Debes' direct commander. The French Army was already culturally alienated from republican politics. With the aristocratic manners of the officer class, the French military had long regarded the republic as an enemy, something exacerbated by the army's public humiliation during the Dreyfus affair 1893–1906. Catholic, conservative, anti-semitic, with many monarchist and Vichy sympathisers, the army stood politically apart from the rest of society. In the absence of strong political control from the chaotic French political class, the army in faraway Indochina avoided, when it suited them, chains of command both downwards and upwards. They developed their own policies and followed guidance from de Gaulle, who had his own quasi-falangist ideas of government and society. De Gaulle's games came home to roost when the culture he had fostered led to the 'generals' putsch' in Algiers in 1961.

Letters to America

Ho made intensive efforts to develop relations with the United States, seeking their good officers to influence France into acceptance of genuine independence for a unified Vietnam. His letters aimed to push at the strongly anti-colonial sentiments in the American administration. There are constant references to British and French imperialism, and the Atlantic charter. His communications are laced with denials of being communist-influenced, hints of economic opportunities to develop Indochina at the US capital, hints as to a naval base for America at Cam Ranh Bay, and appeals for economic, even military, aid. There are nine direct and indirect communications to the US government, the secretary of state and President Truman between 22 October 1945 and February 1946 listed in the Pentagon Papers. It was part of Ho's charm offensive to disarm the Americans, to frustrate any chances for direct or indirect intervention.

A typical communication was the note sent to the secretary of state on 23 October 1945, which talked about how 'two million Vietnamese died of starvation during the winter of 1944 and spring 1945 because of the starvation policy of the French who seized and stored [food] until it was rotted.' The allegations were obviously false because the reason for the famine, despite the efforts of Decoux's Vichy government, was that there were no Japanese ships available to transport the rice from Cochin to Tonkin. There was not enough rail capacity to make a difference. Japanese policies, including orders to Admiral Decoux to plant non-rice crops, exacerbated the famine.

He then goes on to describe Anglo-French perfidy and aggression, including 'street-sniping' in Saigon.

Despite the pleas and the carrots dangled by Ho, Dean Acheson, the secretary of state, was not taken in. He would write an internal communication in December 1946: 'Keep in mind Ho's clear record as an agent of international communism, absence of evidence of rejection of Moscow affiliations.' (Pentagon Papers)

The liquidation of enemies

Despite the *modus vivendi* agreement, in the south the guerrilla war continued, as did the liquidation of rivals. In Tonkin, where Giáp ruled, the war was of a different kind directed entirely at political enemies within. The departure of the Chinese under the Chungking Agreement was essentially a betrayal of their Tonkinese nationalist allies, who now faced the communist-backed Vietminh alone. Giáp moved to eliminate the enemy.

Nationalist troops still controlled key towns such as Lang Son, Viet Tri, Phu Yan and Lao Cai, as well as a strong media presence in Hanoi. All of these places and more fell to Giáp's assaults. At the same time as murdering their rivals, Giáp undermined the nationalists politically by subterfuge, including a staged 'discovering' of faked torture pits and mutilated cadavers and graves at the nationalist headquarters. In Hanoi, the nationalist media presence was shut down by force. About 6,000 nationalists were liquidated in these purges. At a local level, nationalist sympathisers were murdered all over Vietnam. Assassinations took many forms. Shooting was common but a favourite was binding groups of nationalists together and throwing them into the Red River estuary.

A typical case was the murder in Quang Nai, south of Da Nang, of civil servants, Mandarins, Catholics and landowners.[20] Some nationalists fled over the border but many bowed to the inevitable.

In Cochinchina in September and October 1946, there were '436 assassinations of Annamites/356 attacks on military posts/77 attacks – ambushes on communications/209 acts of sabotage on telephone lines etc.'[21] Giáp also prepared for war, setting up military academies and increasing recruitment towards a million-man military force organised at national, regional and village levels. Giáp's memoirs are disingenuous as to the level of Vietminh duplicity and murder. Both sides were preparing for war.

Haiphong October–December 1946

Ho arrived back in Haiphong on 20 October 1946 to be greeted by huge crowds. Whatever his meekness in Paris, Ho soon set about testing the limits of the 6 March agreement. No doubt he did not want to be seen to be firing the first shots and he was probably hoping for changes in the shifting sands of French politics where veteran socialist left-winger Leon Blum was in the running to take over as the new prime minister of France. In Tonkin, the Vietminh promulgated a new constitution with no reference to the French Union. Missing from the National Assembly in Hanoi were any opposition deputies who had apparently been arrested for vaguely described 'crimes against the common law'.

On 28 October, Ho laid the groundwork for a political structure ready for the coming fight. He appointed a new Vietminh-dominated government, where he was the appointed prime minister as well as president. The 30 October ceasefire in the south barely lasted one week when the admiral's French forces started to move into Vietminh areas – an obvious and deliberate provocation. The puppet master was, of course, de Gaulle, who was looking to destabilise the Fourth Republic and push his idea of French glory, while quietly planning a return to front-line politics.

The most important strategic place in Tonkin in December 1946 was Haiphong, the only considerable port of entry to Northern Vietnam. Through it came considerable contraband and, most importantly, arms for Giáp's Vietminh militia. It also supplied government revenue. Not surprisingly it became the focal point for a power struggle between the Vietminh and the French, with the nominal issue being the right to collect custom dues. Already in August 1946, the French had seized the customs house and police station using tanks. It was contrary to the 6 March agreement and Ho complained bitterly to Bidault in a letter on 11 November. Ho's communication to Bidault was delayed for ten days by the French military-controlled post office. In November, the first serious incident broke out when the French navy seized a Chinese junk loaded with contraband petroleum. Shooting broke out and spread around the city. Two hundred and forty Vietminh were killed before the ceasefire was negotiated.

Taking a leaf out of the admiral's book, the French military decided to provoke a showdown. Operating behind the back of the French commander Colonel Debes, who detested Indochina, they issued a general order on 22 November for Vietminh forces to quit Haiphong by 10 a.m. the following day. It was a remarkably short time-frame for such a demand. As the US vice-consul remarked, it is incredible that the French could seriously have wished for a favourable reply to their ultimatum.[22] French journalist Devillers noted:

> *It is probable that Ho had not even seen the ultimatum by the time French heavy artillery from land and sea blasted the civilian packed city. Admiral Battet admitted that 6,000 were killed.*[23]

Curiously, the chairman of the Haiphong Municpal Committee revealed in 1981 that only 500–1,000 died compared to Ho's contemporary claim of 20,000. General Valluy had already informed Colonel Debes of the guarantees that were to be demanded. He even added that he considered it 'indispensable to take advantage of the incidents to improve our position at Haiphong.' The French military were slipping the moorings of political control.

French-flown Spitfires joined in the attacks and machine-gunned refugees and supplies coming into the city. French troops followed on, burning and looting the old town. Then there was heavy fighting and counter-attacks once the surprised Vietminh had regrouped. The French responded with more heavy shelling of outlying villages. By the time restraint came from Paris and the proper chain of command had been re-established, 'All the Vietnamese quarters were utterly destroyed. Dead people were still buried under the rubble.' General Valluy did not consult his government. The French Army had taken matters into their own hands, leaving the politicians to cover their backs. They knew that General de Gaulle would support their position. Operating behind the scenes, de Gaulle instructed General Leclerc to 'show the greatest possible force'. His influence was still pervasive. It was a *fait accompli* that some but not all welcomed. Politicians in Paris did not want to appear as the aggressors. Already the US was beginning to be perturbed by the outbreak of fighting, with the state department warning the French of their concern. The French retorted by raising the spectre of communism, already a sore point in Washington as the Soviets' salami-sliced their way into control in Eastern Europe and advanced in China.

Full-scale war was just a matter of time. The army realised that they needed to take advantage of men and equipment before the Vietminh became more powerful. In the admiral they had a powerful supporter who had shown what could be done by decisive unilateral action in the absence of a strong government in Paris. On 17 December, a general ultimatum was made demanding the disarmament of the Vietminh. An impossible demand, it would lead to war. Clearly not a coincidence, on 17 December de Gaulle received a visit of three hours from the admiral at his mansion at Colombey-les deux Eglises. De Gaulle was flagrantly undermining the elected government.

Taking a last hope from developments in France where Leon Blum became prime minister, Ho anticipated that his recent article recommending 'an agreement for independence' could end maverick decision-making by France's military and political class in Indochina. As usual, Blum found himself in office but not in power, his words were empty, as could be expected of a Fourth Republic socialist politician. General attacks on French military posts and civilians around Hanoi were made on 19 December. Sainteny, who had even to the last tried to broker a peace deal, was badly injured when his armoured car ran over a mine. On the same day the US began its decisive slide over to the French side with the state department announcing that the French occupation was necessary. 'Not only as an antidote to Soviet influence, but to protect Vietnam and South-East Asia from future Chinese imperialism.'[24] As the Chinese Civil War progressed, US policy hardened still more.

Ho Chi Minh, meanwhile, in preparation for war, moved his headquarters and radio transmitters into the jungle, to his former haunts in the north. He was preparing for a long, armed struggle. On 19 December 1946, the war broke out nationwide with attacks on French garrisons and outposts including Toruane (Da-Nang) and Hue. According to one Vietnamese observer: 'The flame of nationalism never burned so bright in the hearts of the people. Vietnamese never united so strongly behind the Vietminh.'

Most of Hanoi was quickly overcome despite the elaborate plans concocted by the Vietminh.

However, the old town, a rabbit warren of Chinese shops and houses, was defended by 3,000 fanatical fighters, who bought two months of precious time for Ho's establishment of the DRV in the jungles of the Bac Kan. A map found on a dead Vietminh cadre shows details of street by street obstacles, French strongpoints, and Vietminh attacking deployment in the old town next to the *petit lac*.[25]

On 23 December 1946, three days after the first fighting in Hanoi, Blum, the hero of the 'popular front', told parliament: 'No stone was left unturned to restore agreement with the Vietnam government,' but his duty was to protect French lives and 'to spare the blood of the people whose political liberty we recognised ten months ago – a people who *must soon take their place in the union of people federated around France*.' (Author's emphasis.)

However, the problem was that the exact definition of 'union' would be French-centric. France would not part with ultimate power. Blum's speech was tacitly approved by *l'Humanite*, the Communist Party newspaper, and the communists stayed in government.

Ho Chi Minh's request for an armistice on 11 January was not responded to by Moutet, the socialist minister of defence. Why was this so? The problem was a split in the French in the colony between the moderate policies being espoused by Sainteny, whose administration believed that Vietnamese nationalism had to be appeased, and the so-called Saigon clique of d'Argenlieu, composed of wealthy industrialists and bankers. The military themselves, with exceptions such as Leclerc, leaned to the more aggressive right-wing and colonialist views of d'Argenlieu. France's government was split on Indochina policy and domestic issues, including intra-coalition government politicking, took priority. Moutet was probably happy not to pick up what was becoming a policy hot potato.

Ho Chi Minh, meanwhile, in preparation for war, moved his headquarters and radio transmitters into the jungle to his former haunts in the north. He was preparing for a long, armed struggle. On 19 December 1946, the war broke out nationwide. According to one Vietnamese observer: 'The flame of nationalism never burned so bright in the hearts of the people, and the Vietnamese never united so strongly behind the Vietminh.'[26] Many radicalised city dwellers, especially middle-class and intellectual supporters, moved out into the jungles. It was the first time for many of them to experience peasant life and the jungle. It was a 'romantic revolutionary experience' that would test their metal once the first enthusiasm had worn off, which was not long. Returnees in 1947 increased the population of the delta by 250,000, and the number of secured villages increased by 636 by August.[27] The Vietminh Army was equipped with an assortment of firearms but precious few support weapons. They lacked training, discipline or uniforms and, according to Ngo Van Chieu writing in his *Diary of a Viet Minh Soldier*, they 'looked more like a gang than an organised army.'[28] However he was assigned to a Japanese-run training camp so that by such hand-to-mouth improvisations, the quality of soldiering was improved. The Vietminh Army would also benefit from Kuomintang-trained Vietnamese officers who had graduated from Chiang Kai-Shek's Huangpu Military Academy in Canton.

In France, public opinion was mainly shaped by de Gaulle and Marius Moutet, the MRP politician. The MRP would, through their hold on the relevant ministries, dominate foreign and colonial policy until 1954. Party leaders Bidault, Pleven and Schuman were implacable imperialists, although the latter would start to drift as the war went on. Popular opinion was also shaped by the propaganda of APF, whose reporting was controlled by the admiral. APF told lies regarding casualties and blame. De Gaulle and the MRP developed another theme as to their colonial rights. Re-colonisation was not just about recovered glory for France, the maintenance of their great power status, but also the civilising mission. De Gaulle declared that France must stay 'united with countries to which she had brought civilisation'. Marius Moutet announced in Saigon what would become the mantra for the next three years. 'Before any thoughts of negotiation, we need to have a decisive military victory.'[29] The problem was, how could you get decisive victory or unconditional surrender from a guerrilla force that had the widespread backing of the populace?

The French storm Hanoi and pretences are over, 19 December 1946

Despite a population that was 'almost completely hostile', the French stormed into Hanoi. Its capture took three days of heavy fighting, although the full subjugation of the Chinese and Vietnamese old city quarters needed a further two months – a vicious conflict that left the old town a shattered ruin. The French had to fight street by street, using artillery at close range to destroy centres of resistance. Contrary to the Geneva Convention, they also used political suspects to clear barricades in the front line. As Mai Elliott reports from her brothers' testimony, thousands died. 'The day after his capture Giu was assigned his first prison duty, working with a group of other prisoners to collect dead bodies from houses in an area that the French had cleared.'[30]

She continues:

> *The Vietminh outnumbered and outgunned were like grasshoppers kicking at elephants. Their soldiers would open fire on the French then disappear inside houses whose walls had been pierced through to create a maze like a rabbit warren. In the street they built barricades – many of which were rigged with crude mines...The French would dispatch gangs of POWs to clear the barricades with their bare hands. My brothers had to do this so many times they became experts at it...And they got used to the deadly fire of snipers and the sudden*

death of an old prisoner who was standing right next to Giu, quietly collapsed like a deflated balloon from a sniper's bullet.

Eventually the French triumphed and the old city was taken. In Hanoi's old town, which fought on for six weeks, many thousands of Vietminh and civilians were killed by indiscriminate shelling and bombing. The French lost nearly 2,000 dead. So much for a civilising mission.

In Paris, meanwhile, another government was falling. Paul Remadier, a socialist, was chosen to replace Leon Blum. It coincided with gradual moves to oust the communists, as the new government was no longer tripartite but contained five political parties including the radicals. The problem with the communists, apart from the allocation of the ministries, was Indochina policy and prices/wages, and economic policy. To satisfy the socialists, Admiral d'Argenlieu was sacked and replaced by M. Bollaert, a radical.

A full debate on Indochina was held in the French parliament on 11 and 18 March 1947. The proposition of the government's Indochina policy was passed with the communists abstaining but the communist minister voting in favour, which allowed them by this formula to stay in government. Government policy was 'resistance to violence and the desire for peace and harmony', linked to the warning that 'there are men with whom it will be impossible to deal'. Delphic, but clearly referring to the communist-backed Vietminh and Ho, the coalition was held together by fictional government solidarity.[31] However, on 5 May, the prices and incomes policy was the battle line on which the communists did eventually choose to resign from the government. Indochina only occasionally intruded on domestic politics in the Fourth Republic and was rarely debated. Where it did intrude, the issues normally revolved around cost, financial scandals or some human rights scandals or massacres reported by the communist daily *L'Humanité*.

Tales from Da-nang (Tourane)

Jean Jacques Bonnaud, *Prisonniers du Mikado*, Temporis, 2022

The war started in Hanoi on 20 December 1946. Giáp and Ho were fully prepared not just for the holding battle in Hanoi but for a general attack across the whole of the north where it was hoped that mass attacks could sweep up outlying French garrisons in places such as Da-Nang and Hue. It was indeed a wholesale attack comparable to the famous Tet offensive in 1968. They were hoping, perhaps, to take advantage of the coming Christmas festivities with French officers being on leave. The French were prepared. D'Argenlieu's letter to General Valluy of 9 November 1946 makes clear that Tourane had to be held as a place for either evacuation or reinforcement of the Hue garrison.[32]

After the 6 March peace accord in 1946 preparatory to the meetings at Versailles in Paris between Ho's DRV delegation and the French government, relations between the two camps had been reasonably correct. French garrisons had been admitted to important French towns, and expatriated professionals such as Monsieur Bonnaud of La Banque Indosuez returned from the compound in Hue to the coast town of Tourane, which was a medium-large place that boasted an important part in Vietnamese history and trading.

Warning signs appeared in Da Nang when:

During the evening of the 19 January there were big explosions, the Vietminh police evacuated without notice…only on the morning at 6.30 a.m. we realised that Hue was also under attack…several civilians there were assassinated and the Viets sought out the commandant of the post to kill him before the attack. My parents rushed to the market to buy provisions before the merchants were evacuated by the police. In Tourane, meanwhile, in his insouciant manner, my father went for an appointment with his Chinese dentist…he noticed in the adjacent road a small troop of uniformed Viets who appeared surprised. He retraced his steps and made it home just as the explosions started. A company of the 3rd battalion of 23rd Tabors reoccupied the post office and the electricity station and dismantled various barricades that had been erected in the night to block the road to the airport.[33]

The small Vietminh garrison that had taken over the post office resisted the French for several hours but were eliminated piece by piece by the deployment of a 57mm cannon. Having killed or wounded with sniper fire two or three soldiers, the 3rd Company led by Captain Mourut engaged the enemy in the rue Jules Ferry and passed by our house with a machine-gun. Resistance by the African army centred on a bunker in front of the museum.

There was a fierce defence of the power station where Sergeant Tardis was wounded and lost his sight, while in the west of the city his brother was killed. By the end of the day the Viets had withdrawn from the central environs but placed themselves in strategic buildings that were fiercely defended. One saw bodies of dead and wounded French, sometimes lying up against trees. Our house received a direct hit from a rocket. We took refuge in the office of my father. Small groups of Viets remained to fight at strategic points. Shooting came from over the river but this was eventually silenced by a French machine-gun in front of the post office…in the night shooting started up again and there was an intensive firefight. We heard the chants of the legionnaires posted at the power station and the factory as they counter-attacked…

In the street next to the cathedral were little shop houses and often a note was pinned to the door saying 'here lives a Catholic family'. A legionnaire entered, marauded through it…he shot at a young Viet volunteer carrying a basket of grenades. He and his grenades were soon captured by a patrol.[34]

After the assault, in which the fighting was intense for two days, there was a clean-up operation for several days, both of the town structures and of the occasional Viet holdout. Civilians, French, Vietnamese and Chinese drifted back to their homes and power was restored after six days. Hue, meanwhile, continued to be under siege.

Gradually, zones of pacification were extended and carved out by the Viet guerrillas who had moved to the hills surrounding these isolated garrisons, which though extended in reach would always be under effective siege even if the main city centres were beyond gunshot reach. Such was the long term pattern established around these garrisons in central and coastal Annam.

As always the retreating Vietminh left behind agents.

Hue, with its 800-man garrison, continued under siege until relieved by several powerful armoured columns landed by sea on the beaches to the east. The Vietminh retreated to their pre-prepared bases in the hills outside the city, including a network of trails, tunnels, defensive positions and listening posts.

Fight for the countryside and military 'sweeps'

French forces moved out from Hanoi into the delta and Tonkin countryside and remote mountain areas where they set up posts and garrisons and started to fall into roadside ambushes. Not long after his arrival, and soon after the capture of Hanoi, Legionnaire Heinrich-Karl Krause went out on his first patrol into the countryside 30km north of Hanoi. On their return, the French were 20km from base when a wire-controlled IED attack exploded some mines along the road. A firefight broke out in which the legionnaires raked the surrounding bushes with machine-gun bursts. Krause took shelter and a little later several armoured cars came to the rescue from Hanoi's guard post down the road:

> *Suddenly there was a faint call from someone wounded in the bushes. Immediately, a few men dragged a young girl out of the bushes, she could not have been any more than 10 or 12. She was barely alive, her underdeveloped chest had a gaping wound, torn apart by an MG bust. It could only have come from machine-gunners Meyr and Minnard, who were distraught. A low groan came from the bloodied lips, her head flopped to one side. Dead! In her right hand she was still holding a piece of electronic wire…I wanted to go home.*

From the first the French had only an ephemeral hold on the territory. Despite this the MRP minister of war, Coste-Floret, declared, 'There is no longer any military problem in Indochina' (14 May 1947). It was typical MRP complacency. Aimless sweeping of the countryside brought little joy as the French set themselves up for being ambushed as a way of fixing the enemy in position. However, the Vietminh could evaporate quickly too. 'Sweeping' was the same tactic used by the legion in the nineteenth century and by the Americans in the Second Vietnam War.

The Vietminh had thoroughly anticipated that the French would take over Hanoi and the delta. They would have to revert to their guerrilla-style of warfare by retreating into the Viet Bac region of hills and forests north of Hanoi. They took with them many people, cadres, technical experts, troops and equipment:

> *They also dismantled machinery they had taken from the shops in the delta and reassembled the equipment in the forest. Small factories sprang up in caves, and using raw materials that had been painstakingly carried into the forest produced soap, matches, cloth, paper, and a few other basic goods. Medical equipment was also carted into the base, along with a small quantity of weapons and ammunition. Makeshift workshops were set up to repair weapons.*[35]

Whole new communities grew up in the jungles. For example:

> *Thang and Hau and the other families settled in a forest clearing, where they shared a long house on stilts – similar to those used by the Tho tribe. A rickety ladder led into the hut…Beyond the fringe was the forbidding forest where boars, bears and tigers roamed among the trees. At night the ladder was pulled up to keep tigers from climbing in… mysterious and menacing, its impenetrable mass pressing down on the tiny hut. There were king cobras and vipers.*[36]

Hau was an agricultural consultant and trainer for crop growing and choosing the best seeds:

> *Throughout the resistance, food would remain as a critical weapon for the Vietminh. When the French entered Vietminh villages, they would destroy rice stockpiles or kill draft animals used for ploughing. When the rice ripened in the fields, they would launch operations to disrupt the harvest.*[37]

Life in the jungle would be difficult and strange for the city dwellers, many of whom would return. The pastoral idyll soon gave way to hunger, boredom and the struggle to survive. Intolerable arrogance of the communist elite and strict officialdom was hardly pleasant for free-thinking intellectuals and cosmopolitan urbanites. Previous condescension over the simple peasant made many town-dwellers feel 'guilty, remembering that we often looked down on the peasants.' Tran Ngoc Chau concluded that a new bond of unity was created.[38] This was a transient feeling in the happy revolutionary phase before it was crushed by cynical careerism and the purges around land reform and the cruelties of the class war.

Hau survived a direct experience of war when he was strafed by a French fighter aircraft while cycling on top of a dike. Miraculously the bullets missed.

For the French, the jungle was a horrible place to fight: 'Scratched faces, bodies and arms, bitten by leeches, mosquitoes...and ants, cut by giant plants.' Major Dr Paul Grauwin complained that:

> *...numberless mosquitos were very persistent: the leeches cold and slimy to the touch – there was only one way of getting them off, to press the burning end of the cigarette into them. These leeches are unlike others; they climb trees and drop down, and then you find them behind your ear, on your neck.*[39]

Heat was also a problem: 'A French soldier suffering from sun stroke had come to die with us in fearful convulsion.'[40] For the lowland Vietnamese, the majority of the Vietminh Army, it was equally detestable and unfamiliar. They caught malaria just the same but had less medicine to deal with it. Forests were the dwelling places for the primitive indigenous people for whom they had so much disdain. Mostly lowlanders from the delta, Vietminh troops were only marginally better adapted to jungle warfare than the French. No one enjoys a soaking rain that pours down in cold rods and the chill that follows, especially in the Northern Highlands.

France's strategy for occupying the great mass of the country outside the Red and Mekong deltas consisted of raising the flag in as many places as possible. Not just in towns, a large number of lonely outposts were created, often on top of hills or in isolated rubber plantations in key areas, for example the Red River valley and Annamite hills, or the Tay Ninh borderland with Cambodia. 'Perfectly isolated in their green world,' they were often small platoon-size posts or even posts with a single NCO. Equipped with a few grenades and a light machine-gun, they were often virtually defenceless and without radios. Every two or three weeks there was some liaison and re-supply.[41] Nor did they have maps. They relied absolutely on local guides.[42] Another problem with the French Army, equipped with the second-hand cast-offs of other nations, was both the paucity of armament and its calibre varieties with concomitant logistics problems.[43]

However, as the French moved out of Hanoi, they were increasingly challenged by ambushes on the roads, in the jungles, in and around villages in the delta, and on the rivers. On one river advance northwards from Hanoi, the flotilla lost seven out of sixteen vessels and dared not make the return journey, so forcing the troops to make the dangerous trek back to the delta area on foot. Dr Grauwin commanded the medics:

> *The pagoda offered a black wall to attack...Suddenly there was a great din, the rattle of tommy guns then rifle fire, all over in a couple of seconds...Suddenly some heavy object rolled across the tiles of the main roof on to the smaller roof of the building alongside to fall into the courtyard. It was a grenade...it did not*

explode. This time there was nothing for it – I gave the order, 'let them have it.' Nedey and Lavasseur from the wall behind the altar emptied their tommy guns into the night. In all the loopholes my orderlies, stretcher bearers and ambulance drivers fired without a break. Odette and Olivette my two nurses fired with their colts.[44]

The struggle for Cochin-Saigon and the Mekong delta

The war in the south took on a totally different personality to the one in the north. The war here was much more scattered and in the nature of a classic hit-and-run guerrilla struggle. It rarely developed into the set-piece battles experienced later in Tonkin. In contrast to the north, in the south the Vietminh were indistinguishable from the villagers, who wore black and sported the typical conical straw hats. However, there were hiding places, cross-border hideouts and inaccessible areas, particular in the waterways of the delta and the Plain of Reeds where the Vietminh established a major base. The Reeds region ran from Saigon in a north-westerly direction to the border with Cambodia, where the marsh system extends up to the provincial town of Takeo. The *Plain des Joncs* network is a seemingly endless swath of tall, swaying reeds, amidst little and large channels of water, interspersed with occasional inhabited mud-mounds with bamboo and grass huts on stilts or even hillocks which, on the Cambodian side, are studded with pre-Ankorian temple ruins of the long-forgotten Funan civilisation.[45]

An adroit observer of the period was the legendary journalist Lucien Bodard, who painted the war in his articles and books with illuminating anecdotes, portraits of participants, as well as incisive critique of the war's conduct. Bodard, who was born and brought up in Kunming had Asia in his DNA. He describes the everyday absurdity, comedy and horror of guerrilla insurgency. Just 15km from Saigon, on the edge of the Plain of Reeds, was the sleepy town of Hocmon. Life for a French family was of constant fear with the wife also doing her duty and defending the family, including two small children. Their bungalow was under constant Vietminh attack. The husband was the French administrator in the town. Grenades and weapons were scattered about the house. 'Just beyond the garden there is a piece of wasteland, covered with tall thick brushwood,' complained the wife. 'The Viets slip into these bushes to fire at the house whenever they choose.'[46] The administrative delegate refused to have the trees cut down for fear of losing face. When absent on business, his wife had on occasions organised the defence of the house with her ragbag of local militia.

For French soldiers going out on search-and-destroy missions, the task was particularly disheartening, especially when one of their number was wounded, because it would take eight men in the swamp and mud to carry him out, at which point the Vietminh would redouble their effort to wipe them out. Like swiping at thin air, the task of trying to find the enemy was near impossible because of some extraordinary tactics of evasion by the ingenious Vietminh. A French lieutenant recounted:

> *...there was no hope of finding them. Some would have turned into bushes. Others would be right under the mud, breathing through hollow bamboos. Most would be in carefully prepared burrows.*[47]

Ex-SS veteran of the Eastern Front, fighting partisans in the forests and the Pripet marshes, Lieutenant Wagemeuller had a method to deal with such sub-aquatic tricks. Wagemeuller ordered gasoline to be poured over the area and set alight. 'The enemy might breathe through canes but he cannot breath fire and smoke,' recalled a grimly laconic Wagemeuller. 'We dispatched thirty guerrillas in that action; half of whom were women, and boys below the age of sixteen.'[48]

Fighting in the Plain of Reeds was a thankless task. The same lieutenant told how an attack on an arms factory on an island in the reeds 'was like an ant-hill that has just been stirred up.' Having struggled through deep mud up to the waist for some hours, the French attackers came within sight of their target. Despite their efforts, the Viets escaped with the most valuable machinery. The rest was smashed and no enemies were taken or killed:

> *...the stocks of rice had been soaked in gasoline and now they were only smouldering heaps...but all the really valuable equipment the lathes for making shells and the electric motors had been carried off in spite of the weight.*[49]

However, many Vietminh were killed. Another officer told Bodard of the delta fighting:

> *...we kill scores and scores of them. But there are always more...often they are just villagers, people's militias, half or even a quarter Viet...Not long ago we got three hundred at one go...we shot them like rabbits.*[50]

But there were losses too, and horrible cruelty exacted by the other side. A wounded man left behind with a medical officer...they were both found decapitated. There was a steady toll of casualties with French officer losses being especially heavy.

Local militias were armed by the French with old-fashioned bolt-action weapons. The French built blockhouses on stilts along the road and the militia and their families would retreat and pull up the ladders at dusk. Occasionally a blockhouse would be destroyed. But life was cheap and there were many more impoverished souls ready to take the French piastre.

At night the Vietminh came out to attack targets of opportunity. Cars and convoys caught on the road late after sunset were ambushed and no mercy was shown to the occupants. From the rooftop bar of the Metropol Hotel, explosions and gunfire could be heard every night in the not too distant countryside and suburbs. Tracer rounds arched lazily over the horizon.

Isolated French or foreigners who went out into the countryside, fishermen or hunters or lovers would be murdered – sliced to death and mutilated. French vigilante gangs, including soldiers, would sometimes go into the countryside and murder whole villages in retaliation:

> *...it was quite commonplace. Yet another village had gone up in flames and forty* nha-ques [peasants] *had been killed. And it was French sailors, recruits who had gone out there.*[51]

Much depended on the quality of the French officers. Those well commanded behaved well while others allowed their troops to run amok.

Finding himself stuck on a deserted road a few miles outside Saigon at dusk when his car broke down, Bodard knew he was in a very dangerous spot and started pushing his car towards a guard tower in the distance:

> *Two hundred yards ahead of me there were some partisans in a tower, and they were making violent signals in my direction. The bullets whipped past me. I reached the tower and darted up the ladder which was instantly pulled up. The partisans laughed...they were firing at a group of Vietminh creeping up behind me.*[52]

On other occasions, captured French civilians, including women, were shot. Such atrocities were often reciprocated and simply added to the spiral of hatred and murder. Two American women who drove out of the city were found murdered in a rubber estate, as were a pair of young French lovers.

In the hills out of sight of the media, the Vietminh wiped out whole villages of local Hmong (Meo), Rhade or other tribes found guilty of harbouring or providing food to French GCMA forces operating behind enemy lines.[53] In the city, the assassination of important civilian officials and businessmen continued apace and of local officials in the towns and villages.

Politically, the problem of Vietnam seemed insoluble. Leclerc in Paris told the new high commissioner, Bollaert, in April 1947 as he was about to fly out to replace d'Argenlieu: 'once more monsieur high commissioner, negotiate, at all costs negotiate.'[54] Already in January 1947, Leclerc had noted that 'anti-communism will be a useless tool as long as the problem of nationalism remains unresolved.'[55] While anti-communism was the main weapon both to mobilise Vietnamese opinion and to bring in US finance and arms, the effectiveness of it would always be blunted to the extent that France hung on to its imperialist delusions. France failed to recognise the shift of history towards decolonisation. Active party cadres were relatively few but, for reasons of nationalism, they had the sympathy and support of the majority of the population.

Weighed down by economic problems at home, the French government was already refusing to spend more money than necessary. By 1950, budgets were actually being cut and just before the RC4 debacle, 9,000 troops were withdrawn from Indochina. American money and equipment had not yet arrived in any large amounts.

North, south and the indigenous tribes' role in the war

They were led by legendary maquis leader Colonel Trinquier, who became head of the GMCA in 1953. His forces may have totalled 15–20,000 tribal, T'ai, Meo, and Moi guerrillas operating in northern Lao and the Vietnamese tribal highlands and led by approximately eighty officers and 250 NCOs. Ironically Trinquier, unlike the phony proletarian and Mandarin bourgeois leaders of the Vietminh, was from peasant stock. Unfortunately, the French high command, starting in April 1951, made a late start in developing this potentially potent strategy but still inflicting some severe defeats on the Vietminh in the north-east. Demonstrating their fear of the GMCA, the Vietminh high command issued an order in 1953, which was intercepted:

> *We need to exterminate at all costs the pirates* [GMCA], *their works can be considered as the biggest machination destined to undermine the Vietminh movement.*[56]

GCMA (or GMI) were not especially well supported by the army and were not listed in the FEC order of battle. Units of 1,000 men were named after the French officers who commanded them. A sprinkling of junior officers and NCOs accompanied these units. It was a hard life but many came to form great bonds of loyalty with their tribal allies. There were constant dangers, and not just from enemy bullets but from poisonous snakes, tigers and disease. If wounded the chances were not good. French medics reported that unless evacuated, seriously injured men always died, 'because it took two or three days to get him to the aid station at Lai Chau and we could never get a helicopter.'[57] Ho was forced to call in the Chinese 302th Regiment to suppress their activities along the northern borders.

General Massu's comment on the indigenous tribes was typical:

> *The curious race of the Moi...gains the sympathy of all my men straightaway. It is evident at first sight that they are not Annamites. Their bronze, powerful corps...is covered by a simple loincloth.*

They were downtrodden allies under 'French protection' who were:

> *Very determined not to let themselves be 'colonised' nor chased any more they oppose the Vietminh with a wild resistance...we will allow ourselves to admire the delicateness, the generous hospitality and the dignity of this little people.*[58]

It was the received romantic view, yet French plantation companies would treat the indigenous as slaves on their rubber estates or inveigle them into misleading contracts as indentured labour in their Pacific islands. Nonetheless, the tribes mainly supported the French.

Hele de St Marc, who organised large Montagnard commando elements in the mountains, revelled in the romance of the tribes:

> *...an ethnic minority and an arm of the Thai people (the languages are very close) who differed from the Annamites. Less fine, better built, more muscled, they wore indigo clothes which they produced themselves on wooden machines. They marched bare-footed...Eventually peasants, often smugglers, always hunters, they were a nice rebel race.*

He described a tribal society little changed to this day, including their wildly drunk festivals:

> *The women and children were always at work. The men decided, walked about and fought. Under a superficial Buddhism animism dominated the spirits. The Tho loved rice alcohol and smoked opium in moderation. The daily life, embedded in a plentiful and exuberant nature...was marked by a great moral liberty.*[59]

They lived in windowless homes on stilts with bamboo walls and matted leaf or straw roofs. Despite the mystique and the fact that most tribes supported the French, many of the Tho tribe on the Chinese border as well as some elements of the Black T'ai were won over by the Vietminh and were well integrated into their army. Vietminh sought to divide and rule by stirring up tribal rivalries.The tribal areas, notably the T'ai Federation, the Hmong, and the Moi of the Central Highlands, was another world entirely. In a semi-pastoral or nomadic life, the Hmong (Meo) lived on hill or mountain tops where they planted opium. With the land worn out after about seven years, they would up sticks and find another hill. Such a hill culture can still be seen along the byways of northern Lao and Vietnam, although many have now settled into more permanent agricultural lifestyles. Lost once in the foothills around the Phan Xi Păng massif in north-west Vietnam, the author is indebted to the three Hmong tribeswomen who found him wandering and lost, then shepherded him through a tricky gorge. Their tribal costumes, knee-length skirt-jackets multicoloured with hand-woven red or blue trimming and underneath homespun black knickerbockers and knee-length socks. On their heads colourful turbans.

Operation Lea in the Bac Kan

On 27 March 1947, Generals Valluy and Salan received policy document no. 3739 from the Remadier government, which said that de Gaulle's policies declared on 24 March 1945 had 'lapsed'. It accepted different states and territories in Indochina, accepted the charter of the Union Francais, and instructed that common interests should be forged, while 'respecting existing French [colonial] Interests'. The document asserted that 'the military conflict had been provoked by Ho Chi Minh's government.'[60] Exclusive French military responsibility would remain, including protection of ethnic minorities, a constant theme and justification for French colonialism. The document was signed by cabinet members, including leading members of the tripartite coalition government, such as Premier Remadier (socialist), Pierre-Henri Teitgen (MRP) and Maurice Thorez (communist PCF). The irony of the ultra-Stalinist Thorez signing off on an imperialist policy document and sanctioning, in effect, the continuation of the war was not lost on many. Thorez always took his party line from Moscow. It pitched the Stalinist PCF against the Stalinist Ho, who also took his orders from Moscow. The policy had everything to do with Stalin's tactical approach to the creeping communist takeover in Eastern Europe.

Despite the escalating war, Ho Chi Minh, in tandem with Moscow's softly-softly policy, continued in his expression of interest to join the French Union, but only as a fully independent nation. He maintained a most unusual correspondence with his adversaries, notably with General Salan, with whom he had travelled a great deal. On 10 June, upon his return to Indochina, Ho sent Salan a letter from his jungle base in Bac Kan:

> *Last year we travelled a lot together, spoken a lot together and on may subjects we were in accord. In a word we became friends. These circumstances which are not our wish have made us adversaries. It is truly regrettable...for the love of humanity and our personal amity, please permit me to ask you to prevent French troops from massacring the civil population, raping women, burning defenceless villages and destroying churches and temples, which is what is currently happening...I send my best wishes for your wife, grandson and baby.*

Soon after this letter, Generals Valluy and Salan were hatching a plan for a major parachute strike on the Vietminh in their Bac Kan heartland. The intention was to bite off the head of the snake, kill Ho, Giáp and the Vietminh leadership, so crushing the movement in one fell swoop. Guerrilla war and the national uprising organised by Ho's Vietminh was already causing significant disruption to France's re-establishment of colonial power and taking a heavy toll on the French Army by constant ambushes, along the length and breadth of the 2,000km-long country. With just 100,000, soldiers it was an impossible job to suppress a national revolt and war that was so widespread. The hope was to cut short what was otherwise developing into an unwinnable war of attrition.

General Valluy, Leclerc's replacement, was a 46 -year-old with a distinguished war record. He realised that time was not on France's side due to limited resources, the possibility of war weariness setting in amongst the general public, and the worrying developments in the Chinese Civil War. He realised that a decisive strike was necessary. His plan was bold and imaginative. Scraping together whatever free resources he had from garrison duties in the rest of Indochina, with about 6,000 troops including eight battalions of infantry and paratroopers, Valluy aimed a three-pronged parachute strike at the heart of the Vietminh in its base area in the Viet Bac. In fact, the attack would aim to pinpoint and destroy the Vietminh headquarters and kill its leadership at their base near Bac Kan. When French intelligence had located the target, Valluy launched the attack. It was a bold move to gather in so many troops and launch such an operation on a shoestring. According to one American marine officer, the FEC was furnished with 'pretty sad equipment.'[61]

Nearly 1,000 paratroopers were dropped onto Bac Kan, simultaneously a French force, which descended down Route Coloniale 4 (RC4) then RC3 from Cao Bang, aimed to smash the fleeing Vietminh from the north-east. Meanwhile, a riverine force of flotilla-borne infantry moved up from the Red River delta along the Clear River to Tuyen Quang to attack the Vietminh base from the south-west. Total deployment was 15,000. It was a good plan. It made strategic sense and on a map the pincer movement looked very convincing. However, as with most French operations in Indochina that aimed at some decisive victory, it was woefully under-resourced in respect of its objectives for an area covering 7,500 square miles. Once again, the map-based French command were underestimating the task and overestimating their operational capacity. Even though the resources would in future years increase dramatically, they would never catch up with the ever-expanding Vietminh war effort. At a moment's notice the Vietminh could drift unseen through the jungle trails while retaining their discipline and cohesion. They could never be pinned down.

The air-drop on Bac Kan was a rare total surprise and nearly a dramatic success, but the paratroopers could only be dropped in three stages over three hours because of the shortage of transport aircraft. They missed Ho Chi Minh and Giáp by a matter of minutes. The pair only survived by squeezing into a tiny hole in the jungle floor covered with leaves and tree branches. French soldiers scoured the ground for secret tunnels and holes, but missed them. After several excruciating hours the pair re-emerged and fled into the jungle. Some of Ho's documents and personal effects were captured. The radio message sent back to high command read: 'The 1st Company has occupied the hospital, treasury, the electric works – stop – enemy losses heavy – stop – Surprise total.'[62]

The Vietminh command had prepared for such an eventuality. Hau, Mai Elliott's brother-in-law, recounted:

> *They also made preparations for a quick evacuation if necessary. Each site was located near trails that would allow escape in several directions. At the first hint of trouble, they would destroy sensitive documents and leave quickly. He could see the planes and parachutes that sailed beneath them like giant umbrellas. But most of the Vietminh managed to escape by following one of the several trails radiating into the forest hills.*[63]

Paratroopers moved into the Vietminh encampment. Some Vietminh were killed, including one leading cadre, but only a few were taken prisoner. Meanwhile, the paratroopers were soon surrounded and coming under pressure from swarms of Vietminh, who regrouped and counter-attacked.

The next problem was the tendency of map-room-bound French generals to make a literal interpretation of what passed for a road on an old colonial map. 'Roads', actually just mud tracks that were never laid with tarmac in the first place, had through years of neglect by the colonial administration never been properly maintained or even graded. The French column from the east descended down the 140-mile 'track', scaling pass after pass and crossing numbers of rivers and rivulets. It became a hard slog involving considerable engineering expertise with grading as well as bridge and culvert repair. All the while they were subject to Vietminh ambush and sniper fire. They arrived at Bac Kan having taken five days to move down the last 50km from Cao Bang. They rescued their beleaguered paratrooper comrades, but the main body of the Vietminh Army had disappeared.

The southern riverine-borne column fared even worse and made no contact with the enemy. Stopped by uncharted sandbanks, the troops had to disembark much sooner than expected. They never made the rendezvous point at Bac Kan, being discovered by the Moroccan troops coming down in the opposite direction. The operation, which was terminated on 8 November, was very nearly a major success and caused significant damage and casualties, perhaps up to 7,000 for the loss of 242 – a victory though not a decisive one.

Concerned to protect the Bac Kan, Giáp and Ho started their strategy of clearing the north-east by focusing guerrilla attacks on the vulnerable RC4 between Lang Son and Ca Bang. The aim was to clear the Chinese border areas and be ready to receive succour from the Red Army after it defeated the Kuomintang in the Chinese Civil War. The first target, though, was the French outpost at Phu Tong Hoa, just 25 tortuous kilometres from Ho's old Bacan base. In a surprise attack at 7.30 p.m. on 25 July in which Japanese

75mm cannon were used to smash in the defences, several hundred legionnaires were nearly overrun. Just clinging on to a few compound buildings, they were relieved a day later. This remote post was abandoned in October.

Nguyên Binh in Saigon

As an itinerant migrant from the north and a laundry worker in Saigon, Binh had enough proletarian roots to be well qualified for the Vietminh. But his first politics was as a member of the ultra-nationalist VNQDD party. At the age of 19, he was arrested by the Sûreté, and tried and sentenced to five years in Poulu Condore. To have been sent there he must have stood out as a particularly dangerous type. On his release he moved back north and became an activist in the working-class areas of Haiphong and the coastal border areas.

Having fallen out with the VNQDD after saving the life of a communist friend during one of the recurrent and dangerous factional brawls at Poulu, Binh started working with the Vietminh. But he did not join the Communist Party. Tall, energetic, rough and violent, he was also flamboyantly individualist. Lucien Bodard described him as 'cruel, indefatigable, pitiless, authoritarian'. One-eyed from the prison fight, Binh stood out by wearing a Japanese helmet and a long cape. He wore a sword at his belt and was always seen sporting sunglasses to cover his injury. He had a talent for leadership and for organisation, so when the Vietminh position in Cochin collapsed under Leclerc's onslaught, Ho and Giáp called upon Binh to go south and save the situation.

Ho Chi Minh wrote to him in 1945: 'The south needs a strategist to lead the Resistance. I am confident you have the ability and so I have proposed you for the south. I hope you will succeed.' In theory at least he became the second highest ranked military commander after Giáp, but he would soon have with him senior communist minders to make sure that the party maintained the upper hand. Distrusted by the jealous upper echelons of the party, he made enemies easily with his flamboyance and brusque manner. His patronising advice to Giáp on the eve of the outbreak of war in the north must have infuriated the communist commander's precious self esteem.

Arriving in November 1945, Binh reorganised large Vietminh formations into seventeen smaller units that would pursue the classic guerrilla terror tactics at which he excelled. Highly organised assassination and terror cell groups infiltrated Saigon and started a reign of terror on elite social elements and grenade attacks on French bars, restaurants and dance clubs. These built up to astounding levels with the murder of seventy leading local businessmen and officials in September 1946 alone.[64] Local magnates, officials, bankers and landowners were especially targeted because they were supporters of the separate Cochinese state. The country entered a bitter civil war phase, not just a colonial war of liberation. This civil war would expand significantly over the next few years both in the north and the south. Local elites were assassinated in increasing numbers. Catholics, the Trotskyists, members of religious sects and many others were liquidated.

In early 1946, General Georges Yves Nyo, an experienced colonial soldier with considerable experience in the Central Highlands in the mid-1930s, took command in Cochin. He immediately set about doubling the size of his army by recruiting auxiliary local forces to support his tiny force of 13,000. Starting with 5,000, this increased to 13,000 by November 1947. He aimed to win over wavering elements and crush the Vietminh. However, his forces were pitifully inadequate for the task of pacifying and normalising the south.

Binh, meanwhile, was improving the number, training and quality of his troops. Communication had been established with Hanoi in December 1946, so the southern command became integrated with overall Vietminh strategic planning. As Vietminh leaders decided to focus on Tonkin, the communist leadership often used the southern 'Cinderella' as a diversionary front to hold down French troops in the south to prevent them reinforcing French forces in the north.

Over the next few years Binh would shake the Cochin regime to its foundations building a very strong revolutionary movement in Saigon. Vietminh cadres launched a creeping takeover of the Saigon government's civil functions, including tax. Binh's troops caused serious disruption to transport links, cutting off roads and rail links and destabilising society with assassinations.

French offensive operations and Dinassaut

Thrown entirely onto the defensive, French forces in the Mekong delta theatre were then weakened by the need to send 3,000 troops north to reinforce General Valluy's 'Lea' offensive. As another stop-gap, the Guard Republicaine Cochinchine was re-established with nearly 8,000 troops by the end of 1947. But short of troops, General Nyo could only hit back with occasional commando raids as well as riverine strike forces (Dinassaut) composed of heavily armed and armoured LCT, LCM and LSI. They were all different types of landing craft with low draughts for the mud banks and variable draughts and tides in the delta. These heavily armed 'Heath Robinson' constructs were ideal, especially as their high conning towers gave excellent visibility over the flat delta region of mangroves, reeds and rice paddy. By 1953 there were four flotillas, with one of them undergoing refitting and training at any one time.

Valluy returned to France and Salan took over to continue the operation. He launched VEGA, a complex operation involving 5,000 troops with land forces on the roads, Dinassaut, artillery and paratrooper drops. The prospects for success looked good. However, it proved to be another swipe at thin air. Some arms workshops were captured, 150 Vietminh killed and weapons and ammunition seized. Most importantly, 600 tons of dynamite were seized and, especially valuable, thirty-two junks loaded with 250 tons of rice were destroyed. Another seventy sampans were captured.

The VEGA offensive was led by Lieutenant-Colonel Sairigne. Shortly afterwards he was leading a convoy of sixty vehicles some 7 miles long on the way to Darlat. Informed of an ambush ahead he continued anyway. According to Bodard, the colonel's pride was piqued so he continued on to his doom. Attacked from higher ground by 500 Vietminh in perfect cover, sixty vehicles were destroyed in the firefight. The colonel and his daughter were killed.

In the autumn of 1948, General Latour, the new commander in Cochin, would be stripped of another 3,000 men to support operations in Tonkin. Latour complained in a communication to command on 1 October 1948: 'Before such shortage of means, how can I maintain the current position and not renounce all the new extensions?' As always, the resources did not match strategy. Latour would soon be replaced by General Carpentier, who was new to Indochina. The 'buggins turn' rotation of commanders in Indochina was excessive and led to a lack of consistency and confusion as strategies chopped and changed.

Cao Dai, Hoa Hoa, Binh Xuyen, Catholic militia, and Khmer Krom

The Cao Dai was established in the early 1920s. An eclectic kaleidoscope of religious influences from Buddhism to Confucianism, Genism and Taoism, plus Christianity, Hinduism and Islam, Cao Daiism is one of the more bizarre religions of the world. The church structure is hierarchical with a pope and cardinals at the apex. Still strong today, the Cao Dai's 'Rome' is located in the city of Tay Ninh, 100km north of Saigon, not far from the Cambodian border and near the great and singular edifice of Tay Ninh mountain.

Cao Dai services in Tay Ninh take place in a vast and garishly coloured cathedral. Services are a theatre and whirl of diaphanously attired Vietnamese women in flowing white *ao dai*-like costumes, in a great snake-columned hall, presided over by augustly robed priests in bright red, yellow and blue before an all seeing large 'eye'. Framed by a triangle, the eye is the centrepiece of Cao Dai iconography. Graham Greene described the scene: 'Christ and Buddha looking down from the roof of the cathedral on a Walt Disney fantasia of the East, dragons and snakes in Technicolor.'[65] Cao Daists have a litany of saints, the leading trinity being Victor Hugo, Sun Yat Sen, and poet Nguyễn Binh Diem. Other minor saints include Jesus, Buddha, Confucius, Muhammad, Lenin, Shakespeare, Pericles, Pasteur, Julius Caesar, Joan of Arc, Winston Churchill,

Charlie Chaplin and the Comte de la Rochefoucauld (whose memoirs inspired Dumas's 'three musketeer' stories).

Fiercely anti-French collaborators with the Japanese, the Cao Dai aligned at first with the Vietminh but became increasingly reluctant to accept Vietminh-communist strictures. Communist assassinations of rivals put them on edge. Eventually, the Cao Dai broke with the communists and accepted the French flag on 9 June 1646. The French supplied them with money and arms, which enabled them to increase their militia and military foothold. France effectively ceded control of Tay Ninh province with the barest of oversight by a French military mission and liaison group. Twenty thousand effective fighters immediately defected from the Vietminh to fight alongside the French Army. Not easy allies, the Cao Dai were a powerful aid to localised pacification. They defeated a communist invasion of Tay Ninh province. Communism was not the only organised religion.

Founded only in 1939, the Hoa Hoa are a fundamentalist Buddhist sect, aligned to the Theradvic branch, which emphasises plain living and simplicity in theology and services. In contrast to Cao Dai's fantasia, the Hoa Hoa sport simple brown gowns. They worship at home rather than in temples. Their founder and leader, formerly a Saigon office clerk, Huynh Phu So, was known as the 'mad monk'. He had an angelic face and wild staring eyes, under threatening eyebrows. He exuded charisma. Hoa Hao were millenarian and somewhat xenophobic.

Their stronghold is the rich rice-growing region alongside the Mekong as it progresses from Can Tho towards the Cambodia border. Bound as they were by common Buddhist belief, they had supported the Japanese then joined with the Vietminh in opposing the French return. However, refusing to conform to secular communist domination, a split was only a matter of time. Covetous of Hoa Hoa rice-growing territory, Vietminh pressure to extract and control rice to feed their cadres and troops led to tensions that were already strained. The Hoa Hoa were reluctant to take orders from a group they deemed to be foreign-influenced and untrustworthy.

When Huynh Phu So's brother and a Trotskyist adviser were arrested and shot by the communists in Can Tho following an anti-Vietminh demonstration on 8 September 1945, the Hoa Hoa took revenge by slaughtering communist cadres. Somehow the alliance staggered on, but when in July 1946 the Hoa Hoa established a political party in a move that challenged the essential communist mantra as to the monopoly on power, the scene was set for a showdown. In April 1947, Phu was kidnapped by the Vietminh as he left Saigon by boat on the way to a reconciliation meeting in the Plain of Reeds. He was executed, cut into pieces and scattered to avoid creating a place of martyrdom. Not intimidated into submission, the movement formed an alliance with the French in short order, putting their seventeen battalions, consisting of about 23,000 troops, at the service of France in return for protection, money and arms. The Hoa Hoa numbered about 1,000,000 in 1944.

The mistake made by Nguyễn Binh and the party leadership was to show their hand too soon before overwhelming strength had been established. Overzealous party hardliners overplayed their hand, so destroying the unity of the anti-imperialist alliance. Supported by the French during 1947–1948, the Hoa Hoa would go on to fight fierce battles with the Vietminh.

Binh Xuyen was essentially a criminal organisation. Members derived originally from pirates and escaped estate workers who had fled to the marshes south of Saigon. They were similar to the triad in China but more brazen, their 10,000 troops even wearing distinctive green berets. Breaking with the communists in 1946, they would in time make a deal with the French to wipe out the Vietminh in Saigon. They controlled Cholon, where they ran the Grande Monde Cassino with its famous hall of mirrors and other gambling, opium and prostitution rackets. Supporting and supported by Bao Dai, they helped make the emperor a very wealthy man. France's Second Bureau said of the Binh Xuyen leader: 'Bay Vien's control over Saigon-Cholon had enabled him to build a multi-faceted business enterprise whose economic potential constitutes...one of the most solid economic forces in South Vietnam.'[66]

The Vietminh broke with the Binh Xuyen for more or less the same reasons as they had with the Cao Dai and Hoa Hoa. They were in competition for power, money, adherents, and territory. Fighting broke out and Nguyễn Binh's assassination squads hunted down the leader, Bay Vieng, who promptly made a deal with the French. France bought his loyalty in return for a free run at the rackets as well as territorial immunity. Knowing the backstreets and wharfs of Saigon and Cholon better than anyone, in alliance with the new Sûreté chief Tam, the Binh Xuyen would play a vital role in eradicating communist assassination squads and agents, using their gang techniques and local intelligence networks. Vietminh cadres were murdered by the dozen, their mutilated bodies left in the street as a warning. The Vietminh-controlled Nam Bo committee was driven from Saigon.

Indochina's Catholic community, both in the north and the south, was generally as nationalistic as any other group in Indochina, being caught up in the same nationalist wave as all other communities. Ho had initially reached out to Catholics. However, communist harassment, intimidation, murder and their desire for total control made the Catholic community suspicious and fearful. Then by degrees, as with all other religious or civil groups, the Catholic community became their deadly enemies. By 1948, the Catholics, who had remained passive when subjected to harassment and murder by the Vietminh cadres, became organised under the lay leadership of Franco-Vietnamese Jean

Leroy, whose power was located in the Ben Tre area to the east of Saigon in what was also a communist hotspot. Catholic militias, the Unites Mobiles de Defense des Christienes, began to combine effectively with French forces. Ben Tre and An Ho were recovered and pacified to the embarrassment of the local bishop. Leroy called his men to fight under the slogan *pro Deo et Patria.* (For God and country.)

So far from the China border, so lacking in heavy weapons or plentiful logistical supply, in terrain that was less supportive to large-scale covert movement, the war would be very different to the one being waged in the north. The defection of four religious militia organisations was to give the French strong local mooring points, hubs and allies for their military activities, even if the wilder, woodier and wetter areas were mainly under Vietminh control.

The Khmer Krom minority in Cochin constituted perhaps 1 million people in 1944. Pushed aside by the Annamites, the original Cambodian occupants of the delta became 'inside-outsiders', despised as inferior, simple and primitive people, a stereotype promoted by early French colonialists but long believed by the Vietnamese. Far from being nice liberators, Vietminh behaviour was as racist, belittling and as oppressive as anything that had gone before, and more so. Khmer antagonism and conflict that developed in these years helped extensive recruitment in French units.[67] Despite Vietminh efforts to develop attractive policies for Khmer recruitment, the translation into action in the far away south was patchy at best. Forced recruitment drives alienated the Khmer community as Vietminh cadres pushed Khmers to 'enlist in the rebellious ranks'. Some Khmer felt forced to 'seek refuge in Cambodia.'[68] However, some were converted to communism, including Ieng Sary, born in Tra Vinh, who became a Khmer Rouge leader in due course and brother-in-law of Pol Pot. Khmer communities and religious structures and priests were attacked by the Vietminh. French attempts to pose as 'protectors' of the Khmer Krom were not especially successful either, but they recruited extensively from a Khmer community that did not feel the pull of Vietnamese nationalism.[69] The French paid and fed them well (with free wine for legionnaires), while Vietminh cadres offered nothing but short rations, no alcohol, inferior status, boring propaganda and death. 'Dialectical materialism' was a poor substitute for an adequate diet.

Lacking finesse, between 1946 and 1948, Binh's brutal power plays and the crude inflexible ideology of Le Duan as the party supervisor led to the defection of most of the important elements of the Cochin resistance. Arrogant, they not only lacked the deftness of touch of Ho, but also his instincts for timing and power. The iron fist was revealed far too soon. Unlike the north, in the south the timing was not right for crude tactics of murder and intimidation against powerful associated organisations. Vietminh tactics backfired. Stabbing allies in the back is a communist tactic taken from the Leninist playbook of revolution. Lenin timed it to perfection when he destroyed the Social Revolutionary Party, as did Ho and Giáp in Tonkin when they destroyed the VQNDD. In the south, Binh and Le Duan failed.

CHAPTER VII

The Time of Grenades

The time of grenades, and the struggle for Cochin

The lack of an ability to fight in formed units was a problem for Nguyễn Binh. Foiled in his attempt to fight a regular war, the Vietminh turned to terror instead to break the will of the occupiers. Suffering heavy casualties from attempts to attack military posts, the choice fell on soft targets. Everyone was fair game and French civilians were targeted by random grenade attacks on cafés, bistros, cinemas, night clubs and restaurants. Inevitably, many Vietnamese civilians were collateral damage in such attacks. Other soft targets were 'collaborators', local businessmen and officials, gunned down by Vietminh assassins in the street. The Vietminh certainly knew their French colonists. What could be more morale-sapping than to be killed while enjoying a long lunch or an aperitif after work? Café society had translated well into Vietnam. There were tree-lined boulevards and colonial buildings, awnings and colonnades, cafés, street corners with umbrellas, wicker chairs, and little marble-topped tables spilling onto the sidewalks. A typical place was Le Paris Orientale along the Rue Catinat. These ex-pat places were not the only ones to suffer, because grenades were also thrown into the crowds in the Asian quarters, at businesses refusing to pay protection money, or even at gaggles of western schoolchildren emerging after classes.

Grenades were tossed by pillion terrorists on passing motorbikes or rolled in under the chairs. A loud explosion or series of detonations if several were thrown, followed by screams, tumbling chairs, bodies, glass smashing, smoke, sobs, blood gushing onto the pavement, white tablecloths stained red. A sudden shock of stillness. The worst atrocities were done by professional killers from Battalion 905. Lucien Bodard witnessed one attack, which felled an entire dancefloor. He ferried to hospital two dying sailors and a wounded prostitute who were gushing blood.

Another attack was witnessed by renowned travel writer Norman Lewis. Upon returning to his hotel a few days after his arrival:

> *…as I pushed open the window, there was a momentary, slight resistance and a violent explosion thumped in my eardrums. Across the square an indolent wreath of smoke lifted from the café tables and dissolved. Two figures got up*

> *from a table, arms about one another's shoulders and reeled away like drunkards who have decided to call it a night...already the wounded were being tended in their cramped attitudes...Within ten minutes every table was full again. This hand grenade, one of eight reported that evening, caused about 15 casualties.*[1]

Nguyễn Binh's aim was to take over Saigon from within. Vietminh cadres were positioned inside all the organs of government and alongside this parallel state there was mass assassination. Fear drove the population into tacit compliance. Potential targets dared not go out. If they did they risked death or kidnapping. The latter tactic enabled the extortion of millions of piastre to finance Vietminh campaigning. This terror campaign was conducted by Nguyễn Bin through the so-called Nam Bo Committee, which was a loose coalition of anti-French resistance groups dominated by the Vietminh.

Some businessmen supported the Vietminh. Norman Lewis describes a clandestine meeting with a group of them, which had been arranged by a Vietminh-supporting 'Taxi' girl:

> *...among them was a prosperous lawyer, a bank director, and a member of the cabinet of the governor of Cochin China. All of these were members of the wealthy landowning class and all were whole hearted supporters of the Vietmin.*[2]

One of their main complaints against the French was the refusal of the exclusive French club, Circle Francais, to allow locals in as members.

The terror attacks lasted several years, unsettling the entire life of the city and seeming to indicate imminent takeover by the Vietminh by *fait accompli*. One famous killing was the assassination of French police chief Marcel Bazin, on 28 April 1950. He was killed in broad daylight as he left home to go to his office. Regular as clockwork, he left his house at 7.30 a.m. and walked to his waiting car. An elegant besuited Annamese with a briefcase emerged from the shadow of a building, took a pistol from his briefcase and began to pump bullets into Bazin. His body 'was as full of holes as a sieve', remarked a detective to the ever-vigilant journalist Bodard, who arrived shortly after. The killer and his team escaped in a fast car. Only a week before, the omniscient Bodard had been told by Bazin, in an off the record conversation:

> *I am fighting for my life...My killers have already arrived in Saigon. I've only a few days to get them...The whole town is riddled with Viet cells. They are everywhere. They kill as they choose and make everyone pay taxes...Clean through it all there is a clandestine administration running parallel with the official one. It is set up in the government and in the ministries and in every district...giving out their daily orders and carrying out their propaganda, spying and tax gathering almost openly.*[3]

No one was too powerful to kill, including the two tobacco kings and other important foreign and Chinese businessmen. Some were kidnapped for ransom. Amidst the breakdown the Vietminh cadres stirred up large pro-Vietminh demonstrations. Even students and schoolchildren held open protests carrying banners supporting the Vietminh, denouncing the French and waving red flags. Fiery revolutionary speeches were made in public gatherings in the centre of Saigon. The puppet regime of Boa Dai and their French protectors was tottering. Lists of traitors were read out in public. Gunfire was heard every night, as well as bombings, mortar- and machine-gunfire.

The defeat of the Vietminh general offensive, March–April 1950

A general attack was ordained by Maoist revolutionary theory, once the countryside was flooded with communism. However, the main reason for a planned offensive in the south was Giáp's intention to divert French troops prior to a general offensive in Tonkin. It was exactly as Bodard's lieutenant on the border at Mon Kai had predicted. The southern leadership hoped for a general uprising in support, but they miscalculated. The population was neither ready or willing to rise up. In fact, many had returned from the countryside to the prosperity and freedom of French-controlled areas rather than face the constant dirge of repetitive propaganda and harsh control by the robotic automatons of the Communist Party. One other factor was the difference in southern culture, which was more free-wheeling and capitalist and open to new ideas and change, something that accounts for and is reflected in the religious and cultural diversity of the population. More importantly, Mao's military mantras did not work in Cochin because the Vietminh faced a tough professional European trained army, not the demoralised and corruptly led phantom armies of the Kuomintang.

For the final act, Nguyễn Binh, whose headquarters of revolution and assassination was just 5 miles out of Saigon in the village of Tan Nhut, concentrated 8,000 regular troops in regular units of battalion and regimental size who had been trained by German legionnaire deserters or Japanese stay-ons, including colonels and majors as well as junior officers and rankers. He launched his Vietminh forces on French outposts across Cochin. Key towns were cut off and their garrisons stranded and under attack, especially at Trà-Vinh, Soc-Trang, and Can Tho in the heart of the delta. This was the third phase of Mao's communist strategy, the final attack after the strangulation and envelopment of towns and cities.

A typical attack in this general offensive was the one made against Trà Vinh, where the Vietminh surrounded and cut off various bastions around this fishing town near the coast south-east of Can Tho. Subjected to a series of

Vietminh attacks from December into January 1950, the coalition of religious orders militia, Vietnamese militia and French regulars held them off but the situation was precarious. General Chanson, having absorbed the pressure, launched counter-attacks. At Trà Vinh he dropped a battalion of Foreign Legion paratroopers and launched a riverine Dinassaut fleet with Moroccan troops against the rear of the Vietminh forces. Badly squeezed between strong bastions and elite troops, the tactically outmanoeuvred Vietminh retreated having lost thousands in this *guerre sans front*. Defeat, which can be compared to the famous Tet offensive in 1966, swung many peasants to desert the Vietminh-held areas and the Vietminh cause.

The general offensive launched across Cochin against dug-in defensive positions manned by hardened German legionnaires failed. Much as the Tet offensive was to be a military disaster for the communists in 1968, so too was Nguyễn Binh's attempt to finish off the French in Cochin in the summer of 1950. Far too premature, the attempt ended in disaster as the naïve new soldiers were mowed down in heaps before the gun-pits of the French. Following their defeat, large regimental-sized units were broken up as the party returned to holding out in remote, malarial jungles and parts of the delta, such as the western Mekong delta, the Cambodian borderlands, and the Plain of Reeds. Vietminh tactics returned to 'hit and run' guerrilla activity, having failed to transition to full-scale modern warfare.

By the time of the failed offensives in 1950, Binh had been effectively neutered and shorn of power. The emerging communist apparatchiks from the north, such as Le Duan, used him as a scapegoat and this served Ho and the communists well. Binh had served his purpose and, unlike Giáp, he was expendable. When Binh was nearly assassinated by his erstwhile allies in the VNDDQ, he took some time to recover in a field hospital where he was at last induced by an attractive nurse into joining the Communist Party. To no avail he was recalled to the Bac Kan headquarters of the Vietminh. On his return he was ambushed and killed in September 1951 by the French-led 4th Bataillon de Chasseurs Cambodgiens. Lucien Bodard, who may well have been privy to French intelligence information, suggests that he was deliberately assassinated by his bodyguards and that Binh was no more than a prisoner by the end. Given the forested and broken ground around Stung Treng where a chance encounter with a Cambodian patrol was unlikely, it is most probable that he was betrayed. It is possible that this was done by his communist rivals or even with the connivance of Ho or Giáp. It is a theory that cannot be totally discounted as such a maverick would certainly have been an embarrassment for the leadership.

Another turning point was the replacement of the weak and ineffectual Nguyễn Phan Long by appointment of Father Huu, an old-school Catholic, as

Cochin's prime minister, whose first appointment was to make Tam head of the Sûreté. Tam the 'Tiger of Calay', whose sons had been killed by the Vietminh, was lucky enough to survive torture at their hands and was fanatically pro-French. He had made a name for himself by wiping out the communists in the district where he was the administrator. 'I did learn about communism and how to detect its presence,' he told Bodard, '...where people no longer went to the pagoda and notables dared not send in denunciations, communism was already in control.'[14] Tam brought in as his deputy Mai Huu-Xuan, a cold-blooded killer who promptly discovered that Tam's secretary was a communist agent. Forced to confess, Huu-Xuan was executed on the same day after telling all. The trail of strings into the communist network was tracked down with a ruthless brutality that matched the communists. Soon, bloodied dead bodies appeared all over Saigon with notices pinned to them denouncing them as communists. Informers who had clammed up began to operate again. Then the big breakthroughs came.

The head office for the Special Assassination Battalion 905 was located in Rue Freres-Louis and the police lay in wait for their leader Van-Linh to return. Storming into the villa at night, the police discovered a large cache of money and arms, as well as a well-known Chinese businessman tied up and waiting for the one million piastre ransom to be paid. After torture of a suspect, forty assassins were rounded up across the city, then the financial committee was arrested followed by a hundred more Vietminh infiltrators in government and society. No mercy was shown. Fresh terrorists and killers were sent in to the city but the game was up. They did not last long. Nguyễn Binh's hold on the city failed when the terror squads of 905 Battalion were liquidated. Networks were smashed, assassins assassinated.

Tam hardly understood the soft ways of the French. When Lieutenant de La Motte discovered a traitor in the plantation in which he was posted, he sent the man down to Saigon. He recalled:

> *I arrested the secretary of the plantation, the most important Vietnamese in this area, because I discovered that he was charged with collecting funds for the Vietminh...the arrested man denied it all... Later Nguyễn Van Tam head of police asked 'But why then did the young lieutenant not simply kill this man?' He raised his hands to the sky when he learnt that it was not my usual style!*[15]

Perhaps this 'softness' was another reason why the French eventually lost. They would make up for it in Algeria.

In falling-in with the Vietminh, Binh had been alienated from his former nationalist comrades in the VNQDDT. They targeted him for assassination. Badly wounded, he was nursed back to health by an attractive young Communist Party nurse, who seduced him into joining the party. But it did not save him.

The conversion was too late and, at heart, he was 'suspect'. Already undermined in his command in the south, only half the new communist battalions were assigned to him. He had to share command with Duong Quoc Chinh and then report to a newly established party headquarters under Le Duan and Le Duc Tho (later to become the famous Vietnamese interlocutor with Henry Kissinger at the Paris peace talks in the 1970s). They acted as his 'political commissars', with detailed oversight on Binh's actions.

Le Duan, an apparatchik and schemer *par excellence* who never worked on practical government matters, and Le Duc Tho plotted to undermine Binh's position from the start. Le Duan was exactly the sort of mediocre but calculating political brain that slides into the slipstream of greater men. Le Duan's extreme secrecy regarding his roots may also have hidden some Chinese blood. Covering his tracks, he sided with the pro-Soviet faction and would eventually supersede Truong Chinh, the pro-Chinese ideologue, as the party's general secretary.

The dirty war

Colonel Le Pulloch, chief-of-staff, and Pierre Messmer, chief-of-staff, were shocked to hear from the high commissioner of the indiscipline of the French Army. French high command sent a secret instruction on 17 April 1947 addressed to all senior and general officers of the expeditionary force:

> *I draw your attention to all kinds of atrocities: looting, indiscriminate reprisals, bombardments or strafing by warships or planes of non-military objectives…I am sure that in almost all cases the responsibility of the officers is engaged… officers compromised themselves in the crimes.*

The Foreign Legion were notoriously tough and ruthless. Although there was a high percentage of Germans, there were not as many SS and Wehrmacht veterans as commonly assumed, with a decline in percentages increasing over time. Most recruits to the ranks were just young Germans looking for adventure and escape from the dour post-war life in the ruins of the German state. But there were still a not inconsiderable number, often at NCO- or officer-level in the Legion, such as Corporal Paul Martelli, formerly of SS Charlemagne, and Legionnaire Heinz Klaus Krause and Lieutenant Hans Josef Wagemeuller, who had fought with the SS in Russia or Pomerania. All of them have published memoirs of their experiences in either English or German. The French press would give such 'mercenaries' more than their due of notoriety.

Wagemeuller termed himself a head-hunter because he had spent the war on the Eastern Front head-hunting for partisans in the forests and marshes behind German lines. As a result, he knew every cruel trick and stratagem of irregular warfare:

> *...we also studied Mao's writings on guerrilla warfare and managed to turn some of his ruses against his own henchmen...we paid off the guerrillas in kind: bomb for bomb, bullet for bullet, murder for murder...it was a war of wits.*[6]

On 29 November 1947, at the village of My Thach in northern Annam, French Army units destroyed over 300 dwellings, raped hundreds and massacred with machine-guns more than 300 women and children who were lined up for execution. It was the most famous atrocity but there were many others. In early 1948, French paratroopers murdered 526 villagers including women and children at My Thuy.

Adrian Liddell-Hart, son of Basil the famous military theorist, became a legionnaire operating in the Plain of Reeds, north of Saigon:

> *We arrived at a row of thatched wooden huts perched on stilts beside a large stream and a couple of crabs* [small US-made four-man tracked amphibious vehicles armed with heavy machine-guns]...*One of them fired a burst of machine-gunfire which was answered only by the clucking of hens...We began rounding up the squealing pigs and chickens. Here and there we shot huge sable cattle...*[the soldiers] *fired the thatch of huts and in a few moments, they were all ablaze, as we waded back to the crabs with our loot...I had been told to take back a small black pig which the Hungarian had captured while he went in search of another...Members of one or two crabs haphazardly chucked propaganda leaflets overboard...*[under the circumstances] *the propaganda was not particularly apt.* [7]

Operating in the Plain of Reeds with amphibious tracked vehicles, the legionnaires burnt as many as ten villages a day, and stole all pigs, chickens and any other valuables. They never met any Vietminh.

The French occupation of Indochina had always been tinged with cruelty, arrogance and oppression. On the other side, nationalism was often tinged with banditry and racist hatred. A spiral of atrocity and unspeakable horror soon built up into the catastrophic bloodbath that would not be assuaged for thirty years. Demonisation or dehumanisation of an enemy allows any barbarity: 'I didn't know what I was doing in Vietnam. I just knew I was fighting communists.' (Heinrich Kleinholz) Later, Kleinholz recounted his actions and defected to the very same communists he had come to fight: 'We were told that we were fighting for European culture, some culture! It destroys everything.'

There were psychopathic and callous killers, such as the legionnaire who shot down innocent civilians as they passed by the post that he was manning on guard duty. Eventually he was posted elsewhere.

One officer on first taking command 'forbade all brutality', but on the first day at his command he discovered that a sergeant had tortured and obtained a confession from a Viet prisoner, an action that saved all their lives by revealing that traitors amongst the partisan militia planned to leave the gates open at night. The officer, formerly a resistance fighter in France, admitted to Bodard:

> *...torture saves lives. It's true. It provides you with the information you need to finish off a few of the men you must kill – the real Viets, the cadres, the political commissars, the militant communists, the heads of committees* [of assassination], *the professional assassins.*[8]

The officer was ruthless by logic, not by nature. He eventually came to believe in calculated and targeted torture but nonetheless complained of ill-discipline and of callous or murderous killing by the FEC, which was rife: 'The high command has not managed to establish any general discipline; everything differs with each unit. Some are irreproachable; some are murderous.' It all depended on the commanding officer.

The war turned dirty at a very early stage, as is almost inevitable in a guerrilla war. The Vietminh wanted to sow terror and fear in the enemy. They fought with asymmetric methods, by ambush, by booby traps, by mines and assassination at close range. Their targets were isolated soldiers or groups of soldiers, on foot or in trucks. Prisoners would rarely be taken. The elusive enemies were 'impossible to find because they disappeared very quickly...here one moment gone the next,' complained Legionnaire Kleinholz. Such tactics only exacerbated the rage of the regular soldier. German soldiers had felt the same anger in the occupied territories of Europe 1940-45.

Often more akin to murder than to war, as such it evoked a bitter response from soldiers on both sides who were driven then by revenge and frustration to exact reprisals. Villages and houses of the suspected enemy would be burnt in the normal course of French 'sweeping' actions. Civilians would be caught in the crossfire. Young Viet men were fair game, it being assumed that they were enemies in civilian clothing. Officers usually directed actions and the men, many of them tough Moroccans or Algerians, had little compunction in complying. Legionnaire soldiers in some units such as Wagemeuller's comprised in the early days of seventy to eighty percent of Wehrmacht or SS veterans, who were already inured to civilian slaughter by their experiences in Russia and occupied Europe. Atrocity piled on atrocity and spiralled out of control, spinning into a macabre maelstrom of tit-for-tat horror.

One legionnaire who recalls being on duty with his comrade nicknamed the Pollak: 'I called him and he didn't answer...then we saw that his head had been impaled on a pole.'

Another soldier remembers:

> *Some friends went for a swim...When they didn't come back we went looking and followed a trail of blood and found their bodies, their genitals cut off, eyes gouged out and their penises in their mouths.*

Legionnaires and paratroopers if captured would be routinely murdered or left to die of their wounds. Hardly surprisingly soldiers would exact a terrible revenge in their turn. And the horror continued into the prison camps. Of the hundred French soldiers captured at Tu-le in 1952 only three survived the war. The prisoners of Dien Bien Phu suffered losses of over seventy percent.

Far away from normal social constraints and tinged by colonial racism, the FEC soldiery regarded the enemy as 'non-human', as 'Viets'. Casualty rates were high and death was never far away. Legionnaire Joachim Schriever recounts: 'Fifteen of us went into a rice paddy and were ambushed...four came back.' Such experiences would not soften a survivor's outlook on taking prisoners, or dealing with 'complicit' civilians.

Veteran legionnaires remember how a patrol might burn several villages with women and children still inside the houses. Young men and boys would be gathered up and beheaded. Gunter Wol admitted: 'There was a firefight and we set fire to everything...that was pretty normal in Tonkin.' Brutality was even institutionalised from the French command level with bonuses paid for heads of the enemy taken. To terrify the population, the legionnaires would leave the headless bodies of the Vietminh in the local marketplace. Such atrocities only encouraged more recruitment by the Vietminh and increased nationalist fervour.

Attacks on convoys were the standard *modus operandi* of the Vietminh, and the country's topography and vegetation was designed for ambushes. In 1947 there were twenty-eight different ambushes along the RC4 conducted by Giáp's famed 174 Regiment. Sent out by the battalion commander to shepherd a convoy to Yen Bay a week after another one had been destroyed, Wagemeuller's way of dealing with 'suicidal' supply convoy missions was to round-up the families of the local Vietminh, put them in vehicles and then advertise the fact through loud speakers. He also tied Vietminh prisoners to the turret of the leading armoured car, a trick that worked when a Vietminh officer with a white flag appeared and asked the column to wait while mines were cleared on the road ahead. Hostages were changed every 10km.[9]

The atrocities would be well broadcast in France by the PCF and their organ *L'Humanite*. Such reporting was particularly difficult for the socialists in government and was used by the communists to split off working-class and intellectual voting. The case of Henri Martin, a young matelot in the French Navy, became a *cause celebre*. He experienced the shelling of Haiphong in December 1946, joined the PCF and distributed propaganda leaflets against the atrocities of the dirty war. When he was arrested and sentenced to five years in prison, there was a torrent of support for him in metropolitan France.

Many of the atrocities were committed by Vietnamese on Vietnamese. 'Exact numbers are not known, but it is reasonable to estimate 500,000 deaths, of which 100,000 to 150,000 were assassinated by the Vietminh.'[10] This was a most deliberate programme of terror to destroy French rule and control of the villages. Minor officials, village chiefs and landlords were especially targeted. Often the killing was accompanied by unspeakable cruelty. Brutality was a recruiting sergeant for both sides. 'Taxim' was an auxiliary given to Sergeant Major Guetre as a translator and guide with the honorary rank of sergeant. 'He detested the rebel Vietnamese who had assassinated his parents; he avowed that he when he had a Vietminh prisoner he would eat their liver.' Much is said of proselytising communists with nationalistic and revolutionary ideals, but the reality is that the peasants, who mostly wanted a quiet life, were coerced into compliance with the Vietminh by terror. Once a village was under control by persuasion or terror or both, the propaganda and brainwashing followed.

Another estimate suggests a wide range of 60,000-265,000 killed by the French.[11] Such killings are by their nature not amenable to accurate quantification. However, indiscriminate killing was an unofficial policy of some army units, and gross negligence or disregard for collateral damage was the norm in army operations.

In Indochina, three types of war co-existed and complemented one another. There was colonial war, where 'justice' was summarily dispensed by both sides.[12] The forgotten war in all of this was the bloody civil war – Vietminh against Vietnamese nationalists, and other militia groupings such as Cao Dai or Hoa Hoa or myriad hill tribes. And then there was class war, the revolutionary war conducted by the Vietminh on their own peoples.

Women in enemy territory or even in friendly areas were routinely raped. That was regarded as a prize of war. For a soldier caught raping a woman the punishment was just six months in jail. In a newsreel, a legionnaire drags away a very young girl. Her fate is unknown. Henrich Kleinhoz recalls that on arriving by ship, 'we went straight to the brothel.' Soldiers were young men already brutalised by war in Europe. Life was lived by the day. An elusive enemy heightened the permanent sense of fear and drove soldiers on to excess. In this faraway land, drink and alcohol fuelled a chaotic and macho lifestyle and fed in to the nihilistic violence of guerrilla war. Journalist Norman Lewis had recorded the history of rape by Moroccans in Second World War Italy and this culture continued in Indochina.[13]

Casual theft of food and belongings was the norm. Mae Elliott recalled:

> *They slit our suitcases with their bayonet. Whatever they found that they liked they would take, like cigarettes and cans of condensed milk. With a knot in her stomach, my mother watched them gulp down the thick and sweet milk hungrily.*[14]

Vo Thi Sau was typical of the many schoolchildren. In 1948, she became a courier and saboteur for a local guerrilla group. Aged 16, on 13 March 1952, she was executed. 'She had been given a grenade with which she managed to kill a French captain and wound twelve French soldiers.'[15]

Le Van Tra joined the youth league when he was just 9 years old:

> *...my job was to steal ammunition, grenades anything I could get. I say it was my job but all the kids did it. We hung around the market place and watched the French soldiers as they came along, waiting for the chance to grab something and run.*[16]

Huong Van joined the Vietminh at the age of 12:

> *Our job was to make propaganda, talking to people in villages and giving musical performances. About a year after I joined, I was sent to a three month course in Marxism. I was taught about dialectical materialism...classes were taught by former political prisoners who had been released from Con Dao prison...Everybody admired the USSR.*

Sometimes Vietminh defected to the French. Lieutenant Wagemeuller described how:

> *Among the prominent Vietminh deserters who had come over to our side was a squat little man. Ghia Xuey, now the honorary 'commander' of Gruppe Drei, working hand in hand with sergeant Krebits. Xuey had been a guerrilla company commander until a tragic mishap induced him to switch sides in 1950. During a raid and the ensuing roundup of French 'collaborators', a neighbourhood Vietminh detachment had executed Xuey's family along with other 'traitors' in a village near Thanhoa.*[17]

Xuey murdered the guilty commander and commissar with a knife then wiped out the offending unit with a machine-gun while they slept.

In the north, French troops hunted out Vietminh suspects as they advanced. Most young men were suspects:

> *Prisoners could be alive one moment and dead the next – shot for being Vietminh suspects... One of the prisoners, a Vietminh security police officer, aroused the suspicion of the French. Right after they finished questioning him, they led him away, shoved him against a wall, and shot him in the mouth.*[18]

This was recalled by Mai's brother Giu, who was a Vietminh supporter but not a cadre. He spoke French and amused his captors. So he lived. As he worked for the French near the front line, he had to run the gauntlet of Vietminh snipers instead.

By 1954, Vietnamese provided thirty percent of French front-line manpower (and well over fifty percent if you included auxiliaries and newly raised units). And this excludes the hundreds of thousands of civilians or PIMs in logistical support. General Ely reported:

> *...the prisoners get fat in the camp; and instead of escaping they asked to become P.I.M. battalion coolies. Only the cadres escape; the other Viets even many regulars prefer to stay.*[19]

In reality communism was not so attractive – many Vietnamese longed to get out of the revolutionary struggle. Used as communist cannon fodder by their senior officers, in turns exhorted with bombast by political commissars who stayed well back, or terrorised into action on pain of punishment by the same party cadres whom they came to hate. When given a choice they usually stayed willingly with the French.

It is a bitter irony that many of the dirty war atrocities involved French colonial troops. As much under the oppressive tutelage of the French as the Vietnamese, they were hired to fight in Indochina. Rugged Algerians or Berbers from Morocco did not come from cultures that respected conquered peoples. Twelve miles from Saigon, an old man cornered Lucien Bodard to complain about a North African battalion recently camped in the area:

> *We understand your soldiers taking our animals and jewellery, our Buddhas; it is normal. We are resigned to their raping our wives and daughters; war has always been like that. But we object to being treated in the same way, not only our sons, but ourselves, old men and dignitaries that we are.*[20]

Civilians were caught in the middle. Legendary American journalist Bob Miller described going on a 'sunset trip' on:

> *...an armoured barge going up a river at ten o'clock one night when three sampans were picked up ahead by search lights. Two failed to stop and were riddled by machine-gunfire. The third gave up and three peasants – an old couple and their son – were bought aboard. They were carrying rice, travelling by night probably to avoid the exactions of local officials. Their cargo was tipped into the river. The boy tried to escape by jumping over the side, he was killed by a hand grenade thrown in after him. The officer in charge was exceedingly young, charming and co-operative.*[21]

A typical problem was posed for military posts, around which civilians clustered both for protection and trade. They were threatened by Vietminh agents that they might be infiltrated and used as a base for mortar attacks or sniping. Reprisals from the garrison on innocent villagers would likely follow.

French garrisons and townships were under unremitting attack. Soldiers lived under constant stress. Norman Lewis describes a dinner with the garrison officers in a provincial town:

> *...we dined in the officers' mess at Tanan. On the previous night one of the hand grenades which I succeeded always in just missing had come through the window and wounded an officer. This time the commandant had posted sentries so that we should all have a nice quiet evening. But no sooner had we taken our seats than there was a series of explosions. The defence towers on the outskirts of the town were being attacked by mortars. A few French 25 pounders joined in. One after another the officers were called to their posts. By the time the entrée was served the commandant and I faced a very junior officer across an otherwise deserted table.*[22]

As the French moved out from Hanoi to take over the small towns and villages of the delta, they feared ambush and booby traps. The Vietnamese civilians were also terrified. Mai's family hid in cellars. When the French arrived:

> *...we all climbed out with our arms raised – men, women, and children – still unsure of what might happen next, the troops laughed when they saw the tiny children coming out with their arms raised in surrender. And they laughed even harder when they saw my younger sister Loan, who had her arms in the air while being carried by her maid.*

Not all of the villagers were so fortunate:

> *...my father and mother passed by my great grand uncle's residence and saw a severed head stuck on one of the rooftops with a cigarette hanging jauntily from his lips. The soldiers said mockingly* 'savez vous ce que cest? C'est la tete d'un Vietminh!' *The decapitated man it turned out was actually not Vietminh, but the rickshaw puller for one of my aunts.*[23]

After these experiences, Mai's family moved back to Hanoi to avoid the dangers of being mistaken for Vietminh supporters. If they had stayed in the country, the Vietminh might well have killed them in the land reform revolution.

Torture was institutional as much as random. French units were widely equipped with electrical equipment. Officers ordered torture as policy even if few admitted it. There were many other methods including 'bastinado' (waterboarding).

Ex-SS trooper in SS Charlemagne Division (French) NCO Paul Martelli witnessed a Vietnamese soldier attached to his African tirailleur unit interrogate a Vietminh prisoner: 'Not getting any answer whatsoever he pulled out a sharp knife and cut off the prisoner's ear.'[24]

Wagemeuller mused on the role of so-called 'non-combatants':

> *In communist-controlled areas there is no such thing as neutrals. Every civilian capable of using his or her arms or legs is compelled to assist the liberation movement...women or children toss grenades or load mortars; old people help fighters by loading empty magazines...lookout, liaison.*[25]

Mines and IEDs

One of the biggest killers in the war were mines, IEDs or booby traps, at which the Vietminh excelled. One day, Lieutenant de La Motte was surprised by a strong explosion:

> *A Jeep pulled up and the colonel* [legion] *told me to hurry. I found it about 5km away, a Jeep cut in two, ten meters apart with the human bits in between. He told me it was a captain and that the Viets had used a radio signalled device. He did not say so but he thought like me that this* [explosive] *charge was meant for him...he was riding behind the captain. The partisans picked up the rest. The colonel was upset because they were short of an arm. I wanted to tell him that it would not prevent the resurrection of the body the next day. Finally, honour was saved because we retrieved the arm which was found in bushes fifty meters away.*[26]

The effectiveness of mines and booby traps is shown by the following figures from African casualties, both Maghreb and black Africans, the percentage of wounds caused by mines or booby traps: 1948 seventeen percent, 1949 twenty-one percent, 1950 seventeen percent, 1951 seven percent, 1952 four percent, 1953 twenty-nine percent, 1954 twenty-nine percent. (Similar figures of about thirty percent applied in the Second Vietnam War.) A common and simple booby trap was concealed stakes in the mud or traps to fall into with poisoned stakes, which caused horrible puncture wounds. Paul Martelli witnessed one of his Senegalese tirailleurs 'step on a sharp bamboo cane hidden in the mud; its tip had been infected with dung and other excrements and this set up an infection that turned into a large wound that refused to heal.'[27]

Falling numbers in the middle years is accounted for by service in the de Lattre lines, in static fortified posts. The Africans on defensive guard duty were replaced by Vietnamese from 1953. Twenty percent of African deaths were due to mines.[28]

Vietminh came out at night to lay mines and this was a constant activity. Karle Heinz Krause recalled that at dawn one morning:

...one of the sentries noticed a sign some 50 meters in front of him. When he went to clear it away, he trod on a mine; this laughable trick nearly led to a second victim but the mine failed to go off. One hour later a Jeep went over a mine between companies one and three. The Jeep was totally destroyed and the driver landed unwounded 15 meters away in a rice field. We immediately searched all tracks and roads looking for mines and found whole rows of them.[29]

Mines or electronically detonated explosives, the forerunner of the IED, were a major factor in casualty numbers. Simple weapons, well camouflaged, they could cause a major casualty event with little risk for the Vietminh. Often but not always it might be co-ordinated with an ambush. For the road-bound French it was a constant terror:

A blinding flash silhouetted the tank in front and an almost simultaneous blast of blisteringly hot air blew me to the ground. Stunned and unable to hear a thing...Amidst the thick smoke vomiting from the open turret, two of the crew emerged...while the muzzle flashes of the enemy's automatic weapons sparkled in the darkness.[30]

Women, children, old people helped prepare and lay mines or even detonate the electronic devices. According to Wagemeuller, 'The majority of booby traps set by the Vietminh were manufactured and planted by non-combatants, often young children...punji stakes, poisoned arrows, and spear guns,'[31] which is why civilians were often slaughtered indiscriminately.

A veteran legionnaire gave a wise piece of advice to new recruit Liddell-Hart: 'Always let someone else go ahead in case there are any booby traps.'[32]

Blockhouse attacks

Picking off isolated bunkers and defence positions in night attacks was the standard *modus operandum* in both the south and the north of Indochina from 1947 through to 1954. A Vietminh account describes a typical attack:

Then they began firing at the blockhouse...the guerrilla commander – his name was Phan Van Phai – and two men ran out from behind the embankment... somehow they managed to get to the front without being shot...Then grenades came flying out. One of Phai's men grabbed it and threw it away before it could explode. Two others followed...Phai's men managed to grab these and got rid of them. The fourth exploded just as it was being picked up. Phai and both men were killed. We were all in a frenzy. Some people were shot down, but others began heaving Molotov cocktails. One French soldier came running out on fire. Phai's men shot him down. The rest were trapped inside. We barbecued them.[33]

On the de Lattre lines in the north, boredom was the main problem, especially when it led to complacency and deadly attacks. In July 1949, Kail Heinz Krause was with his unit of fifty guarding a fortified area around a large pagoda complex near the Red River south-east of the delta near the Catholic region. One of the NCOs, Bobby, was an exceptional leader:

> *...he used to go out at night with a torch to check the bamboo defences, something he enjoyed doing. After one inspection he came back, picked up a machine-gun, called out to all the other posts and jumped into a concrete bunker...we understood immediately and followed him to the bunkers and parapets. Alarm!...we all started to fire at once at the defence zone just 20 meters away...the firing was returned from the enemy but decreased, ours was heavier. Until dawn we did not leave our defences...there were nine dead Viets around the bamboo defences all with satchel bombs in hand; in the full light we saw that they had cut various pathways through the defences.*[34]

Bobby was awarded the *Croix de Guerre*.

The Vietminh also had their tricks:

> *A Viet NCO told me how they blew up our blockhouses; a nine foot bamboo with plastic explosives on the end was gradually advanced towards a loophole; suddenly there was a great explosion...strong enough to bring the blockhouse down on its occupants.*[35]

It was a widely used tactic throughout the war. They attacked at night always and with full intelligence as to the layout of defences and the habits of the garrison down to the minutest detail. Sometimes success would be down to inside information or a spy who unlocked a gate. Women were often used for this role, actively or through pressure using their pillow talk power to pass on help and information. Martelli gave examples of such instances in his memoir *On The Devil's Tail.* He describes how nine Senegalese soldiers and a radio operator were massacred in one outpost with no sign of resistance. They had been rushed at night by Vietminh hidden in pits in the ground while their guard was down.

Sometimes attacks might be regimental-sized, involving thousands of Vietminh against an outlying fortification. Such an attack occurred at the little fort of Zouk To in the Phu Lo district just 20km north of Hanoi near an important crossing of the Red River. Zouk To was a barbed wire defended fort consisting of three bunkers equipped with two machine-guns each and linked by tunnels to a central defensive citadel. The garrison consisted of five European officers and an NCO, thirty Vietnamese and twenty Senegalese. Ex-SS Corporal Martelli, who had considerable building experience from the war against the Russians, added barbed wire and laid mines in a typical triangular pattern. The essential parts of the fort's defence system were the designated artillery 105mm fire zones, 1, 2, 3 spaced respectively at 100, 200, 300m distance around the fort. Artillery cover was provided by the 105mm battery at Phu Lo 3km distant. Paul Martelli was a somewhat typical mercenary recruit to the French Army. Having been trained and seen extensive action against the Russians in Pomerania with the SS Charlemagne Division, he had then served in the French Army before going to work in a forge. A fiery character and tavern brawler, bored with civil life, he enlisted on a three-year contract in 1949 to fight in Indochina.

Knowing that the Vietminh would attack at night, Martelli took the night watch. When a dog in the fort started to become very restless, Martelli went up to the watch tower and switched on the searchlight. '*Mon Dieu,*' gasped the sergeant, 'it's the end. There are a thousand of them. [Vietminh]'.[36] It was a regimental-sized attack launched from the covered jungle fringe just 5km to the north. This was no local initiative but must have been planned by Giáp himself as he sought to take advantage of the strategic and tactical initiative offered by the cover of hills and jungle that ran down from the Vietminh base area in the Bac Kan.

There followed an all-night attack with thousands of Vietminh infiltrating the barbed wire by use of Bangalores and storming the bunker and citadel. Taking on a medieval aspect, the Vietminh used bamboo scaling ladders to storm the tower citadel and were only held off by the generous use of grenades tossed over the top parapet. Attacking the bunkers in waves, the Vietminh were mown down time and again by machine-guns, automatic weapons and grenades.

> *I redirected the machine-gunners' fire which immediately swept out a dozen of the rebels who were sliding charges under the defence wire. The Viet soldiers charged in silence, whining briefly when hit...then the enemy launched their reserves with orders screamed in their shrill, chanting language...I saw them fall in droves, decimated by our bursts, but they had already opened three long gaps in our wire. Against a dozen Vietminh advancing with mines on the end of long bamboo sticks, I let go two MAT-49 sweeps, mowing down half of them.*[37]

Martelli organised the defence, most importantly to make sure that the Vietnamese kept up the ammunition supply to the Senegalese soldiers. This went on relentlessly for hours.

More waves of the enemy were blown apart in the artillery killing zones on the approaches to the wire, although the artillery captain, against strenuous protests from Martelli, was unwilling to risk firing into Zone 1 even when the base was in danger of being overrun after the destruction and capture of No. 2 bunker. After fighting all night, the garrison, having one blockhouse blown up by a satchel charge and running out of ammunition, the situation became desperate as the Vietminh 'were attacking in waves now…forming piles that gave cover…in a scene which reminded me of the Russians in the Battle of Korlin – the same stupid tactic.'[38]

Stupid tactics indeed, but with relatively untrained and poorly educated peasant conscripts there was little alternative for inexperienced Vietminh commanders or ways to finesse tactics when under time pressure as the dawn approached.

'Short on ammo,' Corporal Martelli warned his sergeant. 'If the tanks don't arrive on time it will be a massacre.' Just before the inevitable gruesome end, the Vietminh tried to bluff them into surrender with an amplified appeal, in 'nasal tones' and speaking French: 'Give yourselves up, do not fight against your brothers. Do not serve the cause of colonialism and capitalism!'[39] It was a bluff. Suddenly there was silence.

> *Paul! Tanks…they've arrived…they're retreating…scooting. ….We looked out to see the Vietminh scattering in all directions…our tanks loosed off a few rounds in their midst. Our planes flew overhead…strafing them.*[40]

Martelli would later say, 'I preferred fighting the Russians in Pomerania, the Popovs of Rokossowski and Zhukov.'

Lao and Cambodia

Lao and Cambodia were two backward little kingdoms who added lustre to French pretentions in the name 'French Indochina' and the union thereof, which was the Holy Grail of French regional policy. Originally, occupation was conceived as a way to control the Mekong route to central China, but such ideas faded around the turn of the eighteenth/nineteenth century when it became clear that the topographical characteristics provided insurmountable problems to efficient and profitable commercial exploitation. Cost efficient passage was blocked by the immense, 10-mile-wide expanse of the Khoeung Falls on the Lao-Cambodia border and the rapids at Kratjie. France added the 'Indo' prefix to China, thereby emphasising the French ethnological confusion in their colonial legacy. Indochina was an artificial construct, an adjunct for 'divide and rule' policies. The two countries, Lao and Cambodia, provided a buffer against possible British expansion into Thailand, although it seems that Pavie's opportunistic imperialism rather than deliberate policy led to Lao's incorporation in Indochina. As for Cambodia, the real jewel in the crown was the astounding and vast temple complex at Ankor Wat.

Cambodian communists got their own party, the Khmer People's Revolutionary Party (KPRP), in 1951, but it was effectively controlled by the heavy hand of the Vietminh, something that would store great bitterness in Pol Pot who returned from Paris at this time.[41] Building up to 2,000 party adherents, the armed wing was operated by the Khmer Issarak with a cadre of about 5,000, according to French intelligence.[42] Military operations remained ineffectual and there was minimal impact in the Indochina War, although communist taxation of peasants seems to have been quite effective. As a people the Cambodians were essentially very conservative, as Michael Vickery noted, 'any movement which could unify the right could immediately cut the ground from under the democrats.'[43]

Another point of note is that the French viewed both kingdoms as racially inferior, substantially below the level of the Annamites. In 1858, esteemed naturalist Henri Moot referred to Ankor Wat as '*le tombeau du race morte*' ('the fall of a dead race'), because it was not believed that this extraordinary creation could be the work of the pitifully backward and poor Cambodian race. Ankor must have been built by a most exceptional lost race. Similar patronising and racist comments were made in regard to the Lao. In fact, the temples that arrived much later than the great Gothic cathedrals of Europe were, despite the exquisite carving of stone friezes, comparatively very primitive in their lack of engineering and design finesse.

Colonial administrator Jules Harmand opined with matchless disdain, in 1880:

> *We can count on the Annamites...to colonise to our profit the large part of the valley of the great Indo-Chinese river (Mekong) where they will rapidly supplant the debris of decrepit races which inhabit it...It is necessary that the Laotians be eliminated, not by violent means, but by the natural effect of competition and the supremacy of the most fit.*[44]

While Lao populations reached 1,038,000 by 1936, this number was considerably added to by as many as 100,000 Vietnamese and Chinese immigrants, which was something encouraged by the French for the urbanisation of the key centres such as Thakhek and Savannakhet, as well as providing labourers for the increasing mining activities in Lao's Mekong panhandle. This policy of course led to racial tensions that would be a feature of future wars in Lao. Half the population consisted of Hmong (Meo), T'ai, Leu, Khmu and many other tribes. Government services or administration as such did not touch them in the slightest (and in 2022, Lao's communist government still hardly touched these mountain populations).[45]

The French view of Lao is encapsulated by a remarkably detailed book written by cavalry captain and Lao government commissaire Lucien de Reincarch.[46] De Reinach, who was devoted to the country and lived there many years before having to leave due to ill health brought on by malaria, noted:

They seemed incapable of taking any initiative to get out of their torpor and to recover with the independence, their former prosperity...they were overwhelmed by a kind of fatalism.[47]

De Reinach's very detailed survey saw potential in the mining, plantation and forestry industries if the capital was forthcoming. But in 1911 there was no rail link and the one projected on a contemporary map was never built. These industries did develop but slowly. By 1937, for example, Lao was exporting 1,602 tons of tin concentrate, and by 1926, 60,000 tons of zinc ore, though this rapidly declined to 10,000 tons per annum by 1940.[48] There was one road link to Annam and a second added by Admiral Decoux in the Second World War.

Paul Doumer, who would later become Premier of France, laid the basis of the very highly taxed Indochina system with monopolist levies on salt, opium and alcohol.

The salt and alcohol taxes attracted particular hatred from the populace. In the 1930s' uprising, the government's alcohol warehouses were a particular target for the pyromaniac passions of the mobs. Alcohol burns well.

Fuel for propaganda, it was for Ho a favourite theme. In 1924 Ho wrote in an article entitled 'Condition of the Peasants of Vietnam, *la vie ouvriere*', on 4 January 1924: 'The Annamite peasant is obliged to pay more in taxes on his fields than they can yield.' He attacked France's 'cursed medieval regime, including the salt tax'. At the International Peasants Congress in Moscow, Ho's speech was quoted by Pravda, October 1923, saying that the congress would not be credible 'until it encompasses the peasant masses of the entire east.'[49]

As in the rest of 'primitive' Indochina, i.e Cambodia, in a few partitioned rooms reached by a ladder to the veranda:

...family houses were four to six metres long with columns supporting the houses' beams to a height of one or two metres above the ground...sufficiently comfortable even for Europeans...they were generally placed in the middle of an enclosure which served as a garden, where they plant, coconuts, palms and other fruit trees.[50]

In country areas nothing has changed up to the present day. Under a Cambodian house, which is likely to be higher off the ground due to the seasonal monsoon flood, there may be platforms where cooking is done and where people might sleep in the height of the dry season. Big water jars collect rain. The huts of the Hmong or other mountain tribes are similarly raised but at a lower height, and smaller indigenous people's houses in Indochina are distinctively constructed with bamboo-matted walls and large leaves for roofs rather than wood. Windows in all houses are small and unglazed, making the partitioned rooms dark. There is always one large communal room where the extended family sleeps on thin mats.

Marked out for development and immigration by Annamites as part of an Indochinese political entity, the Lao (Lao-Thai) and Khmer political establishments, unlike significant elements of the Annamite elite, absolutely rejected the idea of an Indochina dominated by Annamites. They were not unaware of the insulting views attached to their races by French imperialists and anthropologists. Visiting Hanoi in March 1931, future Lao nationalist leader Prince Phetxarath, noted petulantly:

> *The Annamese are prone only to think of Annam when they speak of Indochina... all confidence in French promises fades away and the Indochinese federation appears...like an eye wash designed to allow the Annamese to rule over the others.*[51]

The Annamites themselves hardly needed any coaching by the French to regard the Cambodians and the Lao as inferior beings, because they had always looked down on their 'primitive' neighbours. This sense of implicit superiority, racism in fact, was ultimately the *raison d'être* behind the establishment of the ICP and the semi-colonial attitude of the Vietnamese to their neighbours, which is still prevalent although that is today being superseded by the even more arrogant mainland Chinese. Neither minority nation was regarded as being capable of sustaining a serious or effective revolutionary movement without help. In fact, communist penetration into political activism in Lao followed strongly in the wake of substantial Annamite communities that established themselves in the tin mines and in trading/fishing/market communities in Lao's Mekong river towns, notably at Savannakhet and Thakhek along the RC13, which had been extended to Luang Prabang, the capital, in 1941–44. Vietnamese also dominated the Cambodian revolutionary organisation.[52] Vietnamese communist imperialism simply replaced French imperialism and was just as unattractive and racist as the original.

Lao was a Buddhist country, a backward and sleepy Ruritania. The well-known saying 'the Vietnamese plant rice, the Cambodians watch it grow and the Lao listen to it grow' has the ring of truth to anyone who has lived in Indochina. To put it another way, after living in Cambodia and Lao, anyone visiting Vietnam will feel exhausted just watching the visible energy of the Vietnamese going about their business on the waterways, highways and byways of the Mekong delta. Lao is especially slow-paced and Laotian intellectual of the pre- and post-war period, Nhouay Abhay noted, 'until 1940 the Lao with a few rare exceptions scarcely interested themselves in the affairs or their own country.'[53] Politics such as existed revolved around a small and myopic court in remote Luang Prabang. A keen observer of Lao manners was General Salan, who was stationed in remote Laotian outposts for a long time in the pre-war years:

> *The Laotians are a Buddhist people: gentle and idealistic they believe in a life beyond which is better than this one. They accept and are resigned to the evils of the world. The monks preserve and protect their ceremonies which are attended fastidiously. All young men spend some time in the pagoda dressed in yellow or, as soldiers call them, 'canaries'.*[54]

Nationalist resistance before the Second World War in Lao mainly took the form of vicious tribal rebellions in the mountain areas, especially in southern Lao around the Boliven Highlands and Attapu (meaning 'buffalo dung'), in a dusty plain between the highlands and the Annamite mountains near 'the Dragon's Tail' on the Vietnamese-Cambodian border. Revolt involved massacres of the French civilians and officials. Perhaps the main issue that stoked revolt, apart from anti-foreigner feeling, was the French imposition of Corvée labour by way of tax. It was an imposition that infuriated the Indochinese in general and the hill tribes in particular, though the cash equivalent that would later be demanded was hardly more popular. Tactlessly, the French employed officials from minority tribes to collect taxes from other tribes.

These fires of revolt were fanned by a primitive spiritual mysticism that fostered a string of Phu mi bun (holy men). Given the topography of Lao and its immense size, rebellions proved hard to extinguish. They spread like a rash from 1902, particularly in the Champassak and Boliven regions around the southern resort city of Paxse, then continued into the 1930s and 1940s. In the north, instability spread down from China, influenced by Sun Yat Sen's revolution of 1911. A combination of T'ai, Leu and Khmu hill tribes rose in revolt. In one incident the French garrison at Xam Nuea was overrun and massacred, including the French residents. By 1918, the Hmong (Meo) had joined in the revolt led by a local shaman who made messianic predictions of independence. These elements eventually joined with mainstream nationalist movements, which swelled to form the Lao Issarak and later proved to be a recruitment ground for the communist-backed Pathet Lao.

Immediately after the Japanese surrender the Lao Issarak (including the communists) took over and ran the country in tandem with the Chinese, who had been delegated by the allies to occupy Lao and Tonkin. In practice, the Chinese were mainly interested in collecting the opium harvest from the T'ai and Hmong (Meo) peoples as well as looting and theft from the state treasury.

The story of Lao independence politics was one of extraordinary tangled complexity, but it revolved around the three princely brothers, belonging to the second most powerful aristocratic clan in Lao, an offshoot of the royal family. Their wives would play a role in pulling the brothers apart. One of the brothers, Souvanna Pouma, was married to a French woman and became prime minister in due course. He aligned closely with the French. His Oxford-educated elder brother was ambitious nationalist Prince Phetxarath, a long-time player in Lao politics and administration who harboured neutralist and strongly nationalist views. He became prime minister during the Japanese interregnum and was a leading member of the Lao Issarak based in Thailand. He would remain a steadfast nationalist, refusing to compromise with the French and wanting to play off powers against each other. The nationalist movement had realised their goal upon being promoted to independence after the Japanese coup against France in March 1945. Isolated and powerless in Luang Prabang, the king gave in to Phetxarath and accepted independence and the annulment of the protectorate agreement with Vichy France.

However, when Japanese rule ended after Tokyo's surrender, King Sisavang Vong jumped ship again into the French camp, while the Phetxarath fumed about the French colonialists:

> *...only egotists, traitors to their race, in quest of your gold and false honours, follow you...your high promises will dissipate like smoke as soon as you have strangled our brave resistance. Now we have decided to live by immemorial values of our ancestors, values that half a century of French tyranny has suppressed.*[55]

Following Japan's surrender, the Lao Issarak leadership decamped to Thailand after the French reassertion of power in August 1946. Prince Souphouvong, half-brother of Souvanna Phouma, allied himself early on with Ho's ICP. Maverick Prince Souphanouvong, who was a half-brother from a second wife of lower status, possibly a concubine, had a chip on his shoulder from being ignored by the king. His inferiority complex manifested itself in attention-seeking, hyper-competitiveness, vanity and arrogance. Alternatively, he was an energetic, adventurous romantic.[56] A dominating Vietnamese wife who bore him nine children drew him to the Vietminh. The half-brothers were educated at the best school in Hanoi, Lycée Albert Sarraut, where Souphanouvong distinguished himself by becoming an outstanding school goalkeeper – the only defensive thing about the man. Apart from that he was highly intelligent with a facility of speaking nine languages as well as a good knowledge of classical Greek. They both went on to study in Paris. Souphanouvong developed a reputation for aggressive, headstrong and ruthless ambition. Both half-brothers became civil engineers with Souvanna Phouma working in Lao on roads and Suphanouvong building bridges in Annam, the former with a salary seven times higher than the latter.[57] No wonder Souphanouvong was bitter.

He would return with a small group of Vietnamese soldiers who swapped their Vietminh badges for Lao badges and uniforms when they crossed the border in October 1945. Tranh Van Dinh was appointed by Ho as the prince's minder and chief-of-staff. In later interviews he acknowledged that aside from recruiting a few Lao, the prince was a front for recruiting ethnic Vietnamese from the concentrations of Vietnamese immigrants in Lao's central Mekong panhandle. This region around the two major towns on the Mekong at Savannakhet and Thakhet became the prince's power base in the central panhandle.[58] Identifying himself with Vietnamese culture, Souphanouvong sometimes revealed a contempt for the backwardness of Lao, which in 1955 could only count thirty university graduates in the whole country.

So important was this opening to revolution in Lao that Ho supplied 100 out of 240 rifles in the armoury of the Central Vietnamese Revolutionary Committee.[59] The ICP dominated Lao Issarak, whose base and leadership was in Thailand. Increasingly, the movement fell apart as tensions arose over ideological control, personal rivalry, geographic location and money. Issarak factions became increasingly fearful of the communists and their Vietnamese allies. Much of it was informed by racial antipathy and dislike of the large-scale Vietnamese immigration into the Mekong panhandle.

Souphanouvong would position himself on the Vietnamese borderlands close to his Vietminh backers and their supply chain. Lao-Vietminh bases were established along the border and progress was made in recruiting some of the highland tribes whose resentment of the Lao lowlanders was palpable. The future communist-dominated Pathet Lao (equivalent to the Vietminh) became successor to the Lao Issarak.

When Thailand's former military dictator General Phibunsongkhram, who had aligned with the Japanese, came back to power in Thailand via a coup in 1946, the extreme right-wing general would have no truck with the Thailand-based and communist-aligned Lao Issarak group. Thailand was closed to Issarak nationalists, most of whom, except for Prince Phetxarat, returned to be reconciled with the Lao King Sisavonguong, who had agreed to be constitutional ruler under the French Union of Indochina concept by 1949. Mainly under the 'neutralist' leadership of Prince Souvanna Pouma, the Lao government would be a shifting but stable oligarchic coalition that divided government and patronage between competing factions, families and regions.

After this shift, the rebel element of the nationalist Issarak movement was necessarily thrown in the way of the communists (Pathet Lao) under Prince Souphanouvong, who returned to the Lao Vietnam borderlands to cement the alliance with Ho, who had befriended him four years before. Under Vietminh 'guidance', the Pathet Lao was formed from a combination of lowland intellectuals, teachers and Vietnamese emigrants and Meo tribesmen under Phay Dang. Giáp gave them political and military advice:

> *Use the peasants as your eyes and ears and your main source of supply* [and as for the tribesmen] *teach them to shoot, guide them in killing a French soldier and, by implicating them in a crime, you implicate them in the war.*[60]

Souphanouvong became prime minister of the rebel Pathet Lao government after presiding over the first Resistance congress with 105 attendees, including the real powers in the nascent party, Kaysone and Nouhak (a Lao-Vietnamese), at which a twelve-point revolutionary programme and manifesto was established. It seems that the Red Prince was mainly a front for Vietminh power with his vanity being bought off by big titles. Seeking popularity with the hill tribes, the revolutionary government abolished tax on opium. Phay Dang, in a self-congratulatory interview given in 1957, recalled:

> *In place of our poisoned arrows and flintlocks we began to get modern arms... we set up guerrilla bases...later on we were able to form whole Meo companies from our guerrilla bases and attach them to the regular forces formed by Souphanouvong.*[61]

In practice despite the bravado, titles and trappings, the Pathet Lao were weak and Phoui Sananikone for the royal government was probably nearer the mark when he noted at the Geneva Conference in 1954: 'This so-called government does not exist apart from the Vietminh and has no seat other than the Vietminh military command posts.'[62] UN fact-finding evidence later supported this and found that Vietminh-Pathet Lao rule was oppressive involving the usual indoctrination, slave labour and requisitioning of foodstuffs.[63] No doubt the Pathet Lao were useful as guides and for reconnaissance and intelligence. As one veteran recalled, 'We Lao knew the local habits and customs. The Vietminh didn't and, *therefore, feared incidents if they had direct contact with the population.*' (Author's emphasis) But their direct military capability was minimal amounting to 2,000 fighters, most of whom were Lao-Vietnamese from the panhandle, and a few tribesmen.

Eventually, Prince Souphanouvong and the Pathet Lao, following on the coat-tails of the VPA offensive, established themselves in April 1953 inside the eastern borders of Lao, especially in the region of Pongsali in the north and Xam Nuea in the north-east, where they set up a 'revolutionary government'. In the south, the Boliven plateau became a Pathet Lao base. On the edge of the Plain of Jars, French and Lao troops reduced various rebel hotspots. But the base for communist expansion had been established. The Pathet Lao was a puppet of the Vietminh, as one defector noted:

> *I thought I was fighting for my country but the discipline imposed by the Vietminh kept us in constant danger of deportation. The least argument the smallest mistake was greeted by the fatal words 'to be sent to the instruction centre ...no one ever came back.*[64]

Even allowing for some bias, the evidence is that the Pathet Lao had minimal national support or military power and 'slave worker' (Corvée) impositions on the Lao peasanty were the same, or even more oppressive, as those inflicted by the French. Orwell's *Animal Farm* had come full cycle.

From 1946–52, there was only small-scale fighting on the country's fringes. It did not rate as a high priority for Ho and the Vietminh. When Giáp changed to an indirect war strategy in 1952–53, all of this changed. Lao, a large territorial mass some 2,000km long astride littoral Vietnam, became of critical political and military importance out of all proportion to its 1,000,000 population size or economic potential, except for opium production, the capture of which would help finance the war.

Opium and Indochina

The Hmong were an indigenous tribe who lived a completely separate life from the lowlanders. Government hardly touched them and only a tiny number went to school. Life-expectancy was 45. Steeped in their own animist traditions, they led a semi-nomadic life going from hilltop to hilltop, moving on roughly every seven years. *National Geographic* in 1952 described the tribes-women: '... silver rings dangle from their earlobes; numerous silver necklaces, numerous silver necklaces.' Men wore baggy trousers and ornately decorated jackets embroidered with geometric patterns. Cash was hardly used. Unchanged today a typical black Hmong tribeswoman wears thick knee-length socks, a black jacket, with bands of woven colour around the arms and collar. Their heads are topped with the black-blue of red fez-like caps, but without tassels or a turban, of colourful material. Tribal governance involved consensus and debate. The French left them alone after decades of bloody attempts to rule and instead developed a symbiotic relationship based on trade and processing of opium, as well as military employment of the hardy men who had immense physical strength and stamina at high altitudes with loads of 110lb. They practised barter and their medium of exchange was opium, which was their main agricultural activity and *raison d'être*.[65]

The story of opium, the Hmong (Meo) and Indochina are completely intertwined, mainly because taxes on the crop were a vital element in Indochinese and colonial finances as well as the politics of the region and especially of the hill tribes with whom the French administration formed a close bond. The trade operated under French protection and the harvest was shipped to China via Hanoi or Saigon, with a significant proportion being consumed by the large population of users in Indochina. In Saigon, opium was refined at a 1-hectare site in Rue Paul Blanchy, employing twenty-five officials and 250 labourers. According to French historian Vincent Borel, 'it was the most important industrial building in the city.'[66] By 1900, there were 254,000 users consuming nearly 15,000 points of sale. In 1899, the French leased to the empress 82,244 hectares of land for opium production. It contained 962 villages and 175,000 people. This trade in opium continued strongly through the Second World War and the Indochina War 1945–54. France maintained its alliance with T'ai and Meo tribes by encouraging, protecting and sustaining their opium livelihood. Competition for control of the opium crop would lead to the Chinese intervention in 1945–46 as well as the Vietminh decision to move into the T'ai uplands from 1951.

In 1898, France's Kwangchow Wan concession (opposite Hainan Island) was given to France and merged with Indochina. The territory incorporated 200,000 people by 1930 in a place renamed Fort Bayard. By 1923 the opium *entrepôt* there handled 500,000 tons per annum for sale into China and worldwide, especially the US via San Francisco, but also to Marseilles and Bordeaux. Profitability was so great that 1,306 French and 2,172 indigenous tax officials were employed to collect opium taxes and monitor consumption in 1925.[67] As with mainland Indochina, le Banque Indochine was a major beneficiary of the business. Opium-derived revenues accounted for as much as ten percent of Indochina revenues.[68]

Opium was also the key to upland politics and loyalties. A most sentimental Lao lover and habitual opium user, General Salan, explained:

> *...the high mountain Montagnards are friends of those who buy opium. It is for them actually an existential question and the Vietminh understood that. This opium could have been traded with China, but in the current circumstances we needed the Meo to serve in our GMCA* [pro-French partisan] *units so I had to deal positively with this issue by taking the opium on our account.*[69]

Meo specialised in the mountaintop horticulture of opium, moving in a nomadic way every seven years from one site to another in a system of natural rotation:

> *Planted mainly in October, the petals from the pretty multicoloured flowers in fields of grass, fall towards February, one cuts open the pod in the evening and by morning it has formed into a sort of black gum which dries out on large green leaves. Gathered into a cake it constitutes the raw opium.*[70]

Graham Greene describes the delicious, serene, sensory enhancing power of opium:

> *After two pipes I felt a certain drowsiness, after four my mind felt alert and calm – unhappiness and the fear of the future became like something dimly remembered...*[71]

CHAPTER VIII

France and the Home Front

French party politics 1946–1949

From 1947, the communist Eastern European takeover began to be completed. Meanwhile, the PCF's failure to take over France from the inside led the PCF to revert to a harder line, trying to pull the socialists away from the government coalition. The Socialist Party would resist this pull but the effect was to leave the communists in a political ghetto with neither representation in government nor in parliamentary committees. It also split the union movement. Except for one strike in 1953, there was no co-ordination of actions. Increasingly, the PCF moved into opposition on the issue of Indochina with a strong focus and criticism of human rights abuses. *L'Humanité*, primed with plentiful sources from their Vietnamese communist friends, was instrumental in bringing discredit on the French armed forces and to sour public opinion about the war. They infiltrated and controlled the Movement de la Paix, which included all streams of anti-colonial war protesters.[1] Industrial actions looked to hinder war production and logistical support for the FEC. As in anti-inflation demonstrations in 1947–8, and later against NATO in 1952, the PCF organised violent strikes and protests against anti-sabotage laws in 1950. Communist CGT members in French arms factories carried out industrial-scale sabotage. About forty percent of French-produced equipment was found to be sabotaged when unpacked. 'Sugar in gasoline tanks, emery oil in transmission gears, torn or broken electrical wiring.' Typical of the division in French society, others subscribed to public fundraising in several cities for the provision of helicopters to ferry the wounded.

In their anti-NATO stance, the PCF found common cause with de Gaulle's RPF, which was also vehemently opposed to the internationalisation of French defence efforts, especially as it involved 'national subjugation' within the Anglo-Saxon-dominated NATO.

Embarrassingly, the socialists were caught in the middle between their Marxist beliefs and 'realist' political ambitions. As a result, the PCF rallied the working classes and pulled in 25.7% of the vote in 1956 but remained politically isolated. They were unable to appeal to enough centrist votes due to the image related to Sovietisation in Eastern Europe, which acted as an object lesson in what happens to freedoms when the communists are allowed to take over. Weakness showed itself in party membership, which started to slide from 800,000 at its peak in 1946.

The Socialist Party became increasingly caught on the horns of their political pragmatism and revolutionary Marxist ideology. The meekness of their stance over Indochina was an abnegation of the party's ideological commitments when faced with the allure of power. But even in power, the socialists were hardly lions for any policy. In 1944, Leon Blum noted:

> *I have never considered that for the Socialist Party the exercise of power or participation in power has become a necessity or even a normal situation. I consider that, although it is frequently imposed by circumstances, it remains something exceptional.*

In the immediate aftermath of war, the socialists strongly supported the colonial policies of the MRP, radicals and the right. They accepted the bogus mantra of 'association' of Indochina states and sought the re-establishment of French power and reputation, of which the ideal of empire formed a part. It was a paternalist idea that envisaged 'independence' some time in the future, rather like the idea of 'socialism' itself for 'democratic' Marxist parties.

However, Socialist Party policy towards Indochina started to pall under the cumulative impact of human rights abuse, communist propaganda and an appreciation of the genuine national popularity of Ho Chi Minh's Vietminh. Unfortunately for Leon Blum, he found himself becoming prime minister just when the French military launched its war on the Vietminh in Tonkin. Boxed-in by the policy of 'associated states' and by the need to maintain the coalition, he was unable to stop the war. French Army officers were beginning at this point to operate beyond government policy. Effectively, they drew France into their Indochina War by their provocations. The Vietminh were also very willing to be provoked in order to shift the blame for starting the war. Concerns regarding the cost to the national budget where other worker priorities were under threat was another consideration. The socialists were caught between their appeal to the working class and the need for moderated coalition politics.

Political re-evaluation and the start of the end of consensus between the mainstream parties as to colonial policy started to emerge in 1950, when Mendes-France of the Radical Party started to question the Indochina engagement. Efforts to put democratic flesh on the idea of a French Union in the form of the Paris-based Assembly of the French Union proved to be a failure. It was started in 1946 but floundered incoherently as an advisory body. The new assembly first sat in 1947. Vietnam joined in 1950. There would be an equal number of overseas and metropolitan representatives. However, it was impossible to hide French colonialism behind such obviously toothless facades but, politically, such tricks were useful in giving a sop to leftist elements in the government, especially the socialists, whose qualms could be smoothed over with 'talking shop'. Relegated to Versailles, assembly debates were never covered in the press and the National Assembly was not required even to consult it.[2]

When the shock of the humiliating defeat on RC4 in October 1950 sank in, the Socialist Party moved decisively towards opposition to the war and in favour of a negotiated exit. On the centre-left, Mendes-France of the Radical Socialist Party would emerge as an open critic of the war telling parliament frankly that, 'without a military solution the only possibility is negotiation.' Small beginnings, but others to the left and centre, including the small UDSR of Pleven and Francois Mitterrand, espoused *both* closer European ties and the continuation of empire. Mitterrand would become the minister for the African colonies.

This coincided with the weakening of the Socialist Party's electoral appeal such that it would be excluded from coalitions after 1950. However, they would tactically support various MRP, radical, UDSR and right-wing parties in government. Ministries would progressively move to the right even as fighting intensified in Indochina, and the left-wing vote fell. In the 1951 elections, the anti-Fourth democratic parties, communists and Gaullists took forty-five percent of the vote (twenty-five/twenty), but the socialists (fifteen percent), the MRP (12.5%), and the radicals (RGR) (eleven percent) were still able to command a majority. The MRP lost much of their conservative base to de Gaulle's RPF and was reduced from 145 to eighty-eight deputies, and the communists reduced from 179 to 101 seats. The RPF took 117 seats, and became the largest party but it was a bitter disappointment after the forty percent vote achieved in the municipal elections in 1950.

Nevertheless, the right was recovering its power, something that had been boosted by the threatening activities of the Communist Party, whose true nature had been unmasked by Stalin's activities in Eastern Europe. Another unmasking was taking place with MRP voters. The MRP as a Christian democratic party, having been a respectable receptacle for Vichyite and extreme Catholic rightist votes, was now being stripped of a significant part of its voter base, which was increasingly attracted to authoritarian politics. Vichyites were gravitating to de Gaulle, as the memory of wartime divisions faded.

De Gaulle had done much damage to his cause by his clumsy fascistic-style campaign with paramilitary trappings: Jeeps loaded with thugs in berets and black leather jackets. His threats to make a *coup d'état* with a rendezvous on the Champs Elysée was a major campaign mistake. He alienated centre-right, centre and centre-left votes that otherwise would have come to him.

Indochina was a minor issue in the campaign, despite socialist discomfort when challenged by communists screaming, 'Are you or not for the self determination of peoples?' The socialists were moving decisively in favour of negotiation but the issue, though a sore point, was not a major one. Any odium on this issue could be thrown onto the MRP, who controlled the entire administrative and political nexus around the empire, and Indochina in particular. A centrist coalition with a right shift would now dominate French politics. If anything, the imperialist Indochina policy was reinforced by the election result even as the MRP party's popularity plummeted.

The centrist lock on government still held, as it had since 1947, with the exit of the communists, but the emergence of the Gaullist RPF made life more difficult. Forming a government became increasingly fraught as the socialists moved into opposition.

The MRP was the post-war new arrival in French politics. After the catastrophe of war, the MRP with its Christian democratic values was an attractive alternative to the traditional right. Despite the MRP suffering a crashing loss of support upon the entry of the emergence of the RPF in 1947, their balancing role in any coalition remained essential. As a result, the MRP's grip on Indochina's administration and foreign policy was maintained.

The MRP, like any centre party, was always split between its left- and right-wings because they needed to garner votes from both sides of the spectrum. The MRP's left-wing candidates were run in big city constituencies and right-wing candidates in ultra-Catholic small towns and rural areas. On the left Robert Schuman, who was at the heart of the development of the new European integration policy as founder of The Iron and Steel Community, grew increasingly sceptical of the war. George Bidault led the right-wing, which was more orientated to the small-town and rural Catholic voter, and put considerable emphasis on the retention of empire. A part of every ministry in the Fourth Republic, the two men would share the Ministry of Foreign Affairs for almost the entire tenure of the republic.

The very strong Catholic presence in Vietnam, especially in Tonkin, certainly drew the MRP to throw a protective cloak around the Bao Dai regime. The empress was a Catholic.

Economic wreckage

French economic recovery and food supply to the cities was a most pressing need. Not quite on an Eastern European, German or Russian scale of disaster, the French economy had nonetheless been devastated by the war. 'The French economy had been stripped bare.'[3] (McMillan Guardian 2009.) What the Germans had not stolen had largely been destroyed.

A devastated railway network, once boasting 17,000 engines, now had 3,000. Five hundred thousand houses had been destroyed, with whole cities such as St

Malo and Caen left in utter ruin, and a further 1,500,000 houses were damaged. Infrastructure such as bridges had been destroyed in their thousands while area-bombing by Flying Fortresses and Lancasters had wiped out hundreds of factories, not to mention the collateral damage. Coal production for electricity was down to twenty percent of pre-war levels and coking coal had no market because the steel industry had ceased to exist. Agricultural production was still eighty percent of pre-war levels, but food could not be got to market because of lack of transport, most of which was commandeered in any case by the allied military. As a result, adult calorie intake in the cities dropped to 1,050 calories for official rations and elsewhere foodstuff sold on the black market for extreme prices.

Inflation was a constant problem that underlay political instability in the Fourth Republic. It was also a problem of budget, especially as pressing social needs had to be sacrificed for the sake of the Indochina War. A cash-strapped army lived hand-to-mouth and was woefully underfunded. Luckily, colonial soldiers from Africa could be bought cheaply. French officers and men were also attracted to the exotic east, especially as 'all the hopes raised by the liberation (of France) were dissipated,'[4] confessed Legionnaire Robert Schuermans. Additionally, French officers could play the artificial piastre exchange rate to salt away tidy nest-eggs.

Needless to say, the sheer poverty of France meant that their military was living on a shoestring, its soldiers clothed and equipped by an assembly of second-hand weapons, in some cases antique First World War, and hand-me-down American or British clothing. This was the case even six years after the start of the Indochina War. Adrian Liddell-Hart, who served a year with the Legion in 1951–2, was kitted out with 'GI tunics…tucked into French trousers…miscellaneous khaki shorts,' and second-hand shirts. He ended up fighting in the *Plain des Joncs* in the Mekong delta from amphibious tracked machines, 'filled with all kinds of French, American, and British guns, plus bottles of brandy, vin rouge and a rough local concoction fermented out of rice.'[5]

Gaullism and Rassemblement de Peuple Francais (RPF)

In 1944 de Gaulle wrote to Stalin: 'Between France and the Soviet Union there are no matters in direct dispute. Between France and Great Britain there always will be.'[6] On the right a re-alignment would take place following the launch of de Gaulle's Rassemblement de Peuple Francais RFP. The movement that put up the Cross of Lorraine as a sort of proxy Swastika was clearly undemocratic in intention. It developed all the hoodlum razzmatazz of Nazi rallies complete with uniformed armed gangs swaggering around in Jeeps. But it was all a bit down at heel and shambolic compared to the real thing. De Gaulle's language was violent, anti-democratic and falangist in inspiration in emulation of the semi-mystical xenophobic philosophy of Maurras's Action Francais: the glorious dream of a spiritually unified and absolutist French state. He was reverting to the politics of his father.

De Gaulle was vehement in his support for French imperialism. Warm-up acts for the rallies were provided by old Indochina looter and 'Free French' crony Andre Malraux, the 'novelist', charlatan, plagiarist and chancer of the first order. Malraux provided ludicrous melodrama and theatrics. More comic Lehar than Wagner, more tin-pot Falangist than national socialist, Malraux appealed to France's despotic, Napoleonic past. As usual it was all about glory. Malraux would become de Gaulle's longest serving minister (for culture) in the Fifth Republic.

De Gaulle's push for power was underpinned by prices trebling between 1946–49 and spurting again between 1950–52 as a result of the Korean War.[7] Real wages stagnated or declined, from 1950 to July 1951, and the inflation index moved from 108 to 137. As a result, five-year economic planning and emphasis on heavy industry and infrastructure meant:

> *...a structural imbalance had built up as a result of development efforts* [planned economy] *in the basic sectors of industry and transport which had expanded ahead of the secondary sectors.*[8]

Moreover, the budget also came under pressure due to military spending, notably in Indochina where the FEC under General Valluy commanded 100,000 troops.

De Gaulle was helped by the severe socio-economic crisis gripping France as the PCF became rampant in its strike actions. When the CGT (communist trade union) brought out 20,000 Renault workers on strike following Premier Remadier's wage-freeze, the PCF were ejected from government. The violent and long-running strikes in 1947/8 were clearly an attempt to destabilise and possibly overthrow the government. John Foster Dulles, who was travelling in France meeting key leaders, recorded:

> *The situation was indeed desperate. Rail transportation was disrupted. Indeed, the train on which my wife and I travelled had had to be rerouted because the tracks ahead had been blown up.*

In the local elections on 19 October 1947, de Gaulle scored a stunning triumph with forty percent of the national vote. This result was the yearning for a saviour, particularly in the face of a concerted communist effort to destabilise the country by violent massed actions and strikes.

De Gaulle always looked ungainly in the demagogue role. He came from the struggling minor aristocracy who despised the *sans culottes*, and people in general. He could never really hide his misanthropic soul. Not unjustified but exploited for advantage were de Gaulle's warnings of the 'red' threat, both internally and externally: 'The RPF,' he boasted, 'will continue to expand until it embraces the entire nation, with the exception of a few separatists.' In 1948 he expounded that 'the trade union organisation must be thoroughly changed...because there will not be any class struggle inside the association of capital and labour.'[9]

De Gaulle also claimed credit for taking back control in Indochina by sending 80,000 troops, saying France must take a position of strength and give support to Bao Dai, Indochina must be part of the French Union. In the colonies, 'the authority of France yes I repeat the authority must clearly be exercised on the spot,' de Gaulle declaimed. Echoing the refrain of Hitler, Mussolini, Franco and the Spanish Falange, Pilsudski and other tin pot European despots, he wanted a France 'free from political control' by the 'corrupt parliamentary system.' The generals in Indochina, most of whom came from the nexus of the Free French command structure, including generals such as Leclerc, Valluy, Salan, Juin and de Lattre, had taken their cue from de Gaulle and would in the main continue to do so. It was a cabal of St Cyre graduates, with very similar aristocratic pedigrees – except General Salan, the son of a provincial doctor.

With regard to Indochina, de Gaulle as president of the RPF declared in March 1949:

> *...they have allowed the military situation to deteriorate bit by bit...this situation is at the root of everything. They want to replace force with politics, but you cannot make any politics, certainly not politics of grand generosity, if one renounces being strong...In Indochina the solution of Ho Chi Minh that's to say capitulation and after various formalities which last more or less a long time, the destruction of the work of France in Indochina, then that of Indochina itself with its liberty culture and traditions.*

De Gaulle was of course being thoroughly disingenuous as well as showing his ignorance of the military problems. It was a most superficial and glib political statement without meaning, but appealing to the rightist element of the MRP vote and the Vichyites.[10] His policy on Indochina underpinned MRP determination to continue a strong military approach in Indochina without negotiation. France's disasters in Indochina were covered with de Gaulle's fingerprints.

The decline of Gaullist support and the detachment of de Gaulle from his own party in July 1952 made life easier for the radicals, MRP and the traditional right by bringing in the RPF to traditional conservative right-wing majority shorn of some of its Falangist and Salazar-like pretensions.

Instability in the Fourth Republic but stability of Indochina policy

Underlying stability in government policy on key issues 1944–54 is demonstrated by the composition of governments and personnel. There may have been fourteen different coalition governments but in the Ministry of the Interior there were only seven ministers, the Ministry of Finance eight, the Ministry of Defence ten, and the Foreign Ministry two. The Foreign Ministry was entirely occupied by the MRP in this period and the Ministry of the Colonies was similarly dominated by the party. The Ministry of the Interior was controlled by the socialists from 1944–50 and thereafter by the radicals. The Ministry of Finance, apart from a few short spells of socialism in 1946 and 1947, was controlled by conservatives, by Schuman for the MRP, and by the radicals. The Ministry of Defence was split randomly between socialists, MRP and radicals, with a short interlude of three months in 1947 where the communists were in charge. The chart below demonstrates the 'apparent chaos' of the Fourth Republic as well the steady drift from left to right from 1946–54.

The Socialist Party dominated the Colonies Ministry from January 1946 to October 1947. Thereafter the care of the associated states was split off under the control of MRP ministers Paul Costet Floret and Jean Letourneau until June 1953, when the latter resigned due to a piastre exchange rate scandal.

Dates of office – Ministry for Overseas France/Colonies* 1946–54	Minister name	Political party
26 January–23 December 1946	Marius Moutet	Socialist Party SFIO
23 December 1946–22 January 1947	Auguste Laurent	SFIO
22 January–22 October 1947	Marius Moutet	SFIO
22 October 1947–29 October 1949	Paul Coste-Floret	MRP (Catholic-centre) Mouvement Populaire Republicain
29 October 1949–3 July 1949	Jean Letourneau	MRP
3–12 July 1949–3rd July 1950	Paul Costet-Floret	MRP
12 July 1950–11 August 1951	Francois Mitterrand	Rassemblement de Gauches Republicain (RGR) centre-left bloc Union Democratique de la Resistance (UDSR)
11 August–8 March 1952	Louis Jacquinot	Republicain Independente (conservative right) RI
8 March 1952–8 January 1953	Pierre Pflimlin	MRP Mouvement Populaire Republicain
8 January 1953–19 June 1954	Louis Jacquinot	RI

* The names and dates denote the persons and party in charge of Indochina. Administrative responsibility for Indochina was split out from the Ministry of Colonies in July 1950.

Dates of office – Ministry for Overseas France/Colonies* 1946–54	Minister name	Political party
July 1950–28 June 1953 Minister for Relations with the associated states	Jean Letourneau	MRP
8 January 1953–19 June 1954	Marc Jacquet	RPF Rassemblement du Peuple Francais (Gaullist)

General policy remained consistent until the end, but that did not mean that there were no differences at the tactical level or confusion as to policy or adverse underlying shifts in political sentiment on the Indochina issue within the coalition. It led to the sort of imprecise guidance on military grand strategy and political obfuscation over Lao that contributed to the disaster at Dien Bien Phu.

The government comprised a coalition including communists and socialists from 1944 to May 1947. Thereafter the communists were excluded. The socialists were also excluded from February to June 1950, and then again from August 1951. Premierships were dominated by radical and MRP candidates from 1945–1951, then by conservatives after mid-1951 to May 1954, when Mendes-France took over the premiership to negotiate the exit of France from Tonkin after the defeat at Diem Bien Phu. The Indochina War was not once debated in parliament in 1953, even as vital developments were in progress, i.e. the first invasion of Lao, rapidly increasing commitment of American money and equipment, great expansion in local forces, major offensive operations, and the Navarre plan. Behind the apparent consensus, there was certainly a rising scepticism as to the sustainability of the policy, which realistically had always been in doubt, especially after the victory of the communists in China in 1949 and the following RC4 defeat in October 1950.

General Navarre was chosen for the top job because he was close to René Mayer when the political merry-go-round stopped. It marked the recovery of the Radical (Socialist) Party to front-line politics after its demise following the catastrophe of the Third Republic. Mayer wanted his own man under his patronage. A talented finance minister, fairly right-wing and a 'do-er', he had a positive effect on post-war reconstruction. On a visit to Washington on 26 March, he was advised by Eisenhower to avoid the sensitivities of French colonialism in his speeches, which he did by emphasising the joint effort to save western civilisation from communist despotism.

Demonstrating once again the consistency of Fourth Republic policy to Indochina, the Colonies Ministry was held by M. Letourneau of the MRP from July 1950–June 1953.

Bao Dai and the French Union

Born a puppet emperor, Bao Dai's life was tragic in its pointlessness. Regarded as a god by many of the peasantry, at least until they discovered a replacement in Ho Chi Minh, Bao Dai had the added misfortune to be under the sway of his mother, a wizened betel-chewing hag. This wretched woman was addicted to gambling. It was a pastime taken up also by the louche, monarch-playboy, who had at least the gumption to get on the right side of the house by setting up casinos with his cronies. It bolstered his state stipend and gave him more freedom from his French minders.

Photos of Bao Dai show a man with white suit and thick dark glasses, well-groomed and only slightly plump. He led a cosmopolitan life. His education and upbringing were in France, and a lot of time was spent on the Riviera. Captured by the Japanese on one of his solitary hunts in the forest in 1944, he was forced to become emperor of independent Vietnam on pain of death. When the Vietminh took over in August 1945, Ho Chi Minh made him a similar offer but in reverse, which prompted his abdication. In return Bao, now with a commoner name, became Ho's supreme counsellor, which certainly shows Ho's sense of humour. Boa Dai was lucky not to be killed but Ho was wary of trampling on the man's residual mystique, in public at least. In private Ho continued the joke by often inviting Boa Dai to dinner with his driver.

Sent on a diplomatic mission to Chinese warlord Lu Han, Bao eventually escaped from Ho's 'prison of irony' and made his way back to French-controlled Indochina, only to be caught up again in the snake-pit of Cochin politics. Not surprisingly, Bao Dai was to develop various nervous disorders. A compendium of his insecurities accompanied his lonely and feckless life. His essential policy was to do nothing at all and let matters take their course. A *dilettante par excellence*, he perhaps became inured to his utterly frivolous life.

The emperor's arrival at Darlat for a hunting expedition is described by Norman Lewis:

> *...the emperor was first to alight followed by a young lady in black velvet robes, whom from her carriage was even more regal than most Vietnamese girls, I stupidly presumed to be empress. I was later informed that she had been Miss Hanoi in 1949. Several French officers and civilians followed but there were no Vietnamese in the entourage. I was presented to the Emperor who shook hands with reasonable vigour.*[11]

The emperor cavorted openly with his many mistresses. and lived mainly at Darlat when in Indochina, a town described by Norman Lewis, as a 'drab little resort in Haute Savoie.' Otherwise, he spent time in Hong Kong and the French Riviera.

For the French plan of a federated union to work they needed to borrow Bao Dai's 'legitimacy'. There was no other possible unifying candidate to be the head of state in the new construct. De Gaulle's candidate Vanh San was killed in an African air crash in 1945. It would, of course, continue to be a mere front for a French protectorate, which would maintain control on all the levers of power, in finance and most importantly the military. If Bao Dai had been a mere puppet and playboy, then it should have been easy to corral him into line. However, that was not the case. He proved to be a very slippery puppet, because Bao Dai was smart enough to know that he was essential to the plan to bring America onside with support and finance.

There was of course no real intention by the French government to do anything except provide a cloak of respectability to continued French rule. This was the main task of the high commissioner from March 1947–October 1948, Emile Bollaert, a Resistance fighter and Radical Party senator who had never before been to Asia.

French policy was so set in the direction of Bao Dai's restoration that even a peace offer from Ho made on 19 April 1947 was brushed off. Ho and the communists had no serious intention of giving up their claims and goal to gain full independence but they hoped to still play for time while the Chinese Civil War was in the balance. The longer-term intention of the communists would be to throw off their own particular fig leaf, i.e. the Vietminh structure, and reveal themselves as a fully-fledged people's republic with the concomitant socialist revolution. Both the French and the Vietminh were playing a game with the Vietnamese people. However, in terms of popular support, the balance was decisively with the Vietminh in the north, while in the south the French alliance was stronger, albeit with very robust pockets of communist control and resistance in the Plain of Reeds, in the delta, and in the rubber estate country to the south-east of Saigon.

On 6 December 1947, on a warship in An Long Bay, Bao Dai was cornered into signing a protocol containing the word 'independence' for a unified Vietnamese state, which was Bao Dai's ultimate red line. Robert Schuman, the French prime minister, pontificated that 'France recognised the independence of Vietnam *only limited by those matters relating to the Union Francais in respect of being an associated state.*' (Author's emphasis)

Clearly no real independence was intended because the Union would be controlled by France in all essentials. Nevertheless, Schuman's party colleague George Bidault believed that too much had been conceded. High commissioner Bollaert demanded some amendments at a series of meetings that he conducted with Bao Dai in Geneva. Again the 'puppet' did not behave like one. Not surprisingly, no agreement was reached so Bao Dai continued his peripatetic playboy life travelling between Hong Kong, Paris and Cannes. He would not return to Vietnam and play his ordained role unless his demands were met. This dance lasted for eighteen months until a second and 'definitive' agreement was reached at An Long Bay again, on 5 June 1948.

The declaration 'solemnly recognised the independence of Vietnam'. The new state would be free to 'bring about its unity'. This was a key concession to Bao Dai, who wanted to squash any idea that Cochinchina could be a separate element within the Federal Union, something that de Gaulle, d'Argenlieu and his Saigon clique of industrialists and bankers had been pushing for. The Saigon-based colons, in particular, and the Saigon clique press were incensed because it seemed to indicate that France was abandoning Vietnam and ending the war. The prime minister of Cochin, Dr Thinh, committed suicide. The principle of Vietnam's unity was also a major triumph for the Vietminh and is probably the reason that Bao Dai himself was not assassinated. Ho realised that Bao Dai was a useful bastion against French elements pushing for Cochinchina separatism, which is probably why the emperor was not assassinated, which would surely have happened if Bao Dai had ever posed any serious popular threat, which this feckless playboy never did.

Time Magazine reporter Eric Gibb noted: 'In Hanoi, I have seen frozen-faced people watch Bao Dai pass by.'[12]

Minister of War Coste Floret (MRP) reassured the Saigon clique and French business interests that independence would not include diplomacy or military affairs, which was becoming the main focus of government. The reality was that Bao Dai had been sold a lie. He realised immediately and went back to the fleshpots of Europe, refusing to return unless some reality was put on the bones of the agreement. However, the pressure was on to compromise, because his long absences and the negative propaganda about being the absent 'playboy' was undermining his political credibility. Eventually an agreement was signed with President Auriol on 8 March 1949.

American recognition soon followed, with General Shuyler noting:

> *The time has passed when the United States could pursue an attitude of complete neutrality. Our recognition of Bao Dai cast the die. French prestige is at stake and requests from them for assistance will probably be forthcoming shortly.*[13]

In fact, $75m had already been allocated by Acheson out of a general China area budget.

That Cochin China would be integral to the state and not separate was confirmed. Bollaert's successor as high commissioner Leon Pignon was a cast-iron MRP imperialist. When Pignon arrived in May 1949, he made it clear that France would have the veto on any government put together by Bao Dai. Worn down and demotivated by French duplicity, Bao Dai for his part never really seemed to take his role in Vietnam seriously. He took more interest in hunting tigers and girlfriends than in governing. His disinterest was no doubt driven by the fact that his power was very limited. As for appointments, he did not choose the best talent but the most corrupt, on the basis that he did not trust honest or incorruptible men. More interested in making money in the gambling industry than building a state, he absented himself regularly on the Cote d'Azure. Bao Dai's decadence was well-known. He failed to make a political connection to his people. Separated from his wife for most of the time, she lived in the South of France with the heir apparent and refused all French entreaties to return. Shorn of real power, he spent his time collecting money from gangsters and gambling syndicates such as Grand Monde in Saigon.

Bao Dai became so discredited that the Americans, by now concerned about the communist threat, listened to plans to replace him. In January 1951 Gullion, Chargé d'affairs at the US embassy, reported that the Catholic Diem brothers Ngo Dinh Diem and Mgr Ngo Dinh Thuc had 'indicated their interest in a scenario whereby Bao Dai would be replaced by a regency in the name of Bao Long, Bao Dai's heir, managed by the Catholic empress.'[14] It was the start of the American takeover.

The Pignon era 1948–50: Drift and disenchantment

Emile Bolleart resigned his post in October 1948 after being wounded in a failed assassination attempt, and General Valluy was posted back to France. Leon Pignon became high commissioner. An MRP appointment, he was a true believer in colonialism and the project, including using Bao Dai as a front for continued French rule. However, the political reality of Indochina's politics and the decision to deal with Bao Dai meant that the idea of a five-part federated Indochina had had to be given up. The federated Indochina concept was absolutely rejected by King Sihanouke of Cambodia, who represented the wholehearted wishes of the Khmer people to be separated from what had long been regarded as the tutelage of the Annamites along with the Chinese dominated business. Since the British intervention with Sihanouke, Annamites had emigrated in large numbers (200,000), having formerly formed the large majority of French bureaucrats as well as traders, Mekong fishermen and estate workers.

The original Gaullist and MRP concept of five states of Indochina was over. However, this issue was neatly sidestepped by morphing the original concept into The Association of Independent States of Indochina. Coming out of the shadows in July 1949, the communists adopted a new name: the Vietnam Workers Party (VWP), which displaced the ICP, although this did not mean that ideas of a Vietnamese communist-dominated Indochina had been given up. In fact, Ho regarded Vietnamese domination of the smaller states as an axiomatic principle of the DRV, and said so in his last will and testament in

1965. A significant aspect of the VWP was introduced at the Second VWP Congress in February 1951: 'The VWP will combine the theories of Lenin, Stalin and Mao Zhedong.' Ho was already careful to pay homage to both of his political masters. It was a balancing act that became increasingly fraught over the decades.[15]

Valluy's successor General Roger Blaizot, like Valluy, sought the holy grail of total victory in an all-out battle, the very thing that Giáp was intent on denying. Nor in the wilderness of northern Tonkin was it difficult to avoid pitched battle. Also like Valluy, the French command was anxious to finish the conflict before the Red Army finished trouncing the Kuomintang in central China.

Swiping at thin air every time, Blaizot's first offensive *Operation Siren*, an amphibious operation with his entire elite force, achieved virtually nothing apart from small arms caches and a primitive arms factory. Operations *Odine* and *Pegase* were equally futile.

The next great crisis of Indochina was in motion as the victorious Chinese Red Army approached the Indochina border. China's border ran in parallel with the RC4 and its string of French outposts at Lan Son, Donke and Cao Bang. Blaizot was dismissed in 1949 when a unit of Chinese troops came over the border and captured Lao Cai, which lies on the north-western border astride the Kunming railway. This caused a crisis in government, which led to the dispatch of socialist-aligned chief-of-staff General Revers by socialist defence minister Remadier, to make an overall assessment of strategy.

A typically cynical operator of the salon politics of the Third Republic, Remadier's underlying purpose was to use the Revers report to topple MRP-dominance of Indochina policy. Revers' recommendations were that France should withdraw troops from defending the RC4 line in the north-east and concentrate on defending the Red delta. Blaizot agreed but prime minister Henri Queuille squashed the idea, perhaps fearful of criticism from his MRP partners. He may have been reminded of the fall of Jules Ferry's premiership over the abandonment of Lang Son in 1885. However, casualties continued to mount on the winding RC4 along the border to the legion's garrisons at Thatke, Dong-Ke and Cao Bang. There was not enough air capacity to supply more than sixty percent of the Cao Bang garrison's needs, so vulnerable lorry convoys were sent. They were repeatedly ambushed, with heavy casualties, as they drove to and fro along the 100km road from Lan Son. By 1948 there had been 390 major ambushes along the road. By 1948, fifty percent of French casualties in the whole of Indochina had been taken in the Viet Bac in Northern Tonkin and along the RC4, mostly between Loung Phai Pass and Cao Bang.

CHAPTER IX

International Communist Politics

Ho Chi Minh in Moscow February 1950

The years 1945–48 were momentous in the expansion of Russia's communist empire. Soviet armies occupied all of Eastern Europe. Occupied by the Red Army, Stalin did not wolf down these states in one bite. Operating under a strategic disadvantage due to the US's possession of the atom bomb, he proceeded to take them over relentlessly but cautiously. In the words of Hungarian communist leader Myáyás Rákosi, the Eastern European states were taken over in 'salami slices', as they were shorn of their civil institutions, press freedoms and democratic rights. It was a tragedy symbolised by the photograph of foreign minister Jan Masaryk lying dead in a courtyard of the Czechoslovak Foreign Ministry where he had been defenestrated by communist agents on 10 March 1948. In Western Europe, Soviet hopes were dashed despite very large communist voting in France and Italy especially.

The exception in the crushing of Eastern Europe was Yugoslavia, which was not occupied by Soviet troops because Tito's partisans had liberated themselves with Churchill's material aid. After several months of rising tension, and following a failed meeting with a Yugoslav delegation led by Milovan Diljas in February 1948, on 28 June 1948, the USSR decisively broke with Tito when Cominform denounced Tito's mistakes: '...the basis of these mistakes...lies in the undoubted fact that *nationalist elements*' had reached 'a dominant position in the leadership of the Communist Party of Yugoslavia.' (Author's emphasis) Soviet ideological magazine *Kommunist* in November 1948 pointed out that the cause of the rift was in respect of 'the draft of the programme proletarian internationalism' and Yugoslavia's demand for recognition of the equality of nations, which was 'characteristic of petit-bourgeois nationalism.'[1] With the Soviet takeover in Eastern Europe complete and efforts at takeover in France and Italy in retreat, attention began to focus back on the Orient. Picking up from eastern policies developed in the 1920s and 1930s, Stalin asserted in July 1949 that 'the centre of world revolution had moved from west to east.' Mao's victory was complete. Brimming with confidence, the two great communist dictators were eying opportunities for further expansion.

All this ideological verbiage was a smokescreen for the real issue, which was Tito's refusal to bend the knee to Stalin. Yugoslavia left the Cominform and followed its own Marxist-Leninist ideology and foreign policy from thereon. Before Ho's meeting in Moscow, Stalin met with Mao Tse Tung and asked him: 'Is Ho Chi Minh an Oriental, Tito?' In other words, was Ho a petit-bourgeois nationalist? The same question was being asked in the US state department, and it may be that Stalin's question came from the information supplied by a Russian agent there. Ho would have been well aware of the political threat posed by Tito's heresy, because he had been tarred by his enemies for his emphasis on nationalism. In 1950, Ho's government duly denounced Tito as 'a spy for American imperialism'.[2]

Ho visited Moscow, having walked on foot for seventeen days through jungle to Guangxi on the Chinese border. Then Stalin kept Ho waiting for days. He and Mao flew together to Moscow. Ho's main aim was to secure supplies of arms and munitions.

We do not have Ho's impression of Stalin, but we can record Stalin's appearance through Milovan Diljas's meeting in 1944:

> *He was of very small stature and ungainly build. His torso was too short and narrow, while his legs and arms were too long...He had a quite large paunch, His teeth were black and irregular, turned inward. With those yellow eyes and a mixture of sternness and roguishness...a bundle of nerves which never missed the slightest word or glance. Stalin had a sense of humour – a crude sudden humour, he referred to Russia not the Soviet Union...*[3]

Ho had probably met Stalin in 1923–4, but if he did, it is likely that Stalin did not remember him.

Medicine was also on Ho's list, especially quinine, because of the rampant outbreaks of malaria amongst soldiers and civilians living in the jungle. The Soviets produced a lot of the medicine for their own needs. Nikita Khrushchev noted: '...so Stalin went overboard with generosity and said, "send him half a ton".[4] Stalin was not always so gracious. Ho was treated with little courtesy. Stalin, a racist, considered him a minor figure from a minor country. For Ho it was the opposite. Stalin was an icon of communist politics whom he genuinely idolised.

On meeting Stalin, Ho 'kept watching Stalin intently with his unusual eyes,' recalled Khrushchev. 'I would say there was in his gaze a childlike naïveté.' Ho was a sycophant, but he probably needed to be. At one point in the meeting:

> *...he reached into his briefcase and took out a copy of a Soviet magazine – I think it was* The USSR Under Construction *– and asked Stalin to autograph it...He liked the idea of being able to show people Stalin's autograph back in Vietnam. Stalin gave Ho his autograph but shortly afterward had the magazine stolen back from him because he was worried about how Ho might use it.*[5]

Any weaponry secured would have been provided by China. Ho's real purpose was for Stalin to put pressure on China to provide more aid.

Ho was not an 'Oriental Tito'. Yugoslav 'Titoism' was the ultimate heresy at this time. Unlike Tito, Ho had not liberated his country yet and he would need Chinese and Soviet help with arms and advice. Moreover, Ho's Vietnam had a long contiguous border with China. Independence from the USSR-PRC nexus was not possible but there is no real sign that Ho was moving in that direction, though suspicions about his over-zealous patriotism and past denunciations by party enemies to Moscow about his nationalism would continue to haunt him and make him wary of deviating from Moscow's party line.

Stalin gets the 'bomb', Mao wins China, Kim Il Sung invades South Korea

The Russians were astonished when the Americans dropped atom bombs on Hiroshima and Nagasaki in 1945. Japan surrendered eleven days later. The world had changed very suddenly, a world where one bomb of previously unimagined power could win a world war. Although the Russians had been working on nuclear fission for some time, the fact of the American achievement galvanised them into action. Stalin dismissed Molotov, the dour foreign minister, as head of the programme and delegated the function to Lavrenti Beria, the sinister head of the NKVD. Beria was chosen because of his intelligence and organising ability. He was also a trusted Georgian. As head of the NKVD, he commanded a vast overseas spy network that would be of vital importance if the bomb programme was to be accelerated. Stalin felt naked without A-bomb equivalence. However, his reaction to this sudden change in the balance of power was quite the opposite to what was expected by the Americans. Attack being the best form of defence, Stalin made a great show of being particularly difficult and obdurate in negotiations, not at all cowed. Stalin gave Beria a deadline of 1947 to produce a bomb.

Overnight, the production of an A-bomb became the overwhelming priority of the USSR. Nothing could be refused. Scientists were rounded up from all over Russia as well as German scientists who remained in the communist net. Overseas, the NKVD spy networks went into overdrive and were soon penetrating and extracting important scientific information from key bomb scientists, such as Claus Fuchs, the Rosenbergs and Nunn. Tens of thousands of prisoners-of-war were worked to death in new uranium mines. The deadline was missed by twenty months, but on 9 August 1949, the Soviets exploded their A-bomb several years in advance of US estimates. What did this mean for the war in Indochina?

On 10 December 1949, the Chinese nationalist government of Chiang Kai Shek fled the mainland to Formosa. By the end of 1949, Mao's Red Army had completed the conquest of China from the Kuomintang, except for a few hold-outs in Yunnan on the Burmese border. In January 1950, the USSR and China recognised the Democratic Republic of Vietnam. In Washington, Dean Acheson, the secretary of state, immediately noted in an internal memo that it 'should remove any illusions as to the nationalist character of Ho Chi Minh's aims and reveals Ho in his true colours.' (Pentagon Papers) Many inside the administration and diplomatic community had been arguing that Ho was Asia's Tito. This argument was gone, although many would continue to argue that opportunities had been lost by failing to support the Vietminh in the early days.

When the first US aid was delivered to the French in August 1950, Ho wrote: 'We now have one principal opponent – French bandits...and one more opponent...American bandits...' (Pentagon Papers) The balance of evidence is that Ho was a dedicated communist. His flirting with the US from 1945–46 was entirely tactical, aimed at playing for time while the Vietminh were in a weak position. At the same time, the Vietminh were murdering and assassinating thousands of non-communist political opponents. Acheson had already noted decisively in 1949 that: 'The question whether Ho was as much a nationalist as commie is irrelevant. All Stalinists in colonial areas are nationalists.' (Pentagon Papers)

Kim Il Sung of the Democratic People's Republic of Korea (DPRK) immediately jumped on the altered power relations implicit in the Soviet A-bomb development. However, he was too hasty. Stalin sent a message to Ambassador Shytkov in Korea on 24 September 1949[6]:

> *It is necessary to consider that if military actions begin at the initiative of the north and acquire a prolonged character that this can give Americans cause for every kind of interference in Korean affairs.*

Fears of intervention were indeed a worry especially as he had not yet got a battle-ready A-bomb. In the same message Stalin found an excuse for his lack of revolutionary fervour by pointing out that very little had been done to prepare the south politically, including the organisation of partisan groups. However, the real reason for being guarded was his lack of actual A-bomb weapons ready for use. The answer was a 'no' for now. It was one of several requests by the impatient Kim.

In February 1950, Mao visited Stalin in Moscow. At this meeting it was decided to ramp up the pressure and attacks on the West, to keep the momentum of international communism going following their great triumphs in the west and the east from 1947–50. The development of the Russian bomb was a critical release mechanism for Soviet foreign policy. Although the numbers of bombs and the delivery methods were not yet optimal, the fact that he had some bombs enabled Stalin to start to move back to the offensive. Mao was delegated to take care of the operations in Asia. After returning to Beijing, Mao ramped up the international propaganda campaign.

John Foster Dulles, experienced diplomat and the Republican Party's foreign policy 'wonk', was well aware of the significance. Broadcasting on 11 February, Mao called on the peoples of South West Asia to rise up against their present political leaders, who were termed 'colonial puppets' and 'lackeys' of the 'imperialists'. In a broadcast, Mao sermonised that 'the people cannot attain liberation without armed struggle...the liberation movement should take the form of legal and illegal mass struggles proceeding in other more favourable environments.' The broadcast reiterated the leading role of the Soviet Union.

Diplomatic recognition of the Democratic Republic of Vietnam by China and the USSR in January was a highly significant step. Not only was the psychological effect important in lifting morale, but recognition was a means to strengthen legitimacy within Vietnam, so side-lining other nationalist claimants to the mantle of independence. With the sharpening world situation, east-west, communism and capitalism, USSR and US, there was an increasing risk of US intervention in Indochina. 'Recognition' had raised the stakes. The US would have to think carefully about direct intervention. They had not intervened directly in China and the hope now was that the US would be thwarted in any ideas of directly intervening in Indochina.

When the Red Army arrived at the border in 1949, plans were immediately set in hand for extending the revolution into Indochina. Having received Ho's request for aid, Liu Shaoqui called a Politburo meeting for 24 December 1949, but was minded to offer fairly limited help because of China's own post-war problems. However, he was overruled by Mao, who was in Moscow and wanted a more supportive stance. Stalin informed Mao that there would be 'no free ride' and that China had to look after itself and could not expect air cover for the intended invasion of Taiwan. Nonetheless, Mao intended to liquidate any proximate threat to the Chinese revolution and sovereignty. Dealing with this strategic objective was more than revolutionary brotherhood. With Kuomintang elements still active on the Burmese borderlands of the Yunnan, it was the overriding imperative. It would also be imperative in Korea. On 4 August 1950, Mao told the Chinese Politburo: '[We] will take back Taiwan, but now we can't just sit and watch Vietnam and Korea.'[7]

Stalin had given Mao the responsibility to take care of Asian matters. 'We believe it is better for China,' he told Mao, 'to take major responsibility in supporting and helping the Vietnamese...China and Vietnam are sharing the border...it's convenient for China to help.'[8]

By March, the CMAG had been formed, to offer support and advice to the Vietminh.

After sweeping successes in Eastern Europe without challenge, and the victory in China, the main effect was to embolden Stalin and Mao and raise their appetite for aggressive and interventionists actions. The capitalist system looked rotten, weak and ripe for the toppling. Having faced down the nuclear gap for four years while taking over nine countries in Eastern Europe and giving vital support to the Mongolian and Chinese revolutions, Stalin with the A-bomb must have felt particularly confident. After the exploding of a test bomb in 1949, full production was soon underway.

The communist world was on a roll and Mao moved with speed to bring revolutionary war into South-East Asia. China had no doubts about immediately arming the Vietminh. Huge numbers of captured Kuomintang soldiers were building new roads up to the Vietnam border to provide Ho with war supplies. The French garrisons along the RC4 were doomed.

The American reaction was immediate. Despite their long-held misgiving about French colonialism and falling into the political trap of supporting French puppet governments, Truman recognised the Bao Dai government on 7 February:

> *Recognition by the United States of the three legally constituted governments of Vietnam, Laos and Cambodia appears desirable...as a demonstration of displeasure with communist tactics which are obviously aimed at eventual domination of Asia, working under the guise of indigenous nationalism.* (Pentagon Papers)

Recognition represented a dramatic change in US policy because it implicitly recognised French rights in Indochina, so pinning the US to French imperialism, even if that was not intended. The Cold War in Asia was hotting up.

For foreign policy expert John Foster Dulles, who would in due course become Eisenhower's secretary of state in 1953, recognition of the Bao Dai government was long overdue:

> *The French government is, belatedly, trying to work out of the situation by granting a large measure of independence to the Vietnam government of Bao Dai...but the French may have acted too late.*[9]

The quote reveals US awareness that it was not complete independence. He uses the words 'a large measure'. Actually, it was a small measure. Bao Dai's government had minimal power. Resting on the support of the French Army, with political decisions taken largely in Paris and with guidance from Pignon, the plenipotentiary in Saigon, Bao Dai was little more than the 'puppet' that the Vietminh described.

In the US analysis, the Soviet-controlled expansion of communism, both in Asia and in Europe, required, in the interests of US national security, a more active policy in Indochina. The domino thesis was prominent. On 6 March 1950, the secretary of defence wrote to the president:

> *The choice confronting the United States is to support the legal government in Indochina or to face the extension of communism over the remainder of the continental area of South-east Asia and possibly westward.*

Despite this statement, it was a generally accepted proposition that:

> *...regardless of current US commitments for certain military assistance to China* [Formosa-Chiang Kai Shek], *the US will not commit any of its armed forces to the defence of Indochina against overt, foreign aggression, under present circumstances.* (Pentagon Papers)

Most importantly, for the way the next few years played out, was the reaction of Kim Il Sung, the North Korean communist leader, to the developing international situation. He picked up the new mood of confidence in Moscow, craftily playing on the nascent rivalry between Mao and Stalin. He went to Moscow in April 1950, once again to ask permission to invade South Korea. Stalin, although armed at this point with only three plutonium-based bombs, was nevertheless feeling confident enough to give encouragement to Kim, if not an outright yes. According to Soviet diplomatic sources quoted by Henry Kissinger:

> *Comrade Stalin confirmed to Kim Il Sung that the international environment has sufficiently changed to permit more active stance on the unification of Korea...now that China has signed a treaty of alliance with the USSR, Americans will be even more hesitant to challenge the communists in Asia... the prevailing mood* [in the US] *is not to interfere. Such a mood is reinforced by the fact that the USSR now has the atomic bomb and that our positions are solidified in Pyongyang.*[10]

The American mood was indeed becoming more isolationist, but there was the potential for miscalculation nonetheless, as proved to be the case.

Stalin was concerned that the North Koreans should have a quick victory to avoid the risk of American intervention. However, after American failure to protect Eastern Europe, their failure to support France against the Vietminh and their failure to intervene directly in China, Mao regarded the US as weak. What must have astounded and pleased him was the utter failure of the US to use its advantage in possessing the A-bomb.

Then Kim went to Mao, who was also guardedly positive, despite Kim's brazen arrogance. Kim had cleverly egged-on Mao by saying untruthfully 'that

Stalin had approved his plans to attack the south.' Mao was sceptical as to whether Kim had the military power to pull it off and thought the chances of US intervention to support their puppet regime under Syngman Ree were high. However, after his revolutionary successes Mao, like Stalin, was in an adventurous mood, 'and offered to deploy three Chinese armies along the Korean border.' Kim responded 'arrogantly' (according to Mao) that he could manage by himself. Contacting Stalin, his revolutionary mentor, Mao asked for advice. Stalin deftly suggested that he would let Mao make the decision:

> *...the issue should be decided finally by the Chinese and Korean comrades together, and in case of disagreement by the Chinese comrades the decision should be postponed pending further discussion.*[11]

In passing responsibility onto Mao, Stalin left open the possibility to blame or take credit depending on events. It was also testing Mao as to his revolutionary credentials. Given his enormous vanity, as Stalin well realised, Mao could hardly want to be found wanting on this score,[12] even though his policy priorities were to support Ho in Indochina. The reason for supporting Ho as a priority was the fact that a western power supported by the US had a direct and long border with China, whereas in Korea he already had a buffer. Neither did he want to destabilise the Korean peninsula in a place near to China's industrial heartland in Manchuria. Chinese historians put the onus on Stalin for starting the war, but the truth is they were both 'allowing' it to happen, with Mao manoeuvred into it by his own ego.

Mao duly gave the wink and nod and then furnished Kim with 50,000 fully armed Chinese-Korean troops who were part of the Red Army. The communist leaders were encouraged by the fact that South Korea had not been included in the US defence zone and that the US had left just a few weak units in the country. If Kim could strike quickly, he could sweep the Americans into the sea. On 25 June 1950, the North Korean Army smashed into the relatively untrained and ill-equipped South Korean Army. They were quickly driven back to Busan in the south-west before American reinforcements stabilised the front. A counter-attack then developed through the autumn of 1950.

Suddenly Indochina took on a new meaning for American policy makers. Contrary to communist expectations the US reacted to communist aggression not only by mobilising to defeat the North Korean challenge, but by linking the invasion to wide geopolitical issues in Asia. The first sign of this was the vote in the UN Security Council, for once able to make a decision in the absence of the Russian boycott of the institution, to send forces to defend South Korea. Then two days later the 7th Fleet was deployed in the Taiwan Straits to block planned Chinese moves to invade Taiwan.[13] Truman's change in policy, which had previously been one of non-direct intervention in the Chinese Civil

War, signalled a dramatic change in US policy. Communist aggression in Asia (indeed worldwide) would now be aggressively confronted.

Decisively and suddenly the American position had shifted. This was highly significant for France, who until this time had been regarded disdainfully and with suspicion as being a revanchist colonial power, even if there was an undercurrent of support for the anti-communist stance. The US would significantly downplay their distaste for the French imperialists who were now 'comrades in arms against communist aggression'. Accordingly joint planning, plus finance and equipment, would soon be flowing into French Indochina. A brigade of French troops would also be sent to fight with the UN alongside the Americans in Korea.

The decision to begin military assistance to France and the associated states of Indochina was not made under the illusion of great expectations. In April 1950, the joint chiefs would go no further than to say that prompt delivery of the aid would do no more than create the 'possibility of success'. In July 1950, General Erskine, after completing his presidential mission to Indochina, reported:

> *...the amount of aid and the scope of the assistance thus far requested by the French were inadequate to the needs of the situation.*
>
> *The US invasion in Asia can only arouse broad and determined resistance among the people of Asia, declared Mao. 'Truman said on January 5th that the United States would not intervene in Taiwan. Now he himself has proved he was simply lying.*[14]

He was clearly setting out the vision of a regional war with liberation struggles led by China. Indochina was already being groomed for victory with advisors, training and supplies. This would increase. Having wrongly assessed the likelihood of US intervention in Korea, and with US-led UN forces having stabilised their front after the initial shock of the Korean attack, Mao made his position clear in a Politburo meeting on 4 August 1950:

> *If the American imperialists are victorious, they will become dizzy with success and then be in a position to threaten us. We have to help Korea; we have to assist them. This can be in the form of a volunteer force.*[15]

China was put on a war footing and prepared to intervene if necessary. Help for the Vietminh was intensified with increasing supplies of equipment and training.

Of course China's imperative for security and control was also imperialist. Philip Short, in his biography of Mao, steeped in historical knowledge, points out astutely that: 'He yearned for a renewal of its ancient grandeur. Korea like Vietnam, had been for centuries a tributary state...require restoration of that suzerain relationship...Vietnam too had to be brought back into the Chinese fold.' (p.433)

The Cold War escalated in the autumn of 1950 after the American landing at Incheon on 15 September and when UN forces crossed the 38th Parallel on 1 October. Stalin ruled out Soviet intervention but encouraged Mao to intervene which, despite his strategic need, he was reluctant to do without promises of more equipment and Soviet air support. As UN forces neared the Chinese border eventually Mao, having secured the support he needed, told his colleagues, 'The old man writes to us that we must step in.'[16]

On 19 October, the Chinese Army crossed the Yalu and slammed into American UN forces on 1 November, driving them back, south of the 38th Parallel, around which the fighting fluctuated before becoming stalemated. This action radicalised American policy. This 1950–51 period was the high watermark of US fears of direct Chinese communist intervention in Indochina because it was believed that intervention in Korea heralded a wider attack on western interests and possibly an attack in Europe as well. China was also radicalised by their success in trouncing the over-extended and surprised US Army as they approached the Yalu River at the Battle of Changjin Lake November–December 1950, despite paucity of air power and limited Russian support in this capability. American troops suffered 24,000 casualties. 'The Chinese people are now organised, they are not to be trifled with,' boasted Mao.[17] Despite being thrown back and losing Seoul again, the Chinese Army had fought the US to a standstill. Confident in their arms, despite 600,000 casualties, Vietnam was the next target for 'protective' military support, though as with Korea, intervention would at first be limited to logistical support and training. Scarred by their defeats in Korea, the Americans would always have a lingering fear of Chinese military intervention and power, especially as Korean commander Matthew Ridgway was now the head of the US Army. MacArthur had lost his command because of failure against the Chinese. Ridgway would be wary of following his example. Paradoxically, the Chinese, having suffered fearful losses, would also develop a paranoia, which they shared with Ho, as to the likelihood of direct US intervention in Tonkin. This would have important implications for strategy, timing and tactics, as well as the eventual settlement in French Indochina. China's primary goal was the creation of a buffer zone for national security not revolution, which remained a secondary interest. When another Chinese offensive was rebuffed with massive casualties, senior commander of the PLA, Nie Rongzhen, noted: 'Now that we have accomplished the political objective of driving the enemy out of north Korea...restoration of the status quo antebellum would be acceptable to all...'[18]

All US expectations regarding Indochina had originally been underpinned by the joint chiefs' belief that 'attainment of United States objectives in

Asia can only be achieved by ultimate success in China.' (Pentagon Papers) However, communist victory in the Chinese Civil War had changed that and increased the risks of defeat. But with direct intervention from Chinese troops against UN forces, alarm bells went off in fear for the rest of South-East Asia. Suddenly, Indochina was in clear and imminent danger. In regard to Indochina, US NIE5 of 29 December 1950 stated:

> *Direct intervention by Chinese communist troops may occur at any time...it is almost certain to occur in strength whenever there is danger either that the Vietminh will fail to maintain its military objective of driving the French out of Indochina, or that the Bao Dai Government is succeeding in undermining the support of the Vietminh.* (Pentagon Papers)

Fear of direct Chinese intervention never went away and indeed played an instrumental part in shaping American policy during the Dien Bien Phu campaign. Would the US intervene directly in Indochina and would China invade? After the truce in the Korean War, it was a conundrum that would sit heavily with policy makers in both Beijing and Washington.

China had four million troops at its disposal and the American reaction to North Korea's invasion elicited a very hostile response from Mao. He saw the intervention of the American fleet in the Taiwan Strait as a broadening attack on China's interests and sovereignty as hostile interference in Chinese internal affairs. The war in Asia would, as a result, become a regional stand-off between the rival powers in which Indochina became the pre-eminent new battlefront.

Peace movements and the French Fifth Column 1948–50

During the course of 1948–50, a seminal change took over French politics as the Indochina War plummeted in popularity. The most vociferous opponents of the war were the PCF. Paradoxically, they saw their popularity fall from thirty percent to twenty-three percent just as their pacifist influence on the war was increasing, which shows that the Indochina War was not central to French political debate. Communist organisations were suffering defections and decline in membership, publications were being closed, and only *L'Humanité* remained in fairly robust health.

The communist front organisations and the world peace movement caught a popular mood and captured the imagination of many, and not just on the left. A movement secretly promoted by Stalin as a way to undermine and weaken the west, it would encompass the usual legions of 'useful idiots' in intellectual and religious circles who were happy to clap along to the easy melody of world peace. After all, who could be against peace? Jean Paul Sartre, iconic philosopher, novelist and intellectual, and other residents of les Deux Maggots or Floret on the left bank associated themselves with the movement. It was a roll-call of the self-appointed 'intellectual' elite, Camus, Duras, Simone de Beauvoir, etc.

At a time when the USSR still did not have the A-bomb, or they had the bomb but not the capability to produce or deliver many, Stalin also aimed to boost neutralism, which would help prevent the creation of the EDF (European Defence Force) and German re-armament. Strong anti-war movements would lessen the chances of the west using the bomb or even threatening to use the bomb in negotiations. Most intellectuals were horrified by atomic weapons as well as the re-armament of Germany and Japan. A grand coalition of the naïve would gather 500m signatures to a plea for worldwide peace.

When left-wing socialists with connections to the Vietminh tried to block the Bao Dai agreement Victor Auriol, the president, angrily denounced them. 'You are going to ruin everything…only the socialists and the communists together…you will be beaten and you will not have solved the Indochina problem.'[19]

'Indochina would fall to communists and with it the whole of South-East Asia,' Auriol argued. Guy Mollet, socialist leader, fell in with the MRP, but unwillingly. For him, Ho Chi Minh was the only 'authentic representative of their (Vietnamese) aspirations'. However, the socialists (SFIO) recognised Bao Dai as the representative of Indochina in February. The Elysée Accords with Bao Dai, which set up a 'truly' independent nationalist government, were signed on 8 March 1950. France would maintain control of defence and foreign affairs. It was transparently a puppet regime, but it had to be, because with the national army not yet trained or tested and still relatively small, there was no hope for the new regime to defend itself without French help and direction.

When it came to a vote in the chamber, the Elysée Accords were not specifically voted on to avoid a government split and the fall of the ministry. Tensions ran very high in the Chamber of Deputies. When one deputy compared Ho Chi Minh to Ghandi, the leader of the MRP, Robert Schumann, cried out cogently, 'If only Ho Chi Minh had practised the same non-violence. What a pity.' Accusations of treachery and betrayal of the common soldier were flung across the chamber. Socialists and communists had their own insults to throw back, referring to the background of many Foreign Legionnaires. There were accusations that the SS were fighting for France. Avoiding defeat in the vote of censure in which the Gaullists and PCF had allied, for very different reasons (one was anti-war, the other wanted Indochina as a full-blooded colony, not a watered-down protectorate), the government staggered on with its unresolved conflict on the status of the new government in Vietnam. The government won by 348 votes to 202.

The other strand of communist activity to undermine the war was direct action by the communist unions, under the CGT. Throughout 1949/50, Marseilles and all major ports except Cherbourg (non CTG unions) refused to load military cargoes destined for Indochina. This was matched by a similar embargo in Algerian ports, which was backed by a mutiny of 800 Algerian troops. There were also extensive strikes in the coal mines, which were crushed by Moch, the right-wing socialist interior minister. In January 1950, the embarkation of 3,000 troops bound for Indochina was held up for forty-eight hours. At Frangou, 700 troops mutinied, crying out 'no more dirty war'. There was also sabotage in French arms and ammunitions factories. Communist peace propaganda, infiltration, and CGT union activity all combined to unsettle French domestic politics. Legionnaire Liddell-Hart recalled the hostility to the legionnaires shown by the communist sailors on the troop transport ships.[20]

Vietminh intelligence

Intelligence for the Vietminh came from well-placed civil society informants, businessmen, lawyers, secretaries, administrators, prostitutes, waiters or small boys hanging around the soldiers. Another source was communist sympathisers in Paris working in the Administration. When during the negotiation of the Accords with Bao Dai in 1948, Monsieur Bollaert, high commissioner, sent a secret report back to Paris, it was intercepted and published by the Vietminh to the extraordinary embarrassment of the administration: 'It is my impression that we must make a concession to Vietnam of the term, independence,' opined Bollaert. 'But I am convinced that this word need never be interpreted in any other light other than that of a religious verbalism.'

Appointed by a left of centre government, including the MRP, socialists and communists, Bollaert was a radical socialist, Resistance war hero and concentration camp survivor. Like many French politicians of the left and centre, he was blind to the depredations that were done by the French Army.[21] His memo was a clear admission that independence would be a sham.

Intelligence-gathering led to analysis and action in a highly organised and rapid Vietminh chain of command. It operated at every level of society. When he was 13, Huong Van wrote:

> *...we organised as local forces and I was assigned to liaison duty. During the day I hung around the French posts, I talked to the soldiers and made friends with them. I'd got as much information as possible and drew maps of their positions. At night I'd guide the resistance attacks.*[22]

Smaller tasks led to bigger ones and promotion as school students became older.

An important source of information was from tipsy, tongue-loosened officers frequenting bars and the taxi girls who inhabited them. The *Deuxieme Bureaux* was well aware that many taxi girls spied for the Vietminh so:

> *...a discreet surveillance was established in bars and dance halls frequented by troops...they were inveigled into giving away confidences to famous taxi girls, certainly pretty but who were used by the Vietminh for obtaining secrets.*[23]

For the high command and the *Deuxieme Bureaux*, it also became a conduit for sowing disinformation.

Posted on a remote rubber estate, Lieutenant de La Motte realised after being ambushed that the enemy had learnt about his patrol. From that date he changed his *modus operandi*, only deciding on patrols after dark and the closure of the compound gates. He also avoided all the main tracks and took small jungle paths, and with these tactics he avoided future ambushes. Almost all ambushes were initiated by the Vietminh with the French as victims. After one rare intelligence coup, one lieutenant noted that he had been able to round up all the party cadres in one village within an hour, with a 'handful of men whereas ordinarily he could not have entered with less than a company.'[24]

The pervasiveness of Vietminh infiltration, influence and access to intelligence was demonstrated to Norman Lewis when his clandestine taxi girl contacts led him to meet members of the Vietminh-supporting Vietnamese elite.

Giáp claimed that much of French radio chatter was made 'in the clear' during the RC4 campaign and there were plenty of Vietminh with facility in French.[25] German legionnaire units, according to Wagemeuller, had less of a problem.

Red Army on the border 1949–50

In late 1949, Lucien Bodard visited the border and saw matters for himself. He also interviewed one of the legion officers, who understood very clearly what was coming. From a lookout over the town and countryside on the Chinese side, a French officer explained that the Red Army would soon be there, 'And with my handful of men I shall have to say to them, "be so kind as to behave properly".'[26]

It could hardly be forgotten that the communist tide had started in the Soviet-controlled north-east of China and the Shandong peninsula or areas along the Soviet frontier. From this base the red tide swept south through the vastness of peasant China with promises of land reform and smallholding distributions. This and the murder of landowners and village officials had won over the peasanty but they would soon be deceived and denied the benefit of their gains by being forced into co-operatives and an unimagined communist slavery. Islands of nationalist strength in the big cities were swamped one by one. Great and well-armed nationalist armies were surrounded, overrun or simply melted away. This tsunami of change and Red Terror surged ever closer to Indochina and the border town of Mong Cai. Meanwhile, the French chief administrator Pignon echoed the complacency and denial of the higher echelons of the French establishment:

> *There is no sort of hurry. It is not tomorrow that we are concerned about. With the Chinese everything drags on; it is always slower than you expect.*[27]

General Lu Hun, the erstwhile ruler of Hanoi after the Japanese surrender, surrendered to Mao and was given a minor post in the government in Beijing where he eked out a dull and fearful existence. Other nationalist units carried on fighting with their backs to the frontier. Elite nationalist troops, well uniformed and armed, acted as a rearguard while a mob of civilian refugees and deserters piled up on the frontier:

> *…in huge masses, panic-stricken mobs coming by every track and path and down mountainside. As they ran they shouted 'the communists are coming. Hurry! Hurry!' The women were thrust aside, flung into the rice field.'*[28]

They were let though the border in scenes of wild confusion. Arms confiscated from fleeing soldiers were piled up by the roadside. But the terror returned as communist machine-gun bullets ripped into the mob, scything down a legionnaire NCO. In another place a band of communists came up to the border. A fracas followed when they tried to wrench away Colonel Charton into captivity. A firefight ensued and a grave international incident was only just avoided.

On the border opposite Mong Cai the Red Army suddenly materialised. Everything was orderly and correct. Red flags appeared, a few at first, then many, as the main body of the Chinese Army came up and made victory parades in Tong Hin.

Upon reaching the mountainous border area with Indochina, the Chinese started work on their roads and logistic/training bases immediately. All pre-planned, the number of regular Vietminh troops, enough for five divisions, were already located in the area ready for training and indoctrination in the newly established camps.

Of immediate concern to the French high command was the line of four garrisons along the RC4, which were the most accessible to communist infiltration of men and material. General Revers, who was aligned politically with defence minister Remadier's Socialist Party, was sent out from Paris to do a strategic assessment for the French chief-of-staff from May–June 1949. The

Revers report made some sensible recommendations in respect of the RC4 line of fortified outposts – in a nutshell, 'Withdraw! Abandon the string of isolated fortresses!' to defensible lines on the Red River delta. Following Remadier's party line, General Revers also recommended negotiation with Ho Chi Minh about the terms for withdrawal from Tonkin.

Revers was on a political mission to push an SFIO agenda, but Remadier's plot fell apart when Revers was politically knifed in a money scandal. He, together with his report, were catapulted into oblivion. This all blew up into the *Affaire des Generaux*, involving tawdry political shenanigans typical of the Fourth Republic, such as graft and piastre money laundering. Dodgy businessmen were involved as usual. General Carpentier was determined to hold the RC4 line, so the report had no effect on military thinking. Any serious debate was muffled by the scandal.

While the French military politicked amongst themselves the dangers increased. Apparently undetected by French intelligence, tens of thousands of captured Chinese nationalist prisoners were building roads. Trucks carrying PRC troops and supplies were moving up to the border together with heavy artillery, brand-new 105mm American guns captured by the Chinese. Unlike the French high command, the laconic legionnaire captain in conversation with Bodard was attuned to the realities: 'All my agents,' he revealed, 'say the same thing – the Chinese have set to work to build up the Viets.'[29] A few weeks later, the captain ruminated once more on the coming catastrophe:

> *All Indochina is hoodwinked because these Chinese have 'behaved properly' pulling up short at the frontier...The first objective is to expel the French from Indochina...An attack by Mao's army is unnecessary and it would be clumsy. The Viets are perfectly adequate, so long as they are well trained and well driven...We shall never capture a single one of Mao's soldiers; and yet in the end it will be the Chinese who beat us, the Viets being no more than their tools.*[30]

The wise soldier advised Bodard to hurry south to Cochin because, he predicted, the 'Vietminh would launch attacks on Saigon and the delta in order to draw the FEC down south before striking in the north.' Nguyễn Bin's Vietminh offensive in Cochin's Mekong delta was just a few months away in March 1950.

Yet some in Paris had clearly read the runes and understood full well the implications of Mao's victory in China. It was one of the reasons behind Revers' visit. His realpolitik assessment, backed by many in the SFIO, was that they might be on the wrong side of history.

Chinese Military Advisory Group (CMAG)

In May 1950, the PLA started to arm and give munitions to the VPA and in May training began for the 12,000 men of the 308th Division, 60 miles inside China. Leaving their old weapons at the border for their comrades, they were ushered into spotless new dormitories with individual beds, blankets and new towels. In addition, they received new shoes and uniforms, rifles or sub-machine-guns. Training was rudimentary as many of the PLA officer trainers were fairly inexperienced themselves and sixty-seven percent of them were illiterate.[31] Tactics were simple and revolved around the attack *en masse*. But as for any army, discipline and obedience was the main factor in training up the troops. As time went on, more experienced trainers arrived from the Korean War.

Advisers were also sent across the border to directly advise the VPA as well as developing specialist advisory units for logistics, artillery, medical and other, they totalled 570 PLA officers with the senior ones handpicked by Mao himself. Advisers were attached to units from the top down to battalion level. From 1950–51, 8,000 Vietminh officers were put through training courses. Just as important was political education directed through commissars, which had a high priority. There were also training courses for officers and specialists. Senior Chinese officers included Chen Geng, commander of the successful 4th PLA Army Group known for his scholarly and upper class demeanour, and Wei Guoquing, who was made head of CMAG. They fully participated in all high command decisions, both operational and strategic. The Vietminh and VPA commissar system 'was modelled on the lines laid down by Trotsky' in the Russian Civil War in March 1918. The point was, according to the principles laid down by Mao in his Kutien speech in December 1929, 'to offer a good political training to military officers.' The ideal communist political officer should have: 'high class consciousness, [be] very determined and loyal, a regular party member with experience in political education and work…and be an example to his unit…'[32] Reporting regularly to Mao, the great helmsman in his turn reported to Stalin. At the end of the process, Mao would send advice to Ho on key strategic matters.

It is not easy to estimate how much influence the advisers had. Mao took a close interest in the war in Indochina because of his perception of China's vital interests in its close neighbours and fears of having foreign troops on his border, and some of his advice seems to reveal a fairly hands-on and condescending attitude to the Vietminh. For example, Mao was not content to allow Ho's client prince to be left solely in the charge of the Pathet Lao. Souphanouvong was invited to visit China from 1951 and he re-appeared in Indochina in the spring of 1953.[33] This would have been a sensitive matter.

Already the seeds of future dissension were being set because Ho's Vietnam claimed the right to direct control over the Indochinese states in their sphere of influence. Something of an anathema for the PRC, who claimed the right to direct hegemony over all three Indochina states separately.[34] Ironically, it would emerge as a fundamental squabble and then as a deadly dispute between the rival red imperialists.

Reports made from the Chinese advisers in Tonkin obviously tried to impress Mao and make out that they were 'running things' and taking key battle decisions. Chinese historians claim that the great helmsman 'reviewed battle plans and gave specific directions.'[35] Such claims should be treated with suspicion because of the pressures to laud and pander to the leader's ego and the party. Historiography and records relating to Mao himself must be particularly suspect because of the personality cult. Sometimes the report claims would simply parrot the major decisions that were largely made by consensus. Operational and strategic decisions were largely a matter of common logic. Ho and Giáp would have had to have allowed their Chinese overlords the idea that they were in charge. On occasions there were disagreements as to strategy. However, Giáp and Ho had the last word.

The idea that Giáp and Ho were hapless military amateurs who needed the care of the 'experienced' Chinese is clearly wrong. The pair were highly intelligent with a good grasp of strategy. Giáp understood the principals of guerrilla war:

> *Guerrilla war is the war of the broad mases…standing up against a powerfully equipped well trained army… Is the enemy strong? One avoids him. Is he weak? One attacks.*[36]

Giáp understood that transformation was needed in a regular army. He understood the respective advantages enjoyed by each side. When he acquired a trained army and modern weapons, being familiar with Jomini's Napoleonic principles of speed, concentration and initiative, Giáp could orchestrate complex diversionary action by corps marching on different axis as well as logistical factors.

Ho was a master of geopolitical issues – he needed no guidance on this and knew how to put his finger on the political sore points of the French political system. He understood and proposed operations that would tie down and spread French resources. For example, he famously spread his hands and fingers on a campaign map describing how the Vietminh should stretch French resources. Nevertheless, Ho and Giáp were never too proud to learn, so for the most part CMAG advice was appreciated and welcomed. They generally seem to have worked well in partnership but there were tensions. No doubt suffering from Chinese feelings of superiority, Chen Geng described Giáp as 'slippery and not very upright and honest.'[37] At the operational and logistical level, Chinese advice from experienced officers was no doubt very useful. Not least in importance was on-the-spot Chinese Army observation and evaluation of supply and equipment needs. Giáp and Ho were bound to pay attention and treat Chinese advice with reverence, if only for show, because Chinese logistics support was essential. Trung Nguyễn points out, it was 'just advice' amongst many opinions. Giáp mentions Chinese advisers ten times in his collected autobiography of 1,036 pages. However, this is also biased as he was a man with a big ego.

There were disagreements and a culture clash fuelled by historic enmity, although Ho, Giáp and the leadership did their best to smooth relations and relations were generally cordial. Veteran Chinese adviser Lieutenant-General Huynh Thu Truong admitted afterwards that many Chinese officers were arrogant and did not adapt to local conditions. They simply wanted to treat the Vietminh units as just an extension of the PLA.[38] Clearly there was a racist sense of superiority in the condescension of many Chinese officers to the 'backward Vietnamese'. However, there was little difference in educational levels.

Soon Chinese supplies were pouring in through the north-east border to the Vietminh troops hovering around Cao Bang and along the RC4. For example, Giáp was elated by the initial results of Chinese aid. After three months he boasted:

> *Our soldiers have increased their combat effectiveness...it is the first time for our main regiments not to use spears any more during their attack, but to use real weapons...also abundant ammunition. Firepower of our infantry regiments in the past cannot be compared with what we have today.*[39]

Political officers from the PLA would become deeply involved in promoting land reform and in the purging of politicly unreliable elements within the VPA, for example officers with Mandarin or landowning backgrounds. Luo Guibo represented the Chinese Communist Party, which provided 'fraternal' political advice to the Vietminh:

> [Luo Guibo's] *delegation played an important role in advising the Vietnamese on reforming the communist party, purging it of undesirable elements, and strengthening its control over and mobilising the population via reorganised security services, rectification and emulation campaigns, and intensive ideological training.*[40]

In August 1950 Liu Shaoqui, who had responsibility for operations in Indochina, warned in a telegram to Liu Guibo not to impose views and not to take offense if they rejected advice. However, it seems likely that the Chinese, probably under Mao's direction, sought to ally with leftist and anti-Giáp factions in the

VWP, notably with Truong Chin, both to further the radical Chinese political line and to rein-in Ho and Giáp and any drift towards nationalist deviation.

Chinese military intervention represented by CMAG was trumpeted for its fraternal support for fighting colonialism and imperialism, but the primary purpose for Mao was related to China's defensive strategic interests, including defence of China's revolution. It was the primary *raison d'être* for Mao's support for Kim Il Sung's invasion of South Korea (however misguided) and for direct intervention as US forces approached the Yalu River in November 1950. In March 1951, a Vietminh radio broadcast a declaration from an Indochina united front of the three countries of Vietnam, Lao and Cambodia: 'US interventionists are not only plotting to colonise us but intend to use us as a base for aggression in China.'[41]

From the beach: Legionnaire Krause at Phyu Ven, 1949

Typical of many operations on the Annamite coast of the Central Highlands, Carpentier's French command launched a clearing operation on the lowland rice zone between sea and mountain. Landing on the coast to the north of Nha Trang, Heinz-Klaus Krause and his fellow legionnaires marched inland. He remembered:

> *...on the horizon we could see a long column of cyclists, from our binoculars we could see that they were wearing Japanese uniforms and were heavily armed. Regular warfare at last...there was no hiding place for them; it was an uneven battle. they were all dead in just a few seconds. They went down under our machine-guns. The water in the rice field water was red with the blood of 83 Tonkinese.*[42]

Looking to trap the two Vietminh regiments believed to be in the area, Junkers aircraft flew over and dropped a battalion of paratroopers, 1st BEP, behind the township, as they did so:

> *...the accompanying Spitfires peeled off in a wide curve toward the village ahead. That was our attack signal. We were about 200 meters away as the Spitfires came in, with their machine-guns blazing, just 5 meters above the rice field as they hunted down any Vietminh soldiers who were in the open.*[43]

Going through the village, Krause recalled:

> *...we found a great store of mines, and hand grenades in the village. In almost all the houses the Vietminh had been quartered. In one house alone we found 300 backpacks which we burnt.*

They found a malarial Viet officer in bed:

Much to the annoyance of our officers, he was shot while being taken back for interrogation...The Vietminh had taken almost all their dead with them from the area at which Sikolowski's MG had been firing.[44]

A typical village clearing operation had Heinz-Klaus Krause advancing at dawn on the outskirts of a village, treading slowly and quietly along a dyke next to a paddy covered with water, green shoots just breaking the surface of the water. One of the legionnaires lost his footing and crashed loudly to the ground. Suddenly there was the shriek of a young woman who rushed into a nearby hut. The legionnaires, startled by this commotion, which was also an alarm call, opened up on the bamboo village with their machine-guns. As most of the village was made of bamboo, the bullets cut through it and screams could be heard. They moved in to clear the village. As they did so several grenades flew through the air and exploded harmlessly in the water-covered paddy.

The villagers flew out of the back of the village followed by a hail of bullets. As the legionnaires advanced warily through the village, there was suddenly an explosion when Legionnaire Moses from Stettin tried to open a door. It was booby-trapped with a mine. He was thrown against a wall and crumpled down. His blooded body was pierced all over with shrapnel. The medic came up and gave him a shot. He was groaning with pain. Kostal told him to be quiet, then Moses interrupted him: 'I...I...I...know I shall die here and my mother will be totally broken without me, not seeing me again.'[45] He died.

They searched through the wreckage of the now quiet village. 'Here and there we could find dead Vietminh in black or yellow uniforms,' recounted Krause in a poignant passage:

A naked woman lay crumpled in a pool of blood; Kostal bent down and picked up in his arms a new-born baby, perhaps no more than one hour old, then put it back next to the dead mother. He gently put a sleeping mat over both of them. Minard [the captain] *leant his machine-gun against the wall and lit a cigarette.*[46]

Loaded onto planes after being triaged by French doctors, the wounded were flown to Hanoi.

The road to Cao Bang

Route Coloniale 4 weaves through spectacular scenery of jungle-bound passes then through a winding valley of limestone crags and idyllic emerald paddy. In the Cao Bang region there is a famous waterfall with cascades of water below jagged, forest-enclosed hills. From Cao Bang the road runs south-east in parallel with the Chinese border to the main regional city and logistics hub at Lang Son. For the French high command, defence of the road and maintenance of its string of fortified posts on the RC4 (Cao Bang, Dong Khé, That Khé and Langson). They were, it was thought, essential for the territorial integrity of Indochina, and for prestige for the maintenance of the loyalties and morale of hill tribes. It was an attractive notion on a map, but militarily ludicrous because it would just condemn many soldiers in these 'suicide' posts to be overwhelmed and killed with no hope of relief and to no effect. Orthodox high command-thinking believed that if the Vietminh could be boxed up in these frontier mountains, then the revolution could be contained and kept distant from the economic core of the north, the heavily populated Red River delta.

An alternative view that developed was simply to defend the delta flatlands where France's superior weaponry could deal with any menace. However, if RC4 was lost then it opened the spectre of Giáp's Vietminh soldiers sweeping down against all key trunk routes and railways around a vulnerable delta. They would be able to link up and reinforce those other areas of Vietminh infestations inside the delta countryside.

The road had been an increasing problem for some time, with convoys to Cao Bang being destroyed or badly beaten in ambushes by the Vietminh's formidable 174 Regiment. There were so many locations for potential ambushes that it made counter-measures quite impossible. Nor were airstrikes effective, because the Vietminh could fire from numerous mountain caves in the limestone rocks. Convoys then started making a fast run for it one by one, vehicle by vehicle, gunning their engines hectically amid fusillades of bullets.

'I drove those three miles of zig-zags like a lunatic,' recalled one survivor. 'There were bursts of machine-gunfire and you had to go through curtains of bullets skipping off the surface of the road.'[47]

Convoy battles became the norm along RC4, each one being contested at close quarters and even in hand-to-hand combat. One legion sergeant described his experiences on convoy runs to Lucien Bodard:

> *The Viets shoot us like rabbits. I've been in six ambushes already. Twice I've been in trucks that were burnt out – look at my hand. Done rare.*

Each hairpin and constriction in the road had seen vicious close-quarter fighting and dozens killed. Viets would take out the leading trucks and separate the armoured cars at the front of the column. Then the whole convoy would be paralysed. At this point dozens of machine-guns and mortars located in the forest or in caves or behind rocks in the surrounding hills, and already zeroed-in on the spot, would open up on the trucks. Andre Thevenet, a mountain-savvy Savoyard, noted that to make the passage he had to scramble up with his Berbers to a high point above the road every few kilometres to set up a machine-gun post.[48]

Camouflaged Vietminh would spring up from nowhere and rush in from the sides. The sergeant advised Bodard, who was preparing to travel on a convoy:

> *...if we're blocked in like that...get out fast, fast before the Viets attack the trucks. You can't defend yourself inside – you get your throat cut at once. The most important thing is to regroup outside and make little knots of resistance among the Viets...There's hand-to-hand fighting over hundreds of yards, sometimes for miles, on the road itself and the embankments. The battle is all in little unconnected bits, separate engagements. There are countless Viets everywhere... How they howl!*[49]

A French paratrooper battalion commander, the legendary and indestructible Bigeard, experienced the hazards of ambush along the RC4 as he drove in a Jeep at the head of a convoy. 'The Viets ambushed us and they chose the spot well. The terrain with the slope there, is just right,' he said, pointing to the very spot in a television interview forty-five years later:

> *...and there they raked us almost at point blank. Lieutenant de Perrot? My adjutant was shot dead, and the lieutenant medic climbed up there where the undergrowth is. There were two dead in the Jeep, so I dived out and rolled down into that ravine. I just let myself go and they came looking for me but it wasn't easy for them, then I heard the paratroopers coming shooting. It was a tough fight. I spent several difficult minutes there.*[50]

Some bright staffer came up with the idea of convoys with massive accompanying protection. The only problem was that these convoys consumed all the supplies that they were meant to be delivering for the relief of Cao Bang, so much so that the famished defenders often had to share their meagre rations with their saviours. Eventually a whole convoy was massacred with eighty-five out of 110 trucks destroyed. Film shots show burnt-out lorries surrounded by bodies.

'It was a dreadful massacre...we were sent out to recover the pieces,' recalled Andre Thevenet. The convoy system was abandoned. Even then gung-ho General Alessandri hung on to Cao Bang. The colonial civil servant in charge of the town noted that the garrison was held in place:

> *...as a point of honour, for the prestige of the thing and to guard the cemetery... they* [the high command] *just suppose that things are difficult on RC4 but that it's not as bad as all that.*[51]

Dong Khé was the first post to fall on 25 May. However, it was recaptured easily some days later, on 27 May, by a company of legionnaires. But could they hold it?

General Giáp was at the start of his great counter-offensive. By the autumn of 1950, 50,000 raw Vietminh militia were transformed by Chinese training into four regular divisions of the VPA.[52]

There was a great stirring in the mountains across the border from Cao Bang and Lang Son. Masses of Vietminh were processed by the tens of thousands. Each grade of soldier was drilled just enough in the simple tasks of weapon loading, maintenance and basic movement. The next NCO rank received more complex instruction, and so on up the chain, including the commander, Giáp. For reasons of speed, training was rudimentary.

As casualties mounted the reserves were processed from militia and village units. Within a few months Giáp had at his disposal on the Chinese border a crude but disciplined army of 50,000 formed into four divisions. The soon-to-become famous 308th, 312th, 316th and 320th, soldiers who had previously been a loosely organised and untrained rustic rabble fit only for guerrilla war were now capable of army-level attack and manoeuvre. And along with the training was the usual communist brainwashing: constant repetitive slogan-chanting, anti-western denunciation in puerile language: 'dogs', 'lackies', 'hooligans', 'imperialist exploiters', 'rightist elements', 'reactionaries', 'dangerous traitors', etc.[53] Swamped with crude Marxist-Leninism and an admixture of xenophobia, the peasant soldier was imbibed with revolutionary euphoria. The bo doi (foot soldier) courageously attacked again and again in human waves and withstood huge casualties. With their surfeit of captured weaponry, there was no shortage of the means to arm their *protégé* with the latest American small arms, mortars, and artillery of all calibres. All previously supplied and equipped from a multiplicity of captured material, or imported or homemade weapons from hundreds of jungle workshops. Driven right up to the border, the Chinese made sure that supply lines to Giáp's army were both short and secure.

Rumours of Giáp's offensive abounded and journalists challenged the French command's rosy view of the military situation. Colonel Constans, who was to plan the withdrawal operation for the Cao Bang garrison, entertained the journalists to a splendid dinner in Lang Son:

> *...the big bad Viets, Giáp's divisions is an invention of your colleagues, the gentlemen of the press. It's a bluff. They are still nothing but guerrilla fighters, and we shall soon settle their business for them. Don't be afraid for us, but rather for them.*[54]

As usual, bitter political infighting emerged between General Carpentier and the old China hand Alessandri, the hero who had led his men to China when the Japanese attacked at the Second World War's end. Alessandri had successfully suppressed much communist activity in the delta by unglamorous gradualist tactics, cleansing each zone in turn. Suppressed but not gone, the communists would re-emerge at an opportune time. Alessandri wanted a full-scale offensive against VPA forces around the RC4.

Each general had different ideas as to how to deal with the new threat on the Chinese frontier. Carpentier saw the fortress outposts along the RC4 as breakwaters ('brise-lames') that would take the force of the expected attacks on the Red delta and allow the Vietminh Army to be smashed after it had broken itself on the RC4's forward defences. It was a map-based concept that was only attractive in theory. Feisty Corsican Alessandri rejected this believing that if the Vietminh broke through in force to the delta, France's position in Tonkin would be threatened. Equally deluded, he proposed instead to crush them decisively by launching an offensive to attack the Vietminh in their north-eastern lair. MRP politicians in Paris backed each man in turn, but eventually Carpentier exerted his prerogative.

On 16 September 1950, Carpentier, from his map room over 2,000km away, located in the opulent, neo baroque and colonnaded splendour of the Norodom palace, decided on a plan to evacuate the Cao Bang garrison. Even as Carpentier announced his decision to evacuate the region, the 300 legionnaires at Dong Khé on the RC4 were fighting for their lives against hordes of Vietminh after being attacked on the 15th. Ho and Giáp watched the action with binoculars from an eyrie 10km away.[55] To draw off Giáp's forces Carpentier announced, 'I have decided that the evacuation of Cao Bang shall be undertaken as soon as the Thainguyen region is seized.' Forty-five kilometres north of Hanoi, it was a most ineffectual diversion. Vietminh forces simply withdrew into the jungles. Giáp and Ho decided on 16 September to launch their 'new model VPA army' in a region-wide offensive against the other French outposts on the RC4.

Giáp was not tied to his bases but could launch and concentrate his forces freely because his core professional army divisions were highly mobile and could be concentrated with the support of the Vietminh huge porter levée. Giáp and Ho were willing students of Mao's combined military-revolutionary strategy. Like the Chinese communists, the Vietminh had been expelled from the cities but had rebuilt their power bases on the peasantry, which Mao had described as a sea that would swamp the isolated islands (cities) occupied by the enemy.

The Vietminh regular army – first blooding: March–May 1950

The start of the RC4 campaign began not in the north-east next to Vietminh bases but in the north-west. With the new Vietminh regular army in hand, the sheer enthusiasm and impatience of Ho Chi Minh and his Communist Party leadership meant that it would soon be tested. Time was of the essence in case the Americans intervened, as they had successfully done in Korea. The newest 308th Division was sent off to be blooded near Striking in the north-west at the border town of Lao Cai on the Red River. The 308th would be used as a distraction from the main north-eastern objective of the coming campaign at the end of the monsoon season.

Giáp's army was developing from a well-disciplined partisan army into a regular force capable of division-sized operations. The intention now was to step that up to an army-sized operation with numbers of divisions involved in wide-scale conflict. However, Giáp did not give up on guerrilla war, which was an essential component of his holistic strategy of attrition, holding down enemy formations and diverting enemy concentrations. To counter Alessandri's successes in the core Red delta zone that produced the rice for Tonkin, Giáp kept up the pressure:

> *...our units operated in small groups with independent companies penetrating deeply into the enemy controlled zone to launch guerrilla warfare, establish bases...an extremely hard war, generalized in all domains; military economic and political. The enemy mopped up, we fought against the mopping...we firmly upheld local people's power, overthrew straw men, eliminated traitors and carried out active propaganda.*[56]

One of the main aims of the Vietminh was to control rice production and to smuggle it out of the Red delta to supply the needs of the Vietminh Army, which the hill country could not do. Alessandri's policies had indeed caused supply disruption.

General Carpentier's confidential memorandum on 21 March revealed his analysis of the military balance in Tonkin. Even as the new divisions, newly armed and trained, rolled off the Chinese assembly lines, even as the 308th prepared for attack, the general commanding in Indochina wrote, 'The situation in Tonkin has definitely been clearing up in the past few months.'

This statement seems at odds with the actual situation as presented to the American ambassador in Paris. Desperate to ease their budget burden due to home front pressure, on 16 February, the US ambassador was informed at the Quai d'Orsay:

> *...that the effort in Indochina was such a drain on France that a long-term program of assistance was necessary and it was only from the United States that it could come. Otherwise...it was very likely that France might be forced to reconsider her entire policy with the possible view to cutting her losses...that France could not continue indefinitely to bear this burden alone if the expected developments in regard to increased assistance to Ho Chi Minh came about* [i.e. Chinese aid]. (Pentagon Papers)

In May 1950, President Truman announced an aid programme.

Simultaneous with this news was a new direction for France. Robert Schuman announced his famous plan, the Schuman Plan for European Union. He was clearly making a strategic choice. When speaking at Thionville on 9 May 1950, he declared that 'European integration' based on the Franco-German axis was 'indispensable to the maintenance of peaceful relations.'

The 308th Division in the north-west

There was a sleepy post, a log redoubt bastion, on a picturesque hillock by a lake in the Red River valley some 30km south-east of Lao Cai. Situated in a basin of dense jungle, the company-sized citadel was overlooked by huge limestone peaks, a landscape not dissimilar to the Cao Bang-Dong Khé-Lang Son region of the north-east. Suddenly, 308th Division swarmed over the area. After a ten-day running fight, they took over the mountains that dominated the little outpost. A furious attack was launched, with 75mm mountain guns, heavy machine-guns and mortars operating from caves and hidden positions impenetrable even to air attack. The new model Vietminh Army, no longer a lightweight guerrilla force, was supplied by sampan fleets operating along the Red River. Despite paratrooper drops and an attempted relief expedition from nearby Lao Cai, the post was overrun, its occupants disappeared without trace.

The paratrooper drop, which was at most a forlorn hope some 30km on the wrong side of the river, was only a gesture of no value whatsoever. Small in size and led by a mere lieutenant, this force immediately found itself hounded and in a firefight with two battalions of Vietminh regulars, with thousands more regular VPA troops nearby and moving their way.

'We could see thousands of Viets…swarming across the river to join in the kill,' complained the young Lieutenant Planey, who escaped and was later accused of cowardice and loss of nerve. 'I never stopped telling the chiefs "the Viets aren't any longer the same; these are really tough ones".'

After another escape a few weeks later, a captain of 3rd BCCP declared: 'Planey, you're right, I had no notion of Viets like that.'[57] While the soldiers on the ground understood the change from a small lightweight guerrilla force that would break and evaporate on first contact, to a disciplined regular force that would keep on attacking and outflanking in large numbers, the generals in Hanoi and Saigon refused to believe their testimony.

Giáp's diversionary attacks became the hallmark of his generalship. Intended to throw the French off balance and induce them to commit their forces away from Cao Bang and the RC4, having made their mark in the Red River valley, the 308th suddenly disappeared.

A personal war on the Cambodian border

Lieutenant de La Motte was posted to Indochina and immediately made the commander of a company of Vietnamese-Khmer soldiers in an isolated rubber estate in the north of Tay Ninh province bordering on Cambodia.

Treated as an employee by the estate manager, La Motte was even ordered to find the manager's pet otter when it became lost in the jungle. There are other stories about tigers and a large and beautiful python under his bed. Mostly he feared buffalo but the Vietminh became an increasing problem:

> *I have mixed feelings about buffalo. Generally buffalos hate whites and charge at the first opportunity. You can only stop them with a rifle shot…the problem being the odour of soap which they hate.*[58]
>
> *One morning we noticed a troop of Vietminh four or five hundred metres away, less numerous but well-armed. The Viets hid and laid down a reasonable rate of well-directed fire. I put the least experienced of my men up front to gain experience under fire…both sides were dressed in black except I could see my opposite number who was attired in immaculate white civilian clothes, standing still leaning on his cane in a contemptuous manner. I could do no less. We deployed our men as if they were chess pawns…I learnt that they were a school for Vietminh NCOs…for two months we would come across them quite often but at distance.*[59]

During his posting he realised that 'the primary Manichean objective consists of killing those on the other side of the water'[60] (i.e. his white-suited rival).

However, the situation was becoming ever more dangerous. 'Returns from patrols became ever more rapid, only speed would allow us to evade an ambush and an unequal combat.' And then the inevitable happened:

> *…all of sudden five or six machine-guns opened up on us supported by rifle fire and sub-machine-guns…we were a little over twenty lying down in 40 centimetres of water which hid us quite well. I shouted out to see if anyone was dead; bullets made little geysers in the water in front and behind me. I awaited the final assault which is the climax of all well mounted ambushes…suddenly I felt a shock in the leg and the water turned red, I could barely move my limb.*[61]

'Why don't they assault?' he asked himself repeatedly.

> *It was necessary to keep them occupied with the French grenades received three weeks before; they exploded in the trees and would have produced a disagreeable effect. Hon got up and as if on exercise threw grenade after grenade with great precision in the places where the machine-gunning was coming from.*

La Motte had used up all his grenades and was later criticised for profligacy by the commissary officer when ordering a new supply.[62]

In the engagement, La Motte's command suffered twelve wounded and none dead...Learning was the essential thing – to keep a step ahead of your enemy. 'I reflected on the experience and started to use even longer patrols with even greater rapidity.'[63]

Under new tactics, to avoid the leakage of information, patrols were only issued orders after dark when all gates had been locked. They would set off at 1–2 a.m. in the morning.

> *One time we seized some Viet papers which admitted that they had no idea of my plans. Viets started putting grenade traps along the small jungle paths to sound the alarm when detonated.*

Failure to learn and adapt was fatal in Indochina. The complacent assumption made by French commanders that the enemy would not adapt was a fatal flaw that led to the major disasters of the war.

On one patrol, after about one and a half years in the post, La Motte's men captured a Vietminh bo doi, who promised to take La Motte to kill his rival enemy commander. It was a place 20km away and in the middle of the Viet zone. To catch him and get away, one had to arrive at 5 a.m. in morning.

> *...We arrived at a point where the Viet said we were 3km distant and that the area was well guarded. I went forward with my five best scouts. We took astonishing secret paths which we would never have discovered. We advanced very fast...In less than an hour we came out into a little clearing still well hidden where we could see several huts. From the central hut a guy rushed out... the scouts fired in unison, he must have been dead before his body hit the ground. In the hut we found files of documents, no arms and we left...we rejoined the command and retreated running...my war was over; I had killed the person who had authority on the other side of the water* [the regional commander]. *I caught typhus and this took me out of combat.*

CHAPTER X

Route Coloniale 4, October 1950

Cao Bang evacuation, 3 October 1950

As Colonel Charton in Cao Bang prepared for evacuation, 20km further south of the RC4 a relief column of 3,000 French troops advanced. The aim of the column was to meet with Charlton's retreating column and shepherd them back to safety in the fortified township of That Khé. A secondary aim was to re-establish a French garrison of legionnaires at Dong Khé, which had recently been overrun again on 18 September after a heroic legionnaire defence against 8,000 Vietminh.

The loss of Dong Khé in heroic legion-style reminiscent of the Battle of the Camerone in 1863, was a shock. Only fourteen survivors made it back, the rest being captured or killed. Vietminh film footage shows a wrecked bastion full of dead bodies and a few bearded, disorientated legionnaire prisoners. That fifty percent of the defenders died is testament to the ferocity of the defence. They accounted for 500 Vietminh, according to VPA figures, so even on their reckoning, total casualties must have been much higher.[1] Vietminh soldiers' tactics still consisted of fairly crude charges *en masse*.

Despite their dissent to the Revers analysis, Generals Carpentier and Alessandri decided that Cao Bang and Dong Khé were no longer tenable strongpoints as they were beyond the formidably dangerous Loung Phai Pass. Cao Bang had to be evacuated. The line of strongpoints along RC4 had been held for reasons of prestige. The can had for many months been kicked down the road, perhaps to save the career and embarrassment of General Carpentier, who may have hoped that the decision would be taken by the next in line for the 'buggins turn' of Indochina command. However, with a 25,000-man deficit in Indochina's complement, the decision now had to be taken especially as it had been decided by high command to shift six battalions to the Mekong delta to attempt a pacification in this vital economic zone.[2]

The orders for the relief advance had been given on 30 September by Colonel Constans, Carpentier's man on the spot. Carpentier had bypassed the theatre commander General Alessandri in Hanoi. Simultaneously, Colonel Le Page was ordered to march along RC4 from That Khé to recapture the fortress of Dong Khé by 2 October. To maintain secrecy, as if it was a secret to the all-knowing Vietminh commanders, nothing was mentioned about the link-up with Charton. Le Page was totally in the dark, and not happy about the prospects for the mysterious mission.

Colonel Le Page was an artillery officer with little experience in fighting and field operations command. A dour career soldier lacking in leadership qualities, Colonel Le Page failed to inspire confidence in any degree. However, he did realise that the mission was suicidal because the That Khé base was already closely invested by Vietminh forces. 'My only hope,' he moaned, 'is that the Viets are not holding Dong Khé. Otherwise, I do not see how we can set about taking it.'[3] Requests for a delay were refused. He set off with his four battalions, the elite 1st BEP parachutists, two Moroccan 'tabor' battalions and 8th RTM, which was a scratch unit of bits and pieces.

With a sense of impending doom, the column advancing up the RC4 set off from That Khé on 30 September. For the first few days there were no incidents whatsoever. There was no ambush even at Loung Phai Pass, which would normally have been a point of resistance. So ever wary with foreboding at the apparent ease of their advance, they were led on into the jungle, further from their base, sanctuary and supplies. Wishful thinking aside, officers could hardly have been under any illusions as to what was to come. The Vietminh were known to be in the region in increasing strength. To make a dangerous mission still more risky, at this time of year during the monsoon season the clouds hang so thick and heavy over the narrow valleys and tangle of Khast mountains that the likelihood of fighter-bomber support was negligible.

Most surprisingly no one, including Colonel Le Page, had any idea what the expedition was about, that this seemingly aimless expedition was related to the Cao Bang garrison break-out. Spies in the town were fully aware of the loading of vehicles and preparations for departure by the civilian population.

So, the irony was that General Giáp, sitting a few kilometres away in the mountains, had a much better idea of French intentions than the commander of the column going to the relief of the Cao Bang garrison. The Vietminh were now formed into regular units, including the recently returned and battle-hardened 308th, and supported by 70,000 porters and road labourers.[4] Enjoying new weaponry, newly trained troops and plentiful supplies near to the Yunan base areas, Giáp and his Chinese advisers, after some heated argument (according to Chinese historical sources), realised that there was an opportunity for a major set-piece attack under optimal conditions. Mao himself was involved and drafted a telegram on 6 October saying, 'destroy the enemy reinforcement on the hills south-east of Dong Khé first, and then attack the withdrawing enemy force from Cao Bang.'[5] It was like cats playing with a mouse.

Woefully provided with intelligence, the French were advancing into an ambush by vastly superior forces who would be fighting in jungle and mountain terrain where few of the French advantages in training, firepower, and air control could be deployed. Moreover, the Vietminh were now well equipped with 75mm mountain guns, mortars and machine-guns. Fighting close to their base, there would be few problems of supply. All four divisions would be deployed in a rapid and secret concentration under the cover of jungle. Following Jomini, it became Giáp's standard operating procedure.

What surprised the French was the sheer speed with which the new Vietminh regular army had progressed. By August 1950, the new army had been trained and equipped with everything except heavy artillery and anti-aircraft guns, although training for these last two categories was being planned. By mid-1950, the Vietminh had everything they needed, including 14,000 additional small arms, 1,700 machine-guns, 150 cannons up to 75mm, large numbers of mortars of varying calibre, tens of thousands of grenades, and 200 Molotova Russian-made trucks. Sitting on the border in safe base areas they also had 2,800 tons of rice in hand, although the rice ration had to be reduced due to General Alessandri's successful occupation and squeeze on the Red delta, which meant that rice yields from the area had dropped by half.

On just a few days' notice Colonel Charton, pipe-smoking, straw topee-wearing and crusty colonel of the legion, was perturbed by the prospect of his troops' retreat along RC4. A renowned fighter worshipped by his men, even he knew that the task was impossible. 'It is madness,' Charton told General Alessandri, who agreed. 'I can't see how you can possibly succeed.'[6]

Rene Mary recalled that Colonel Constans had sent a ludicrous order for 'the destruction of the post without fire or smoke'. Ludicrous because the Vietminh would obviously be forewarned by spies. Colonel Charton hung on to the last moment till 3 October, hoping desperately that 'the order to evacuate would be countermanded'.[7] The garrison of Cao Bang blew up its stores, including 50 tons of munitions. The big bang announcement of Colonel Charton's departure would have been heard in China. So when they set off, the Vietminh horde was forewarned already by their spies, although the timing took Giáp by surprise, so his reaction was somewhat delayed. In Charton's column there were 2,500 plus a ragbag of 500 camp followers, prostitutes, cooks, and families of his indigenous T'ai soldiers and guides.

Despite the obvious dangers, the legionnaires, eighty percent of whom were German,[8] had high morale as they took the road that snaked into the densely forested mountains of north-east Vietnam. The high peaks towered above them to the east, and beneath them were jagged limestone crags and sharply undulating foothills and ridges. A threatening green mass merged into shades of purple with successive ridge lines to the solid dark blocks of the mountains that form the watershed on the border with China.

Charton, against orders, trailed several heavy weapons. He was expecting to be attacked and he did not care what the armchair generals in Saigon thought. Nevertheless, he found himself pinned down by well-placed machine-gunfire from the tops of limestone hills about 30km from his Cao Bang fortress. After exploratory attempts at turning the position and deploying his two heavy weapons, Charton realised that there was no practical way forward along RC4, which was occupied in force by Giáp's regulars.

The legionnaires did have options apparently, because anxious radio signals from Constans' command in Hanoi informed him of the Quangliet trail, which ran off on a direct and shorter route that cut out a big double loop in the RC4. The only problem with this idealised vision from an old map was that none of the guides knew about it. The map was old and in Vietnam trails can disappear within a year or so due to the rampant growth of jungle plants. After some searching, a thin and overgrown trail of sorts was found. So with jaunty optimism, the Charton column plunged into the dense jungle, so dark and hemmed-in by foliage that there was no visibility beyond a few feet. Heavy weaponry was destroyed, excess baggage discarded, and trucks set on fire. With the air heavy, thick, musty with the stench of rotting plants, stagnant and clammy, no breath of wind could penetrate the mass of foliage. The column spread out in single-file on a narrow, overgrown trail for over 3 miles. Radios did not work so command and control became an exacting and imprecise matter of runners and written messages from Charton, who placed himself in the middle. Around them the Viets closed in. In their extended order the column was extremely vulnerable to ambush because their line could be rushed and broken into segments.

The Vietminh were also on the move. As the porters, most of them women, struggled forward in their tens of thousands with weapons and munitions, many were met by a dishevelled old man with a stringy goatee beard. Ho, dressed in local peasant garb, walked amongst the porters. He had always liked young women and enjoyed flirting so he must have revelled in the opportunity. No doubt his appearance and friendly chat and enquiries after their welfare would have inspired the Vietminh host. He was infinitely calculating but in a way that was charming and natural. He knew that stories of his presence would proliferate around the army. Morale would be raised. Simple, homespun, saintly Uncle Ho, the mystique and legend was in the making. On one occasion, having heard complaints about the rice quota, he ordered, 'the rice quota must be increased to 900 grams,' (about a thirteen percent increase).[9]

Route 4 and Cousin Luc

After Vietminh officer training, Mae Elliot's cousin Luc was appointed to a staff job helping to plan operations and assist in their execution, to observe and report back what had gone right and what had gone wrong:

> *That night before his unit went into action, Luc made an entry in his journal, noting the pale moonlight and recording his excitement and his indifference to death. He felt like a romantic lead in a war movie. But when it came combat was anything but romantic. It was frightening and chaotic.*

Attack on Dong Khé, 1 and 2 October 1950

On 1 October, leading units of the 1st BEP tried to rush Dong Khé, but they were soon pinned down by accurate mortar- and machine-gun fire, which was zeroed-in on the approaches to the fortress. They withdrew.

As Le Page's main column reached the high ground above Dong Khé's valley it met the first resistance from the Vietminh. From the heights dozens of Khast hills and ridges could be seen floating above the thick jungle on all sides. On 2 October, Le Page directed the 1st BEP to attack the position on the right and sent the Moroccans to attack the left, by climbing small Khast peaks at Na Keo and Na Pa respectively: 'We were climbing up but then we were unexpectedly attacked from behind,'[10] recounted Andre Thevent and Legionnaire Joseph Del Magro, the latter of whom added, 'It was a brutal fight with grenades and knives.' The legionnaire parachutists battled large Vietminh troop concentrations in thick forest, spending several hours in a firefight at close quarters before extricating themselves. Giáp s VPA forces were clearly looking to curl around Le Page's right flank to block any possibility of retreat back down the RC4. Retold by Mae Elliott, Vietminh officer Luc recalled:

> *At ten o'clock shrouded by mist and guided by the moon, his unit began its assault. Suddenly, deafening explosions rent the silence and bright flashes of light sliced through the darkness. Everyone on both sides was yelling. Bullets whizzed by Luc's head and his dead and wounded comrades were collapsing next to him. He saw a close friend rush forwards and then fall down, killed by a bullet, Luc lay flat on his back, scared out of his mind, trying to make himself as small a target as possible, but holding on to his field radio. His unit beat a hasty retreat when the platoon commander was killed. It was a defeat, and for Luc a rather humiliating experience.*[11]

Meanwhile, the Moroccans were blocked by heavy machine-gunfire in the valley emanating from the blackened and wrecked defences of Dong Khé.

With seasonal low cloud hanging over the hills there was no chance of using air power to blast their way through.

With their rebuff at Dong Khé, General Alessandri in Hanoi tried to take back operational control from Constans, who took orders directly from Carpentier. There was grotesque political infighting while the battle raged. Alessandri sought to cancel an operation from which he had been side-lined in flagrant breach of 'chain of command principles'. He was right to try. Unlike the 'map men', Constans in Lang Son and General Carpentier in Saigon, Alessandri knew the mountains well. Rapid retreat to That Khé was the only practical course. 'Cancel everything,' Alessandri pleaded to Carpentier. 'If you carry on it will be a crime.' Meanwhile, on 3 October, Giáp was sending an encouraging rallying message to his troops: 'It is a rare chance for us to annihilate the French elite forces.'[12] Giáp aimed to keep the two French columns apart, then crush them by turns.

But they did carry on. Map-bound Constans and Carpentier in their cosy headquarters ordered the column to move west across trackless mountains and jungles to link up with Charton's evacuation column along an obscure trail. The mooted trail bypassed the RC4 to the west and came out near That Khé. It was a crazy order because Le Page's column would lose all form and defensive shape in the tangle of uncharted limestone crags and jungle. The two 75mm cannon, which had just been parachuted to Le Page, would have to be abandoned immediately. One of Le Page's legionnaires commented afterwards:

> *We plunged into the mountains on a trail which was a trail only in name…we were all beat, for we had practically no sleep since leaving the base 4 days earlier. Climbing, then descending several times each day on these sharp steep slopes fully loaded with packs and equipment, was backbreaking.*[13]

Trekking for days through thick untamed jungle in thick humidity is an exhausting business. Surely the best alternative would have been to try to retreat back down the RC4 and attempt to break through Giáp's anticipatory blockade by Regiment 246 at the foot of Loung Pai pass. A difficult task but the best of two terrible options.

Giáp launched his entire army to overwhelm the French, intending first to destroy Le Page's column and block its junction with Charton. Charton's column would be slowed down while the weight of Vietminh attacks fell on Le Page. Then Charton's Cao Bang column would be destroyed in its turn.

At this moment Le Page got official instructions for the real objectives of his mission: to link up with Charton's retreating garrison from Cao Bang. In fact, his troops already knew because a Moroccan radio operator had picked up news of the Cao Bang evacuation on Singapore public radio.[14] However, with large Vietminh troop concentrations on his eastern flank, Le Page's troops would find themselves pushed to the west in the dense jungles and rocky crags around the Coxha Gorge. From his map room, Colonel Constans blithely and erroneously informed Le Page that there was only one small ridge between him and Charton. Soon Le Page was pleading for parachute reinforcements, but this was refused. All the while thick mist and low cloud of the monsoon season hung over the valley. Le Page deployed his troops in three long elongated columns too far apart for mutual support. In dense jungle they were constantly ambushed. Normal weather for the time of year, there was no hope or expectation that it would clear to allow air support, which was the only way in which the coming catastrophe might have been mitigated. Not that napalm would have been very effective in a damp and sodden forest.

Vietminh troops came rushing down from the bases on the border, so brazen in confidence that at night the French could see thousands of twinkling lights in a forest that was alive with four Vietminh divisions racing to smash and slice into the thinly deployed columns with close-quarter ambushes. The two French columns faced being annihilated and overrun by this vast human swarm. Casualties mounted and the wounded had to be carried on the backs of soldiers through appalling terrain. For Giáp the race was on to stop the disparate columns of Le Page and Charton from linking up.

Charton's trail of tears

On 4 October, Charton received a panicked order from Colonel Constans in Lang Son: 'March without stopping. Get to Laparge within a few hours, this very night.' In this terrain the order was complete fantasy. Charton's column could only move 6km in atrocious conditions on a trail that petered out. They were then forced to follow an overgrown stream. On the 5th, the stream also ran out and the disjointed column blundered about, lost and map-less in the dark, but eventually emerged into the picturesque valley of Quangliet where a patrol moving along the paddy terracing was subjected to machine-gunfire from the heights above the valley to the west.

Charton knew that he could be wiped out if he proceeded through the valley, so he decided to stay in the forest and traverse a ridge line with successive peaks, the first objective being Point 590 on the map. The Moroccans eventually reached the peak and dug-in, but a patrol that went out in the direction of Le Page to the east ran into a Vietminh ambush, which delayed the retreat now aimed at Point 515 below That Khé. There were two other high points at 477 at Banca. Another delay was caused by a breakdown in communications along the long column. There was a halt and a few hours were lost bringing up several lagging companies of legionnaires. But as they were found and proper orders given, the Vietminh attacked in waves from the sides of the trail, killing many civilian evacuees. Legionnaire Rene Maury remembered:

> *You just had to go, go on, leaving the dead and wounded on the trail...they attacked us from the front, right and left and from behind rocks.*[15]

Troop losses were still fairly light. Point 590 was held and the Moroccans moved on to Point 477. Other partisan units held other heights, including the Banca peak. The way was still open so Charton, who had been put under Le Page's command, requested permission to make a break for That Khé to collect reinforcements. He believed that there was a narrow gap in time and space. Le Page refused permission. Charton was in a desperate situation. *Sauve qui peut* was less interesting for him, than *sauvez moi.* The chance was lost.

On 6 October, a gathering of journalists in Lang Son was officially informed by Colonel Constans' press officer that:

> *...now it can be said that the hardest part is over, that the daring operation of withdrawal from Cao Bang has succeeded. Even in their own domain, the jungle and the mountains, the Viets have not been able to prevent the movement of two isolated French columns...very far from their bases.*[16]

The Vietminh Army of 40,000 was now in position all around the two battered and exhausted French columns of 5,000 men in total.

Conditions were tough for the Vietminh too. The idea that this region was their natural habitat was nonsense. Jagged crags and dense jungle were no one's habitat. The Vietminh had to be driven to it just as much as the French, and after six days of non-stop trekking, hunting and fighting, they too were exhausted. 'Why should we rest now?' demanded Ho Chi Minh, who revealed his clear-sighted ruthlessness. 'We are tired but the enemy is ten times more exhausted. A runner at the finish line in a race cannot rest.'[17]

Giáp chimed in to berate the regimental officers who had been complaining of their men's exhaustion:

> *I am sure that the enemy is hungrier and colder than you. He has suffered heavier losses...Therefore you must put in greater effort to wipe out the enemy. We have the added advantage in rain and fog.*

The Battle of Cox Ha Gorge

The Battle of Cox Ha Gorge became the crux of the RC4 campaign. It is perhaps one of the most remarkable battlefields of the world, although the use of the word 'battlefield' is certainly misplaced, except by conventional usage. As they struggled west through the jungle, little did Le Page or his troops know that another even greater topographical ambush lay in store for their increasingly desperate and bedraggled band. The gorge itself is an 8km-long gash of steep and sheer limestone cliffs with slices of jungle running obliquely across them at intervals.

The Cox Ha Gorge cuts north-south in parallel with the RC4 but curls towards the Loung Pai pass at the southern end. It would have to be traversed to be able to link up with Charton's force along the forested hills beyond it. The place where the traverse needed to happen on the straight line to Charton was the most severe and steepest, with limestone walls rising 300–400m from the bottom of the gorge, slashed with ribbons of immensely steep jungle.

The scene was set by the orders given to Le Page from Saigon (*vis* Colonel Constans in Lan Son), to make a junction with Charton's evacuating garrison, by making their tortuous and tortured trek over successive forested peaks running 5km parallel with RC4.

On a map there seems no particular problem. But that is only for those ignorant of the topography in this region. In fact, the terrain to be traversed is some of the worst that could be found in South-East Asia, consisting as it does of a kaleidoscopic tangle of thickly forested and jagged Khast peaks. Looking at them from the RC4 in the Dong Khé Valley, one is filled with awe and wonder at the insanity of the idea.

Anyone familiar with the terrain, such as General Alessandri, Carpentier's sidelined deputy, knew that it was utter madness. The author can confirm that the order was even crazier than that given to the light brigade at Balaclava.

A mere trek of several days through this jungle morass would physically destroy any formation, let alone a fighting withdrawal against overwhelming numbers, when weighed down by heavy equipment, munitions, water, wounded on stretchers and victuals. The French Army from a logistics standpoint was a road-bound army. It was not trained or attuned to such jungle manoeuvres.

The two French columns were fighting with all the disadvantages of French methods of warfare and none of the advantages. Colonel Callwell in his 1896 classic 'small wars' – a tactical textbook for imperial soldiers – points out:

> *Lines of communication are in fact a necessary consequence of elaborate and systematic organisation, of modern armament, of the extensive requirements of the soldier 'day to day' and of the conditions under which a regular army operates. The enemy on the other hand in most small wars works on an altogether different system.*

The problems of the French Army fighting in Indochina were to be fully exposed by the October 1950 RC4 campaign. It was a road-bound army struggling through the jungle.

However, Callwell's analysis was only true for pre-1950 Vietminh because, by the time of the RC4 campaigns, the VPA was operating as a well-resourced, well-armed, modern hybrid army, with an excellent logistics system.

The distance to be travelled by Le Page's column would take at least three days, all the while hounded, ambushed and harried by the fleet of foot Vietminh regular army of 40,000–50,000 men and supported by a similar number of porters.

Between the two French columns lay 5km of exceptionally dense jungle and the barrier of the Cox Ha Gorge, which would involve a difficult and precipitous descent followed by another jungle traverse to the heights of 477m and 533m, in which vicinity Charton was waiting for them.

Le Page's force consisted of two groups of two battalions, the left and right flanks of his attack on Dong Khé. The two groups moving west from the RC4 towards the gorge would pass consecutively through the high point of Hill 765. The 1st Tabor and the BM8 RTM were in the lead and reached the bottom of the gorge, a perfect amphitheatre at about 5 p.m. having set off in the early afternoon.

The 11th Tabor and the BEP faced even greater difficulties. Due to a hasty departure, broken terrain and poor decision-making, the BM8 RTM (the left flank) lost the link to the following two battalions and left Hill 765 unoccupied and available for occupation by the Vietminh. So, when the 11th Tabor and the BEP showed up, they were ambushed and suffered significant casualties in getting through. Their path to Cox Ha was cut off.

From this moment the two lagging French battalions faced a terrible ordeal to join Le Page's column. 'The progression was extremely slow,' wrote Captain Jeanpierre, 'because of the wounded who had to be carried on men's backs at certain points because it was impossible to stretcher their companions.' During the night of 4 and 5 October, only 2km were covered. They had to skirt point 765 and cross the gorge to the north of Le Page's group.

As the French retreated, 'some coolies tossed wounded and medical material into a ravine to escape and save themselves. Constant ambushes and you had to change porters every half hour,' according to Jaques Romain Desfosses. 'Twelve combatants were needed for one wounded.' Some of the wounded were abandoned. It was a terrible but necessary decision to avoid compromising the entire column. (Legendary Colonel Bigeard would do the same when fleeing from Tu Le in 1953.)

On their Trek from RC4, a company of Moroccans and Goumiers was sent back to That Khé via the Lung Pai, and thirty made it through after meeting a Vietminh block. But this suggests that the whole column could have escaped to That Khé if they had decided quickly enough and been so ordered. However, this has to be qualified because French movements were ascertained already from radio communications that were made in the clear, so this derogation from the known plan may have led to the Vietminh underweighting the blocking guard on the Lung Pai pass section of the RC4.

The problems of the French Army fighting in Indochina were to be fully exposed by the RC4 campaigns. It was a road-bound army, so if it took to the jungle for any length of time, inadequate logistical capacity and lack of local porterage would soon degrade its efficacy. A report on the battle from the head of the 11 Tabor made on 10 March 1951 noted:

> *The problem of porterage imposed on us seriously…it is hardly possible in this country to ask men to carry more than 15 kilos. Therefore, you cannot carry all the heavy arms or the munitions that are army regulated. Many companies left their encampments with only half of their complement of 81 mortars and machine guns, our rifle companies were only armed with submachine guns. Our enemies in contrast to us carried double the quantity of heavy arms and had virtually inexhaustible supplies of ammunition, which was far from the case with us.*

In contrast, porterage by tens of thousands of the local populace supported the crack VPA and regional units that could draw on vast quantities of munitions and supplies from the nearby dumps on the Chinese border.

A further advantage for the Vietminh was that the abandonment of Cao Bang had left the use of the 40km of road from the provincial capital to the VPA at Dong Khé. From their Chinese border bases, they could easily run down supplies to their troops by using 200 Russian Molotova trucks, porters, carts and bicycles.

Le Page with two leading battalions scrambled down vegetation on the sheer rockface. While under attack from behind, Le Page's troops had to lower themselves branch by branch, creeper by creeper, down these ribbons of green. It looks more than daunting from the bottom and must surely have been terrifying from the top. Luckily the troops were hardened legionnaires, paratroopers and mountain-hardened Moroccans, mostly Berbers.

Towards the bottom of the cliffs was a 50m drop, soldiers had to descend into it by hanging on to vegetation and trailing creepers. By 5 p.m. on 5 October, they reached the bottom.

After descending, troops milled around in disorder with officers trying to restore some military cohesion to their units. The pursuing Vietminh Army did not dare emulate their descent but rather trained their rifles and machine-guns at the scurrying dots below.

On the morning of 6 October, as the light came up, Vietminh machine-gunners and Tommy-gunners started pouring fire into the gorge, shooting down the herd of soldiers whose organisation began to fall apart, particularly the Moroccans, whose officers had mostly been killed.

The only reasonably passable exit from the bottom of the gorge where the French had descended is a narrow gully with a stream running through it, which debouches from the western side. The gully winds for several kilometres and runs through to a line of moderate peaks along which Charton's troops were trekking. Even in the dry season the forested and shaded gully is a very muddy watercourse. However, the entrance, which required the negotiation of a steep incline, was blocked by Vietminh machine-gun positions.

The 1st Tabor and the BM8 RTM had been in the lead of the column and reached the bowl at the foot of the gorge at about 5 p.m. However, the 11th Tabor and 1 BEP had to face the difficulties of being the rearguard on the approach to the sheer cliffs of the Cox Ha Gorge. They became separated from the lead battalions at point 765.

When the Goumiers of 11 Tabor and 1 BEP showed up at the rendezvous, they were ambushed by the Vietminh, who had taken up occupation of 765 after it had been mistakenly abandoned. The track to Cox Ha was cut off. As they retreated, the legionnaires and Moroccans had another battle with five VPA battalions.

They would have to skirt around to the north and take a more northerly descent down the gorge rockface from where they marched southwards along the bottom of the limestone gorge to eventually rendezvous with Le Page in the early hours of 6 March.

We should not imagine that all was plain sailing for the VPA. Losses were high and fatigue was also taking its toll. Unfamiliar themselves with the jungle morass, directing troops cannot have been easy. Mistakes must also have been common on the side of the Vietminh. Information from Luc (Mai Eliott's cousin) indicates a relapse in morale after the first contact and ambush attempt, leading to a temporary defeat by the French right wing in front of Dong Khé. But with the enemy on the run morale improved. On the Vietminh side:

> *Luc's next assignment was to join the offensive against the border garrisons, taking part in ambushes against the retreating French column. Each attack ended in a rout for the French, and remnants of their units fled for their lives into the hills where they hid, usually without food.*

In the bowl beneath the cliffs at Cox Ha Gorge, battalion commander Delcros informed Le Page: 'The men have lost their strength marching in this chaotic terrain, a convoy of stretchered wounded had become a veritable calvary.' They were three days without sleep. One medic talked of 'medical assassination' to alleviate the suffering of the wounded and reduce the logistical burden.

Not surprisingly eye witness testimony in the horror and confusion of a jungle fight in appalling climate conditions and terrain where an ambush threatened from behind every rock and tree cannot be fully relied on for accuracy on time or place. Knowledge of the terrain and geography was in any case imperfect to non-existent. If it had been otherwise, the orders from General Carpentier and Colonel Constans to march cross-country would not have been given.

A visit to the site through a gully that connected the two French columns, from the gorge to the Quang Liet valley, is the most difficult and remote terrain requiring a tortuous motorbike ride along narrow steeply undulating trails, through thick forest, along precipitous tracks, muddy banks of streams and along riverbeds. Even today this remote part of northern Vietnam has never been visited by villagers only 8km distant who only vaguely know its location. A small government plaque at the bottom of the Cox Ha Gorge gives the correct locations.

Having descended into the gorge by a more northerly route, the two lost battalions turned south to join Le Page's battalions in the late evening. On the morning of 6 October, Le Page's column was at the receiving end of machine-gun and small arms fire directed by the Vietminh from above.

Exhausted and transfixed in failure, Le Page seemed locked into a stupor of indecision until approached by angry paratroopers from 1 BEP wanting to know how he was going to get them out of this mess. The exit from the depths of the gorge under the limestone rockface was to take the narrow exit on the west side and head east to join Charton's column.

Unfortunately, Le Page's delay and the wait for 1 BEP to arrive allowed the Vietminh time to reinforce and block the one exit to the west, which was heavily defended by the time the paratroopers came to unblock it.

This gap at the entrance to the gully, bristling with Vietminh machine-guns, was stormed by surviving 1 BEP legionnaires. Using grenades and tommy guns, they succeeded in breaking open a passage for a broken mob of Moroccan and French soldiers who followed behind.

The confused, mostly leaderless units, largely without military order, rushed through this gap and would after a few hours rendezvous with Charton in the saddle of point 477 and point 533 (Ban Ca).

As for Charton's command, which had held in place whilst waiting for Le Page, peaks were lost and re-taken in bewildering confusion. Charton's command from the beginning of their Quiang Liet trail odyssey had a problem with communications on their strung-out column several kilometres long. Radios were not working and messengers got lost or they brought commands or information that was already out of date. Unfortunately, the confusion in Charton's long trail of troops and refugees from Cao Bang had led to leads and lags in the column, sometimes overextended and vulnerable to ambush and sometimes bunched up.

Communication was by runner because the radios were not operating. Ambushes by Vietminh broke up the column, causing casualties and yet more chaos. In the gorge, Le Page was transfixed by indecision, and in the saddle, Charton was immobilised by orders from high command to wait for Le Page. But the Vietminh net was closing and chances of escape were draining away.

Having broken through Le Page's column, troops found themselves in a narrow, forested gully with a stream running through it. The gully winds for 3–4km, with an occasional slim clearing of paddy. Near the end of the gully the broken detritus of Le Page's column stumbled into contact with Charton's hard-pressed scrum of troops. They milled around in the saddle between point 477 and Ban Ca (point 533), where the best legionnaire unit 3/3REI had battled along the ridge-line against increasing opposition. Meanwhile, Vietminh units, unseen in the jungle, began their stealthy approach to finish off the French Army. They closed in as if hunting down a dangerous and wounded animal.

The final hours

Unfortunately, Charton's column was in a confused bunched condition when Le Page's mob of soldiers met it. There was crowded chaos with the Vietminh pressing all around. It was a situation made worse by the loss of Hill 533 to the Vietminh by the flight of an officer-less Tabor company. Driven by fear, the disorderly mob stampeded down into the milling crowd of soldiers. The two columns were now bunched in a miserable and disordered mass without room to properly re-organise. Ironically, 533 was recaptured by a partisan unit soon after but too late to stop the panic.

Worn down by heavy losses, by midday on 6 October what was left of Le Page's column was a hapless, dazed and demoralised mob. According to a witness:

> *...these broken men were afraid; they spread fear all around them among our people. Soon we were no more than a quiet dejected herd. Everyone was thinking how the Viets were crowding nearer, somewhere out of sight, for an enormous ambush.*

What had been a coherent and effective fighting force twenty-four hours before was now wrecked and scattered. Le Page himself staggered into the mass and blurted out to Charton: 'And I who thought I should have my fifth broad stripe this year!'

A weeping Charles Henry Arnoux de Pirey recounted in his documentary interview, 'The dead and the dying were laid out in rows.' And, 'A priest who had come from Cao Bang gave the dead and the dying benediction. He was taken prisoner to Dong Khé and never seen again.' Charton sought to bring control but with so few officers left, the task amongst the panicked, starved and thirsty Moroccans was hopeless.

Giáp had failed to stop the junction of the two French forces but by now it hardly mattered, because Le Page's force was broken and his shattered and demoralised Moroccan troops infected morale of the Moroccans in Charton's command.

Charton's last stand

Meanwhile the dispositions made by Charton had begun to crack. Banca Peak was lost by partisan troops and, worse, a cliff-top position was abandoned disgracefully when a French officer deserted his men. It led to flight by exhausted Moroccans. 'I saw the Moroccans run for it when the Viets were still hundreds of yards away,' complained Charton.

A mob of soldiers gathered on a saddle between Point 477 and Banca Peak. Andre Thevenet recalled that having escaped the Coxha Gorge where his company was 'slaughtered within a quarter of an hour', he expected that he 'would die on the 8th of October in appalling circumstances.'[18]

Legionnaire Regis Leboeuf noted that bayonets '*l'arme blanche* were used to kill' and recounted that 'the wounded had to be left behind'.

Another surviving lieutenant recorded what happened next as Charton jauntily led the way towards freedom and safety 20km away. Calling out to his men to follow, Charton found himself followed by just four legionnaires and a mob of leaderless and officer-less troops. Wounded by a grenade, Charton fought for his life. Suddenly thousands of Vietminh rushed out of their ambush positions firing into the mob. A survivor recounted:

> *...for a few minutes the column fought back furiously...breaking into thousands of separate personal battles in the midst of this wild tumble of rocks and greenery...But there were too many Viets: the ones who were killed didn't count – there were always more coming from behind every bush and every rock...we were attacked with everything that could kill – there were shells coming in, but they* [the Vietminh] *were now reaching point-blank range. And then it was the grenade and the knife.*[19]

Charton was knocked down, his batman was killed, and a sergeant cut in half beside him by an exploding grenade. He was only saved from a forest of bayonets by a political commissar who took him prisoner just in time.

There was slaughter on both sides:

I saw a captain weeping...There were officers who got their men to shoot them. Some completely surrounded Moroccans charged singing a battle chant until they were all killed. There were last farewells.[20]

Suddenly it was over:

There was silence over the destroyed column; and a smell. That silence you know with groaning on it and that smell of bodies which comes after there has been a great slaughter – they are the first realities of defeat.

A few dozen escaped to reach That Khé, where they were promptly captured because the Vietminh had taken the place after it had been precipitously abandoned complete with untouched stores, food and munitions. A handful more, including thirty wounded, had earlier been able to breach the blockade by 246 Regiment and leave in the last lorries out of That Khé. Surprisingly for the French, there was strict discipline from the Vietminh. No massacres, no cruelty but an orderly clear-up and treatment for the wounded.

Other fragments of units escaped to the west in small groups fighting through ambush after ambush. 'We started with fifteen,' remembered Robert Schuerman. 'After three days there were three of us.'

Not having eaten for nine days, Andre Thevenet's group came across a village making red rice. They went in and ate and were promptly rounded up by the Vietminh. Similarly for Regis Lebouef.[21]

Luc's testimony from the Vietminh side supports this account:

After three or four days, all Luc's unit had to do to induce the famished soldiers to come out of hiding was to brandish a handful of rice. Since he could speak French, Luc was given the job of interrogating POWs...Luc received a Garrand rifle[22] *as a reward. The capture of French supplies in Lang Son and elsewhere exceeded the wildest dreams of the Vietminh.*[23]

But this was not the end of the French tragedy of RC4. Amongst Charton's final radio pleas was a call for a battalion parachute-drop. On 8 October, the 3rd BCCP was dropped near That Khé, waiting to support Charton's 1st BEP as it emerged. But what had once been an elite unit was now a tired and under-strength battalion of 380 men after punishing tours in Laos. A dreadful military decision, they gathered in some human flotsam before having to flee themselves. The rescuers of the rescuers and the rescued fled through the jungles, thickets and jagged rock outcrops, just as the Le Page and Charton columns had done. Hunted through mountains and forests and paddy, they became lost and went in circles. After successive ambushes they were destroyed. Only forty from the two parachute battalions escaped.

At the Vietminh victory banquet hosted by Ho, Giáp 'felt drunk for the first time in my entire life: he was celebrating the opening of a new phase in the evolution of our long resistance.'[24] While Giáp reeled drunkenly in gleeful celebration, the French high command and government reeled in shock.

Jeanpierre's odyssey

A few kept their heads. Captain Jeanpierre of 1 BEP held his troops in hand enough to command them to break out. All the time hunted by the Vietminh, only twenty-three escaped the combined Charton and Le Page forces and got back to Lang Son after an epic flight of daring and endurance. Jeanpierre became a legendary legionnaire and was installed in the Pantheon of Heroes after his death in action in Algeria 1958. Another group of 200 Moroccans managed to reach That Khé before it was evacuated. Other determined groups also broke out but they were all captured or killed over a period of several days, some of them wandering hopefully unknowingly into an already Vietminh-occupied That Khé.

Novelist Marois remarked of Jeanpierre, 'a heroic soldier but a detestable character. This makes the perfect leader.' Such was the voice of a dilettante Paris intellectual who opposed the colonial wars. Legionnaires followed the leader who fought from the front.

A few hundred metres beyond the exit of the cross gulley from Cox Ha into the Quang Liet Valley is the modest monument to the Vietminh victory over the French. Dien Bien Phu gathered the laurel leaf of victory, but having opened up France's defences as if it were a sardine can, the war was mostly won in the RC4 battles.

Conclusions on the RC4 Campaign

The RC4 campaign and France defeat rivalled that of Dien Bien Phu in size. In many ways, it was a far worse defeat against an enemy still inexperienced and not equipped with heavy cannon. The defeat would stun France's political elite and call into question the whole project of holding on to Indochina. The rapid decline in popularity of the war and increasing pessimism as to its outcome dated from this catastrophe. In the subsequent parliamentary debate, Pierre Mendes France would issue his blistering attack on the failed logic of France's policy. They either had to increase the military budget quite massively or quit the war and negotiate. As financial expert and chairman of parliament's financial committee he understood that the war was not sustainable: 'France must choose!' Like Zola's article *j'accuse* in respect of the *Affaire Dreyfus*, where the target was the establishment and the reactionary military, 'France must choose' became the *bon mot* of the day at a seminal moment in the history of France. This time the target was colonialism and French Indochina, although the bloody Madagascan revolt 1947–49 had already demonstrated the moral and political bankruptcy of colonialism.

The defeat stunned and panicked the French military, civilian administrators, and Parisien politicians. Lang Son's abandonment was a completely unnecessary secondary catastrophe that handed to the Vietminh a vast treasure trove of resources that was not destroyed as would be usual military protocol. There was so much ammunition and equipment stored in Lang Son that any garrison could have held out for years. The Vietminh would be able to equip many more regional units with high quality weaponry. Losses included 11,000 tons of ammunition, 10,000 75mm shells, 4,000 sub-machine-guns, and huge amounts of petrol.

Moreover, Lang Son could have been resupplied and reinforced. From Hanoi, there are hills around 75km from the Lang Son but not of a height or intensity to prevent a column getting through, especially if air-covered and with firebase support at key points. There is a huge series of Khasts bordering on the road for a few kilometres, but so high and sheer as to make military usage by the Vietminh impracticable. The last 20km would have been more challenging with the road hemmed-in by steeper hills, but firebases on either side would have dealt with that.

For Giáp and Ho, the loss of Lang Son meant that Chinese supplies of munitions, arms and victuals could be shipped by road right down to the edge of the Red delta, which would facilitate a fast transfer to a new offensive to destroy the enemy's hold on Tonkin while they were still off balance and panicking.

The French hold on Tonkin and Indochina was tottering. There was talk of evacuation. Civilians left. It was the beginning of the end. A few days later in parliament, Pierre Mendes-France pushed at the reeling edifice of Indochina imperialism – many others would follow. Opinion polls showed that in 1950, twenty-seven percent of French people still supported a military solution, down from thirty-seven percent in 1947. The number would fall to fifteen percent in 1953.[25] However, in 1950, the end was to be delayed by nearly four years. There was a most unexpected recovery. About eight weeks after the RC4 debacle, General Jean de Lattre de Tassigny flew into Saigon.

Flapping fish

Stretched so thin and recently reduced in number by the politicians in Paris, there were no reserves left to hold back the Vietminh tide. The soldiers that should have been holding That Khé were being slaughtered in the jungle.

On 14 October, journalist Lucien Bodard flew in to Lang Son. He found a garrison in shock. Amidst defeatism was a determination to save honour. 'There is only one thing left for us,' said one captain, 'to do our duty according to the traditions of the French Army and fight honourably to the last man.'[26]

In a war fought to restore France's honour after the Second World War humiliation, Colonel Constans continued to be a blustering humbug to the bitter end. Promising to defend the frontier citadel, he boasted, 'So when Giáp's divisions charge I shall crush them with my guns and fighters…I have huge reserves of stores and ammunitions.'

However, the defeat on RC4 precipitated a complete panic and collapse all along the frontier. Not only was That Khé abandoned but such was Colonel Constans' funk that he now decided that the main garrison fortress and magazine at Lang Son should also be ditched. Defeat had rolled open the frontier like a sardine can.

The next day, when Bodard landed back in Hanoi, he heard that the abandonment of Lang Son had been ordered. Constans had lost his nerve and persuaded Carpentier to vacate the town. It was quite unnecessary. There was no immediate threat and the town was eminently defensible, especially as there were vast stocks of supplies including 11,000 tons of munitions, 10,000 75mm rounds, and 4,000 sub-machine-guns, and much more besides. The decision was widely regarded as a disgrace to French arms. When Constans landed back in Hanoi in an immaculate uniform, Bodard observed, 'You would have said that he was a conqueror.'[27] Glad-handing everyone and sporting a sunny smile, the shameless Constans claimed credit for the 'timely' withdrawal from Lang Son.

It was a major turning point in French policy and public sentiment. General Yves Gras remarked:

> *…the disaster was mostly of a moral nature. The basic fact is that the French troops considered to be the best, were crushed in the open countryside by an army of Vietnamese peasants who we used to scorn. The shockwaves go well beyond the physical outcome.*[28]

Legendary General Juin was sent out by a panicked government to steady the situation and report back on the disaster and make recommendations. The FEC was drawn back to defensive perimeters along the Red River. It could no longer be stretched in penny packet garrisons that would be overrun by Giáp's overwhelming troop concentrations. The temptation to have as many pins in maps as possible had always been too great for the map-men of the general staff.

The air arm had to be bolstered considerably. Another shibboleth was killed off by Juin: 'I believe that the solution to the Indochina War lies in the strength and the faith of a Vietnamese Army,'[29] i.e. arming the locals. Fears that it would be used against them by the national government gave way to the reality of troop shortage.

But the disaster did not stop at Lang Son. Soon Lao Cai, the railway junction on the northern Chinese frontier, had to be abandoned. This opened up the north-west of Tonkin and the road to Lao. Hoa Binh, the strategic market town and Meo tribe capital, was also abandoned. The French-dominated Red River delta was being surrounded. Infiltration and strangulation would be next, followed by the overwhelming attack. It was the Chinese model of extermination. French Hanoi would be strangled then drowned by the incoming communist tide.

Only Mon-kai on the coast by the Chinese border was held. The sea was a French province so it was protected. Lai Chau, capital of the White T'ai and the T'ai Federation, was held as the only garrison in the north-east. Unfortunately, this led to France giving too much preference to the White T'ai, something that allowed the Vietminh to make inroads and divisions in the T'ai Federation, pulling away significant numbers of Black T'ai, Meo and Yao. The Tho tribe of the north-east was already mainly Vietminh-aligned.

Perhaps the most important consequence of the RC4 debacle was the quantum shift in public and political opinion in France most notably symbolised by the defection of Pierre Mendes-France and the Radical Socialist Party from the coalition consensus on a continuing form of Indochina protectorate. Radical socialist leader, Jewish intellectual and former Free French ally of de Gaulle, Mendes-France broke ranks on 19 October 1950, just three days after the abandonment of Lang Son. He declared:

> *...the entire policy on which our Indochinese policy is based is misconceived because there are inadequate military resources to achieve a military solution and our policy is not convincing enough to win the support of the* [Vietnamese] *people.*

An isolated figure at first, just a few years later, in May 1953, he would fail to become prime minister by just fourteen votes.

His thesis was clear. If France could not afford to triple its military commitment to get a military victory, then negotiation and withdrawal was the only viable option. Mendes-France's analysis and conclusion were spot on, but radical changes in international affairs and in US government policy towards French Indochina were about to offer France an alternative way forward with the resources required to fund it.

In a major and well reported speech made on 30 December 1951, Pierre Mendes-France threw another argument into the mix by linking the Indochina conflict to developments in Europe and to internal issues. Perhaps for the first time from a non-communist, he pushed on the essential dichotomy facing France:

> *...you will never organise national defence in Europe so long as you have your cadres in Indochina, as long as you lose a large number of officers every year, so long as you send 500 milliards a year – which...only add to the inflation in France, poverty and higher prices.*[30]

The essential point was that you had to choose between costly and probably hopeless imperial glory or an economically sound and better-grounded future in Europe. 'A choice was necessary.' These views were anathema to the MRP, and Bidault's wing in particular. During the MRP's May 1951 party conference, it was clear the party was becoming hopelessly split with the left led by Schuman increasingly looking to a Franco-German future in Europe. Conversely, Bidault's rural Catholic wing was fighting to maintain the imperialist dream. Typical of Bidault's idea of the French empire was his speech on 25 September 1951, where he trumpeted the illusion that the majority of colonial citizens supported French rule. Talking mainly in respect of Tunisia and Morocco, Bidault declared that the rebels and nationalists in these countries were 'happily a minority'. All that was needed was a much 'neglected social progress and political evolution based on a communal plan for the indifferent masses on whom we can rely on for support to block the agitators.' At the same party congress, even the more left-wing Schuman posited the view that there should only be a progressive move towards 'internal autonomy'.[31] Following the RC4 debacle, the MRP right needed to fight hard for their position because there was rising scepticism about the possibility of winning in Indochina.

Influential MRP deputy and former senior Free French officer Pierre de Chevigne was already sceptical as to the future of colonialism. Becoming involved as a government advisor to MRP colonies ministers over serious rebellion in Madagascar, he '...hoped that one could give the impression that there were options other than indefinite repression.'[32] As a centrist MRP deputy, he carried forward this sentiment to the Indochina war.

Meanwhile, the new Vietminh Army was on the march, victorious, blooded and confident. Returning from injury, veteran Ngo Van Chieu remarked on the change that had overcome the former rabble of guerrillas fighters:

> *...we continue to march through mountains and jungle. Thousands of coolies accompany us. An amazing change has taken over the army. The roads leading from China echo in the night with the noise of trucks bringing weapons and ammunition.*[33]

Under advice from Chinese General Chen Geng, and following Mao's theses on revolutionary war, they were headed for the Red delta to finally sweep the

French into the Gulf of Tonkin and reclaim the capital at Hanoi. Having swamped outlying garrisons, under Maoist theory, now was the time to strike. This advice was followed by Ho and Giáp, who were also enamoured with and well-read in Mao's military teachings.[34] 'It is as if the people were the sea and the army a fish…should the water recede or become dry then the fish cannot escape sure death.' Hanoi was seen as the fish that was flapping around waiting to be picked up as the water receded.

The advance to the Red delta would need more transport, both on the Chinese side of the border and for the roads to the delta. Responding to Ho's pleas, Mao urgently negotiated with Stalin for 1,010 trucks: 'Among the vehicles, please ship 505 in January to March 1951, and the other 505 in July–August.'[35] For the moment Giáp would have to rely on human porterage.

North, West and Central African troops

North African troops had suffered very serious losses in the RC4 campaign and there was certainly an effect on morale with increasing incidents of insubordination. But generally it was the wear and tear of constant or extended operations without enough rest leave that was the most damaging to troops' morale. It was often small matters such as food, which lacked variety and fresh vegetables, or the question of promotions or battle honours, that most vexed the troops. Certain climates did not suit either. Black Africans, mostly used for garrison duty or security sweeps in the Red delta, disliked the cold mountains, and the Magrhebians (mainly Berbers) detested marshland such as the Plain of Reeds.[36]

Senegalese Tirailleurs numbered 14,500 in 1951, peaking at 20,000 in 1954. They formed BMTS units or were parcelled out in mixed colonial units, RIC, or in the air force for ground duty. A few were at Dien Bien Phu. They were controlled by white French officers or NCOs on three year 'mercenary' contracts, who were recruited from the French Army, either serving or former soldiers.[37] French military personnel and conscripts could not be drafted to Indochina unless they volunteered on special contracts.

Of 130,000 North African troops sent to Indochina in 1947–54, fifty-two percent came from Morocco, of whom sixty percent were infantry or auxiliaries.[38] Perhaps fifty percent were of Berber rather than Arab origin. According to Michel Bodin, from 1950 morale problems increased as veteran Second World War troops finished their contracts and returned. At the same time fatigue was setting in from overuse, and casualties were rising, as was the effectiveness of enemy propaganda. Increasingly, troops failed to respond to or accept French-only speaking officers. Indiscipline and insubordination increased. There was greater awareness too of inequalities in pay conditions and awards with French troops.

However, high command was not unaware of problems. From 1952, policy changes allowed those soldiers who merited it permission to visit Mecca on their return.[39] Other enacted policies included respect for major religious festivals, attention to diet, and multiple sorties, in special intervention units, and in the quiet times entertainment was laid on. Drawn from rural areas, ninety percent were illiterate. Aliens in this strange land, according to the commander of 10th Tabor:

> *...the goumier does not understand the nuances and his traditional contempt for the Chinese* [a term of abuse in Arabic] *makes him ill equipped to grasp the subtleties of our policies.*[40]

Performance as fighters was excellent and they formed major components of elite Groupe Mobile formations. However, if leaderless, after losing their officers or NCOs, as at Coxha George in the RC4 debacle, or on occasions at Dien Bien Phu, units could fall apart. In the final radio call at Dien Bien Phu, de Castries would complain, 'Three companies of Moroccan Tirailleurs, but which are no use at all, you realise, no use at all, which are completely demoralised.'[41] Obviously unfair comments tinged with racism.

Vietnamese opinions on the components of the French Army were as varied as experiences:

> *On the whole they* [the Foreign Legion] *were more disciplined than those from the expeditionary corps, whose soldiers were recruited from Morocco and other French African colonies, whatever they found there they kicked. French colonies in Africa. Vietnamese had never seen dark-skinned people before, and in general felt uneasy in their presence, especially that of the black soldiers whose faces bore the criss-cross scars of tribal rituals. Ignorance of these people and their culture bred fear.*

Suicide levels for Africans were relatively high for cultural reasons:

> *Hallucination indicated a mental derangement. Africans, sometimes alone in their ethnicity in their unit, assumed that they were victims of sorcery, which condition could infect their families; to escape this and to turn back the spell of the sorcerer* [in their tribal belief] *they would prefer suicide.*[42]

Disciplinary infringements had the usual variety of causes. In 1953, alcohol was responsible for forty percent of violations, fifty percent of mutinies/disobedience and forty-four percent of attempted murders.[43] Murder was not uncommon. Former SS soldier and military policeman with the Senegalese Tirailleurs Paul Martelli witnessed the body of a Vietnamese woman:

> *...half naked in a puddle of blood. Her head had been severed from the body and rolled away from it. Nobody dared touch it. She had been murdered by a jealous Senegalese soldier who had caught her being unfaithful. He was arrested and sent back to Africa.*[44]

Moroccan and Algerian troops carried with them their reputation for rape from the Italian campaign in the Second World War and continued to deserve it.[45] African troops were infamous for rape and other such undisciplined behaviour, something that is alluded to by Bodard.[46] The fact that French soldiers earned approximately two-and-a-half to three times more than Africans[47] would also have meant less access to bordello women for African troops.

Only half of twenty-nine North African battalions were fully manned, and only two of eighteen West African units. Discipline could be a problem in these unfamiliar lands:

> *...more trouble was expected because a ship full of Africans had arrived...In the suburbs the streets were full of them, the Senegalese wandering like lost children in the posts they had just taken over – the black heads of processional giants carried jerkily above the oblivious Asiatic crowd.*[48]

A typical problem for African and North African units was described by the commander of 27th BTA (Algerians):

> *...arrived in Laos 15th December 1953, I spent the week of Christmas fighting against an enemy in all respects superior...I blame our poor performance on mediocre and inefficient command, due to insufficient men, both in quality and in morale. After the losses on the 20th to 25th* [in Lao] *more than half my effectives, and despite the promises of the commanders, there were insufficient replacements especially poor in quality. Captains were replaced by lieutenants, adjutants by sergeants.*[49]

Despite all of this, desertions at 416 between 1948–54 were very low. Desertion was relatively low in any case at 1½ per 1,000 for North Africans and 3.2 per 1,000 for other Africans. Ninety-eight percent of officers in African units were French and approximately two-thirds of NCOs.

At Dien Bien Phu, Colonel Langlais was sometimes dismissive of Algerian and Moroccan reliability, but these exhausted and overused units were short on leave and rest. His opinions were probably touched with common racism of the era and a sense of elitist para superiority and so lacked objectivity. North African colonial units sometimes broke but, in general, their performance was excellent so long as there were enough French officers and NCOs still standing. North African troops made up about twenty-five percent of the regular army in Indochina. Initially they comprised excellent Second World War veterans, especially Algerian and Moroccan units that had fought in Italy with General Juin, where they had won the Battle of Monte Cassino and Rome by their advance and breakthrough in the Aurunci mountains. Performance declined as veterans returned. At Dien Bien Phu, the performance was mixed. But where there was failure it was failure of overstretch, fatigue and shortage of officers. Some units had been constantly in action for nine months. Sometimes they cracked. Central African units, especially the gunners, who fought round the clock at Dien Bien Phu, performed to the highest level despite heavy losses and huge stress. Witnesses attest to their frenetic performance under fire, black bodies glimmering with sweat in the torrid climate. They were often all that stood between the enemy and precipitate defeat. As casualties mounted, many replacements were dropped into the valley of hell having had no previous parachute experience. Their story and that of the mainly illiterate Magrhebians is little told, and we have no memoirs. Under-resourced and operating in extremely challenging terrain and climate, France's African soldiers were integral to the generally excellent performance of French arms in Indochina. If only they could speak and tell us their stories.

However, we know that there was jealousy and resentment at the inequalities in status and pay. Paul Martelli, the ex-SS soldier, was forced to confront a drunken Senegalese who threatened the Europeans with an MAT49 submachine-gun in a drunken rant. 'We stay longer than you...we get less pay than you...we eat less than you whites. No access to canteen for black soldiers.' With laconic humour, former SS soldier Martelli recalled:

> *...that type of weapon* [the MAT49 SMG] *has a hair trigger – a slight touch and it would spray bullets. I thought I was about to pay in person for the inequalities perpetrated by the French colonial authorities.*[50]

CHAPTER XI

Enter General Lattre de Tassigny

The actor 'Roi Jean'

'I have never seen an actor who has made such an entry as de Lattre in Indochine,' declared Lucien Bodard.[1] The whole world of officialdom was there at Saigon Airport, including High Commissioner Pignon and the commander-in-chief, General Carpentier, as well as the political *introducteur* from Paris, colonies minister Letourneau. De Lattre was dressed in a new tropical white uniform immaculate with razor-sharp creases. Rows of medal ribbons rippled across his chest. He carried the glittering and large Rhine Danube Star on his left breast and various other honours on his arm, including one from the legion. His khaki peaked cap carried the four stars of a Marshal of France. With delicious sarcasm, Bodard painted him as 'a mannequin of Grandeur'. After the defeats of the RC4, he was there to stop the rot. 'Le Roi Jean', as Bodard famously dubbed him, had arrived.[2]

He did the rounds of the 'other' monarchs in his realm, feigning deference to them in their Asiatic regal pomp. Bodard gives an account of the audience with King Sihanouk, who had a squeaky high-pitched voice:

> *...it recalled images of naivety in former centuries when one saw white plenipotentiaries arrayed in audience in front of an oriental despot who they are trying to civilise...de Lattre put on a show of grandiose benevolence which was somewhat paternal but this was not a role that he could play with any finesse.*[3]

He was indeed more regal than them. Despite the deference and the pretences of independence within the French Union, France was still the boss, and de Lattre was the boss of bosses.

The meetings with the monarchs of Indochina were for show and confidence building. However, the most significant visit to a 'monarch' was the conversation that de Lattre had with General de Gaulle prior to departure from Paris. On the flight from Paris, de Lattre informed Salan and the other team of generals and staff officers:

> *General de Gaulle approved my decision to leave for Indochina...'we have received a grave setback in Tonkin, but we must win this war, because it sustains the integrity of the French Union,' he told me.*[4]

President Saurrat, the same former colonies minister who had recognised the danger of Ho at the start of his career and had failed to win him over as hoped, had counselled him that Bao Dai represented a tradition and that de Lattre should support his efforts and build up the national army. De Lattre had also consulted with Admiral Decoux, who suggested various appointments with administrative experience in Indochina. On an operational level, de Lattre's main plans involved the formation of Groupe Mobiles as rapid reaction forces and acceleration of the build-out of the so-called de Lattre lines around the delta: a fortified chain of concrete blockhouses.

From the entry of de Lattre into the conflict following the debacle on RC4, increasing emphasis was put on three issues: Firstly, the defence of the Red delta and the eradication of communism within it; Secondly, training local forces to take on a greater role; And thirdly, exploiting the Cold War fears generated by the Korean War as a way to extract greater resources from the US.

De Lattre immediately ordered the construction of the de Lattre line, which was a series of concrete blockhouses around the triangular-shaped delta. Apart from defence and suppression in the delta, its primary focus was to stop the flow of rice to the Vietminh, for whom food supply was always a critical problem.

De Gaulle exits politics

In a bitterly divided France, de Gaulle's messianic calls for unity made a huge appeal and won him forty percent of the municipal elections. His expectation was to do even better in the 1951 general election.

On his tours round the country in the 1951 elections, his rallies were pale and shabby imitations of Nuremburg rallies. He was accompanied by convoys of Jeeps loaded with thugs in leather jackets and berets. Malraux was a warm-up act for de Gaulle's election rallies: 'Think of the soldiers of Valmy,' he blathered histrionically. 'Those were the days when the whole world gave herself to France!' At his rallies, the Cross of Lorraine was paraded with the reverence of a swastika. Despite his amateur falangism, de Gaulle was nevertheless not quite on the same level of psychopathic fantasy as other dictators, much as he would have liked to become one. In the event, his antics as well as a recovering economy led to him gathering only twenty percent of the vote.

In 1952, part of his parliamentary faction deserted him to support conservative Antoine Pinay for premier. 'I did not save France,' intoned de Gaulle with customary grandiloquence, 'to hand her over to this Monsieur Pinay.'[5] The drama queen of French history had exited politics again.

Pride would not allow him to stoop to anything other than absolute power, so he disengaged from his own party and retired to Colombey-les-deux Eglises. In splendid isolation and full pomp, he would wait for the call.

He craved total power. He covered his retreat with the usual lachrymose pomposity:

> *Perhaps it is my mission to represent the history of our country in a last upsurge to the lofty heights. Perhaps it is my destiny to have written the last pages in the book of our greatness.*[6]

In due course, his fascistic political appeal, which always has some traction in France, would be taken up by rabble-rousing Poujade and the UDCA, which counted Jean Marie Pen as a member. De Gaulle's memoirs accept no blame whatsoever for the Indochina catastrophe and he avoids mentioning his role in undermining French democracy by encouraging military insubordination.

Giáp's plans to swamp the French in their Red River bastion

Having cleared the French outposts from his north-western base area on the border with China and taken the major provincial city in the area, Lang Son, the strategic path was clear for Giáp's regular army to move down through the mountains and jungle to the edge of the Red River delta, which was essentially the heart of Tonkin.

Giáp enjoyed both the strategic initiative and the momentum of success. The French were isolated in a sea of jungle. It was time to swamp them. He could concentrate his forces in secret in the mountains and jungles of Tonkin, then strike at the thinly held rim of French forces defending the delta, bringing overwhelming numbers to bear against particular points before the French could react and bring up reserves. It would be difficult for the French to estimate whether an advance on a particular point was indeed the main attack or merely a diversion to screen the major effort from the enemy.

With the French in panic and Hanoi being evacuated of women and children, an offensive aimed at Hanoi was an obvious strategy to follow and one that was eventually approved by Mao, whose troops were smashing the Americans back from the Yalu River. However, Chinese sources, having claimed the victory of RC4, indicated that the Vietminh under Giáp were too inexperienced and advancing too quickly. As Giáp was now to suffer three successive defeats, this looks like the manipulation of history by PLA Generals Chen Geng and Wei Guoquing, according to sources. They wanted credit for the victories but not the defeats,[7] complaining, 'We had to agree with them [Giáp and Ho] soon after they presented their new plans.'[8]

Giáp's plan entailed a major tactical change. Vietminh regular forces could dominate in the forests and mountains even when the skies were clear enough for French aerial forces to support ground troops. Being able to concentrate greater numbers with superior jungle craft and numbers, the Vietminh would aim to overwhelm the French forces, who were tied to single roads and a vulnerable logistical trail. The French Army (a western-style army designed for formal warfare) was wedded to a heavy and inflexible logistical system but was short of air transport capability relative to its commitments. However, in the open plain the situation reversed. French asymmetric advantages in artillery and air power could devastate concentrations of the enemy moving in the open and destroy their supply system. Resting on the defensive in the delta and pulling in their outposts was the logical defensive strategy following the RC4 defeat.

As the French retreated into the Red delta, their supply lines became very short and, conversely, the Vietminh supply lines became long and tortuous. After the Battle of Vinh Ven, Major-General Trupnell of the US supply *Operation MAAG* was able to boast, 'Material was rushed from the docks of Haiphong to the battlefield of Vinh Ven.' Operating on interior lines while Giáp had to operate on exterior lines gave the French a distinct advantage in switching their reserves and supply chain from place to place at short notice. As for the air war, French aircraft would be within minutes of their bases so able to respond quickly to support roles as required, or they could loiter with intent over the battlefield., to attack targets of opportunity such as Vietminh troop formations, supply lines, or command posts.

The de Lattre lines

After the debacle of RC4, the arrival of the renowned General de Lattre soon restored order and morale to the FEC. Armed with plenipotentiary powers, he not only replaced Carpentier and Alessandri but also High Commissioner Pignon. All talk of abandoning Hanoi was quashed. Mainly basing himself in Hanoi rather than distant Saigon, unlike other French commanders he was close to the action and the troops in the front line of the threatened delta. On his first exit from Hanoi, he emphasised his commitment to holding Tonkin by announcing, 'I am leaving behind my wife.'[9] He ordered the acceleration of training and recruitment for indigenous units, who would replace French troops garrisoning the forts, so releasing elite troops for mobile and offensive actions.

From 1951, a typical fortification on the de Lattre lines was a rectangular or polygon concrete construction, depending on terrain and importance.[10] In a typical post, in 1953 120 riflemen of 1/24th RMTS with ten machine-guns and four mortars occupied a concrete fortification that defended a perimeter of 1,275m. Before de Lattre, bunkers and redoubts had been made of dry bricks in some places and wood and sandbags in remoter regions. The first emphasis on the build-out of the de Lattre line was along the Red delta's north side where attacks from the Vietminh were expected as they descended from the Bac Kan after the RC4 battle.

The most famous post was Ven Vi on the Day River, which repelled major attacks by several Vietminh regiments. It comprised five pill boxes and a central redoubt all of concrete. It disposed of eighteen machine-guns, and two turrets armed with 37mm cannons.

Defences along the north side of the Red delta were generally more solid than those on the south side because it was from the north that the main threat would come from the Vietminh. The lines were 378km long, defended by 1,200 blockhouses in 250 clusters of three to six each with two 105mm cannon in each. Canon sizes varied with the size and importance of the garrison. For close support and for immediate intervention, their presence could be vital, as when Corporal Martelli, firing the post's 57mm cannon, saved a retreating patrol of Senegalese tirailleurs. 'You deserve a drink!' exclaimed the Senegalese sergeant. 'Without your cannon it would have been the end for all of us.'[11] Each blockhouse had at least ten men to man machine-guns. They were surrounded by barbed wire and minefields. Information about the new defensive lines was given out by Tassigny de Lattre on 17 September 1951 at his first meeting in Washington.[12]

Bastions, however well-equipped and protected, were vulnerable to being overwhelmed in surprise attacks. What saved French positions from much greater losses and massacre of garrisons was the supporting fire of French 105mm firebases some 10km+ distant. Such 'firebases' – a term later coined by the Americans who used the exact same tactics – were established across the de Lattre lines to support clusters of bastions within their arc of fire. A firebase with a battery of four 105mm guns would, assuming a range of 10km, cover an area of 314 square kilometres ($A = \pi \times r2$). Killing zones were established around each fort with pre-set co-ordinates.

Such defences in 920 static posts held down 82,470 troops in January 1954 and huge amounts of supply, treasure, and armament that was rarely used. An example given in General Ely's 1955 Post-War Performance Review noted that in one district just two battalions of Vietminh in effect held down 7,000 troops within their radius of operations, and 100 military posts. They were largely undisturbed because the posts posed 'no harm'[13] or 'then one night the post falls like a gangrenous bone…' The French controlled more troops than Giáp, but they were on the strategic defensive. By 1954, Giáp had built a strategic strike-force of 60,000 regular VPA troops with substantial reserves. France's strategic offensive capacity only went beyond 20–30,000 for limited periods.

Giáp held the strategic initiative and, due to the terrain surrounding the Red delta, could concentrate his forces in secret. De Lattre understood exactly both the strategic problem and the solution. Borrowing from German

Kamphfgruppe concepts at the end of the Second World War, he created self-contained Hanoi-based GM (Groupe Mobiles), which included armour, artillery, engineers, medics, logistics and motorised infantry. Still thinly held the bastions had to delay Vietminh offensives until the GM arrived along radial lines of communication.

Three Vietminh divisions, 308th, 312th and 316th, were positioned in the Viet Bac region of northern Tonkin and one division, the 320th, was placed south of the delta in the Day River area. With the arrival of de Lattre, the well-briefed Giáp was under no illusions as to the quality of his opponent. At Vinh Ye, they would find themselves within a few kilometres of each other on the same battlefield. It was a very personal contest that might have come from a different era.

Skewered by a lance

In the early phases of the First World War in 1914, Jean Tassigny de Lattre was lucky to make it past his first experience of warfare.

The lieutenant, from the 12th Dragoons, had cut a dash as he charged forwards in an early skirmish with German Uhlans in 1914. His uniform of blue, with brass buttons, bright red trousers over long black boots, and a plumed cuirassier's helmet, looked little different to the cuirassiers commanded by Marshal Ney as they circled and sought to break into the British squares at Waterloo. Before being skewered by an Uhlan's lance, he had sabred three of the enemy cavalry. To remove the lance impaled deep in his chest, a comrade stamped on his upper torso then used both hands with full force to extract it. At this point, de Lattre was probably not contemplating a long soldiering career.

Recovering from the grievous lance wound, de Lattre would go on to fight a different type of war at Verdun where he was highly decorated for his actions in this battle of artillery and high explosives. Surviving the trenches, he served the rest of the war on the general staff and was marked out for a stellar career. He served in the Riff wars in Morocco, where he was wounded again, and he battled with distinction following the calamitous retreat of the French Army in the Second World War.

Commanding French troops in Germany at the war's end, he disobeyed orders and took Ulm and Stuttgart, whose capture had been allocated to the Americans. It was typical of the desperate French attempt to recover military honour to prove themselves, to show that they were relevant to winning the war. He joined with Montgomery, Eisenhower and Zhukov in Berlin in celebrating the allied victory, and was included in a famous group photograph of the war's three leading generals. De Lattre is shown smoking a cigarette. He would die of lung cancer.

Born into a poor noble family from the Vendée, a region steeped in royalism and anti-republican sentiments, he grew up in a rambling tumbledown manor house. His was the career of a d'Artagnon. From such a humble aristocratic background, the army offered honour, adventure and escape from an impoverished Vendée region with its rolling hills, barren soil and stone-built villages. It is still a poor province and was the last hold-out against republicanism after the revolution. A bedrock of Catholic conservative and monarchist beliefs, these traits stayed with him. He detested communism. Bedecked in pomp and circumstance, for which he earned the nickname 'le Roi Jean', his character was bounded by unbridled confidence, pomposity and arrogance that certainly matched his counterpart Giáp.

He was an imperious martinet who terrorised his officers. However, his confidence and swagger were infectious. Egocentric certainly, but he inspired his troops. De Lattre's ability straddled both tactical command and strategic operations at army level. He was also politically attuned to geopolitics. He would launch his fiercest verbal offensive on American policy-makers, using anti-communist rhetoric and charisma as if they were heavy artillery. Before accepting the post in Indochina, de Lattre demanded and received plenipotentiary powers, which allowed him free reign over domestic affairs. This power was used liberally to both court and strictly control the press. He even felt free to expel diplomats he disliked, such as Trevor Wilson, the British consul in Hanoi.

With US troops fighting for their lives against the Chinese in Korea, it was a message that was well received in Washington's powerful anti-communist lobby, where China was regarded as the new Satan-in-chief, taking a starring role in that drama previously played only by the USSR.

Like Juin and Revers before him, de Lattre understood that the only real hope to save Vietnam was large-scale intervention and support of the United States. The Korean War, which started on 25 June 1950, was France's great chance to save their empire. He injected great impetus to the raising and recruitment of French-officered Vietnamese units which, within a short space of time, became thirty percent of the total manpower.

Battle of Vĩnh Yên, 13–17 January 1951

Encouraged by success, Giáp and Ho decided to sweep the French into the Gulf of Tonkin. It made sense to exploit the RC4 victory after the French-panicked collapse in the north-east. But with de Lattre the panic had stopped. However, Giáp's supplies were rapidly building up from just 20 tons per month to 250 tons in 1952.[14] Giáp had also captured copious quantities from the French in Lang Son and on the battlefield. The most obvious place for an attack would be on the north side of the delta, closer to the Chinese bases. Giáp would strike from a place that offered the most mountain and jungle cover in proximity to the lowland and tree-sparse Red River delta area. The French awaited the attack, which was bound to come; but from where? French patrols on the edge of the jungle were the forward antennae to pick up movement.

These mountains could be infiltrated by large forces, with the attack being sprung by surprise. The most obvious line of attack would be the RC3 descending on the nearest line of attack to the north of Hanoi, but another possible venue for a major attack to break into the Red River delta and smash into Hanoi was at Vĩnh Yên, where a pointed spur of hills (the Tam Dao massif) and jungle swept down from northern Tonkin hills. The launch point for an attack from jungle cover would be just 15km from Vĩnh Yên, which was 30km from Hanoi.

General Salan noted in his memoirs that the Vĩnh Yên command picked up some unusual signals when 'villagers were seen herding their buffaloes into the foothills of the Tam Dao massif and then many Vietminh soldiers were seen assembling in the area.'[15]

Vĩnh Yên seemed to be the place of attack, but was it a typical Giáp feint? GM3, which consisted of many North African troops, was already in place. Salan sent them over to the west of Vĩnh Yên to meet the first column of Vietminh, which was descending down the RP12 from Bao Chuc to Dong Dao to the west of Vĩnh Yên.

For the first time the Vietminh would be fighting in the open and 30,000 front-line soldiers of the new army, supported by the efforts of 60,000 porters who would bring down 5,000 tons of supplies, would test their metal in open array against the French main army.

Another diversionary attack was made on the night of the 12th, the day before the main offensive. Attacks from regional forces to the north of Nam Dinh would attack RN1 and link up with 304th Division.

Giáp launched his main feint attack with the 308th Division to the left of the French positions at Vĩnh Yên, which worked to the extent that a French column, Group Mobile 3, became ensnared in an ambush launched by elements of the 312th Division. 'Suffering severe losses,' they were only with difficultly able to disengage after several days of hardship. The French lost a whole battalion in this fight, some 550 men who had advanced against the initial threat against Cam Trach on the RP12 on 13 January. They were outflanked and cut off by rapidly moving Vietminh infantry advancing a further 5km down the RP12 to attack Vĩnh Yên directly.

Following this gambit, Giáp struck in the centre of the French position at Vĩnh Yên, hoping to draw French reserves into a sack that could be sealed off. In a rolling and staggered offensive west to east, Giáp's real punch was made further to the east of Vĩnh Yên. This angle of attack brought the Vietminh closer to Hanoi, which was the key element of Giáp's plan to cut off French forces by interposing the main Vietminh forces between Vĩnh Yên and Hanoi, thus blocking French lines of retreat, supply lines and passage over the Red River at Huong Canh. To stop this dangerous flanking movement, the battle now moved to the series of low hills east of Vĩnh Yên.

Reacting quickly, de Lattre abandoned the plush high command centres in Hanoi and Saigon with their large map rooms, banks of telephones, red-tabbed staff officers, fine luncheon rooms, and pretty secretaries. He flew into the battle zone in a little Morane light aeroplane.

Just a few kilometres from the front, de Lattre took personal tactical command at Vĩnh Yên, petulantly pushing Salan aside amidst the reeling cannon and punching noise of heavy mortars. Giáp was also in tactical command just a few kilometres to the north. At Vĩnh Yên, in the crisis of battle, de Lattre is shown in a laudatory newsreel consulting closely with Salan over a map laid out on the ground. In another scene he is conferring with GM commander Colonel de Castries. Roi Jean wanted to see the battlefield, which he did by climbing up a ladder to one of the look-out towers on his fortification line. He decided to quiz his colonels directly. Meeting with Colonel Redon, he said, 'So, Redon, this incident is not yet finished.'

Redon, whose GM had been badly cut up, gushed with melodramatic self-pity. 'We will die at Vĩnh Yên if necessary, but we will not quit our post.'

De Lattre was told the facts of the dire situation amidst a scene of some chaos as wounded men streamed back from the front. De Lattre, who was in a foul mood, closed his eyes and took Salan by the arm saying, 'We need a general here.'

To which Salan replied, 'Mon general, have confidence believe me. Giáp has lost this game by failing to exploit the situation on day one.'[16] However, an estimated eighteen Vietminh battalions were still attacking.

De Lattre's exhausted troops were about to be overwhelmed but he held off committing his reserves because he was concerned that this was a diversion. So, when de Lattre realised that the attack east of Vĩnh Yên was the main one and not a diversion, he committed his reserves. 'I am going to send all of my mobile groups.'[17] It was a considerable risk because he could not be completely sure that Giáp's attacks were not a strategic diversion from the one he had previously expected against Hanoi directly from the north on the RC3. To add to the confusion, a Vietminh force erupted from the jungles around the Ba Vi Mountain range to the south-west. In a feigned strategic pincer movement, they attacked the town of Son Tay along RC21 some 20km south-west from Vĩnh Yên.

Checked at Vĩnh Yên, Giáp shifted to the east on 15 January and the night of the 16th, throwing his forces against the key town of Huong Canh, which controlled the Ca Lo River crossing and direct access to Hanoi along the RC2 as well as the hill line that sits above the RC2. This enabled them to cut off the retreat of the French forces at Vĩnh Yên. If the hill line and Huong Canh River crossing were lost, the French forces between Vĩnh Yên and Huong Canh would be bottled up with no escape route. Cut off and short of supplies, the plan was that they would be swamped by superior forces. Giáp's tactics would normally have won under terms of firepower equality, but he was operating in the open without heavy artillery cover, with no air force and no tanks or armoured vehicles. He was also facing Salan and de Lattre, whose decisive reactions and early warning intelligence set-up had foiled Giáp's strategic and tactical plan.

Discovering that no fighter bombers had been sent in to support his troops, de Lattre raged at those around him, first picking on a young air force officer. Having discovered that he had been alone at Vĩnh Yên for one week he exploded:

> *…and you have been* alone *guiding the fighter bombers. You are an even bigger idiot than I thought. Who are the idiots who chose you to be sent here?* (Author's emphasis)

Without waiting for a reply, de Lattre addressed Salan, his preferred victim. De Lattre discovered that an instruction had indeed gone out the day before for more air force liaison officers, but that did not save Salan's blushes: 'But you weren't obeyed,' snapped de Lattre. 'And you tolerate that! Your Hanoi HQ offices are full of Johnny-idles who don't do anything.'[18]

GM3 was furthest over to the east having been sent there by Salan after the first inklings of the attack and GMs 1 and 2 were ordered up from reserve to attack the communists from the east. They drove to the battle front west from Hanoi along RC2, which came to resemble Indochina's *voie sacre* (of Verdun). The hills to the east of Vĩnh Yên were re-taken but Giáp counter-attacked using Chinese mass attack tactics and recovered them. French forces attacked again and supported by artillery and aeroplanes wreaked havoc on exposed Vietminh columns as they swarmed over treeless hills.

Napalm was widely deployed. Its effects were devastating to astonished Vietminh troops out in the open. At Vĩnh Yên, Ngo Van Chieu:

> *…hell was brought by a strange looking egg…a great ball of fire leapt out hundreds of metres in all directions, reaping havoc and terror in the ranks of the soldiers. Under this deluge of fire that spread out and consumes everything in its path the troops could not hold. The flames leapt up all around, and were*

> *accompanied by machine-guns, mortars, and artillery which in a matter of minutes turned a small forest into a burning tomb.*[19]

A Vietminh commander recounted:

> *Fire storms descended from the sky. Everyone felt the great heat, suffocating and frantically trying to escape, but only a few could escape. That is the napalm bomb.*[20]

Ngo Van Chieu described his troops' reaction 'as an instant, an immense wall of fire running for hundreds of metres terrorised my men.'[21] Van Chieu's men ran for their lives. 'The French infantry now attacks, we can hear their screams.' He instructed the reserve platoon to 'try to delay the French' while he rallied his men behind a hill. He shouted orders 'but who listens to me?'

Napalm was a petro-jelly that burned for longer than gasoline at extremely high temperatures and its properties included 'clinging' to its target, which made it a fearsome anti-personnel weapon. Some Moroccans who were too far forward were also caught. Napalm was dropped in tumbling oval canisters that upon bursting would flow into the hollows, bunkers and trenches of Vietminh infantry, splashing and boring relentless phosphorescent fingers of death through the bodies of the enemy.

French strongpoints in the hills were taken and re-taken in counter-attacks. The French held Hill 201, which clung on after reinforcement by GM2, but lost Hill 101 when the ammunition ran out. However, the flanking hill to the south, Point 157, was maintained with the help of GM3. Several days of heavy fighting followed, including a final mass-attack by Vietminh infantry in Chinese-style human waves on 16 and 17 January. When three battalions of French reinforcements came up, Giáp was forced to withdraw his troops and abandon attempts to smash through the de Lattre line. They quickly disappeared under the jungle canopy.

De Lattre was conscious that this napalm terror weapon was controversial for the sheer horror of its effect. 'This war in Indochina is a real war – which we have to win with all means possible.'[22]

A key element in the victory was de Lattre's deployment of hard-hitting elite Groupe Mobiles as well as adept use of the increasingly important Dinassaut riverine flotillas, which speedily delivered thirty percent of the reinforcements, as well as adding firepower.

Giáp withdrew, having suffered as many as 10,000–15,000 casualties. That casualties were high is a matter of logic. If infantry attack *en masse* against defensive positions in open field without the benefit of thick forest canopy and mountains, or without air cover, artillery or tanks, then the result will be carnage. Two front-line Vietminh divisions had been crippled and would need to be rebuilt in the back areas. However, replacements flowed in from the training camps on the Chinese border and the redoubtable 308th and 312th would soon be ready for another offensive.

General Yves Gras noted that the French won because:

> *...artillery and air power added considerable firepower...on the terrain of Vĩnh Yên a favourable combination of material, organisation of logistics and proximity to their bases.*[23]

In open conventional warfare, the French had scored a major victory against far larger numbers.

Meanwhile, de Lattre bathed in the glow of victory quoting expansively at a press conference the number of Viets killed, 6,000, and 10,000 wounded. Bodard wrote laconically: 'After all, you cannot have a victory without lots of dead.'[24] 'Telegrams of congratulations by the kilo' poured in from around the globe, including from John Foster Dulles, secretary of state, the Pentagon, and President Eisenhower.

De Lattre also sought to rally the French nation behind the struggle in Indochina. In front of the Committee of National Defence on 17 March 1951, he declared: 'If we can hold Indochina, we will remain a great power. If on the contrary we fail we will become the sick man of the second half of the twentieth century.'[25]

Moving on from France, he flew to the United States to repeat the message of victory, and to gather in more pledges of arms, munitions and money. He would play strongly on the anti-communist message to dispel fears regarding France's imperialist ambitions – quite the opposite message that he had conveyed in Paris. Following the opening of the Korean conflict, France and America were allies in the same anti-communist war.

Battle of Mao Khé, 23–29 March 1951

The entire supply and logistics of French Tonkin depended on Haiphong. Once again Giáp chose a line of attack that offered a covered approach from the north along the Dong Tieu massif whose forest fringe was very close to the chosen target of attack. Unlike Vĩnh Yên, French logistical access to the battlefield would be limited. On this occasion too, Giáp prepared by launching preliminary and diversionary attacks using his relatively untested 304th and 320th Divisions to the south of the delta on the Day River axis.

After the victory at Vĩnh Yên the French high command knew that the game was not over and that Giáp would strike again. First thoughts were that Giáp would move 20km to the west at Viet Tri on the convergence of the Red and Black Rivers. Troops were shifted accordingly. But de Lattre was wary of feints because he already understood Giáp's method. He asked General Salan to find out the real direction of attack. Salan sent out air patrols but nothing turned up. The jungle canopies of the Bac Kan retained their secrets. Likewise, when Salan ordered his intelligence team *ancienne antenne du S.R.I.* (old antennae) to send out jungle patrols they drew a blank. However, on the 13th and 14th there were intercept indications that 'the main body of the VPA was moving: But where?' Suddenly Salan's team were brandishing decoded telegrams. 'It's to the east.' The 308th was making a move east in the direction of Massif du Dong Trieu and an element of the 312th Division had appeared at Luc Nam.[26]

Vietnamese officialdom responsible for the northern delta confirmed the intelligence and on the air waves there was increased enemy 'chatter'. The French high command was aware that 'Giáp was going to attack us at what he considered our weak point.'[27] With the intelligence in hand, Salan ordered his command to use 'every means, lorries, boats, to carry everything to Mao Khé.'

Salan recounted how, in their search for intelligence before the Mao Khé battle, 'we took prisoner the SR (intelligence) leader of Battalion 36 of the 308th Division just days ago…he cut off his own tongue to prevent himself from speaking.'[28] Such was the fanatical single mindedness that faced the French attempt to retain its colony.

Mao Khé was a small town on de Lattre's northern defensive ring. Giáp's attack here was well chosen because it was located just 30km north-north-west of Haiphong. If Haiphong were to fall, so would French Tonkin, because the port was the only port of entry and the main depot for the FEC. Mao Khé was also hard to reinforce because the RF18 runs along the forest line, so it was easy to cut and prevent reinforcements moving along it. Groupe Mobiles sent out from Hanoi could easily be stopped and ambushed *en route* and troops coming from Hongay to the east from the coast would also be cut off by Vietminh emerging from the adjacent jungle. The RC5 between Hanoi and Haiphong ran parallel to RF18, some 15km distant along its length but with no lateral connecting roads, and criss-crossed by muddy inlets and waterways, a miasma more or less impassable to heavily laden bodies of troops let alone tanks or trucks. Mao Khé was an isolated post that would have little chance to defend itself against the might of the 312th Division. If the Vietminh were to fully establish themselves in the area of Mao Khé, they would soon be acquiring a base for infiltration attacks on the key RC5 highway running between Hanoi and Haiphong.

Mao Khé was chosen for attack because it was the nearest town along the north side of the delta that could offer a direct approach to Haiphong. Go further west and any eruption against a defensive point would only bring an attacker against the wide estuary of the Da Bac River, where the French Navy ruled. What Giáp probably did not realise was that the estuaries of the Bach

Dong and Da Song Dac had enough draught at 5.2m to host a light cruiser and destroyers, which enabled the French Navy to offer fire support to Mao Khé's defensive positions. If Giáp had attacked further west, he would have run up against the heavily defended Hanoi section of the line. Mao Khé, which was only defended by 400 troops, was therefore the perfect place to attack and, once again, tactical surprise was achieved due to the forest canopy. To deflect the attention of the French, the 304th and 320th Divisions were launched at the south of the Red delta. But with their intelligence reports in hand, the French were not for a moment deceived.

Attacking against the RP18 on the 23rd, the French outposts in the low foothills in front of the jungle were overrun in a ferocious night attack by the 312th and 316th Divisions. To the west of Mao Khé, fortified outposts in front of the de Lattre lines, at Bai Tho and Ben Tram adjacent to the RF18, were taken and Hoang Xa on the road itself was attacked. To the east, various hamlets were attacked and the important town of Yen Lap cut off from Hongay.

One outpost where the attack failed was the coal mine 3km north of the town, which was defended by a French-officered local Vietnamese company. This company was led by Lieutenant Toan, a rare example of a St Cyr-trained Vietnamese officer whose troops came entirely from the north-eastern Tho tribe. Ironically this tribe had been mostly won over by Ho Chi Minh and the Vietminh who used Tho territory as a base. The Tho troops at Mao Khé had an incentive to fight because capture would probably have meant execution as traitors. Lieutenant Nhgiem Xuan Toan was:

> *...a huge man, his head rested between enormous shoulders, a large face between the prominent pitiless eyes like black stones and, when he wished it, a wide gay smile.*[29]

Partly Chinese, Toan came from a distinguished Hue family, while his grandfather had been governor of Lang Son. Coincidently he had also been a translator attached to General Salan. His father was a famed poet and his uncle the first Baron of Annam. He had attended the elite Lycée Saurat in Hanoi and military school at Saint Cyr in Paris.

Vietminh troops worked their way through the mine diggings and channels to move close to Lieutenant Toan's military post. They launched their attack at 1 am on the 23rd, but Toan's men hung on even though two French NCOs were killed and Toan himself wounded. Attacks were also made along RP18 to the east to cut off the road and reinforcements that might be filtered in from the French-controlled seaboard. However, reinforcements were delivered in LSSLs, LCMs and LCTs, which could reach Ha Chieu and Mao Khé just a few hundred metres from the main centre of fighting at Mao Khé. As hordes of Vietminh emerged from the jungles during the day of the 23rd, and subsequent days, a Morane spotter plane circled above them directing fire from the naval flotilla anchored a few kilometres away. Inland, the Vietminh stepped up diversionary attacks on the Hanoi-Haiphong highway and destroyed the freshwater reservoir serving Haiphong.

Amazingly, Toan's small command of ninety-five indigenous Tho auxiliaries held on for four days and did not retreat on their main defences at Mao Khé until the evening of the 27th, after being subject to heavy shellfire. In the meantime, the weight of the 312th Division attack had washed round them, focusing on the main defences at Mao Khé, which held out around the fortified church. Mao Khé itself was defended by about 300 troops comprising a Moroccan armoured car unit, a Senegalese infantry company, and another contingent of Tho partisans.[30] Fifteen kilometres further to the east, Vietminh attacks captured the village of Bi Chou, so closing off any hope of relief along RP18 from Hongay on the coast, although the fortified post at Uong Bi 5km to the east held.

By-passing the mines, the 312th smashed into the fortified village of Mao Khé with mass attacks supported by 75mm and mortar-fire. The centre of the battle focused on the Catholic church surrounded by bunkers and pierced by loopholes. In fierce close combat, the Vietminh suffered 400 dead and the colonial troops 200 casualties, including forty dead around the collapsed wreckage of the church. Armoured cars were destroyed and buried in rubble. Cannon-fire from the batteries at Dong Trieu had saved the Mao Khé bastion, but more attacks followed. However, General Salan singled out the Tho partisans round the church for special praise, noting that they 'fought with the energy of the damned.'[31]

Unsure as to the definite point of attack, de Lattre cautiously responded by sending in parachutists of the 6th BPC. Legionnaires were also sent by road having forced their way down the RF18, which was subject to attack. As the Vietminh continued their advance from the hills their attack was suddenly hit by a deluge of naval gunfire from the cruiser *Daguay Touin* with its massive 8x155mm guns. Included in the flotilla was the destroyer *Savorgnan de Brazza*, which added to the mayhem with its 3 x 136mm guns, 4 x 37mm guns, and a landing-craft fleet with their 76mm guns. Admiral Ortoli had been requested to move his flotilla up in support by General Salan as soon as the intelligence reports indicated a move on the RP18 in Mao Khé.

To the west at the Dong Trieu bastion, there was a firebase with twenty 105mm cannon that provided a curtain of fire around the beleaguered outposts from 8km away. Salvoes of deadly naval and army heavy artillery held the Vietminh at bay. Meanwhile the French Air Force blasted Vietminh base areas on the edge of the jungle with napalm.

Within a few days the town itself was well defended by the paratroopers, local militia and a platoon of armoured cars. Shaken by the resistance, Giáp reorganised and consolidated his troops for an all-out assault, which began early on the 27th and lasted a full twenty-four hours. On the 28th, de Lattre, who had been constantly in contact by radio from Paris, landed at Haiphong and resumed operational command from his deputy Salan. Further heavy attacks were made in the early hours of the 28th and on the night of the 29th.

Vietminh troops from the 316th Division attacked in waves, but once again close air support, artillery and naval gunfire swept the enemy from the field. Further attacks spread out to the west of Mao Khé over the following days, but the battle was nearly over. Giáp tried to counter the artillery and logistical support for Mao Khé by trying to take the village on the other side of the Son Bac narrows by infiltrating over the RP18 to attack Ha Chieu on 5 April. On the same night, attacks were made on Dong Tieu, the key town and bastion to the west of Mao Khé, which was the artillery base pouring shells into the Vietminh around Mao Khé. If Dong Trieu fell, Mao Khé would be indefensible. However, these attacks were all repelled although attacks in the Dong Trieu sector continued until early April.

Giáp retreated on 6 April, leaving 1,200 dead on the battlefield, according to General Salan, with estimates of 2,000 wounded.[32] However, many more dead were probably removed by the Vietminh or died in back area hospitals.

The attack had been foiled by unexpected resistance, but the essential mistake had been to underestimate the ability of the French Navy to quickly bring in huge fire support and reinforcements up the Da Bac River. It was a capability lightly dismissed by Ho when visiting the cruiser *Jeanne d'Arc* in 1946.

Defeated again, Giáp's reputation must have suffered but no doubt Ho, the Chinese adviser, and the party leaders had been closely involved in the decision-making. Nevertheless, the Vietminh retained the initiative. The regular army had been bloodied and trained by experience and valuable lessons had been learnt. Giáp the autodidact would study the lessons closely.

De Lattre had another victory. He celebrated by making a trip in his Morane to congratulate the troops. On return, he ordered the pilot to fly low over the jungle next to the RF18. He brusquely ordered the terrified pilot to fly for one and half hours at extremely low altitude over the jungle canopy, which was smashed in places by artillery or burnt by napalm. But of the Vietminh he saw nothing. Giáp was gone. On his return to Hanoi, de Lattre made a great show of visiting Lieutenant Toan's hospital bed and awarding him the *Legion d'Honneur*.

For Lucien Bodard, this battle showed the determination of the Vietminh. It was the moment when he realised that attrition would be the Vietminh's method of war: lost battles were just part of the process.

Battle of the Day River, 29 May–18 June 1951

It took several months for Giáp to change the battle front to the south of the delta. There was a logistical buildup behind the shelter of the idyllic Khast mountains at the extremities of the Red delta furthest from Giáp's northern supply bases. Supplies had to skirt the French defensive ring and the ever-watchful air force that patrolled the rivers. It meant riverine movement at night and superb camouflage during the day. A double bluff, the French would not expect attacks from a quarter so distant to the Chinese supply bases, which involved several hundred kilometres of extra tramping over difficult terrain. The logistics feat was considerable. Giáp had studied the reasons for losing at Vĩnh Yên and Mao Khê. This time every tactical device would be exploited to mitigating French advantages in firepower and mobility.

On the south-west side of the delta some 50 miles south of Hanoi there is a long Khast mountain range running 23km in parallel with the Day River just 3km distant. Jagged sharp edge limestone crags contain myriad caves and cavities created by water seepage over centuries, which provided excellent storage places for food and munitions. Waterways and channels cut through the emerald green of paddy producing its second or third rice crop made this one of the most beautiful battlefields in history. The Khast mountains (a UNESCO heritage region) to the west of Ninh Binh, which would be the fulcrum of the offensive, are like islands of stone in a vast green Zen garden with silvery winding channels. It would be excellent cover as an assembly area for the 304th and 320th Divisions.

While the dry season remained, Giáp used the opportunity to bring round supplies from the north and store them in caves in the Khasts close to the Day River as well as sending the ubiquitous 308th as an additional reserve. The river towns of Binh Dinh, Phu Ly and Phat Diem would be the focal point for attacks that would be more spread out than previously, the three focal points being some 35 and 10km apart. Giáp's three divisions, 304th, 308th and 320th, would each take a target. Dispersed attacks would lessen the target for French artillery and aircraft. The main objective was the Catholic enclave of Phat Diem and neighbouring Biu Chu, which the communists decided to crush in revenge for their failure to make any inroads in this region.

Ho's wooing of the Catholics had failed despite their fiercely nationalist agenda. As in the south, it was time for armed terror to smash a rival organisation to a communist party that would abide no competitors. So Giáp's operation had both military and political objectives. The Catholic diocese was ruled by 54-year-old former Franciscan monk Bishop Tu Huu Le, and chubby and cheerful Bishop Pham Ngoc Chi, whose combined lands encompassed 2,600,000 people from which they organised 5,800 militia and a regular force,

General Mobile Autonome, of 1,700. Only a quarter of the population was Catholic, the rest Buddhist.[33] With only a third of the troops armed, this percentage increased sharply as French aid increased. A convinced nationalist, Bishop Tu Huu Le had at first sided with the communists, even becoming supreme counsellor to Ho Chi Minh in 1945. Tu Huu Le claimed:

> *...being supreme counsellor to Ho Chi Minh was only an expedient. I realised from the first that he was communist, but I used to tell him if you are a nationalist, I am for you and your government, but if you are a communist I am against you.*

When ruthless communist duplicity became apparent, he changed sides and supported Emperor Bao Dai and his Catholic empress. The bishop's troops' flag and cap badge consisted of a mitre and cross keys.

Giáp also planned for troops to advance into Thai Binh province to consolidate their hold on the region to the south-east of Hanoi. The area on the south-west of the delta is flat paddy. In the early monsoon season, the water looks like sheets of plate-glass framed by dikes. Intersected by channels, the area would not be easy for movement or for tanks, which would be restricted to roads, of which there were few. Moreover, the low cloud and mist at this time of year would reduce France's fighter-bomber advantages. Giáp was hoping that all these factors would help support a conventional military attack. The region was the furthest from Hanoi in the delta area and Giáp must have been hoping that the GMs and artillery would be slow to come down from Hanoi; a journey for an armoured column of about eight to twelve hours (it would take about two and a half to three hours today). Vietminh units in the delta's interior were positioned to interdict French reinforcements. Given that the GM would not be committed before the true focal point of the attack was clear, there could be a considerable delay before they arrived and they were to be slowed down further by local ambushes, by which time Giáp hoped to have taken his objectives.

Another tactical variation for Giáp was his involvement of Vietminh regional units within the delta to rise up and attack the French from the rear. Their main mission would be to block reinforcements from reaching the strongpoints that were under attack. Giáp had organised the Vietminh throughout Vietnam at various levels of operational capacity. There were local forces based in villages and, since 1949, there were regional forces available for wider reaching operations. Local forces would tend to operate at night. This effectively meant that the French only controlled the roads and the countryside in daylight. At night, the Vietminh irregular forces would pick off stragglers on the roads, or attack French outposts, or blow up unprotected facilities. In addition to these irregulars, Giáp also infiltrated into the delta the 64th Regiment of the 320th Division, which reinforced the recently amalgamated regional force named the

42nd Independent Infantry. They would block French reinforcement at choke points on the road from Hanoi to the strongpoints on the de Lattre line.

Attacks from regional forces to the north of Nam Dinh would focus on RN1 to the north of Phu Ly and link up with 304th Division. Other units would operate from base areas in the Thai Binh and Hung Yen area. The attack on Nam Dinh aimed to hold down GM1, which was based there (the Groupement Mobile Nord Africain because of its Algerian composition, plus the 64th West African artillery). In the event, the Vietminh regional units performed poorly, failing to hamper GM1's movement to re-take Ninh Binh and reinforce the Catholic militia. The problem was that the terrain was flat and open, so ambushing the heavily armed and armoured French forces was very difficult. In the open, Vietminh advantages disappeared. Moreover, the local and regional troops lacked training or sufficient infantry support weapons such as mortars or light-machine-guns.

After a feint attack by the 312th in the north-west of the delta, the offensive started against the towns of Phu Ly, Ninh Bin, and Phat Diem, a cathedral city in a strong Catholic area. Its loss would be a blow to one of the main French supporting areas. There was a failure of intelligence because General Salan admitted:

> *...in Hanoi our intelligence functioned badly, there was total surprise as the battle lit up across the broad front of the Day River...suddenly some of our posts despite the efforts of the Dinassauts, were overrun.*[34]

Vietminh crack Divisions 304 and 308 slammed into the centre of the French defence lines at Phu Ly and Ninh Bin respectively. Serious losses were sustained and an entire marine commando unit was destroyed.

De Lattre was not impressed by the diversionary attack on the north-west side of the delta made by the 312th, who then moved on up the Red River valley to threaten an important French base in T'ai country, the city of Nghia Lo. De Lattre would not be completely drawn out, but to counter the threat to the T'ai Hills he did have to throw in three of his elite parachute battalions out of the nine available to him in reserve. This may have looked like a straw in the wind, but Giáp was actually beginning to develop a new strategy of indirect warfare aimed at the French allies in the T'ai Hills and, more importantly, the associated state of the kingdom of Lao beyond them.

The battle started with assaults against Phu Ly and Ninh Binh. Diversionary and strong attacks in themselves, they were followed by assaults on the main target at Phat Diem. Various lodgements were made on the north bank of the river, but ferocious defence kept the enemy at bay. In fierce fighting at Ninh Binh on the evening of 29 May, de Lattre's only son was killed on the first day of fighting. His unit was under orders from the general to hold at all costs until the GM arrived. He and two comrades mounted the 98m-high Nui Ninh Binh, one of the rocky Khast crags that are dotted along the Day River, to defend this imposing position against the expected Vietminh attack. To reduce the impact of French artillery still more, Vietminh elite regular units attacked in force across the river at night, supported by heavy mortar-fire. Bernard de Lattre, the commander's son, a tall lanky soldier, was killed instantly by a mortar round, pierced through eight times. A French riverine flotilla moored in the area also came under heavy attack. It survived, but only nineteen out of eighty marines and sailors were left alive at the end of the day. The next day the Algerians of GM1 counter-attacked with an armoured squadron of the 1st Chasseurs a Cheval, recaptured the crag, and recovered de Lattre's son's body. De Lattre, who doted on Bernard with fierce affection, was devastated by the news of his death. Recognising at once the import when an ashen faced subordinate burst into a conference, the aghast general with sudden terrible premonition blurted out, '*Bernhard est mort!*' 'Bernard is dead!' His morbid and melodramatic reaction to his son's death must surely have been enhanced by the guilty knowledge that he had posted Bernard from Hanoi to the Vietnamese unit in a remote spot, to remove him from the affections of a beautiful but 'unsuitable' Vietnamese, a former consort of Bao Dai. No doubt there was a fear of Vietminh intelligence infiltration because honey traps were commonly used by the communists.

Giáp's gambit at the Day River started to fail for various reasons. Decisive use was made of French river flotillas. They forced their way along the Day River under heavy fire from both banks of the river. River monitors from Dinassaut flotillas with heavy and light-machine-guns, 40mm cannon and with their substantial combined firepower of heavy and medium machine-guns in armoured turrets or encasements, plus 3-inch cannon, blasted their way through. They were able to disrupt and punish the Vietminh badly. Sampans, other wooden boats, canoes and rafts on which Vietminh logistics relied, were blown out of the water. Members of the Vietminh infantry were left stranded and short of supplies on the east bank of the Day River. It was the decisive moment in the battle. Chinese adviser Tain Dabang recalled:

> *French firepower from these gunboats was very strong and accurate. They not only stopped our attacks against the French defensive positions but also inflicted heavy casualties on the Vietnamese troops.*[35]

Even more important, with VPA units straddled across two sides of the Day River, French riverine naval units (the Dinassaut) were able to disrupt communications, reinforcements and resupplies.

At To Phu Ly, the Vietminh crossed the river, destroyed a bridge and set-up ambushes for the expected French counter-attack. GM4, 2nd BPC (colonial paratroopers) and a VNA battalion descended from Hanoi and swatted off the ambushes. South-east of Ninh Binh, in an area difficult to access by road, the French dropped 7th BPC, who severely damaged a Vietminh battalion as they advanced south to attack Phat Diem.

The Vietminh found themselves both fractured and outgunned. Vietminh forces placed in the delta behind the French lines proved much less effective than expected in holding up French road-bound GMs, and logistical and reinforcement capacity, while a surprise factor was the solid performance of the Huu Tu Le and Pham Ngoc Chi's Catholic militias.

As the initial thrusts of the Vietminh were parried and destroyed, Giáp launched the 320th Division at Phat Diem to the south of the Day River line on 5 June. It was Giáp's last gambit in the battle. They were fended off by the bishop's militia backed up by French troops and, as matters became desperate, French reinforcements arrived by LCM transporter.

De Lattre was not impeded in his reinforcement plans. His logistics hub at Nam Dinh, at a communications crossroads, was 20km behind the battlefront. From here along a radial road network, de Lattre fed in supplies and reinforcements from his elite mobile groups to blunt the main points of attack. Other reinforcements came in with the flotillas or down the main highway from Hanoi. The battle dribbled on but petered out finally on the 18th. The Vietminh lost around 2,000 dead and about 10,000 further casualties. Cut off on the east bank, 1,000 Vietminh were taken prisoner.

As the battle closed, the Vietminh became very short of all sorts of supplies and their 40,000 porters could not keep up or ran short of food. Moreover, French riverine flotillas along the Day River were blasting the Vietminh supply vessels out of the water. Senior Chinese adviser Luo Guibo reported urgently to Beijing on 17 June, the 18th and the 22nd that the 'troops are starving'.[36] Beijing responded quickly by sending 1,800 tons before the end of June, but it was too late to save Giáp from defeat.

After his son's death, de Lattre immersed himself in self-pity. He lamented to Salan, 'I came to Indochina to protect youth…I was not even capable of protecting my own child.'[37] Turning to pomp he arranged a requiem mass at the cathedral in Saigon with required attendance from all senior officials. He ostentatiously wore a black armband for weeks. He maintained the armband during his US trip. It was a potent message to take to America along with his anti-communist rhetoric. 'I failed you, I failed to protect him,' he wrote to his wife. However, from the point of view of many of his officers, the ostentatious and self-indulgent displays of grief and self-pity were perhaps a little misplaced for an army commander in the context of the many thousands, indeed tens of thousands, of other mortalities since 1945.

Despite the victories and the hard-earned stabilisation of the Tonkin military situation, Giáp still held the initiative and, as de Lattre's deputy General Raoul Salan noted in his memoirs, 'This was terrible because we knew that thanks to increasing Chinese aid, the Vietminh reforged its units and started to create new ones.'[38]

The French were also forging new units, rapidly building up the Vietnamese National Army, equipping them with a deluge of American supplies. For de Lattre, this was a vital development in the drive to hold back the communist advances and to reduce reliance on overstretched French units. Elite units could be relieved from guard duty to build up the mobile reserves. He also toured educational establishments to encourage Vietnam's youth to fight for their freedom. Attending a prizegiving event at the Lycée Chasseloup-Laubat, de Lattre intoned:

> *...if you are patriots fight for your country, because this war is your war...it is in fidelity to the idea represented by S.M. Bao Dai that you can find your truth...I believe that Vietnam will be saved by you!*[39]

The problem was that Bao Dai, the louche playboy and French puppet, had such limited traction in the national psyche. A patriotic motive to fight was lacking and there was a natural reluctance to give their lives in support of a corrupt playboy and Vietnamese national administration.

Political consequences of failure and trouble in the party

The communist offensives of 1951 were an abject fiasco. Their attempt to drive out the French invader, break into the delta and capture Hanoi had failed. Heavy casualties of about 35,000 had badly damaged Giáp's elite divisions. In the DRV zone, the increasingly ugly face of communism within the Vietminh movement, its excessive propaganda and ideology, its carelessness with people's lives, its martinet discipline, and oppression of non-communist groups and individuals, was taking its toll on communist popularity. Moreover, the party was experiencing bitter internecine warfare between factions with the issue of class background being used to denigrate party rivals. Defeat only accelerated the internal strife. Maoist thoughts on class war pushed by Chinese advisers was beginning to have a poisonous effect on the broad front Vietminh coalition.

Both Giáp and Ho were to come under attack from leftist ideologues on account of their middle-class-landowner and Mandarin backgrounds. Revealing testimony as to long-running internal strife was given by Hoang Huu Quynh – educated in the Moscow technical institute – who later defected:

> *...in 1947 or 48 there was a conflict in the resistance between the intellectual and proletarian factions. In Quang Ngai south of Hue they even murdered each other and it was during this period that my father was assassinated.*[40]

During this period the classification of people began in earnest. It was a signal for the increasingly sharp ideological developments in the communist-controlled Vietminh as the sham of the Vietminh's broad nationalist coalition was exposed. Nguyễn van Hun:

> *I was twenty-eight years old when I received my draft notice. My father had been a deputy village head under the French regime, so I was classified as a 'middle farmer element'. This was an undesirable classification and of course my father had worked with the French.*[41]

Increasingly such classifications would lead to active discrimination, persecution and eventually to murder in many cases. Van Hun's story is typical. As Chinese influence increased so did the ideological and factional struggle under the guise of class war.

Ever since the nineteenth century there had been active discrimination and pogroms against the Catholic minority. Buddhists also began to be persecuted. The venerable Giac Duc, who would eventually flee to the south after the Geneva partition, recounts:

> *I went for two reasons – one personal one religious. My family had a long tradition of anti-French politics. My father one of Ho Chi Minh's nationalist opponents had been killed by the Vietminh. So, I was afraid of the communists because of my background. Secondly, we thought that the communists would make life difficult for Buddhists in the north – there were already indications of that in areas that had been communist strongholds for a long time.*[42]

An entire Buddhist intellectual movement relocated from north to south at the time of the Geneva Accord partition.

Although the Communist ICP had been dissolved in 1945, no one was under any illusion as to who was running the Vietminh. Nationalist non-communist sentiment was reinforced by communist failure. The war was being fought at a political level, not just a military one, and the result was by no means clear. Penalties for being on the wrong side of power could be quite severe.

Giáp kept his position despite the failures. He no longer had much credit left in reserve from his extraordinary successes at the start of the war and the RC4 campaign in particular. Most importantly for his survival, he was closely aligned to Ho Chi Minh. Ho had the utmost confidence in his general and defence minister and was his ultimate protector. The risks of the offensives must have been well-known and Giáp would have pointed this out to his Politburo colleagues before a collective decision was made. Giáp was an astute politician, so he would certainly have covered himself from blame, as he did later in the highly risky Dien Bien Phu campaign. Ho could have employed an experienced Chinese general, but it was politically impossible to have a Chinese person in this position, though they were maintained as advisers, which was part of the price of taking Chinese equipment and training. Besides, who else but Giáp had the knowledge, experience, capability and trust in this fledgling state to carry off both the roles of defence minister and commander-in-chief?

If the French were not enough as an enemy, Giáp's main problem as Chinese arms supplies developed was his relationship with his Chinese advisers. Mao's logistical largess did not come free. He expected influence as well and even aimed at outright control. The Chinese did this by identifying 'clients' within the DRV Politburo and central committee. Notable among them, Truong Chinh, on the pro-Chinese left of the party, had been a close friend and associate of Giáp's in the 1930s as they did journalistic and editorial work for party newspapers. However, jealousy and rivalry developed as they ascended the narrowing pyramid of party hierarchy. Truong and others constantly sought to trim Giáp's powers and prestige as well as hobble his independence in military matters. Giáp's extensive powers over the army and the war economy of the DRV elicited considerable jealousy and even fear. Revolutionaries always feared military takeover. Fear of Thermidorian reaction or Bonapartism has always been present in communist party thinking. The same innuendo had been exploited by Stalin against Red Army commissar Leon Trotsky, and in future years Mao would purge or even kill leaders with strong military links, such as Lui Shaoqui, Deng Xiao Ping and Lin Piao.

Apart from fears of Thermidor, there was also the Stalin-inspired witch-hunt in the communist world against the new heresy of Titoism following accusations of nationalism and Yugoslavia's break with the USSR and Cominform in mid-1948. This crisis built up into a Stalinist purge from 1950–53 against 'nationalist elements', as Stalin looked to consolidate his grip on the bloc. Dozens of leading party figures in Poland, Czechoslovakia, Hungary and Rumania were arrested, shot or imprisoned, including prominent leaders Gomulka, Kostov, Slansky, Clementis, Kardar and Ana Pauker. These expulsions, which saw thirty percent of party members being ousted in Eastern Europe and hundreds of thousands of citizens imprisoned, were accompanied by accelerated land reform and collectivisation. Even in faraway Indochina, under the watchful eye of Mao, Ho and Giáp would be buffeted by these events. China, following Stalin's lead, also launched extreme land reform policies and mass eliminations, including the use by Mao of arbitrary regional terror quotas that resulted in up to two million deaths.[43] Even if he had wanted it, Ho's policies could not have been immune from these trends.

As part of the internal checks and balances, the Politburo appointed one of Truong's acolytes as army political commissar. It might have been debilitating but Giáp dealt with that challenge by winning over the friendship and trust of the man who was supposed to spy on him. More serious were charges brought by the Chinese that Giáp was bourgeoise with a French lycée and university education. (Never mind that Mao and Zou En Lai also had bourgeois backgrounds.) This was a serious attack and leading Chinese military adviser General Chen Gen led the complaints.

An important part of the attack was the launch by Deng Yifan of a widespread political education and thought movement, which was aimed at propaganda and politicisation of the army to enthuse the troops in the struggle against imperialism. The campaign started in August 1951 and ran to the spring of 1952. It was followed by another campaign launched by Ho on 11 May 1952. It was the start of the Chinese-inspired leftist move and would be followed by land reform and intensified class struggle against bourgeois and landowning elements.

This was all part of a Chinese ploy to move into an ascendant position within the army, but it was blocked by Ho who normally acquiesced in most of what the Chinese wanted. The essential issue was, of course, Giáp's talent and brilliance, qualities that will always attract the special vitriol of mediocre competitors. Ho had to protect Giáp because the left faction was also trying to weaken Ho by removing his acolyte. Criticism of Giáp was, by proxy, a criticism of Ho, who also had a Mandarin background. The duo had to tread warily because they were in the line of fire on three dangerous issues: nationalism-Titoism, bourgeois background and, for Giáp, Thermidorism.

De Lattre in America

De Lattre travelled to the US in September 1951. The crisis in the Red delta having passed and with the monsoon season in full onset, it was a good time to go and, apart from that, France needed to get more money and arms from the US to try to draw them into the Indochina conflict to share the burden. Stopping over in Paris on the way to Washington, he lectured the government on the need for more resources. De Lattre was in his element. He loved the pomp and ceremony, the panoply of power amongst the great and mighty. With victories behind him, his ego was bigger than ever.

Newsreels of him speaking in English in America on 20 September 1951 show a man of confidence and charisma. Speaking plainly he came straight to the point in asking for American help, making the powerful and logical claim that 'We are making war against communism…the war in Korea and the war in Vietnam is the same war against the same enemy.' His manner was grave and determined but there is no mistaking the urgent nature of the plea, its underlying emotional sincerity, and the level of desperation. It was the pleading of a realist, who had been at the front in Tonkin, who realised how desperate was the situation.

He understood America and how to talk to American policy-makers, directly, confidently: 'If Hanoi is lost,' he declared, 'the road will be clear all the way to Suez.' (20 September). De Lattre was able to build the sense that (following the Korean invasion) the US and France were in it together on the front line against communism. Suddenly, perceptions in the US changed. What had been viewed as a colonial war had turned into an anti-communist crusade and given France a kudos that had formerly been lacking. As to the issue of colonialism, he tackled it head on announcing emphatically in a radio broadcast that was also filmed, 'That story is over.' The future was 'the association of states'. America lapped it up. Here was an ally that fought side by side with America with a Cold War commitment far greater than any other power. For the US at this moment, the special relationship was with France, not with Britain. Indeed, considerable concessions were made to self-governance a few months after the RC4 disaster. However, his peremptory tone and use of plenipotentiary powers in Indochina contradicted the assertion about the freedom of the Indochinese governments.

Returning to Hanoi, he told his subordinates that the army must remain mobile, ready to take the initiative to break up Vietminh concentrations. Touched perhaps by de Gaulle's grandiosity, in his maudlin fog de Lattre confided to Salan:

> *...this was a great chance for the French Army to have its rendezvous with history. If we lose everything will be finished. Asia, North Africa perhaps France itself. Thousands of young officers have paid with their blood...Bernard my son himself died for this cause. He did not die for France...he died for Vietnam.*[44]

Jack and Bobby in Indochina October 1951

John and Bobby Kennedy made a world tour in October 1951 as part of John Kennedy's aim to burnish his foreign policy credentials on his way to run for the presidency. Indochina was for the Kennedys the most interesting part of the trip, as it was in the front line of the Cold War. In India, Nehru had indicated to them his neutral stance, which leaned strongly to the anti-colonialist Vietminh side. But as democratics with Irish roots, the Kennedys also had a natural prejudice against colonialism.

From the rooftop bar of the Majestic Hotel, the brothers heard the sound of cannon-fire and machine-guns and saw the flashes of gunfire out in the Mekong delta. They were joined for a drink by respected AP correspondent

Seymour Topping, who informed them that the people supported the Vietminh and that the French attempt to hold the country was doomed. Quizzing senior foreign correspondents, de Lattre and others, the brothers soon came to the conclusion that the war was probably not winnable, that Ho Chi Minh was overwhelmingly popular, and he would win any national poll. Bao Dai, who met the brothers off the plane, they regarded as a lightweight, decadent French puppet.

In his diary, Jack Kennedy wrote fearfully that 'we [US] are more and more becoming colonialists in the minds of the people.' For JFK, the way to defeat communism was by economic and social policy to act on poverty and inequality. Bobby Kennedy was concerned that:

> *...our mistake has been not to insist on definite political reforms by the French towards the natives as prerequisites to any aid...we are becoming more and more involved in the war to a point where we can't back out.*[45]

They held some fractious meetings with de Lattre.

An increasingly influential senator, Jack Kennedy rapidly became a key opinion-former on Indochina matters. On his return in November 1951, he reported to congress:

> *In Indochina we have allied ourselves to the desperate effort of a French regime to hang on to the remnants of empire. There is no broad, general support of the native Vietnam Government among the people of that area. To check the southern drive of communism makes sense but not only through reliance on the force of arms.* (JFK presidential library)

CHAPTER XII

Giáp's New Strategic Directions – Death of Stalin – Land Reform

Battle of Nghia Lo, 3–10 October 1951

When Giáp threw in the last of his set-piece and failed attacks against the Red delta's de Lattre line, he had tried to distract the French by launching the 312th Division on a feint attack against the key hill town of Nghia Lo in the T'ai Highlands on 3 October. Heavy attacks on the French redoubt, which was commanded by a mere captain, were repulsed. At the climax of the battle flares lit up the approaches to the barbed wire as seven fighter bombers swooped in catching thousands of advancing bo doi in the open. This was followed by a B26 attack with napalm. Then de Lattre followed this with a drop of two elite paratrooper battalions astride the 312's logistics trail amidst the auxiliary coolies.

It was typical of the war, which the French were coming to call *la guerre sans front* (war without a front), in which French mobility triumphed on this occasion with the paratroopers acting as the hammer to Nghia Lo's garrison's anvil. Trapped between the defences of Nghia Lo and the paratroopers, the Vietminh's 312th Division suffered severely, leaving 300 bodies behind. In a complex firefight over several days, they suffered about 3,500 casualties.

The third phase of the strategy that Giáp had outlined along the lines of Chinese communist experiences with the nationalists had clearly been premature. Maoist military theory had been applied mechanistically. The time was not ripe for moving from the defensive to the destruction of the enemy. Vietminh hubris arose from an overconfidence borne of the triumph on RC4 and the desire to exploit the momentum of victory. It seems likely that the urgency of Giáp's attacks was related to the need of the political imperative to score a decisive victory quickly before the Americans and their allies decided to intervene directly in Vietnam, as they were doing in Korea. Moreover, the Politburo would have calculated that time was on the French side given the impressive build-up of US-supplied arms in addition to the rapid expansion of the Vietnamese National Army (VNA). In terms of modern arms, the DRV had the advantage from early 1950 after the Chinese communists took the border regions. But this advantage seemed to be dissipating as the US logistics train channelled Korean War US-Army surpluses into Indochina. Giáp's attacks followed the formulaic concept of Mao as to the timing of the overwhelming attack to finish off the enemy. Mao's concepts had worked well against the demoralised and corruptly led Kuomintang armies, but the French Army was cast with different metal.

Despite the huge casualties, the metal of the new VPA was being forged in blood and a necessary transition was being made from guerrilla war to formal-modern war. As Mao instructed his military advisory group:

> *...your duty is not only to teach the Vietnamese about guerrilla war, but also to help them to fight a modern war against the French. You must teach them how to organise a professional army, use modern weapons and provide military aid.*[1]

A change of strategy was essential. The Vietminh, even when concentrating vastly superior numbers at certain pressure points, could not hope to win in the open field in the Red delta because as long as it was well handled, French firepower from defensive positions and total command of the air would always win. As yet the Vietminh had neither been supplied or trained with 105mm heavy artillery, nor did Giáp yet have anti-aircraft guns, though some light 22mm AA weapons were on the way. From now on Giáp would play to his strengths, which were rapidity of deployment and secrecy of movements, to concentrate on French weak points and to disperse French resources. If the French tried offensive movements that inevitably tied them to a particular road, Giáp would trade space for time and concentrate forces to wipe them out either *in situ* or when they withdrew.

At the same time the political work would continue. The Vietminh expanded control over liberated areas, including those within the supposedly French-controlled Red River delta. Infiltration of the delta villages was the major triumph of the Vietminh high command in the 1951–52 period, even as they were being defeated in open battle. About half the villages in the delta were under Vietminh control where they even deployed formed militia units. Perhaps only twenty-five percent of the delta was under government control. The balance was mostly Vietminh controlled or contested.

An increasing element of Giáp's strategy was the push to dominate the western hill country in a determined move into the north-west. Giáp intended to suppress French-led Meo and Tai partisan units and make an opening towards Lao to start to threaten that country, whose monarch was an active supporter of the federated states concept. The development of the communist Pathet Lao, under the leadership of 'The Red Prince' Souphanavong, followed the same broad national front tactics as exploited by the Vietminh. It represented the opening of a fourth front against the French after Tonkin, Annam and Cochin. It was all part of a Vietminh plan to force the French to spread out their forces in mountainous and wooded areas where the VPA would enjoy tactical advantages. The French government and high command were to become very sensitive to the need to prevent the takeover of Lao as well as protect their allies in the hills of the T'ai Federation and the Meo. All credibility in the union of Indochina and the protectorate concept would be lost if the FEC failed to come to the defence of Lao. If Lao were to fall, communism would outflank French Indochina's strategic edge along Vietnam's border. Giáp's indirect strategy was something that military theorists Captain Basil Liddell-Hart or Major J.F.C. Fuller would have heartily approved. It would eventually pay extraordinary dividends.

The French could be satisfied with the victories over the Vietminh in 1951. But while they were enough to stabilise France's position in Indochina, France still had no war-winning strategy.

Blockhouse attacks

Picking off isolated bunkers and defence positions in night attacks was the standard *modus operandum* in both the south and the north of Indochina from 1947 through to 1954. A Vietminh account describes a typical attack:

> *Then they began firing at the blockhouse...Then grenades came flying out. One of Phai's men grabbed it and threw it away before it could explode. Two others followed...The fourth exploded just as it was being picked up. Phai and both men were killed...We were all in a frenzy. Some people were shot down, but others began heaving Molotov cocktails. One French soldier came running out on fire. Phai's men shot him down. The rest were trapped inside. We barbecued them.*[2]

On the de Lattre lines in the north, boredom was the main problem, especially when it led to complacency and deadly attacks. In July 1949, Karl Heinz Krause was with his unit of fifty guarding a fortified area around a large pagoda complex near the Red River in the south-east delta near the Catholic region. One of the NCOs, called Bobby, was an exceptional leader:

> *...he used to go out at night with a torch to check the bamboo defences, something he enjoyed doing. After one inspection he came back picked up a machine-gun, called out to all the other posts and jumped into a concrete bunker...we understood immediately and followed him to the bunkers and parapets. Alarm!...we all started to fire at once at the defence zone just 20m away...the firing was returned from the enemy but decreased, ours was heavier. Until dawn we did not leave our defences...there were nine dead Viets around the bamboo defences*

> *all with satchel bombs in hand; in the full light we saw that they had cut various pathways through the defences.*[3]

Bobby was awarded the *Croix de Guerre.*

The Vietminh also had their tricks:

> *A Viet NCO told me how they blew up our blockhouses; a nine-foot bamboo with plastic explosives on the end was gradually advanced towards a loophole; suddenly there was a great explosion.*[4]

It was the standard assault method against blockhouses. They attacked at night always and with full intelligence as to the layout of defences and the habits of the garrison, down to the minutest detail. Sometimes success would be down to inside information, such as a spy who unlocked a gate and left it open. Women were often actively used for this role or via pressure using pillow talk to pass on information. Martelli gave examples of such instances in his memoir. He describes how nine Senegalese soldiers and a radio operator were massacred in one outpost with no sign of resistance. They had been rushed at night by Vietminh hidden in pits in the ground.[5]

Sometimes attacks might be regimental in size, involving thousands of Vietminh against an outlying fortification. Such an attack occurred at the little fort of Zouk To in the Phu Lo district just 20km north of Hanoi near an important crossing of the Red River. (Martelli p263) Zouk To was a barbed wire-defended fort consisting of three bunkers equipped with two machine-guns each and linked by tunnels to a central defensive citadel. The garrison consisted of five European officers and NCOs, thirty Vietnamese and twenty Senegalese. Ex-SS Corporal Martelli, who had considerable building experience due to the war against the Russians, added barbed wire and laid mines in a typical triangular pattern. There were three designated artillery 105mm fire zones, respectively 100, 200, 300m distant around the fort, with cover provided from an artillery base at Phu Lo, 3km away.

French citizen Paul Martelli (of Italian-German descent) was a somewhat typical mercenary recruit to the French Army. A true believer in the new empire of the Fourth Reich, he joined the SS and saw extensive action against the Russians in Pomerania with the SS Charlemagne Division. He then served in the French Army before going to work in a forge. Bored with civil life, he enlisted on a three-year contract in 1949 to fight in Indochina. He stayed until 1954 and the defeat at Dien Bien Phu. He was a notorious and inveterate tavern brawler and lothario who nearly got himself murdered in an off-base village when he became enamoured with a beautiful Vietnamese. Another time he survived a poison attack by a food stall chef.

Knowing that the Vietminh would attack at night, Martelli took the night watch. When a dog in the fort started to become restless, Martelli went up to the watch tower and switched on the searchlight. '*Mon Dieu,*' gasped the sergeant. 'It's the end. There are a thousand of them [Vietminh].'[6] It was a regimental-sized attack launched from the covered jungle fringe just 5km to the north.

There followed an all-night attack with thousands of Vietminh infiltrating the barbed wire using Bangalores and storming the bunker and citadel. Taking on a medieval aspect, the Vietminh used bamboo scaling ladders to charge the tower citadel and were only held off by the generous use of grenades tossed over the top parapet. Attacking the bunkers in waves, the Vietminh were mown down time and again by machine-guns, automatic weapons and grenades:

> *I redirected the machine-gunners' fire which immediately swept out a dozen of the rebels who were sliding charges under the defence wire. The Viet soldiers charged in silence, whining briefly when hit...then the enemy launched their reserves with orders screamed in their shrill, chanting language...I saw them fall in droves, decimated by our bursts, but they had already opened three long gaps in our wire. Against a dozen Vietminh advancing with mines on the end of long bamboo sticks, I let go two MAT-49 sweeps, mowing down half of them.*[7]

Martelli organised the defence, most importantly to ensure that the Vietnamese auxiliaries kept up an ammunition supply to the Senegalese soldiers. This went on relentlessly for hours.

More waves of enemy were blown apart in the artillery killing zones on the approaches to the wire, although the artillery captain, who was in touch by radio from the nearest firebase, against strenuous protests from Martelli, was unwilling to risk firing into Zone 1 even when the base was in danger of being overrun after the destruction and capture of No. 2 bunker. After fighting all night, having one blockhouse blown up by a satchel charge and running out of ammunition, the situation became desperate as the Vietminh:

> *...were attacking in waves now...forming piles that gave cover...in a scene which reminded me of the Russians in the Battle of Korlin – the same stupid tactic.*[8]

Stupid tactics indeed, but with relatively untrained and poorly educated peasant conscripts, there was little alternative for inexperienced Vietminh commanders.

Short on ammunition, just before the inevitable gruesome massacre, the Vietminh tried to bluff them into surrender with an amplified appeal, in nasal tones and speaking French: 'Give yourselves up, do not fight against your brothers. Do not serve the cause of colonialism and capitalism!'[9] Suddenly, there was silence:

> *Paul! Tanks...they've arrived...We looked out to see the Vietminh scattering in all directions...our tanks loosed off a few rounds in their midst. Our planes flew overhead...strafing them.*[10]

Martelli would later say, 'I preferred fighting the Russians in Pomerania, the Popovs of Rokossowski and Zhukov.'

Just before the attack the live-in Vietnamese girlfriend of the sergeant commanding the fort slipped away from the post. She was never seen again.

The Hoa Binh campaign: October 1951–February 1952

Why Hoa Binh?

Before Giáp could launch a new offensive as well as starting his advance into the T'ai uplands, de Lattre took the initiative. By this time the magic of de Lattre seemed to be wearing thin. His huge ego and pretensions did not make him popular, and his irascibility was wearing on his staff. He had early on acquired the title 'King Jean', a name popularised by Lucien Bodard, who developed a close relationship with the general despite retaining journalistic detachment. Graham Greene, who was entertained by de Lattre a number of times despite the general's paranoid suspicions and accusations that Greene was still spying for British intelligence, recalled:

> *...he was an altered man. His rhetoric of hope was wearing painfully thin; his colonels were openly critical of him even to a foreigner. They were tired of his continual references to his sacrifices*[11]*...[and] the general, whose speeches were too long, whose magic had faded.*

No one knew that he was dying of cancer.

De Lattre arrived back from his successful visit to the US on 19 October. Having assessed the situation, he met with General Salan and Colonel Linares on the evening of 4 November. After he had complained to Salan about the politicians in Paris, who had criticised him for his lack of aggression, he outlined his plan. 'Attack, attack,' repeated de Lattre. 'I shall go to Hoa Binh and cut the Vietminh in two.'[12]

Why Hoa Binh? It was the spiritual and tribal centre for the Meo, France's tribal ally, which had been abandoned into Vietminh hands the year before. To save face, he needed to recover it on behalf of France's Meo (Hmong) allies. Accessible by road, the RC6 and the Black River, Hoa Binh was 75km south-west of Hanoi. Just 20km beyond the de Lattre lines surrounding the core Red delta region, the town was set amidst the usual jungle-covered Khast hills. The place was strategically important for the Vietminh because it was the main route through which arms and munitions passed south while recruits and victuals, especially rice, were brought north to the food-poor regions along the Black and Day Rivers and the Bac Kan nexus. Such would be the disruption that the Vietminh would be forced to counter-attack in force.

Generals Linares and Salan were against the plan, the former because he wanted to concentrate elite troops on the delta, and the latter because he preferred to let the enemy attack the French on terms advantageous to the FEC. But de Lattre overrode them. 'Believe me,' he exclaimed. 'It must be done! Until now we have never taken the initiative, have always been content to allow the fire to be lit by the Vietminh. I am throwing out a challenge to Giáp, I believe he will accept it.'

The movement of rice was a strategic priority for the Vietminh, so they were bound to attack and be drawn into de Lattre's heavy artillery and napalm. De Latte was perfectly aware that much of the terrain along the Black River and the RC6 and RC21 to the basin of Hoa Binh would favour the Vietminh and would inevitably lead to widespread and difficult fighting. Nevertheless, with control of the air and the establishment of important firebases at Hoa Binh and along the river, de Lattre believed that he could force the VPA to attack and inflict unacceptable casualties. It was an attack-defence strategy. General de Lattre realised he needed to do more than just hold the Red delta behind fortified lines and always allow the enemy to take the initiative. That would be a dangerous and complacent way to proceed and bad for morale. Just waiting to be attacked was not a winning strategy, as the Maginot experience showed. He would attack in November at the beginning of the dry season, which meant he would have air cover and not the mists that had doomed Leparge's column on RC4.

De Lattre had been looking for a battle, but so had Giáp. From Giáp's perspective, Hoa Binh was better suited to the Vietminh tactical capacities than the last three battles in the delta. In jungle-clad and mountainous Hoa Binh, French superiority in firepower, including artillery and air power, would be mitigated. The hills and jungles protected his approaches. Moreover, the French lines of supply ran along 33km of jungle-covered mountains and thick vegetation, which would be vulnerable to ambush. Alternatively, there was the river route where it was easy to ambush the Dinassaut flotillas that shepherded supply convoys. Luckily, according to the post-war review, the Vietminh were quite naïve about marine operations and were 'invariably surprised…by the density and extent of our [French] return fire.'[13] Despite this naïveté, the VPA would inflict some significant defeats on the heavily armed Dinassauts above Hoa Binh.

The Hoa Binh campaign was the result of de Latte's tactical and strategic thoughts and would foreshadow both the battles of Ná Sán and Dien Bien Phu, where his successors Salan and Navarre would look to his example of applying the tactical defensive to the strategic offensive. Similarly, the aim of the Hoa Binh offensive was to establish a grinding battle of attrition where Vietminh forces would suffer disproportionately heavy casualties by attacking fortified French positions. Fought over a period of four months, it would lead to the most prolonged and complex battle of the French Indochina War.

Giáp, for his part, had, with his Chinese advisers, thoroughly re-evaluated their strategy and come to terms with their tactical limitations. Remarkable mobility and the ability to concentrate in secret at high speed by using the forest paths, roads and tracks would enable Giáp to triumph. French firepower in defence, tanks and air power would be neutralised by the terrain, the jungle, the jagged pinnacles and ridges of limestone and clouds, which limited the effectiveness of air power. Even dreaded tumbling napalm canisters would be much less effective in broken and forested terrain.

Giáp's new theory of war, for which he drew on his hero Lawrence of Arabia and which closely resembled the Chinese model that had won the civil war, was put like this: 'The countryside was to encircle the towns, the mountains were to dominate the rice lands of the plain.'[14] Essentially, Giáp's plan was to try to disperse the enemy and pick off isolated positions along the lines of supply with overwhelming numbers before the French could react or escape. It was in fact a return to the successful policies of 1950, which culminated in the RC4 victory. Hoa Binh was an opportunity to swamp a powerful French detachment and win a major political victory. If Giáp could beat France's best general, France, which was already tottering politically, would surely give up.

The battle would rage around the routes of supply for the French garrison at Hoa Binh. There were three main scenes of fighting reflecting the battles of logistics. The Dinassaut supply convoys were the preferred line of supply, mainly because it was a very efficient way to move heavy goods and because heavily armed and armoured Dinassaut were deemed more defensible than soft-skinned trucks. This fight would involve intense and confused warfare, the typical *guerre sans front* in the forested slopes on the north and west side in areas adjacent to the east bank of the river along a 50km stretch. Secondly, the Vietminh would aim to close down or impose unacceptable losses on the French using the road. Thirdly, attempts would be made to close down the air route to the airstrip at Hoa Binh and to use their new 22mm AA guns and 120mm mortars to hinder JU52 supply runs.

De Lattre launched the attack, but he would soon return on medical leave to France and never return. His place would be taken by his deputy general, Raul Salan.

Salan

Salan was a capable general and he knew Indochina better than any other French senior officer. Taking over from de Lattre was not easy and unfortunately de Lattre had had the advantage of teaching the naïve VPA a few lessons, which Giáp had learnt from by the time Salan took command. An interesting character, veteran of Verdun and Syria where he was wounded, Salan spent many years in Lao and learnt the language, probably 'on the pillow'. He also developed an opium habit. A romantic, he loved Lao with a heartfelt passion, even using a whole page of his memoir to describe his favourite Lao meal of fermented rice-vermicelli and a marmite of slow-cooked mixed meats. Lao food is indeed delicious.

Salan's real fame and notoriety would be in the future when in 1961 he would lead a *coup d'état* in Algiers against President de Gaulle's Fifth Republic. Salan then became head of the OAS terrorist organisation, for which he was sentenced to death. Luckily for him, the sentence would be commuted. Son of a provincial doctor from the Tarn, not an aristocrat, unlike most of the other generals, Salan was a soldier's soldier and with forty-one different awards he was the most decorated officer in the French Army. Behind the scenes in Paris the ground was shifting below the feet of the Bidault faction. MRP deputy Pierre de Chavigne was made secretary for war on 11 August 1951. He would serve under Pleven's new government and maintained his position under the successive governments of Edgar Faure, Antoine Pinay, Rene Mayer, and Joseph Laniel, until July 1954. With the strategic clarity of a soldier, he recognised that Indochina was doomed unless the PRC desisted in military support. Rather naively, in February 1952 he flew a kite to suggest that China might desist in return for recognition from France, which would allow China to join the comity of nations. As a soldier amongst politicians, de Chavigne would be influential in his opinions on the military situation.

First moves: setting up firebases and Klaus Klause cruises up river to Hoa Binh

The Battle of Hoa Bin started on 10 November 1952 with preparatory attacks to clear RP21, which met considerable resistance that was broken by air power. On the 13th, *Operation Lotus* began to clear the RP21 traverse road that reached to the crossroads at Apa Da Chong, which was set up as a firebase. Confused fighting flared around this strategic entry point to the west side of the river and would last into January with the French needing to parachute in reinforcements at critical moments. Salan, who directed operations, launched elite parachutists on 14 November at the main target, Hoa Binh. On the 14th, a second paratrooper battalion, 2nd BPC, followed by 1st BPC and 7th BCCP, were dropped in by JU52. After light skirmishing, they cleared the town and the immediate area, including the airstrip between 2 and 5 p.m. for the loss of just ten men in fighting estimated to have cost the Vietminh some 600 troops. At this point, de Lattre instructed Salan that 'the difficult part will now commence; watch out for the Vietminh counter-attack, dig-in, prepare your fortifications.'[15] The second prong of the offensive saw GM moving down the Black River from the north from the Pu to Tu Vu, where firebases and fortified positions were established. Also, on the other side of the river, four firebases were established including the Rocher de Notre Dame position on the east bank. Containing batteries of 105mm cannon, they would be able to enfilade any attacks on the French positions or riverine convoys. Three batteries of 105mm cannon were transported into Hoa Binh. The third prong of the offensive was made from Xuan Mai on the Day River along RC6 going west, which would be the land route into Hoa Binh.

Shortly afterwards, de Lattre announced that he had to return to France for medical reasons on 19 December, and instructed Salan to take over the operation and wished him luck. Accompanying de Lattre to the airport, Salan received an uncharacteristically affectionate handshake from the departing general.

As de Lattre had predicted, when Giáp heard about the French offensive, he immediately accepted the challenge. It was not only necessary to maintain his logistical link to the southern delta and Annam, which was a major rice supplier to the VPA, but it was too tempting to resist attacking in terrain that was much more favourable to the Vietminh than the flat lands around the de Lattre lines in the Red delta. He decided quickly. By the 21st, French intelligence decoders had discovered that the 312th Division was on the move south from the Red River.[16] Soon not one but three elite divisions were mobilised for the attack. Giáp decided to destroy the French with an overwhelming force of three divisions launched at the city, using the 308th, 312th and 304th, some 30,000 trained, some three-quarters of the best VPA troops supported by 40,000 auxiliaries. The second strand to Giáp's strategy was to infiltrate more regular units into the Red delta behind the de Lattre lines while France's elite units were otherwise occupied. Having disassociated themselves from the delta battles, Chinese military sources retrospectively claimed full credit for the strategy at Hoa Binh,[17] which 'coincidentally' could be claimed as a victory even if that was by no means clear cut.

The VPA moved through the jungle as if it were a river, like a frenzy of ravenous piranha smelling red meat. In the past the Vietminh were lightly armed with rifles, machine-guns, sub-machine-guns, and light mortars. But heavier equipment, such as 75mm recoilless rifles, captured 120mm mortars,

75mm mountain guns and bazookas, were beginning to arrive down the supply chain from the Yunnan, along with some 22mm anti-aircraft guns. These would begin to alter the balance, but as yet there was still no heavy artillery to match the 105mm guns of the French.

Meanwhile, following the parachute-drops a strong French column, comprising fifteen infantry battalions, engineers, artillery and tanks, advanced along RC6. Other reinforcements poured in along the Black River. Klaus Klause, with his battalion of the 13th Legion demi-brigade, was on his way to Hoa Binh in a big Dinassaut convoy on 11 November, but not without incident for Klause's section. Their LCT went ashore to make a reconnaissance of the locality. Section leader Bobby, winner of the *Croix de Guerre*, took a shine to a local stray dog but Bobby went missing. The LCT waited a further ten minutes but, despite their calling, he did not turn up. With the vessel beginning to attract Vietminh fire, they had to leave without him. Klause writes laconically, 'We hope he had a good legionnaire's death. One shot and all over.'

A tragedy befell the village the legionnaires had briefly occupied. After retreating to their LCT:

> ...*the Vietminh started to fire on the village, regardless of the fact that the village was totally unoccupied* [by the French] *with at least 1,000 women and children who wanted to avoid the fighting.*[18]

Apart from RC6, de Lattre had three other possible methods of supply: the air field at Hoa Binh; parachute-drops; and the Black River, with the support of two Dinassaut. This latter prong of attack of supply was supported by the northern operational group, which descended as far as Tu Vu on the west bank of the Black River. The multiplicity of supply routes (air, road and river) was an essential de Lattre understood well. At Dien Bin Phu there would only be one method of supply, and that would be badly impaired on day one.

Once established at Hoa Binh, the parachutists were mainly withdrawn by air and replaced by the demi-brigade of the Foreign Legion (DBLE) to which Klaus Klause was attached. The battle would be different this time. Legionnaire Karl Heinz Krause and his company 'were cautioned by our captain that we would have to reckon with Vietminh artillery. For the first time we dug deep bunkers.'[19]

One problem for the French on RC6 was that the road had to be repaired as they went along. Moreover, there was no time to clear the dense foliage on either side of the road to open fields of fire and prevent ambushes. As the difficult part of the road was 33km long, it was impossible to defend along the entire stretch. So the French established fortified defensive positions and firebases at key topographical points along the RC6.

Similarly, the 50km-stretch of the Black River tributary off the Red River needed defending with a series of fortified firebases on the left and right banks along its length at La Pu, Dan Te, Rocher Notre Dame, Ap Da Chong, Xom Bu, Ap Phu To and Tu Vu. Caught by surprise, it would be three weeks before VPA forces were in place to start putting pressure on the French riverine lines of supply and the Hoa Binh garrison itself.

The first months of the siege until mid-January were mainly taken up with a tussle for control of the river with the forested and hilly region of Bai Trai between the Mount Hui and Ba Vi Mountain ranges being a constant battle between elite GM, Moroccan units, parachutists and Hmong battalions, against the 304th and 312th Divisions The north-western slopes of Ba Vi Mountain were heavily contested as each side tried to cut off and surround its enemy. Fierce planned or encounter battles surged around Ap Da Chong, the northern and southern slopes of Ba Vi Mountain, around Van Mong and Yen Le and further over on the RC21. The importance of the river route came into sharp focus because as Klause attests, about 100 trucks were destroyed in two separate ambushes on the RC6 once the Vietminh divisions had arrived in the early weeks of the offensive. With uncleared shrubbery and forest running alongside the RC6, the vulnerability to ambush was palpable. Salan poured significant resources into keeping open the river route.

Attacks on river supply route

The 308th would place itself on both sides of the river, looking to pick off the French mini-fortresses and firebases dotted along both banks. The battle for Tu Vu would be an immense bloodletting, but the more bitter and hidden battles would rage in the forests of Bai Trai and on the western slopes of Ba Vi Mountain adjacent to the eastern side of the river in a *guerre sans front*. The French expended their energies through parachute drops and jungle thrusts to try to destroy Vietminh units who hovered around the mini fortresses on the east bank of the river. However, the VPA always slipped through or turned to hunt down the hunters. Nonetheless, they were deterred from their objectives in storming and closing down the riverine fortresses and firebases because interlocking fire from the firebases prevented storming attacks on French positions. Changing tactics, Giáp would focus on the weak links of the French operations along their extended communication and supply routes, both RC6 and the Black River. On the 22nd, a French Dinassaut convoy lost four vessels, one of them a large, armoured landing craft (LSSI). Dinassaut convoys bringing up supplies were subjected to increasing attacks and casualties from short-range ambushes all the way along the 50km stretches of the Red River from the confluence with the Red River at Trung Ha Bridge. After the abandonment of La Pu, by 9 December there was only one major fortified position left on the west side of the Black River, Tu Vu. But it did have artillery cover from the French-controlled east bank at Notre Dame.

At Tu Vu, a fortified village on a strategic bend in the river, a strong French outpost was overrun after several days of vicious fighting on the 11th. The strongpoint on the west side of the Black River was evacuated late at night after an all-day bloodbath. Droves of Vietminh soldiers were left hanging on the wire, mown down by machine-guns and blasted to bits by direct French artillery from Notre Dame's firebase. Things might have been worse for the French but for intelligence as to a simultaneous attack on Notre Dame from the surrounding jungle, which allowed the French to forestall it with their own counter-attack on the 10th supported by fighter bombers. After heavy fighting, the 1st BPC withdrew, suffering eighty-seven dead and many wounded. Simultaneously, GM 4 (about 3,000 troops) and 7th BPC attacking from the east cleared the south-eastern slopes of Ba Vi Mountain in confused firefights.

Supporting fire for the defenders of Tu Vu was so effective that an astonishing ninety percent of VPA casualties were caused by artillery.[20] In all, 5,000 shells were to be fired by the Notre Dame firebase alone.

Three hours later, on 11 December, waves of Vietminh of the 308th charged at the Moroccan manned Tu Vu strongpoints on the west bank. A platoon of five French tanks fought to the bitter end with hatches closed as Vietminh soldiers crawled and clawed at them like a swarm of red ants on a dying animal. Spitting fire and grinding the bodies of the enemy into the mud with their tracks, the tanks eventually succumbed. VPA troops fired bazookas at point-blank range, then set the tanks on fire with Molotov cocktails. The crews were incinerated. Protected by a thick river mist, the remaining Moroccans, with no space to retreat, jumped into the river and waded over to a large sandbank midstream. There were still 400 dead Vietminh lying around the defences when they returned the next day. The Vietminh were gone by the time the Moroccans re-occupied the Tu Vu. According to prisoners, an entire Vietminh battalion was wiped out. The FEC suffered twenty-five dead, mostly tank crew.

The experienced Salan had adroitly used French riverine power to its maximum potential to provide river transport to Hoa Binh. The armoured flotillas provided withering fire from the heavy machine-guns mounted on its gunboats, LSSI monitors, LCM and LCT.

However, on 12 December, the Vietminh launched a massive attack on the south-bound convoy 15km north of Hoa Binh, in a location where hills and forest on a spur of the Ba Vi Mountain came down close to a narrow stretch of the river. Elements of the 312th attacked from the east bank and the 308th from the west bank. From a thirty-vessel flotilla, three support vessels and a heavily armoured LSSI were sunk. The rest were badly damaged and withdrew back up the river. The battle for control of the east bank hinterland increased because Salan was determined to keep open his best and most efficient line of supply. But on 22 December, an entire convoy was sunk. This and the fact that low water in the dry season was making the passage ever more hazardous meant that the Black River supply route would be abandoned. In consequence, Salan was forced to 'stop this traffic' along the Black River.[21]

On the 24th, a major attack was launched against the Notre Dame firebase. The final straw was an attack on a river convoy on 8 January, when the Vietminh sank four patrol boats and one armed LCT, although the French withdrawal from the Black River front, including Tu Vu, had already started on 6 January after failed attacks on 23 December when the 1st BPVN was dropped into Ap Da Chong and Notre Dame areas to support major attacks by 5th BEP and 1st RTA across the west Bank sector. The attacks continued on Christmas Day. Heavy casualties were inflicted but VPA units remained in the area. A major extension of the offensive was then planned for 5 January.

Supply convoys would now need to travel by road on the RC26 and it was to this sector that the battle now moved. The Vietminh response was swift. On the RC6, elements of the 304th wiped out half a company of French troops and destroyed ten supply trucks. The first major attack on 2 December was made near Moi Ngoc, 15km north of Hoa Binh where a convoy of twenty out of forty trucks were destroyed along with the four lorries of troops assigned to shepherd convoys on the last leg to Hoa Binh.

Meanwhile, 70 miles south-east in the delta, the Catholic stronghold of Phat Diem came under attack by the 320th. This was typical of diversionary tactics by Giáp. Some Vietminh units did breach the defences of the Catholic militias and were only turned back eventually when Salan ordered drops by two paratrooper battalions.[22]

At a command conference on 1 January, Giáp' announced the reorganisation of his plan and order of battle. His three divisions were assigned specific zones of operation.

- The 308th would cover the west bank of the Black River from Hoa Binh and its environs up the Trang Ha Bridge at the confluence with the Red River, 55km distant. The task was to hem-in the FEC around Hoa Binh as well as attack French outposts on the Black River and Dinassaut-protected supply convoys heading down from the Red River to Hoa Binh.
- The 304th Division was to attack French supply lines and outposts from Ao Trach going east along the RC6 and on the eastern side of Ba Vi range.
- The 312th Division was to cross over and take charge of the east bank of the Black River and to attack the French supply convoy along the RC6, west and south of Ao Trach, as it bends through rivers from Ben Ngoc to Hoa

One careless driver? The French chain of command at Castor, Dien Bien Phu before the battle; left to right Generals Navarre, Cogny and de Castries. The 'family' shot hides bitter politicking between Navarre and Cogny, his deputy in Hanoi.

A caricature of a playboy, Emperor Bảo Đại, with General de lattre de Tassigny, inspecting French-led Montagnard troops, 1951. Unlike Ho, Bảo Đại lacked political rapport with the Vietnamese people who regarded him as a puppet. Neither of them had a good rapport with Indigenous Montagnards.

At Dien Bien Phu, Vietminh troops dug saps to within 10–20m of the French defenses and suddenly emerged to attack the French from close quarters with satchel bombs, grenades, and Russian-designed sub-machine-guns (PPsh-41 'burp guns').

Day one of *Operation Castor* 20 November 1953, a paratrooper of Colonel Bigeard's 6 BPC, wearing the distinctive forage cap, gives covering fire with an LMG FM 24/29 across paddy, having just unharnessed his parachute.

French troops at Huguette 5 were located to the east of the runway and near the central zone. This bastion of mud would be the scene of very fierce fighting towards the end of the battle, April-May 1954. Note the abandoned Dakota C-47 cargo plane in the background.

Ex-Carmelite monk and acolyte of de Gaulle, cynical Admiral d'Argenlieu, high commissioner 1945-7, was prompted by the general to start the war, behind the back of the Fourth Republic's elected government.

Ho and Giáp with America OSS operatives in 1946 – Giáp the dandy in white during his playboy phase. Ho developed excellent relations with them but was unable to convince Washington of his *bona fides*, despite efforts to pain himself as a nationalist rather than a communist.

At Nà Sản, 23 November–2 December 1952, a constant stream of Dakotas brought in supplies. French 105mm guns and Nà Sản's interlocking network of machine-guns and barbed wire defenses was too much for the Vietminh: Giáp learnt from his failure to close down the runway.

According to Graham Greene, de Castries had 'the nervy histrionic features of an old time actor', he probably suffered a nervous breakdown during the fifty-six-day battle where his defensive planning was negligent. He never left his bunker.

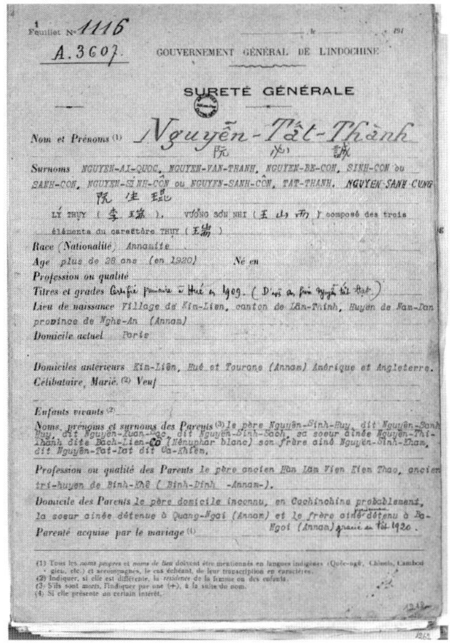

Feuillet N° 1116

A. 3607.

GOUVERNEMENT GÉNÉRAL DE L'INDOCHINE

SURETÉ GÉNÉRALE

Nom et Prénoms (1) Nguyễn-Tất-Thành 阮必誠

Surnoms NGUYEN-AI-QUOC, NGUYEN-VAN-THANH, NGUYEN-BE-CON, SINH-CON ou SANH-CON, NGUYEN-SINH-CÔN ou NGUYEN-SANH-CÔN, TAT-THANH. NGUYEN-SANH-CUNG 阮生瑞

LÝ THỤY (李瑞), VƯƠNG SƠN NHI (王山而) composé des trois éléments du caractère THỤY (瑞)

Race (Nationalité) Annamite

Age plus de 28 ans (en 1920) Né en

Profession ou qualité

Titres et grades Certifié primaire à Huế en 1909.

Lieu de naissance Village de Kim-Lien, canton de Lâm-Thinh, Huyen de Nam-Dan province de Nghe-An (Annam)

Domicile actuel Paris

Domiciles antérieurs Kim-Liên, Huê et Tourane (Annam) Amérique et Angleterre.

Célibataire, Marié (2) Veuf

Enfants vivants (2)

Noms, prénoms et surnoms des Parents (3) le père Nguyên-Sinh-Huy, dit Nguyên-Sanh Huy, dit Nguyên-Xuan-Ngoc, dit Nguyên-Sinh-Sach, sa soeur aînée Nguyên-Thi-Thanh dite Bach-Lien-Cô (Nénuphar blanc) son frère aîné Nguyên-Sinh-Khiem, dit Nguyên-Tat-Dat dit Ca-Khiêm.

Profession ou qualité des Parents le père ancien Hàn Lâm Viện Kiểm Thảo, ancien tri-huyen de Binh-Khê (Binh-Dinh -Annam-).

Domicile des Parents le père domicile inconnu, en Cochinchine probablement, la soeur aînée détenue à Quang-Ngai (Annam) et le frère aîné détenu à Ba-Ngoi (Annam)

Parenté acquise par le mariage (4)

(1) Tous les noms propres et noms de lieu doivent être mentionnés en langues indigènes (Quôc-ngữ, Chinois, Cambodgien, etc.) et accompagnés, le cas échéant, de leur transcription en caractères.
(2) Indiquer, si elle est différente, la résidence de la femme ou des enfants.
(3) S'ils sont morts, l'indiquer par une (+), à la suite du nom.
(4) Si elle présente un certain intérêt.

French secret police (Surete) report on Ho, who was tracked across the world. Arrested in Hong Kong 6 June 1931, he would be saved from extradition and the guillotine by 'leftie' British lawyers, including Sir Stafford Cripps.

After failed negotiations, Marius Moutet, French socialist, agreed with Ho on a *Modus Vivendi*, 14 September 1946, pending further negotiations. Ho as a head of state would have been deeply insulted by having to negotiate with the French colonies minister.

Such French outposts were dotted around the country, so giving the illusion of control. When the Vietminh emerged as a professional, well-armed army in 1950, these posts would be easily overrun.

Up to his waist in waterlogged paddy, a paratrooper hauls in his chute. Note the para-issue MAS 36 carbine with folding aluminium butt. Only about ten percent of 300,000 French troops in Indochina were mobile and available for offensive operations, with the rest in garrisons. Deployed to cover multiple crises, parachute battalions were at the forefront of French offensive operations or emergencies. Dien Bien Phu consumed seven of France's elite paratroop units, about ninety percent of available paratroopers. Paratroopers have barely been used globally in operational drops since Dien Bien Phu 1954. Elite troops of many nationalities, there were only about 3,000 in Indochina, but they suffered more than their fair share of action and casualties.

Ho (bottom right) meets Trotsky, *circa* 1923. A dangerous liaison, the photo could have cost him his life in the 1930s purges, perhaps saved by his eulogy of Lenin in Pravda and his usefulness to the Comintern.

De Gaulle's exuberant return to Brazzaville 1966 after his famous 1944 speech which was full of high-toned braggadocio promising French return to imperial glory.

Pictures showing France's tactical and logistical advantages: Bailey bridge; landing craft near Hue; Light Chaffee tank; Arromanches aircraft carrier. Despite unsuitable terrain, the nine tanks at Dien Bien Phu proved very useful as mobile firepower. Sir Anthony Eden holding forth at the Geneva Peace Conference May 1954. Eager for peace, Eden and Churchill sided with Molotov and Zou En-lai against Dulles, who 'subjected them to a prolonged and heated onslaught…' (*Eden Memoirs*)

Ho was a prolific reader and a masterly writer of polemics. Note the photos of his idols Lenin and Stalin. But Stalin regarded him as a potential 'Titoist', as did some in the US State Department.

Operation Castor (Dien Bien Phu) 20 November 1953, American C119 Boxcar offloading paratroopers from their back ramps. For cargo drops they were more efficient than Dakotas, needing only one run over the drop-zone target.

Like First World War trench warfare, French troops digging out defences, probably a machine-gun nest or mortar post, at Huguette 5 to the west of the runway.

Vietminh troops swarm over de Castries' bunker at the end of the Battle of Dien Bien Phu, 7 May 1954. De Castries simply said 'Don't shoot, I surrender.' Vinh recalled, 'I pushed my rifle into de Castries' stomach…forcing him to put his hands up.'

After the emperor's abdication in August 1945, Ho 'hosted' Bảo Đại in Hanoi for some months before the emperor escaped while on a Vietminh-sanctioned mission to Hong Kong. The unease on their faces is palpable.

In July 1954, 'the Angel of Dien Bien Phu', nurse Genevieve Galard, received the Congressional Medal of Honor from President Eisenhower at the Rose Garden following a ticker tape parade in New York.

Author's photo taken from RC4 shows the scenery between Dong Khe and Cox Ha Gorge, a dreadful terrain for Colonel Le Pages's 3,000-man column to march and fight through while surrounded by 30,000 well-supplied VPA regulars. 3–7 October 1950.

As Giáp's VPA divisions emerged from the jungle and mountains of northern Tonkin to attack the French Red delta defences at Vinh Yen on 14 January 1951, de Lattre, bright-eyed and eager, set off in his Morane light aircraft for the centre of the battle.

Author's photo (near Dong Khe on the RC4) of the 300–400m-high limestone cliff at the bottom of Cox Ha Gorge, where le Page's column was picked off by Vietminh troops from the top of the cliff. The gully exit and escape from this photo location is some 500m north-west of this point (the cliff is to the east and Dong Khe is 3km further north-east).

In the RC4 campaign, tens of thousands of female porters with heavy wicker baskets provided the logistical backbone for the Vietnam People's Army (VPA), which expanded still further to hundreds of thousands for the Dien Bien Phu campaign, and 800 Russian trucks.

Eleven thousand French prisoners-of-war marching north from Dien Bien Phu. Seventy percent died on the march and in captivity. The survivors were released after four months in July 1954 following the Geneva Accords. The French Army at Dien Bien Phu: Vietnamese thirty-six percent, French eighteen and a half percent, Africans nineteen and a half percent (Algerians, Moroccans, and a few Senegalese-mainly gunners), Foreign Legion twenty-six percent (*circa* seventy percent German).

Vietminh troops drag a 105mm cannon through the jungle. Contrary to popular belief, French intelligence knew by 1 January 1954 that some heavy artillery were on the way. The French would be surprised at how many cannons were deployed by the VPA, by their ability to hide them, and by the amount of ammunition available.

Binh. Other targets would be the capture of high points in the Ba Vi range and the 1,931m-high Mount Hui, 30km to the north on the east side of the Black River.

In *Operation Violet*, 7–9 January, the French launched a clearing operation on the western slopes of Ba Vi to cover the abandonment of Notre Dame, Xom Bu and Ap Da Chong. The riverine route of supply was no longer tenable. Salan ordered a diversionary attack to clear the Bi Vi northern slopes and distract the Giáp whilst the east bank bases were abandoned. Apart from the river convoy loss, Salan had decided that it was too costly to be involved in this jungle-bound battle of attrition along the Black River supply route. It was an important tactical and psychological victory for the Vietminh. Giáp began to dream and plan for another RC4-style victory with the garrison at Hoa Binh becoming the hostage to fortune and the albatross around the neck of the FEC just as the Cao Bang garrison had been the siren of French fortunes along the Chinese border.

On 11 January, Salan launched an airborne drop of the French-officered 1st BPVN on the east bank of the river to combine with other French paratrooper battalions and an Algerian unit to forestall another assembly of 5,000 VPA in two regiments who had occupied the Bai Trai Forest, preparatory to attacking riverside bases, especially Notre Dame. Once again it was *la guerre sans front*. There followed a confused firefight with attack and counter-attack in the jungle in which the increasingly effective French ground/air co-ordination caused large VPA casualties, including 300 confirmed dead. However, the Vietminh stayed on.

Attacks along the RC6

The second region of battle ran alongside the RC26 to Hanoi. With many similarities to the RC4 campaign, it would be a struggle that neither soldiers nor their commander in Hanoi could look forward to, especially as hills and scrub along the road made it ideal for ambush and camouflage. The RC6 passed through the de Lattre lines at Xian Mai then struck into the hills for about 33km. Bi Vi Mountain reared up on the north side and overlooked any convoy using the road. It and the road would become the second major battleground of the campaign.

Heavy fighting also took place along Route 21 and in the highlands as French forces pushed west.

There were dozens of attacks on the fortified positions along RC6 as Vietminh troops worked behind and along the flanks of the French advance. Meo Phe was a particularly prominent position, the loss of which would seriously endanger the French supply lines and avenue of retreat. On 8 January, a whole VPA regiment, about 2,500 men, attacked a Foreign Legion battalion of the 13th Demi Brigade. The defenders at Meo Pheo consisted of 400 men in good defensive positions surrounded by a minefield and rings of barbed wire. However, on 8 January, the deftly camouflaged Vietminh nearly overran the place by tagging behind the minefield-meandering of a returning French patrol who only discovered the ruse at the last moment. There followed a furious cannonade and massed attacks on three out of the four strongpoints. Special Viet satchel bomb teams raced through wire that was blown through by Bangalore torpedoes. Bunker after bunker was taken, with the Vietminh both inflicting and suffering heavy casualties in their turn.

These were all new tactics that would be refined and further developed at Dien Bien Phu. The Vietminh infantry attack was supported closely by recoilless rifles, machine-gunfire and bazookas from undetected camouflaged bunkers that had been created at night. As usual, the VPA infantry benefitted from extraordinary capability in field-work, camouflage and tactics, which allowed them to approach undetected. Eventually the Vietminh, who had penetrated the wire, were massacred to a man by the defenders' last desperate bayonet charge. Just one survivor leapt like an Olympian over the wire and raced in a weaving pattern downhill:

> *'I think I must have emptied a whole clip into him,' recounted a legionnaire. 'He fell but was still rolling his way to safety when Sgt Thomas, one of the few survivors of the 1st platoon, touched my shoulder...and...raised his carbine; a single shot rang out and the enemy's motion stopped. It was 1st Platoon's revenge.*[23]

Seven hundred dead Vietminh were counted around the stronghold.

Already forgotten, on 11 January, de Lattre died of cancer in a Paris hospital.

With Salan now focusing on resupply by road along the RC6, the battle now switched to the southern slopes of Ba Vi Mountain as they abutted the RC26. Despite a repeated sweep operation through the jungle and brush beside the road, the FEC could not prevent massed attacks on their fortified posts at Meo Pheo, Kem Pass and Ao Trach.

There were ambushes and fierce fighting on 12 January when a French offensive on the south side of Ba Vi was halted.

On 28–29 January, Algerian troops stormed key heights on Ba Vi occupied by the Vietminh. It was a covering attack aimed at disrupting VPA units on the north side of RC26 prior to withdrawal of the Hoa Binh garrison, which Salan had decided was necessary to avoid attrition, heavy losses and perhaps another disaster.

Attacks on the garrison at Hoa Binh

Containment was the main priority. Giáp did not want to drive out the French immediately but instead focused on their logistics and communication. By the end of the year the Vietminh had reinforced their positions round Hoa Binh with thirty battalions and, for the first time, an element of their heavy weapons units.[24] As time went by there was increasing pressure and firepower from 75mm and 102mm mortars. On 7 January, the French suffered a significant weakening of their defences when a Vietminh commando infiltrated the wire and destroyed four 105mm cannon.

At Hoa Binh, the French infantry came under 75mm artillery and heavy mortar-fire. Legionnaire Klause complained: 'We received little help from the artillery.'[25] He was more impressed by the effectiveness of napalm dropped from navy Hellcats and Bearcats that devastated several Vietminh assaults. Attacks against Hoa Binh increased. Apart from the artillery the big surprise for the French was the deployment in February of 22mm anti-aircraft machine-guns that forced their planes to fly higher. Ex-Luftwaffe Ju52s, which had been used as napalm-dropping bombers, were too slow and vulnerable in the face of Giáp's newly acquired 22mm AA. The Ju52s were old aircraft, and the method was primitive, but as Legionnaire Krause commented: 'France was poor...Because of the heavy flak they [the Ju52s] could not attack any more.'[26] Even the fighter bombers had to stop dropping napalm, 'otherwise it would be suicide.' One hit on a napalm canister and the aircraft would blow up.

Krause also witnessed the downing of a Hellcat fighter bomber, which was the first plane destroyed by the Vietminh in the war. A Bearcat from a flight of twelve that attacked Vietminh positions amongst the khasts and caves around the Kessel was hit by 22mm AA and slammed into the rocks. Klause complained:

> *...there were hardly any fighter bombers; we could see that when a division of Vietminh crossed the runway which was black with ant-like people...if only we had two fighter bombers with napalm, thousand would have been destroyed.*

Ground attacks on the Doa Binh garrison were resisted in the usual fashion, behind blockhouses equipped with machine-guns and barbed wire defences with artillery in support. The Vietminh made a determined effort to try to bring more firepower onto the battlefield, even breaking open old crates of weapons captured in the 1950 RC4 campaign. One VPA platoon found itself training on two fairly decrepit 120mm heavy mortars several weeks before the battle. An artillery man recounted his experiences to Pham, who had noticed the inscriptions on the mortars:

> *...victory at Hoa Binh 22nd February 1952...They lacked tripods so the cross of the trellis made from bamboo had to hold mortar no 1 in place.*[27]

There were other defects in the firing mechanisms and no oil to grease them, but the difficulties were overcome in a Heath Robinson fashion.

The mortars were brought by lorries camouflaged with tree branches close to the battlefield some 30km from the front. During the night of the 21st, they moved to the front. With the help of engineers, they ranged and sited the angles of the weapons. In a comedy of errors, they could not find a flat enough space on the hillock opposite the French positions, so one mortar had to be positioned on the road. Ordered to open fire at 11 a.m., they found themselves firing smoke rounds instead of explosive ammunition. Eventually they located some live ammunition for 105mm mortars which, incredibly, still worked. An opening salvo scored a lucky hit on a blockhouse, scattering French troops like rabbits into their dug-outs:

> *When there was a pause, they leapt out again to recover their weapons and retreat down route 41 in the direction of the delta...Their fighter-bombers arrived to start pounding us but we were well camouflaged and they were not on target.*

The day before the victory:

> *...we were on foot when we chanced upon General Giáp who helped us target the mortars against enemy blockhouses at Ba Vanh. Luckily, we were not let down. The second shot in particular was perfect!*

The fighting commenced again at 7 a.m. when the Vietminh bombarded Ben Ngoc on the Black River as the French forces were crossing. 'Stopping to eat at 3 p.m. we were dirty but happy...there were only six bags of rice but the cook got some manioc from a local village.' Pham's recounting of the story is typical. Food was never far from the thoughts of the common soldier as soon as there was any break in the fighting.

As the fighting continued the colony minister, Letourneau, came under powerful attacks in parliament about the cost of the war, citing casualties of 26,000 dead and 36,000 wounded between September 1945 and 31 December 1951.[28] Other parliamentarians called for a commission of inquiry or a reference to the United Nations for mediation in the settlement of the conflict. Such parliamentary criticism and scrutiny, *irritantes et désagréables*, only added to the disgust felt by most of the French officer class for the political class.[29]

Retreat from Hoa Binh and Legionnaire Krause, February 1952

Salan's forces had fended off many attacks, causing heavy casualties to the enemy as usual. But in this terrain, with its covered approaches and so detached from the delta, there was the possibility of being overrun. With the monsoon season setting in, air cover would become even more precarious or impossible. Another significant event in this campaign was the first downing of a French plane by Chinese-supplied anti-aircraft guns – a foretaste of a more difficult future for French fighter-bombers that had provided very useful support in stalling Vietminh attacks, at least when the weather was good enough. French forces had fought the Vietminh to a stalemate but prospects for the forces, which were spread out in about twenty isolated positions, were not good.

Moreover, there was simply no benefit to hanging on to Hoa Binh, as Giáp was exploiting the commitment of French elite forces to the Hoa Binh region as an opportune moment to insert elements of the 316th and 320th Divisions into the delta where they linked up with regional forces, independent 42nd and 48th regiments. Soon the no-go areas inside the delta were expanding even further. With sixteen elite units held down in the Hoa Binh area, and in fortified strongpoints along the RC26, Salan's ability to commit reserves to other danger areas became severely impaired. Operationally hobbled, he claimed the decision was caused by *a la faiblesse de mes reserves.*[30] In other words he was overstretched, especially after two parachute battalions had been committed to save Phat Diem. He had to withdraw. It was a bitter pill to swallow, but a logical one.

Elite troops could not be held in place indefinitely as 'garrison troops' without relief and rest. A typical problem for the French was that all their offensive operations involved GMs whose operational time was limited. Tempted to use them in every operation, the French could not afford to become involved in battles of attrition. So it proved that in operation after operation the FEC found that its 'appetite was bigger than its stomach'. Moreover, key elite colonial units became progressively exhausted, and their veterans reduced as their terms of deployment ended. This would in time become a serious problem that introduced stress fractures in French military deployment.

With pressure in France to limit the military budget in Indochina there was no political will to increase resources. Moreover, General Salan did not have the reputation and prestige of de Lattre, a five-star general, to bully his way to extra funding and resources. Salan was an outsider to the French elites, an old colonial soldier steeped in his love of Laos where he spent so much time in the interwar years. He had no pull in Paris, either politically or amongst the aristocratic military elites.

With two divisions placed on the east side of the Black River amidst the jungle- and scrub-covered Ba Vi Mountain, these prominent points had been captured by the 312th Division on the 29–30 December 1951. Clearly, Giáp's intention was to focus attacks on the vulnerable communication and logistics routes of Hoa Binh's garrison, starting with attacks on inbound convoys along the Black River. Having starved it of resources, Giáp intended to cut off and destroy the French column as it retreated, as he had done on RC4 in 1951.

Also, on the 29th and 30th, elements of the 304th developed a new focus of attack on RC21 running north from Xian Mai.

On 29–30 January, the 141st Regiment of the 312th Division captured Mount Hui, part of the Ba Vi Mountain range, which extended down to run parallel to the RC6 on its south side and RC21 on its east side. Holding interior lines in the centre of the salient by controlling Ba Vi Mountain and Bai Trai Forest meant that French supply convoys could be attacked at many of their vulnerable points either on the river route or on RC6 and 21. With pressure now building on Hoa Binh itself and increasing numbers of troops needed to hold open the supply route, French strategy was becoming untenable.

Meanwhile at Hoa Binh the air field was beginning to come under direct fire from Vietminh artillery. Aeroplanes on the runway were destroyed so the supply route by air was also being severely threatened. The noose around the garrison was being tightened. After the fall of Tu Vu and the abandonment of river convoys, attacks on the French central position were stepped up from the redeployed Vietminh divisions. With the Black River route cut, the logistic supply route by air increasingly threatened, and the RC6 tenuously held and briefly cut off by an attack on 8 January, withdrawal was the sensible option.

Salan's tactic of setting up central artillery bases that could fire in many different directions was a key innovation that helped to repel Vietminh attacks. However, VPA infiltration of the Red River delta was an increasing concern, particularly as the elite forces needed to deal with it were at Hoa Binh or protecting the RC26. This and the stress of maintaining the supply routes led Salan to give the order on 21 January. Serious casualties had been inflicted on the Vietminh, but the FEC was forced to retreat. Krause saved the life of a friend in a neighbouring unit by making sure that he got a place on the last Medivac plane out.

Under the command of the capable Colonel Gilles, there followed a hard-fought retreat, with the Vietminh pressing and rushing in on the sides of the retreating column in the typical cowboys and indians style of Indochina fighting. Giáp's aim was to break up the column into manageable segments that could then be chewed up piecemeal as he had done on RC4. The French force had to progress down RC6 to escape.

As usual, the heavily armed and encumbered French needed to hug the road while the Vietminh swarmed through the jungle. Under the command of veteran Colonel Gilles, it took the column eleven days of constant fighting to reach de Lattre's lines at Xuan Mai, and even here there was fierce fighting around the flotillas as the Vietminh sought to prevent evacuation. Salan's retreating troops had to walk down one thin road surrounded by the enemy at every turn attacking from both sides of the road. As they were retreating, 200 Meo suddenly came through their position. Krause recalled:

> *The old, women, children, 2–3 cows, all with bamboo baskets and full bags. The Muongs* [Meo] *wanted to retreat with us but we let them go ahead as we could not afford to get mixed up with them…Five minutes was a long time. We were the last 30 soldiers.*[31]

One battalion of paratroopers was flown out but the Moroccans, the 13th Legion half brigade, and Klause's legionnaire battalion, set off on foot. Krause's company came under attack with the rearguard. 'Our vehicles stood in the open,' he recalled:

> *Others stood in a burnt-out half circle…many were burning, munitions exploded, petrol canisters flew in the air. it was an inferno.…We were the last to come through…the Viets waited for us…legionnaires first class Krausemann and Hansen met their end.*

Some took their comrades' dead bodies with them, such as the beloved Stary, the Cossack who had joined Vlassov's German Army unit and had been a member of an SS unit in the Balkans.

The Hoa Binh's attack force had to retreat by the RC6 to the Black River and the safety of the Red River delta zone. Although heavily armed and protected by intermittent fortified positions such as Xom Pheo, the column would be subject to constant ambush, often at close range from the shrubs and tall grass close to the road. The road was held open by 2nd BEP. The 'parachutists were amazed that another section of 5th Regiment was coming through.' Having eaten and 'grabbed one hour's sleep between burnt out vehicles,' Klause continues:

> *In the morning we left the paras behind so were no longer the rearguard, but it was a thirsty trek because all the springs were spoilt by napalm and the dead… Around 6 p.m. we cleared the mountains and were met by trucks with tea, beer and something to eat. Seldom had we been so gratefully blessed.*[32]

The retreating French force of 20,000 reached safety. It was a professional and well executed withdrawal. During the overall campaign, the French had been roughly handled and suffered several thousand casualties, including 600 dead (regulars, partisans and auxiliaries), according to Krause,[33] who reckoned that the campaign had been a bad defeat. However, despite camouflage and ambush positions, the Vietminh had suffered 10,000 casualties in the extended battle. These high casualty rates were caused by artillery directed from firebases and close support aircraft, factors that extricated the French forces from multiple ambushes and tight spots and kept the VPA masses at bay.

Postscript to Hoa Binh

The definition of victory has always been possession of the battlefield and the retreat felt like a defeat. But a factual analysis suggests that de Lattre's strategy was broadly vindicated.

It was claimed as a victory by Giáp but if it was, it was a pyrrhic one. Giáp had learnt that even in unfavourable terrain, the French could use their firepower to inflict heavy casualties and escape destruction. Nevertheless, the Vietminh had drawn off many of the enemy, which enabled them to exploit the battle by infiltrating even more soldiers from the 316th and 320th Divisions into the Red delta, so undermining still further Hanoi's control on its immediate hinterland.

General Navarre commented critically that the battle 'permitted the infiltration of the delta *en masse*...the enemy brought back the echo of a major victory.'[34] But criticising a predecessor was an established tradition of the French Army. The Vietminh withdrew. In the five battles since de Lattre's arrival the French Army had killed and wounded over 50,000 elite Vietminh troops, which was almost equal to the entire strength of the new Vietnamese regular army. They could be replaced for now by new recruits and transfers from regional forces, but for how long could this rate of attrition on the politically committed elite be tolerated? Eighty percent of VPA troops had been Communist Party or Communist League cadres.

The French were also suffering from attrition, which was less about casualties, severe and constant though they were, but more about the lack of rotation and rest due to constant fighting and limits on numbers. Veterans in north African units were returning home. Attrition was also sapping political will in France, amongst the public and the political class.

The French lauded the Hoa Binh campaign as a victory. They pointed to the body count. However, the fact they could not hold territory between 75km from Hanoi and just 25km from the de Lattre lines should have been a reality check on any celebration. Moreover, the denuding of the Red delta of reserves had allowed the infiltration of an entire Vietminh division into the region to consolidate their hold on at least fifty percent of the villages inside the de Lattre lines around the delta. President Auriol awarded Salan the *Croix de Guerre*, describing him as the *Vainqueur a Hoa Binh*. It was certainly a victory, an achievement, to extricate his Hoa Binh garrison without an RC4-type debacle.

Salan noted with pride: 'We succeeded in taking away 20,000 men and considerable materials of war with just 66 killed and 250 wounded and the loss of just 15 vehicles and two LCM.'[35]

Overall, campaign losses were 436. Further, the FEC had shown that they had learned how to fight in the forest, albeit with fighter-bomber support on occasions. From a fixed defensive position, the French had pulverised the enemy, who had been drawn onto French firepower and suffered devastating casualties. Salan estimated Vietminh casualties at over 10,000 with 3,450 killed. However, it was also a defeat in that the FEC had shown once again its inability to hold territory just 30km from the delta defensive zone.

Salan's responsibilities included command over the whole of Indochina, but he was sanguine as to the situation in Cochin where 'the sects helped us and were still a necessary part of the military plan.'[36] Nevertheless, he needed to bring them into line when their actions amounted to outright brigandage. On the other side he had to protect them from the demands by Bao Dai's government that they should come under Vietnamese national command. Nonetheless, the military situation in the south was stable.

Huge losses had been inflicted on the Vietminh, and the enemy had been disrupted along their key supply routes. Giáp's attempt at an RC4-style victory was crushed. Despite throwing three divisions at the French forces in Hoa Binh and RC6, he failed. On the other side the significant moral advantage gained was the satisfaction that they could throw the French out of any mountainous area which, given Vietnam's topography, was significant. Ho claimed victory, but he warned his cadres 'not to underestimate the enemy'.[37]

However, there was stalemate on the battlefield. Giáp could not win in open combat in the delta. While the French were learning to hold their own in forested and hilly country in the dry season and with air support, they could not win or hold territory in the great mass of mountainous and forest-covered Tonkin. For Giáp it was time to develop further the change to an indirect strategy. He planned to take the T'ai Highlands and invade Lao, so extending French forces much further. From the French perspective, victory would be won with vastly increased US aid from Eisenhower's new republican administration. Much of the aid was aimed at arming and training the Vietnamese National Army, something that had been stepped up under de Lattre.

The Battle of Hoa Binh represented a transition stage in the French Indochina War, transition in tactics, in weaponry and strategy. Both sides could draw some positive conclusions from the outcome. Which side would learn and adjust better? Both sides would change their approach to the war.

Symbolic of the change, the iconic and very antiquated JU52 would be replaced within a few months by the American Dakota C47. Meanwhile, over the Chinese border, the VPA were graduating from use of the 75mm cannon. The 351st Heavy Division was being formed, being trained and equipped with 105mm cannon (guns supplied to and captured by the Red Army from Chiang's Kuomintang Army), the same American model used by the French. In addition, 37mm AA of Soviet design were being supplied. The first heavy artillery regiment was formed on 16 January 1953, after which they were provided with 122 vehicles including multi-wheel heavy trucks. Special Chinese trainers with Korean War experience were delegated to train 1,000 Vietminh AA gunners.[38]

Inspection tour

In October 1952, secretary for war de Chevigne was making a tour of Indochina and experiencing for himself conditions in waterlogged Tonkin on patrol with French troops. Back in Hanoi on the evening of his field trip, there was by surreal contrast to the mud an opulent banquet given in his honour by the governor of north Vietnam. He inspected the Ná Sán battlefield, which was being prepared, and took time to meet Major Bigeard, who had just returned from his suicide mission. De Chevigne awarded him the Ribbon of the Commander of the Legion of Honour as well as decorating other officers and soldiers.[39]

Upon his return, de Chevigne made his pessimistic report to President Auriol, along with his views and those of others, and became pervasive in the French establishment with only the MRP right and the conservative parties holding out. A consensus was emerging that France would have to negotiate with Ho and the Chinese. De Chevigne explained to Auriol that in respect of the military and political situation there was 'no chance of an amelioration in the coming years.' On the contrary, there was likely to be a degradation in a situation that was 'static and defensive'.

The authority and credit of Bao Dai 'was non existent over there'. In his view, the 'interests of France required it to extricate itself from indochina.'[40]

Fall of the T'ai country, Tu Le and Bigeard's escape

On 18 October 1952, Bigeard and his 6th BCP were dropped into Tu Le on their mission to draw off the three Vietminh divisions (312, 308, 316), about 30,000 regulars who had advanced suddenly under the jungle canopy against French garrisons located north-east of the Black River. These included the important T'ai market town of Nghia Lo where the French had scored a significant victory during the Giáp's Day River offensive. Taken by surprise, the French initially thought this was a diversionary attack.

Following a meeting between Mao and Ho in Beijing in late September 1952, the strategic move to the north-west and Lao was agreed. Giáp would plan to sweep the French out of their T'ai Hills garrisons, open the way to Lao and liberate the borderlands with China.[41] This was in line with Mao's primary strategic goal creating a defensive buffer zone beyond the Chinese border. Again, Giáp followed the Napoleonic concept of speed, strategic initiative and overwhelming concentration of forces. For the 700-man garrison at Nghia Lo, it meant a fierce defence using pre-set mortar- and cannon-fire around the barbed wire defences against mass infantry attacks on 17 November. Salan realised that the line of fortified posts in the T'ai Hills west of the Black River line could not be held. Realising the scale of the Vietminh offensive, Salan ordered a consolidation and retreat to the west side of Black River.

Colonel Bigeard, who was familiar with the area, was soon under orders to gather in the various garrisons and fleeing detritus from a string of garrisons including Tu Le, Gia Hoi, Lang Chang and Muon Chen around the Tu Lu fortified base. He would then lead them back to the Black River some 25km distant. Clearly a suicide mission from the outset, Bigeard was the right man for the job, his motto being, 'If it is impossible, it will still be done.'[42]

Situated in a small, isolated valley, a mere 6km long and 2km wide, the Tu Le post was atop a little hillock in the middle of the valley. Trenches were dug, and barbed wire laid out as they waited for the attack. They listened to the ominous sounds of gunfire in the distance. Other fortified points were overrun, including Nghia Lo with its 700 defenders, which succumbed after repeated attacks by a full VPA regiment. Tu Le would be facing two Vietminh regiments, about 10,000 men (regiments from 308th and 312th) while the paratroopers dug-in, slower moving regular infantry battalions of Moroccans, and a T'ai Mountain battalion scampered back to the cover of the Black River 25km to the south-west.

Attacked in overwhelming force on the night of the 19th and 20th, Bigeard had by 6.30 a.m. on the 20th repelled three major attacks. The post was deluged by fire from mortars, recoilless rifles, bazookas and machine-guns. Air support could do little to winkle out the high angle mortar positions hidden in deep clefts of rock. Waves of Vietminh tried to pour into the position but were mown down and forced to retreat. But Bigeard knew that they would be back with even greater force. He decided to retreat while he could. The 100 wounded had to be abandoned to the care of military chaplain Father Jeandel. In such circumstances it was normal to finish off the seriously wounded with an overdose of morphine, but it is unlikely that there was enough to go round.[43] Only three of them, including the uninjured padre, who volunteered to stay behind, would survive capture and imprisonment. Most were murdered. Other diversionary attacks and a paratrooper drop were made at Ho Huan on the eastern flank of the Vietminh line of the attack. Code-named *Operation Lorraine*, it was General Salan's offensive against the vital Vietminh magazines at Yen-Bay that underpinned Giáp's Clear River offensive.

The Vietminh were not impressed by *Operation Lorraine* despite the large commitment of 30,000 men, four groupes mobiles and two dinassault flotillas. The VPA continued their attacks, merely refusing the flank by lightly screening the flanking threat. Such a threat might have seemed impressive on a map to a commander and staff officer in Hanoi or Saigon, but in the topography of north-west Vietnam, with its thick jungles, tangle of steep jungle-covered hills and mountains, rivers and streams, it was no threat at all. Though a good concept, *Operation Lorraine* was just another hostage to fortune when the time came to retreat. Knowing that the thrust was time- and resources-limited, Giáp ignored it. He set an ambush on their retreat in a narrow gorge of Chan Muong on 17 November, where the French armoured column had to run the gauntlet in a storm of shot and shell. In this engagement they suffered 300 casualties and the loss of twelve vehicles, including one tank and six half tracks, to add to the other 900 casualties.

Significant amounts of Vietminh stores were captured and destroyed but the expedition fell short by 15km of the main supply hub at Yen Bay.

Meanwhile, retreating over a series of 1,500m colls and steep inclines, Bigeard just managed to outrun the Vietminh. He brought the bulk of his battalion back to safety having sacrificed one of his companies in a rearguard. action. Another company-strength hilltop post, which he passed through on the retreat, was sacrificed in yet another suicidal rearguard action at Muong Chen. It was here where eighty-four T'ai partisans under Sergeant Peyrol were ordered to delay the whole of the 312th Division. Having fought every part of the way back, fending off ambush after ambush in deadly short-range actions involving for the most part grenades and submachine-guns, Bigeard eventually brought back sixty percent of his men. He had been expected to be wiped out. As for Peyrol, he made a miraculous escape in mountains swarming with the enemy. He staggered back with just sixteen men. Bigeard became a legend. A defeat, but his heroic retreat was a much-publicised morale-boost to cover a serious defeat for France. Thirty-five outposts in their beloved T'ai hills, with over 1,800 losses including 1,200 captured.[44]

Dien Bien Phu, which was defended by a small and weak Lao unit, fell to the Vietminh on 30 November 1952. Above the Black River line, only air field-supported strongholds at Lai Chau and Ná Sán remained in French hands in the north-west quadrant of Tonkin. The three Vietminh divisions converged on an isolated French base at Ná Sán.

Priests

Chaplains played a vital and unsung role in the conflict and seem to have drawn great respect from the troops. Apart from conducting services and giving pastoral advice, they stayed behind with the wounded when capture was imminent and arranged the funeral details of the dead. Giving the last sacraments was a sacred and special duty. At Dien Bien Phu, Dr Grauwin describes how the priest would run through heavy fire to reach a dying man before he expired. 'In the terrible days of the beginning of May Father Heinrich administered the last rites hundreds of times.' Running around under fire, 'he would appear, red in the face and out of breath, but always with a smile on his face.'

It was a miracle of courage.

He also describes his earlier years in the conflict when a dying soldier was administered to by a badly wounded priest. Father Faugerson 'turned painfully on his left side. Stifling his own pain, he applied the holy oils to the dying man's forehead and hands. A few seconds later there was a jerk, a rattle in the throat and terror in the eyes.'[45]

In the Cao Bang retreat, the padre stayed behind with the wounded and was never seen again.

During an ambush of a convoy containing women soldiers Corporal Martelli, in a scene that would haunt him, witnessed a Catholic priest get up from cover and appeal for a truce, 'with his hands raised to the sky…he said in a loud voice, "I offer you peace brothers…the most precious gift…" He fell forward heavily, with a single bullet through the forehead.'[46]

Operation Lorraine, October 1952

After Hoa Binh, Salan continued a policy of disruption, always looking to be on the offensive to keep the Vietminh off balance. An important aim was to disrupt Giáp's advance offensive westwards over the Red River into the T'ai Hills following the attacks on Gia Hoi and Tu Le by sweeping through his lines of communication and supply. For *Operation Lorraine*, the French deployed two elite GM, the 1st and 4th, as well as several smaller armoured groups, a reconnaissance group and two Dinassaut flotillas of forty vessels. A parachute-drop was made on the main targets. In addition, the French deployed three engineering battalions to repair the road and construct bridges over culverts and streams. This was a necessary addition as General Salan calculated correctly that the retreating Vietminh would sabotage the road to slow down the French advance. In all there were 30,000 FEC troops who advanced on a single road on 29 October 1952, reaching their end targets by 4 November.

As Giáp predicted, the offensive ran out of steam within a week. French tanks had battered through to create a long thin corridor. At Yen Binh and Tuyen Quang, arms depots were captured amounting to some 200 tons of munitions. including 40 tons of mortar bombs, 35,000 grenades, shells, and thousands of recoilless rifles and small arms. Several new Russian Molotova trucks were also captured. These were all important captures but not in any sense decisive, as it was not the Vietminh's main magazine in the area. There was a much bigger magazine at Yen Bai. Strangely, Yen Bai, a few kilometres to the west of the main line of attack, was not made the focus of the operation, because stores captured there may have been a multiple of five- to ten-times those captured along the 80km road to Phu Yen Binh from Viet Tri. However, lack of resources and further topographical difficulties made the extra 15km impossible. As ever, in Indochina map distances are deceptive. The targets of the attacks were accessible by Dinassaut on the Clear River (Phu To), which offered much better navigation than the Red River to Yen Bai on this stretch, where the monsoon drop-off was creating too many difficult and unpredictable sandbars. The French were tied to their road or riverine routes of supply.

Intended as an extended raid, the French would have to retreat down the same road. As expected, the Vietminh were waiting for them as they retreated through a narrow gorge. The French suffered 500 dead and perhaps 1,000 other casualties in the stiff fighting to regain de Lattre's lines. Most of the fighting was on the retreat in the Chang Muong defile, where twelve French vehicles including a tank and six half-tracks were destroyed.[47]

Salan's *Lorraine* offensive was a clever move aimed at undermining Giáp's strategy, but Giáp showed his mastery of generalship by refusing to be distracted from his plan. Not panicking, he correctly calculated that the French effort must be short-lived and that the loss of stores and the Molotova had to be accepted in the exchange. Like a chess master he sacrificed a few pieces in order to win the game.

Riverine war

L'Adjudant chef Jean Guetre (sergeant-major), a veteran of the Second World War, fought in the backwaters as a marine operating from LSTs and launching rescue missions for beleaguered outposts and villages in the jungle, or patrolling along the coast or riverbanks of the Red River, or amongst the islands of Halong bay, where they would be attacked almost daily.

A typical mission began with a call out to save a friendly and heavily fortified village called San-koi on the Day River. This region was a Catholic bastion near Phat Diem. Two LSTs were soon loaded up with sixty men each. The battle began in early March 1954, just a few days before the denouement at Dien Bien Phu.

Differing from the officer class, Guetre writes in the jaunty and earthy language of a long-term working class professional soldier. It is rare evidence from an NCO:

> *Suddenly a 'sixty five' whistled over my head…it came from the right bank of the river. Simultaneously the Viets opened up with mortars and masked machine-guns…the sailors returned fire with their large ordnances…we heard the zip of a thousand so bullets overhead and the ping of bullets hitting the LST's side armour.* [Upon landing on the steeply banked left side of the river] *we were soon amongst them fighting man to man, and just before me were some Viets loading a heavy machine-gun. I emptied my tommy gun into them. Suddenly out of nowhere a Viet armed with a rifle appeared, and not having tome to reload my sub-machine-gun, I slashed at his neck with my army knife. Nearly decapitated he crumpled abruptly.*
>
> *An assault was launched, and a few Viet survivors were soon dispatched. Around us were twenty Viet bodies contorted in death in more or less grotesque positions. We recovered a 75mm recoilless rifle, 2x60mm mortars.*

The ambush in the far south eastern section of the Red River delta was a typical Vietminh ruse: attack a pro-French village or outpost and wait to ambush the relief force. More than that this attack in force by the Vietminh was one of many intended to distract the French and French reserve formations from the upcoming onslaught at Dien Bien Phu.

> *The marine commandos approached the village* [of San-koi] *silently. The leader of the company got on the radio to tell* [Guetre] *to lead his squad against the back door while he assaulted the front;* [he was met by a fusillade of bullets.] *As I tried to find an entry into the back of the village, we came face to face with a dozen Viets who were trying to flee but too late; we cut them down with a few short bursts. A few others ran back into the village were similarly dispatched.*
>
> [Inside the Catholic village of San-koi Guetre discovered,] *a real butcher's shop, the men, about twenty of them were completely carved up; testicles removed and decapitated. My heart and all feelings of compassion was completely shut down; there would be no prisoners on this mission. The hate and this ferocity is completely unimaginable.*
>
> [Guetre met the company commander, who ranted] *'My God, my God, what can we do in this fucking country…we always arrive too late with too few troops, tired equipment, our means are non-existent, and we lack helicopters which would be more rapid and effective in such operations.*

> [With two dead and four injured] *for such an operation we had got off lightly. We had run into a company of regular Viets reinforced by local militia. We also recovered a considerable quantity of material, heavy machine guns, cannons and mortars.*[48]

It was the small change of constant guerrilla war. Guetre does not give a body count, but from his evidence, Vietminh losses were obviously very considerable and much higher than French ones.

Korean armistice and Pierre Mendes-France

Neither side seemed able to win, but with French public opinion moving against a seemingly unwinnable war, there was pressure for a peace conference to achieve some sort of settlement. It was not just the public who were sceptical about victory. Socialist premier Paul Ramadier returning from Indochina on 3 October 1953 noted, 'I believe that it is a crime against France to maintain this haemorrhage that is the war in Indochina.' President Auriol agreed.[49]

Eisenhower and his ideologically anti-colonialist secretary of state John Foster Dulles had by the end of 1953 persuaded Laniel's coalition government to grant full independence to Lao, Cambodia and Saigon, instead of the associated states concept. Agreed in principle, the concept had not yet been enacted in 1954 in the face of backsliding recalcitrance on the part of members of the coalition, especially the right-wing of the MRP.

France's main coalition parties, the socialists, radicals, MRP and RPF, were all hopelessly split on the matter of Indochina, while the communists of Thorez were the largest party but excluded from government. One common theme of coalition governments of all stripes was the idea that there should only be negotiation with Ho's communists from a position of strength on the back of military success, but this aspect of the mantra was proving elusive. However, the French government believed that they had one important advantage in negotiations, which was that the US had promised not to make a separate peace with North Korea and China.

The French still clung to their ambitions for a dominant post-colonial role via the French Union of Indochina. Given the threat of China to the north, France could reasonably assume that there would be a continuing role for defence needs. The fight for Indochina was to defend a French idea of Indochina's future and the economic interests that went along with it. Much emphasis was put on cultural ties also, and while this could be dismissed by cynics as a fig leaf, the emotional commitment by France to Indochina, whether through Catholicism or other cultural links, cannot lightly be dismissed. 'King rubber' was only one of many aspects of imperial interest. Glory, self-identity and the sense of French 'civilisation' were also important. These sentimental interests had always run alongside the cynical ones.

The main communist powers were also looking for a pause in their global fight. Their economies were wrecked by the Second World War and the Korean adventure had been a costly draw. Stalin died in March 1953 and, despite infighting, all of his potential successors, including Beria, the NKVD chief, Georgy Malenkov, the premier, and Nikita Khrushchev, CPSU party secretary, were all inclined to more moderate polices and a softening of the economic hardship on their peoples. This was reflected in a more restrained foreign policy as both sides in the Cold War began to search for some sort of stability. This would require reduction in tension and mutual accommodation. Mao, who at this time carefully followed the lead of the USSR, started to move towards a similar position. Chinese losses in Korea (*circa* 600,000) had been huge and their economy was in need of modernisation. More importantly, the Chinese were desperate to prevent direct US intervention in Indochina.

The Korean armistice was signed on 27 July 1953 at Panmunjom. Its effect on French public and political morale was devastating, not least because the Truman administration had promised France not to make a separate peace. France felt that they had been abandoned, betrayed and left to continue the struggle alone against Chinese communism. They realised that the full weight of Chinese resources, logistical and technical, would now be focused on them. Having believed themselves to be in a common fight against communism, the US had negotiated unilaterally with the communist enemy and left them in the lurch.

Mendes-France's ideas for negotiations began to gain ground and even the MRP were shifting their position in the face of popular opinion. So as the FEC fought this bitter war and outposts fought to the last man in desperate lonely battles in the jungles, swamps and mountains of Indochina, some of the political class were preparing to sell them out. When Eisenhower was elected on a ticket that emphasised disengagement, lower taxes, withdrawal from foreign adventures, and direct military actions, the French began to sense equivocation in American support, for all their anti-communist bluster.

Hero of the anti-war left-centre in French politics, Mendes-France issued one of those famous press articles and papers that mark modern French history. *J'accuse* by Anatole France had electrified the cause of Dreyfus. Mendes-France's article *France can stand the truth* similarly enthused the left bank intellectuals, anti-war and anti-colonialist political groups. Mendes-France's candidacy for the premiership on 21 May 1953 won 301 votes, just thirteen short of a majority. The Gaullists did not support him nor, ironically, did the communists. If the communists were added into the anti-war parties, the socialists, the radicals, then there were 406 members of parliament who were against the war. A considerable majority. Politically the war was on a knife edge. With blockage in parliament, a non-entity called Joseph Laniel, an independent deputy from Normandy, was elected premier after a hiatus of thirty-six days. A wealthy man, he was the empty vessel that the Fourth Republic needed to resolve a stalemate between the parties. Bidault, who had also failed to raise a majority for his second premiership candidacy, continued in his role as foreign minister. MRP continuity in Indochina policy was maintained. But even that continuity was bending to reality. Navarre was instructed to win a victory, or at least not lose, to enable France to negotiate a way out at Geneva. It was beginning to be understood by many in Paris that a French-dominated Indochina might no longer be politically or militarily tenable.

French bitterness towards the US pull-out of the Korean War and support for France only in monetary aid led to radical socialist Edouard Daladier's rasping comment in the *Chambre de Deputé*: 'One of the party brings dollars, whilst the other presents its blood and sons.'[50] As the US had recently spent blood and treasure liberating his country, it was a typically ingrate, sour and cynical comment from the former premier who had led France into the Second World War. However, memories are short, and it had popular resonance. France, it seemed, especially their elites, liked the idea of glory and empire, but not the pain that went with it. The war and the quest for lost honour was being replaced by the need for economic recovery. Losses of men and money to this faraway place played little part in the new dreams of the post-war generation in which the vision of European unity played an ever-increasing role.

Very few Frenchmen were dying in the conflict, because most of the troops were colonial or local. Nonetheless, the cost in officer lives was very high with the equivalent of the yearly intake of St Cyr Military Academy being killed each year. Informed of FEC torture, massacres and rape by the left-wing press and the 'left bank' intellectual cohort, weariness had set in with the general public, as well as the consciousness of cost, even though this was increasingly and overwhelming underwritten by the US.

However, there were considerable political and personal vested interests tied up in the continuation of the war. The Saigon clique, including the bankers, were making huge fortunes. Apart from the arms and logistics trade involving military contracts, the main scam was the trade in piastre, which was fixed at a different rate in Indochina compared with the rate in Paris. Transfers of funds for all sorts of reasons, e.g. artificial commercial trades on import export, which required a license, could be used to rig the system and make enormous risk-free profits. Army officers, traders, the Corsican Mafia, Chinese magnates, Chinese triads, the Vietnamese elite and bankers were all in on the game. So were politicians, especially the MRP, radicals and socialists, who funded themselves personally and politically. Journalist Bourdet wrote in *Tempe Moderne*:

> *...the war itself became a vast racket...the MRP were now too deeply committed, knowing full well that any peace negotiations and even any change in personnel would show up certain of its most eminent members.*[51]

A book called *Traffic des Piastres 1953* published by former French Indochina official M. Dupieuch caused a national outcry because of the scandals revealed.

Huge big business profits were exposed by communist deputy Georges Cogniot, who revealed in the National Assembly on 18 May 1953:

> *...the* Banque de l'Indochine *admits a profit of 502 m (fr) in 1951 against 53m in 1947, the* cie de Cambodge *717m against 44m, the* Plantations des terres *107m against 100m etc. Forty-five capitalist societies whose balance sheets I have before me admit to have pocketed 10,101m fr in 1951 against 1,250m in 1947.*

The *Affairs des Genereaux*, which led to General Revers' downfall, was a typical drama in the Fourth Republic in the hothouse world of money, political funding and political scheming between coalition elements. It was scheming, vicious salon politics in continuity with all the problems of the Third Republic so detested by de Gaulle.

Yet, amidst the corruption and pettiness of the Fourth Republic, the country had already launched into impressive new directions. On 9 May 1950, MRP finance minister Schuman announced the so-called Schuman Plan for economic and political integration with Germany, starting with the iron and steel community. It was a shock for the political system and offered a remarkable and idealist new vision of a federated Europe. It was a vision that seemed relevant, modern and practical in contrast to the Indochinese empire, which was exotic, distant and apparently in the interests of a small, greedy minority and the aristocratic army. Initially the plan was not welcomed by Bidault, the MRP prime minister, but it gained traction and even popularity as a policy that could unite the centre block of parties and give a vision of hope in Europe around a common Christian democratic ideal. The idea of ending the possibility for war had resonance for the French people and, indeed, in Europe.

The European ideal offered a new vision of France, a Franco-German axis that ironically embraced a Vichy idea,[52] for a new path to glory and co-dominion in Europe that did not involve the morally dubious and troublesome idea of empire. Schuman's European vision hastened the detachment of the French from the self-identity and pride in imperial achievement.

The beginning of the Lao problem

Salan understood that Giáp's offensive in the T'ai Hills was aimed not just at the tribal uplands but at Lao. 'Northern Lao,' he noted, 'and particularly the region of Xam Neua required all my attention.'[53] He was soon visiting the king in Luang Prabang to pre-warn and consult. At Lai Chau near the Lao border to the north of Dien Bien Phu, a whole Senegalese battalion fell into an ambush and were wiped out. In a preview of the thinking that would take the French to the Battle of Dien Bien Phu, Salan issued an order to the commander of the post:

> *...monitor this communication route into Lao and reconnaissance mission by the enemy and in case of a heavy force try to slow down the inevitable enemy advance on Northern Lao, however do not deploy more than the necessary forces for these reconnaissance missions and avoid at all costs becoming encircled.*[54]

Salan was aware of the vulnerability of Lao, not least because their national characteristics were so Buddhist and peace-loving:

> *...a people gentle and idealistic who believed in the better after life and were not fearful of death...they accepted fate...in the face of evil the monks...prayed for protection and took religious ceremony with the utmost seriousness.*[55]

It was not the ideal material from which military units could be formed. However, French-officered Laotian units were to perform surprisingly well in defence of their homeland.

Land reform, class war, terror and civil mobilisation 1952–3

'Carrying out Agrarian Reform', in the Lao Động Manifesto, Hồ Chí Minh's policy strategy was implemented to:

> *improve the living conditions of the peasants and to mobilise the majority of the people, that is, the peasants, to participate actively in the armed resistance, to increase production and ensure supplies.*[56]

As the situation in the war became more desperate and the fear of US intervention increased to frenzied levels, so too did the programme of land reform and terror. Land reform marked the move towards a total war economy in the DRV.

In 1949, as the final victory of the Chinese Communist Party was approaching and the remnants of Kuomintang forces were being mopped up, Mao declared, 'The socialisation of agriculture is necessary for the complete consolidation of socialism.'[57] With victory complete, Mao was soon launching into the first of his great campaigns of terror and social revolution, which reduced the impoverished peasant masses into virtual slaves and prisoners of the state – more impoverished than ever. This revolution and the crushingly repetitive mantras of communism would be pushed down the throat of the Vietnamese people. Fed by Chinese arms and money, the Vietnam revolution, which aped the Chinese one, was the price to be paid. Not that it was done unwillingly by fanatical Vietminh communist cadres, most of whom were only too willing to learn from the great helmsman.

The course of the land reform terror was outlined by defector Hoàng Văn Chí in his book *From Colonialism to Communism: A Case History of North Vietnam*.[58] The land reform programme had two stages: land rent reduction campaign (1953–1954), and transformational (radical) land reform campaign (1954–1956).[59] Both stages involved violence, murder, compulsion, extreme social bullying, and confiscation. But the level of violence and murder increased substantially in the second phase. The atmosphere was sharpened by pressure from the Chinese advisers who were influential in all aspects of government, including economic, political and social matters. This included 'Agitprop', the mindless banal sloganising that was rammed into village communities by crude loudspeakers and endlessly repeated in political meetings in order to stoke up the hysteria of hatred and class war.

Chinese advisor Luo Guibo was not only an advisor but also a highly influential policy-maker. Many leading Vietminh communists followed his advice and pushed their own political agenda at the same time in their factional struggle, which included Ho and Giáp as targets. Land reform was a political issue as much as an economic one. Luo played a big role. A financial team was established in early 1951 to help North Vietnam formulate regulations on tax and rice collection, which was the most critical strategic issue of total revolutionary war in Asia.

It seems likely that Ho, with his bias towards a more nationalist agenda, regarded land reform as a distraction from the goal of freedom from France. Not that he disagreed with socialist ideas. However, 'whoever pays the piper calls the tune.' Necessary deference had to be given to the Chinese. For Ho, if national liberation required following the Chinese line on agriculture, and 'eating shit', so be it. Party official Bui Tin recounted that 'large numbers of Chinese advisers arrived.'[60]

After the defeats in 1952 and checks in 1953, the push for a more radical agenda increased as if revolutionary fervour in the political arena would win battlefield results. Even though some voices urged caution in the middle of the war and the need to maintain the fiction that the Vietminh were a coalition of political views, this view was overwhelmed. In the sharpened atmosphere of crisis, especially after the string of defeats in 1952, Chinese pressure meant that the socialisation of agriculture was seen as a way of boosting the war effort, as well as supporting rather than hindering it.

Peasants, it was argued, would be bound to the regime by their participation in the oppression of class enemy landlords. They were encouraged to lead the way in judgment on their fellow villagers. The party took a back seat while organising and pushing the masses to take a leading role. Land reform was an expression of political insecurity. Poor peasants were led to believe that they would benefit from class war and the redistribution of land. Forced collectivisation would later come as a rude shock. Land reform was not really about justice or economic redistribution, but it was an extreme ideological struggle that deliberately inflamed class war, resulting in the unleashing of the most vile, base instincts of the mob. As in all communist revolutions, the worst criminal elements quickly came to the surface: psychopaths, criminals, and opportunistic chancers. The terror and class mobilisation of land reform and redistribution was meant to, and did, allow the communists to impose a total war economy. Most particularly this meant the militarisation of all labour for war purposes, something not unknown to western societies, including Britain, in existential total wars.

In May 1953, Luo Guibo forced Ho to allow the public humiliation, assault and public execution of wealthy Vietminh supporter Nguyễn Thi Nam. For the Chinese it would be an example and signal for a wider purging of landowners. Ho pleaded: 'We should not open the campaign by shooting a woman, especially one who had fed communist soldiers…Ho knew it was not right,' according to a close advisor, '…but he did not dare tell [the Chinese].'[61]

So Ho stood aside. After 5,000 people screamed at and physically abused the old lady for eight hours, she was shot in the back of the head. It set the tone for the harsher second stage.

Giáp also climbed aboard the circus of class war. He could do nothing else because he was also a suspect. Besides, he was a believer. As he said to his generals, land reform was necessary 'because in the face of an enemy as powerful as he is cruel, victory is possible only by uniting the whole people.'[62] Throughout 1953, under Chinese guidance and Truong Chin's leftist faction in the ICP, the VPA purged bad elements in the army, i.e. the Mandarin class and land-owners such as Giáp. The victims were mainly officers and the punishment for their class crime was dismissal, imprisonment or execution. In some case they had to 'disown parents, cut family ties and even change their name.'[63] If they passed through the inquisition, bearing the unbearable they often had to accept without complaint the torture and murder of their parents even as they risked their lives for the revolution. Political repression accompanied land reform and even artists were subject to punishment for wayward thoughts. Artist Tho Ngoc Van, director of a fine arts institute, argued publicly at a convention in 1948 with party general secretary Truong Chin about the value of proletarian propaganda art. He would duly be sent for re-education in a village to artistically record the struggle against landlords. Phan Kế, by contrast, was tasked with drawing anti-colonial caricatures on the walls of French-occupied territory. A style that lends itself easily to communist polemic, he became a politically correct artist who was asked by General Secretary Trường Chinh to join The Truth (Sự Thật) newspaper and given the title of commissioning editor. Socialism in action was all about the micro-management of individual thoughts and actions.

Mass mobilisation had begun with Ho's creation of youth shock brigades in 1950. Tapping into the enthusiasm and naïveté of youth the Vietminh used these auxiliaries in a role that blurred the distinction between front line and auxiliary. Although we are familiar with the bright and smiling propaganda photos of the youth auxiliaries, François Guillemot's book *Death and Suffering at First Hand: Youth Shock Brigades During the Vietnam War (1950–1975)* gives the lie to this happy communist picture that so beguiled useful idiots in the west. Such innocents were used and abused and suffered terribly in the wars.[64] They were just 'two-bit soldiers'.[65]

Uncle Chinh

The land reform experience of former Mandarin official Uncle Chinh was typical. Mai Elliott's Uncle Chinh had 260 acres of rice in hilly territory in the midlands, with several thatched homes to accommodate his family and support forty peasant livelihoods. He had bought the land many years before when working as a magistrate in a nearby district. He rented out the land in exchange for ten percent of the crop. He also owned an orange grove. Representative of the broad Vietminh coalition, Chinh was a typical nationalist supporter of the Vietminh, even representing his region at a conference with Ho Chi Minh, who he met and was photographed with. Mai Elliot tells the story of her uncle:

> *In spite of his background as a big landowner and Mandarin, the Vietminh approached him. They invited him to serve as vice chairman of the province committee of the Lien Viet, an organisation they had set up to attract the middle-class people and intellectuals into their ranks…my aunt and uncle immersed themselves in these activities, supporting the resistance as ardently as the poor peasants.*[66]

In 1953, a series of decrees and laws on land reform were released. The VWP central committee assessed the possibility of moving on to the last phase of land revolution: redistribution of agricultural land. This was followed by a radical land reform law publicised on 19 December 1953. Soon after being passed in National Congress, a wave of land reform took place between December 1953 and March 1954 in Thai Nguyễn province, following trials that were apparently successful. A Central Land Reform Committee headed by Pham Van Dong was set up on 15 March 1954.[67]

Chinh was targeted in the first wave of 'moderate' land reform. Mai Elliott, his niece, takes up the story:

> *Already my uncle, as provincial leader of the Lien Viet front, felt it his duty to set an example. In 1950, when he attended a front meeting, Ho Chi Min himself took him aside and warned him to get rid of his land because land reform was coming...his wife insisted on holding onto 250 acres.*[68]

In early 1953, with the slow development of rent reduction policies, the pressure really built up on Uncle Chinh, who would enter the Kafkaesque world and horror of class war. Full-throttled communist oppression was on the way.

Chinh believed he would be protected because of his loyalty and service to the Vietminh and would get fair treatment. But the Vietminh:

> *...now required not only to reduce rent, but also to return to their tenant farmers the excess rent they had collected over the years...teams of zealous cadres (trained by the Chinese) were sent into the villages from outside to enforce the new policy.*[69]

Since 1953, for facilitating mass mobilisation and a rent reduction campaign, more than 100 North Vietnamese cadres were sent to China for training. Spring 1953 saw the creation of the policy group known as the Land Reform and Party Consolidation Section. It was headed by Chinese delegated advisor Zhang Dequn, who had other colleagues responsible for training. Similar to Chinese experience, social organisations such as peasant, youth and women's leagues, were established. Cadres were trained to practice a Vietnamese version of the banally named Chinese 'three together system', while peasants were mobilised to 'pour out grievances, suffering from landlords and French collaborators.'

When the land reform team arrived to a friendly welcome 'their threatening demeanour and harsh accusations stunned my uncle,' he signed papers they put in front of him 'confessing his wrongdoing.'[70]

The cadres employed for the task were ideologically trained but had little knowledge of the region and no interest in the background history or circumstances. In a typical story, Chinh was classified as a rich landlord farmer and that was the only thing that mattered for the class warriors. He was promptly ordered to pay back sixteen years of rents up to 1952, with the proceeds going pro-rata to the tenants. It was equivalent to 80 tons of rice. Accusations of hiding followed, and his wife and children were interrogated separately. The cadres took all the stored rice and animals, leaving them with nothing. To pay the fine, Chinh collected 10oz of gold through relatives in Hanoi, but the courier stole 9 out of the 10.

Chinh and his family had to subsist on one meal a day of watery rice and boiled veg. They were destitute. His land was confiscated, and he was allowed to farm 4 acres but was forbidden to hire labour. He attempted to sell his orange grove, but the potential buyer, a regimental commander, pulled out for fear of being associated with a criminal landlord. Chinh was arrested because he could not pay the back-tax assessment. Taken into the jungle prison, he was leniently treated by the police who knew him. Concerned for his destitute family, he sent away five of the seven children to walk to Hanoi to live with relatives. Uncle Chinh was in jail for three months.

The radical phase of land reform

This meant revolutionary radicalisation and land reform, which involved the sending of teams of cadres into the villages backed up by police and military. Mass rallies, games and entertainment drew the masses in and the political message was interlaced with the pomp, the show of red flag processions and revolutionary dance troops with their 'shouty' and banal cultural offerings. This went hand in hand with competition between villages and groups to compete for certain economic or social targets. This was not a new policy. The socialisation and new heroes policy had already begun in 1948 as part of a Chinese-inspired emulation campaign. But from 1953, the policies of class war, land reformation and liquidation of certain class enemies began to sharpen.

It was all part of the dual and parallel purpose of total war and state building. Only total control and galvanised societal effort could deliver the logistical requirements that would be needed for a victory at Dien Bien Phu.

People's courts were set up by decree on 12 April 1953. Decree after decree followed with the most radical saved till last on 19 December 1953. Under the orders of the party, courts were run by uneducated peasants with party cadres pushing from the sidelines. Tactically deft, the idea of the Communist Party was to tie in the peasantry to the revolution by aligning the party's interests with those of the peasant majority. Peasant courts descended into organised lynching. Onlooking crowds and the 'tribunes themselves' were whipped up into a frenzy of murderous hatred. Radical expropriation and punishment 'courts' comprised peasants who knew nothing about law. They were formed according to Decree 150. There was, of course, no recognisable due process. Sentences varied from the death penalty to years of hard labour. Despite their service, many soldiers serving at the front would discover that their landlord parents had been murdered in their absence.

There were indeed some bad landlords: 'On one occasion the landlord in the village came to my house and demanded paddy in a threatening manner. My parents had to hastily prepare food and wine.'

They had to sacrifice an egg-laying hen and 'When he finally left, his face crimson with all the drinking, I broke down and cried in anger…' Her brother was arrested by puppet officials and the landlord hit him. 'He was not the only one who was tortured…'[71]

The label of landlord was dangerous. According to Hoang's memoir, as soon as a man was defined as a landlord, whether a good or a bad landlord, he and his family were isolated from their fellow human beings, and nobody was permitted to talk to them or even have any contact with them.

Ho was clearly the most important leader in the north, but he did little to moderate or stop the policy, though anecdotal evidence suggests that he had doubts. He seems to have intervened in a few cases, including that of Uncle Chinh. Democratic centralism had to dominate. If he did have an inclination to intervene, he would have tempered that intervention in the knowledge that his party enemies on the left often working in tandem with the radicalised Chinese would attack him for *petit bourgeois* nationalism, rightist tendencies and class betrayal. The problem for his enemies was that his popularity and personality cult were the basis for regime legitimacy.

Ho's overriding interest was the protection of the revolution and independence for Vietnam. If this called for people to be massacred and oppressed in huge numbers, he was certainly willing to pay the price in blood, including the blood of innocents. He was a Marxist-Leninist. Stalin was his hero. Having lived extensively in Moscow with many contacts at the top, he was completely familiar with the ruthless logic of communist power, the maintenance of power and the uncompromising demands of democratic centralism. Ho must have been well aware of the murderous outcomes from class war, collectivisation and land reform in the USSR, because he lived through it whilst in Moscow:

> [Chinh] *became a prime target for any peasants seeking to vent their resentment on the landlords. He would be forced to kneel on a raised earth platform built at the foot of the hill with his head bowed. His accusers would take turns stepping up to the platform to denounce him, violently pushing his head from side to side. or jabbing at his forehead with their pointed fingers. The mood would be ugly.*[72]

This was the normal ritual based exactly on the Chinese model and repeated thousands of times in liberated areas. But the charges were dropped just before the trial. Perhaps Ho had secretly stepped in to save him. For those hoping to mitigate Ho Chi Minh's support for mass murder, this possible evidence of his munificence is thin gruel indeed. His later crocodile-teared criticism of leftist excess in 1956 was only a criticism at the margins, not of the substance of the land reform process.

According to Hoang, the DRV authorities never stated the number of dispossessed landlords in any of their official publications. Expropriation was occasional during the first campaign, but it was universally practised during the second. As soon as the confiscation ceremony was over, an exhibition of the landlord's removed personal belongings was organised, and in doing so, class awareness was intentionally provoked by illustrating the sharp contrast in living standards between peasants and landlords. The Chinese quota system for executions by district was introduced. This led to excesses as revolutionary cadres in the countryside sought to ingratiate themselves and impress their leaders at party centres with their plan fulfilment or over achievement.

Calculations as to the numbers of casualties of land reform are necessarily difficult to pin down. Official sources are inevitably going to be inaccurate because communists will hide or diminish uncomfortable truth. It is the habit of governments and not just communists. Declassified documents from Vietnamese and Hungarian archives indicate that the number of executions was much lower than reported at the time, although likely greater than 13,500. However we have to treat any communist sources with great suspicion. Economist Vo Nhan Tri reported uncovering a document in the central party archives that put the number of wrongful executions at 15,000. The implication from this is that there were many executions of landowners, simply for the crime of being landowners, who were therefore 'justly' executed. That number is not given. From discussions with party cadres, Vo Nhan Tri concluded that the overall number of deaths was considerably higher than 15,000.

The facts, or at least many of them, have been admitted by official Vietnamese government agencies, in particular the Institute of Economy. The Vietnamese Institute of Social Sciences stated in a report in 2005 that 5.8% of the population was classed as landowners. An impossibly high number but if that number was used by the cadres the victim numbers may have been very high indeed. In December 1953, Ho admitted that landlords comprised only 0.1% of the population. This means that eighty percent of people were wrongly categorised.[73] Redistribution affected forty-five percent of the land and 10 million people. Professor Julia Lovell estimates that 10,000–30,000 people were killed. Other estimates of unlawfully killed citizens – not just in land reform – have been estimated at between 100,000 to 700,000, and a six-figure total for this wider category is likely, given the known policies and evidence. Some Maoist apologists, active in the 1970s, and propagandists who similarly downplayed Pol Pot's Cambodian holocaust, put the figure for deaths at 2,500 or less. They have been discredited not least by the evidence of Ho, Giáp and DRV/SRV sources.

One participant in the mass atrocities, Vu Yhu Hien, reflecting on his guilt tried to find some rationale for the land reform campaign, but could find no rational reasoning or scientific or economic study underpinning the campaign.

Ho, as if he had been oblivious to the fact, was quoted in the 1956 *Land Reform Journal* as saying, 'the frenzy seemed to have become uncontrollable… too many leftist measures were implemented.' These are sly and disingenuous words indeed from the powerful head of state who was at all times aware of the horror, injustice and illegality of the mass murder that he and his cohorts had set in train.

China had already led by example. Estimates for the number of executions during China's land reform range from 200,000 to 800,000 to higher estimates of 2 to 5 million for the years 1949–1953, along with 1.5 to 6 million people being sent to 'reform through labour', camps where many perished. There were policies in certain regions of China that required the selection of 'at least one landlord, and usually several, in virtually every village for public execution'. Such estimates exclude the hundreds of thousands driven to suicide during 'struggle sessions' of the three-anti/five-anti campaigns, which also occurred around the same time.[74] Land Reform in Soviet Russia had been similarly bloody in outcome if less focused on quotas of either the dead rich or farmers. It was often enforced with machine-guns. Armed intervention and the murder of Kulaks in Russia was followed by mass starvation, especially in the Ukraine. Stalin's murderous land reform policy made him a hero to Mao, and they were both heroes to Ho Chi Minh.

In Tonkin, Duong Thu Huong recalls seeing bodies as a child of eight when he went out to water vegetables:

> *Right in front of my house was a hanged man in the year of the land reform. When I was eight years old, I had to accompany the students to public locations where landowners were dishonored and tortured…In the back of my house lay another dead man who had been wrongly classified as a landowner. He cut his own throat by laying it on the railway track.*[75]

Terror and murder had already been extensively used to liquidate opposition and class enemies, but the time was right to take this much further. The reasons are clear:

1. To liquidate centres of potential political opposition.
2. To mobilise support in the countryside for the widening and intensification of the armed struggle by distributing land to landless and poor peasants who formed a majority of Tonkin population. (It was estimated that twenty-five percent were landless, a particular problem in the overpopulated Red River delta. Their position was desperate and there was recent memory of

mass starvation in 1945/6, which only sharpened the class war anger against the smaller minority of landlords and landowners.)

3. To carry through the communist programme and prepare the way for future collectivisation, which it was thought (wrongly) would raise production.

In December 1953, the third national congress passed a land reform law that set out the route to land reform: step by step to wipe out feudal system relying on poor peasants, by uniting against middle and rich peasants.

As is always the case in top-down communist purges and class war programmes, the process led to excesses as local officials tried to impress their superiors by overfilling the quotas. The system was chaotic and lawless. The net was cast wider and wider. For example, Tran Kim Anh's father, uncle and grandfather were all staunch supporters of the revolution in the northern province of Thai Binh. They belonged to the National People's Party, which became a designated enemy organisation during the land reform period:

> *My father was determined to deny his being a member of the National People's Party. He was then tortured by having his two toes tied by two ropes that hung him to the ceiling. The ropes were pulled up. This hurt him badly, so he cried hard and asked them to pull down the ropes. Down he was pulled. However, he still cried wildly due to his great pain. They then stuffed cloth into his mouth.*

Journalist Xuan Phong, who had been sent for re-education in the countryside, took part in the land reform process in Bac Ninh province:

> *...the loudspeakers announced progress in the land reform campaign. Soon no one would be able to escape it. My brother-in-law the vice minister is from Nghe Anh, like Ho chi Minh...where the reform raged stronger than in other places. His affiliation with government did not stop his parents from being condemned to death. Every day we learn of new executions.*[76]

Supporters of nationalist minority parties were murdered, and Catholics and Buddhists were particularly targeted for oppression.

Estimates of the number of people affected by land reform are 4 million, with 150,000 properties redistributed. Actually there were no scientific studies or survey but hastily rigged local lists drawn up by local cadres, who filled in names to satisfy the arbitrary quota set from the centre, a number that had no statistical or intellectual basis but can only have been a figure drawn from the ideological ruminations and prejudices of functionaries working at the party centre: 'To set the ratio at 5.68 percent of the population as landowners is "far too high to compare with the actual situation",' according to an official publication.[77]

There were political risks in the land reform policy. Excitement soon faded. The harsh face of communism and its brutal and violent methods were revealed.

Many resented becoming slaves to the new system, quietly at first but the resentment was there. Peasants were given expropriated land and then forced into co-operatives. It was anathema to the peasant mind because it removed their freedom of ownership, the very thing that they wanted above all else.

As always with communists, the new elite of party cadres made sure that their nests were well feathered. This was noticed. Soon exhortations grew stale, and hypocrisy became evident as the ones making the speeches were mostly not those making the sacrifices. Moreover, the party attracted careerists, opportunists, criminal elements, psychopaths, bullies, as all communist parties or totalitarian structures do. Even the good or ideologically committed become corrupted by power and the money that comes with it. The author of this book, when flying after a business trip from Vientiane to Hanoi, sat next to a tycoon whose father had been a senior cadre in the powerful Communist Party Secretariat. Discussing the political system, he said, 'My father was a senior official in the party secretariat. My father told me, "Communism is just a label stuck on an empty bottle".'

Not surprisingly, Giáp and Ho regarded political work as equally important as military operations, as Giáp spelled out: 'a spirit of unreserved sacrifice are fundamental questions for the army…the political work in its ranks is of first importance. It is the soul of the army.'[78] This work was always backed up by 'persuasion', administrative methods, punishments, instillation of fear or, at worst, the firing squad.

Conscription had been available in the DRV since 1949, but it was often not needed because of the persuasive power of the Communist Party apparatus. In practice there was conscription and Corvée labour. Anyone refusing risked being denounced as a traitor.

Former Hanoi government official Nguyễn Minh Can, who was in the team that oversaw the ending of the reign of terror, said: 'The land reform was a massacre of innocent, honest people, and using contemporary terms we must say that it was a genocide triggered by class discrimination.' (Radio Free Asia.) Tran Manh Hao witnessed the land reforms: 'I saw the extreme horror, and I wondered what kind of regime this was, that had no other method than to repress and annihilate people…It took them to "people's courts" and shot them on the scene without a fair trial and even without any evidence. The land reform campaign was a crime of genocide like that of Pol Pot.' R.J. Rummel estimates unnatural death from all causes between 1946–1954 are in the range 242,000 to 922,000. Statistics are impossible to verify, and much would in any case depend on definition. The best evidence for the statistics and horror of land reform have emerged from within the DRV and subsequently the SRV. Ho talked of the 'frenzy' and noted that through torture euphemistically called 'corporeal punishment', 'we caused them [the landlords] so much pain they had to admit their guilt even though they were innocent.'[79] The number murdered was 172,008, as given out by Professor Nguyen Manh Tuong of Hanoi University, from a total of approximately 5.68% of the population who were landlords, i.e. 568,000. Of those killed, apparently 26,742 were 'properly' killed, though there was no due process whatsoever. This is all culled from a total DRV population in liberated areas of 10 million.

CHAPTER XIII

Genevieve's War

Genevieve's path to Indochina

Genevieve de Galard-Terraube was a Parisian. Born on 13 April 1925 into a *haute bourgeoise* minor aristocratic family. She grew up in the exclusive 17th arrondissement in a comfortable apartment in Rue de Levis, the same apartment in which she lived out her long life. She attended a traditional Catholic girls' school. Her love of maps and a certain romantic vision of Indochina as well as a touch of tomboy antics in tree-climbing, bicycle tricks or hanging upside down on the railings of bridges predisposed her to an adventurous life. She could never have guessed what extreme adventure fate had in store for her. Her formative and memorable days were spent in the Haute Garonne, 80km from Toulouse. It was a time of big families, cousins, long summer holidays and countryside adventures, riding an Arab stallion bareback, jumping off haystacks, bicycle races, grape-picking, and mushroom-hunting. That her grandparents' house was a chateau is not in doubt as she refers to an orangery and a collection of coaches stored within. In another epoque, she would have been a candidate for the guillotine.

Genevieve's family on both sides were steeped in military tradition. Duty and defence of country were etched into her DNA, as it was and still is for the very large number of French aristocrats who continue to dominate the upper reaches of the elite in the military, commerce, finance, and administration. They formed a considerable element of the political establishment and still do. During the Second World War, Genevieve's family suffered from hunger and cold when they moved to the country. However, her education continued at a convent school. Like many of her class she came from a Petain- and Vichy-supporting family, though as the war progressed, and allied victory became more assured, support for the Resistance increased as the name of de Gaulle became more familiar.

After the war, she eased back into a gay social life in Paris and mixed with the military set, with which her upbringing associated her. In the course of 1951, Genevieve felt the call of duty and adventure and through a friend she learned the existence of the Air Force Nursing Corps. She had discovered her *metier*. Her sister had married already, but Genevieve felt that life should offer more. A plain girl and already 26, she may also have been looking for a husband in the target-rich Indochina environment.

Indochina appealed to her sense of the exotic. There were many army officers there who belonged to her class and friendship cohort. She had cousins serving there including one who would be stationed at the Isabelle Bastion of Dien Bien Phu. Like many of her class, she was appalled by communism as a secular creed. Disgusted by the antics and propaganda of the communists in France who were encouraging sabotage in arms factories and anti-patriotic attitudes, she also felt a certain ideological motivation to go to Indochina. The rights and wrongs of colonialism she never considered. After agonising over whether or not to leave her mother alone, she spent a weekend in prayer at a convent in the Paris suburbs. She started her new vocation in 1952, and after several trips around Africa, she was posted at last to French Indochina in 1953.

Saigon – Dolce Vita

By the time Genevieve flew into Saigon for the first time in April 1953, the time of terror, assassinations and grenades had passed. Saigon had returned to its exotic and charming life. The threats were still around and about the city, so countryside excursions were not possible:

> *When I landed in Saigon, after a tiring flight, I was struck by the intense, humid heat…I was quickly taken in charge by one of my cousins, who took me to visit the whole city.*
>
> *I was fascinated to discover this large city built in the European style in a tropical landscape, with its districts of comfortable villas surrounded by verandas in luxuriant and well maintained gardens; its wide avenues bordered by sycamores or rubber trees; its pink Cathedral crowned by two soaring steeples; its majestic white governor's palace encircled by an immense garden filled with flamboyant frangipanis, and multicoloured flower beds; its rue Catinat, running between the lovely European style boutiques and shaded by tamarind trees; and its Continental Hotel with its terrace, in these years of war, as famous as the best known Parisian cafés.*
>
> *…the sampans glided silently in front of the wooden pier at the point of the Jokers. Our tour extended to Cholon, the Chinese city teeming with life. From every alleyway came the odours of cooking food, prepared in the street by ambulant merchants. The aromas of nuoc mam and Chinese soup mingled with the scents of sandalwood and incense. I was intoxicated by all these aromas, the spices and perfumes of the orient of which I had dreamed so long.*

Marguerite Duras also remarked on the smells of the city:

> *Whiffs of burnt sugar drift into the room, the smell of roasted peanuts, Chinese soups, roast meat, herbs, jasmin, dust, incense, charcoal fires, they carry fire about in baskets here, it's sold in the street, the smell of the city.*

Little has changed.

Saigon is 'a city of pleasure that reaches its peak at night', especially in the bustling Chinese quarter in Cholon where there were, according to Duras:

> *...those Chinese restaurants on several floors, they occupy whole buildings, they're as big as department stores, or barracks, they look out over the city from balconies and terraces. The noise that comes from these buildings is inconceivable in Europe, the noise of orders yelled out by the kitchens. No one ever merely speaks. On the terraces there are Chinese orchestras.*[1]

The Chinese quarters of South-East Asia are much the same today, except for electronic amplification and the traditional orchestras replaced by ballad singers in tight red cheongsam dresses.

Not everyone was enamoured by the place. Legendary travel writer and political radical Norman Lewis had a different reaction:

> [Saigon is] *a pleasant colourless and characterless French provincial city, squeezed on a strip of delta land in the South China Seas. From it exude strangely into the surrounding creeks ten thousand sampans, harbouring an unaccounted native population. To the south the once separated China town of Cholon has swollen so enormously as to become its grotesque Siamese twin. The better part of the city contains many shops, cafés and cinemas and one small plain cathedral in red brick. Twenty thousand Europeans keep as much as possible to themselves in a few tamarind shaded central streets and they are surrounded by about a million Vietnamese and Chinese.*[2]

Unlike Greene, Genevieve or Duras, Lewis's snide views on Indochina are those of a suburban prig. Who could not be charmed by the sheer exoticism, the bustle, colours, smells and energy of Saigon and Cochin in general? Or the oriental diaphanousness of the ao dai-clad young women whether on foot or flowing from a push-bike?

There was little time to acclimatise. Genevieve went into action immediately. There followed an exhausting round of flights in Lao and Vietnam, from one point of danger to another. Wherever the fighting was the most intense the ambulance air arm went into action.

Genevieve in Hanoi and the medivac tour

Genevieve landed in Hanoi on 5 May 1953 during the crisis of the first major Vietminh attack on Lao. She was soon thrust into the thick of the medical action with flights to Luang Prabang, the charming temple-rich and Ruritanian capital of Lao. Then she flew into Xam Nueva just before its garrison was overrun. Later, Genevieve landed in the mysterious and strategically important Plain of Jars, a unique verdant and unforested pastoral upland with its hundreds of enormous stone jars at three main sites lying in clusters at all angles, in all shapes and sizes. But there was no time for sightseeing. Near Xieng Khouang the provincial market town, where the French had an air field and base, there was heavy fighting. She would be evacuating the wounded detritus and remnants of the doomed retreat from Xam Nuea. Flying in Junkers 52 planes, with their distinctive boxy corrugated-iron look, was not ideal for intricate medical work, nor for casualty comfort. She would remark on the extreme noise and juddering of the craft caused by the third engine in the nose of the plane.

Pierre Schoendoeffer's film *Dien Bien Phu* (1992) takes the audience to Hanoi's classical opera house (which still operates) and the beautiful soprano voice of the performing diva. The music is romantic and sorrowful. He shows us the café terrace and restaurant life of the colonies at its decadent best, but the soldiers are on standby, passing the time in bars with the local women, or the occasionally feted French women, ready to dash to the airport and jump into any desperate maelstrom that required the urgent attention of the elite paratroopers or GMs. The contrast is well drawn with the brutal realities of jungle war and the filth of battle at Dien Bien Phu. In Hanoi for the first time, Genevieve recounts:

When I arrived at Petit Lac, I was enchanted by a flower market, its stands spilling colour, and the mirror of the water, a small pagoda. The light shadows of the trees along its shores and reflections of clouds passing over the water enhanced the charm…I would return some evenings to pass young lovers drawn by this romantic spot and admire young girls in their spotless ao dai, with their long black hair drawn back on the nape of their necks. But that day I continued my way to the old Vietnamese quarter. The street of the silk and the street of cotton, their display windows glistening with colour under the shade of the flamboyant trees. Enveloped in the scent of the Orient, the women went about under their conical hats, bearing their pendulums across their shoulders. They trotted along in their typical mincing steps, carrying large baskets of fruit or vegetables. Most of them wore black satin pyjamas with short white vests.

Men passed by, carrying on their balancing poles all they needed to prepare pho, a soup of rice noodles flavoured with strips of meat and served in a highly spiced bouillon.

Our friends, soldiers, officers posted at Ná Sán, were delighted when we were on leave to rest. We would go with them for a drink at the well-known Metropol Hotel or Splendide.

In those places, since the start of the war, one would run into an animated and cosmopolitan clientele of many journalists and writers from Europe or America covering the Indochina conflict, including Jean Larteguy, Jules Roy, Graham Greene, Lucien Bodard, Max Olivier-Lecamo, Max Clos, Fred Spark, and Jean Francois Chauvel.

Most VIP visitors would pass through the colonial fantasy of white-washed colonial portals, colonnades, louvred doors and windows, brass fittings, chequered marble tiles, bamboo armchairs, and the overflowing verdancy from planters of a tropical luxury hotel. Visitors of the era included Jack Kennedy and brother Bobby, Pierre Trudeau, and Richard Nixon. Nixon reminisces about Hanoi: 'We drove down wide tree-shaded boulevards, and through ornate wrought-iron gates I caught glimpses of large villas set amidst lawns and gardens.'[3]

The Metropole Hotel, the finest establishment in Hanoi (and still is), is near the opera house by the lake. It is the essence of colonial ease with grandeur in its white classical looks, with louvred green shutters, art nouveau filigree iron work and green sun canopies, colonnaded verandas, planters sprouting the verdancy of the east, delicate bright orchids, soft-pillowed ratan furniture, brass, checkered black and white marbled floor or highly polished mahogany or teak, sharp shadows cut by light and the unobtrusive glide of immaculately creased, white-liveried hotel servants. One can almost hear the clink of tall glasses and hear the chatter and guffaws from groups of officers or the more raucous outbursts from the drink-merry members of the foreign press. In elegant side rooms of white soft furnishing, ladies in cotton and chiffon surrounded by explosions of colour from the flower bouquets sip champagne or the latest American cocktail.

Bernhard Fall describes it:

Opposite the residence of the governor and next to the massive Bank of Indochina building it was at the Metropole that one could find the wealthier of the French merchants, those among the journalists who had got tired of the professional in-breeding resulting from an overlong stay at the Press club, and the senior officers of the northern command who were on leave from their posts in the paddy and who needed a shot in the arms of French civilisation before returning to the bunkers, leeches, and stench of Hung-Yen or Nam-dinh…the commanders of the Groupe Mobiles by virtue of their particular assignment, were an element quite apart from the rest.[4]

The Groupe Mobiles were the dashing free-wheeling elites – the inheritors of the cavalry tradition of the French Army. Colonel de Castries, later the commander at Dien Bien Phu, was one of the GM commanders. Fancying themselves as modern cavalry, they were constantly in action dashing from one trouble spot to another.

Ná Sán

As the French garrisons north of the Black River were collapsing in 1952 following the storming of Nghia Lo, General Salan set up Ná Sán as a large Dakotable aero-terrestrial base in November. It would compensate for other losses in the T'ai Hills and give a rallying point for the T'ai and Hmong partisan populations whose French-led GCMA units were a scourge of Vietminh military infrastructure and personnel.

In November 1952, Giáp's aim, having drawn French forces to many points around Vietnam, was to strike with a massive concentration of force at Ná Sán to snuff the French out of the T'ai Hills once and for all. It seemed that the Ná Sán defence zone was his for the taking; it would be a triumphant conclusion to the Black River offensive. Giáp and Ho were confident of victory. A document found on a dead political commissar, which was signed by a high party functionary, Tran Kim, declared:

> *The enemy has lost the initiative and is passively encircled...we shall destroy them, and this will be very influential in the coming Battle of Lao...each soldier needs to be informed of this before the battle.*[5]

The Chinese were also enthusiastic for the Battle of Ná Sán as a staging post for Lao, because the Chinese leadership believed it 'the weakest link of the enemy force; and it will have strategic significance later.'[6]

However, this was a battle induced by Salan and already thoroughly thought out. Not uninfluential in Salan's thinking was the successful experience of the British with air-supplied defensive 'boxes' in the Burma campaign in the Arakan, at Kohima and Imphal and at Meiktila 1943–45. Salan was visited by Sir Charles F. Kneightly, British commander-in-chief in the Far East, who advised:

> *The situation was similar to the British operations against the Japanese in Burma* [who] *believed that 'base aeroterrestial' tactic* [boxes in British parlance] *were indispensable in the analogous situation in Indochina.*[7]

Not passive at all, Salan had been preparing for a 'defensive ambush' between 16 October and 30 November when the airstrip at Ná Sán received 1,267 civil and military flights that landed every ten minutes during the day, bringing in eleven fresh battalions and 2,500 tons of military material, food, munitions, four artillery batteries of 102mm cannon and barbed wire. It was an audacious and calculated risk aimed at bringing Giáp to his guns and reckoning on

Vietminh overconfidence. Salan was meanwhile fending off the idiotic concepts from the armchair generals in Paris, who were still thinking in terms of strategic defensive lines and were concerned that battle was being offered on 'unfavourable terms…I was sent a barely serious message by the defence ministry…they complained that my dispositions were not linear.' It was a war without fronts, *sans fronts*, in mountainous jungle. The map-bound politicians were out of touch. Unfortunately, many of the French generals were also map-bound.

Giáp sent three divisions of 30,000 elite front-line troops to crush the Ná Sán fortress. Included in the battle order were the 308th, 312th and 316th Divisions. He decided to attack because his information was that only 2,000 troops manned the defences, which were not complete. Advanced elements of the 308th, bypassing some outer defences, launched a surprise night attack at 8.30 p.m. on 23 November 1952 on strongpoint 8 on the inner line of strongpoints, which had a ring-side view of the airstrip. Strongpoint 8 was commanded by a company of 5th REI (Legionnaire Infantry) led by the formidable Captain Lestestu. When the Vietminh infiltrated the double wire defences and got into the trenches, there was a furious hand-to-hand battle with grenades, automatic artillery and spades. The enemy were ejected but leaving thirty percent of Letestu's company dead or wounded. A second attack followed and was met by French mortar fire. The assault was held off until relief came at 11.30 p.m. Sixty-four dead Vietminh were left behind on the wire.

Following the attack, Salan flew in further vast quantities of defensive building materials, barbed wire, reinforcements and three batteries of 105mm cannon. Colonel Gilles developed an outer ring of defences to absorb the enemy attacks and provide interlocking machine-gunfire. By the time his other divisions came up, Giáp was to be met by eleven elite battalions. French defences consisted of thirty-one interlocking strongpoints surrounded by barbed wire and minefields. Heavy artillery was zeroed-in on the approaches to the defences. At night, French patrols swept inside the perimeters and between the strongpoints to check for Vietminh infiltration.

There were three T'ai battalions, one battalion of Foreign Legion cavalry, Moroccan troops and a Vietnamese battalion. Elite parachute battalions included the 1st and 2nd BEP and the 3rd BPC. Salan reckoned that this key strategic position and the isolation of the French would be too tempting for Giáp. It was and he accepted battle.

Six nights later, on the 30th, the 308th attacked outer defence strongpoint 24, manned by companies of T'ai and Moroccans. They were overrun at 3 a.m. but an all-day counter-attack by 2nd BEP and a Moroccan infantry unit supported by ground attack Bearcats and Hellcats succeeded in retaking it.

Captured plans found on a dead VPA officer confirmed the obvious: Giáp was looking to set up a mortar-firebase to try to close the airstrip. General Navarre should have taken note when looking at the defences for Dien Bien Phu.

Giáp's divisions launched wave after wave of infantry attacks. Genevieve described the geography of the situation:

> *Situated in a mountainous region on T'ai land, the position* [Ná Sán] *could only be reached by air. Many civilian aircraft from Autrex, Aigle Azur, Cati, and Air Vietnam had been requisitioned to bring in troop reinforcements and evacuate casualties.*[8]

Her evidence again underlines the extent to which France's military efforts ran on a shoestring, something that was exposed when the FEC overstretched on major operations. The logistical tail of the French military was under-resourced and undermanned,[9] as the French military strained to boost the number of front-line troops without corresponding development of auxiliary services.

On the night of 2 December, the 312th Division launched mass diversionary attacks on strongpoint 21 bis. The main attack was against strongpoint 26, which ran along an 800m ridge overlooking the runway from an enfilading position along the length of it. If captured, Giáp's 22mm AA batteries could shoot down the flight path of the Dakota supply planes as they were landing or taking off, and mortars could easily target the runway. A serious situation developed when strongpoint 26 was nearly overrun by three battalions of the 312th.

Massed human wave attacks were launched on the Ná Sán defences at night using significantly improved firepower capability, including heavy mortars and recoilless rifles in close support.

The VPA launched four night-assaults against strongpoint 26. However, the long-lasting flares dropped from circling aircraft or fired by the defenders constantly illuminated the battlefield, so nullifying the benefits of darkness. The approaches to the position were plastered with artillery fire, which Colonel Gilles described as 'an indescribable deluge of fire.'[10] Attacks by two battalions on stronghold 21 bis led to the same result. Hundreds of Vietminh dead were left behind.

In the Ná Sán campaign, the Vietminh were never able to shut down the aero-terrestrial system. Supplies and men came in, medical cases flew out. One thing the Vietminh learned at Ná Sán and in the Lao battles was the incredible attention that the French paid to the treatment of the wounded and the resources put into that aspect of war. Genevieve was often in attendance there. Giáp was to exploit this as a weakness in due course.

Genevieve recounts medivac flights from Ná Sán:

> *On the military aircraft that were not pressurized (Ju52s), it was particularly crucial to give oxygen to the wounded and to sustain their blood pressure…One day after a serious battle, we were warned to expect many casualties.*

Genevieve spent the nights 'helping nurses prolong the "disconnections", intravenous injections of Phenergan Dolosal, a process that had been perfected by Dr Henri Laborit to reduce the effect of shock from the injuries.'

With ammunition and food running short, in desperation Giáp had launched the costly mass attacks because his logistics were in crisis. It was the final act of a commander who could not sustain a long siege. At the height of the battle and in despair Giáp yelled at his Chinese advisers, 'Where are our artillery guns?' Apart from the lack of artillery, there were no heavy calibre AA guns and the Vietminh had to watch in frustration as the planes landed unchallenged, one after another. The Vietminh withdrew and the 316th Division prepared to move west over the T'ai Hills as Giáp prepared to invade Lao. 'The troops were not yet well trained,' Giáp claimed. 'It wasn't a defeat, but we suffered losses.' Losses may have been as high as 7,000 against about 1,000 casualties suffered by the French.

Vietminh reaction to defeat at Ná Sán, and American criticism of Salan

The Vietminh were severely handled. Thousands were mown down by concentrated machine-gun- and shell-fire. Only one of the thirty-one defensive strongpoints was taken, then lost. Attacking well set defensive positions had again proved impossible. There were lessons to be learned. Firepower needed to be increased, which meant much greater logistical effort. It also needed to be hidden. How could the Vietminh take on strongly constructed defensive positions that were impervious to mass attacks even with 10–1 odds in favour of the attacker?

The conclusions reached from their analysis were to have a profound effect on Giáp and Ho's military and political strategy. Giáp needed a much better supply chain to provide for a longer siege with more men, and most of all he wanted firepower, i.e. the heavy artillery of the 315th Division, which was in training across the border. This would necessarily mean a human porterage system beyond even the large civilian porter armies that he had collected already. Not just guns would need to be transported, but tens of thousands of artillery and mortar shells and huge quantities of rice. Such a quantum increase would have profound political consequences, requiring the total war commitment of the entirety of the DRV's civil and military society where as many as a million civilians would be inducted into the supply chain (porters) and ancillary services. This from a DRV population in the north of about 6 million.

Mobilisation of the necessary logistic capacity would require the long-term establishment of the hated Corvée systems, i.e. forced labour and conscription for men and women. Moreover, forced conscription was also necessary to replace the volunteers who had been mowed down in their tens of thousands since 1950/1. Much of the elite of the resistance to France were dead already. Even with considerable enthusiasm in places, harsh discipline, terror and coercion might well be needed. This meant land reform, social revolution including bringing women into the total system, and heightened political activity including propaganda. The reward for the peasants would be land reform, notably the forced distribution of farm property assets in a process that was meant to bind the peasantry to the state.

Giáp and Ho were taking big risks. Launching a major social revolution in the middle of a war was politically dangerous. It could backfire and throw the essentially conservative peasantry into the arms of the nationalist Vietnamese government.

So why did Giáp, Ho and the Politburo take such risks? There were three fears. Firstly, the Americans were rapidly increasing aid intervention with arms shipments. Secondly, following de Lattre's change of policy, the French were successfully and rapidly building up American-equipped Vietnamese national forces that were beginning to show themselves, at least in parts, as capable fighters. And thirdly, there was the fear of direct American intervention following on from the Korean War. Ho and Giáp needed to seize their chances now. And at any cost.

This accounts for the extraordinary haste and impatience in Vietminh military decisions and their willingness to take big risks and suffer enormous casualties. There was a feeling that time might not be on their side. If Giáp could wear down the French quickly, or score just one more decisive victory, such as the RC4 battle, then maybe France could be knocked out of the war before the Americans had time to react or before the national government had established a credible military backbone that the Americans could support.

The Vietminh leadership was well aware of political developments in France, of increasing war weariness, political fragility and the rising popularity of Pierre Mendes-France's Radical Socialist Party's anti-war policies. Just fourteen votes short, he would come very near victory in securing the premiership in May 1953. One more push, Ho must have felt, and they could topple the Laniel government and the MRP faction that had controlled colonial policy since 1945. Meanwhile, de Gaulle and the RPF seemed to be in decline and de Gaulle was losing interest in the democratic process. The communists were already in the anti-war camp. The French socialists were teetering. Ho needed just one more major victory.

Soon after the fighting at Ná Sán ended, Salan needed to order the abandonment of Dien Bien Phu near the Lao border as large Vietminh forces descended on it. This was a further blow, undermining the French hold on the T'ai Federation territory, as well as opening the door to the invasion of Lao. However, it was only to be a temporary withdrawal. Salan's Directive No. 40 (issued on 10 January 1953) stated:

> *The reoccupation of Dien Bien Phu must constitute in the forthcoming period the first step for regaining control of the T'ai country and for the elimination of the Vietminh from the area west of the Black River.*

It was not a realistic objective, but it was on record as an agenda item when Navarre took over.

Meanwhile, at Ná Sán, the French celebrated their victory (*Time* 12 January 1953):

> *...in the underground mess (at Ná Sán) Gilles passed out cigars and liquor to staff and declared 'we have done a nice job here' while in Hanoi officers celebrated by dining sumptuously.*

The ordinary troops were not excluded:

> *Fresh bread, Algerian wine, and three thousand bottles of champagne – one for every four men in the embattled camp. Vietnamese troops got frozen meat, dried fish, and rice, while North Africans received wine, live sheep, and goats, all brought in by airlift.*

Even Bao Dai was flown in to celebrate the victory with senior officers. A photograph shows a slightly bemused emperor incongruously squashed up in a command bunker with his victorious army officers – all of them French.

The Americans at Pacific high command, CONCPAC, concluded sniffily that it was 'an inconclusive battle in a mountain wilderness.'[11] Morally appalled at Salan's lifestyle and the perceived decadence in the FEC, the prudish Americans were determined to show their power and started a campaign supported by Eisenhower in person to get rid of him.[12] The JCS complained that the French command and plans 'lacked determination and vigour'.[13]

For Salan, having taken a major gamble, this was a great triumph, but it was also his undoing because in the American view he failed to send his troops to pursue the enemy. He drew enormous criticism from Admiral Radford, the American chief-of-staff in Washington. An armchair admiral's criticism, he had no understanding of the terrain and logistics *in situ*. Salan understood well that with his inflexible road-bound logistics and the Vietminh capacity for ambush in places where all his firepower advantages would be negated, a pursuit would have been both impossible and, indeed, suicidal. It was not just the Americans who were gunning for Salan. In Paris, secretary of war Pierre de Chevigne was also critical from an earlier date, similarly describing Salan as too timid and always looking to Paris for political cover.[14] However, the most likely reason for de Chevigne's disapproval was a cultural one. Salan, with his petite bourgeois background, was not 'one of us' in the aristocratic and haute bourgeois club, which typified the senior officer's cadre. Having spent much of his career in Indochina, he was also out of tune with the Europe-centric army cadre.

The American high command is depicted in Graham Greene's book *The Quiet American*, which features Pyle, the self-righteous know-all, management school and 'scientific' prig. A mini-McNamara, it set the old world against the new world. Americans, it seemed, knew everything but understood nothing. The Second Vietnam War was just seven years away.

When the Americans from their Pentagon map rooms on the other side of the world demanded Salan's removal, the French government meekly complied (Pentagon Papers). With Salan removed, the French lost their most experienced soldier in Indochina and a victorious general who had shown deft handling of his command in difficult situations. They received an office-bound 'technocratic' General Navarre in return, an officer with minimal combat experience and none in Indochina. Be careful what you wish for.

In August 1953, Navarre decided to pull out of Ná Sán. A good decision. The position had been completely bypassed by the Vietminh 316th Division in its attack on Lao and since the hectic battle of November 1952, the Ná Sán garrison was simply swinging uselessly at anchor. The evacuation had to be done discreetly. It was. Considerable organisation and skill were involved and some luck because for once Vietminh intelligence failed. France's defensive resources were deficient. Not realising before it was too late, the French got clean away by air.

The aero-terrestrial system had been proven. The French were bound to try again and Giáp was bound to try to come up with iterative solutions to the problem. A stage had been set for Dien Bien Phu. Giáp, fully informed on French strategic perspectives and sensitivities, now started to follow the concepts of indirect warfare so beloved of Colonel Lawrence. Giáp would still maintain his Napoleonic concepts of speed and concentration. A concept soon to be complemented with heavy artillery.

Giáp's aim would be to intensify and extend the strategy of widening and stretching France's defensive resources. France's commitment to protect Lao as a key strategic and political interest would be fully tested. The threat to the T'ai Highlands and to Lao would be the bait to tempt the French again into another cauldron where Giáp hoped to spring on them various tactical surprises, new weapons, and troops trained in siege warfare supported by a powerful logistics train. When Ná Sán was evacuated by Navarre in August 1953, Giáp sent in his engineers and specialists to study the French defensive systems.

> *One especial difficulty under which the regular army labours in this class of warfare (asymmetric war) – care for the wounded…the wounded are almost always a special case of anxiety to regular troops…strategically as well as tactically the disciplined army is at very serious disadvantage in this respect.*[15]

Giáp understood well the problems both in logistics and morale that would be caused by cutting off medivac flights. He would follow this cruel logic at Dien Bien Phu.

US pressure for more aggressive actions

American pressure on France focused on localised military effort alongside a move to genuine self rule. Following Letourneau's visit to Washington to meet with Dean Acheson in June 1952, the state department sent out a press statement on behalf of the secretary of state:

> *I have been particularly impressed by what M. Letourneau has told me of what is being done to enable the people of the three associated states to play the constantly greater role in their own defence to which they rightly aspire. Much has been accomplished toward the creation, training and equipping of the national armies. Units of these armies have distinguished themselves in battle and are performing vital security functions in many parts of the country.* (Pentagon Papers)

At the same time, the Americans were pressurising France to make independence more of a reality. The next part of the statement cannot have been entirely frank, because the Americans knew full well that the French were dragging their feet on the transfer of real power. Boa Dai was a puppet, and everyone knew it. The American government recorded in the Pentagon Papers:

> *M. Letourneau's account of the manner in which these new member states of the French Union are envisaging and meeting their responsibilities was heartening. I do not think it is generally realised to what extent these new states in fact control their own affairs. Only a limited number of services related to the necessities of the war remain temporarily in French hands.*

This was clearly naïve or disingenuous, or both. Letourneau, who had behaved like a despot in Indochina, would have to resign ten days later having been implicated in another *scandale de piastre*, one of the recurrent exchange frauds so often involving officialdom and influence. He was replaced as secretary of state for the associated states by Gaullist politician Marc Jacquet of the RPF.

The reality behind Letourneau's demise was more complex. His strategic plan for winning in Indochina was rejected by the Americans as being too lacklustre. Chief-of-staff Admiral Radford and Dulles were putting heavy pressure on France to be more aggressive, and funding would be withheld unless they came up with a suitable plan. Admiral Radford's internal memo was written on 28 August 1953:

> *...the joint chiefs-of-staff believe that additional U.S. support should be situated and conditioned upon continued implementation of French support, demonstration of French intent by actual performance in Indochina, and continued French willingness to receive and act upon U.S. military advice.*

The same memo approved of the Navarre plan as well as a French promise to send two more divisions in line with Navarre's US-supported request. There were only minor adjustments to the Letourneau plan. But there were reservations. Admiral Radford's note was also a tough criticism of dilatory French efforts to implement the plan and a threat to withhold aid if France's performance did not improve. The report's negative drift is mainly directed at the French government:

> *...if the Navarre concept is vigorously pursued militarily in Indochina and given wholehearted political support in France, it does offer a promise of military success sufficient to warrant appropriate additional US aid required to assist...Information received from Indochina indicates the French are not pursuing agreements reached between General O'Daniel and General Navarre (including the Navarre concept) as vigorously as expected...the French have 'no plans for a general fall offensive beyond limited objective operations designed to keep the enemy "off balance"...additional US support should be conditioned upon continued implementation of French support.'*

Such information would certainly have been leaked to put pressure on the French high command and particularly on the French government, whose trustworthiness on political reform in Indochina, including the transfer of powers to Bao Dai's government, was in question.

No doubt Navarre's surprising and premature decision to seek battle at Dien Bien Phu at the end of 1953 was a defensive act of a general (and behind him the French government) desperate to fend off American criticism and, most importantly, to keep the aid rolling. They had got rid of Salan, and Navarre might be next if he was not aggressive enough.

It seems likely that American pressure helped persuade Navarre to bring on the Battle of Dien Bien Phu. Bao Dai, like the Americans, was also pushing for more power to control the Vietnamese National Army, which was building up rapidly. In a meeting with General Salan, he pushed hard but Salan prevaricated because the VNA was not ready.

CHAPTER XIV

Lao – France's Achilles Heel and the Navarre Plan

Giáp attacks Lao, April 1953

The road from Dien Bien Phu climbs and winds up through thick jungle towards the border with Lao. An occasional clearing gives a panorama onto the valley, a patchwork of lush green paddy. It meanders on slowly through the village of Sop Noa for a further 30km along winding mountain roads, then falls sharply into the Nam U River basin with the overgrown village sitting on a bluff peninsula on the opposite (west) side of the river. The peninsular is formed by the Nam U confluence with the Nam Pak. However, the bluff slopes down to a large sandy beach on the bend in the river.

In April 1953, Giáp launched the 316th Division on a surprise two-pronged offensive aimed at Luang Prabang, the ancient capital of Lao, as well as the French positions on the strategically placed central plateau in the Plain of Jars. It was a politically astute thrust as the Lao government was edging towards becoming the first government to sign up to the Union of Federated States of Indochina in a series of treaties between 14 July 1949 and December 1950.

Not only a political move to boost their brothers in arms, the invasion of Lao was also the first signpost of Ho Chi Minh's intention to become the Big Brother to revolutions in South-East Asia. In effect, to create his own Indochina protectorate with France replaced by the DRV. The French general staff believed that the loss of the Mekong River line would be a threat to France's strategic flank in the north-central Indochina – Hue – the Central Highlands, Cambodia, and Cochin. The fight for control of Lao's Boliven plateau, laced with spectacular high waterfalls, would be particularly acute in the coming decades. Eisenhower regarded Lao as a key asset equal to that of Vietnam because it opened up the rest of South-East Asia to communist infiltration through its borders to Thailand, Burma and Cambodia.[1]

The French position was weak. There were a large number of scattered outposts throughout Lao in terrain that made rapid support for threatened places impossible, unless there were major deployment of elite paratrooper units. Luang Prabang was defended by just three French battalions. Some fairly fresh Lao units defended Xam Nuea. If the French reserves were committed in Lao, they would not be available for defence around the Red River delta.

However, the immediate problem for General Salan and the French high command was how to react to this Lao attack, and to react quickly. That Lao needed to be saved was not in doubt. It would be politically very difficult to throw to the wolves the only state that was enthusiastically willing to join the association of states of the French Union. This was the new name that was entered in Article 61 of the French constitution, which belied the idea of the willing protectorate the French were promoting to the Americans. There was a political imperative to save Lao, but at what cost? Could France afford to save the kingdom?

How would it look if the French protectorate could not be protected? But the reinforcements needed would take a huge amount of aeroplane capacity. It could not be done quickly. There were no practicable roads. Orders went out to French outposts and forts across northern Lao to buy time for Luang Prabang and Xan Nuea, holding on as long as possible against enemy attacks. French Dakotas and JU52s would soon be landing battalion after battalion of French troops in the Plain of Jars base at Xien Khouang. But it took time to build up to eleven battalions.

The first and most important of the significant outposts was at Sop Nao on the border. Further on, there was Muong Khoua, located on the juncture of the Noum River, which runs from north to south, and the main road from the border town of Dien Bien Phu in Vietnam, just 30km away. Moung Khoua is a sleepy village on the Nam Ou River that runs north-south for much of Northern Lao. It is an important market hub for the Leu tribe. If you picked up a dug-out boat at Moung Khoua, you could go with the flow of the river for several days through the Khast mountains to then reach the vicinity of Luang Prabang within two days. This is exactly what the Vietminh did as they bypassed Moung Khoua and headed for the ancient capital. Today you have to stop after one day's boat ride and pick up a mini-van at Nong Khiaw for a five-hour ride to the holy capital of the Laos. Luang Prabang is a tranquil town of exquisite temples and a modest royal palace besides the Mekong.

On 3 April, a Vietminh battalion attacked at Sop Nao under the command of Lieutenant Grezy, who was given orders to fight to the last. Captain Teullier took command of Muong Khua on the same day.

Remarkably, against overwhelming odds, the post held out until 9 April, at which point a breakout was ordered. Hunted through the jungle by two Vietnamese companies, Lieutenant Grezy managed to escape the ambush set for them by taking a long northerly route of some 100km to the market town of Pongsaly. In this steeply undulating jungle-covered terrain, the distance was much further. Two unshaven scarecrows in rags eventually reached Pongsaly fourteen days later.

A few days after the attack on Sop Nao, the first sign that a Vietminh attack was underway at Muong Khoua was the cutting off of contact from the villagers. Tribespeople no longer came down from the hills to go to market. Teullier, realising that the attack was imminent, arranged a convoy of dug-out boats. On 12 April, he decided to make a dash for Muong Noi 40km downriver but, too slow, they were turned back by an ambush just 600m on. The siege had started.

Teullier might have objected to the order he received from the commanding officer of the French forces in Lao, Colonel de Boucher de Crevecoeur:

> *You are to hold the position at Muong Khoua for a minimum of fourteen days with all the means at your disposal. You will be re-supplied by air-drop and receive adequate air support.*[2]

The order was already largely superfluous. Giáp had sent the bulk of his troops around the town.

On 18 April, Salan visited the king at Luang Prabang to explain why Xam Neua had to be abandoned. Salan found the sleepy capital fully prepared for defence with monks' prayers for divine help. Just in case the prayers did not work, Salan flew in four elite battalions to fight alongside French-officered units of the Royal Lao Army.

Meanwhile, the main village at Muang Khoua became a deserted no-man's land in which both sides probed and patrolled or where the French set ambushes for unwary incoming attackers. By 27 April, the outpost was already a legend. The *Legion d'Honneur* and other medals were parachuted in. Newspapers began to take up the story. While the 173rd Regiment was battling against Muong Khoua, other elements of 316th Division pushed deep over the forbidding waves of jungle-clad mountains towards Luang Prabang. They had reached within 30km of the capital, but even the toughened Vietminh found the going hard and their logistics stretched.

As the 316th Division approached Luang Prabang, King Sisavangvong refused to move. Encouraged by a Buddhist sage, Pra Sathon,[3] who predicted that the capital would not be taken, Luang Prabang began a Buddhist festival in praise of the victory even before its realisation. With divine help and French reinforcements, the leading columns of the 316th pulled up short of the Lao capital. The Vietminh attacks may have failed, although it is unlikely that Giáp expected it to fully succeed, but the main purpose had been achieved. Too fragile in logistics and confronted by fresh and well supplied French troops, Salan reckoned that their troops 'were too exhausted to prevail against well ordered troops in their bases areas, and with no chance of an overwhelming victory.'[4] It was also a divisionary offensive.

Muong Khuoa was still holding out in early May when the Vietminh forces began their retreat from their advanced positions near Luang Prabang and the Plain of Jars.

At Moung Khoua, by the morning of 18 May, Alpha position had been wiped out and Pi was a mass of exploding ordnance. Only four from 300 survived. At 12 noon, the red flag was flying over Pi. They were one of many scattered posts destroyed in the deluge, the detritus of which washed up at the remaining French posts. More assaults were launched on the main defences until the last defenders were cornered and forced to surrender around 3 a.m.

Xam Nuea Campaign

On 12 April 1953, Giáp launched three divisions along three prongs into Lao, against Pongsaly in the north, Muong Khuoa-Luang Prabang, and Xam Nuea, with the 308, 312 and 316 divisions of 30,000 men. The ultimate goal of the attack on Xam Nuea was to take control of the Plain of Jars. The Plain of Jars is a high upland plateau entirely different in topography to the rest of Indochina. Largely treeless, it is gently rolling landscape, with paddy fields stepped into the dells below lush grassland hills. It takes its name from the hundreds of mysterious stone jars of all shapes and sizes that litter the plateau. In this vast country the plain is about 20km by 20km and is kidney-shaped. (An important strategic area that dominates northern Lao, the region would become a major battleground for the US and North Vietnam 1958–73.)

When it was clear that 10,000 Vietminh were descending on the 2,400 French garrison at Xam Nuea, 700 elite French troops were airlifted out just in time. However, 1,700 of the French-led Laotian troops of 1st Laotian Parachute Battalion and the 8th Battalion of Laotian Chasseurs remained, and they were faced with trekking 200km through jungle and mountains to the French fortified base at Xieng Khouang, with the fast-moving VPA in close pursuit. Vietminh pursuers in their turn were also harassed and ambushed by partisan units amongst the Meo tribesmen *en route*.

Captain Desfarges described the help offered by pro-French Meo:

> *After dropping out of Sam Neua towards the Plain of Jars...the Meos offered themselves to serve as our guides, telling us that a channel had already been established and that the French from Sam Neua had already passed and had been directed towards the south. Between each village, tracks were made by the inhabitants, tracks sometimes along rivers in the bed itself and impossible to find by the VM...the village chief had us build a hut hidden in the middle of the bamboo and where they came to bring us food. It was in Ban Ban, south of Phu San, that one hundred VMs were reported in the area, the villagers went*

into the forest, in groups of two, to look for hidden weapons to be able to set an ambush, which has certainly yielded results.

The Meo would carry on killing Vietnamese and Pathet Lao communists for another forty years. Short on supplies, the three VPA divisional probes pulled back in May 1953. Ambushed at Hua Muong, only 220 exhausted and wounded men survived. At the Xieng Khouang base, many were medevacked on Ju52s, tended by nurse Genevieve Galard.

Fifteen out of twenty-two French officers were killed or captured. Vietminh units overran the pretty Buddhist pilgrimage town of Xieng Khouang, but by the time the Vietminh reached the military base, it was well defended by elite French units. The Vietminh, who were at the end of their supply chain, retreated. French and Lao troops retook Xieng Khouang village. (According to Graham Greene, the local Xieng Khouang No. 1 was the finest quality of opium.) Attacking against six entrenched battalions on the open Plain of Jars, the Vietminh, having lost all the advantages of jungle cover, had been comprehensively repulsed with significant losses by 13 May. By the end of May, the French recovered their territorial losses. Except for Xam Nuea and Pongsaly, where Ho established permanent Pathet Lao bases.

French stockpiles in key garrisons and deployments or supply by air had trumped the Vietminh's capability on this occasion. One of these air components was the flight ambulance service to which Nurse Genevieve was attached:

I arrived in Hanoi on May 5th and took off again to accompany a flight nurse to Luang Prabang in Laos. We were to evacuate a number of soldiers who had tramped through the brush on an exhausting march of sixty kilometres. They were the survivors of battles at Xam Nuea and the entire region around Luang Prabang…during the following days these evacuation missions took me to Xieng Khouang and to the Plain of Jars where many battles were occurring.[5]

Many of these deployment and supply missions were carried out in the iconic Ju52 transport plane, planes that had been taken from the Wehrmacht at the war's end. The Ju52, distinctive with its corrugated metal fuselage, was the workhorse of the French Colonial Army until replaced from the end of 1953, as US Dakotas were supplied in large numbers. So stretched were French resources that Ju52s were even used in bombing roles, including napalm drops.

Although defeated tactically, Giáp's strategic purpose had been served:

…either they try to extend their strongpoints once again, with their depleted manpower, in which case they spread themselves too thin, or else they move out of their strongpoints, which frees territory and population for us.[6]

It was the abiding French problem in Indochina. To maintain security over wide areas with static defences whilst developing large enough mobile reserves to launch offensives against the elusive Vietminh main army. Giáp had launched his Lao offensive from his marshalling base in the Dien Bien Phu valley. The following year, General Navarre would remember this as he considered how to block Vietminh attacks on France's vulnerable ally.

The constant pressure, stretch of resources and attrition launched by Vietminh forces across Indochina in 1953 is revealed by the frenetic schedule of Nurse Genevieve, after one extremely stressful flight with a double-leg Vietnamese amputee:

> *The following day I flew to Xieng Khouang to fetch* [the] *wounded. It was a stressful period. We were flying two missions a day. After Xien Khoang, it was Luang Prabang. On my return to Hanoi I scribbled a few quick lines to my mother: 'Barely back from Luang Prabang, I leave in a few minutes for Ná Sán.*

Already pro-French because of his wife, King Sissavangvong and the Laotian government were being encouraged to signed the Treaty of Friendship and Association with France, which they did in October 1953. It was an important political event for the French government because it was to be a first step on the road to the formation of the French-controlled association and would put pressure on King Sihanouke's and Bao Dai's governments to follow suit. Most significantly for future developments, Article 4 of the treaty stated that French troops would 'guarantee the defence of the frontiers of Laos in collaboration with the Lao Army'. Article 7 reiterated that the defence of Lao was France's responsibility.[7] This commitment became an essential political and strategic commitment for France, on which considerable political prestige rested. It was also an albatross around their necks.

Churchill on Indochina

While Eisenhower and the Americans believed that the invasion of Lao was a decisive indicator of the communist block's aggressive intentions, Winston Churchill, in a speech on 11 May 1953 in the House of Commons, saw things quite differently:

> *I ought to say that, in my opinion – I am venturing to offer my opinion – the sudden advance of elements of the Vietminh forces, or their foraging parties, towards the Siamese frontier ought not to lead us to conclude that it is a Soviet-inspired move inconsistent with the new attitude of the Soviet Government. This may unhappily prove to be the case, but also it might well have arisen from local circumstances and impulses, and from plans made many months ago*

> *and now, perhaps, reversed. We should at least not be over hasty in drawing a conclusion in an adverse sense.*[8]

Churchill's interests were quite different from those of the Americans. He had no real feel for the Far East, having never been there, and even in 1952 he had speculated that France could not hold Indochina. Nor did he care. He was even pessimistic that British Malaya could hold off the communists. His main concern was that France at that time should be strong in Europe and part of the EDF to confront the Soviet menace. In contrast to the views of senior British military leaders, such as Field Marshal Slim, the domino theory held no terror for him. His foreign secretary also had a different outlook and agreed with his advisers and the British military that South-East Asia was threatened. Churchill would go along with American policies in Asia including an active engagement in Korea so long as he had a predominant say in Middle Eastern policy.

After the death of Stalin in March 1953, Churchill's views on the international situation had changed. The reasons for his opinions were based on his profound understanding on the change in Soviet foreign policy stance brought on by Stalin's death. In the USSR, the new leaders emerging from the Politburo had been genuinely frightened by Stalin's adventurist foreign policies and the debacle in Korea caused by Kim's risk-taking. For the new Politburo the priorities had to change. Not as inured to revolution as Stalin or obsessed by revolutionary stature, the new men in the Kremlin were predominantly dour apparatchiks. Malenkov was the new man at the helm. For Khrushchev, the party secretary, and others in the party leadership, the main issue was how to deal with the rising power of NKVD (KGB forerunner) chief Lavrenti Beria. As Khrushchev relates:

> *I wasn't just weeping for Stalin. I was terribly worried about the future of the party and the future of the country. I already sensed that Beria would start bossing everyone around and this could be the beginning of the end.*[9]

Beria wielded, it seemed, a vast amount of power through the NKVD, the NKVD military units, and the camps as well as control of the atomic weapons program. However, Beria, vile murderer and serial rapist though he was, became a moderate in policy matters. Immediately upon Stalin's death, which some Russian historians believe Beria hastened by stopping medical support during his dying seizure, he became a reformer in domestic politics. The collective leadership believed that consumer goods and de-Stalinisation were essential. This inevitably meant *détente* and peace policies if the emphasis of the economy was switched from guns to butter.

Malenkov was quoted in *Izvestia* on 13 March 1953 as saying that nuclear weapons 'threatened the end of civilisation.' This was a very clear signal but only Churchill understood its significance.

Churchill's new fixation began to revolve around the developments in the USSR:

> *The supreme event which has occurred since we last had a debate on foreign affairs is, of course, the change of attitude and, as we all hope, of mood which has taken place in the Soviet domains and particularly in the Kremlin since the death of Stalin. We, on both sides of the House, have watched this with profound attention. It is the policy of Her Majesty's Government to avoid by every means in their power doing anything or saying anything which could check any favourable reaction that may be taking place and to welcome every sign of improvement in our relations with Russia.* (Churchill, Hansard, May 1953)

Here there was the chance for world peace and a new balance. Churchill, in his declining years, after a lifetime of belligerency, was now seeking to play the peacemaker. Not least in his thoughts was the destructive power of the atom bomb.

He had previously 'wanted the Americans to have a *show* with the Soviet Republic before the Russians had the bomb,'[10] but that option was all over due to the acquisition of the bomb by the USSR. For 'show' read 'war' or 'threat of war'. The allies had not exploited their atom bomb for asymmetric superiority to negotiate political gains over the USSR. While this asymmetry was present, Stalin had conquered Eastern Europe and secured the triumph of communism in China.

Peace and the reduction of the danger of nuclear war were to be Churchill's main focus as his health declined and thoughts of resignation started to crop up. He had mellowed with old age and illness.[11] Rapprochement with the Soviets was the means to this end. This would be his last gift to history. Churchill and Eden would soon become fixated by the idea of an international summit of the superpowers to fix world peace. It would be a grand finale to Churchill's political career and the launch pad for Eden's premiership.

But what did the UK matter? Exhausted by two world wars, it was a power in rapid relative decline, but at this point in history, the UK still mattered a lot because Eisenhower and the US congress held the British leader in very high regard. The warm glow of the 'special relationship' was still very influential. Not just rational, the relationship was emotional between allies that had gone through the hard times of the Second World War. Eisenhower would also let out that: 'No one has treated me so well as Winston Churchill. He knows I love him. Sometimes he takes advantage of that.'[12]

The US congressional elite felt the same way about Churchill, long since regarding him as a sage even more so after his Fulton speech on the Iron Curtain. They would not readily go down an interventionist path without the United Kingdom and Churchill at their side. However, while the US became more interventionist in respect of Indochina, more hawkish in their view of communism and the Soviets, the UK became less so. How would this play out in respect of France and Indochina, a place where the Cold War seemed to be hotting up and where the military focus of ideological confrontation had shifted after the truce in Korea?

The other crucial and parallel international issue of the moment was the proposal, strongly backed by the US and the UK, for a European Defence Force (EDF) as a way of strengthening European defence against the Soviet threat and at the same time bringing Germany in from the cold by allowing her to re-arm and so contribute to European defence. Even for a party such as the MRP this was a difficult call because the idea of German re-armament was anathema to most of the French people. The MRP's more conservative voters were being tempted away by de Gaulle's rampant RPF, which was vehemently against the EDF. To the left of the MRP, the Socialist Party were loath to give ammunition to their communist rivals. For the US and the UK, the problem was that compared to the huge Red Army they simply did not have enough troops in Europe, nor could they afford the cost and political cost of maintaining even the current level, especially with the French and Germany economies recovering from the wartime disaster. US defence spending had already shot up from $14 billion in 1949 to $52.2 billion in 1953 and Eisenhower, as a republican, was reluctant to increase taxes.

It meant that a nuclear attack on the USSR would be the only response to a conventional attack on Germany. And that would mean mutually assured destruction (MAD). Hardly a good option. The convening of the three-power conference in Bermuda for December (US/UK/France) was, it was hoped, to be the crowning of the EDF policy, or a last desperate attempt to get the French to change course.

Overshadowing everything was the atom bomb and then the hydrogen bomb, which had been successfully tested in November 1952. Churchill noted in the Commons on 3 November:

> *The rapid and ceaseless developments of atomic warfare and the hydrogen bomb – these fearful scientific discoveries cast their shadow on every thoughtful mind.*

And on 3 December he noted:

> *There was a time when the western powers could have used the atom bomb without any reply by Russia. That time has gone.*

Churchill, in opposition to the American view as shaped by Dulles and to the views of Foreign Secretary Eden and those of the military, believed that the new post-Stalin Soviet leadership wanted peace and improvement in the material lives of their subjects. He believed, therefore, that the Soviet leadership would be amenable to some rapprochement. Churchill's instincts would be proved correct. Meanwhile, Churchill was against any policy or actions that would threaten the chances for peace or risk atomic war. That said, earlier in the year he had agreed with Eisenhower to the use of atom bombs if the Chinese and North Koreans reneged on the Panmunjom armistice and renewed their attack.

Before Bermuda, there was considerable debate in France on the Indochina question despite the subject not being debated in parliament for a full year. There was a general sense amongst the centre-left, except in Bidault's MRP faction, that something radical needed to be done. Meanwhile, another government, that of Premier Mayer, had fallen over the EDF and German re-armament question. A government crisis lasted from May to June 1953. It seemed that it was the turn of Mendes-France. The biggest issues were to do with budget and the EDF. Indochina was a smaller issue, though important for the MRP and the right. Mendes-France tried to be emollient and vague on all of the issues, which pleased no one. On Indochina, in order to woo the MRP right-wing and the RPF, he was less forthright in his anti-war stance than previously. But his direction was clear nonetheless:

> *France is today using up in the Far East a large part of its human material and military resources...At Bermuda we must impress on our allies that the Indochina War imposes a crushing burden...we shall submit to them* [the Vietminh] *a precise plan with a view to solving this painful conflict.*[13]

He lost by thirteen votes, mainly due to the hostility of the MRP's Bidault and his diehard (Indochina-Catholic) wing. There were 151 votes against from Gaullists, who also wanted a hard line on pursuing the Indochina War and maintaining the French empire. De Gaulle, in splendid isolation at Colombey-les Deux Eglises, was distrusting of Mendes-France's views on the EDF and found his Indochina views 'disquieting'.[14] Despite his disingenuous biography, de Gaulle was still the imperialist who wanted to hold on to empire and fight on.

Mendes-France would be joined in his anti-war stance by François Mitterrand, who rebelled against colonial policy and resigned from the government on 2 September. His book, published in July 1953, *Aux Frontierrres de L'Union Francais,* advocated closure of the war in Indochina and rued the loss of wealth that it entailed. The preface was written by Mendes-France.

The agenda for discussion at the upcoming Bermuda conference included the following:

1. Securing the future of the EDF and French agreement to German re-armament.
2. To review the state of relations with the Soviets and to discuss Churchill's proposal for a four-power conference to reach a *détente* with the post-Stalin leadership.
3. To discuss the Indochina conflict – and for France to plead for more aid.

General Navarre arrives

Navarre's appointment in 1953 was intended to give fresh impetus to the FEC campaign in what was a deadlocked and increasingly unpopular war. France needed to find a way out and negotiations about negotiations were already underway. Having little battle experience, and none in Indochina, Navarre developed clear strategic and tactical precepts amidst a defeatist, overstretched command that lived from hand-to-mouth, reactive to Vietminh strategy but with no clear plan for victory.

Henri Navarre was appointed by premier Rene Meyer, who made it clear that his role was to extricate France from the Indochina War by winning battles and allowing France to go with strength to the negotiating table. Meyer believed, as did most Frenchmen by this time, that the war was not winnable. France should focus on the EDF and their future in political economic alliance with Germany. Navarre was a strange choice because his career had been mostly wrapped up with intelligence work, staff appointments, and as an officer and commander of France's occupations of Germany after respective world wars. He had come to Meyer's attention because of this role in Europe and Germany, which was Meyer's main focus of interest. He had some intelligence work experience in Syria and Lebanon, but his operational experience was limited to commanding a tank regiment in Juin's army of liberation for a few months at the end of the war. He was decorated seven times for bravery. Jealous rivals were quick to point out his lack of experience and utter ignorance of Indochina, but that is unfair. Great commanders adapt and demonstrate a decision-making and leadership flair that sets them apart. For some it is a gift. Navarre was highly rated for the knowledge and truth[15] of his analyses.

A political general, Navarre was 'an individualist, but cold and aloof and imperious'. To be plucked from relative obscurity from an office and a sort of diplomatic-military posting in Germany, then parachuted into Indochina as supremo, might have gone to many men's heads. It certainly went to his. Pathé News reels depict an officer immaculately coiffured who sported an air of studied insouciance. He revelled in the media spotlight. He can be seen on camera surrounded by staff officers grandly sweeping his hand over a wall map of Indochina, then studying a table map, then poking the ground with his stick to describe some attack or other in the earth as everyone watches on with feigned interest.

In 1953, Navarre's high command would issue a quite ludicrous document criticising commanders for being road-bound with 'motor complex', but in reality there was no alternative because roads allowed the transport of the necessary firepower to deal with the greater numbers of Vietminh. There was no way out of that conundrum.

Unlike de Lattre or Salan, Navarre acted the grand theatre commander, isolating himself in Saigon away from the crucial battles around the key Red delta, where General Cogny commanded. He was unlucky in his subordinate, who briefed and leaked to the press and was constantly politicking. Salan said of Coligny, 'He had a tendency to ignore orders and create disagreeable frictions. Above all, he wanted to be Number One in Tonkin.'[16]

The first mistake was made by Cogny, who caved in to pressure from his most experienced colonel in siege warfare. Colonel Gilles, who had successfully defended Ná Sán, pleaded not to be appointed to command at Dien Bien Phu. On 22 November, Colonel Gilles wrote to General Cogny, the commander of the Tonkin region under Navarre: 'At Ná Sán I spent six months of my life like a rat. Use me in the open air.' Unfortunately, Cogny surrendered to the old boy network and not rational judgment. Giáp, by contrast to Navarre, moved to be near all his major battles, including Dien Bien Phu, the deciding battle of the war. More importantly, unlike Navarre, Giáp was flexible according to circumstances. If needed, he could adapt to the level of regimental commander.

Navarre was also given responsibility for the defence of Lao and was informed of the great importance of defending the only country that had wholeheartedly accepted the association of states concept. Unfortunately for the French Expeditionary Force, the Lao tangle would lead Navarre to overweigh Lao's significance in his strategic thinking. In his account of the campaign after the war he noted: 'When I discussed the matter in November, the commissioner general informed me that there was no question of not defending Laos.' Further, Secretary Marc Jacquet, secretary of state for the associated states, in November was adamant that 'if the Vietminh succeeded in reaching the Mekong, the shock would knock France out of the war.' (*Navarre Memoires*) This was a fąirly weak exculpatory post-war effort by Navarre as the officials were not particularly senior. He should have had clear written and official directions from the government. What is surprising is his lack of requests for clear written political guidance on this most important issue. This suggests one of two things. Either he wanted to 'fly solo' without government interference, and/or his story about Jacquet's verbal advice was exaggerated or plain nonsense.

Obviously, his first and overriding duty was not to be defeated and to maintain the integrity of key areas of Indochina until the Geneva Conference.

While Navarre pored over his maps from well-appointed colonial mansions in Saigon, Giáp was just behind the front lines living in a cave, quizzing individual bo doi on intelligence reports or regimental commanders on tactics. Giáp at Dien Bien Phu, armed with Ho's mandate, understood what was at stake at Dien Bien Phu. He invested time and resources accordingly, but Navarre did not.

Navarre's plan envisaged the following:

1. Remaining on the strategic defensive in the north where the Vietminh were strong, but launching disruptive raids.
2. Being active in the south where the French were relatively stronger and supported by Buddhist sect militias such as the Cao Dai and the Hoa Hoa.
3. *Operation Atlante* to pacify the Central Highlands in the 1953–54 fighting season ahead of the Geneva Conference and 'blooding' newly trained Vietnamese forces.
4. Rapidly building up local forces (a continuation of de Lattre's policy) and handing over the defence of the south and centre to Bao Dai's government.
5. Looking for an opportunity to challenge and defeat the Vietminh in the north using a mobile elite reserve that would be built up for the purpose, in the 1954–55 fighting season with a view to decisive victory in 1955.

This plan was soon known to Ho and Giáp.

Overall, the situation for the French was not dire. Since the debacle of RC4, the French had not suffered a major defeat and had bested the Vietminh in four set-piece battles, drawing a further one at Hoa Binh. The Vietminh had lost tens of thousands of their best men in these battles with losses far outnumbering those of the French. The key Red delta was still French-controlled, albeit with substantial Vietminh ingress. However, in the south the main centres of population were under French control and the Vietminh had much less traction than in the north. Vietminh units there, at the end of a 2,000km supply chain, focused on small-scale hit and run tactics.

US reaction to the Navarre plan and the political situation in Indochina War

The US had become the major funders of the Indochina campaign with a special increase in commitment at the onset of the Korean War. What they thought about French plans was therefore important, 'as he who pays the piper calls the tune'. US politicians wanted to know what their taxes were paying for, that they were getting value for money and commitment from the recipient. Generally, there was a recognition of the value in having the French fight their war, tempered with specific criticisms about the lack of aggression or a war winning strategy.

There were complaints about inefficiency, for example the French Air Force only managed twenty-five hours air time per aircraft compared to seventy-five hours for the USAAF on the same models. It was also an example of the inadequacy of auxiliary services, where the ratio of such supporting personnel to the number of front-line troops decreased significantly as a percentage of the total manpower in the last three years of the war, from 9.1% to 5.3% (1947–March 1953).[17] In the Second Vietnam War, US forces would have a ratio of about fifty percent, which was not efficient either. Such personnel would include aircraft maintenance, truck drivers, medical staff and motor mechanics. By the end of France's First Vietnam War, only 21,700 service personnel were supporting 407,000 troops. Recruitment of such skilled personnel was very difficult, especially with the post-war economic recovery.

There may have been other cultural factors for lack of efficiency: long lunches with wine; siestas; alcohol at breakfast. One article written by Dennis Duncan of *Life* magazine, depicted a decadent French military: 'Staff officers kept hours that would delight a banker…troops, following the example of their commanders take long siestas.'

Officers frequented the many fashionable bars and restaurants. They went to parties, found local girlfriends or mistresses, or went to the officer-only section of the large military-run bordellos. Mobile bordellos accompanied them on campaign. On the other hand, American General O'Daniel, head of the US military mission, praised the Navarre plan and felt that it was 'capable of achieving military victory.'[18]

Mike Mansfield, later to become a giant figure in the US Senate as head of the foreign affairs committee, had just become a first term senator. He had a particular interest in foreign affairs. In February 1953 he wrote in the *New York Times*:

> *Indochina is at this time the most important area on the continent of Asia its loss would start up a chain reaction extending to the Persian Gulf and would give the Soviets and their satellites, the rubber, the tin and the oil which are in short supply in the Soviet Union.*

A year later, President Eisenhower was talking about the domino theory, but the essence of the fear had long been established by Mansfield and others. Mansfield would later visit Vietnam and was fulsome in praise for the Navarre plan.

American media continued to be mixed in its reporting. *Life* magazine exclaimed that 'in the background of this war is a society that has become corrupt.'[19] Other journals, such as the virulently anti-communist *Time* magazine, were in contrast overgenerous in their praise of France as the title of their 28 September 1953 edition read, 'France is fighting the good fight.' This edition carried a full picture of General Navarre on the front page: a rare honour and a sign that international media was focusing on the sharpening confrontation in this exotic land, which was far more photogenic than grey and devastated Korea. Foreign correspondents liked going there for interesting assignments. With French restaurants, bars and café life, it was delightfully decadent.

On 27 October 1953, Wei Gaoquing returned from China, going straight to Ho's headquarters in the Viet Bac, where he delivered the great helmsman's twelve-point strategic suggestions as well as a copy of the Navarre plan, which had been picked up by Chinese intelligence. It is unlikely that Ho and Giáp did not already have the details from their agents or fellow communist travellers in Saigon or Paris. In any case, the intelligence was about to become irrelevant because the plan was about to change radically.[20]

In the US, the mood was positive overall and the war situation had not even been discussed at Bermuda: 'There are indications that the stalemate was coming to an end,' reported Senator Mansfield. The main fear on the US side was that China would again intervene to aid their ally if the French looked like winning. What would the US do then? Mansfield's report to congress posed the issue: 'Only outright Chinese communists would be likely to rescue the Vietminh from defeat.' (Pentagon Papers)

Nixon had visited Indochina on 31 October 1953 just as the fateful decisions were being made. 'The tide of aggression has reached its peak and has finally begun to recede,' declared an ebullient Nixon in Hanoi. He thought the Navarre plan was a winner. However, he was concerned that more effort should be made to move more powers to the Vietnam national government and to build up local forces. Twenty years later he would be calling for 'Vietnamisation'. In private he noted:

> *I saw immediately a basic problem of the war. The French did nothing to hide the disdain they felt towards the Vietnamese.*

It was an attitude 'which kept the French from dealing with the Vietnamese in a way that would have allowed a working partnership.'[21]

Nixon was sent off by General Commissioner Dejean with a sumptuous dinner at his residence:

> *Except for a sprinkling of Vietnamese faces and the lush palms and orchids in the garden outside the occasion might have been a mayoral banquet in Dijon or Toulouse, with starched linen napkins, sparkling crystal goblets, and silver candelabra.*

Nixon had mixed feelings about his visit and was obviously uncomfortable with the overt and distasteful French colonialism.

However, he also understood the fundamental problem of non-communist nationalism, which was that without the French it would be overrun by the communists in short order. It was the essential dilemma of US involvement with the French in Indochina. Only support for an essentially unreconstructed colonial power and the associated states concept could provide a military solution:

> *Deep down,* [argued Nixon, Navarre and other commanders] *have very little faith in the ability of the Vietnamese to fight separately in independent units that don't have French non-coms...as far as the Vietnamese and the Cambodians and the Laotians are concerned...their only hope to remain independent is to have their independence within the French Union...which the French are now willing to give.* (Pentagon Papers)

Nixon's analysis of the issues was spot on. However, the nationalist government, Bao Dai and their supporters still hung on to the illusion of complete independence, which was unrealistic with the PRC sitting on the northern border.

Others were more sceptical of the Navarre plan, including John F. Kennedy, who also visited Indochina with brother Robert in 1951. Kennedy was more in favour of building up the 'third force' and was no doubt influenced by Catholic nationalist politician Diem, who he later patronised. Diem visited Washington in May 1953. He lectured airily that there was a lack of a 'rallying point between the communists and the French.'

Kennedy, who had recently been so close to Joe McCarthy on the hysterical anti-communist right, was now shifting left. He played to his Irish Bostonian roots and the 'anti-colonial' card. The Kennedys thought the French were losing. This despite JFK's admiration of the Frenchman's drive and ability. JFK enjoyed an ugly tangle with de Lattre, which left the Frenchman fuming. 'In Indochina,' JFK intoned, 'we have allied ourselves to the desperate efforts of the French regime to hang on to the remnants of empire.' Not wrong in his analysis of the French, although the French position was rapidly developing under pressure of public opinion, JFK missed the point, which Nixon got, which was that it was the French with their army and their imperial troops who stood between the Vietnamese nationalists and complete and rapid communist victory. In the end it was political posturing not practical outcomes that was interesting to JFK. When he came into power, his actions in Indochina in respect of what in 1962 had become a US satellite would be little different to those of the French.

Congress approved a subsidy of US$400 million for 1954 and this was boosted by another US$385 million, which was re-allocated from existing foreign aid budgets. As much as eighty percent of the FEC's military budget was provided by the US. Two ships a week arrived in Haiphong or Saigon. The French Army was almost entirely equipped by the Americans, so much so that they looked exactly the same as the GIs, including their weaponry, helmets, jackets and battle fatigues.

On the Vietminh side, Chinese logistical support stepped up rapidly. Supply for the Vietminh increased per month by the start of the Battle of Dien Bien Phu. Supply increased so much during the battle that by the end it was running at 4,000 tons per month.

And what of the nationalist government, which was meant to be the 'independent government' within the French Union of Federated States? Visiting dignitaries were introduced to Vietnamese politicians such as the 'prime minister' Nguyễn Van Tam and 'head of state' Bao Dai, who were wheeled out to prove that the 'association of federated states was working'. However, nobody could have any illusions. The Vietnamese were in office but not in power.

Nevertheless, Nguyễn Van Tam was as effective as he was allowed to be. Pro-French, his son was a French Air Force pilot in the Battle of France in 1940. We have seen that his fierce anti-Tam and other nationalists perfectly understood the unrelenting and fanatical nature of the enemy they were facing as well as the mainspring of their support in the Vietnamese village:

> *The most important thing is winning the village populations over to the cause. Our nationalist fervour has got to match the Vietminh's.*[22]

Tam also believed that nationalist ruthlessness needed to match the communists. Another prominent nationalist, Nguyễn Van Hinh, a holder of French citizenship, had played a leading role in developing an effective national army under de Lattre's orders and command.

Large elements of Vietnamese society detested communism. Other elements who had experienced communism and the iniquities, arrogance and brutal repression involved in land reform hated it too. In the course of 1952, 45,000 Vietnamese had uprooted and left Vietminh areas for the freedom and safety of nationalist areas.[23] Communism was vulnerable and losing popularity. Vietminh prisoners happily worked for the French and rarely defected. Only thirty out of 2,400 deserted their posts at Dien Bien Phu (1.25%). There is evidence from Ná Sán of PIM volunteering to load mortar tubes to replace wounded gunners. Legionnaire Klause speaks of shared comradeship with PIM. As we have seen, the bright communist propaganda about the youth brigades hid the fact of oppressive Corvée labour and deep resentment by many victims of Ho's totalitarian regime.

Defeat and bitter memories of coercion and destruction of village traditions brought seething and hidden bitterness, as did enormous casualties and food shortages. Many peasants living under communism soon saw through the phony charade of revolutionary songs, the conformity and numbingly boring political rhetoric screamed at them through loudspeakers by a party cadre that was ever more corrupt and arrogant. Most of all the peasants soon realised that the hated but occasional Corvée labour system of early French imperialism had been transformed by the communists into full time slavery. Soon after the victory at Dien Bien Phu there would be peasant revolts, which required major troop deployment to quell. The political victory of communism was not inevitable. It had to be implemented and maintained at the point of a gun.

Tactical and strategic issues for both sides and the decision to occupy Dien Bien Phu

In November 1953, Navarre developed a scheme to drop a mobile force into Dien Bien Phu as a way to block Vietminh moves and logistical chains into Lao, with which France had signed a Treaty of Guarantee. As a mooring point or base for elite forces, mobile units would fan out in all directions attacking Vietminh communications in the rear and creating havoc. It would be taking the fight to the Vietminh and tying up resources behind their front and exploiting French air power and strategic flexibility. It looked good in the map room.

Vietminh moves against Lao, which was known to be a target for the Vietminh high command, would be blocked and its logistics train interdicted. By fortifying Dien Bien Phu Navarre could achieve all his objectives in one fell swoop. Block Vietminh attacks against Lao, provide support to the T'ai minority in the T'ai Hills and their French-led guerrilla bands, and give an opportunity for winning a set-piece battle if Giáp should choose to try to confront them. If Giáp was drawn off it would mean less pressure in other areas, including the Red delta.

The only problem with this elegant concept was that it was based only on false premises:

> *Navarre…had failed to realise that there are no blocking positions in* [a] *country lacking European-type roads. Since the Vietminh relied largely on human porters for their front-line units, they could easily bypass such bottlenecks as Dien Bien Phu or the Plain of Jars while bottling up the forces contained in those strongholds.*[24]

Anyone who has actually travelled in the region would be aware of this impracticality of relying on the few tracks or roads that could always be intercepted, blocked or subjected to ambush in a topography that overwhelmingly favoured the Vietminh. The premise on which the Dien Bien Phu operation was based was completely flawed because it assumed that the Vietminh were as road-bound as the French.

When the Vietminh reacted so aggressively to the Navarre plan, it started to become clear that a major battle was building up a year earlier than planned. After Ná Sán and Hoa Binh, no one should have been under any illusions that Giáp would react in the same way as he had to all previous incursions. In contrast to Navarre, for the Vietminh a battle in 1953–54 would meet their plan, and it would be on ground of their choosing. Having over-committed to the Dien Bien Phu landings, Navarre would find himself prematurely sucked into a major battle. Almost from the start withdrawal was not an option, because they were so quickly hemmed-in by superior forces. By 1 January, Navarre knew he had to either accept a major battle or beat a humiliating and costly retreat into Lao, with the Vietminh snapping at his heels and storming in from the flanks in a relentless series of ambushes. He also knew by early January that he would be facing at least some 105mm artillery supplied by the Chinese as well as 37mm AA. Moreover, from intelligence reports received on 27 December, he knew that 49,000 Vietminh including 33,000 Vietminh combat troops were on the way, not the two divisions he had reckoned on. Navarre thought that he would have more guns and ammunition with which to crush any enemy. French high command could not imagine that the Vietminh could haul across the mountains enough guns and especially enough ammunition.

Dien Bien Phu was hemmed-in, loosely but strongly. Every patrol ran into fierce resistance and pulled back helter-skelter to the base defences. The big battle was coming and everyone knew it. There was something almost medieval in this contest, something almost formal and public in the 'challenge'. Press from around the world on both sides, Russians on one side, French, English and Americans on the other, were invited to witness the spectacle and revel in the preparations for battle.

The risks at Dien Bien Phu were much greater than those accepted at Ná Sán. First and foremost was the size and capability of the French Air Force transport fleet, which would have to supply Dien Bien Phu. There were only seventy-eight Dakotas. The size of the garrison would be constrained by the logistical capacity of the air force which, due to inefficiencies and lack of maintenance personnel, was operating at only one-third optimum strength. Yet the force at Dien Bien Phu had to be of a size large enough to withstand the weight of the whole DRV Army. Colonel Jean Nicot, head of the French transport air arm, objected to the plan on 11 November. It could not be done because he did not have enough aircraft to cover Dien Bien Phu and other needs, such as *Operation Atlante*, which began in November, and operations in Lao. A key factor in this assessment was the fact that Dien Bien Phu was

400–500km from French air bases, double the distance of Ná Sán. Secondly, Dien Bien Phu was in the mountains and poor weather would reduce flights, even before the rainy season, which was due to start in April.

Working out the size of the garrison for Dien Bien Phu was a complex matrix between the transport capacity needed and the area to be defended, the distance to air field bases and the requisite needs of the base's equipment and building materials for defences and ammunition reserves. Capacity was required after heavy engagements for rapid stock replenishment.

In February, the capacity of the Dakota fleet decreased by sixteen percent. On top of that, supply fell by forty-six percent from the previous months – a figure contributed to by seasonal bad weather and the needs of Lao where French forces were being redeployed to fend off the invasion by the VPA's 312th Division. The net result was that stocks were lower than planned and building materials, wire, etc., were only a fraction of what was needed. Navarre's problem was that the footprint and topographical requirement for perimeter defence and occupation in an area of hills 500 to 800m high was too big for the force in place. However, it was simply impossible to consider having more troops there because they could not be supplied, and this meant that the key sentinel Beatrice and Gabrielle strongpoints stood alone with little in the way of close interlocking supporting fire, although they had plenty of artillery cover. More hills should have been occupied and defended, but this was not possible due to logistical constraints that limited the size of the garrison, which ideally should have been at least thirty percent larger. The defensive system was brittle because there was no defence in depth to absorb initial attacks. A comparison to Ná Sán is instructive because positions benefited from being much more numerous and having interlocking fire. A fall of one position in forty was less devasting than one in nine.

Giáp remembered:

> *Wei Guoqing and I agreed to launch the attack against isolated positions of the enemy where they were weakest, or relatively weak, but which they were not able to abandon…we also agreed on the choice of Lau Chau, the middle and lower Lao would be the principal focus of our next offensive.*

The policy was decided at a Politburo meeting in September 1953, where, according to Giáp:

> *Uncle said, 'the enemy is concentrating his mobile forces to create great strength. We have nothing to fear! We will force him to disperse his forces. Then his strength will evaporate.' With this, his cigarette in his mouth, Uncle spread his hands so that each finger pointed in a different direction.*[25]

As it happened, the French commander, with his Atlante offensive, which started on 20 January 1954, fell in exactly with Ho and Giáp's strategic plans. Navarre's decision to occupy Dien Bien Phu was not expected, but was exactly the opportunity Giáp was seeking.

Navarre was adamant that the FEC had to take the initiative and take the fight to the enemy. American equipment had improved both mobility and firepower so Navarre was determined to marry this capability with the French 'genius' for aggressive offensive action: 'We shall give back to our troops the mobility and aggressiveness they have sometimes lacked,' he boasted. Navarre looked to pep up the morale of his troops. His attempts were the gauche efforts of a man trying to dumb-down to his men with vulgarities he thought might be pleasing to the macho self-image of the French soldier: 'Victory is a woman who gives herself to those who know how to take her.'[26] Coming from the cold and aloof Navarre it rang false. He lacked the common touch, but he did not lack bravado. '*La victoire est certaine.*' War minister de Chevigne would with hindsight reflect, a good time afterwards, that 'intelligence could not substitute for inexperience allied to too high self-confidence.'[27] Navarre's adornment of the front cover of *Time* magazine hardly diminished his self esteem.

Contrary to post-event exculpatory allegations against Deuxieme Bureau intelligence, Maurice Dejean in his post-mortem report of 28 July 1953 confirmed that Navarre had been informed of Vietminh capability in heavy weapons, which Navarre knew were going to be deployed at Dien Bien Phu. However, Navarre misread the situation, because:

> *The Command was convinced that the enemy could not deploy sufficient means to take such defensive systems. Indications received as to the movement of diverse amounts of munitions including 75mm, 105mm and 37mm did not cause the Command to modify their thoughts.*

Operations *Hirondelle* and *Atlante*

Navarre had an early success upon taking command. *Operation Hirondelle* was an astute and well executed operation that combined the FEC's two major strengths: its mobility with elite paratrooper units, and naval power. Lang Son had become a major Vietminh supply depot near the Chinese border in a place that had previously been the hub for French military stores and operations in the north-east. Intelligence reported that it was not particularly well defended.

Additionally, the main stash for munitions and weapons and trucks had been pinpointed in bomb-proof natural caverns on hills just to the west of the town. Two elite paratrooper battalions, including the legendary Bigeard's 6th BEPC, were dropped into the area on 17 July 1953. The massive hoard of military goods including arms factories and Molotova trucks in the caverns was destroyed. Before any reaction force could be assembled the French escaped. They made their way to the coast, which was just 70km distant, where the French Navy covered their retreat with their guns and evacuated them.

Exploiting mobility, air and naval power, Navarre was tempted to use the same combination again for a large operation to take place below the 16th Parallel to clear a large coastal area with a force mainly composed of newly trained VNA troops. He would gain territory, at least nominally, prior to the Geneva Conference, and 'blood' the new divisions. However, he might have noted the previous coastal operations that had not given a good return on resource deployment, for example *Operation Camargue*, where French forces found themselves swiping at thin air in tangled coast swamps, fishing villages and waterways astride RC1. Nguyễn Hoan lived in a fishing village:

> *...so French soldiers and the mercenaries would come in on sweep operations, to arrest people or round them up for labour. My father was killed during one of these sweeps before I was born.*
>
> *One morning when we were going out to work, word spread that a French ship was coming into the harbour...people running around to gather up kids and grab whatever rice they...when we came back the village was wrecked. Most of the houses were burned down...we found my baby sister, crawling round next to my older sister's body. Her chest was a mass of dried blood.*
>
> *And once in a while the planes would come, bombing and strafing. One of these times...my best friend Huu was lying on the ground, burned by napalm. She wasn't dead, but she was dying. We sat around her at night watching her. Her body glowed with phosphorus.*

Operation Atlante was meant to clear up and take control once and for all, along with all of the communist vipers' nests along the narrow coastal plain behind Da Nang and Nha Trang. Launched in January with fifty-three battalions, the blooding of the nascent Vietnamese Army achieved nothing concrete. 'I was too optimistic,' declared General Ely, the French chief-of-staff in Paris. The region had no strategic importance at all, except perhaps as a tenuous but not essential link for the Vietminh in the north to those in the south. At a time when the French were trying to build up their logistics and defences at Dien Bien Phu, *Operation Atlante* absorbed large amounts of air transport and air cover. The *Atlante* operation fitted Giáp's strategy perfectly because it spread out French resources and diverted significant resources away from the crucial battle at Dien Bien Phu.

Graham Greene in Dien Bien Phu

When Greene visited Dien Bien Phu for twenty-four hours on 5 January 1954, on assignment for the *Sunday Times*, de Castries was still gung-ho with the offensive spirit even as the Vietminh net was closing around him and making his offensive patrols increasingly hazardous and costly. De Castries wrote that Greene 'had the nervy histrionic features of an old-time actor.' In a diary entry he recorded a remarkable incident at lunch with de Castries, Colonel Piroth and other officers. When artillery commander Colonel Piroth started to boast about the victory at Ná Sán and how the Vietminh would get the same treatment if they tried it at Dien Bien Phu, de Castries violently responded, '*Tais toi!* [be silent!]. I will not have Ná Sán mentioned in this mess. Ná Sán was a defensive post. This is an offensive one.'[28] For this offensive posture, de Castries had a mere ten tanks that were entirely unsuitable for offensive action in the mountains surrounding the small valley let alone the flooded paddy in the flat valley, which would also be impassable for tanks during the monsoon. But de Castries, the dashing cavalryman, had a macho reputation to keep up. His aristocratic manners, his prolific womanising and sporting prowess as a world champion show jumper and the holder of the world horse high jump record, lent him a stallion's aura.

That de Castries was still working to notions of offensive action in January 1954 that were long out of date is highly significant. He should have been preparing defences and making provision for counter-attacks in terrain where armour could not be used, not dreaming of offensive gallivanting. However, as a Group Mobile commander, he was absolutely unqualified and unfit for a defensive battle where the fate of French Indochina would rest in his hands. Others, such as Colonel Gilles, were at hand but not appointed. What is astonishing is that intelligence information and the actual experience of trying to take patrols out of the bastion already made it clear that offensive action was out of the question. That Dien Bien Phu was only a defensive fortress was clear to everyone except de Castries himself. This delusion no doubt accounts for the somewhat lackadaisical and complacent approach to defence planning, especially in respect of the Beatrice bastion, where no plans were in hand for rapid reaction counter-attacks. This, despite the advice from Colonel Gilles that the Vietminh would target outlying strongpoints that were vital for air field defence.

The junior officer attending to Greene on his visit to Beatrice offered far more insight than de Castries and the high command. The guide acerbically told the author after lunch that for offensive action in this terrain they needed 'a thousand mules not tanks'. As it turned out, the tanks would prove very useful in both a defensive and limited counter-attack mode within the defensive perimeter.

Many French journalists were not impressed by the French defences or the strategy expressed by de Castries, who contrary to his offensive-minded chat to Greene, to Guillan of le Monde (February 14 1954) he said that he aimed to 'Get the Vietminh down into the basin. Once he's come down, we'll catch him.'

Guillan wrote in his notebook, 'One had the impression of being trapped and surrounded…The enemy knew all about us, we knew nothing about him. A feeling of being in the lion's mouth…'

Writing in *France-Observateur* on 18 March, French military correspondent Paul Rossel noted: 'Instead of being a "fixation point" for the enemy, it [Dien Bien Phu] became a fixation centre for the expeditionary corps. It was the French not the Vietminh who were "bogged down" at Dien Bien Phu.'

Back in Paris, as the Geneva Conference set for early May approached, Bidault and the government were paying lip service to peace, according to correspondent Alexander Werth. On 9 March, Mendès-France picked up the point saying, 'Can these people really be trusted to pursue a peace policy which is diametrically opposed to that which they have pursued until now?'

As so often occurs in Indochina, an aspect of the war well understood by Lucien Bodard, the junior officers often had a better idea of the strategic and tactical truths than the senior officers. Although the truth of Dien Bien Phu's predicament had not yet dawned on de Castries, within a month the harsh reality had been accepted by the French high command, who now shaped their strategy in quite different terms to the original one of 'active defence of Lao'. In fact, de Castries, who was quite slow-witted and more macho than membrane, did not know that the day before Greene's visit Navarre had ordered contingency planning for an evacuation of the camp. This would involve going east into Lao in an operation known as *Xenophon*. On Christmas Day, Navarre had received intelligence on the number of Soviet trucks moving towards Dien Bien Phu. French intelligence estimates put the number available at 1,000, driven by Chinese, although the actual number was 628. They were maintained and repaired by Chinese trained mechanics.[29] The PLA had supplied 30,000 labourers for road-making and supply duties.

Amazingly, with the Dien Bien Phu battle shaping up into a major confrontation needing all of the FEC resources and energy, map-man Navarre decided to continue to execute his major offensive below the 17th Parallel, *Operation Atlante*.

In fact, he had already decided to accept battle on 3 December, when he issued 'Personal and secret instructions for the conduct of *Operation 949*.' So even at that point it was clear that offensive action was not contemplated. Only battle from and behind set positions, drawing on the Vietminh to French artillery killing zones, barbed wire, machine-guns and air attack, would even up the fight against Vietminh numbers.

On 21 February, by which time the FEC at Dien Bien Phu were well and truly hemmed-in and under effective siege, Navarre had officially changed his tune. He boasted to Heath, the US ambassador, that the encampment was 'a veritable jungle Verdun'. This was not a very happy analogy for a battle where 'impregnable' Verdun fortresses, such as Douaumont and Vaux, were quickly lost.

CHAPTER XV

Theatre of Battle, Strategies, and the Road to Bermuda

The theatre of battle

The essential facts are that French forces, including paratroopers, crack Algerian and French-trained T'ai (tribal) forces (local tribesmen) and Vietnamese ('puppet soldiers' according to the communists), about 11,000 in all, were dropped or flown into Dien Bien Phu from 19 November 1953. Resistance from a Vietminh unit stationed there was short and sharp. Another 5,000 troops would drop or fly in at a later date. The first flights brought in steel matting and equipment for levelling and producing an all-weather runway. When this was finished, a continual stream of Dakotas started to land their cargoes of military stores, munitions, barbed wire and construction equipment.

The settlement was located in an elongated oval-shaped plain of rice paddy, running north-south along the Noum Yam River and surrounded on all sides by peaks of about 1,000 to 1,500m. It is about 12km directly or 33km by road from the Lao border, 200km south of the Chinese border and 55 tortuous kilometres (as the crow flies) from Tau Giao, which was the pivotal point of the Vietminh supply system on the north-south RC41. Between them is the small upland valley at Mung Ang, whose dimensions and surface area were about one third of those of Dien Bn Phu. A vulnerable flat and open area, it was traversed at night by Vietminh supply columns.

Genevieve set the scene from her Dakota-eye-view as she came into land in January on her first trip:

> *When I first arrived in DBP the camp appeared to be already denuded. From the air it was a universe of tunnels, trenches, and shelters whose entrances were revealed and reinforced by logs and sandbags. Machine-gun posts were spotted on the hillsides, and on the plain, as we descended to land, I could see the brown tarps that still covered the shelters. Once I landed, the hills, green and wooded hills seemed suddenly less hostile than the vast jungle universe we had flown over with its menacing density. In the distance a few rice fields still quivered in the wind, but the camp was closed in by a threatening jungle where paths must be carved out by machete. Since November 1953 DBP had become the*

main mission of the flight nurses stationed in Hanoi. Each day two of us were assigned to go into the remote camp and evacuate the wounded whose numbers increased when the battalions affected a sortie.

The size of the battlefield, as defined by the French porcupine's footprint, would be 16km long and 6km wide in a valley that measured about 19 by 7km. It is only one of two significant valleys in the whole north-western region of Vietnam, the other being Lai Chau 120km (as the crow flies) to the north. At the time of the parachute-drop into Dien Bien Phu, Lai Chau was garrisoned by 2,500 French-officered North African and local T'ai soldiers.

Dien Bien Phu bastion was far too large an area for the 16,000 French troops to occupy in depth, so they would build a series of forty-nine strongpoints grouped in eight distinct defensive bastions on hills or slightly raised ground named after French women, reputedly the mistresses of Colonel de Castries, the French commander at Dien Bien Phu. They included Beatrice, the key bastion to block the Vietminh access to the airport and the nearest defensive position to the Vietminh line of supply. Gabrielle, situated to protect the north end of the runway was vital for the same reason as was Anne-Marie, a cluster of positions to the east of the runway. Isabelle was an isolated defensive position 5km to the south of the main bastion areas. Dominique and Éliane positions covered the so-called five hills area to the east of the Yam Noum River. In descending order, they were: Dominique 1; Dominique 2; Éliane 1; Éliane 4; and Éliane 2. The central area bastions and positions were Claudine and Huguette. Other positions and *ad hoc* add-ons were created throughout the battle. Strategically, the holding of Beatrice, Gabrielle and Anne-Marie was critical for the protection of the runway and maintenance of air supply. Without direct air transport for supplies, reinforcement and evacuation of wounded, the odds on the survival of fortress Dien Bien Phu would fall dramatically.

Most of the significant hills and main French positions in the valley were on the east side of the airstrip, east of the Nam Yam River. These hills stood about 12km from the much higher surrounding mountains, which were several thousand feet above the French positions. The common but mistaken legend of Dien Bien Phu is that this basin was a death-trap because of the surrounding mountains. In fact, the high mountains, which enveloped the valley on all sides, were a benefit in so far as they made Vietminh logistics very difficult. The high mountains were not the problem, rather it was the plethora of smaller foothills in the valley, especially on the north and east sides. Ideally, key hills in this group, such as Hill 781 to the east of Dominique, or Mount Fictif, should have been occupied. A costly raid on Hill 781 led by Colonel Langlais demonstrated that it was too well defended and too distant to hold. There were far too many hills for the French to occupy them all, so the Vietminh could range freely amongst the foothills below the high mountains and draw close to the French bastions whilst under cover. Of the outlying and isolated bastions, Gabrielle, Isabelle and Anne-Marie enjoyed relatively good 360-degree free-fire over flat paddy fields. The bastions of Dominique and Éliane were hemmed-in by a surfeit of nearby hills that gave ample cover for hidden approaches by Vietminh units and dug-in artillery.

However, there was one serious disadvantage to being in the valley, which was that the enemy could see everything that you were doing. Every new trench or stronghold could be noted. Dang Quan Thuy, the officer charged with setting up an observation post, noted that they could look down on:

> *The tank depot, the French artillery battery positions, each and every movement…we could see nearly everything. In looking from on high I had the impression that I was hovering 'over the head of the enemy'. 'I know what you are doing,' I said to myself.*[1]

A lack of communication equipment and training meant that artillery spotting could not be exploited by the holding of high ground. Nonetheless, the Vietminh enjoyed a significant advantage in troop deployment, concentration and initiative. The French could not know exactly where and when the blows would fall. Giáp himself would go up to the observation point and assess the field of battle. He even witnessed French reinforcement paratrooper drops. Giáp positioned himself near the front. Navarre and Cogny were respectively in Saigon and Hanoi.

Each defensive block would in due course become a legend for horrific close-quarter fighting. Ideally the bastions of the porcupine, which were mainly located on hilltops, would be able to give mutual supporting covering fire. In practice some of these bastions were too widely separated, such as Gabrielle, Anne-Marie and Beatrice to the north, and Isabelle far to the south. Not surprisingly Giáp noted this weakness and the fact that these bastions were essential for protecting the integrity of the airstrip and the central core. If these bastions were lost, then the integrity of the whole landing zone would be threatened by infiltration and strangulation by trench warfare and siege tactics. Aircraft landing would be entirely compromised and the area for targeted parachute-drops would also be severely restricted. It opened the way for the Vietminh to operate a successful battle of attrition where logistical capacity would be the key to victory.

Road communication for vehicles from the Red River delta/Tonkin was practically non-existent. Only a minor dirt track no more than 1m wide connected Dien Bien Phu with the market town of Tau Giao, about 100km to the north-east. From a small tribal settlement that would soon turn into a major depot, better roads ran out across more hills in various directions. One road led to the north-east and the conduit to the Bac Kan-Chinese border areas. Another road followed the Day River Valley through Son La to Hoa Binh, where it connected to the Black River. Hoa Binh was the vital connecting hub to Hue and north-central Vietnam and the Central Highlands below that. Another road ran north towards the 3,143m Phan Xi Pang Massif around Sapa and Lai Chau.

As for Lai Chau, whose province contained Dien Bien Phu, there was no proper direct connection except via Tau Giao and a rudimentary track running south, optimistically called the Pave Road after the explorer. Dien Bien Phu was, in essence, a small tribal township, a market town, serving as an important *entrepot* for the opium trade. Even today the direct road from Lai Chau is primitive and tortuous, though currently being upgraded. The road from Tau Giao was often blocked by French bombing so Vietminh supplies would have to cross extraordinarily difficult sharply undulating mountainous jungles and rivers. The map reveals that the only conceivable retreat for the French Army was by way of Lao on foot, because the narrow tarmac road today was just a track in 1954.

French tactical plan

- Strongly fortified bastions surrounded by wire would draw the 'tactically inept' Vietminh into killing zones, where they would be destroyed by pre-set French artillery, mortars and machine-guns. By offering a seemingly tempting and isolated target, the Vietminh would be lured into a firepower trap.
- French 155mm and 105mm artillery spotted by light aircraft would destroy any artillery capability brought up by the Vietminh.
- Interlocking defensive positions would deliver supporting fire, including Isabelle to the south, which would act as an artillery base offering flanking fire to VPA approaches to the Élianes.
- Close support air power would also destroy enemy infantry formations as they formed-up and attacked. They would also suppress AA fire.
- Fighter-bombers and medium B26 bombers would attack and close off Vietminh supply lines and troop concentrations, and blow-up bridges or cause landslides to block tracks.
- Cargo aircraft, mainly Dakotas, would keep the fortress supplied by the air-land system.

In essence, massive superior French firepower would destroy the VPA in a set-piece battle on ground of French choosing.

Navarre's tactics and strategy were not unique and it was indeed the only way to bring the Vietminh to battle. To attack them at DBP, the Vietminh had to think they had a reasonable chance at victory. But that involved a much higher level of risk than sitting behind the defences of the de Lattre lines. Navarre's plan also assumed that Giáp had not learnt anything from his defeat at Ná Sán.

Navarre's plan assumed huge American logistical support, which had seen a quantum leap after US chief-of-staff Lawton Collin's visit in October 1951. Between May 1950 and the end of 1951, 239,000 tons of supplies had been delivered, with 53 million rounds of ammunition, 800 vehicles, 650 tanks and armoured cars, 200 aircraft of various types including fighter-bombers and Dakotas, 14,000 automatic weapons and 3,500 communication radios. In 1952, aid totalled US$616 million. According to the Pentagon Papers:

> *Through 1952 and into 1954 the MDAP shipments to Indochina increased steadily: by February 3, 1953, the United States had shipped 137,200 long tons of material (224 ships' cargoes); by July 1954, approximately 150,000 long tons had been sent, including 1,800 combat vehicles, 30,887 motor transport vehicles, 361,522 small arms and machine-guns, 438 naval craft, 2 World War II aircraft carriers, and about 500 aircraft.*[2]

'You came like a crusader,' lauded Collins of America's French allies:

> *...few of your campaigns have created enthusiasm that is comparable to that which you raised by your visit to America. No one has ever shown, as you showed, in such simple language, all that is at stake in Indochina...to our peoples you have rendered a great service.*[3]

By spring 1953, the French could count about 300,000 troops, 60/40[4] FEC/associated states. Additional arms were needed to modernise the French Army, but also to arm the increasing number of Vietnamese conscripts. By the end of 1953, Navarre had an army at his disposal of nearly 500,000 including associated states troops. In a young army, quality was mixed. They faced 300,000 Vietminh of whom some two thirds were regulars of various grades, including regional units.

Developments in US policy and communist tactics, the Cold War

The domino theory was already in development before the famous domino speech was given by Eisenhower in April 1954, one month before the fall of Dien Ben Phu. Similar ripple-effect analogies were already common.

In Indochina there was stalemate. As the parties moved towards negotiation in 1953, there was an increasing need to either avoid battlefield defeats or secure victory, but only in circumstances where victory was assured. If extra leverage could be obtained by a battlefield victory, then so much the better. Both sides were aware of this. Navarre was under instructions to produce a plan whereby France could disengage victoriously but with honour in Indochina while Giáp was told by Ho Chi Minh only to risk a major battle if victory was absolutely certain. The propaganda myth of Dien Bien Phu is that it secured the freedom of French Indochina. In fact, key government and political elements in France, by the time of the battle, were already recognising that they would probably not win an outright victory, that both the time and tide of history was against them.

In January 1953, Dwight Eisenhower became president of the United States. He appointed anti-communist hawk John Foster Dulles as his secretary of state and Allen Dulles as his director of the CIA. J.F. Dulles was an experienced diplomat, having attended the Versailles conference in 1919. He was the foreign policy advisor to Dewey, the loser to Truman in the 1949 election. The president came into office on a rising tide of fear and anger in the US following a succession of communist victories around the world, especially in China. It was anger mixed with fear and paranoia, which was soon to result in the McCarthy purges. Dulles had made clear his views on foreign policy and communism in an extremely forthright book published in 1950, *War or Peace*. He commented with raw vitriol on the methods used by international communism:

> *The party* [communist] *stirs up class war, civil war, or guerrilla war wherever it seems propitious. This technique has been successful in China, and is now being followed in Indochina.*[5]

His understanding of communism was simple but accurate. He was well-read, in Soviet history, ideology and tactics. He was particularly impressed by their use of tactical retreat: 'In this respect Soviet communism is far more formidable than Hitler's Nazism,' he noted. Dulles' reputation preceded him. He was well aware of the power of Soviet propaganda recounting:

> *Secretary Marshall and I were portrayed in the 1947 Moscow May Day rally as chopping down the Tree of Peace, and Mr. Churchill and I have been caricatured as two torpedoes launched from a pirate submarine to sink the ship of peace.*[6]

Stalin and Lenin were indeed masters of the tactical retreat, as was Ho.

Vietminh strategy

Vietminh strategy, which became known as Winter Spring 1953–4 Strategy, was conceived directly in response to accurate intelligence reports about the Navarre plan, copies of which were even received through embedded spy networks in France's civil administration and from China via Soviet

Intelligence, who had obtained copies from spies at senior levels in the US camp. The French administration and its multiplicity of parties in government meant that confidential military information was impossible to keep secret, not least because party ministers in coalition liked to leak against each other for the purpose of political infighting. Francois Mitterrand, for example, would be accused by right-wing deputies of leaking French military plans to the Vietminh and causing the defeat at Dien Bien Phu.[7] Although it was strongly denied, it demonstrates the atmosphere of the times. Poisonous infighting and leaks while trying to present common government were typical of both the Third and Fourth Republics. As de Gaulle well understood, coalition politics was deadly to the formation of clear policies.

Ho Chi Minh's strategy aimed at tying up French forces around Indochina, including in Lao where an important strategic link with the Pathet Lao was already operating in the Lao border areas. Having soaked up General Navarre's reserves, the Vietminh would seek an opportunity to overwhelm some French garrisons in a set-piece victory somewhere in the north.

Towards *détente*?

On 4 July 1953, the Foreign Office's Sir William Stang discussed with Churchill the French desire for a three-power conference to win support for continuing the French struggle in Indochina. Churchill was pushing for a four-power summit with the Russians: 'I thought you and I might form our own impression of Malenkov,'[8] he wrote to Eisenhower. Churchill already had some positive feedback about Malenkov's disposition from diplomatic meetings with the new leader who was well noted for his fine erudition in contrast to the crude Khrushchev. Malenkov's sentiments expressed on the atoms bombs in Izvestia in March exactly tallied with Churchill's horror at the prospect of nuclear war. This was the genesis of the Bermuda Conference and the subsequent international conferences in Berlin and Geneva.

Colville noted in his diary of Churchill:

> *...still very wrapped up with the possibility of bringing something off with the Russians and the idea of meeting Malenkov face to face. Very disappointed in Eisenhower whom he thinks both weak and stupid.*

This continued through the summer. Lord Salisbury visiting Washington found Eisenhower:

> *...violently Russophobe, greatly more than Dulles, and believes the president is personally responsible for the policy of useless pinpricks and harassing tactics the US has been following against Russia in Europe and the Far East.*[9]

Eden and the orthodox Foreign Office view was to keep close to NATO and the Western Alliance and not ruffle feathers in Washington. Churchill was depressed by Eden's attitude, 'because he thinks it consigns us to years of more hatred and hostility.'

Taking the goat in Bermuda

In Bermuda, where Churchill flew on 1 December 1953, Eisenhower told Churchill that if there was a deliberate breach of the Korean armistice, the US 'would expect to strike back with nuclear weapons.'[10]

On this point Churchill concurred. Bidault lined up with the Americans. He doubted any new-look USSR. Churchill countered, saying, 'Let us make sure we do not too lightly dismiss this possibility.'

France's fragile ego following the humiliations of the war years was to suffer greatly at the hands of an attractive goat. The French press, ever looking for a sharp story to browbeat the lacklustre premier Laniel, took note of Churchill's behaviour at the airport as they waited for Eisenhower. The Band of the Welsh Fusiliers was playing as the two premiers waited. Churchill noticed that the regiment's white goat mascot was on hand so, in a playful humour, he made a great show of stroking and talking to the beast whilst turning his back on Premier Laniel. A mischievous French press loved it and moved rapidly from humour to lampooning the unfortunate premier. Perhaps the weakest of the Fourth Republic's premiers, Laniel, an obscure independent deputy from Normandy, had become prime minister because the voting was deadlocked. He was the last-resort Buggins' turn candidate. Laniel, the French backwoodsman, was ready-made for satirical hilarity. 'Churchill apparently preferred talking to a goat.'

Much of the discussions were taken up by the bullying of Laniel and foreign minister Bidault about getting EDF over the line. They became, according to the French press, the butt of slightly condescending and derogatory remarks. For his part Bidault fished for more support from the Americans. From the French point of view, with the armistice concluded in Korea on 27 July 1953, there was a fear that France would be left in the lurch to fight the communist hordes on its own. The French wanted political and material support, with as few strings attached as possible with regard to their Indochina political set-up.

The Americans were upbeat on the prospects in Indochina. Now that American money and arms as well as advisers were being shipped in, they were feeling gung-ho. Navarre's plan delivered to the Americans with all the vim and assurance of a cocky general had hit exactly the right note to appeal to the American 'can do' approach to military action. Brimming with confidence after the victory in the Second World War, the Americans had reached the point of hubris, something only a little dented by the experience in Korea. Navarre's optimism about victory also appealed to the foreign policy peccadillos of the new Eisenhower-Dulles administration, because it fitted exactly Dulles' belief that the communist influence must be rolled back, not just contained. 'Passivity' was the main criticism of democratic foreign policy in respect to the Russians and the contagion of communism. Indochina was on the verge of developing into what would become a project for the way in which post-colonial societies could be rescued from communism with democracy, American values and American money.

By 1949, even the Truman administration, having lost China and Eastern Europe without challenge to the Soviets, was beginning to be concerned by South-East Asia. A national security council paper published in 1949 noted:

> *In any event, colonial-nationalist conflict provides a fertile field for subversive communist activities, and it is now clear that South-east Asia is the target of a co-ordinated offensive directed by the Kremlin...The extension of communist authority in China represents a grievous political defeat for us: if South-east Asia also is swept by communism we shall have suffered a major political rout.*

It was a short step to start providing arms and aid to France.

Dulles strongly encouraged the French to continue the war. For Dulles, France was a very cheap catspaw in their game with the Soviets. Vast amounts of army surplus could be shipped to the French. Delivered free, this surplus had already been paid for and was a wasting asset surplus to requirements. Written down as scrap or valueless inventory, in reality much of the aid would be a costless gift...

At dinner in Bermuda on 4 December, Churchill, well-oiled with the usual rounds of champagne, cognac and whiskey, regaled the leaders with stories and had a fine time exchanging reminiscences with 'Ike'. Laniel, 'the French PM looked abstracted and as bored as Anthony [Eden].' On 5 December, there were discussions about the developments in the Soviet Union and possibilities for engaging with Premier Malenkov and the new leadership. Churchill was shocked when Eisenhower described Russia as a tart. 'Despite the bath, perfume, or lace, it is still the same old girl.'[11] At the conference on 5 December, Eisenhower did not believe there had been any change in the Soviet's 'long term purpose [of destroying the capitalist free world]. From their writings it was clear there had been no change since Lenin.'

Objectively, some things had indeed changed. Armistice talks for Korea were nearly finished. NKVD chief Beria had been purged in July when Marshal Zhukov, by pre-arrangement with coup leader Nikita Khrushchev and the other Politburo plotters, had burst into a Politburo meeting with a pistol and arrested him. Prisoners were soon streaming home from the gulags.

Beria would be shot on 23 December, although this would not become known for a while. Churchill argued so cogently for the need to approach post-Stalin Russia that after the meeting Ike, according to Churchill, 'said there was a lot in what I said.'[12] The conference was dominated by the matter and, to an even greater extent, by the EDF issue.

Indochina was barely covered except in lower-level technical discussions but did appear in the communique. Britain and the US declared that they supported France's struggle against communist aggression in Indochina. 'We salute the valiant contribution of France and the three associated states of Indo China with the French Union.' (Communique, December 1953) This communique must have heartened Bidault because it was tantamount to recognition of the French constitutional settlement and continued dominion in Indochina. It noted that the three had studied proposals 'that would hasten the outcome of the war in satisfactory conditions' and would lead to 'the re-establishment of peace'.[13] A typical reaction to the conference came from J.J. Servan Schrieber, writing in *Le Monde* on 21 July: 'Bidault had given Dulles a blank cheque' on France. France was offering 'blood for money'. Nevertheless, a contrary view might have found that the blank cheque had been written by the Americans in respect of France's constitutional settlement in Indochina. Certainly, that was the view developing in some parts of the Democratic Party, and even with some republicans.

But even as the Bermuda Conference progressed there was great complacency about the situation in Indochina. At the Vietnamese Workers Party meeting of the Politburo on 5 December, the formal decision for battle at Dien Bien Phu was made when Giáp's request for 35,000 troops was approved, as well as supplies for forty-five days. This implied that a short sharp overwhelming attack was contemplated. The campaign was already underway. On 7 December, the French left Lai Chau, the capital of the T'ai Federation, as Vietminh forces advanced.

From the Anglo-Saxon perspective, the failure of the conference was palpable. Churchill and Eisenhower were bitterly disappointed by France's continued resistance to EDF: 'The Americans talked about pulling out of Europe,'[14] and Churchill said if they pulled out of Europe so would the UK.

Churchill opined that 'in refusing EDF the French may have thrown away the last chance of saving France.'

CHAPTER XVI

A Nation on the March

'We must win at all costs'

Informed through his excellent intelligence network, Giáp knew that:

> *In the autumn of 1953, the French commander calculated that the Vietminh were too far from Dien Bien Phu and could at most send only two divisions.*[1]
>
> *When the enemy occupied a position of strategic importance, we saw this not as something to worry about but as an opportunity to destroy them…after the parachute-drop at Dien Bien Phu, the north-west really did become the principal focus, as already outlined in our plan.*

Giáp met with Ho at the end of December 1953. They decided to destroy the French at Dien Bien Phu. What was at stake was the future of Indochina. Navarre had thrown down the gauntlet and the DRV had picked it up. The prize was to go into the room at Geneva as victors. It was a price worth massive sacrifice. An entire nation would be mobilised and concentrated on one single objective. With France's will to win already tottering, now was the time for the *coup de grace*.

Ho Chi Minh declared:

> *You are the battlefield commander. I give you complete powers. It is a battle of huge importance and we must win at all costs. Attack when you are sure of victory. If on the contrary you are not certain, abstain from attacking.*

Ho Chi Minh's words made a strong impression on Giáp. He could be in no doubt of the huge geo-political consequences for victory or defeat in this battle.[2]

Upon news of the French landings at Dien Bien Phu, Uncle Ho and the Vietminh leadership had immediately seized on the opportunity to score the crushing defeat they desperately needed following those suffered since 1951. They needed a great victory such as the one at RC4 in 1950 to re-energise their liberation movement and launch a fiery propaganda campaign both at home and overseas. With the French home front obviously beginning to crack following the rise of Mendes-France and the shifting in the position of the Socialist Party, one more big push was needed to secure the geo-political victory that was needed to get the French out of Indochina, comprehensively and for good.

Ho also needed to impress his Chinese and Russian allies to get them to push for Vietnamese unification under Vietminh leadership at Geneva. Ho realised that the Russians and Chinese would not necessarily support their interests in full. The danger was that some compromise would be reached behind their backs, giving voice to the aspirations of the old Saigon clique for a separate Cochin China-based political entity built around the Catholic minority and virulently anti-communist Buddhist sects, such as the Cao Dai and the Hoa Hao. There was the danger of a partition.

Ho issued a command ordering that the FEC at Dien Bien Phu should be crushed. This was the opportunity envisaged in the 1953 Summer Strategic Plan. There was a determination not to hand the French another Ná Sán-type victory, letting the opportunity slip away.

Marching with Pham

Giáp, the architect of the great national mobilisation was awe-struck by his own creation:

> *Just there, plunging in the darkness, the forests of the north-west suddenly became full of life, the night brought uninterrupted artillery trains, lorries, interminable files of men moving rapidly...columns of bicycle transports seemed like herds of young elephants...one also saw members of the logistics teams driving herds of pigs...all converged.*[3]

A high-definition satellite overview of Tonkin in January, February and early March 1954 (if such had existed) would have shown a great stream of human movement like armies of ants swarming in multiple streams towards a great new colony to the east of Dien Bien Phu. A nation in arms on the move. The streams started off as small thin lines, gradually thickening, then merged on the wider concourse of main routes, then again into broad thick torrents as they entered the last 70km of the route. Some of these streams had started in little dribbles from as far away as 400km; not ants but parties of individual men and women in small groups. Much less than half of them were front-line soldiers. The majority were men and women carrying food, arms and munitions, both for the soldiers and the armies of porters, civilian levees, drivers, propaganda dance troops, cooks, and road workers who toiled in difficult and arduous conditions in remote mountain areas. To ease the burden on logistics, each soldier also had to carry a 5kg bag of rice in addition to their other equipment. As they marched, they were cheered and often fed and feted by local villagers with food and fruits, delicacies that were a rare and almost forgotten treat for those who had spent years in the thick forests and on the rocky crags of the borderlands. The Vietminh mobilised 20,000 bicycles, including East German imports, for the transportation effort, along with 34,000 porters.[4]

Do Sam, born in 1931, was a gunner from the 45th Regiment of the 351st Heavy Division:

> *In 1952 I went to China for technical instruction as an artilleryman. Following that I was then deployed in the first heavy artillery unit of the Vietminh popular army. At the start of 1953 we were ordered to transport the cannons by road from China to my country* [Vietnam DRV].

Moving in secret, it was the start of the great campaign of Dien Bien Phu, a logistics and artillery battle that started not at Dien Bien Phu but on the Chinese border. A momentous event, it presaged not only a rare achievement but one of the greatest army-scale ambushes in military history.

One of the young soldiers on the march was Pham – better educated than many and a gifted artist. In February 1954, Pham Thanh Tam was 22 years old but had already spent seven years fighting for the Vietminh from the jungle bases on the Chinese border around Cao Bang. Part of the 315th Heavy Division, he was ordered with his unit to make his way to Dien Bien Phu. Equipped with a crude backpack, a bag of rice, and wearing simple sandals, he set off. In his baggage he carried the diary that would make him famous. He had been training as an artilleryman in one of the Chinese camps adjacent to the border in southern Yunnan. His trek started on little tracks through dense forests and ravines and over rocky limestone crags, all infested with mosquitos and other dangers of the jungle such as snakes. Eventually he reached the main track, which was under construction as a conduit for the guns, men and food supplies destined for Dien Bien Phu. He was 400km from the French encampment. His unit's 105mm cannon would be carried by lorries while the gunners marched on foot. 'I was not afraid of sacrificing myself,'[5] recounted Pham after the war.

Tran Do explained:

> *...our march took fifteen nights; more than 400km. During our expedition, nothing was left to chance. We were assured of good and sufficient food, resting areas, and reasonable conditions along the route, making sure that both men and equipment arrived in good shape.*[6]

The phrase 'sufficient food' covers a multitude of defaults. Poor quality rice stored in north-western warehouses 'was already spoiled' by the time it reached the battlezone areas which, according to Pham, meant that 'eating in Dien Bien Phu was a very miserable experience...stored rice had lots of cockroach droppings mixed in.'[7]

Pham would walk through mountains then cross areas of paddy on the fringes of the Red River, which itself must be crossed. Its main crossing points were constantly under threat from French aircraft, but it was already witness to the passage of 6,000 men per day, a flood that fighter bombers could not hold back. Before reaching the Red River, they had to cross the Song Chay River where the bombers were also active. On arriving at Be Ngoc, he found:

> *...the French...had already bombed the place destroying everything, including decapitating the trees...the river was high for the time of year. Clouds of crickets were flying north as they do every season and underneath them the river looked white with their reflection.*[8]

Typical of Pham's diary, his military descriptions often wander off into poetic description. Hemmed-in by communist orthodoxy, Pham's romantic spirit and humanity shines through the dreary dirge of communist propaganda.

Having crossed the river Pham continued walking to the west. He noticed 'children in vivid colours singing' while crossing a field 'and on the march there were fresh papaya. So long since Pham and his friend Lanh had seen them that they ate four at a single sitting.'[9]

He spent a night with his brother-in-law and his family, whose farm they were passing. They gorged on delicacies. 'They were warmly welcomed. The father-in-law went into the orchard and cut more papaya and fresh sugar cane.'[10] Crossing the river they re-joined the RP13, which was a branch of the RC41, the main Vietminh supply route the French had often tried but failed to cut – notably during the FEC's Hoa Binh campaign. He noted:

> *...thousands of kilometres of road had been constructed in secret...and additionally bridges were assembled, disassembled and then reassembled at the passing of every convoy.*

Volunteers and civilian workers, gangs of young men and women, all were collectively enthused about this great national enterprise. Everyone was involved in the great struggle. Everyone understood the objective...victory at Dien Bien Phu.

In the stream there were Chinese-supplied lorries, often of American make, captured by the Chinese from the nationalists, as well as Russian Moltovas.

Bicycle-loads of rice or munitions were pushed by black-clad peasants. Hand-carts and bullock-carts creaked over rough paths, gun-carriages and mortars being pulled along in all manner of means, or just individuals with mountainous loads on their backs. In typical communist fashion, the achievement of Stakhanovite individuals was lauded for their porterage feats.

Some bicycle-loads were recorded at as much as 220kg, but this was a Stakhanovite hero-load. Normal loads would have been about 150kg at most.

The party encouraged such hero-worship and competition between groups or individuals to achieve and overachieve. This was all part of a belief in communist societies that transformation of individuals into social units, into 'new people' as the Khmer Rouge would call them, was really possible and part of the inexorable progression to socialism. Propaganda posters copied the same Asia adapted stereotype as the lantern-jawed, muscle-rippling, dungaree-wearing Soviet industrial or agricultural co-operative farmer in the USSR. They were very similar to Nazi posters of the period.

Moulding, shaping, pushing, encouraging, prodding, threatening and forcing people into the great utopian system of communism was the dystopian goal of the multifaceted party programme of indoctrination and brainwashing. Ho, who had lived through the ludicrous era of heroic proletarians in 1930s industrialisation in the USSR, was familiar with such methods and copied them.[11] The abused had become the abuser:

> *By the end of 1953, the market town of Thanh Hoa, like many others, sent a huge contingent of pack-bicycles to carry food supplies to the Dien Bien Phu battlefield. This was repeated in towns and village the length and breadth of Vietnam.*

Pictures of the time show lines of East German, Czech or Chinese-made bicycles *en route*, loaded down on both sides with bulging sacks of rice, front and back, and with sundry accoutrements strapped on. Each is adorned with a branch and leaves for camouflage. Competition prizes and awards were all part of this great scheme. Pham describes how Duy from Phu province carried 87kg on his back. He was awarded the hero medal third class and a flag in honour of Ho. Targets and quotas were set. Civilians were dragooned into civil works battalions for porterage or road-building. An entire society was militarised.

On the road the soldiers felt a huge sense of belonging to something momentous and glorious. They were feted along the way. Young girls deserted their families to join patriotic dance troupes to support party propaganda and entertain the soldiers (bo doi). As they reached the Red River delta the streams of traffic merged. Pham fell in love and drew the picture of a pretty dancer. Sex-starved Pham had been living in the remote north-east jungles for seven years and was:

> *...astonished to see a gaggle of young women...visibly too young to officially take part in the campaign...one of them, sister Bau, was a totally innocent beauty... who came from a very poor family.*[12]

His censoriousness as to her age shows a sweet concern for the victim of his affection, and an implied criticism of the party for its excessive campaign, which had inveigled this very young poor girl away from the natural affections of her family. She, a simple peasant girl:

> *...had been seduced by the dancing and singing which was part of the political organisation in the village...having pleaded with her parents to let her join up, however she had cried more than once during the long march as she carried the regulation 20kg on her back.*[13] [Note: These sentences with their implied criticism were edited out of the 2005 edition.]

She and her troupe would accompany Pham and his friends for several weeks.

Not all women had such a glamorous opportunity to serve the nation and it was mainly the pretty ones who were chosen for the dance troupes. The Communist Party was not just about 'bread and circuses', but sex as well, though it was not advertised as such. This aspect was hidden by the usual puritanical rhetoric and hypocrisy of the party's priggish revolutionary culture. It was, of course, the political commissars and more senior party officials behind the front line who had first pick of the entertainment troupes, just as Ho was provided with women by the party. For the citizens and lower party officials, strict proletarian morality was the order of the day. Pham never had a chance.

Women played a major role in the porterage of supplies along RC41 and even up to near the front lines. That this is so is no surprise at all in the context of South-East Asia where women are not just the backbone of family life but of economic activity as a whole, whether in planting rice before harvest or reaping or milling, tending vegetable gardens, looking after the shop, or earning extra cash by sewing or weaving. (Recognising the key role of women in South-East Asia led Muhammad Yunus and his Grameen bank to create the famous microfinance model based on women's groups in villages.)

About 10 million Vietnamese came under effective communist rule in 1953 and 1.7 million were used for porterage. An estimated 250,000 took part directly in the Dien Bien Phu campaign. Given that the young men were being drafted into the army it seems likely that more than half of the porters were women. Theirs was a dual function:

> *On the way to the front we took munitions, and on the way back the wounded. We clambered up and down steep slopes of mountains and over passes. Just one box of munitions needed two volunteer porters...we were sleepwalking sometimes when we carried supplies and munitions because we were so exhausted.*

Efficiency of porter operations were enhanced by giving the porters a return cargo:

On the return journey each wounded man had two helpers in attendance, stopping every few kilometres to give them a drink or let them relieve themselves. We pressed water on their lips. A lot of soldiers were in great pain; and moaned aloud.

Having no professional medical training, all the nurses could do was give encouragement. 'Sometimes the soldiers died later or on the road. Travel was by night and rest by day,' recalled Dao Thi Vinh, who was 25 years old when she experienced the hell of war as part of the great organic backbone of the regular Vietminh Army.

Pham admits that 'without the leadership of Uncle Ho and the organisation of the party the young men who acted as porters would never have volunteered for such work.' It is an admission that they were forced labour, a system of Corvée work that was anathema under the French. Enthusiasm played some part but the prolific effort of the Vietnamese nation could only be achieved through the despotism of social control, discipline and coercion.

There were privations. Pham describes meeting a 16-year-old youth who had not eaten for two days who beat on a metal can without cease as a means to distract from hunger. Others struggled day after day with 45kg on their backs. Lorry drivers drove for eighteen hours a day. All the time they were surveyed by enemy spotter planes, who on the open road could not fail to see battalions of bicycle porters moving towards the front.[14]

Pham and his friends could not light fires to cook rice for fear of drawing attention from enemy planes. However, the mood was celebratory. 'Everyone was singing and dancing. The atmosphere was so gay and full of emotion that we hurried towards the front.' In the evening various party delegates and political commissars would boast optimistically about the battle to come, even laying bets as to who would capture the first enemy flag, little realising that the French Army had moved on from Waterloo. Pham describes meeting a brigade of young volunteers who all came from poor rural homes. Mostly aged between 18 and 25 but many just 16 or 17 (as Pham had been when he joined up), 'with the faces of innocent children they only dreamed of one day being able to wear the uniform of Uncle Ho's soldiers.'[15]

Although Pham concentrates on the positives and the uplifting enthusiasm and spirit of the times, he is not blind to the fact that not everyone is participating in this revolutionary spirit. There were many for whom Corvée labour was as much an onerous and unpleasant imposition, whether it was being ordered by officials working for the French or the communists. For the most part people shared, but Pham met some surly road workers smoking tobacco one night. They refused to share their pipes. Other soldiers greedily consumed depot supplies meant for troops yet to come through. It was all testament to the fact that human nature, not totally transformed by revolutionary spirit, was reasserting itself amidst the general euphoria.

Rivers were crossed, first the Red River and then the Black River after traversing some steep mountains. Always there was the threat of aerial attack because this great stream had not gone unnoticed. Crossings were choke-points and any river traffic was assumed to be a military target especially along the western sections of the Red and Black Rivers, the well-known thoroughfares for Vietminh logistics. French bombers would swoop down from time to time like great birds of prey. Graham Greene snagged a ride on an attack mission when he visited Indochina in 1951. Squeezing into the cockpit of a fighter bomber meant for a two-man team he described how:

> *...we made fourteen dives. It was most uncomfortable, coming up rapidly and diving steeply from 9,000 to 3,000 feet...coming back down to about 200 feet & shot up a sampan on the Red River.*[16]

On 26 February, Pham reached the Black River where 'the mountains were reflected in the tranquil river. Further off on the high peaks fires burnt in the villages of our indigenous compatriots, the Meo.'[17] He was naively optimistic about mountain people such as the Meo and the T'ai, who regarded the Vietnamese lowlanders with disdain because of their arrogance and the history of exploitation and oppression. Pham was infected by Vietminh propaganda. Just as the Vietnamese were rebelling against the French so the hill people were in many, even most, instances, allying themselves with the French against the Vietminh in revenge for long-held grievances. The tribes joined French-led partisan groups who conducted a constant guerrilla war on the Vietminh, so tying down large numbers of troops. Some T'ai or Meo units even became semi-regular units within the French Army. They were well represented at Dien Bien Phu. For the most part indigenous people did not relish Vietminh victory because, as proud and independent people,[18] it would leave them defenceless against a new and more rigorous communist oppression. The French exploited this. At the political level, the protection of the hill peoples served as a prime justification for continued French rule in Indochina.

The infantry suffered as much as anyone else on the marches, which for many included gruelling treks deep into Lao. 'Our men die in many ways,' recounted battalion commander Colonel Bui Tin. Malaria and snakebites were common, but drowning or being crushed by falling trees were not unusual, or even death by tiger attack. Conditions were mitigated by rigid discipline on matters of hygiene, for which Giáp was especially concerned:

> *Drinking water was to be boiled. Troops were to use clean socks after washing their feet in warm water and salt. They should have hot rice with adequate meat and vegetables at least once a day, and sleep at least six hours every night.*[19]

Given conflicting demands of speed of march and military objectives, these regulations must have been hard to maintain.

On 27 February, Pham's group split from the dance troupe, who went off in another direction. 'We said our farewells with big smiles but it warmed my heart,' recounted the slightly love-sick Pham. Further along the RC41, as they mounted the hills on 2 March they passed through the beautiful valley of Co Noi where on each peak they came across the vestiges of former French camps, including the battlefield at Ná Sán, strewn with rusting empty food tins and equally decaying coils of barbed wire.[20]

On 5 March, they passed over the mountain of Son La, another destroyed enemy encampment. Just the façade of a brick bunker remained and the ubiquitous litter of tin cans. Pham passed through empty villages the jungle was reclaiming. Tribal people had fled the terrors of war, most probably French-supporting villagers who felt it sensible to avoid the Vietminh. 'Soldiers collected tamarind fruit from abandoned trees to refill their bamboo tubes as provisions for the days to come.'[21] On 6 March, they climbed a steep and dangerous part of the road over the highest point in the track. Pham recorded 'the beginnings of spring as flowers burst out on the trees by the side of the road; blooms of pink and blue covered in butterflies.'[22]

To shelter from French bombing or reconnaissance, the Vietminh became experts in camouflage. One trick was to knit together the canopy of trees over the roads. On patrol Legionnaire Hans Wagemeuller had watched labourers fill planter baskets with earth. They could then be moved on to roads in the daytime when vehicles had passed. Also observed were Vietminh troops who appeared to be wading 'across the river as if it were only ten inches deep. They certainly had a bridge there,' recalled Wagemeuller, 'built to remain under water. Otherwise the reconnaissance planes would have spotted it long ago.'[23]

Along the way there were tragedies and sacrifices. One of the toughest challenges was hauling the huge 105mm cannon up and down steep mountain paths. Tran Do remembered:

> *One time the ropes tore. The cannon started to fall back without enough time to place chocks under the wheels. To Vinh Dien, in a sublime gesture, threw his body under the wheels. His body blocked the cannon's descent. He died for us all.*[24]

Pham met a chief of engineers who was constructing the road. The details reveal impressive feats of road-widening, which allowed the passage of heavy artillery. Engineer Thuy told him how they 'worked at least twenty hours per day and had to forage for wood and bamboo for the road up to 16km away.' There had been significant air raids on 6 and 16 December and for the first ten days of January, which clearly indicated that the French were well aware of the mass of forces descending on Dien Bien Phu.

Engineer Thuy noted that the fighter bombers dropped hundreds of delayed action and butterfly bombs, which were particularly deadly as each one contained a minimum of 50 bomblets. That meant a total of about 1,000 bombs per night. Just before General Giáp's passage to the front, bombs had destroyed part of the road. To finish the road before the arrival of Giáp and the artillery, all 100 of his men had worked fifty hours without a break to remove 3,000m^3 of earth manually, or 30m^3 per man in order to fill in the bomb craters. There were many near misses and on one occasion a delayed action 250kg bomb made a monumental explosion. Observation posts on the top of hills were attacked by air.

Another time, at a place where vegetation was sparse, they were caught in the open and a bomb fell just 20m from Pham and his comrades. One infantryman was killed. French airmen knew exactly the right places to trap the unwary or unlucky convoys. However, the activities of the French Air Force were nothing more than mosquito bites on the vast animal that was the Vietminh logistics machine. While devastating if used against targets in the open, in set-piece battle where flak was limited and there was no air opposition, the impact against logistical targets moving along hundreds of kilometres of jungle trails through mountains was much more limited. Not least of the problems was the weather, where clouds in the mountains and mist in the valleys simply prevented flying let alone target identification. Had the French Air Force been five times bigger than its 300 machines then it is unlikely to have made much difference, as the Americans were to discover when they brought their massive air fleets to Indochina yet failed to interdict the huge flows along the Ho Chi Minh trail in the 1960s.

Closing the doors

Upon hearing of the size of the paratrooper drop into Dien Bien Phu on 19 November 1953, Giáp immediately understood the significance:

> *...there were about 4,500 enemy soldiers comparable to Ná Sán. In the first phase the 316th Division should attack Lai Chau an operation which should finish in January. After twenty days rest they should attack Dien Bien Phu. In the second phase the attack on Dien Bien Phu should take about 45 days.*[25]

After being surprised by the French landings at Dien Bien Phu, the Vietminh quickly assessed the situation. When the French started to dig-in it was soon realised that there was another Ná Sán-type of opportunity for a major victory. Could they learn from previous errors and win this time? From the first it was decided to hem-in the FEC with enough troops to prevent them retreating and to restrict any possibility of an aerial rescue. It was immediately understood by Ho Chi Minh and Giáp that the French had to be locked up in the valley yet not so threatened that they would try to retreat before he was fully ready to block them. Giáp worried that the enemy might decide to retreat. 'Would the enemy stay at Dien Bien Phu or not? We wanted them to dig-in at Dien Bien Phu.'[26] The build-up for a major battle and the logistical effort to support an overwhelmingly large force had to be kept as secret as possible.

The initial plan envisaged an offensive against the French in mid-January. Having failed at Ná Sán to prevent the French retreat, Giáp was determined to thoroughly invest Dien Bien Phu to prevent any withdrawal. The main strategic aspect of his plan was completely Napoleonic in vision, i.e. to concentrate rapidly an overwhelming force to achieve strategic surprise and a decisive war-winning victory, even if that meant stripping every available man from northern Vietnam and mobilising the entire nation in the fight.

Operation Castor, opening gambits

Vietnamese accounts of the war are laudatory as to the magnificent feats of their intelligence service and the fact that Navarre's plan had been so completely rumbled. However, their historical hagiography wilts a little on acquaintance with the facts because, on their own admission, Navarre's decision to throw eight battalions of his finest troops (10,814 men) into the weakly held tribal village of Dien Bien Phu on 19 November was a complete shock to the Vietnamese leadership. Four more battalions were added in the course of the battle, 4,291 men and, in addition, there were about 2,400 PIM (Vietnamese prisoners-of-war who volunteered for auxiliary tasks).

The French immediately started to dig-in on the string of hills to the east of the Yam Noum River and build a series of strongpoints. Major Andre Sudrat, the chief engineer who had been one of those to advise against the Castor plan, was aghast at the logistical problem. He knew that one battalion alone needed 200 tons per day in supplies, but he could not supply a fraction of that. To deliver enough barbed wire and defence equipment alone would require five months' continual air operations at full capacity. For his estimated needs (36,000 tons), he was allocated just enough space for 3,000 tons. Meanwhile, Navarre's *Operation Atlante* would divert many precious transport resources. Deshaux, who was in command of the air arm, was also against the Dien Bien Phu build-up because he knew that his transport resources were inadequate to the task. By the time the battle started in earnest on 13 March, the French had only built-up reserves equivalent to eight days' needs.

Reacting quickly to the French move, Giáp sent in two divisions of 10,000 men each to hem-in and screen the French, whilst a third division joined up with the Pathet Lao and invaded Lao in the direction of the capital, Luang Prabang. Both sides probed and skirmished in the vicinity of Dien Bien Phu, with the French suffering over 1,000 casualties prior to March. Whenever the French moved out on deep patrols, they were attacked and bundled back into the bastion. The Vietminh's task was to hem them in tight enough to make it impossible to think of withdrawing, particularly on the south-western route through the village of Muoang Khua in Lao on the key crossing of the Nam Oum River. The FEC in Dien Bien Phu would not be the envisioned mobile force that would gad about, smashing up Vietminh rear areas and blocking attacks on Lao. In any case, Giáp's 308th Division, under orders to invade Lao, was about to show how ludicrous were the map-bound concepts of Navarre and the politicians in Paris, because the occupation of Dien Bien Phu would not hinder the French attack on Lao.

Some large-scale patrols did go out on 5, 13 and 20 December, but they found themselves constantly being ambushed and harried back into their base. The northwards patrol on the 13th had linked up with the remnants of the Lai Chau garrison while the probe on the 20th, which headed in a south-westerly direction, had linked up with the long-range French Mobile Group from Luang Prabang in Laos. The purpose of this latter probe was to prove or test-run a possible FEC evacuation in the direction of Lao. The troops met with a great propaganda fanfare, but it was meaningless. Having marched to the top of the hill they marched down again amidst a swarm of Vietminh, who snapped at their flanks and rearguard. When the French force eventually emerged into the valley of Dien Bien Phu from the jungle after their gruelling excursion, the first man was shot dead by a sniper. Giáp, of course, was well aware that the French were probably doing a dry run to establish an exit route in case of emergency. That he did not make a greater effort to destroy this column was probably to lull Navarre with the illusion that an Exit Plan B, a strategic withdrawal through Lao, was a realistic option.

By 1 January, Navarre knew two very important facts. Firstly, his force at Dien Bien Phu was shut-in and could not move out without a major battle in unfavourable terrain, and that evacuation by air or road back to the Red delta base area, unlike Ná Sán, was not a viable option, i.e. there was no Plan B unless it was an escape over brutal and unfavourable terrain under constant attack to Lao. Casualties would in such an eventuality be very high with the possibility of disaster. Secondly, in the second half of December, the military balance at Dien Bien Phu had become precarious. Writing to Secretary Jaquet on 1 January 1954, Navarre noted:

> *During the past few weeks serious intelligence informs us of the arrival of new resources* (37mm AA guns, perhaps heavy artillery) *and motorised equipment; and if these really exist and the enemy succeeds in getting them into action, then I can no longer guarantee success.*[27] (Author's emphasis.)

Such an analysis should have provoked much more serious concern than it did both in Paris and Saigon. The decision made in Paris to break promises about supply shipments on 13 November should have been reversed, but were not. Nor were the Americans asked for more help at an early stage, nor were serious contingency plans put in hand. With utter naïveté as to the political realities in France and internationally, Navarre was even boasting with unalloyed callousness to Ambassador Heath that the loss of ten battalions would not be 'mission critical'. Reported to Dulles, the question has to be asked why he did not immediately step up logistical and other support to the utmost. The most likely answer is complacency as well as the 'crying wolf' syndrome, of which the French Army had often seemed guilty as they sought ever more equipment and finance.

The Lai Chau debacle

A harbinger of doom was the fate of the French garrison of Lai Chau: about 2,500 men in a similar valley bottom beneath the towering 3,000m Mount Phan Xi Pâng, roughly 120km to the north of Dien Bien Phu (as the crow flies but possibly 200km in actual travelling distance), which takes eight hours on improved roads even today. It came under attack from a detached Vietminh division, the 316th. The division, which was based at Tuan Giao, would have to cross 80km of steep mountain passes and descents on old roads that were in a very poor state of repair following years of neglect during the Second World War and Japanese occupation. Pham Quang Vinh, the 98 Regiment's political commissar, noted a general mutiny. After 40km of terrible bumping on the unmetalled road:

> *...most of our soldiers were soldiers who had never ridden in a vehicle...In the bouncing lorries they were sick and hammered the sides of the trucks exclaiming 'let us out!' Everyone got down and continued to Lai Chau on foot.*[28]

Along the way there were several firefights with pro-French White T'ai forces officered by the French, one of whom was captured. This side campaign from the Dien Bien Phu struggle emphasised the fact that the Vietminh were operating in a region completely foreign to them.

In fact, the French and their T'ai allies had an advantage in knowing the area better. Company commander Vu The Chau admitted to leading men who were not the fittest for such terrain:

> *It was the first time that we had come to this country, whereas the enemy were composed of local T'ai who had a good knowledge of the region and who in addition possessed horses and mules to carry their loads.*[29]

Like Dien Bien Phu, Lai Chau had an airstrip set in a large plain beneath a towering mountain, the Phan Xi Păng massif (Fansipan). In the plain there are dozens of steep conical-shaped hills. So close to the Chinese border, and adjacent to new Vietminh supply lines from the north, it was impossible to think about defence. The Vietminh were bound to want to snuff out this irritant as a precursor to the Dien Bien Phu battle, which they duly did by sending in a division of regular troops. As it was a main base for France's T'ai troops and special forces operating along Vietminh supply lines, the taking of Lai Chau was a precursor to an increased effort to suppress this guerrilla activity. Hopelessly isolated, there were not enough planes available to extricate them all and several thousand troops were ordered to break out south on foot to the base at Dien Bien Phu. Besides, they were mainly colonial troops (Moroccans, Algerians and T'ai) rather than French regulars. However, the ancestral chief of the T'ai Federation and the White T'ai, Đèo Văn Long and his family were airlifted out from Lai Chau to Hanoi on 8 December,[30] as his troops scurried southwards braving a succession of Vietminh ambushes.

Apart from the obvious fact that they were surrounded by a far more numerous enemy, the major problem with the Lai Chau breakout plan was that the Vietminh knew exactly the direction in which they were going. Anyone familiar with the terrain must have known that the breakout was a suicide mission. They would have to trek down to Dien Bien Phu alongside La Piste Pavie. Following the track along the Nam Yam River was not an option because it could easily be cut and ambushed. Moreover, various river crossings on tributaries that ran into the main stream would be impassable because the bridges were down. These waterflows would have to be crossed further upstream. The track is long and winding, an appalling and arduous journey by road even today. But of course, because of the danger of ambush, it would have been madness to use the track itself, with surrounding jungle on each side and sharply undulating hills and deep ravines running off a massif of higher peaks at a distance of 5–10km from the river. Habitation along the river was very sparse as the hill tribes preferred to establish settlements higher up (and still do).

The breakout parties would have to follow mountain paths or hack through jungle under the guidance of indigenous scouts. Separating into small groups led by French officers, in a vicious jungle war of encounter-skirmishes, they were harried, ambushed and overwhelmed by large numbers of Vietminh regulars. In one skirmish at Muong Pon, 15km north of Dien Bien Phu, a unit of the 316th Division had tracked a T'ai-French troop using the trail left by donkey and human droppings, and blocked their path. An officer commanding a company, Vu The Chau (Company 674 Regiment 174), was wounded and forty percent of his 100-man command was killed or wounded. But the T'ai escaped.[31]

A French rescue attempt, led by Colonel Langlais, on 13 December, penetrating 18km north of Dien Bien Phu, was itself nearly wiped out as Vietminh regulars savaged them from all sides. The French failed in their mission, arriving too late to save one group of colonial soldiers holed-up in a village near Muong Pon. That 175 T'ai soldiers made it through to the encampment was a remarkable feat. Others dribbled in a month later, and many of the T'ai troops melted away to their villages.

For the Vietminh there was a deficit in tactical intelligence, notably in the availability of detailed maps. Only useless administrative maps were available. It was a most desperate need for Giáp and his staff as well as for the junior officers. They were fighting almost blind because the mountains of the northwest were as foreign to them as to the French, probably more so because there were many French-officered T'ai regular and irregular units operating in the region. Then luck stepped in. When de Castries' portly chief-of-staff ventured out on patrol to reconnoitre another potential bastion, he was ambushed and mown down by a Vietminh tommy gunner, who snatched his satchel of prized maps and documents. Then at Christmas 1953, a distinctive red parachute was recovered from beyond the wire. Inside was a zinc box full of accurate maps from aerial photography plus twenty-five detailed relief maps to 1:25,000 scale, with accurate contour elevations, wells and rivers. Due to Giáp's instructions on the importance of maps that had been filtered down to junior levels, the reconnaissance unit understood their vital importance and were overjoyed at their luck. Giáp was elated. The troops were well rewarded in due course, and the maps, which were extensively copied and distributed, would prove invaluable for ground troops and for the artillery who would accurately be able to gauge ranges and plot zones of bombardment.

The other main imponderable intelligence question was this: 'What were French intentions in positioning troops in such remote and tangled mountains?'[32]

US political opinion

In the US, fear of communism and the consequences of French defeat kept government and congress strongly committed despite doubts in some quarters as to France's staying power. Even J.F. Kennedy, speaking in January 1954, was concerned about the consequences of losing Indochina:

> *...undoubtedly within a short time Burma, Thailand, Malaysia and Indonesia and other new independent states might fall under the control of the communist bloc in a series of chain reactions.*[33]

Influential Mike Mansfield of Montana held similar opinions but strongly supported Navarre's plan. It was exactly the same as the dominoes analysis of Eisenhower, Dulles and Admiral Radford, the chief-of-staff, as well as that made by Truman's national security council in 1952.[34] For the moment there was little practical difference between democrats and republicans in congress, but no calls for direct intervention had yet been made. It was unclear how the politics of congress and the president's policy would develop if such pleas for help were made.

Berlin, February 1954

The timetable for Giáp's attacks at Dien Bien Phu was decided in Berlin in December 1954. Berlin was to be a four-power foreign ministers' conference. Indochina was on the agenda. It would pave the way for a full-scale conference in Geneva in May, which would aim at settlement of the Korean and Indochina questions. In a Western-centric world, neither China nor Taipei were to be represented. The USSR would speak for its proxy China, with whom communist foreign policy was co-ordinated. Ho was inevitably suspicious of the convening of such a multilateral conference where DRV interests would only be represented by third-level proxy. Given that the USSR regarded Indochina as a Chinese zone of influence, losing control to this degree was not Ho's ideal negotiation. Much better a one-on-one negotiation with France. Who knew what the Soviet Union might bargain away in their own interest?

American policy was still taking shape but with a major battle shaping up at Dien Bien Phu the direction was in favour of military intervention of some sort, notably air strikes using its ninety-strong B29 super fortress fleet at the Clark air base in the Philippines and its carrier force. Despite this there was significant opposition to Admiral Radford, Dulles and Eisenhower by the treasury secretary and General Ridgeway, head of the army, who had a longstanding opposition to further armed interventions after his miserable experience in Korea. With an admiral as chairman of the joint chief-of-staff, his army opposition was almost guaranteed in any case. For now, more B26 bombers and other supplies would be fed into the French military machine. Behind Ridgeway's negative stance was the thinking that was later admitted by General James Gavin, his chief of research and planning:

> *...the more we studied the situation the more we realised that we were, in fact, talking about going to war with China...the Chinese would very likely re-open the fighting in Korea.*[35]

Ridgeway and his team, having been part of the successful effort to defeat communist aggression in Korea, were running scared. The analysis was also palpably not based on fact because the Chinese had not shown any sign of moving over the border in scale since arriving there in 1950, nor being ready to do so.

Moreover, the air power intervention was quite different to a land-based intervention, which had been the trigger issue when UN forces approached the Chinese border in 1952. British foreign secretary Sir Anthony Eden noticed the turmoil, the fact that they had difficulty to 'find a realistic policy towards China'. He lamented that the US would not be able to sit down with China in a big four meeting. Accommodation of China and peace in Indochina as part of a global ratcheting down of global Cold War tensions would be Eden's primary concern over the next months.

Eden was a member of the British squirearchy. Self-aggrandising, smug, loftily acerbic, he had a breezy charm and a narcissistic regard for his good looks – the self-assured arrogance of the English elite that foreigners hate. He was lucky to survive the First World War, earning a Military Cross at the Somme in 1916. Dapper and elegantly clothed he could have been a male model or a Harrods shop-window mannequin. Beneath this glamorous exterior he was essentially a loner, a dull man wedded to clichés in which he excelled, and a 'skill' he consciously cultivated.

His languor hid a highly stressed psyche, with a tendency to garrulous pontification. His political enemy in the 1930s, Lord Halifax, and his mistress Baba Metcalf-Curzon had dubbed him 'drafty mouth'. Surprisingly for a squire from Durham, Eden was cultured and remarkably gifted in languages, being well-read in both Persian and Arabic. After three tenures as foreign minister, he was a seasoned diplomat but frustrated that this was Churchill's area of policy interest. He could hardly wait to take over from the ailing old man, the only survivor of the 'big three'. Ironically, given his pre-war alliance with Churchill in the conservative anti-appeasement camp, his policy for China rested on pragmatic acceptance of Chinese regional power, i.e. appeasement. 'Acceptance of the facts of the situation, the avoidance of provocations.' Apart from the global peace angle, something that chimed with the mood of the British public in the H-bomb world, to contain and recognise China and bring her in from the cold seemed the best way to save Hong Kong.

That France's Indochina tenure depended on the US was anathema to de Gaulle – better to lose it and focus on colonies closer to home. 'We have no real dirt interest in China…that is a reality. What is taking place there now is merely a prestige war.'[36] Now that only seven percent of the French public favoured continuing the war, even the MRP under Bidault was looking for a negotiated settlement. Premier Laniel favoured Chinese participation in any international conference. They were desperate at least to show willing to negotiate. Eden noted: 'He [Bidault] feels that the bottom will fall out of the French home situation unless he does something here to indicate desire to end the Indochina War.'

The Soviets, still guided in foreign policy by that most dour and cynical technocrat Molotov, author of the infamous Molotov-Ribbentrop pact in 1938, understood the tensions between the allies and pushed for China's inclusion. Russian policy at this juncture in international politics was to dampen tension. New leaders in Moscow included Malenkov, Molotov and Khrushchev, although the latter was progressively undermining his Troika rivals. Since the trial and execution of vice premier and NKVD chief Lavrenti Beria in December 1953, the Soviet leadership were intent on sorting out the legacy of Stalin and fighting their internal battles.

Eden would have expected Dulles' emphatic refusal. However, he divined that Dulles might accept China if Korea was on the agenda. Eventually Korea would come on to the agenda. By 18 January, Eden had managed to bring all the parties together on a consensus agenda, place and timetable.

'With continued US economic and material assistance the Franco-Vietnamese forces are not in danger of being militarily defeated by the Vietminh.' This national security council document NSC-177 was approved and signed by Eisenhower on 16 January 1954. The tone is complacent and, in light of events to take shape within weeks, plainly wrong. There were two points of misunderstanding and failed intelligence. Firstly, defeat could come quickly due to the failure of political will in France given faltering popularity for the war amongst the French public. French commitment to the war was hanging by a thread. By the end of the Berlin Conference on 18 February 1954, Dulles understood the precariousness of the French position. But would Eisenhower move decisively to shore up the situation? If he did not, Indochina would be lost. At Berlin the permanent security council members convened, excluding irrelevant Formosa. Attendees included Dulles, Bidault, Eden and Molotov. China was excluded. It was agreed that talks at Geneva would cover the Korean situation and Indochina: 8 May 1954. The meeting itself was a sign of thaw in the Cold War, but the exceptional event was the gift of Austria to the west and the removal of Soviet troops. Stalin would never have agreed to this concession. However, nothing was given away in respect of free and fair elections in East Germany. Wearing a double-breasted overcoat with fur collar, Eden looked a picture of smug contentment as he left Dulles' residence in Berlin.

A significant localised defeat would not change the military balance much in Indochina, but it would change the outcome because France would certainly walk away from the conflict. Ho and Giáp clearly understood this, but the Americans did not. With their pure and sharply honed instincts for power,

Ho and Giáp would pour the fervour and resources of a nation into one single purpose: the defeat and destruction of the French Army at Dien Bien Phu before 8 May.

On 18 February, captured sketches found on a Vietminh prisoner showed plans for hidden hillside artillery emplacements. At the conference to discuss these artillery emplacements, Colonel Piroth at Dien Bien Phu was warned that counter-battery-fire on which he was relying would be difficult.

On a visit on 19 February, the French defence minister Pleven, accompanied by chief-of-staff General Ely and secretary for war de Chevigne, inspected a supremely confident army at Dien Bien Phu ready to smash any Vietminh attack as they had at Ná Sán. However, air force chief General Fay encouraged Navarre to evacuate the position. On 11 March, de Chevigne told the Committee of National Defence: 'The military situation is fragile…the eventual success of Navarre's plan will weaken the enemy but will not enable France to impose peace.'[37]

In private de Chavigne was even clearer, noting that though the camp was well situated to protect Lao, it suffered from irremediable handicaps in topography and logistics and had been invested in the winter by the Vietminh, who had demonstrated remarkable organisational strength. The camp was a sort of pot de chambre around which the Vietminh occupied the high ground and it would quickly become untenable.

He was not the only one of the visitors to be horrified by the sight of the high enemy-controlled mountains overlooking the narrow valley. It was a common fear and observation raised by many military visitors, as well as by journalists, cameramen and politicians who were paraded through the encampment. However, Navarre gushed optimism, something the Americans and the media always relished. 'A year ago none of us could see victory. There wasn't a prayer. Now we see it clearly – like light at the end of the tunnel.'[38] A cliché that Eden would have been proud of. Why did de Chavigne not tell the truth to the Committee of National Defence? He was an MRP politician. If he had told the truth it would have been leaked to the press, to the embarrassment of his party and with great detriment to his political career.

The Berlin Conference had set the timetable for battle and for the prizes to be won in Geneva, prizes so great that soon both sides would be fighting to the death in a ghastly battle of attrition. However, unbeknown to the participants, the Berlin Conference set off a chain of backdoor negotiations that probably made the outcome of the battle irrelevant. Churchill's instincts were entirely correct. The Soviets wanted peace.

By early March, the Soviets had squared off the Chinese, who also wanted a return to peace and stability after the shock, the huge losses and near disaster caused by American intervention in Korea (Chinese losses in Korea have been estimated at 600,000 by Chinese Army expert John Gittings). On 6 March, the PRC's Foreign Ministry position paper posited the following:

> *Even though the United States will try everything possible to sabotage reaching all kinds of agreements favourable to the cause of peace, we should still go all out at the Geneva Conference to strive for some agreements…Regarding Indochina…we must try our best to make sure that the Geneva Conference will not end without any result;* [we] *should create a situation characterised by 'negotiating while fighting,' thus increasing the difficulties inside France and the contradictions between France and America.*[39]

The great fear of the communist block and of Churchill and Eden was that America was in an aggressive foreign policy mode, readying itself to sabotage the move to *détente*, a move that should be crowned at the proposed Geneva Conference. Instead of peace Eisenhower and Dulles wanted to roll back the communist tide and promote the Navarre plan aimed at total victory in Indochina. Nor had the US given up the idea of beating the Chinese in Korea, despite the armistice.

However, in understanding early on what was at stake at Dien Bien Phu, the focused Vietminh held a decisive advantage over American complacency. The Americans may have wanted an aggressive foreign policy but their missteps made sure that their objectives were not matched by their actions.

The great convergence

Soon, Vietnamese units from all around the northern delta and central Vietnam began converging on Dien Bien Phu, despite numerous attacks from French bombers and fighter bombers at embarkation points on the Red River. In mid-December, the 308th arrived at Son La.[40] They trekked on foot with each man carrying according to his size and strength between 30–40kg plus a 12kg bag of rice and a short digging implement. Pham Van Nham, platoon leader in the 312th Division, also carried his mandolin. Marches took place at night until 1 or 2 a.m. It was a hard routine, especially for some educated city boys such as Le Hai, who was a self-confessed:

> *petit bourgeois* [who] *had no familiarity with manual work. This annoyed his comrades who had to pick up his slack in manual tasks but in exchange he found a way to compensate them by relating stories, such as plots from films, westerns or from* Les Misérables *by Victor Hugo.*[41]

Meals consisted mainly of rice and dried fish but were regularly substituted with haricot soup seasoned with salt and a bit of bacon.

The Vietminh operated to a tough timetable, but not surprisingly in the appalling terrain it was falling behind. Giáp immediately calculated that the campaign would require 4,200 men just for carrying the rice for the approximately 70,000 soldiers who would need about a kilo of rice per day each. In addition, he would need 100 tons of vegetables, 100 tons of meat or dried fish, 8,000kg (eighty quintals) of salt, and 12 tons of sugar, all of which would have to be carried 500km.[42] These requirements did not include those for the civilian workers, porters, etc. in the supply and road gangs, whose numbers would dwarf those of the army. This might be offset by some attempts to source locally, but given the terrain, lack of habitation and the few valleys, the largest one of which would in any case be a battle zone, local production was very limited. Local families of T'ai indigenous people cultivated for subsistence, not as a cash crop and, although efforts were made to develop more local fields and increase production, this would hardly dent overall needs.

Giáp had at his disposal about a million civilian auxiliaries and, in all, about 300,000 for the specific Dien Bien Phu campaign. Human porterage was necessary to overcome the deficiencies in transport and passable roads. The sheer numbers may seem huge but the porters themselves consumed as they went, so much in fact that they sometimes consumed ninety percent of what they carried. Load factors were therefore carefully calculated by Giáp's general staff: one man = 55lb of rice/or 40lb of munitions and 15½ miles per day on flat terrain or 12.4 miles at night. In rough or mountainous terrain, the figures were 38/22 – rice/munitions – and 9 miles or 7½ at night. Buffalo carts carried 770lb. and could travel 7½ miles, horse carts 473lb and 12.4 miles. Bicycle porters could carry about 150kg.

Roads that had fallen into serious disrepair would have to be hurriedly upgraded, notably the 80km connection between Tuan Giao and Dien Bien Phu, which came to be known as Route 41:

> *The Tuan Giao Dien Bien Phu road had long been abandoned. It was only passable by foot...each company was allocated 2–3km and charged with improving and enlarging the road in about 2–3 days.*

The road had to be widened to 3m then later to 3.5m. Road workers constructed 9–10m passing points for lorries and extra-wide cannon pulling vehicles.[43] Work began in early December.[44] Sixty kilometres of road was finished in short order.[45] This work as well as the transport by bicycle and other means of carriage required the mobilisation of tens of thousands of civilian draftees. They would also have to be fed in more or less the same ratio and Giáp calculated that up to 300,000 persons, soldiers and civilians were required for the effort, excluding the farmers, who would need to supply the rice from the fringes of the Red River delta, i.e. those areas not under French control. Smuggled rice from within the Red delta was also an important source of supply. It was a logistics effort that would consume the attentions and economic energy of the entire North Vietnamese liberated populace, not to mention their Chinese allies. Only a militarised society could have delivered the victory at Dien Bien Phu. What the populace did not know was that it would carry on being militarised for another fifty years.

Other Vietminh testimony notes the comic attempt to hide the fact of artillery movement towards Dien Bien Phu, with the introduction from on high of transparently infantile open radio communication code. Dan Quan Thuy, major-general in the operations department, remembered:

> *The artillery convoy was called the convoy of comrade Bich who was passing with a party of 'schoolchildren'. Every morning as the convoy of artillery progressed the high command would ask over the radio 'how many students have passed by?'...We did not know who invented such a ridiculous code.*[46]

Giáp's crisis, delay and reversal of strategy, January 1954

When Giáp arrived at the battle front in mid-January, it was to review the preparation for battle and sign-off on the offensive that was due to launch on 26 January. In a confident mood, he had received news a few days before of Navarre's launching of Operation Atalante on coastal regions around Hue. Such dispersal of resources would strain France's logistical and manpower resources. Of the situation at the front, Giáp noted:

> *Our soldiers had done a miraculous job...The road to Tuan Giao and Dien Bien Phu was eighty-two kilometres long. Before, it had been a one-metre-wide path, but now our engineers and volunteers* [more likely conscripted labour] *had opened a road so we could drive artillery to within fifteen kilometres of Dien Bien Phu. Then we would have to haul by hand the last 15km.*[47]

They had to drag guns over peaks of more than 1,000m. Two whole engineering divisions of about 15,000 men plus up to tens of thousands of civilians were assigned to the task, trying to cope with slopes of 30–60 degrees. Film footage from Russian cameramen shows soldiers pulling in unison on command of an officer. They chanted as they pulled.

The idea of a 'fast strike, fast victory', which was the slogan of the campaign being pushed by the senior Chinese adviser, was becoming a worry in the face of the rapidly strengthening enemy defences, increasing manpower and firepower. Of particular worry was the fact that there were only 2,000 105mm artillery rounds in position. Hardly enough for a day of heavy shelling, let alone an extended campaign against multiple French bastions. Giáp had already noted that 'the entrenched camps were rigid and passive…the component sectors were separate…we could limit the enemy's ability to counter-attack.'[48] Under enormous pressure, which induced appalling migraines, Giáp suddenly realised that a premature attack in waves *en masse* would likely be defeated as it had been at Ná Sán. Logistical preparation was not yet enough to sustain a prolonged attack if the mass assaults on multiple strongpoints failed, which Giáp deemed likely. With the Geneva Peace Conference approaching in May, Ho's strict instruction was to be absolutely sure of victory before ordering an attack. He was also conscious that the Vietminh infantry were still short of training for open-field attacks without jungle cover against powerful fixed defence systems.

In response to this new information and intelligence analysis Giáp, having secured the support of the battlefield Chinese adviser Wei Guoquing, decided on a significant postponement from the scheduled 26 January date. Attacking *en masse* in this way was simply playing into French hands, as he would have learnt from a French officer captured in late January near to Beatrice (Him Lam). Under questioning, the officer confidently told his interrogator, Bui Xuan Linh of the 316th:

> *You cannot succeed. We can lay down such a curtain of fire that Vietminh assaults will be blocked, without counting three battalions of artillery, two based in the central redoubt and another at Isabelle* [bastion to the south].[49]

Giáp also had intelligence through a radio intercept that the French had divined the exact date of the offensive from a captured Vietminh soldier. This fact was so important according to Le Trng Nghia, the 312th's director of signals, that against all normal protocols Giáp 'visited the signals bunker and insisted on speaking directly to the signals technician who had intercepted the enemy transmission.'[50] Giáp even chased down the likely source of the leak, discovering that there was indeed one missing soldier from the 312th Division. On getting confirmation Giáp remarked briskly, 'that's sufficient.' Rigorous attention to detail was his hallmark. These typical incisive actions show Giáp at his best, cutting through wishful thinking to go to the heart of the matter with objective honesty, even if his memoirs are less than objective and suffer from egotism. In battle he did not let preconceived notions, inertia or ideology infect military decision-making.

In a supercharged atmosphere, there followed a bitterly contested meeting of the battlefield war council. A final nail was hammered down in favour of postponement when Dang Kim Giang, in arguing for a going ahead, chose the wrong argument by saying: 'Heaven! Just for a battle of three nights and two days there is not sufficient rice.' Insufficient rice was the main reason for the retreat from Ná Sán.

He thought it was an argument in favour of an immediate offensive. but Giáp exploited the slip. 'Exactly,' he countered. 'Rice is the commander.'[51]

Another leader at the meeting was Le Liem, the head of ideology (and Agitprop) who was naturally concerned about morale: 'More than 50,000 men are ready to attack, so if we order a retreat now just before the offensive start date, it would be as if the sky had fallen on their heads.'[52]

With rice running out a decision had to be taken immediately. Giáp summed it all up: 'The situation is urgent. Under the plan we are due to open fire this afternoon. Attack or not we have to decide now.'[53] Giáp then made his decision, covering it by quoting Ho Chi Minh's words of warning.

Giáp realised that there were simply not enough stocks of munitions or food to sustain a long attack. If the short, sharp attack failed, then he would have to fall back in defeat simply for logistical reasons, as they had done at Ná Sán. Against well dug-in defenders, Giáp realised that a quick victory was unlikely. It was too risky.

It was a tough decision to take. As head of logistics, Dang Kim Giang had a vested emotional interest in the action. He was loath to pull back now, especially because a long postponement would require the artillery and front-line troops to be pulled back from their forward positions. 'No one can be one hundred percent sure of victory,' Dang argued.[54] Others pointed out that if they delayed further, the French defences would become even stronger, that more troops could be landed. Another argument was simply the geo-political time factor, because the Anglo-Soviet-sponsored Geneva Conference on Indochina was due to start in May. If they delayed, they might run out of time. A ceasefire might be agreed amongst the superpowers behind Ho's back. It was the toughest of calls, because the momentum and impatience for action was intense. Facing criticism for delay from his enemies, Giáp would also have feared for his political future in case of a failed attack. In his brilliant calculation of the odds and the courage to stand up to the consensus, Giáp was at the apogee of his powers as if his whole life had led to this one decision. The decision was made and the troops immediately started to pull back to their logistical bases some 20km behind the front in the Mong Ang valley, or all the way back to Tau Giao.

Despite the loss of face, Giáp was aware of Ho Chi Minh's warnings and the need for absolute certainty in victory. 'There's no choice but victory. We must not lose. If we lose, we'll have no resources left.'[55] Despite the troops being at their jump-off positions, he decided to pull back, regroup and retrain, to give time for the logistical effort, notably to bring up more artillery shells. His army needed time to adapt to the new plan for a long attritional campaign, which he felt sure would bring victory with much less risk. As was to be expected the decision to postpone was a shock and disappointment for the Vietminh troops:

> *...the order to withdraw the artillery fell on us like a blow from a heavy weight. The soldiers were depressed and angry...many of them demanded to know why.*[56]

Another anecdote revealed by Hoang Ming Phuong, Giáp's Chinese interpreter, described the reaction to the 26 January retreat order:

> *...the order was given to pull back and this was reported to the divisions waiting in the valley, quite a number of the combatants did not understand its real intention. Some of them protested 'why decamp? we should be wary of Vietnamese traitors! Who is the fellow who ordered the retreat?' they did not know that it was their commanding general.*

Not the least of the reasons for anger was the necessity of pulling back from forward positions and dragging back the heavy artillery having expended so much hurried dangerous and backbreaking effort in getting it into position.

Giáp records:

> *...to respect exactly the principle of attack followed by certain victory, it was necessary to modify our plans; instead of 'attack for rapid victory', 'steady attack, steady advance...' our troops had to go back to their bases to regroup and pull back their artillery. Political work should monitor rigorously the order to retreat, to communicate the new order of battle. The logistics must make preparations to follow new directives.*[57]

Giáp always understood the political element alongside the military one and, while active communication and propaganda could not entirely assuage the disappointment, it does not seem to have unduly diminished the Vietminh's appetite for battle.

It took nine days and nights to pull back the AA artillery to a point at the 62km mark on Route 41 in the Muong Ang valley. This was the point at which our gunner Pham met his frustrated comrades following Giáp's decision to postpone the attack at Dien Bien Phu. An AA artillerist, Nguyễn Quang Thuan, in the same 351st Heavy Division, described how he had helped save an artillery piece when it slipped its mooring on a slope. He was wounded and an older comrade was killed:

> *Two soldiers were ejected into the void. The piece continued to slide and pushed me violently, as we arrived at a cliff, I braced with all my strength to stop the piece from flying away. Everyone thought I was dead. Such an AA gun weighs 2.4 tons.*[58]

He had some help. Up to 100 men were required to manhandle each gun down the difficult slopes.

The significance of Giáp's momentous decision was well understood at the time. Memoirs of the event see it as a turning point in the story of Dien Bien Phu and, indeed, in the history of the Vietnamese people. Trong Lan, sergeant-major of anti-aircraft artillery of the 351st, recounted: 'The more I think about this period, the more that I find this decision to change tactics to be clairvoyant. If we had attacked on 26 January we would have been totally defeated.' Pham Sinh, political commissar in the 98th Regiment of 316th Division, reflected:

> *...thanks to the* volte face *we won the battle, and we were later able to take on the Americans, the Khmers and the expansionist Chinese*[59] *and finally spend our last years with our families.*

Fine on reflection, but Giáp must have known that his decision was risky politically. However, he was able to take it because he enjoyed the absolute confidence of his commander-in-chief, Ho Chi Minh.

No doubt covering his back and showing necessary obeisance to the great leader Mao Tse Tung, Wei sent a request on the 24th asking for advice from the Chinese Politburo. But by the time the reply came on the 27th, the decision had already been taken. Perhaps Giáp took the decision ahead of any possible rebuff from the Chinese leadership.

Under the new battle plan, French bastions would be snapped off piece by piece, strongpoint by strongpoint, bunker by bunker, trench by trench, as artillery and troops focused on one target at time. Giáp had already noted that 'the entrenched camps were rigid and passive...the component sectors were separate...we could limit the enemy's ability to counter-attack.'[60] Vietminh units would train for incremental siege tactics, the lessons of Ná Sán and even French trench systems there would be studied. It would be a slow strangulation by attrition in a style of warfare not seen on a large scale since 1914–18.[61] Giáp applied a new slogan for a new strategy, 'Steady attack, steady advance.'[62]

The 308th's Laos excursion, January–February 1954

Having delayed the offensive against Dien Bien Phu on 26 January, Giáp sent the 308th Division on a lunge towards Luang Prabang.[63] Once again it was a diversionary tactic aimed at confusing the enemy and putting them off guard and dispersing their resources. He hardly needed to have worried on that score because Navarre, poring over his grand maps of campaign, went ahead anyway with his Atlante attacks in the Central Highlands, which frittered away the strength of some of his elite forces who, together with France's local Vietnamese units, were roughly handled and failed to win back territory that was meant to be used as a bargaining chip at the conference. In his memoirs, Giáp noted:

> *...the offensive against upper Laos proceeded simultaneously with the liberation of Kontum* [a town in the Central Highlands] *followed by attacks to liberate Tha Ket and the Boliven Highlands* [in southern Lao]. *And the concentration by Navarre of French troops in the end unbalanced the enemy's mobile forces.*[64]

Even as the Berlin Conference was coming to an end, Vietminh troops were beginning their raid in force on Lao, with the 308th Division leading the way.

The second invasion of Lao was all part of a choreographed exercise in indirect warfare. The aim was to befuddle and confuse the French high command rather than hold territory. Simultaneous with the postponement of the offensive, Giáp ordered the 308th Division, supported by two regiments of the 316th and the 148th (both recruited from highland populations), to advance down the line of the Nou Oum River to make a show of capturing the Laotian capital of Luang Prabang. The Nou Oum River runs from north to south, and from Muong Kua to the point at which it reaches the route to Luang Prabang is 200km. In seizing this river line and the few garrisons dotted along it, for example at Muong Ngoi, Giáp was denying bases for any future relief column for Dien Bien Phu.

On 13 January 1954, when Graham Greene was visiting, he recorded:

> *Where Vientiane has two streets Luang Prabang has one, some shops, a tiny modest royal palace (the king is as poor as the state) and opposite the palace a steep hill crowned by a pagoda which contains so it is believed the giant footsteps of the Buddha. Little streets run down to the Mekong. There is the sense of trees, temples, small quiet houses, river and peace. One can see the whole town in half an hour's walk and one could live here one feels for weeks, working, walking, sleeping,* if the Vietminh were not on their way down from the mountains. (Author's emphasis)

He did not know it but this was an opening move in the Dien Bien Phu campaign. Surprisingly, Lao, a landlocked, impoverished and remote country with a tiny population, was becoming an important focus of attention in the latter stages of the war. The 308th stopped in the environs of Luang Prabang, where they halted on 24 February.

Other elements of the invasion, like the spreading fingers of Ho's hand, reached down to the Mekong at Thakhaek with its large Vietnamese population, and to the French base at Xeno near Savannakhet. France's air base at Muong Sai was also threatened. Attacks spread over hundreds of kilometres were to divert not hold territory. Further south, another probe took Attapatu and the Boliven Highlands.

Like a good chess player, Giáp was planning and contemplating many moves ahead to the point when the French might choose to scuttle from the field, as they had done at Hoa Binh and Ná Sán. Knowing that Navarre must have prepared an escape plan, Giáp wanted to counter it in advance by removing some of the covering outposts in the Lao borderlands.

Navarre had indeed prepared a plan. It was named 'Xenophon' after the famous retreat to Greece from Asia minor. But a realistic Plan B was never achieved. Giáp intended to wrap the French force at Dien Bien Phu in a tangled web as a spider would its victim, before moving in for the kill.

The troops

The Vietminh possessed a seasoned professional army of trained troops who were highly ideologically motivated. At Dien Bien Phu, Giáp deployed 49,500, plus 31,500 support troops. An additional 23,000 support troops and personnel were strung out along logistical lines. Behind them was another 300,000 mobilised peasant auxiliaries. Eventually, sixty percent of the VPA would be thrown into the battle. Morale was high. Memoirs of the period are full of patriotic puff and propaganda. 'We worked night and day,' remembered Tran Thinh Tan, an official in the victualling department. 'Joyously singing popular airs with modified words, we have just one sentiment; not to return home until Dien Bien Phu is no longer occupied by the aggressors.'

Despite such revolutionary 'proletarian realist' exaggeration, morale and patriotic spirit was high. Hatred for the French was common and encouraged by propaganda. Only troops with exceptional morale could take the punishment sustained in the capturing of France's fortified bastions in Dien Bien Phu valley. We should also remember that these Chinese-trained divisions were the hand-chosen elite and it must be doubted that such *élan* extended in the same proportion to the great mass of conscripts and the huge army of civilians subject to Corvée and military discipline.

Vietminh cadres contained many educated officers, including skilled engineers. French education was to be turned back on the colonists with a vengeance. Despite class war structures, the Vietminh were not slow to exploit the intellectual capacity in their ranks – something that would be quite at variance with Pol Pot's Cambodia where the communists killed anyone with education or professional skills. An example of applied intelligence was the Din Hoa group of twenty-four officers, set up to study strategies of attack and the methods of the enemy to learn from successes and failures including the setbacks of 1952 against General de Lattre. The defences of Ná Sán were revisited for the purpose of study and to develop infantry tactics to deal with them.[65]

Lessons drawn from these strategy sessions were widely disseminated in the form of manuals or direct training down to the lowest levels. One example of insightful tactical training was to instruct ordinary soldiers on target prioritisation. Firstly kill the machine-gunners, then officers, then radio operators, i.e. take out firepower, leadership and communications, in that order. High losses in French officers that caused senior commanders great anxiety proved that the lessons were learnt and applied.

The French Union employed a third of its infantry forces in Indochina keeping roads and waterways open to traffic. Both sides had about ninety battalions in Tonkin, but the French assigned sixty-four of theirs to protecting lines of communication and rear areas, leaving only twenty-five battalions for mobile offensive operations (approximately twenty-five percent).[66] If we included associated states forces and look at Indochina as a whole, probably no more than seven to ten percent of total French forces were a truly mobile reserve.

General Navarre commanded a polyglot colonial army, of whom only about twenty percent were French. There were three good Algerian Tirailleurs and a Moroccan unit at Dien Bien Phu, but they had been overused and were exhausted. They were also short of the leavening of French officers and NCOs that turned these units into very effective formations. Seasoned veterans from the Second World War were declining and replaced by lesser, greener recruits. Even the legionnaires were not immune. There were some divided loyalties amongst the German troops reflecting the partition of the country. Subjected to constant Vietminh propaganda, a not inconsiderable number defected for both political and personal reasons. Elite legionnaire paratrooper units added to the ethnic mix. Weaker units included some indigenous units, such as a company of Catholics from Phat Diem and a battalion of French-officered T'ai tribesmen. By the beginning of the battle, there were 13,200 soldiers, of which 7,000 could be counted as front-line. Overall, there was a battlefield advantage for the Vietminh in a ratio of 4:1. If we look at the odds in terms of front-line troops, it was about 7:1. By the end of the battle, due to killed in action (KIA), wounded and internal desertions, this ratio had probably changed to about 20:1, despite reinforcements, assuming a steady 50,000 for front-line VPA units who replaced the fallen with reserves.

In all, 32,000 (out of 38,000 total deserters in the entire nine-year war) deserted from the French Army during the last six months of the war, a sharp increase on 1953 when there were just 2,187 desertions, less than one percent of the FEC total, about half of whom were indigenous Vietnamese or tribal recruits.[67] Though anti-colonial propaganda is thought to have influenced many in their future fight against the French in Algeria, it seems that most deserters did not do so for ideological reasons but just to get out of the war.

Legionnaires and the Camerone

Ex-legionnaire Christian Jennings noted that the barracks' wall at Sidi Bel Abbès in Algeria was painted with the words:

> *Legionnaires, you are soldiers in order to die, and I am sending you where you can die* [because] *anything he had done in his past life was immaterial. He only became whole on becoming a legionnaire.*

Recruits were inculcated with the special traditions of the legion based on the story of fighting to the end, the Battle of the Camerone on 30 April 1863, where one-armed Captain Danjou and his company fought to the death. Celebrated every year with considerable alcoholic festivity, it toasted the fight to the death of sixty-five legionnaires in Mexico who had sworn to fight to the death on the wooden hand of their Captain Danjou. The hand is still the most precious relic of the legion and is paraded once a year.

On a plaque at the end of the barracks' corridor is written, '*Lui qui est devenu fils de France, non par le sang reçu, mais par la sang versé* – you have become a son of France not by blood received, but by blood given.'

Foreign Legion units, including paratroopers were mainly foreign with perhaps thirty to eighty percent being German with a good leavening of east Europeans. Many were ex-SS and Wehrmacht soldiers. Variances in the calculation of percentages of Germans was probably due to the fact that legion units also contained as many as half who were white beret Vietnamese. As Vietnamese they did not have the white kepi privilege. Legionnaire numbers did not exceed 20,000–30,000 at any one time but, as elite troops, they were prominent in fighting rather than in guard duty, so casualties were heavy. Legionnaire Adrian Liddell-Hart noted that in his barracks, 'out of twenty men thirteen were German or Austrian,' a typical ratio that would be diluted by indigenous recruits in Indochina. After roasting pigs and chickens looted while on patrol, they would: 'Sit around the dying embers of the log fire. The Europeans sang *Deutschland uber alles* or sad melodies from distant lands.'[68]

Liddell-Hart signed-on at Fort St Nicholas in Marseilles. He was not required to use his real name. From the depot they were sent in an overcrowded cattle ship to the legion's base and training camp in Algeria. On arriving in Saigon, Liddell-Hart was attached to the Foreign Legion cavalry battalion, where he became a machine-gunner in small amphibious tracked vehicles nicknamed 'crabs'.

One German legionnaire defected to avoid the predatory attentions of his homosexual commanding officer. Willy Decker says of the matter: 'I was a good-looking guy at this time and our commanding officer was a total queer; as it was not my kind of thing...I shot him.' It was not a fatal shot but he felt it politic to get out of harm's way so he defected to the DRV. It was usually a way to desert and obtain repatriation rather than a political statement as such. The Vietminh used deserters for propaganda and training or for special military functions, for example on one occasion dismantling machine-gun nests from the turret of a captured armoured train. German legionaries were sent home via Moscow. Lauded on the one hand for propaganda reasons they would also be politically suspect on the other.

Defections were a minor part of the legion story. Foreign Legion combat record in Indochina is outstanding for bravery and fighting to the last in the tradition of the Camerone. Legionnaires still hark back to the battle honours gained in Indochina at Phu Tong Hoa on 25 July 1948, at Dong Khé on 16–18 September 1950, and on the RC4 in October 1950. The legion would perform great feats of resistance in 1951 at Hoa Binh and at the Battle of Xom Pheo on the RC6. Dien Bien Phu 1954 was to be the epic finale to their service in Indochina. Legionnaires singing their battle song as they stormed Éliane 1 is an epic moment in the legion story amongst many. During the First Indochina War, legion losses were high. For example, 13th DBLE (Double Brigade) lost eighty officers (including two of its commanders), 307 NCOs and 2,334 legionnaires, which meant that it turned over its own size in dead legionnaires.[69]

However, there was also the record of unbridled brutality, which is amply described in memoirs and remembered in the memories of the victims.

The roads, logistics and air power

To avoid French aircraft attack, the Vietminh built five new roads from Tau Giao, totalling 100km of new road and 200km of upgraded track. The existing track was blocked by French air attack, but the new road wound over mountains of up to 2,000m and through jungle. At the highest mountain passes, 75,000 lowland civilians unaccustomed to these temperatures toiled in the freezing winter cold to construct the vital supply highway. Often hidden by jungle canopy and camouflage, these tracks proved essential for the huge supply effort to provide food and ammunition for the 65,000 troops and artillery. Only massive civilian mobilisation and extraordinary political-technical mobilisation by well-educated cadres could achieve these feats of engineering and planning. The VPA was supported by 15,000 military engineering troops in specialist units. The scale of the organisational achievement can be measured not just by the movement of military hardware but by the 220,000 shells used in the campaign. Food supply required not just a kilogram for every soldier per day, but four times that amount because of porters and auxiliaries in the logistics train.

The Vietminh's secret weapon was mass mobilisation of the people whose enthusiasm was encouraged by propaganda, organised and channelled efficiently:

> *My sister Hau saw the peasants in her province become energised and filled with ardour. Thousands of labourers left to carry rice and other supplies to Dien Bien Phu, filling roads at night. Young able-bodied men in my brother in law's station left to join these labourers who trekked on foot across 400km to reach the front. The trip would take a month.*[70]

Hau was a romantic communist who no doubt saw things through rose-tinted spectacles. Nevertheless, there was genuine enthusiasm in many conscripts.

Camouflage was a vital method of keeping the communications intact but even more importantly keeping secret the extent of Vietminh logistical operations, for what was to be a major strategic level ambush. Pham Than Tam wrote: 'The preparation of the campaign was laborious, and no doubt the Vietminh mobilised more than courage to bring every piece of artillery, every rifle and every rice ball from the hinterland to the front.'[71]

By 7 March, Pham had reached the key junctions that saw the road branch in three, towards Dien Bien Phu 89km away, Lai Chau to the north, and Son La to the south. The junction was a mass of activity: soldiers, engineers, civilian porters and workers, youth volunteer brigades, gunners and their cannons. By 10 March, Pham was just 10km from the front, having marched more than 25km per day over three days. On this day as Pham approached the battlezone, he met up with his comrades from the 804th Company of the 45th Artillery Heavy Regiment. They recounted to him how they had been forced to withdraw from the battlefield in January just before the expected attack. Now the order was to go forward again. Each company had four guns in each of four batteries.[72] The company had just suffered the effects of Giáp's order to retreat and regroup at the end of January. Pham's colleagues were numb with exhaustion and now they were ordered to retrace their steps. Just as they did so the enemy planes spotted them, wrote Pham in his diary: 'Bombs fell 100m away.' Then they continued to toil all night without sleep.

French attack planes were the least of the problem for Pham and his gunner comrades. It was the exertion and danger in manhandling the guns that threatened life and limb. Not a few soldiers were hurtled into the void by careering heavy guns. 'Exhausted, rent by hunger, eyes dizzy with fatigue, the guns teams continued to haul their load,'[73] recounts Pham. 'One time the cannon slid forty meters toward the bottom of the hill. It took a superhuman effort to stop it.'

Happily, a political commissar was on hand to offer his trite and patronising homily: 'Cannons are so terribly precious that the party and the people trust you with them. Remember the number of times that you had to fight without them!'

'Despite everything,' recalled Pham, 'dead or alive we had definitely decided not to leave our cannon.'[74]

On a similar occasion they just avoided the cannon plunging into the fast-flowing river, 'palms of hands burnt on the ropes.'[75] Cine pictures of the campaign shot by propaganda units equipped with Russian cameras show straining winches, teams of men tugging on long ropes, and guns inching up precipitous slopes.

Artilleryman Tran Do remarks:

> *Dien Bien Phu was the first campaign where we used batteries of 105mm... getting them there was not an easy matter. Each piece weighed two tons. On the road they were pulled behind trucks but, in the mountains where there were only inclines, they could only be manhandled with brute human force.*[76]

Tran remembers:

> *...a road just wide enough to fit the wheels wound round the flank of the mountain. It was necessary to tackle three passes over a ten kilometre stretch. In the ascent we had to make sure that the cannons did not tip over into the precipice.*[77]

Rivers became a major conduit for Vietminh logistics. Feats of skill, engineering, and derring-do to effect this were recounted in a 1984 magazine:

> *The river was cut by rapids 105mm howitzers had to be transported over 90klm of this waterway. The only way to do it was on bamboo rafts...the guns had to be taken apart...our men had to train very hard, taking the howitzer apart, studying the pieces, reassembling them, testing the gun and doing it again.*

Each 105mm cannon weighed 2 tons and the accompanying lorries also weighed 2 tons. Progress was slow, at as little as 10–20km in a whole day, so that only at the end of April had all the guns arrived.[78] Using the Black River from the Lai Chau region, the Chinese developed another logistical avenue for victuals due south from Yunan, with 6,000 rafts carrying salt, rice and horses.[79]

As the trail reached the mountains and got nearer to Dien Bien Phu the attention from French spotter planes and fighters increased. Sometimes the great canopy of forest would give way to a clearing where it was impossible to stitch together an artificial canopy over the road. Here in the open they would be vulnerable and exposed. Pham describes one bombing attack:

> *...the ground shook violently but we did not let go our hold on the cannon*[80]*...the planes then descended very low and emptied their machine-guns on us...in our battery six comrades were wounded...four of them, To, Nhu, Dan and Phuc,*

> *grievously, some had their arms cut off, another with intestines torn open – fatal wounds.*[81]

Afterwards, a spotter aircraft appeared to track their progress. Pham's comrades continued to pull and strain up and down steep hills burnt out by napalm. 'Good work, keep it up,' exhorted the political commissar.[82] With lack of cover in the burnt-out landscape the planes had an easier target. Tran Do writes with some heroic and melodramatic prose probably in a style learnt from the high-flown Vietminh propaganda:

> *On those twelve kilometres of steep slopes, the arms that had hauled those tons of steel were now lowering them…The forest threatened us with its unhealthy humidity and its beasts with poisonous bites. We had only rice to eat, which was served to us either charred or almost raw.…A young carrier who was knocked to the ground by a bomb blast had the courage to recover her load of paddy immediately and to resume her journey.*

Eventually, they arrived having crossed 9km of creeks and ravines and pulled the guns by hand. Pham remembers that 'I was in a truck the last two miles. I didn't care how cramped we were.' They manhandled them into casements already constructed by comrades just 3km from the front. They stockpiled ammunition as it came up and constructed dug-outs. All of this was done under the noses of the French and in plain sight on the forward slopes, something that the French had calculated to be impossible without discovery and destruction by the French heavy artillery, including not just their 105s but the four 155mm.

When fetching wood from the forest, Pham and his comrades were caught in a French barrage and thrown to the ground. A number of Pham's comrades were killed. A few days later as they were constructing another dug-out, enemy fighters swooped down low and machine-gunned his position. Luckily no one was killed that time. That night Pham went on a reconnaissance mission to within 100m of the French positions to check on targets for the attack.

The Vietminh guns were positioned in impregnable casements fronting French-occupied Beatrice. Facing the mountains, the cannon would be fired direct over open sights at the French positions, so nullifying their lesser experience and technological/communications deficits. However, there were indirect fire possibilities as well, especially as the runways of the airport of the central defensive and artillery zone of the French encampment could be targeted with ease. So target-rich was the crowded French encampment that even misdirected salvoes could cause damage or score direct hits on vulnerable targets.

Air power, for both logistical mobility and for tactical and strategic offensive purposes, was a vital and asymmetric French advantage. However, Brigadier-General Dechaux of the French Air Force was against the Dien Bien Phu project because he was sceptical that he had the resources to supply the laager, and he would have been aware of the extreme weather problems in this part of Vietnam as well as the distance from his air bases. Vietminh commando raids on air fields at Haiphong and Hanoi on 5 March resulted in the destruction of seventy-eight aircraft in early March, but these could be readily replaced by the Americans from the vast stocks built up during the Korean War. However, the stock of planes was not substantially added to, despite pleas for more help, so the transport fleet in particular became increasingly inadequate and run-down in the course of the battle. However, the main problem was the shortage of air force mechanics and auxiliaries. For tactical offence, the French also deployed Hellcat dive-bombers and Corsair fighters from the carrier *Arromanches* in addition to their B26 bombers. Bearcat fighters, the stubby and tough planes that served the Americans well in the Second World War, were the mainstay of fighter bombers in the French Air Force. The main methods to counter the French aerial monopoly were camouflage, multiplicity of road routes, and repair teams *in situ*, to restore damaged bridges or blocked roads. The newly established AA capability would only be unveiled once battle commenced.

In total the French Air Force deployed 388 machines at its peak and 10,000 men, of whom 434 died in the course of the war. They were reinforced by the US Civil Air Transport (CAT) flying C119 Boxcars during the war and the Dien Bien Phu campaign. Sixty-two planes were shot down during the 10,000 sorties that were flown during the Battle of Dien Bien Phu. Hundreds of US technicians would be flown into the Haiphong base and US pilots in limited numbers would also take part, though only two died in the conflict. The 100 Dakotas were the mainstay of the transport fleet, although the sixteen US-piloted C-119 Boxcars were more effective in getting large amounts of cargo out of the plane quickly via their back door in a single pass. As the perimeter shrank, the ability to offload quickly on a drop run was a key benefit to prevent loss of cargo to the enemy or repeated runs under heavy AA fire.

The other main deterrent to French control of the air was the deployment of twenty-four 37mm anti-aircraft guns, twenty 20mm and a host of .50 calibre tripod-mounted machine-guns to throw a curtain of fire in the path of the French aeroplanes. France was only armed with American turbo prop fighters and ground attack aircraft, which were stable, effective and rugged gun platforms. They could come under dangerous crossfire if they flew low at targets between peaks and along mountain valleys. The flight of lumbering supply aircraft was absolutely predictable because to avoid the peaks they had to fly along the north-south axis of the valley, and their position over the target could not be varied. To drop their loads they had to fly straight into the mouth of the waiting guns.

However, the key focus of the AA guns was not defensive but offensive – to block resupply to the FEC. Giáp's revised strategy developed in mid-January, as part of his decision to delay the Vietminh offensive on 26 January aimed at winning a long battle of attrition in which overmatching French logistical, firepower and material advantages were a key factor. So, deployment of 37mm and .50 calibre machine-guns around the approaches to the airstrip had the aim of strangling French supply operations once the runway had been put out of action, by preventing accurate low-level supply parachuting.

Transport aircraft were forced to fly above 4,000 feet. However, at this height, accurate parachuting was impossible, and supply would be haphazard and at the mercy of variable winds. The ceiling range of the twenty-four 37mm AA guns was 14,000 feet. These AA weapons could fire 180 rounds per minute and were described by Janes as being 'a mobile weapon with highly respectable performance.' As a result, supplies from 82,000 parachutes were dropped into enemy hands or were not delivered at all because of cloud cover above 4,000 feet. Supply canisters fell into Vietminh hands, perhaps as much as sixty percent by the end of the siege, and many other canisters fell into the wire or no man's land and were irrecoverable except at great risk and human loss in retrieval. Slowly the FEC supply line was being strangled. By the end the French artillery was short of ammunition and spare parts. Machine-gun ammunition and supply of grenades, the vital weapons of trench warfare, ran short or ran out.

The result of weather, AA activity and the closure of the landing strip meant that supply barely reached 100 tons a day against a requested minimum need of 200 tons per day. Operating in good weather on three days from 20 to 23 November, the French air fleet was able to land 240 tons per day on average, with 248 flights. This rate of supply was exceptional and would reduce to a trickle in bad weather. Clearly, they would be stretched to maintain this rate, especially as other sectors in Vietnam also had needs and bad weather would often close off the airstrip. Requirements for servicing maintenance and repair to aircraft would cut operational capacity by a further fifty percent. By the end of the campaign, a combination of strangulation of the drop-zone, lack of plane capacity and bad weather would reduce supplies actually received by the FEC to less than one third of the minimum required rate of 100 tons per day. Lack of supplies meant reduction in defensive capability. Air supply to besieged forces was not a magic formula for success but a carefully calibrated gamble with a record of failures and successes in recent history. Successes include: Demyansk pocket (Russia) 1942, the Arakan boxes-Kohima-Meiktila (Burma) 1944–45, Ná Sán 1953 had to be balanced against failures such as Stalingrad 1943 and Arnhem (Holland) 1944.

Even before the monsoons, the weather is not good for aerial warfare in December, January and February, because fog covers the valley bottom and does not start to burn off till late morning. Then comes the rainy season. This affected both transport and offensive operations. It was rare for there to be good weather in both the take-off and the target zones simultaneously. The fighter bombers were also flying at the limits of their range so could not hang around over the battlefield for targets of opportunity, or standby for battle support. The air force reported that Dien Bien Phu 'has a serious deficiency from an aerial point of view; its distance from the delta country, where our aircraft are based.'[83] France's forty-eight B26 bombers managed to close vulnerable parts of the main track on occasions, by causing large landslides, but they were generally repaired within hours by armies of civilian workers. Again, the bombers were weather-hampered.

To counter air-raids on the supply route, the Vietminh built blockhouses on key high points defended by machine-guns. Pham records how having built such a hilltop defensive point, they beat off attacks by three aeroplanes, for which they were awarded a medal, third class.

Air power was Navarre's weapon to constrain Vietminh logistical efforts. It proved relatively ineffective but, in contrast, the Vietminh heavy artillery were able to crater the runway. Their high-powered AA guns were extremely effective in constraining French supplies, not by shooting down many planes but by keeping the transports at high altitude. This was the decisive matrix of the battle. Even by January, Navarre knew of the massive Vietminh logistics build-up because he started to intensively lobby both his government and the Americans for increased supplies and transport aircraft. But these requests became caught up in bureaucracy and politics. It was too late, and even during the battle the French government thought that there was special pleading, which should not be taken seriously. French forces could not be increased because they could not be supplied. And only paratroopers could be used for reinforcement. There was a limited number of elite paratroopers in Indochina, numbering no more than about 3,000.

French defences

Beatrice (Him Lam), the sentinel bastion on the north-east point, Gabrielle (Dôc Lâp), which dominated the road to Lai Chau, and the post at Anne-Marie (Ban Keo) were each occupied by a battalion. In the centre was located de Castries' command bunker. There were thirty fortified positions grouped in seven main bastions and 5km to the south at Isabelle (Hong Hum) there were twenty fortified positions. There were thirty-one strongpoints grouped in eight main bastions. The defensive base at Ná Sán had fifty.

As for the artillery, 155mm and 105mm cannon as well as 120mm mortars were grouped centrally in shallow and wide guns pits, which allowed for 360 degree firing north, south, east and west. Zeroed in on the killing zone approaches to all the strongpoints, the French had no doubt that if an attack came, they would finish off any Vietminh who survived the artillery and got through the triple barbed wire bands laced around Beatrice's bastion with machine-guns and mortars.

However, if the Vietminh were able to bring up heavy guns, the open and very wide French gun-pits would mean heavy casualties for gunners and guns, which could be picked off by Vietminh artillerymen in the hills. The French high command supported by O'Daniels considered that the 'fortress of Dien Bien Phu' was 'impregnable'. They were particularly proud of Beatrice, the sentinel fortress to the north-east, which was the main site of all the endless inspection tours made by French ministers and visiting dignitaries. Isolated and unsupported by crossfire from any nearby bastions, it was obvious that it would be the focus of Vietminh attacks. Beatrice would be defended by just one battalion of the Foreign Legion – about 450 men. They were about 2km from the nearest supporting units and perimeter defences.

The French considered that the logistics of moving cannon and enough munitions over steep mountains was impossible, and that they would in any case be destroyed by air power. The number of Vietminh troops needed to attack Dien Bien Phu would be huge and the French estimated that only two divisions at most could be supplied over such distances and terrain, giving only a 2:1 advantage, which would not be nearly enough. However, the Vietminh would have the high ground to the east. An old adage of Saint-Cyre opined that 'he who controls the heights takes the low ground', but without artillery this adage would not work. In the event, the Vietminh were able to haul 100 guns (105mm and 75mm) and the necessary men and supplies. And they were then able to exploit their occupation of the heights around Dien Bien Phu, notably hills such as 518, Mont Chauve and Mont Fictif, which faced the critical Beatrice and 5 Hills chain of defences. Behind these hills Giáp could martial his troops with reasonable impunity, except for occasional bomber attacks.

A typical bastion's defence consisted of two circular lines of zig-zag trenches in double rings around the top of a hill dotted with reinforced concrete machine-gun pill-boxes, with connecting trenches and a trench-line bisecting the defence system. Command, control bunkers and the last defences were at the top of the hill. Around the trench rings were thick lines of barbed wire and minefields to a depth of 100–200m. The zones between the defence lines were zeroed-in on grid references for artillery-, mortar- and machine-gunfire. Prizes were awarded for the best defensive system. It was won by an Algerian battalion at Gabrielle.

To reduce these defences would require heavy artillery, siege tactics, and a willingness to accept heavy casualties. Fighting would be vicious and at close quarters. One problem of the defensive system was the location of the command bunkers which, being at the top instead of on the reverse slopes, could be knocked out easily. Moreover, there were no bunkers on the reverse slopes to hold reserve troops, either to reinforce the defence or to launch counter-attacks.

The bastion construction used 21km of barbed wire (50 tons) and 7,000 wire-holding stanchions, which were brought in by plane between November and January. Deficiencies in concrete and building materials meant that the blockhouses were not strong enough nor as numerous as necessary.

Other needs for food, ammunition, troops, fuel, etc. also had to be satisfied. When the shells rained down from the Vietminh artillery, which was not supposed to be there, trenches, dug-outs and barbed wire were blown apart and French defences soon lost their coherence. What the shells did not achieve the monsoon completed as trenches dissolved in mud. Lieutenant-General O'Daniels, the American adviser who reported on Dien Bien Phu, warned that just a few batteries of enemy heavy artillery could make French positions untenable.

However, the dignitaries who visited Beatrice during the phoney war were impressed. The secretary of state for defence declared the place 'impregnable', and the French minister of defence said it was like 'Verdun', a stupid analogy repeating Navarre's previous comments, because Fort Douaumont at Verdun was captured on the first day.

Beatrice was a long way from the base area and reinforcements. If it fell, counter-attacks would have to be launched from a distance and could be blocked by infiltration between bastions. But the complacent French had not planned for any counter-attacks to re-take or reinforce the bastion.

Modern war defensive tactics developed during the First World War required defence in depth. At Dien Bien Phu, there was no depth. If Beatrice or Gabrielle were lost, the whole encampment would be lost because of constraints on logistics.

Robert Guillain, special envoy of *Le Monde*, published an article on his return from Dien Bien Phu on 15 February 1954 in *Metropole* magazine. He was talking about 'the Beatrice' bastion when he wrote:

> *...each of his movements must be perceived by the enemy, who looks down from above, while he himself, behind the curtain of the forests, is nowhere visible to us...But soon a reassuring feeling arises: that of entering a formidable system. It is a sort of gigantic and complicated trap, bristling with spikes, swollen with structures, mined, dug-out, compartmentalised, ploughed over square kilometres, and more inhabited than an anthill.*

But Guillan's reports also revealed doubts and misgivings about the gung-ho confidence of the troops post-Ná Sán, who constantly boasted of breaking the Vietnamese while the journalist fretted that Dien Bien Phu was 'Dangling in the mouth of a wolf'.[84]

The French public and indeed the world was being told by the FEC, 'bring it on!'

Figaro's correspondent Etienne Anthérieu[85] commented on the mood of optimism in the French camp and noted that five months would be needed for Giáp's preparations because of the problem of logistics in such an environment. The enemy did not know where the next attack would come from and Navarre was apparently unceasingly attacking them, harassing their rear. In reality, all of the French probes in the area around the valley were met from the first with fierce resistance from significant bodies of Vietminh waiting in ambush on the flanks, and even threatening to cut off large scale French patrols. After each attempt at offensive action, the French would soon scamper back into the central defences bringing their dead and wounded with them.

Dien Bien Phu was from the first a most public affair, so much information and publicity attended the creation of the French base there that the Vietminh hardly had need of intelligence. Navarre literally threw down the gauntlet. Britain and France recognised the associated states, but the developing world, especially the newly decolonised nations of Asia, such as India and Burma, were siding wholeheartedly with the Democratic Republic of Vietnam. Ho Chi Minh had thoroughly captured the moral high ground as had Marxist-Leninist doctrine, which became the natural home for all groups struggling against colonialist powers or indeed newly liberated nations. It would from the first be the most public battle in world history. Millions of television viewers around the world watched a film of the preparations for the coming battle or saw it on Pathé News at the cinema. The Battle of Dien Bien Phu became a global gladiatorial spectacle.

The artillery duel

Apart from underestimating Vietminh logistical capacity, the great surprise of the campaign for the French was the extent of Vietminh heavy artillery and AA with a reasonably good supply of shells. However, the French were definitely not outgunned – the excuse used later to explain defeat. The other surprise was that French counter-battery-fire was ineffective. These surprises were despite good intelligence on these points.

On 18 January, the French received definitive intelligence information as to 105mm artillery and 37mm AA at Dien Bien Phu. That ex-US supplied Kuomintang 75mm cannon were around had already been evident for several months. Nonetheless, anyone familiar with the topography of the region would have some sympathy with the views of the French general staff and their artillery commander *in situ*, the one-armed Colonel Piroth, that deployment of large numbers of heavy artillery with enough shells was impossible. However, given prodigious feats of Vietminh logistics in other campaigns it should have been expected after their logistical achievements to support the offensives around the Red delta in 1954.

The figures for the number of guns are not clear but it seems that the Vietminh were able to drag across the mountains about 130 medium-size guns and heavy mortars, notably twenty-four mountain 75mm short barrels (standard French calibre of First World War field artillery), and twenty-four 105mm cannon captured by the Chinese in the Korean War.[86] There were twenty-four 37mm anti-aircraft guns and sixteen 75mm heavy mortars. There were an unspecified number of 20mm AA guns, but at least seventeen, because that was the number captured by a French attack on 28 March. They had many recoilless rifles, plus twelve Katusha multiple rocket-launchers, which only reached the battlefield on the penultimate day. Due to the lack of communications equipment, the guns had to be dragged close to the targets for direct firing over open sights or for individual gun command. This required excellent camouflage over the gun ports and casements dug into the hillside, an art in which the Vietminh excelled. If that was not enough, Giáp arranged for decoy smoke flares to be emitted on automatic fuses some 50m from the gun emplacements, to be set off at the same time that the cannon fired.

The arrival of the cannon was a matter of great joy to the Vietminh soldiers, from the humble bo doi to senior officers. The infantry already understood the devastating impact that artillery made. The Vietminh were highly encouraged to have something that could reply to the French, who hitherto had dominated the battlefield with their guns and pulverised their battalions around the Red delta:

> *After dinner we went to the road to see the cannons with our own eyes, having only today been informed of their existence...when we saw the towing lorries in the distance everyone exclaimed 'there they are, our cannons!'*[87]

One colonel even asked if he could 'touch' a cannon, as if it were some holy icon.

The French had sixty cannon, including twelve 155mm, twelve 105mm guns and eight 102mm mortars, which were very effective in breaking up attacks in killing zones in front of the porcupine bastions on co-ordinates already mapped out in advance of the Vietminh approach. French gunnery also included TOT (time on target) ability, whereby barrages could be co-ordinated to land and explode together. Unlike the Vietminh artillery, the French artillery were exposed in the centre of the French position and lacking even shields to protect the gunners. They needed to be sited in the open to enable all-round fire to the various points on the compass from which attacks might be expected against the bastion. The French artillerymen suffered heavily and many gun parts and gunners had to be replaced by parachute. After 13 March, munitions supply depended on parachute-drops, a highly unsatisfactory method but, luckily, substantial inventories had been established.

Towards the end, the French artillery would be overwhelmed, short of ammunition, unable to replace spare parts or gunners. As effectiveness declined, it was not enough to offset the huge manpower disparity.

Colonel Piroth, the artillery commander at Dien Bien Phu, patently gave wrong advice, to the effect that the Vietminh could not bring heavy weapons to the battlefield or enough ammunition in case they did. Navarre had also miscalculated. The latter noted airily that peaks are 'at 10–12km…this distance is greater than a useful range of a possible artillery attack.'[88]

De Castries also remarked, 'We will demolish the Viets when they come down from the hills.' Optimism from high command spread down into the lower levels, including Major Dr Grauwin's bunker where everyone knew that 'The Viets are going to attack…the mood was frankly optimistic.'[89]

Pham Thanh Tam noted VPA engineers were building bunkers for artillery just 300m from French positions at Beatrice: 'We worked in absolute silence.' The French were assuming that artillery would be deployed in a classic fashion, but the Vietminh had other ideas. Contrary to logic, they placed their guns not behind the hills but on the face of the hills in front of the French positions to allow for direct fire. Had the guns been placed behind the hills, the French would have won the battle. With relatively unsophisticated gunners only recently and quickly trained in the Chinese camps, direct fire was more effective.

This was all a tremendous morale boost for the infantry, who were due to storm the fortress of Beatrice. Pham noted: 'I really had the impression that the infantry sensed that here at Dien Bien Phu the artillery was behind them in a way that they had never before experienced.'[90] Close-range direct artillery-fire made possible the quick overrunning of Beatrice and prevented the rapid formation or planning for a counter-attack.

Pham's diary shows quite clearly the priority in Giáp's strategy for victory, and that was to interdict logistic supply at the airport. If the French lost their sentinel at Beatrice, then the airport could be completely shut down.

The French commanders

The officer commanding at Dien Bien Phu was Christian de la Croix de Castries, who in medieval style sent a chivalric letter of challenge to Giáp before the battle. Clearly enamoured with his ducal ancestry, he dined on white tablecloth service throughout the battle while his men lived in mud up to their waists with mostly cold rations. Genevieve de Galard described him as a 'man of medium height, rather thin and pale with sharp aquiline features and an aquiline profile.' He was a taciturn man who would suffer some sort of mental breakdown after the catastrophes of mid-March. After the battle started, he never once left his bunker to visit his troops except for a visit to the hospital in the last few days. It was not as though he was indispensable.

His nervous disposition was already somewhat apparent when Graham Greene had lunch with him in his bunker several months previously. Lacking in communicable charisma for his men, he is little commented on by de Galard, in marked contrast to her warm remarks for Colonels Langlais and Bigeard. She spent nearly six weeks of the battle in close proximity to de Castries' command post. Typical of her class, de Galard is scrupulously and honourably discreet, but it is in the *absence* of comment on de Castries that we must look for the truth. Similarly, with his fellow officers Langlais and Bigeard, with their discreet military code of honour. It is on these latter two that the affection and devotion of the Dien Bien Phu veterans falls. Every soldier knows that mental breakdown is possible and that it should not be censured. It is an injury or a war-induced malady. It is not an issue of courage or failed duty. De Castries was a casualty of war.

De Castries spent the entire battle in his bunker, never venturing out to visit his subordinates or direct counter-attacks in person. Tactical control was lacking and the quick fall of key bastions at Beatrice, Gabrielle and Anne-Marie showed that something had gone badly wrong. It seems that at this point early on in the battle, after the loss of the three key outlying bastions, de Castries' deputy Lieutenant-Colonel Langlais took effective command, following which there was a marked improvement in tactics, including readiness for counter-attack against fallen positions. In de Castries' defence, not a convincing one, we could point out that he had to stay at his command post to handle vital radio traffic as well as to supervise the unglamorous business of logistics, which is what in essence this battle of attrition had been reduced to. Given his personal cavalry self-identity sense of dash and glory, this diminished role must have been humiliating. Under the hammer of battle, de Castries withered as a leader. Others with real leadership charisma filled the void.

The command structure was not optimal. De Castries reported to General Cogny in Hanoi, who reported to Navarre in Saigon, who acted as Indochina theatre chief. Cogny had a prickly and volatile temperament. As the situation deteriorated, vicious arguments broke out in front of the entire command with Cogny openly insulting his commander in faraway Saigon or making poisonous off the record briefings to the press. There is justifiable speculation that Navarre kept Cogny in place to take the blame for failures while Cogny was intent on avoiding the fate of 'the fall guy'.

Hill 781

When five extra Vietminh regiments moved into the valley between 5 December and 24 January, the net started to tighten.

Away to the east of Dominque and Éliane was Hill 781 (or Doi Xanh, the green hill). It was occupied by the Vietminh 316th Division with 75mm mountain guns dug into its western face for close support and direct fire. To celebrate spring, the 75mm cannon were fired at the enemy, causing the loss of one Morane spotter plane at the airstrip. This would obviously bring on a response by French fighter-bombers looking to suppress this fire. In anticipation of this, various light AA weapons were set up with the intention of ambushing Hellcat or Bearcat planes arriving from the north-west. Three planes attacked and one of them 'visibly stuttered in flight, was engulfed in flames then exploded into the side of the hill. It was our first victory for our AA,' noted bo doi do Van Tinh proudly.[91]

But the French did not like to be bottled up. Provoked by this artillery attack Colonel Langlais, de Castries deputy, launched a spoiling assault against Hill 781 on 5 February. It was decided that a foray should be made to find and destroy the gun batteries that they believed were on the reverse slope of the hills facing Beatrice, of which Hill 781 was the most prominent. He took with him a mixed force of legionnaires and Moroccans. Cameraman Pierre Schoendoerffer accompanied them. Bearcat fighter bombers flew in support, some of them armed with napalm cannisters.

First shots from Schoendorffer's film show troops on top of Beatrice. The view of the plain of Dien Bien Phu is impressive and then the camara pans around the panorama of high mountains, sweeping the five hills to the west – the Dominque and Éliane positions. Then it tracks on round to the high T'ai mountains to the east, over which the Vietminh have come and where Giáp was sitting in a cave opening, surveying the valley.

Film footage of the action shows soldiers marching Indian-file through thick brush and long elephant grass. They are T'ais and legionnaire paratroopers or Moroccans all dressed in loose-fitting American fatigues and with accoutrements. They wear American helmets with net covering but, unlike the Vietminh, there are no camouflage leaves or branches in them. Some of the troops wear slouch hats. Weapons are a mixture of American- and French-made carbines. Fold-up MAT49 sub-machine-guns for paratroopers, or the stubby bolt-action paratrooper rifles (MAS36), or the American M1 carbine. There are French light-machine-guns (MAC29) with the curved magazine on top, or belt-fed American medium Browning machine-guns with aerated vents. Dakotas flew low overhead dropping supplies by fast-opening parachutes. The chutes open and their cargo swings crazily, then thud into the grassy hillside.

Infiltrating through Vietminh pickets, then cutting through thick shrub and jungle, de Langlais' force reached the lower slopes of Hill 781. It was here that they were spotted for the first time. Machine-gunner Dang Duc Song sprang into action and started firing his light machine-gun. He received fire in return. Dang Duc Song recalled this sharp skirmishing at close quarters. When the enemy were just 10m away, he:

> *...cried 'attack' then threw several hand grenades...not daring to raise my head for fear of snipers I threw several grenades in return, then seeing several enemy soldiers on the left I fired at them killing one and wounding another. Then I hurled three more grenades and heard the cries of wounded men when they exploded.*[92]

After that Dang saw a parachute officer sporting a red beret driving his men forward with his cane. He was accompanied by a radio operator. Dang remembered target selection instructions that stated:

> *...first light machine-guns, second officers and third radio operators...I turned my sights* [of the gun] *on the officer who folded under my firing then tracked the radio operator, fired and watched his body fall over that of his officer.*[93]

At Dien Bien Phu, officers would increasingly dress and arm themselves so as not to stand out. Moving around the trench system, Dang gathered up other survivors of the French onslaught, encouraging others and throwing grenades. Many of his comrades were killed.

Surviving the firefight, he noticed that his metal water canteen had been hit several times, possibly saving his life. The canteen now adorns the Fame Hall of Regiment 98 of 316th Division of Military Region 2.

In Pierre Schoendoerffer's film, the action cuts to smouldering bare slopes consumed by napalm. Vietminh bodies shrivelled and burnt to a carbon crisp are amongst many passed on the slopes. There are pictures of men firing uphill and scampering down for cover after coming under fire. The slopes, bare from burning, are so steep that soldiers scramble up slowly on all fours. A soldier is hit and suddenly limps downhill into the arms of comrades. Light and medium machine-gunners give covering fire. Others fire with M1 carbines. A wounded man is treated by his comrades. Shot in the foot he smokes a cigarette with a laconic look on his face – a lucky one. He will be evacuated but his wound is light so he was probably parachuted back again. A T'ai soldier with a bad leg wound is being bandaged. A legionnaire with chiselled German looks sits next to a man with a throat wound. Another is bandaged round the mouth where the jaw has been shot away. Finally, the film cuts to a US helmet on a cross overlooking the panorama and to another more formal funeral where a priest holds a burial service.

After that darkness descends, then the French shell the hill, to further cover their retreat and prevent pursuit. Nothing much had been achieved and no 75mm guns were found, because there were none on the reverse slope.

Divided objectives/divided counsels

Giáp, in his *Memoirs of War*, notes:

> *As is widely known, in the master plan to solve the Indochina War worked out by General Navarre and adopted on 24 July 1953 by the French Council of National Defence under the direct chairmanship of President Vincent Auriol himself, Dien Bien Phu was not initially considered to be an important strategic position, from a political as well as military viewpoint. Yet only four months later, on 3 December 1953, General Navarre in person declared he would accept battle in North-west Viêt Nam with Dien Bien Phu as centre.*[94]

There was discord at the top of French high command. Navarre had wanted a base for offensive operations whereas Cogny wanted another Ná Sán.[95]

Lieutenant-Colonel Jules Roy, who had volunteered for Indochina in 1952 but resigned his commission in June 1953, wrote informed commentary on the Indochina War. He described a poisonous atmosphere in the army of Tonkin under the command of Cogny where officers constantly covered their backs by acting only on written orders. Cogny was the ultimate plotter and schemer. Roy says of him:

> *...if the operation had succeeded Cogny would be able to take the glory, and if it failed, the reservations that he had expressed would protect him...Cogny who pressed and repressed his arguments and words. The adversary was less the Viet than the commander-in-chief* [Navarre].[96]

The remarkable point about the FEC's high command is that it was full of brave and intelligent men, with extraordinary records of war service. But they were often dysfunctional as a group and this tendency was accentuated under Navarre and Cogny.

French intelligence analysis and GMI (GMCA)

In January, Giáp received a vital and pleasing intelligence report that Navarre planned to commit two-thirds of his mobile units and one important parachute unit to *Operation Atlante* in the Central Highlands on 20 January.

While the French had some inkling of an impending attack at Dien Bien Phu, they did not understand the size of the threat, nor its logistical depth, and believed they could handle it. On 20 February, a French probe discovered pre-prepared gun emplacements at Dien Bien Phu, a clear warning of what was to come, although they may have assumed that these were for the 75mm mountain guns that occasionally peppered the French base areas to reinforce the French delusion that the Vietminh had some artillery but not much.

Intelligence gathered, patchy though it was, was enough for Navarre to realise by 1 January 1954 that the balance of advantage had appreciably changed in favour of the Vietminh, including the likelihood that 105mm artillery was on the way. He conveyed his fears in a stark report to Paris and the matter so shocked the war council that a special delegation, including de Chevigne and chief-of-staff General Ely, with plenipotentiary powers was sent out to make an assessment. Navarre had made a back-covering political response to the new intelligence, not a military response. Despite ample prewarning, they all failed to react to the massive extent of Vietminh mobilisation until the battle had started, even though they had picked up radio intercepts, on 6 December 1953, of Giáp's orders for a general mobilisation. As if dazzled in the headlights, there was no appropriate response to the intelligence, which should have led to massive reinforcement and cancellation of *Operation Atlante* or withdrawal through Lao.

As the 351st Heavy Division had returned from training in China in September 1953 with large numbers of 105mm guns, 120mm mortars and twenty-four 37mm anti-aircraft guns, the failure to pick this up on radio transmission is also surprising. In fact, there was intelligence, but the quantity of the movement was not understood. In his post-war analysis and post-mortem, General Ely estimated that French Intelligence was eighty percent correct. However, he also noted that the GMI French-led irregular units failed 'to interdict the Viet communication routes that in the region…[over] a distance of 400–500km in a heavily forested mountainous zone.'[97] General Ely was being unfair with his map-based criticism and showed the typical prejudice of military establishments against irregular forces. In fact, it was the GMI who first revealed that heavy AA guns were on the way to Dien Bien Phu. It should also be understood that GMI had only been active for about two years and were underfunded and understaffed with an inadequate ratio of officers and NCOs.[98] Extremely strong in the north, the GMI were weaker in the Black T'ai country along the route of supply to Dien Bien Phu, where there were split loyalties. Political mistakes were made in alienating elements of the Black T'ai by clumsy favouritism for the White T'ai. However, Pham noticed the villages were empty, so any potentially hostile tribes had been driven away along a route that was well guarded by VPA regulars. There were successful attacks at Lai

Chau and Lao Cai in September 1953, where the key towns were occupied and a Vietminh battalion destroyed with 150 killed.

Such attacks were repeated during the battle. As to effectiveness, Giáp admitted:

> *In mid-March* [1954] *our army's general staff had to transfer its 9th Regiment… and detach our 176th Regiment from the campaign forces and send them to Lai Cau to sweep away the phi* [a Vietminh term for bandits] *and the general admitted Dien Bien Phu would have fallen sooner had those infantry units fought in the final offensive.*[99]

Despite this, the implication is that there was a failure in generalship. A former French officer in Indochina, Roy wrote that Navarre was taking military decisions, 'without realising that he was staking the whole war on a single throw of the dice.'

Another glaring intelligence mistake was made by the French Air Force, who confidently asserted just before Giáp's opening attack on 13 March that the Vietminh did not possess 37mm anti-aircraft guns. When belated probes in the direction of the main Vietminh line of advance on 20 February did confirm the fact that heavy artillery would be brought up, Navarre began to lobby strenuously for more air transport resources, which was the main limiting factor on the size and fighting capacity of his army at Dien Bien Phu. After the loss of over a thousand men since the November landings, Navarre must have also realised that major Vietminh resources had been committed. He failed to get the necessary additional resources in time and also failed to reconsider the whole 'base aero-terrestrial' concept in light of new facts. There was no Plan B, except for 'Xenophon', which would only be enacted *in extremis*, and which was not a robust plan. Navarre's 'certain victory' was becoming a high-risk gamble. Pride and politics prevented Navarre from making a painful decision to withdraw at an early stage when the facts started to become available.

Pham waits to attack

Vietminh soldiers were as close as 300m from the French, so construction took place in absolute silence for fear of discovery.[100] They were to wait quietly for twenty-five days before the attack.

For the enthusiastic Vietminh soldiers there was no shortage of humour and hijinks in the early stages of the campaign. Pham's comrade was on watch and observation duty one night overlooking Beatrice when he called out to his colleagues, 'Mmm…I can see a pretty pair of twins and a very sexy little wench.'[101] Morale was high. Other military objects received nicknames. For example, Dakotas were referred to as 'old ladies' and tanks as 'crabs'.

One day Pham climbed up to the observation point on top of the hill. He could understand the geography easily. They had an excellent view and estimated that the enemy's cannon were about 5km away. 'The plain of Dien Bien Phu was covered in a thin mist through which a pale plume of smoke trailed upwards.'[102]

In the weeks before the attack, while the Vietminh gunners waited, observed, stockpiled shells and put the finishing touches to their casements, the infantry were involved in a deadlier game of developing saps[103] to a point near enough to launch attacks on the appointed hour. This was a twenty-four-hour-a-day operation. French troops watched as the saps, marked by earth piles, drew closer. It was the part of the 100km of trench-lines that were gradually drawing in on French bastions all around their perimeter. Digging at night was clearly safer, but there was a constant glow of light from torches or parachute flares dropped by the French reconnaissance aeroplanes overhead. The saps would act as launch pads for infantry attack. Positioned just before the wire, the leading elements would place Bangalore tubes under the wire, some of which would already have been cut to allow the long explosive charges to be better placed. Everyone knew that an attack was imminent. De Castries, however, does not seem to have prepared for contingencies such as reinforcement or counter-attack plans. It was negligence. A failure of detail in contingency planning, borne of complacency and inexperience.

As the battle date grew nearer, so did the intensity of the 75mm shelling and sapping as well as the deep penetration raids into the French positions, including one that damaged the airstrip. Captain Nicholas of the 3rd Legion Battalion was aware of the intensification of Vietminh activities: 'The entire day had been spent trying to fill in the Vietminh approach trenches.'[104]

In the days running up to the first attack, Pham recorded the successes of the different 75mm gun batteries:

> *C801 destroyed objectives on the enemy post. A spotter aircraft was set on fire… C803 destroyed an enemy artillery position! All our targets at the north end of the runway were destroyed. Then C801 picked out post 307a* [a French bunker each given a code number], *C802 picked out 307b, C803 fired two salvoes from six tubes and hit an airplane. A Dakota caught fire on the runway* [C800s were codes for batteries of artillery or mortars in the 351st Heavy Regiment].

For the attack itself, orders were given to Pham's artillery unit to concentrate on counter-battery efforts aimed at preventing effective fire against Vietminh infantry. The French, in anticipation of the battle, had moved six heavy mortars of the Foreign Legion to the base of Dominique 1 (coded Post 201 by the Vietminh) to zero-in on the approaches to Beatrice where Vietminh infantry waited in their saps ready to spring into action just 400m from the French defences. Because they were being pinned down by accurate fire from the French mortars, the Vietminh gunners were given orders to 'fire on Post 201 to help our infantry advance. Bombard the high hill [Dominique] at its base.'[105] French troops sniped at bobbing pith helmets and mortared the enemy as they approached. Piroth's artillery blasted the ground and scored occasional direct hits, or there would be raids against some of the more advanced saps. Vietminh casualties were heavy even in this build-up period. But gradually and intimidatingly the saps drew nearer. However, not all the saps were as far advanced as they should be. One bo doi recounted how they took over a sap about 400m out and started digging Indian-file.[106] Working on difficult terrain, one night they only completed 20m by morning and similarly the next night, 12 March, even then they only managed to dig to a depth of only 30cm. 'Discovered by the French, several salvoes were fired in our direction, killing three soldiers and wounding one out of our 12 man platoon. Towards four in the morning, we had to retreat,' recounted Pham Van Pham, head of a Bangalore torpedo group.

The French were very aware of the effectiveness of numerous Vietminh 75mm cannon and 120mm mortars that had already created damage to the steel mesh runway. On 12 March, two DC17s had been destroyed and one spotter plane. Medivac evacuees, including a well-known journalist, had been killed as well as aircrew and personnel around the landing strip. The main aim of Giáp's artillery in the days preceding the first major offensive was to impinge reinforcement and the delivery of supplies. If the runway was closed by shellfire, then victory was theirs, because air-drop supply and reinforcement would be very difficult. The choice of Beatrice as a first objective was exactly related to Giáp's strategy of winning the battle of logistics. From the top of Beatrice, Giáp's artillery would have a perfect observation point over the plain and much of the air field.

As always, the Vietminh attack was preceded by the shrill and melodramatic incantations of the political commissars. This time there was a message from Ho himself, which was read out to the troops:

> *I instruct you to start the fight. I await news of your exploits so that I can reward the most courageous units and individuals. I hope that you attain a great victory. I embrace you all.*[107]

Not to be denied their own verbosity, the political commissars would then add yet more rhetorical gloss. For example, political commissar Tong Tu of the Heavy Artillery Regiment added, 'We are participating in an historic battle. Comrades bring back victory!'[108] For the communist commissars it was always 'bring back',[109] because while they stayed in shelter behind the lines, they were sending out the bo doi to death or mutilation.

On 7 March, Chinese advisers reported to the Chinese high command in Beijing that:

> *The VPA ground works will reach a point 500–1,000m from the enemy external defensive positions. All the artillery positions have been completed and all the guns began to move in position today.* [The VPA] *will begin their artillery bombardment against the airstrip on the 12th to block the enemy airlifting.*[110]

Diplomacy on the road to Geneva

On 11 March, Zhou En Lai sent instructions to Ho Chi Minh telling him to prepare documents to be ready in Geneva from 26 April. He indicated clearly that a ceasefire was in the offing and that a partition of Vietnam along an armistice line of the 16th Parallel was likely:

> *As a matter of a fact, the line for ceasefire today is possible to become the demarcation line in the future. Therefore, this is an issue quite big, and it will also depend upon the development of the military situation in the future. Where should this line be drawn and at which parallel? This should be considered from two aspects: on the one hand, it should be favourable to Vietnam; on the other, it should be acceptable to the enemy side. The more toward the south the line can be drawn, the better. It seems that the question of* [drawing the line at] *the 16th Parallel could be considered as one of the options…Please come to Beijing at the end of March or in early April, and then go to Moscow to exchange opinions with the Soviet Party Central Committee…At present, the headquarters should assign some people to specifically work for preparing for the negotiation, but the main strength should still be placed on commanding combat operations and mobilising the masses.*

This document shows clearly that Ho was not independent but in thrall to the USSR and the Chinese, and that a partition deal had already been agreed with the British. The exact drawing of the line would depend on the military outcome, though it seems that variances would only be at the margin.

Most interesting was the concern that France should be accommodated. This was almost certainly the result of the overriding Soviet and Chinese desire for peace as well as the wish to split the French from the Americans, who it was feared were on the way to intervening directly in Indochina. As the battle began, Ho knew that the result of Dien Bien Phu would only be marginal to the outcome at Geneva, so the emotions and blood to be spilt on the battlefield would barely make a difference, perhaps moving the parallel from the 17th to the 16th if the Vietminh won. The 16th Parallel would give the ancient capital Hue and Ho's home town to the communists, so there was still much to fight for.

CHAPTER XVII

The Battle of Dien Bien Phu, 13 March 1954

First general offensive, Beatrice (Him Lam), and closing the airstrip – 13 to 14 March

The first isolated domino to be knocked down was Beatrice (Him Lam Hill), about 2.5km from Dominique, the nearest part of the central porcupine. Clearly, the communications between Beatrice and the central bastions could be interdicted by Vietminh infiltration. Beatrice was also hemmed-in by other hills and was close to the Vietminh-embedded gun-line of 105mm cannon in those hills. From the top of the hill you can see most of the valley and the airstrip. Beatrice seemed an impregnable position and de Castries had always made a point of showing visiting dignitaries around it. Was it an assumption made in ignorance of the mass of heavy guns being brought up over the mountains and dug into impregnable encasements?

Despite the protective hills to the north and south-east of Beatrice, which gave cover to the Vietminh as they assembled, Vietminh troops still had to cover hundreds of metres in the open. Emerging from saps near to the first wire, they had to penetrate minefields and three rows of deep French wire entanglements. They would incur huge losses covering the ground from the saps to the wire, especially as much of the wire would likely remain uncut despite the use of high explosive shells from their 105mm guns. Multiple saps and communication trenches were dug forward, as if many moles were in action. They were the width of one man and ran in zig-zag or oblique patterns to avoid enfilading fire along the length of the trench.

On 13 March, the officers and men at Beatrice knew that an attack was coming. One of their listening posts with four men in it had disappeared. Weapons were prepared and double-checked, cold rations were issued to posts. At 3 p.m., Vietminh troops disgorging from their bases behind the surrounding hills were spotted swarming over the hill crests to the south and down through the light canopy of brush and trees. This must have been reported to de Castries, so why was Dien Bien Phu's command caught by surprise and relatively unprepared? Why was French battery-fire so slow and ineffective in the first minutes of the Vietminh attack? Colonel Langlais was so unprepared that he was caught in the open having a shower. The most significant oversight was the undermanned Beatrice garrison. Less than 450 of the 517 complement were present, the rest being absent for one reason or another, including being wounded, missing, on rest rotation, or guarding de Castries. Total available troops were probably 428 legionnaires of the 13th Demi Brigade. Given the importance of Beatrice, it would be no exaggeration to say that the future of the entire Dien Bien Phu bastion and of the war in Indochina was in their hands. If this domino fell so might all the others.

The command at Dien Bien Phu failed to take action over Navarre's observation that the positioning of the Beatrice command post at the top of the hill made it extremely vulnerable. Navarre should have followed-up. Perhaps such details were beneath him.

The start of the attack was not the artillery barrage launched on Beatrice itself but the barrages against the airstrip and French artillery positions that preceded it by an hour. Secondary objective targeting was intended to draw French counter-battery-fire. Fire against the airport was also aimed at keeping French fighter bombers and artillery spotter planes grounded. Giáp's plan was for a simultaneous attack by two regiments from two different directions, against the north and south-west respectively, against the two easterly positions B1 and B3 of the Beatrice bastion. Having converged, they would roll over the westerly positions B2 and B4. Ground attacks were timed to go in at 5.30 p.m. after the artillery barrage.

At 4 p.m. on 13 March 1954, Giáp's Vietminh Army launched the greatest artillery ambush in the history of warfare. Until this moment the French, despite intelligence information, had been unaware of the extent of Giáp's access to such immense firepower. Giáp had not used his 105mm cannon nor had these guns been spotted in the vicinity of Dien Bien Phu. They were only deployed on the day of the first attack. It was the day of reckoning that Giáp had long awaited.

The 13th Heavy Regiment was ordered to fire:[1]

> *Soon the reports of success were coming in. C801* [codes used for different gun positions] *hit its first target and all the shots from the three salvoes from the third hit the target* [Isabelle], *one of the French lorry's* [sic] *was destroyed. C802 the first two salvoes hit the enemy who counter-battery-fired at our* [dummy] *wooden cannon.*

The Vietminh ruse worked. At C801, 'twenty-five percent of targets hit. Five rounds fell on the airport in the helicopter zone.' New orders came through for C801, C802, C803: 'continue to pulverize the enemy artillery when they open up.' But the Vietminh high command was more immediately concerned to interdict the runway, particularly for use by spotter planes. When two spotter planes were reported on the runway by C803, the command came down: 'Okay, bombard the runway and don't let any planes takeoff or land, keep firing at the same place.'[2] Just then the French artillery counter-attacked from Isabelle. However, within their mountainside casements, the artillerymen were well protected.

Pham's gun battery C803 continued to fire, reporting the destruction of French artillery post 203, which set off the spectacular explosion of a munitions depot. C802 pulverised the enemy artillery post 307. A spotter took off towards the south (i.e. away from the north of the runway, which it could do because it was a light plane), while the French towed their Bearcat fighters into sandbag revetments. It was a minor victory in that they would not be active in strafing the Vietminh infantry as they attacked. But the spotter would be directing artillery fire over the battlefield. 'At 5.25 a brave French helicopter pilot landed near to post 307'. Such was the military dialogue of action and response in this opening artillery duel. Several Bearcats were destroyed in their revetments. Down in the valley, French troops were in shock. Paratrooper Pregnon exclaimed, 'It's not possible. I said to Bastian, they have artillery. Listen to that its 105mm…we're finished.'[3]

The ground attack started on 13 March at 5.10 p.m., heralded by a mass artillery barrage of 9,000 rounds, including 105mm shells. The legion commander and all of his staff were killed by a direct hit on the misplaced command post:

> *…when during the first hour of bombardment, a 120mm* [mortar] *shell with a delayed fuse penetrated the command post…as the bombardment had completely disorganised our telephone and radio network.*

Captain Nicholas, commanding position B2, recalled:

> *I was only informed of Major Pegot and Captain Pardi's deaths half an hour after they occurred…*[we] *could not mount a co-ordinated defence, each legionnaire fighting individually and finally taken in the rear by the enemy.*[4]

The first that de Castries heard of the disaster was when a German legionnaire stammered out the words over the still functioning radio set, '*alles tot*,' (all dead). Three other company leaders were also killed or wounded. It was akin to an ambush because the French were ignorant of the presence of so many Vietminh heavy calibre weapons. Luu Trong Lan, major of the 351st artillery, reported: 'one could say that the Vietminh heavy artillery created total surprise on this afternoon of the 13 March.'[5] Moreover, there were a lot of guns and all well-supplied with ammunition.

'During this violent preparation, the Vietminh re-opened their trenches and pushed them up to the wire under cover of the thick dust raised by the explosions.' The extent of the massive barrage by heavy guns was a shock as trenches, gun positions and men were obliterated.

Dr Grauwin, who was counting, noted that: 'The shells were still falling, about sixty a minute.'[6] The artillery fire was co-ordinated with concentrated fire from 12.7mm heavy machine-guns aimed at the main French positions, the aim being to keep down the heads of the French infantry as the Vietminh stormtroopers rushed through the wire.[7] One legionnaire recalled in a diary entry a few days later:

> *Thousands of Vietminh troops dashed forth and up the hillside. Mines and barbed wire did not impede them. Our machine-guns cut many of them down, but soon we were about to be overrun. We gradually retreated. I helped cover my comrades' retreat. I'd hurl a grenade here or there; shot the closest enemy gunman, dash 50m or so, then repeat...Once, an enemy grenade fell within two meters of my feet. I quickly kicked it away and threw my body to the ground.*[8]

The deluge of fire also extended simultaneously to Dominique 2 bastion, which was the closest one for offering supporting fire, as well as Isabelle, whose 105mm battery was able to lay down zonal protective fire on the Vietminh lines of approach. However, counter-battery-fire was ineffective, as was the attack by a squadron of French bombers who seemed to drop their load aimlessly, 'without any precise objective.'

Vietminh infantry leapt from their saps with leading elements composed of pioneers who rushed forward with their Bangalores. These Bangalores were meant to blow up the thick barbed wire defences to allow a path for the infantry. However, two hours after the battle began, wire obstructions had still not been cleared. Many of the pioneers were dead before they could release their charges. The situation remained tense as losses mounted from French machine-gunfire and shelling, although the latter was strangely delayed, perhaps due to the communications problem or even Colonel Piroth's shock at what had just happened. Piroth had been directing the fire of his battery of 155mm cannon for counter-battery purposes against targets that he could not see or identify because they were hidden in caves. Only too late did he switch their fire to the obvious priority of pre-set co-ordinates on the slopes of Beatrice, through which the Vietminh infantry were passing. Artillery- and heavy mortar-fire was Beatrice's main defensive weapon. Given the warnings on the day, the tardiness of the entire garrison, excluding the Beatrice legionnaires themselves, is testament to a failure of leadership.

According to Pham Van Nham, satchel bomb explosives pioneer platoon leader, 11th battalion 312th Division:

> *...the only practical means of fighting was to advance without hesitation; in any case we would certainly die if we stayed lying down. So we bounded out of our saps at high speed and hurled ourselves toward the wire where we picked up*

the explosives of our fallen comrades and continued. It took 37 charges and one hour to blow a way through the last 20m of wire defences.[9]

All of this was done under intense machine-gun, artillery-, small arms-, grenade- and mortar-fire. Some of the attackers leapt over the barbed wire where the defences had been damaged, but others were blocked or pinned down. 'Some enemy artillery fire from Muong Thanh bombarded our infantry,' recorded gunner Pham Than Tam. 'It prevented the 209th Regiment from passing the wire which encircled the base of the hill. The 141st Regiment was able to pass through with thanks to Bangalore torpedoes!'[10] After bursting through the defences, the human wave of attackers stood a good chance of overwhelming the remaining defenders with sub-machine-guns and grenades, as well as satchel bomb teams who took out concrete blockhouses. Despite excellent planning and breach of the wire defences, the attack would cost the battalion half their manpower in dead and wounded, about 250 men. 'We were all very downcast.'[11]

Their communications smashed in the first moments, disorganised legionnaires were fighting attacks from all directions against their three rings of trench defences. Only supreme skill, discipline and unit morale could sustain them against overwhelming odds. Fighting was hand-to-hand, from trench to trench, bunker to bunker. Remarkably in the carnage and deafening noise of war, a truce was arranged at 10 p.m. to enable both sides to evacuate the wounded. Both sides exploited the truce, the Vietminh to rush up reinforcements to fill the void left by the annihilation of their leading elements, and the French to bring up ammunition, which was in very short supply. As an exchange it was about even.

The battle continued with ferocity. According to Captain Nicholas, Vietminh attacks were stopped with enormous casualties by a well-positioned machine-gun:

...the Vietminh put a recoilless rifle in place to neutralize it and the machine-gun was completely destroyed. With the breach opened, the enemy horde burst through and stormed the summit.[12]

Tran Do recounted that their artillery did not support them in the close attack for which they had to rely on small arms, but even then:

...our two machine-guns had been put into position when the enemy artillery sited them. The gunners were killed and the guns buried under clods of earth.[13]

Legionnaires at the base of Dominique had been giving essential supporting fire with their 120mm mortars in the face of heavy Vietminh artillery barrages. With open gun-pits, it was highly risky and, inevitably, amidst the deluge there was a direct hit, not just on the gun. The ammunition dump of 5,000 mortar rounds blew up. Twelve gunners were immediately killed with three others severely wounded, nearly half of the thirty-six-man battery crew. Only two mortars out of six were left functioning. Given that the floor space needed by a mortar was very small, unlike an artillery piece with a big trail, it seems remarkable that the gun-pits were not of a silo form and spread out and that the ammunition dump was not more distant. It smacks of poor organisation and complacent leadership.

As if fate had not been unkind enough to command posts, Lieutenant-Colonel Gaucher, commander of the 3rd Legion battalion whose post was located at Claudine, was killed by a shell that ripped off his arms and opened his chest. He asked for a drink and miraculously lived long enough to receive the last rites. His staff officers were also killed. This tragedy happened while Gaucher was planning the relief of beleaguered troops on Beatrice. Responsibility for planning and executing the counter-attack fell on Colonel Langlais. Langlais and his staff were meeting to discuss a counter-attack to relieve the bastion when their dug-out was collapsed by a near miss, and a dud that luckily failed to explode. While not injured the officers had to dig themselves out and precious time was lost as well as communications. By the time the planning was done, Vietminh troops had infiltrated into strong positions interposed between the base area and Beatrice.

This striking of two key command posts was probably just bad luck, though Vietminh reconnaissance infiltrators had located the highest priority targets by the number of radio masts emanating from the top of bunkers.[14]

Adding to the mayhem, a spectacular explosion lit the valley when the main napalm and aviation fuel dump received a direct hit.

Due to the complacency and lack of foresight by de Castries, as well as the lucky hits on the French command posts, no effective counter-attack was launched until it was too late. In the early hours of the 14th, when French paratroopers of the 1st BEP Parachute Battalion tried to advance to Beatrice's relief, they were stopped by heavy fire from dug-in Vietminh infiltrators who had been in places undiscovered since some time prior to the attack. A shocked de Castries, meanwhile, sat in his bunker and waited for news.

It was also hell to be a legionnaire on the receiving end of mass artillery attacks, the like of which had not been experienced by most of them, excepting those German veterans of the Eastern Front in the Second World War. One of those Eastern Front veterans, Sergeant Bleyer, found himself 'confronting the Viets and greeting them with shots from my Colt pistol. A grenade exploded between my legs.' He escaped. There was a lull toward the end as the last legionnaires rearranged their defences in front of the wire where hundreds of Vietminh hung motionless in contorted shapes or in bits and pieces. Then the human wave of attackers poured through to overwhelm the exhausted remnants. The last legionnaires' radio operator even called down artillery fire on his own position when the situation became hopeless. A bo doi infantryman:

> *…crept through the barbed wire, leapt up forwards then dived to the ground. He threw a hand grenade and machine-gunned a blockhouse. Weaving over the uneven ground to maintain cover to avoid the enemy fire, he crawled closer then hoisted the Vietminh flag, followed by his men.*[15]

Bedraggled survivors consisting mainly of a reduced company of Algerian riflemen came down from the hill in the early morning.

Even as the French were being forced off the mountain on the 14th, Pham and eighty Vietminh comrades were being ordered onto it to recover the ammunition that the French had left in their bunkers. It was still a very dangerous job, as the French were still shelling. After walking 4km, they had to pick their way through 200m of barbed wire, minefields and the detritus of war even as the fighting was still going on and with shells falling around them. On reaching the captured enemy munitions bunker, Pham's team formed a human chain down the mountain to pass out the captured 75mm shells one by one.[16] As they started the work:

> *French fighters dropped down from the sky to attack the hill. They swooped over the minefield like gigantic birds as they emptied their machine-guns. Three de-mining personnel were hit.*[17]

With the double danger from the air and French artillery the recovery crew worked with extra vigour. 'Hurry up, get on with it, pass more quickly,' were the cries that went down the line. Also passing down the line were the bodies of two comrades wrapped in parachutes.[18]

In total, Pham's team took 200 75mm shells from the mountain. These were 200 shells that would have required about 100 bicycle trips, using 100 men (at two shells per bicycle) for the 450km from the Chinese border. The feeding of these men would have required yet more bicycle trips to carry the rice.

The happy excitement before the battle was quickly wearing thin in the face of war's harsh reality, 'since the start of the battle', lamented Pham:

> *I have not stopped losing friends. During the operation on hill 6 a delayed action bomb killed two of them. We had made the journey together from the Yunnan training camps. It was the first time that I saw a friend killed in front of me…I decided to stop crying. I did not have enough tears; it took too much energy. That is war.*[19]

The routines of life had to continue, and Pham had quickly become hardened to the cold realities. 'In battle there is no choice, nor the right to hesitate, each action becomes a question of life and death.' And people had to eat and sleep. The hierarchies of life take over. Meals consisted of 'vegetables, a little boiled buffalo meat, salt, pepper and sticky rice.'[20]

Others becoming hardened on the French side included the indomitable Dr Grauwin in the central medical facility: 'The square hole was full of dead; outside...there were a hundred corpses, pell-mell thrown on stretchers or onto the ground, stiffened in grotesque tragic positions.'[21]

From the 13th Demi Brigade holding Beatrice, only two junior officers and 111 men came off the mountain. One hundred and twenty-five were killed and the rest captured and wounded to varying degrees. Following a truce, some of the more seriously wounded were returned, a cynical policy because it caused many problems for the garrison. However, it gave them a chance to live because there were virtually no medical facilities on the Vietminh side.

Aftershock

Maurice Dejean, commissaire general in Indochina, post-mortem report, 28 July 1954:

> *On the morning of the 15th after the loss of the north-eastern outworks (Beatrice) it was clear that the battle* as conceived and desired *was lost. The airport was under direct force of the enemy artillery. which was at least as powerful as ours, in underground bunkers cut into the hills, difficult to find and practically escaped our cannon and aircraft. Our bunkers did not stand up well to 105mm shells. Trenches dug at night right up to our wire reduced considerably the value of the defenses.* (Author's emphasis)

There is too much hindsight in this analysis, but the fall of Beatrice radically changed the odds.

The Vietminh suffered heavily for their human wave attacks over the last 150m of their advance, against fixed positions, machine-guns manned by crack troops and with pre-set artillery zeroed-in on the approaches. Bad luck in the loss of command and control functions as well as the dependence on just one radio after the others had been destroyed crucially led to a lack of co-ordination in defence and, more importantly, to a less than optimum artillery response.

The loss of Beatrice was a shock defeat for the French command. This was also a triple shock because suddenly de Castries realised that the Vietminh firepower consisted of significant numbers of 105mm heavy artillery and was seemingly well provided with ammunition and even more significantly was invulnerable to counter-battery-fire from superior French gunnery, including their battery of 155mm cannons. To add further gloom, the high command was awakened to the newly unveiled reality of high-powered 37mm AA guns that could track the pre-ordained flight movements of the cargo fleet. The Vietminh also outnumbered him five or six to one with five divisions, contrary to assumptions that only two could be sustained logistically. Cogny and Navarre had always predicated the strategy on absolute artillery dominance. The mood in Hanoi headquarters was more than glum, and it would soon be added to by the closing of the airstrip to all flights except emergency Medivac planes due to the close range of Vietminh artillery fire. From the heights of Beatrice, the Vietminh had a view in plain sight of significant parts of the air field and encampment area.

Even from 11 March, the use of the airstrip had become precarious. Many planes were destroyed on the ground. However, negotiations with the Vietminh permitted Red Cross flights to resume for a while, but suspicions (correct ones) as to the French inbound use of the flights, i.e. to bring in ammunition and supplies, meant that this privilege was soon stopped. It would have been clear to Giáp that a build-up of useless mouths at Dien Bien Phu and appalling conditions for wounded men would reduce morale as well as increase de Castries' logistical difficulties. A cruel but normal tactic in siege warfare that has been used since time immemorial.

The ending of these unhindered Red Cross flights coincided with the launching of the main battle by Giáp on 13 March. Up to this point, Giáp's soft policy approach had been about making sure that the French were not encouraged to retreat. Giáp did not want the French to break out and retreat to Lao. Miraculously some flights continued to come in. Casualties were flown to the French base at Muong Sai just thirty minutes away in Lao.

On 14 March, a Beaver light aircraft took out six people, including de Castries' pretty secretary.

Next, the high command had to try to evacuate the nine Bearcat fighters before they were destroyed, and their crews stranded. In any case, the fuel dump had been destroyed. Three of the stubby fat-looking little aircraft managed to take off before the inevitable barrage, guided now with accurate observation, came crashing down to obliterate the other six, whose shattered carcasses were left burnt and smouldering – more victims of the greatest artillery ambush in history. Quick-reaction close-support air cover was now a thing of the past. Fighter bombers from Hanoi or Haiphong air fields and the aircraft carrier *Arromanches* would have to make a 600km round trip or more. They now had to look for targets of opportunity as they arrived, rather than being integrated into a coherent offensive or fast reaction tactical structure.

The airport control tower (still visible from the top of Beatrice today) was knocked down with the first shots. This meant that supplies and reinforcements would mostly have to be parachuted in and the wounded could not be evacuated. In a war of attrition, this was a deadly blow because parachute-drop supply was less effective and supplies would need to be dropped to support those 'useless mouths' of increasing numbers of wounded. Nor could exhausted troops be rotated.

Additionally, Beatrice had a commanding view of the whole valley and all the other adjacent defensive bastions. Dominique could now be put under pinpoint fire at close range. AA guns (small calibre 20mm) were drawn in nearer.

The fall of Gabrielle (Dôc Lâp)

Giáp was ruthlessly logical in the way that he approached the reduction of the French porcupine. In accordance with the tactical plan, Gabrielle had to be attacked as the second priority because it was the other key to keeping the airstrip closed. It also allowed the Vietminh the chance to considerably reduce the drop-zone territory (DZ) occupied by the French so aiding the process of strangulation by close siege. There were no defences between Gabrielle and the northern end of the airstrip just a few kilometres away, so its capture would mean that Vietminh 75mm artillery and heavy mortars could be brought up on the secret artillery road that came down from the mountains and cut about 500m to the south of Gabrielle. Vietminh artillery would be able to fire on the runway and the central French encampment over open sights with no danger of being attacked in their rear.

Gabrielle is a significant hill rising about 50–60m above the plain to the north of the valley. It was a long thin mound running north to south some 170m long, defended by double layers of barbed wire and connected trenches between the defence positions. The defensive positions were well built and protected by iron-wood logs, with a complement of 877 Algerians and still including a good sprinkling of Second World War veterans. Sited on the reverse central west side of the bastion, the command centre could deploy a reserve of forty men as well as mortar and flame-throwers platoons. Gabrielle, like Beatrice, was a sentinel mini-fortress isolated from close support by other French bastions except Anne-Marie which, from 1km to the south-west, would be able to provide a modicum of support. But this was only really relevant if the Vietminh attacked from that quadrant, which they did not.

The most crucial support would be from pre-arranged artillery fire from the central French 155mm and 105mm batteries that could zero in on the lines of approach to Gabrielle. Unfortunately for the French, the small size of their force in comparison to the area that needed to be defended was immediately exposed by the inability to extend the defences to defend low hills both to the west and east of Gabrielle. There was open paddy all around, but nearby low hills to the east and west would provide fire support positions and covered approach for the Vietminh's attack forces.

When the attack came according to an Algerian officer, 'They came down the hills 604 and 702 like termites.' The opening Vietminh artillery barrage was a 'damned deluge'. To the west, the dominating height was 800m away and a hill to the east just 500m. This geographical factor allowed the Vietminh to martial their forces in secret in the shadow of neighbouring hills for a two-pronged attack on the key bastion. Nguyễn Manh Quan, commander of the 308th, recounted:

> *...during the night of 14 March, when we opened fire, the enemy riposte was violent but relatively ineffectual. By the time the French succeeded in organising their firepower, we were already close to the enemy positions.*[22]

This seems to have demonstrated again a problem with the command and control of the French batteries. Nevertheless, as the mass attacks went in, Vietminh units were destroyed by a combination of artillery- and mortar-fire that rained down on the attackers, as well as the staccato blizzard from heavy machine-guns.

On the night of the attack, 'we approached in silence towards the launch positions...the least noise could be fatal. If the enemy discovered us their fire would rain down on us.'[23] Before the attack, the French position suffered the same deluge of heavy artillery fire as Beatrice. Suddenly, the hillsides lit up with yellow flashes and the sky was set alight by streaks of tracer. Huge bursts of exploding yellow lit up the hillsides of Gabrielle. The French radio command post was blasted and destroyed along with its occupants.

'My recoilless cannon [bazooka] spewed out shells until the barrel glowed red,' recalled a Vietminh gunner. 'I was the number one aimer of the team and I occupied myself with sighting. In the dark I could not see so I just aimed at the gun flashes of the enemy.'[24]

As a cannon operator serving behind the front-line wave of Vietminh infantry, he was lucky to survive. Most of his division's front-line infantry were killed or wounded.

The attack was made by two elite regiments from the 308th (88th) and 312th Division (165th), which drove in from the north-east and south-east after the Vietminh artillery barrage, which had begun at 6 p.m. on the 14th and was lifted at 7.45 p.m. When waves of Vietminh troops rushed in there were still enough Algerians left to eviscerate them with machine-guns, hand grenades and flame-throwers. From the base area four-quad heavy machine-guns (four-barrel machine-guns) drenched the south-eastern approaches of Gabrielle with tracer fire. Particularly effective was the air burst cannon-fire directed at the Vietminh second wave assembly areas, which severely disrupted the second assault and probably saved Gabrielle from being swamped. As a result, after six hours of constant fighting, the Vietminh attack slackened. However, the French 81mm mortar platoon had been destroyed.

The 308th Division was away in Lao when the rest of the army was withdrawn for training and indoctrination in the new tactics of siege warfare, which had been applied so successfully at Beatrice. Moreover, the 308th were late in taking up their positions around Gabrielle. They were also exhausted and somewhat depleted by casualties and sickness after their extended jungle trek. It was noted before the attack:

> *The enemy were more vigilant after their first defeat. When we returned from Lao we were exhausted, our numbers reduced and disorganised but despite that we were enthusiastic for our offensive mission against Dôc Lâp* [Gabrielle]*...we were agreed on tactics; to attack the enemy at points which were unattended.*[25]

Despite this, they made a human wave-style of attack that was learnt from the Chinese. Vietminh soldiers advanced and were mown down on the wire with many of the leading pioneer elements unable to explode their TNT-filled bamboo Bangalores. Like a wave breaking over a sea wall, some did get through and the massed barrage had an effect too in helping to open gaps in the French wire defences, as well as knocking out strongpoints. Nevertheless, there appears to have been less close-quarter and hand-to-hand fighting on Gabrielle compared to Beatrice.

Heavy losses were also reported by another regiment of the 312th, who arrived at the end but still suffered 100 dead, not to mention the wounded. French sources also noted the heavy casualties inflicted on the Vietminh as well as the human wave tactics that overpowered them. 'For every ten that fell... another fifty kept on coming. Viets have reached our wire, Viets are pouring through the wire, Viets within our positions.' When the second wave came, the Vietminh adjusted tactics to emphasise small group actions and infiltration. This was effective against a defensive system that was now broken, patchy, depleted in reserves, and suffering communication problems. After two attacks, the Vietminh were established in the northern half of Gabrielle's bastion.

Colonel Langlais, replacing the dead Gaucher as de Castries' deputy, soon realised that a relief attack and reinforcement was needed. The legion-led force that was assembled would be guided across the open ground from the main base by three tanks. The latter would be useful in overcoming the Vietminh infiltrators, who were expected to try to block the reinforcement column between the base area and Gabrielle to the north. A particular choke-point was the village of Ben Khé Phai, which guarded the approach to the west side of Gabrielle. It had been strongly entrenched by the Vietminh and heavy fighting was needed to clear it. Only two companies of one BEP (Foreign Legion parachutists) were deployed for the attack because the accompanying unit, a Vietnamese parachute battalion, which had dropped just the previous evening, was late in arriving. The tanks provided an essential role in the attack, which could not have been made without them. After taking Ben Kai Phai village they were a mere 600m from Gabrielle.

However, the wounded in the command headquarters mistranslated the message as to the relief force. Half picking up a signal that seemed to suggest that the French force coming towards Gabrielle was just to 'retrieve', not 'relieve' and 'reinforce' the survivors, the Algerian remnants were led down the hill, just as they were about to be reinforced by the crack legionnaire paratroopers. The situation was not irretrievable but when the 1st Barowan Vietnamese paratroopers went to ground and retreated, it spelled the end for Gabrielle. The Vietnamese paratroopers' advance had started badly. A Vietminh soldier, Kieu, described how:

> *...a Jeep at the start of the column exploded and the occupants were tossed into the air. Others fled towards Muong Thanh to seek refuge by the air field. As they got out onto the runway, we fired our cannon at them. They fell pell mell one on top of the other.*[26]

The previous day the green Vietnamese paratroopers had had to march 10km from their drop-zone to the positions around Éliane and had spent most of the night digging-in. Then they were ordered from the far side of the battlefield to launch an early morning attack on the opposite end of the laager. Nonetheless, against a storm of advice Langlais had decided to deploy this unit in the most crucial battle of the campaign. It was a grievous error. He was perhaps worn down by sleeplessness and general exhaustion. Having been put in operational command of the camp the day before, he was still finding his feet.

Diversionary attacks made by Giáp on the Dominique bastions had distracted Langlais from pulling over his crack troops to Gabrielle.

Demoralised, the French-led Vietnamese paratroopers would not advance to the counter-attack, fell back and even fled. They could not be induced to attack any further in the face of concentrated artillery fire directed from the heights to the east. Miscommunication and poor command decisions had led to a debilitating reverse.

French troops coming off Gabrielle talked of walking on a carpet of Vietminh dead with dozens also hanging on the wire. On the Vietminh side, when Dinh Van Dinh, a member of the operational instruction team, returned to base after the battle he found the battalion chief in tears, 'Hardly anyone has returned for his rice ration,' he cried.[27] Le Pham Pong admitted that of his company of 100, two thirds were dead.[28]

Further ahead but lacking in numbers the relief force legionnaires could only watch as the Algerians abandoned Gabrielle. Of the Algerians and legionnaires on Gabrielle, just 114 escaped out of 877. Of the balance, 540 were dead or missing and 220 captured.

Transfixed with shock, de Castries withdrew into an aloof cocoon inside his bunker. Colonel Langlais would take over as effective garrison commander. Another of the mentally shell-shocked was artillery commander Colonel Piroth, who went around muttering to himself, apologising to all and sundry. He was put under the chaplain's pastoral watch.

Gabrielle's loss was a second devastating blow to French morale in two days. In Hanoi, a sense of doom took hold and General Cogny began to distance himself from the project and from Navarre, referring to it as a 'gamble'. He privately briefed Paris-based journalists against Navarre. It was not long, of course, before the well-connected Navarre was being informed of the exact words of his sly subordinate.

Vietminh gunners, including Pham, were well aware of the reasons for their victory:

> *...they* [the French] *found themselves at the bottom of a plain while our artillery over looked them from the mountains...this gave us the advantage that we needed because their artillery was more powerful than ours.*[29]

This was the plain truth. The Vietminh had weaker artillery because their communication/observation systems were weak and their ammunition stocks were much lower. But these points were compensated by positional advantages including their hidden gun encasements. By contrast and by necessity, the French guns were placed in wide circular open gun pits, with only sandbags for blast protection. On the evening of the victory, the Vietminh gunners in Pham's unit were feted. They partied:

> *The singing troupe were invited to spend the evening at the command post; there was even some sugar and tobacco available with the meal; poems were read and songs sung together with Madam Minh and Madam Ty, who made admiring and flattering comments about our cannons and shells.*[30]

After the great victories, many officers and some in the party leadership pressed for resumption of the offensive to keep up the pressure and wipe out the French altogether in an overwhelming attack. Giáp, however, knew that it was not over and that complacency could become the greatest enemy:

> *...as some comrades, unaware of the actual situation and the forces involved, show subjectivity and underestimate our adversaries, from which comes a weakening of our combat organisation that can easily lead to defeat.*[31]

Dang Quan Thuy, sergeant-major in the operations department, explained the tactical concepts used in the destruction of Beatrice and Gabrielle:

> *You have to make several complementary attacks to destroy the chain of the enemy defences...in other words, it is necessary to apply simultaneously three attacking principles: attack from the exterior to the interior, penetrate deeply and suppress the artillery fire of the enemy. When the offensive is launched prevent reinforcement coming from neighbouring positions.*[32]

These were exactly the tactics executed by the VPA and the reason for their success.

In de Castries' bunker there was no jollity, but a deep gloom as realisation slowly sank in that the FEC at Dien Bien Phu was facing defeat and humiliating surrender. Barely suppressed panic buzzed to and fro over the radio links to Hanoi and to Saigon and from Saigon to Paris. Smouldering munition dumps, mangled guns and dead gunners in the inadequate and open gun-pits were testament to the catastrophe now staring them in the face.

The Vietnamese paratrooper battalion who fled or refused battle were purged of 130 troops. Expelled by Captain Botella, in due course they would fight well and the miscreants were re-admitted to their unit where they would 'die well', according to their commander.

The mood was also dire in the Saigon and Hanoi commands. There was already a toxic relationship between General Cogny in Hanoi and Navarre in Saigon as each manoeuvred to shift the blame for the coming disaster. In a letter of 21 March to Marshal Juin in Paris, Navarre understated the morale problem, saying:

> *There was a certain drop in morale due to the surprise of finding themselves facing much worse conditions than they expected. The command echelons had been too confident.*[33]

This was a sly way of making an accusation of complacency against those under his own command, from the man who had claimed that 'victory is certain'.

The pause in the battle was due to exhaustion. Both sides needed to replenish artillery shells, both needed reinforcement and rest for their units. The French needed to drop in some replacement 105mm artillery, but the eight destroyed heavy mortars were never replaced. Navarre also needed to replace various senior fallen officers as well de Castries' chief-of-staff, who had suffered a nervous breakdown, and Colonel Piroth seemed likely to go the same way.

Both sides started digging. Thousands of Vietminh began worming their way towards the next bastions in line of sight at Anne-Marie at Huguette. A French prisoner observed that 'so many men were used that a considerable distance was accomplished in one night.'[34] The tendrils grew as rapidly and remorselessly as a rampant cancer. Their ominous progress was tracked regularly by aerial photography. For his part, Langlais was also busy organising PIMs to build new defensive positions on the north and south of the west bank of the Nam

Youm. Junon was established in the south-east area of the camp, and a quad position called Sparrowhawk was constructed on the west side to protect the rear areas of the five hills and the bridge crossing the Nam Youm River.

Anne-Marie

After the fall of Gabrielle, the Vietminh turned their full attention on the Anne-Marie bastion, which was defended by T'ai tribal units. Undermined by enemy propaganda, morale collapsed after the sudden fall of Gabrielle. Most of the garrison deserted on 18 March, leaving the airstrip even more exposed and reducing the French area of control to the inner core of the Huguette and Claudine. Over 200 of the T'ai soldiers deserted their posts at Anne-Marie 1 and 2. Their officers and NCOs retreated back to a rump at Anne-Marie 3, which was incorporated as an outpost of Huguette. These fighters were excellent soldiers but only in their own environment, the jungle and mountains. Siege warfare was not for them. After the battle, Pierre Langlais noted:

> *Yet they did not join the Vietminh...Some even asked their lower European cadres for permission to leave...If they heartily detest the Vietnamese in general and the Vietminh in particular the sense of nation is alien to them: their land is their village. Now, the Thai of the BT3 originate for the most part from the region of Sonla and Moc Chau...this earth of Dien Bien Phu is not theirs. In addition, the type of war which took place since March 13 is not the one they are used to...So the Thai left.*[35]

Given that their unsuitability was well-known to the French high command, why were they there? Why not replaced already?

When de Castries' chief-of-staff was flown out following a nervous breakdown, Colonel de Castries summoned Colonel Langlais and offered him the job. 'You shall take overall command!' This decision was confirmed in due course.

'Yes, my general.' Consequently from this moment, there were two sector commanders. At Isabelle there was Lallande. De Castries informed Hanoi of his decision.

Piroth had promised that any Vietminh heavy guns would be silenced by his counter-battery-fire, just as he had done at Ná Sán. He had more than enough guns to deal with the Vietminh, he boasted. A naturally cheerful man, a man of old school honour, he exclaimed on 14 March: 'I have been dishonoured.' He knew that the battle was lost and said so. After a tongue-lashing from Colonel Langlais over the poor handling of artillery on 15 March, he retired to his bunker and blew himself up with a hand grenade held to his head. Being one-armed, he could not cock a pistol.

Contrary to international law, his replacement was flown in on a medical evacuation flight.

Pause and replenishment

Giáp did not continue his attack because he had run out of ammunition. Stocks of shells for all calibres had been almost completely exhausted with nearly 15,000 expended from a stock of 16,000. It would take some weeks to make good the deficit. He was also running out of veteran troops. Reserves were increased to 25,000 and pulled in from all around the country after the initial 9,000 reservists had been used up. Raw recruits from regional units with little or no experience.

One of the great myths of the Dien Bien Phu siege relates to Vietminh artillery preponderance: the excellent study on arms and ammunition stocks/usage done by Boylan and Olivier in *Valley of the Shadow*. The siege of Dien Bien Phu puts this thesis to rest.[36] In all, there was rough parity in heavy weapons with both sides deploying twenty-four each of 105mm cannon. However, the French had four powerful 155mm guns firing shells with three times more explosive power than a 105mm shell. The Vietminh were overmatched in the 75mm weapon by twenty-four to ten. Heavy mortars 100mm–120mm were at thirty-two Vietminh against twenty-seven French. In light mortars there was rough equivalence, and in medium-sized pieces the Vietminh, at 162, deployed twice as many as the French. However, this does not tell the full story because firepower has to be measured by the amount of ammunition available. Firepower is a matrix of the number of guns, the available shells, the accuracy of delivery and the rate of fire. The French used 103,000 shells in the campaign, of which 70,000 were for 105mm guns, compared to an estimated 20,000 105mm shells for the Vietminh guns.[37] Boylan and Olivier point out that as many as forty percent of Vietminh ammunition were duds because of their age. In a major re-assessment, these figures suggest that firepower available to the French was about four to five times that of the Vietminh. Moreover, the French cannon at Isabelle could fire with little counter-battery challenge because of the Vietminh ammunition shortage. Their flanking fire against the threat to Éliane 2 was decisive in holding this vital position throughout the battle.

After Gabrielle, the French discovered that their rate of fire was double what was planned. Stocks of shells needed to be urgently replenished and this caused delays to reinforcement by two paratrooper battalions because shell-resupply had to take precedence. There was not enough transport to do both. This was because artillery shelling was the most effective weapon of defence accounting for sixty percent of battle casualties in modern war, including the First World War.[38] Although this number does not seem to have been calculated, the conditions of trench warfare were similar to the First World War and the increased effectiveness of projectiles, particularly finely calibrated air-burst ammunition with proximity fuses probably led to casualties from shelling at least as high as the First World War example, and possibly much greater.

However, the Vietminh had some advantages in the exchange. Their heavy gun positions were hidden and therefore virtually impervious to counter-battery-fire or even air attack. Air sorties, mainly by fighter bombers totalled 1,048 from 6 to 30 April, but only twenty percent were directed against counter-battery work. In May, counter-battery airstrikes accounted for just forty out of 333 strikes. Priorities were focused on the matrix of priority and effectiveness, which meant direct infantry support and flak suppression. It was not easy to hide flak positions because they needed a 360-degree sweep for their guns.

French positions were in a tight target-rich space and the guns could not be moved or hidden. Moreover, sandbag emplacements were highly inadequate to protect the guns or the gunners because of the long trails that needed to be manoeuvred around 360 degrees to cover the entire perimeter at any point of attack. By the nature of the weapon in the context of the French positions, 105mm cannon could not be hidden in one-directional hillside caverns. This meant that the gun-pits were large and relatively easy to hit. Gunner losses were high. Replacements had to be regularly parachuted in.

Trench warfare 16–17 March

By the start of the Battle of Dien Bien Phu, a trench-line of circumvallation some 30km long had been thrown around the French bastions and several new military roads had been constructed to give supply access to the north end of the battlefield. With the fall of the outer bastions in the north, the main focus of Giáp's campaign was to draw the trench system tighter to the French lines as if to strangle the life out of the FEC. Eventually, there were 100km of trenches, in a Kandinsky-like confusion, wriggling and zig-zagging in seemingly random configurations across the plain. Digging was a form of attack and less costly than human waves. After the immense losses at Gabrielle and Beatrice, Giáp needed to rest his crack divisions and bring them up to strength with replacements who needed training. He had to draw on other units from all over Vietnam and this took time. It was estimated that Giáp eventually deployed sixty percent of his armed forces at Dien Bien Phu. This compared to four percent of forces deployed by the French at Dien Bien Phu (but seventy percent of elite paratrooper forces). The core fighting power of Giáp's elite veterans was heavily diluted through the battle. This probably accounts for morale problems that emerged as well as the reduced performance of Vietminh units, which led to the slowdown in progress over the fifty-four days following the fall of Beatrice and Gabrielle.

Once they had been captured, the way was open to the Vietminh to infiltrate around Anne-Marie and Huguette and to close-in on the central defensive areas around the northern end of the airstrip. However, the losses inflicted were so severe that new tactics were adopted that involved siege-type zig-zag sap approaches and trenching screened by rolling rope buffers to absorb bullets. Assaults would be increasingly made from close-range in short rushes rather than in large-unit formation. In essence, there was no difference to the approach works used by besiegers from early modern times. Captain Lucciani (1st BEP, YouTube interview) compared it to the First World War with trenches, barbed wire, machine-guns, grenades and heavy shelling. But for the French it was far worse than the First World War when units would be relieved after a few days in the front trenches. As there was no rear area to go to at Dien Bien Phu, there could be no rotation of units in the line, no hot food in the later stages, and no comfortable hospitals in case of being wounded. It was 'hell in a small place.'[39]

The end game in the battle was long and bloody. It did not finish until 8 May. However, the French had, without outside help, become the probable losers of the battle on 13 to 15 March, just two days after it had started. But like a tiresome opponent in a losing position in chess, the French ran down every piece, pawn by pawn, exchange by exchange, desperately hoping for something to turn up: a mistake, a stalemate, a miracle. In desperation, Generals Navarre and Cogny threw in their elite paratroopers under Colonel Bigeard.

Taking part in these battles for the air field in the north was gunner Dang Hung Manh of the 308th Division:

> *Once the battle commenced, we lived permanently in the trenches. These works were so complicated and the area over which they were built so immense that it was important to take note of the sign posts to stop getting totally lost.*

The rainy season had not yet fully started, but early rain storms were beginning to arrive. Dang noted: 'When it rained the bottom of the trench became a swamp with the consistency of a bowl of rice congee [thick rice soup].'[40] These appalling living conditions would last for the duration of the campaign and become much worse as the monsoon and the campaign developed. The rice crop was flowering and ripe for harvest. Having been abandoned by the villagers the Vietminh left their trenches at night to collect it. Luckily, Dang came from a peasant family and was familiar with the work and its processes. Other off-duty hours were spent rooting for manioc in the forests and hunting down pigs that had been left to run wild. By contrast, Legionnaire Issert recalled: 'After 13 March, the great attack, there was no rest…'[41]

The AA battle

Meanwhile, the French Air Force, particularly from 17 March, became very active in observation and attack. Positions where the French believed the anti-aircraft batteries to be located were repeatedly bombed. Later in the afternoon of the 17th, the fighters were joined by B24 and B26 bombers. 'The anti-aircraft guns answered back and the barrels glowed red, while the leaves over the camouflage netting began to burn like torches.'[42] Tran Quoc Chan, anti-aircraft platoon leader, 351 Division, remembered: 'Suddenly, two Hellcats whizzed through a gap in the mountains and dropped two bombs on the first platoon. The whole command post was buried in earth.' Chan extricated himself, but several, including the company commander, his adjutant and numbers of soldiers, were killed. The political commissar survived with seven others, but in a profound state of shock. Chan took over the two remaining guns as provisional company head.

Tran Quoc Chan and the AA batteries were subject to intensive attacks during the lull in fighting from 17 to 19 March. They were highly vulnerable, necessarily being in open 360-degree gun-pits with wide vision (in essence the same problem faced by the French heavy gunners). As Tran Quoc Chan indicated, they suffered heavily from direct hits and cluster bombs that riddled the gun teams so badly that untrained auxiliary troops had to be drafted in to cover the losses. Batteries 829th and 828th were crippled and 383rd suffered heavily. Five 12.7mm guns were destroyed at the light battery of the 818th. Twenty-four of the crucial heavy 37mm AA guns were put out of action but repaired. Most AA guns were withdrawn from the battle only to be redeployed after repair and crew-training at the start of the second offensive. Having done their job, only thirty-three out of 845 French combat missions from 16 to 31 March were for flak suppression.[43]

Actual losses of planes were significant but relatively small given the extent of the campaign. Air power was constrained by the narrow flight corridors down which French military and transport aircraft transport were necessarily funnelled, although brave fighter-bomber pilots could surprise their targets by weaving unseen through the knot of hills in front of which the AA batteries were placed. While 158 aircraft were damaged, only fourteen were shot down, of which six were fighters/dive bombers in close support, and just five cargo aircraft. Twenty-one crewmen were killed and fifty-five missing, which means they either died, were murdered after bailing out, or succumbed in prison camps.[44] However, the effect of the AA was to make it necessary to drop at night, which meant higher losses of supply drops.

Bigeard has landed

Colonel Bigeard landed at Dien Bien Phu with much fanfare amongst the demoralised troops of the shrunken and defeated garrison. Not only did he bring with him his elite paratroopers of the 6th BEP, but also his personal aura of invincibility even amongst a host of commanders of reputation. There were many legends and charismatic colonels in the FEC as well as dashing leaders of the Group Mobile. But since his escapades on RC4 and miraculous escape from a suicide mission at Tu Le, his reputation had surpassed those of the other great characters of the war. If Bigeard comes we won't be overwhelmed here… Bruno [Bigeard's call sign] is not a type to let himself be locked up here.' was the typical feeling of relief and hope that greeted his arrival.[45]

Born to a lower-middle-class family, his start in life was inauspicious to say the least. After an undistinguished schooling he became a minor railway official like his father. When war broke out in Europe, he was conscripted into the ranks and was captured on the Maginot Line at the surrender, like so many others. From this point on there was a sort of inflection point on his dour, unremarkable existence, which was to lead to a life of adventure and fame.

Lionised by the popular right-wing press after Tu Le, he would become the talisman of resistance and hope for Dien Bien Phu's beleaguered garrison. A soldier's soldier, Bigeard's reputation at Dien Bien Phu stood above and contrasted with the bickering, backstabbing and exculpatory yapping of general staff officers and politicians.

Bigeard's fighting qualities were soon recognised. Langlais called him in after a few days and handed him responsibility for organising counter-attacks. Langlais would command at the centre, deploying reserves on request, while Bigeard organised the fighting on the spot from just behind the front line. Had this partnership been there at the beginning, Beatrice may well have been properly reinforced and the counter-attack at Gabrielle would not, for want of on-the-spot leadership, have descended into unco-ordinated catastrophe. Legionnaire Cledic described the new hands-on system of command that Langlais and Bigeard established once de Castries' incapacity was obvious:

> We were in permanent contact with the battalion but also with central command. It was always with Bigeard. We had direct permanent contact with Brechinac and Bigeard…and there was always on hand a communications artilleryman to regulate shell fire…we asked for precise pre-registered firing in advance against pre-set zones.[46]

The path to Isabelle

Isolated Isabelle, 6km to the south, with more than 1,000 legionnaires, Algerians, Moroccans and French paratroopers, had long been cut off by infiltration between the outlying bastion and the core of the camp. On 22 March, the French launched a battalion-level attack backed by tanks to clear the way, losing 150 dead in the process. However, the bastion was soon isolated again. Isabelle came under heavy attack, so much so that ammunition supplies ran down to near exhaustion. At this point a breakout was planned and defeated. Aerial maps of the time showed a tangle of trenches growing around the Isabelle porcupine. Its tendrils grew faster than Japanese knotweed, constricting then constricting again. All part of Giáp's tactical plan to squeeze the oxygen out of the French defences. As a bastion it served little strategic purpose and was largely ignored until near the end of the battle. Tactically, however, it still had a major role as a gun base to support the defence system around the main base area, and the five hills in particular.

Pham recorded the hard life of a fellow artilleryman who was less fortunate in his location on the battlefield because his gun position was in the open plain around Isabelle. It was an unhappy stage of his campaign. When their positions were marked by artillery smoke rounds for the French fighter bombers to swoop on them, one gun position was destroyed. Several friends died. To add to his misery, he had suffered a case of unrequited love when he once again fell for a member of a dance troupe in the back area but was too shy to express his feelings. It must have been a common problem for soldiers who had not had female company for five years. Possibly that was the best outcome because it is likely that she had already been snagged by a political commissar, as he would discover when he went to look her up after the war.

Political commissars were always at the back and out of the worst danger, hectoring, lecturing and spouting puerile communist propaganda while having the time and opportunity to groom the best girls from the dance troupes. After the fearsome toll on the troops their verbal drivel must have palled somewhat on the simple bo doi, and the sheer hypocrisy was no doubt a part of the morale problem that was to become so acute after the failure of the second offensive on 30 March. Nothing undermines morale more than the thought that management is having it soft while the grunts are being sacrificed. Constantly under battle pressure with comrades falling right and left, fatigue and cynicism began to creep into the souls of survivors.

The mood was more sombre now. Pham's sunny optimism evaporated. Many had died, and that was in the well protected artillery units. For the infantry, the battle so far had been a massacre. Most units entering a battle came out of it wrecked.

French fighter-bombers responded to the developing threat to Isabelle by swooping in and dropping napalm on the Vietminh positions, which had already been marked out in advance by smoke shells. This dreadful gel-like substance would burst in long flaming lines of death scorching everything in its path, burning up wooden fortifications and telephone lines. The napalm poured into any hole in its path. Several of Pham's comrades, whose covered foxholes lay in the path of the deadly molten flood, were instantly incinerated. In another bunker both radio operators were torched together.

French relief attacks sometimes cleared the way to Isabelle, but these operations only gave temporary relief and were so costly in lives and to such little lasting effect that they were abandoned. The Isabelle porcupine would be perfectly sealed in a web of Vietminh trenches, like a fly in a spider's web, waiting to be eaten.

Sniping around Isabelle mid-March 1954

The war of strangulation by trenching was especially severe for the isolated bastion at Isabelle. Although the Vietminh had decided to simply screen off this post, it did not mean quiet times for the garrison. Vietminh trenching wrapped itself like a python around the lonely bastion and its outposts. Constant pressure on the beleaguered French hemmed-in on all sides made sniping a greater problem and a terrible stress on nerves and morale. The French were in the more static positions, on the inner ring of the battle and less able to take the initiative in sniping. Giang Van Tue, aged just 20, from 304th Division, was a sniper tasked to the Isabelle front. True to Soviet military dogmas, sniping was a vital element in Vietminh military operations aimed at disrupting the enemy and reducing morale.

Normally, Giang and his fellow sniper team would seek out positions about 200m from the target area but from an oblique angle because this would trap more targets:

> *We used the interior of a banana tree trunk. The distance from the first out ring of barbed wire to our position was 40–50m...the least little bit of carelessness and everything would be ruined...well camouflaged, laden with rice balls, each member of the three-man team would find their hideout.*

Giang noted the regular movements of the garrison looking for weaknesses:

> *...the first outpost of the enemy that we chose was held by Africans and Europeans. They used to go looking for water in the Nam Youn River. We learnt their routine and we came to an agreed order of firing...On the first day they did not come but on the following day, the first day of the new moon, I saw four*

> *soldiers creeping down to the river. We fired together; three enemies fell to the ground.*
>
> *Giang was given another mission, which was to eliminate a machine-gun nest that comprised three weapons. After three nights of reconnaissance and observation they found suitable hides about 120m from the target.*

The Vietminh then showed their innate cunning, because they set a trap by arranging an artillery strike, so feigning an imminent attack. The machine-gunners emerged to man their weapons as predicted, 'two minutes later they were all dead.' However, it was not a risk-free occupation. Giang laments:

> *...on the same day Luc died. He was probably spotted. We found his body when we were pulling back...Over a one month period I shot nine of the enemy in total.*[47]

Bigeard's attack on the western front, 28 March

On 24 March, Bigeard was invited to de Castries' bunker. De Castries offered him a scotch then asked him to plan and lead an attack against the battery of .50 calibre anti-aircraft guns on the west side of the porcupine. Mounted on tripods they could launch a hail of heavy calibre bullets into the path of slow-moving Dakotas. Orders had come down from Hanoi where high command was increasingly concerned at the AA-fire against the Dakotas coming in to land to evacuate medevac casualties. De Castries promised him complete control of the operation and whatever resources he needed. Bigeard realised it was a desperate and dangerous gamble with a garrison that was already severely depleted. De Castries wished him luck and expressed his confidence in his abilities.

Huguette 5 would be the launchpad for the attack. Bigeard prepared carefully for a three-battalion attack with one battalion held in reserve. In all about 1,000 men in depleted units would take part. He would have heavy artillery support, a short barrage, then the attack. Three Chaffee tanks were also involved. They were to come up from Isabelle 5km to the south. They added considerably to counter-attacks and the squadron of twelve would be used extensively over the coming months.[48]

The attack was fast and furious and took the Vietminh entirely by surprise. One legionnaire described how he lost contact with his section but charged on ahead. Suddenly he confronted a Vietminh. They were both in momentary shock, but he recovered first and shot him. Moving on he threw a phosphorus grenade into a bunker with one of the AA guns. It was destroyed. In a daze still, he threw another phosphorus grenade into another bunker. There was a huge flash and explosion because it was a munitions magazine for the battery.

Berated by his officer for getting lost, the action soon started again and he found himself throwing more grenades and shooting down attacking Vietminh.

The success of the attack was in the balance but the tanks that had been delayed by enemy action between Isabelle and the Claudines suddenly appeared, spraying death and destruction into the ranks of the Vietminh and enfilading them along their trench-lines so sealing the success of the operation. Bigeard controlled the battle out in the open from the edge of the air field. In total the Vietminh lost around 400 dead, and seventeen AA guns were destroyed. It was a significant success and boost to morale.

Despite this minor victory, the grim reality changed little, not least because the large 37mm guns remained active. However, a great effort was made to supress them too with French fighter bombers launching repeated attacks. On account of heavy losses, Pham was by this time commanding a 37mm gun team. He described how on 15 April:

> A squadron of French planes headed straight for us. I counted 18 planes altogether – eighteen planes, eight hellcats, two b24s, 1 eight 1b26s … Nuhuan the no 1 batery commander was hit, no, killed! The sky was clear blue but the smell of sulphur from the cannons and bombs was suffocating. The sun was in our eyes. We were blinded. The fighter bombers took advantage of it and came at us from the direction of the sun. The gunners opened fire with their machine-guns…bombs, bullets, smoke, flames, earth and dust blew up into huge clouds that covered the whole battlefield. For five hours we fought. I counted nearly 300 bombs which had exploded around us.[49]

After the loss of a Dakota on 26 March, low-flying parachute-drops had been banned. Despite French efforts, the AA noose around Dien Bien Phu's logistical throat tightened yet more as the drop-zone shrank.

General Navarre launched complaints at Colonel Jean Louis Nicot, who had been charged with guaranteeing fifty supply flights a day into the encampment. However, the logistical underpinning of the French air-drop effort was just too weak, so the target was not nearly reached. Having had his advice ignored in the first place, Nicot faced carping criticism from Navarre. 'I think nevertheless that it is not working properly because after investigation it has been impossible to determine where the responsibilities lie.'[50]

Apart from the reduced flight numbers from the levels hoped for, there was the loss of parachuted supplies that fell behind the enemy lines. As much as ninety percent of medical supplies was being lost let alone the tons of ammunition for 105mm cannon, exactly the same calibre as the guns being used by the Vietminh. Shells were delivered to Giáp's doorstep instead of by a tortuous and dangerous 500km journey from the Chinese border. Many supply drops were faulty and sloppy logistics management infuriated the commanders at Dien Bien Phu. De Castries wrote bitterly:

> *The electric generator requested was poorly packed; arrived smashed and beyond repair. The gasoline parachuted in fully filled jerry cans burst on hitting the ground. Not enough gasoline to fill the tanks' reservoirs.*[51]

Pham's war and the monsoon

In the western hills, Pham and his comrades busied themselves with repositioning their guns for the next offensive against the western hill line of Dominique and the Élianes. The mood was more serious now. Hopes of a quick victory had evaporated. As if the risks of French planes and artillery were not enough, nature also had to have its share of the killing. Two close friends died when their truck bringing up munitions slid on the approach road and crashed into a ravine. Three more were killed when an enemy shell exploded at the mouth of their casement. Another friend was blown apart by an exploding enemy shell. A few days later two more friends were killed in a trucking accident, crushed under boxes of ammunition. For devastated infantry divisions such as the 308th or 312th, the atmosphere must have been heavier still. Reinforced by multitudes of young new recruits who were shuffled between the heavily depleted units, the survivors must have felt that their whole world had been destroyed. Pham chose to shut down his emotions and dedicate himself to the revolution.

Pham was moved for a while to the Gabrielle position, which looked down the runway. It was a fire support position for the attacks that were taking place around Huguette, but also for firing on the central French positions and the reverse side of the five hills. There were constant air attacks by French fighter bombers, with occasional cheers when a Bearcat was shot down. His diaries became generally more wooden and propagandistic. He repeats the somewhat exaggerated claims of the political commissars as to French casualties and Vietminh successes. Now a battery commander, he became serious. His unit suffered high casualties, even though as artillerymen they were in a much safer place. He had lost his youth and innocence.

Nonetheless, Pham breaks out occasionally into his more romantic and poetic nature, with a description of the simple pleasures of life at Gabrielle. He walked round to the other side of the hill one day and discovered a serene arcadia, hardly believing his eyes at the tranquillity and beauty of the mountain river that snaked toward the central French position. Here soldiers bathed and dozed under trees during the day.[52] His words match his romantic 'poetic realism' style of painting, evocative and influenced by impressionism. Towards dusk they roused themselves and trekked off once more into the maze of trenches, once more to kill the French or dig their saps ever nearer to the enemy. They burrowed at night around or under the barbed wire defences. Far more time was spent digging than shooting. Soldiers worked shifts of up to eighteen hours and could dig as much as 50m in one day. Covered in slime, they would repair to their riverside to wash, to sleep, to doze in the shade of trees, or to idle before starting over. 'We were sinking into the mud,' recalled Pham. Troops were so weary that 'they fell asleep as soon as they finished eating…black toes sticking out of rubber-soled sandals that they didn't have the strength to take off.'[53] Pham was struck by the charm of the scene and its Manichean contrast to the ghastly ritual of battle, night and day.

Vietminh dug-outs typically had a narrow opening. Behind it the 'living quarter' was covered in wood, on top of which was thrown mounds of earth. Wooden supports around the entrance gave way to assemblies of wood running crossways and acted as a buttress. Inside the living area was white silk parachute material that had been scavenged from the battlefield. It was festooned around the walls, which helped keep out the damp and gave the place a more homely feel. Whatever the circumstances, soldiers will try to claw at the essentials of life to create hearth and home even amidst the horror of war. With his delightful charcoal portraits, Pham the artist, diarist, humanist and battery commander, captured the lives of the bo doi in their simple humanity. Not so much the heroics of war but the humdrum struggle for camp-side normality.

Before the Battle for the Five Hills, Pham moved to his gun battery opposite D2 (Dominique 2) positioned at the top of the hill in a direct fire position facing the enemy. Less protected than in the previous battles, on 31 March Battery 4 suffered heavy casualties during the attack against Hill D when an enemy shell exploded at the opening of the shelter.[54]

From 15 March to 7 May, there was bloody and vicious fighting from bastion to bastion as the two sides fought an ugly war of attrition in conditions that became increasingly horrendous as the rainy season set in, turning the battlefield into a disgusting and squalid quagmire of filth, excrement, and human detritus. With latrines being too dangerous to visit many had to relieve themselves where they could. So the trenches became stinking cesspits. Added to this were blood, guts and body parts, from shells that churned and sprayed out the rotting flesh of old and new bodies in all directions. Rats and flies took over. The valley bottom took water from all directions. Except for the Nam Youm River, there was no place for it to drain off. 'From mid-April it rained a lot. The trenches were inundated. We were in the mud up to our knees,' noted Duong Van Liam.[55]

Genevieve flies in

Despite the raging battles and artillery shells that rained onto the runway, medivac flights continued both during the day and later on at night until the last flight on 28 March, which carried in the woman who would soon become an international legend to rival Florence Nightingale or Mary Seacoal: the angel of Dien Bien Phu. Helicopters and planes had by this time evacuated about 300 wounded, but they could not keep up with the numbers flowing into the central hospital and field stations. Wearing a bulletproof jacket, Lieutenant Genevieve de Galard, the French Air Force flight nurse, was on board one of the last Dakota flights in, but technical problems led to a delayed take-off, after which her plane was destroyed.

> *...fog protected the plane and rendered it invisible to the Vietminh. Alas it cleared around 10 a.m. and their artillery went into action. At 10.30 on the fourth Salvoe, our aircraft was hit. With emotion we watched the flames and smoke envelope it.*[56]

Genevieve de Galard-Terraube, the 26-year-old daughter of a patrician aristocrat and stalwart Catholic of the anciene regime, had flown into history.

Genevieve soon settled in to life in the encampment. She was surprised that life was not quite as bad as she had been led to believe:

> *I imagined it to be catastrophic. In fact, during those last days of March, one could still walk about the camp freely, though once in a while I heard a mortar explosion, so I scrupulously wore the helmet I was given.*[57]

She was graciously entertained. Nevertheless, there was fierce fighting raging just a few kilometres away at Huguette 6, where the enemy made a determined effort to isolate the legionnaire-held post by relentless trench-digging. Bigeard was in the process of mounting a relief counter-attack, and the wounded were coming in. They included Lieutenant Loulou Martin, twice wounded already and now suffering a wound that left him with a gaping hole for a mouth. He was one of the last to be evacuated by helicopter.

On 13 April, Genevieve dined with Colonel Langlais in his bunker. She also met Colonel de Castries, describing him briefly as:

> *...thin and pale...In truth Colonel de Castries did not want command of a defensive base, but General Navarre had assured him that it would be on the offensive.*[58]

She soon discovered that the Dien Bien Phu base was cut off from within. Upon applying to make a social call to her cousin, Louis de Chatenet, at Isabelle, she was informed that this was impossible because the route was blocked.

General Ely goes to Washington, 22 March 1954

After the fall of Gabrielle, the French high command in Paris panicked, and for good reason. General Ely was soon in Washington pleading for help. More guns, more planes, more money. But most of all, France needed direct US intervention. Realistically, in the urgent time-frame created by the debacle at Dien Bien Phu, this meant intervention by the US Air Force's 100-unit B29 fleet based in the Philippines and aircraft carrier units. The concept was named *Operation Vulture.*

Pictures of General Ely in Washington meeting with American leaders show a man grinning broadly and looking at President Eisenhower, who grins too. Admiral Radford, chief-of-staff of combined forces, a fervent interventionist, smiles broadly into the camera. Ely has reason to grin. In the opulence of the Oval Office, Eisenhower has just told him that he should not be glum about the situation in Indochina. Comparing it to the bad times of the Second World War he said, 'but we won in the end and we will win again.'

Admiral Radford had added, 'The French are going to win. It is a fight that is going to be finished with our help.'

But there were no specifics on what to do about the crisis at Dien Bien Phu, the urgent question in hand. Focus soon shifted to what concessions could be gained from France in return for support. Dulles, the hard-nosed lawyer, insisted that intervention, which he supported, should come at a price. There must be joint war-planning, joint training of the VNA and more positive moves to granting full independence and political commitments from Paris. So began the US takeover of the Vietnam War. Know-it-all 'scientific' Yanks and their money knew how to win a war. McNamara was not in office yet, but his spirit was.

General Ely was more interested in immediate help for Dien Bien Phu, which was at the centre of the crisis. His conversations in private with Radford focused on practical actions such as bombing from the Clark air base in the Philippines, or from the carriers located in the Gulf of Tonkin. Radford promised him strong support. For all his lawyerly negotiating, savvy Dulles was extremely positive for intervention.

The problem was the president. While Eisenhower strongly supported intervention, declaring at the NSC meeting on 25 March, 'The collapse of Indochina would produce a chain reaction which would result in the fall of South-East Asia to the communists,' he also showed his caution by tying the decision to the will of congress, who 'would have to be in on any move by the United States to intervene in Indochina.'[59] Eisenhower was truly out of his depth in understanding the interconnection between Dien Bien Phu and Geneva: that the loss of Dien Bien Phu would certainly mean the loss of Tonkin and probably the loss of Indochina. There was no time for finessed politics, arcane diplomacy, complex negotiations or conversations with congress. Only urgent military actions could save the situation. The fate of Indochina was indeed in Eisenhower's hands.

Elements on the right of American politics wanted isolationism and lower taxes, but they also wanted strong anti-communist actions. On the left there was a real reticence about propping up French colonial fantasies. Congress was equivocal on intervention and the numbers were finely balanced. Senators Lyndon Johnson and John F. Kennedy were among many sceptics. While Admiral Radford and Vice-President Nixon were hawkish and determined to support the French. Believing it to be a cheap and effective way of intervention, they faced opposition from the chief of the army, General Ridgeway, and the treasury secretary, who took a myopic view of the situation. Ridgeway claimed that the army was under-resourced, which meant it was incapable of intervention. He also believed that Indochina was not a vital US interest. The domino theory apparently did not interest him. Most of all, he feared Chinese intervention.

In addition to the B29 fleet, several US aircraft carriers were heading towards the coast of Vietnam. They packed a heavy punch and would be invaluable in the ground attacks and close-support role. Ready to strike on command, carriers *Essex* and *Boxer* would arrive in the Gulf of Tonkin on 11 April. Such an intervention could possibly have been decisive.

Massive carpet-bombing plus targeted bombing by the carrier's tactical aircraft in a densely populated, target-rich environment would be devastating to the Vietminh and would probably have turned the course of the battle. That was also the opinion of a US specialist who went on reconnaissance missions over the area. Massive losses and logistic disruption would be deadly for Giáp's plans and would likely force a withdrawal. Apart from the packed valleys with encampments full of troops behind Mount Fictive and at Huyen Tuan Giao, the crossroads and logistics/assembly base 76km to the east. The third plan was for a nuclear strike at the Vietminh key targets.

Rather than the fear of Soviet escalation, it was the concern about Chinese air attacks, something warned of by French intelligence, which provided more concern, as well as the general fright as to Chinese intervention with land forces that would create another Korea. Such points are also made by historians, but the reality is that Chinese air intervention would have been quickly eliminated by the vastly superior US carrier-borne fighter planes. As for direct land intervention, it would have taken months for the Chinese Army to mobilise and develop enough logistical capacity, as was shown in the Third Indochina War twenty years later.

Meanwhile, Dulles and Eisenhower tried to convince congress of the 'Vulture' option. Eisenhower did indeed refer to Dien Bien Phu when taking soundings from congress leaders on 29 March. 'Within the space of forty-eight hours,' he told them:

> *...it might be necessary to move into the Battle of Dien Bien Phu in order to keep it from going against us, and in that case I will be calling in the Democrats as well as the Republican leaders to inform them of the actions we're taking.*

Dulles took up the theme of the communist threat on a grander scale in a speech on the same day. But even as Dulles spoke, the ground was shifting and shaking beneath his feet.

In a speech in New York at the Overseas Press Club, also on 29 March, Dulles warned:

> *...if the communist forces won an uncontested control of Indochina or any substantial part thereof, they would surely resume the same pattern of aggression against other free peoples in the area.* (i.e. capitalist allies of the US)

For the benefit, no doubt, of the US business lobby, Dulles noted that South-East Asia:

> *...is the so-called 'rice bowl' which helps to feed the densely populated region that extends to India and Japan. It is rich in many raw materials, such as tin, oil, rubber, and iron ore.*

It was a worldwide threat playing to the republican right's phobia about Red China. He made sure to remind congress and the American people of Chinese arms, training and direction of the war effort in Indochina on Ho's behalf. The American press was convinced that the US were going to intervene directly, and soon.

For Dulles, his eyes were fixed on the prize of intervention and fighting alongside France's well established expeditionary force (FEC), in a coalition that recreated the one that had just fought the Chinese to a standstill in Korea. He actually had less interest in saving Dien Bien Phu *per se*. For Dulles, the result there was an irrelevance in the bigger picture. In this he was quite wrong. Surrender at Dien Bien Phu, and the Laniel-Bidault government would fall. France would exit the war entirely, most likely under the leadership of Pierre Mendes-France. Within twenty-four hours, Giáp launched his second great offensive, which came within an ace of capturing Éliane 2, a loss that would have doomed the FEC encampment in short order.

On 3 April, at the state department, there was a gathering of the most important house and senate leaders from both parties. Admiral Radford strongly backed the idea of intervention by giving a presentation on the hard facts of the situation in Indochina, with especial emphasis on the desperate situation at Dien Bien Phu. Dulles backed this up by pointing to the dire consequences of the fall of Dien Bien Phu and French defeat in Indochina: 'It was only a question of time before all of South-East Asia falls along with Indonesia.'[60] He pleaded further for support of the president to be free to 'use air and sea power in the area if he felt it necessary in the interest of national security.'

Despite strong support for intervention, Eisenhower felt constrained politically. His senate majority was just one and his house majority just seven. In an age when party loyalties and voting were more fluid, he could not rely on republican votes either, with senators such as Knowland of California being both isolationist and a vociferous opponent of French colonialism. The democrats also resisted intervention. They resented the fact that ninety percent of the Korean War had been fought and financed by Americans.

The decision for action, which was entirely in his gift, could have been made almost immediately. But Eisenhower was a political general, had only experienced action from 'on high' and had never experienced close combat or the need for quick and decisive actions that are sometimes necessary in a close-run battle. A map-room general nervous of the political situation, he dithered.

The low Élianes and Dominique

These positions were constructed to protect the rear areas and communications between the Nan Youm River and the five main hills (D1, D2, E1, E4, E2). Especially important was the control of the Bailey bridge over the river, which connected the central area with its depots and the five hills. E10, E11 and E12 were clustered around the Bailey bridge approaches, but E3's main function was to protect the vital E2 from attack from its southern flank and rear. Another key defence post was Dominque 3. It was a defensive position and a firebase for a battery of 105mm cannon under the command of Lieutenant Brunbouk, a veteran of Ná Sán. Set up along the river, it had a company of Algerians for close defence. It was essential because Vietminh troops could easily infiltrate or even burst *en masse* through the gaps and dells between the hills. If the major peaks at D1 and D2 fell, the way would be open to the bridge and the central zone.

The others: PIMs, camp followers, coolies and river rats

Less feted were the camp followers, including the mobile bordellos. All through the battle, two mobile 'comfort units' of Algerian and Vietnamese women and hundreds of local porters and prisoners-of-war continued to serve. Many of the prostitutes acted as nurses during the battle. Sadly, we don't have their stories.

Another large group of unsung heroes were the captured enemy personnel PIMs (Prisoniers Internes Militaire), who were several thousand-strong, plus civilian auxiliaries. These were drawn from pools of prisoners-of-war and civilian porters, who supported the French war effort in the construction of roads, bridges, blockhouses and the supply and logistics train. There were about 100,000 deployed by the French in Indochina. At Dien Bien Phu there were 2,400, of whom only thirty deserted during the battle.

Through the muck and mire, though torrents of shelling, men hauled munitions and food up to the front line. On the way back, they would carry the wounded soldiers. Many died and their tragic stories of pain and suffering go unrecorded. One extraordinary fact is the devotion of these peasant soldiers to their French masters and other colonial troops. While some may well have deserted or joined the so-called 'rats of the Nam Youm' (a phrase conjured up by Colonel Bigeard), the fact is that most served with great courage and loyalty. The Vietnamese peasant was inured to authority of any sort, as are peasants in South-East Asia. In his post-war report, General Ely quoted a certain Commander P of the FTNV, who noted that PIMs 'almost always became dutiful and extraordinarily faithful auxiliaries for our troops.' According to an infantry captain, 'many asked to become partisans,' i.e. armed. At Camp X between 1952–4, of 2,000 prisoners, 900 went on to serve with distinction in the Vietnamese national army.[61] This is very significant evidence that the DRV peasant was not enamoured with the communist system that the new elite were unveiling and imposing on Vietnamese villages.

There were also several thousand internal deserters, both soldiers and auxiliaries, who dug pits into the riverbank and skulked and scavenged.

The ferocious heat and humidity, the climate and the heavy terrain of muddy paddy and forest, led the French high command to assign PIMs to French units to act as porters and carry heavy loads. It was something the troops had mixed feelings about at first. However, they produced good cooking and fresh vegetables, including luxuries like palm heart. Krause's legionnaire group received twenty-five 'kulis' (coolies) per company:

> *Were they Viet prisoners who would flee at the first opportunity? We didn't know. Therefore, we treated them differently, like second class people even though many could speak French. After a few days of mistrust things changed when we found two cooks who could prepare dishes with vegetables and rice which was most delicious even with dried fish sauce over it. In our company none of the Kulis deserted. they were trusted so much that we even gave them our weapons to carry.*[62]

Such relationships, fellow feelings and bonding under fire, also built up at Dien Bien Phu.

CHAPTER XVIII

The Second General Offensive

The Battle for the Five Hills, 30 March 1954

Giáp's second major offensive was a co-ordinated attack meant to take the five hills overlooking the French central positions at Claudine. The hills were Dominique 1, Dominique 2, Éliane 1 (C1), Éliane 2 and Éliane 4. Giáp aimed to burst through then launch a deep penetration into the heart of the encampment, so forcing a quick surrender. The question was, if they could burst through would there be enough momentum and strength to get through the French secondary-reserve positions that the French had set up behind their main front? These positions were not reconnoitred or prepared by VPA infiltration teams and were to some extent unknown.

The essential and final key to the entire battlefield was Éliane 2 (A1). Once taken and with the Vietminh literally hovering over the central French encampment with de Castries' command post only about 1km away, the French fortress would have become untenable. Surrender would follow in short order. The geography of the hills is a set of peaks that arc in a north-easterly direction away from the north-south axis of the French position and the runway. Dominque 1, a large hill with a fairly flat summit, pointed in the direction of Beatrice and was the most isolated of the positions.

Unlike his first offensive, which involved picking off the two key sentinels, Giáp aimed to attack with overwhelming force on a number of five hills' targets simultaneously, knowing that he would outnumber the French four or five to one. At this point in the battle the French had no more than 3,500 front-line troops holding the entire Dien Bien Phu porcupine with another approximately 1,400 trapped uselessly at Isabelle some 5km to the south. Giáp commanded perhaps 50,000 front-line troops, with plenty of reserves on hand to replace losses and perhaps the same number of auxiliaries. With hidden heavy artillery and the dominance of the high ground around the French positions, the situation was indeed desperate for the French high command. Giáp could also throw in diversionary attacks at other points in the ring to draw off reserves and prevent counter-attack and reinforcement of threatened strongpoints. He must have been confident as he called in his commanders the day before the battle to galvanise and quiz them on their preparations in detail, down to the composition and morale of the assault platoons:

> *I asked them again: 'Do you have confidence?' 'Yes my general,' Vu Lang replied rapidly.*
>
> *'How long will it take you to take C1* [Éliane 1]*?' '45 minutes!' I turned towards Nguyễn Huu An,* 'Et pour A1 [and for A1], *how long do you need?' Nguyễn Huu was embarrassed because of the timetable proposed by Vu Lang. I interrupted, 'A1 is more difficult, two hours should be sufficient?' He replied to me joyously 'My general, that is agreed!'*[1]

Despite their obvious reflective and exculpatory nature, Giáp's comments on the problems of the five hills battle are worth noting. Giáp writes:

> *...the number of our units engaged was larger but the number of targets had also increased. Besides the five main objectives on the Eastern hills, there were other secondary targets...*[Unlike Beatrice and Gabrielle] *This time we were a sector composed of several centres of resistance, defended by many battalions, who could provide mutual support.*

At the same time Giáp was quizzing his commanders, General Navarre in Saigon was writing a critical letter dated 29 March to General Cogny, the theatre commander in Tonkin, in response to Cogny's constant complaints as to lack of resources, 'the resources at your disposal are entirely adequate to fulfil your present mission.'

Navarre was preparing the ground to put the blame for any disaster at Dien Bien Phu on his subordinate. Cogny was doing the same. Navarre blamed Cogny for his excessive concentration on the Red delta. He pointed to the lack of co-ordination with the air force, poor use of artillery, and bad planning of the defence. Navarre had reserves of paratrooper battalions, but he would not commit them. The government in Paris also held reserves and resources in metropolitan France and other parts of the empire but did not deploy them. All the while his *Operation Atlante* was continuing on the coast between Na Trang and Da Nang. It tied up 30,000 troops and required the support of air-drops, using Dakota capacity that could hardly be afforded in the circumstances.

Aware that an attack was imminent, Colonel Langlais made an inspection of the five hills. What he saw concerned him. On Dominique 1, the defending Algerian battalion seemed to have poor morale. Their commanding officer was sick and most of the officers had been killed or wounded or were down with malaria. They were relieved by half a company of Algerians sent from Dominique 3. However, there was no time to improve the poorly laid out defences and inadequate bunkers. Recognising that Dominique 1 might easily be overrun, the six 120mm mortars of the legion were removed to Dominique 4 in the nick of time. Unfortunately, there were still only 100 defenders. On Dominique 2, one position was held by Vietnamese troops, barely trained

Catholic militia from Phat Diem armed with Lee Enfield rifles. Éliane 2 was held by a Moroccan unit and a T'ai battalion, whose reliability Langlais doubted. Langlais ordered the 5th BPVN (Vietnamese parachutists) to replace the Algerians while a legion company was ordered up to reinforce the Moroccans on Éliane 2.

In New York at the Overseas Press Club, Dulles made a speech pressing the case for intervention and united international action. It was no doubt aimed at the British. He admitted that there were 'serious risks. But these risks are less than those that will face us a few years from now if we dare not be resolute today.'[2]

The general assault and Éliane 1, 30 March

Nurse Genevieve was due to fly out of the encampment at 12.30 a.m. on 30 March, but a rain storm combined with the slippery, treacherous and badly damaged runway meant that the air traffic controllers would not permit her plane to take off. Landing was forbidden. She had missed the last flight out of Dien Bien Phu:

> *...at four in the afternoon shells from mortars and 105mm howitzers started to fall. By five the artillery fire had reached an unbelievable violence. Never even on March 13 had Dien Bien Phu endured such concentrated bombardments. I felt as if it was the end of the world. The impacts shook the bunker. Pieces of earth fell from the roof and we wondered how long it would hold. Nobody said a word.*[3]

The second general offensive started at 4 p.m. on 30 March. Whereas concentration had been the order of the day on 13 March against Beatrice and then Gabrielle, Giáp's tactics changed. Attacks were made against all of the five hills, something that would stretch the limits of the bastion's thin reserves. Assault groups rushed forwards through wire that they hoped had been broken by high explosives, or they used Bangalores to blow a passage through. Other specialist teams carried satchel bombs to toss through the vent- and firing-holes of blockhouses. Mixed arms teams with light machine-guns and bags full of grenades moved forward, hugging the ground or rushing in waves, hoping to overpower the French machine-gun positions. Each assault group was assigned its tasks. Individual French blockhouses and bunkers had been the subject of reconnaissance. Each had a designated code name, each had heavy artillery zeroed-in on them, each was assigned spotters to record the fall of shot.

Despite the preparations, the bo doi were mown down in droves by a blizzard of machine-gunfire or blown apart by French artillery called down on pre-set zones in front of the wire. If they penetrated the first ring of wire defences the radio operators called in that the wire had been breached and artillery ranges were reset to pre-arranged target areas. All of this was done in the mud and slime of the hills churned by artillery fire and sluiced with the monsoon downpours from the heavy clouds now sitting permanently over the mountains and valley. Of course the barbed wire, which was thick and in layers, was not all cut, or if it was, the assault teams had to find where it had been. All the while their numbers would reduce, as men fell dead or wounded under the scything sweeps of machine-guns or the rip of high explosive.

The French knew where the breaches were, so they trained their fire on the assault teams bursting through or leaping over the remains of wire defences at the gaps. As the fighting continued from the first line of wire, and then the second line, the distance to the French bunkers, blockhouses and trenches reduced to 30–50m.

For the French there were also problems. Apart from the incoming assault groups, the heavy artillery, mortars and heavy machine-guns trained on their positions, as the Vietminh assault groups rushed up hill they could see the heads and shoulders of the enemy above the trench parapets, often picked out against the skyline. An easy shot. There were lots of depressions in the ground or dead zones where Vietminh assault groups could find cover and hide from the bullets. Shooting down was not so easy either with the mud-spattered Vietminh hard to see, especially the machine-gunners or snipers who gave fire support to the attacks. Enemy gunners manning recoilless rifles or bazookas or even 75mm mountain guns were also engaged at short ranges to take out French positions. Enclosure in a blockhouse hardly gave comfort either. As targets for artillery, the gun slits would be peppered by machine-gunfire. As the enemy crept up on the flanks, they tossed in grenades or satchel bombs through the gun slits. No survivors in an enclosed concrete space.

At close quarters the main weapons were grenades, lots of them, flying in both directions. Chinese-made grenades were not especially good, often causing little damage. Had the bo doi been equipped with good grenades, the battle would probably have been shorter.

Dominique 1 was attacked at 7.45 p.m. Vietminh sappers had already undermined the barbed wire stanchions in some places and earth-filled bamboo mats were rolled over the wire in other places. Pre-planned defensive artillery fire overshot the VPA attackers. The fighting on D1 lasted four and a half hours, by the end of which almost all of the D1 garrison were dead, wounded or captured, including the fifteen European officers and NCOs. Given that attacks were non-stop for four and a half hours, Vietminh casualties must have been very heavy.

When the enemy salvoes stopped, the FEC were faced by wailing masses of Vietminh charging in waves, and sometimes emerging from secret positions some 30m away, having already undermined the wire. In other places, large straw mattresses were thrown across the wire to allow the Vietminh soldiers to clamber over. Defensive mortar and artillery fire was too slow to adjust to the tempo of the attack, so the Vietminh rushed in on badly demoralised defenders. It was too much for many of the Algerian soldiers, who fled the hill leaving the defence to the fresher Vietnamese, the one remaining Algerian NCO and the legion mortar company. Orders to shoot the runaways had little effect.

At Éliane 1, Viet platoon leader Dang Duc Song had lost touch with most of his men, the majority of whom were already dead. However, he discovered Comrade Niem, all alone and wounded in an empty blockhouse. He was joined by others:

> *I found a place to position the light machine-gun. I took an earth filled sandbag to use as both cover and a resting point for the weapon, so that the enemy would not be able to see the weapon…'stay here and fire when I give the signal.' They advanced towards another blockhouse. We scrambled over the bodies of our brothers in arms. Arriving at a trench about 150m from our objective, we met a wounded man holding a grenade. He told us; 'the French are in that blockhouse up there.'…From time to time, I saw an imprudent Frenchman who got up above the parapet. I signalled to Niem to fire then throwing two grenades and firing burst from my sub machine-guns I launched my attack. Thin followed behind. In the blockhouse I found one dead and two wounded. I then dived into another trench and threw some more grenades. The surviving enemy fled to the base of the hill.*[4]

Survival was a matter of luck, but the odds could be narrowed by experience, skill in attack and use of the ground. Experience helped Nguyễn Don Tu, but comrade Quan was killed by a stray bullet after Éliane 1's (C1's) capture, while Don Tu soon fell ill with dengue fever.

Éliane 1's capture took about three hours.

Dominique 2 and Éliane 2, 30 March

The attack on Dominque 2 started at 8 p.m. and fifteen minutes later than on D1.

After its capture at around 9.50 p.m., D1 was used as a Vietminh centre for battery-fire for either 75mm guns or mortars. Radio communication was an essential part of the battle. Information came in by radio and orders came out. Commands or orders were varied in nature, but target selection and prioritisation were key elements.

The head of a mortar team, Nguyễn Huu Chap, recounted his experiences:

> *We stayed on the hill for one month and four days. If we just fired one round of our mortar, we'd get dozens in return. We were under constant air attack. Two of my mortar group were killed and three wounded...tension, fatigue, lack of sleep.*[5]

Although covered with sandbags and well dug-in, they also suffered from counter-battery-fire. One battery whose opening for the cannon was too big 'suffered twenty minutes of bombardment from a tank, which destroyed two pieces of artillery, killed seven gunners and wounded eleven more,' recalled Van Khau.[6] However, the Vietminh sitting up on the hill were much better protected and they could see the enemy distinctly in the valley below.

Battery commander Pha Van Khau recounted the constant round of tit-for-tat counter-battery-fire. Ordered over the radio to take out a French gun position with four 105mm guns, his battery destroyed one where he could see a Frenchman brandishing a flag at the side of his piece. It was the first chosen target and was soon destroyed, but there followed a maelstrom of shelling and firing of all sorts on their position. With the next shot they hit a munitions centre and then destroyed a second enemy cannon with two extra shots. Coming under machine-gunfire from another direction, they quicky had to turn the cannon. One shot and they saw the machine-gun spinning in the air. Another effort at counter-battery landed so close to the gun port that Van Khau was knocked out. Fire was then redirected on a tank crossing the bridge below. But one by one the gunners were wounded. Van Khau succeeded in silencing all four of the enemy guns, but at the end of the day he was alone at his gun. All the others were injured.

The French on their side had no possibility of providing fresh cooked food to their soldiers. They lived by eating out of cold tins. The Vietminh fared better:

> *Meals were brought up the mountain by kitchen teams, everyone had some water, a stalk of bamboo, and a bowl of rice with dried fish, fish sauce. On the 13th of April a whole group of kitchen staff were killed by a shell as they were coming to feed us.*

After an initial defence, a similar stampede took place on Dominique 2 as on Éliane 1. Small handfuls of troops low in morale, hungry and under massive attack by two regiments of the 312th, 316th and half of the 308th, were likely to run. And so they did. The command post on Dominique 2 was overrun within a few hours.

'A1 (E2) was regarded as the magic eye on the west side of the French encampment.' (Bui Xuan, Linh) Éliane 2 was the toughest of the hills, better defended with perfect fields of fire over large distances along the so-called *Champs Elysée*. Tensions in the Vietminh camp before the battle were palpable.

At a conference, the commander of a battalion in 316th Division challenged another commander to a bet on who would capture their objective first. 'I said to myself what bet? What competition? Combat is not a game,' complained battalion commander Van Dinh Hoa:

> *I pronounced some neutral words about victory, but to tell the truth I was a little angry. Combat is a question of life and death...We do not have competitions to gamble away our men on the battlefield.*
>
> *Before the departure to the front line before the attack a group of entertainers visited and presented us with a flag to plant on the summit...Cu, a company commander, was of a taciturn disposition and when the artists continued to sing and dance around us he turned to me and said, 'Brother Hoe, going into combat with these women dancing all around is not a good omen. Tell them to stop!'* (Hoe, battalion commander 249, 174th Regiment 316th Division)
>
> *We thought as we prepared to attack from the launch site that this would be easier than last year's attack on Moc Chau. We had to attack the north-west face of A1.* (Éliane 2)

It was not easier. The Vietminh were shot down or blasted in their hundreds. The batteries located at Isabelle some 5km to the south were particularly effective in raining down flanking fire. Vietminh troops found that much of the barbed wire was intact. When they did find gaps, they found themselves raked by machine-gunfire as they ran through them across open ground. Casualties were very heavy on the first day of the attack. One company commander remembers 'walking in trenches filled with bodies of our comrades.'

Survivors pinned down on the hillside scoured the bodies of their comrades looking for food, because every soldier carried a bag of fried rice. 'Even though the rice was soaked in the blood of our brothers, we devoured it nonetheless.' Destroyed, they were relieved by the 174th Regiment. Platoon leader of 102nd Regiment 308th Division, Sy Trinh, recorded that his battalion of 300 had been reduced to seventeen men.[7]

Van Dinh Hoe, commander of 174th Regiment, advanced to the attack with his 500 men but in such an attack at night:

> *...it was impossible to maintain tactical control, which devolved in practice to the attacking spirit and capability of platoon or section leaders.*

The attack failed after a furious counter-attack by the French. Coming back off the hill with a leg wound, Van met with the commander of the first battalion, who said to him with a shocked voice, 'I don't have any soldiers left.'[8]

On Éliane 2, the Vietminh poured over and through the defences of the toughest hill. They were slaughtered too but nonetheless succeeded in occupying the greater part of the hill, leaving the survivor of Beatrice, Major

Nicholas, and his legionnaires holding the rest. The 1st BEP paratroopers were sent up to reinforce and assault Vietminh positions on the hill. Numbers of lightly wounded paratroopers were treated and went back again. Lieutenant Rolin was shot in the leg as he mounted the hill then wounded by a grenade fragment. He was treated by a medic and hidden in a bunker until it was safe to bring him down. Fighting followed a similar pattern of grenade, parcel bomb and submachine-gun attacks by Vietminh, met by machine-guns, grenades, artillery and mortar fire. Mini tactical battles in small areas took place around individual trenches, sandbagged machine-gun positions and blockhouses. It was bloody, fast and merciless. All around them tracers fizzed in slow arcs through the sky, shells exploded, light from flares burst open and died. Then quiet, as the mini battles resolved themselves and the exhausted victors counted their dead friends, bound their wounds and searched bodies for food and ammunition.

One Vietminh section leader found himself alone:

> *On the night of the 30th having occupied the radio bunker of the enemy I found myself alone in a profound silence…I had lost a lot of my men…I called out is anyone there?* 'Moi' *called out Hong from a neighbouring fox hole, he was a strong and experienced company commander – I was so happy! It was in this moment that I understood how precious a human voice is. My mood was lightened because some of my brothers in arms had survived.*

In the back areas the remnants of units had to be reconstituted with new soldiers. Volunteers as young as 16 were thrown in to replace the seasoned veterans whose bodies were rotting on Éliane 2. Many did not know how to fire a rifle. Surviving NCOs had to show them how to sight weapons. Many of these youngsters in the 316th Division died in their first combat, remembered Phan Than Tung of the 174th's logistics team. 'These young were entering the war and no one had the time to even know their identity or to make any record about their fate.'[9]

One of the jobs of political commissars during the battle was to organise the collection of bodies. Commissar Nguyễn Nhu Thien of the 102nd Regiment in the 308th Division remembered seeing bodies lying on the hillside from a covered bunker 500m away. He sent a company of soldiers to collect them. They had to wait for rare moments of calm on the battlefield:

> *…many of the bodies could not be identified because for new recruits we had not had time even to register their names, age or place of birth. There were still many bodies on the hill that we were not able to recover.*[10]

The Vietminh high command could not understand why they were failing in their attacks on Éliane 2. Rumours started to go around that the French had constructed a tunnel that passed through the mountain. It was big enough for a tank to pass through and attack the Vietminh in the rear. One intelligence officer, Bui Xia Lin, head of intelligence in the 316th Division, was instructed to find it. In the course of the furious battle raging on the higher reaches of the hill, he and his troops scoured the mountain on his ludicrous quest. He even sent men to infiltrate the rear areas of the hill behind enemy lines. When he found nothing, he was severely criticised.

The Vietminh failed to take the hill. Toeholds on the top were re-taken in the counter-attack led by several tanks, including those of Captain Hervouet. Hit twice, both his arms were broken. After treatment he returned to the battle leading the tank counter-attack with his arms in white casts waving around uselessly from the tank turret hatch.

Colonel Bigeard's headquarters was positioned at Éliane 4. The fifth of the hills, it was just behind Éliane 1 and to the south of Dominique 2. Created by his paratrooper battalion, it was a perfect central point for a forward command post. From this point Bigeard tried to supervise the battle by directing supporting fire, including artillery and dropping in reinforcements.

'My memory of Eliane 2…the Viets were on all sides,' recalled Legionnaire Pregnon. 'They came on without stopping. Even when we descended they were everywhere…'[11]

Bigeard was able to reinforce the toe hold on Éliane 2 with German legionnaires who clambered into battle singing a German marching song. He also sent Lieutenant Lucciani with a mixed force of paratroopers and Moroccans. The French held on. Éliane 2 was cleared with its western slopes covered in the dead of both sides.

Lieutenant Brunbouk stands by his guns

The fall of Dominiques 1 and 2 led to the most dangerous attack yet sustained by the garrison of Dien Bien Phu. There is a gully between the Élianes and the Dominiques and through this gully rushed two regiments of elite Vietminh soldiers (about 4,000 men). Having taken the French positions on D2 the Vietminh, thrilled with the chance of victory, charged on, aiming to cross the bridge and pour into the central area of the French porcupine. There was nothing to bar the way except the four-gun 105mm battery by the river at Dominque 3, manned by indomitable West Africans commanded by Lieutenant Paul Brunbouk. A mere company of Algerian infantry covered his battery.

Brunbouk was about to conduct one of the legendary artillery actions of military history:

> *This tall and athletic boy with an angular face hid behind the irony of his blue eyes and his mocking causticity, a soul steeped in faith and patriotism at the mercy of the trials of his youth. Born in Roubaix* [Lille] *in 1926 into a very large family, orphaned at a very young age, raised by an older sister, he entered Saint-Cyr among the elite.*[12]

When the French front along the northern hill line of D1, D2 and E1 collapsed, Algerian and Vietnamese paratroopers scampered down the steep hillsides. Brunbouk readied his gun teams. They had been toiling all night firing about 450–500 shells per gun at the pre-set targets on the approaches to the Dominiques' defences. As described by Dr Grindrey, they were faced by:

> *...the howling surge of thousands of Viets. These see themselves victorious and throw two regiments of Division 312 towards the position by the Nam Youm. The heart of the defence is there, a few hundred meters away, and, they believe, there is nothing left, no one to stop them, apart from a battery of four 105 HM2* [howitzers] *from the 4th RAC, a very small obstacle.*

Algerians fleeing from the Dominiques and Éliane 1 came through his position. Brunbouk arranged a triage of courage. Those willing and able to actively defend were put into the line, while others whose nerve had gone after the horrors on the hills were thrown out.

Attacks of D3 began at 10 p.m. In the gun-pits, Brunbouk barked out his order to the gunners who, with their spanner, turned the nozzle of the shells to the required setting: '*Debouches á zero.*' (Set to zero.)

When 4,000 Vietminh came charging in, Lieutenant Brunbouk ordered the barrels to be lowered. Then he opened fire. The reports of the guns were almost instantaneous with the airburst explosions tearing into the waves of Vietminh troops. Still they came on and still the guns fired. They were stopped dead. Further waves charged on into the wall of whirring steel fragments and high explosive.

Two quad .50 calibre machine-guns with turntable mounts, on the other side of the river in position Epervier, swung round their fearsome four-barrelled harbingers of death and turned their attention to the human waves charging towards the guns and the bridge. Amid the airbursts from the guns, a withering hail of machine-gunfire ripped across the Vietminh line toppling, spinning, killing the onrushing Vietminh. Bodies littered the ground.

Told to withdraw several times, Brunbouk refused orders from Colonel Langlais and stayed in position:

> *The order is given – twice repeated – to blow up his cannons. Brunbouk sharply refuses: – Gang of Cons...send me infantry ammunition and, tomorrow, I will bring my equipment!" Colonel Langlais, the heart and soul of the defence, famous*

for his harsh and uncouth language maintained his calm, was dumbfounded for a brief moment and exclaimed admiringly.[13]

'I take my hat off to the gunner!' exclaimed Colonel Langlais. A singular compliment.

Several hundred survivors of the storm of shot and shell sought cover in the riverbed below the river bank, where they were annihilated by the electronic triggering of minefields Colonel Langlais had ordered to be buried there. The crisis was over. The Vietminh regiments had been utterly obliterated. French high command now understood that the position at Dien Bien Phu was desperate because they had lost three out of the five hills. Luckily, by supreme effort, they had been able to hang on to Éliane 2. They also held Éliane 4 where Bigeard's headquarters was located. Dogged and courageous defence had held off the waves of the enemy whose bodies littered the field.

Dominque 5 was a reserve position between D2 and E1, but with those two positions gone, the Vietminh fell upon the isolated position defended by a T'ai company and officered by yet another minor aristocrat, Lieutenant Lunet de La Malène. Having not prepared the assault the Vietminh were mown down at the wire. Their attack launched at 11 p.m. failed, so preventing a rampant exploitation of the breaches in the French defences and limiting the attacks on Lieutenant Brunbouk's position at D3. Another reserve position below D1 was held by a T'ai company equipped with several medium and light machine-guns. They provided further flanking fire and slowed down Giáp's intended *coup de grace* on D3 and the central encampment. The Vietnamese paratroopers on D6, which had no defences, were led into an orderly retreat to the river.

Meanwhile, there were concerns about the logistical situation, which was tight. Just on 30 and 31 March, the French expended 13,000 105mm, 1,200 120mm and 855 155mm shells. Between the start of the siege and 31 March, the French had used 32,000 105mm shells, outmatching the Vietminh by two times.[14] By 6 April, there were just 7,000 105mm shells left. Firing had to be rationed by both sides, though the French ration was much higher. However, shortage of shells could rapidly lead to defeat, because it was artillery that kept the Vietminh hordes at bay. Artillery was the main weapon of defence. In the First World War, artillery caused sixty percent of casualties and, by analogy, we must reckon that at Die Bien Phu it was a similar if not greater percentage. Urgent messages went out for reinforcements and more shells on both sides.

Another crack battalion of paratroopers under Colonel Bréchignac was dropped into the maelstrom on 1 April. Corporal Sibbile remembered:

It was like a fireworks display with tracers passing on each side of us. We were heavily laden with leg bags, supply sacks, machine-guns, and 60mm mortars. [On landing] *I found myself on my back, caught on the barbed wire. Then I was*

> *hit in the leg by a shell fragment. There was a first aid bag nearby…A wounded Vietminh soldier and I reached it at the same time…we shared its contents.*

Colonel Bréchignac also landed in the wire. He arrived cut up at headquarters.

Altogether, reinforcements dropped into the bastion over the course of the battle included 1,398 French, 962 legionnaires and just under 2,000 Indochinese, together with a clutch of African gunners. The next day, 2 April, the air force managed to drop a significant tonnage over the zone, one of the best of the campaign at 221 tons, but unfortunately over twenty-five percent of it was a miss-drop, including large amounts of 105mm shells, which were put to good use by the Vietminh. Between 30 March and 15 April, miss-drops accounted for ten to fifteen percent of the total. After the capture of Huguette 1 and the abandonment of Opera, miss-drops increased to thirty to fifty percent as the drop-zone contracted. The bastion was only receiving about twenty-five percent of its daily minimum needs. Drops varied according to weather conditions and generally became much more difficult because of flak and the height at which the plane had to fly.

Such were the shortages of equipment, ammunition, food, cannon and medicines that supply drops had taken priority, despite the desperate shortage of fit, unwounded soldiers. Fifty percent of French gunners, most of whom were West Africans, had been put out of action. Reserve gunners had to be dropped in at short notice. Not trained as paratroopers this would have been a harrowing experience in probably the most dangerous drop-zone in history.

There was increasing frustration too over the accuracy of the drops. De Castries fumed impotently over the radio link to Hanoi. Eight hundred shells had been accidently dropped on the enemy, a huge bonus for them because their stocks had also been heavily depleted. Giáp's account of the battle boasts about shelling the French with their own munitions. Despite this, the second offensive was at an end. The Vietminh troops were exhausted and the casualty lists huge. Except for the air-dropped bonus, they had run out of munitions for their big guns.

In the main medical centre, the need for space meant that surrounding bunkers housing troops had to be taken over for the medical needs, so troops had to live in the open and for shelter they burrowed into the walls of trenches. The shelters were soon filled with the wounded. A particular favourite for Dr Grauwin was the irrepressible triple amputee Heinz:

> *Every morning he nearly broke my heart by saluting each with his right stump… his vitality and gaiety never varied.*[15]

Lieutenant Brunbouk would die towards the end of the siege. Mortally wounded when a shell crashed into his command post, he died slowly and agonisingly in the central medical unit. His good friend and surgeon, Dr J. Grindrey in the central medical unit, would be there to treat his shattered body and close his eyes when he passed:

> *On Tuesday April 13, Holy Tuesday, a direct hit from 105 crushes his combat shelter and seriously injures him. He feels that he is going to die, confesses, takes communion, then gathers his last strength and exhorts his men to fight with all their energy, with all their courage, with a vehemence, a harshness that strikes everyone. Then, only then, he is taken to the surgical antenna, just in time for him to know that my friendly hands will close his eyes, after the big farewell that we had time to exchange, under the eyes of my friends. Nurses, twisted with emotion.*[16]

Genevieve wept.

Casualties at dawn

FEC medical facilities for forty-two were swamped by 4,000 wounded soldiers. They were stacked and treated in appalling filthy conditions. Medicines, chloroform, medical alcohol, antibiotics, bandages and other medical supplies ran out. Genevieve recorded:

> *...by dawn on the 31 March the unit was already full...the corridor of the unit was immediately blocked with stretchers that one had to step over to get past... outside on the rampart at the entry to the unit men waited on their stretchers until room could be found for them. Some receive new wounds and others were killed at the door of the unit. It was utter hell. The sound of the artillery was deafening and the wounds of the injured had dirt mixed with their blood. As the wounded were brought in the PIMs cleaned them up as best they could.*[17]

PIM orderlies, referred to by Grauwin as coolies, were themselves being killed and wounded in large numbers. 'By the middle of April two-thirds of the medical orderlies were either killed or wounded.'[18]

Nurse Genevieve was put in charge of the severely wounded and spent much of her time doing intravenous injections with the painkiller Pheergan Dolossal: 'How can I describe the uninterrupted flow of injured, the heartbreak at our inability to shelter all of them and to operate fast enough?' Dr Grauwin conducted the triage.

> *This posed terrible choices, because an abdominal operation took as much time as five or six amputations and he had to make his decision according to the most urgent cases. Dr Grindrey was operating without a break...With each explosion, the earth shook and debris fell from the ceiling of the operating room.*

An experienced doctor, Dr Grauwin, formerly a prisoner of the Germans, was a rugged chain-smoker not averse to drinking wine when the opportunity arose. A veteran of eight years in Indochina, his account of the battle, written in a stream of consciousness style, *A doctor at Dien Bien Phu*, is a tough read even for this author, who spent months reading and listening to transcripts and court testimony of the Khmer rouge holocaust in Cambodia. A deeply religious man, his faith and professionalism carried him through the endless grotesquery of war.

A confident man, Grauwin dealt with triage and supervised the most seriously wounded. He and his young associate surgeon, Dr Grindrey, who did the majority of the operations, worked bare-chested in the stifling and fetid underground bunkers, 'underground bowels – humid, hot and foul smelling.' They were supported by a polyglot team of nurses and Jeep ambulance drivers, including Vietnamese and North and West Africans. Some of the prostitutes from the bordello mobiles acted as nurses.

His memories are filled with the horrors:

> *My orderlies brought in a Moroccan sapper on a stretcher. A mortar shell had exploded only two or three yards behind him. There was a single huge hole in the middle of his back. His vertebrae were shattered and the spinal cord destroyed. In the few seconds before he died I seemed to read a reproach to me in his eyes.* (p.164)
>
> *Another legionnaire, Muller, of the First Battalion, second Foreign Infantry, had a compound fracture high up on the left thigh and an enormous wound in the buttocks and loins making it impossible to use plaster. Complex splint with 40 lb weights attached to force the bone into place.*[19]

Genevieve was especially moved by the death of Lieutenant Chevalier in Bigeard's colonial paratrooper battalion. Shot in the head during a counter-attack:

> *...the bullet had severed his spinal cord and paralyzed him...the anguish of Robert Chevalier increased moment by moment. His paralysis progressed, first his legs, then his abdomen, his chest, and his arms. His breathing became more and more feeble. 'Genevieve, promise me I won't die?' I turned my head without answering and felt desperately helpless.*

Twice a day Genevieve gave him soup with a teaspoon.[20]

But there were successes in the fight for life. Haas, a young German legionnaire, was:

> *...horribly mutilated by shell fragments, both arms and one leg had to be amputated. To avoid risk of infection, the stumps were left open. Each change of*

bandages caused him to howl in pain. To be eighteen in Dien Bien Phu…and a triple amputee for the rest of his life.

Conditions were quite disgusting underground. The floors squelched mud, human detritus, excrement and urine, and blood. Genevieve describes how:

Mud invaded the tunnels and the shelters and we had to raise the lower-level beds. Water seeped into certain places; the engineers dug sumps to collect the runoff and on one night…I fell in mud up to my hips.[21]

The heat became unbearable – the heat of the roof baked by the sun, the heat of fifty electric lightbulbs, the heat of the lamp in the operating theatre, the heat of two hundred living creatures unable to keep still, the heat which encouraged mushrooms and other growth to appear all over the place on the walls and on the beams of the roof. At the end of April it was worse. Water was trickling everywhere and only evaporating very slowly. The heat became damp and smelly. Blood, vomit and faeces mixed with the mud made up a frightful compound which stuck to the boots in thick layers. A pair of shorts was the only possible uniform. Sweat pored constantly from the forehead and back, dripping from the armpits to the hands and from the chest to the stomach.[22]

Dr Grauwin describes the scene of the battlefield at night, beauty and death combined:

I had a look towards the Éliane positions on which our fate depended. If they were lost it would be all over. There were explosions here and there, with vivid flashes of light. Flare followed flare in the sky…an ordinary shell makes a quick flash, followed by a cloud of smoke and that is all. But this was a magnificent fountain of silvery sparks…I suspected that it was a phosphorous shell.

Soon the stretchers were coming in. They found the phosphorescent wounds on the victims by turning out the lights in the operating theatre as the 'burning 'anthracite-like substance' bored into the flesh.[23]

Abdominal cases, the most humiliating type of injury, became Genevieve's special responsibility. Special care was needed because:

In Indochina nearly half the abdominal cases die a few days or a few weeks after the operation – intestinal flora, two hours to a unit, lowered resistance to illness and infection.[24]

Nearly all had a piece of intestine protruding with a slit in it through which faeces gently flowed. Their dressings were constantly fouled and had to be changed two or three times a day. Genevieve did this…She was always smiling and reassuring.[25] *Captain Boisbouvier was in for a second time. After an injection and some rum, he trotted off, 'really nothing broken? Well goodbye till the next time.' Yes I was to see him for a third time – but that would be the last.*[26]

Dr Grauwin's job in triage was the essential first step in the induction of casualties. His first priority was to stabilise and save the men who were on the edge of dying. As the stretchers came in after a battle, he was constantly barking curt orders: 'The stream of usual orders issued from my mouth Dolossal Phenegan, anti-tet-tox, anti-gangrene, haemostatics, resuscitation.'

Flies became a major problem. Maggots festered on wounds and under bandages causing intolerable itching. Dr Grauwin described the worm horror: 'It was shocking to see these revolting little white maggots crawling over hands, then faces and the ears of the wounded as they slept.'[27]

French high command

As the crisis was developing on the 31st, General Navarre flew up from his Saigon headquarters to Hanoi to confer with General Cogny. When Navarre arrived at night to the French high command in Hanoi, Cogny was not there. He had gone to bed following a social engagement. Navarre was quite naturally furious at such laxity when Dien Bien Phu was fighting for survival. Navarre ostentatiously busied himself throughout the night with the huge traffic flow brought on by the crisis, including preparations for reinforcements and air-drops. In the morning when Cogny eventually re-appeared there was a furious argument during the course of which Cogny made clear his views on his commander, the same things that the loquacious Cogny had been saying behind Navarre's back. Cogny would then put on record in a written statement a rebuttal of all the accusations made against him. It was altogether an unedifying spectacle given that men were dying in mud and slime at the bottom of a valley at Dien Bien Phu.

It was obvious that the French position could collapse at any time, so Navarre prepared contingency instructions for the destruction of equipment and for a final resistance in the central areas of Claudine and Isabelle. A message to the garrison declared that they were 'defending the honour of France and Vietnam…the whole world has its eyes fixed on it.' Navarre promised one more parachute battalion and a 75mm gun crew, but said he would not commit his entire airborne force, 'unless I am convinced that their intervention would provide us with victory.' Navarre's attitude was already defeatist. Had extra reserves of troops been made available then the hills may not have been lost and counter-attacks could have forced off the Vietminh.

Navarre and the French political elite simply lacked focus and conviction, as did the Americans. The French had committed just three percent of their troops. The battle was now, the war would be won or lost in Dien Bien Phu. It was the only thing that mattered, yet the French command was still thinking in terms of maps, garrisons and their wider strategic commitments in Indochina.

Dien Bien Phu became expendable as the battle progressed and thoughts turned to damage limitation and blame games rather than victory.

Negative rightist thoughts

The French were not the only ones at breaking point. There may have been anger and recrimination in the French camp, but a sombre mood also descended on the Vietminh encampments. In mid-April, after the blood bath of the second offensive, morale sagged still further in the Vietminh Army. We do not know the Vietminh casualty figures for their attack on the five hills but anecdotal evidence, including the losses taken in front of Lieutenant Brunbouk's guns, suggest that a figure of 8,000–10,000 would be reasonable.

The French had recaptured Éliane 1 so the massive losses seemed to be in vain. Pham visited a command post behind the front and was shocked by the collapse in morale. On the front line the joys of the mass movement towards Dien Bien Phu and the early victories had been replaced by doubt. One can only imagine the feelings of those few veterans who remained alive in front-line units such as the 308th and 312th Divisions, and how their enthusiasm now turned bitter under the shadow of the hollow bombast and hectoring criticism of the political commissars. Remaining veterans were exhausted and demoralised. Fatalistic despair was as deadly as a virus and Giáp stepped in with harsh measures to deal with it. We do not know all the details of his measures, but the communist way is typically more indoctrination, firing squads and terror: deserters shot; malingerers shot or harshly punished. Unit commanders were demoted and sacked. We do not know if they were also imprisoned or shot, but that would have been the usual Soviet method.

For Giáp and the communists, defeatism was a 'rightist deviancy', which had to be stamped out by the harshest means. Giáp refers archly to the problems and emphasised political work or AGITPROP in 'Soviet-speak':

> *To maintain and develop this determination to fight and to win was a whole process of unremitting and patient political work and ideological education and struggle.*[28]

To the uneducated in the language of class struggle and democratic centralism, this means 'brainwashing'. He admitted that after the early victories:

> *...we found in our ranks signs of underestimation of the enemy. By criticism we rectified this state of mind in good time.* [Further,] *after the second phase of the campaign, when attack and defence were equally fierce,* negative rightist thoughts cropped up again *to the detriment of carrying out the task...we opened in the heart of the battlefield an intensive and extensive struggle against*

> *rightist passivity, and for the heightening of revolutionary enthusiasm and the spirit of strict discipline.* (Author's emphasis)

From this communist drivel, read 'brainwashing and terror', the classic double-punch of Marxist-Leninist orthodoxy. According to Giáp, ruthless enforcement through the commissars 'led the Dien Bien Phu campaign to complete victory.'[29]

The massive losses, far greater than admitted by the Vietminh and by most historians, could only be sustained by such brutal methods. The timetable of Geneva and the greater good demanded it. But the costs and morale damage were very serious. Losses were compounded by the awful provision of medical services where one doctor and six nurses cared for 50,000 troops. According to a Vietminh medical officer, this desperate situation was made worse by the paucity of transport. Most wounded were 'carried out on foot…[it] often resulted in wounds becoming infected and the men either die or become permanently disabled.'[30] Poor treatment of wounded Vietminh soldiers also caused demoralisation. Sporting pith helmets rather than metal helmets, head wounds were numerous and normally deadly due to infection.

In Washington

In April 1954, Eisenhower publicly threatened China with nuclear attack over the threat to the Taiwanese islands of Quemoy. Eisenhower said he would use nuclear weapons, 'exactly as you would use a bullet.' However, in respect of Indochina, Eisenhower talked loudly but carried a very tiny stick. At one point in April, he mulled over a request by foreign minister and MRP party leader George Bidault with the idea of lending a few atom bombs to the French, but the idea ran into the sand. The concept of making tactical nuclear strikes was not as alien or repugnant as it might now be considered.

As a political general he hated to be forced into a difficult decisive action – to alienate any factions completely. He would rather give something to everyone. Compromise was his style. But there are moments in history when compromise is entirely the wrong style. In failing to decisively use his presidential powers, surrendering to congress and London the veto over his decision, Eisenhower effectively doomed the beleaguered garrison at Dien Bien Phu and the people of Vietnam.

On 16 April, Vice-President Nixon said that he 'would personally support such a decision [for intervention].'[31] Even if it was politically unpopular.

Meanwhile, at Dien Bien Phu:

> *Towards the middle of April injuries dating from Gabrielle. Beatrice and Dominique attacks were well on the way to being healed…so I sent back to their*

fighting positions hundreds of wounded who were well on their way to being cured – abdominal cases, thorax wounds, and those who had lost an eye. Nearly all of these were wounded a second time and I am sure a third were killed in the blockhouses in the course of the final week.

They were sent back to units where they mostly joined in the fighting, even amputees propped up on crates or the one-eyed, manning machine-guns.[32]

Izvestia calling

In London, Churchill thought *Izvestia*'s 8 April article calling for a ceasefire was confirmation of changed Soviet attitudes.

The extent of fear in the Politburo at the military setbacks was demonstrated by Ho's panic-stricken pleading in Moscow as he worked with Khrushchev and Zhou En-Lai to prepare for the Geneva Conference. Ho was, according to Khrushchev, desperate for a ceasefire. Zhou En-Lai informed Khrushchev that:

Ho Chi Minh has told me that the situation in Vietnam is hopeless and that if we do not obtain a ceasefire soon, the Vietnamese won't be able to hold out against the French. Therefore, they have decided to retreat to the Chinese border if necessary, and they want China to be ready to move troops into Vietnam as we did in Korea.

Zhou En Lai told Khrushchev that China had no intention of intervening directly. 'We've already lost too many men in Korea – that war cost us dearly. We're in no condition to get involved in another war at this time.'[33] They decided not to tell Ho the truth, and simply humoured him by saying they would help if necessary. Zhou En Lai and Mao had deeper strategic reasons for their non-intervention position. They were desperate to keep the US out of Indochina. A partition would suit them by keeping the French in control of the south. Still suspect for his 'nationalist tendencies', it would also keep Ho's Vietnam as a keen client state safe from the temptations of Titoism.

The fear of losing at Dien Bien Phu after the abandonment of the second general offensive on 5 April and the unravelling of all of the Vietminh gains would lead to the official Soviet news organ *Izvestia* calling for a ceasefire in Indochina on 8 April.[34] Ironically, the French were also discreetly casting around for a meeting with the Chinese to discuss a ceasefire as well as pressing Eden to ask the Chinese to pressurise Ho about allowing medical evacuation from Dien Ben Phu. At a meeting in Moscow on the 22nd with Malenkov, Khrushchev, Suslov and Ho Chi Minh, a common approach to the Geneva Conference was agreed.[35] Ho was forced by the Soviets and China to accept the idea of an armistice and partition – something that was a mixed blessing. Agreement on partition would secure him from his fear of losing the war and prevent US intervention, but was also putting the great dream of a unified Vietnam in jeopardy – something that would rankle and sour relations with China for decades to come.[36] Giáp's victory would make little difference to the armistice agreement.

Eden thought the truce proposal was a diplomatic trap. He was wrong. The truce should have been grabbed immediately. It was another failure by the British and Americans, both in analysis and in intelligence. However, as April developed and Eden's diplomatic meetings with Molotov increased, it became apparent that Churchill was right. On 26 April, Eden was introduced by Molotov to Zou En Lai. They shook hands.[37] The communist camp was set on peace both in Korea and Indochina. It was the Americans who were out of step in looking to intervene in support of the French. Bidault's position was firstly to ally with the US so long as they intervened aggressively to save Dien Bien Phu, which would save him and his government politically. Failing that, Bidault would tuck in beside Eden, because a compromised peace and armistice was better than total collapse in Indochina.

Why did the Soviets and the PRC agree to a partition on terms very generous to the about-to-be-defeated French? Apart from war weariness, there are two reasons. Ho was still suspected of 'Titoist-petit-bourgoise nationalist heresy.' Keeping Vietnam split would keep Ho hungry, dependent and loyal. Secondly, France and Britain could be split from the US, and France in particular could be kept sweet because of its Gaullist potential for disruption within the capitalist camp and as a preventative to German re-armament (EDF).

French rations

Meals in the central part of the encampment were better than for those in the trenches for whom a cooked meal was a rarity. Just as their compatriots were doing on the other side of the hills, PIMs trudged up the hills with rations or slipped and slid along trenches exposed to shellfire and snipers. However, paratrooper Cledic noted that most days 'we had rice, we ate hot rice, with sardines or with a bit of beef, until May 1st…'[38] According to Genevieve, 'our meals were composed of canned goods such as corned beef, but some vegetables and mixed salads were sometimes parachuted to us in packs.' Sometimes treats such as chocolate and rum were parachuted in. Wine was available in cartons. 'Vino gel' needed water to be added to it. But there was never enough and receipt of a carton depended on a lucky parachute recovery.

'We were always talking of food,' remembered paratrooper Suaudeau. 'Steak and chips, bottles of Beaujolais and camembert![39] Moroccan rations were particularly popular with all the troops.[40]

First Battle for Huguette 6, 4–6 April 1954

Given that Giáp's stock of shells had run out, the method of attack would need to be different. It was not an option available on the five hills. Vietminh troops and their auxiliaries would revert to digging their way to victory by wrapping French bastions in a spider's web of entrenchment. Creeping right up to or under wire defences, the Vietminh burrowed into the heart of French defences then sought to swamp them from close range. This would strangle French positions one by one, so negating French defensive advantages, especially artillery. Elements of these tactics had already been employed but Giáp now accelerated a process that could allow him to attack without massive shell expenditure. A tactic now turned into a strategy.

Having failed in his five hills attack, Giáp's exhausted and depleted units on that front could do no more, so Giáp suddenly switched the axis of attack to the north-west quadrant of the battlefield using his 'fresher' units in that sector. It was an offensive that would continue for several weeks.

Formerly part of Anne-Marie, Huguette 6 was positioned in the north-west corner of the battlefield. Since the early loss of Anne-Marie, this position had been vital in holding open a large area of land for gathering in supply parachutes. It was a small mound of trenches and bunkers surrounded by thick layers of barbed wire. A key strategic outpost, Huguette 6 acted as a sentinel guarding enemy approaches into the north-west quadrant of the battlefield and defended by a mere eighty-six legionnaires and one officer. A vulnerable and obvious target because it dominated so much territory, its loss would bring the Vietminh a great step nearer to the heart of the French encampment.

The great Battle for the Five Hills had only just finished when Giáp, like a boxer using combination punches, first left then right, slugged at the FEC's underbelly. In the early hours of 4 April, Giáp launched four battalions at Huguette 6, whose defenders were the remnants of the 13th Legion Demi Brigade, which had been devastated at Beatrice. They included amongst them Staff Sergeant Bleyer, who had survived both Stalingrad and Beatrice, where he had fought his way out of his bunker through a throng of Vietminh using just a pistol. Driven on by political commissars and officers cowed by Giáp's ruthless demotion of those who failed, the Vietminh stormed the Huguette in waves. But they were thrown back. Those few at least who were not blasted by artillery salvoes were mown down by automatic and machine-gunfire at close range, left hanging on the wire or stiffened in jumbled contortions of death.

The situation was desperate because by the end of the 5th there were only twenty fit legionnaires left to defend the last trench. Bigeard was tasked to rescue the position and save the encampment. First he launched an attack from the east, by driving along the Vietminh-built trench that connected their positions on either side of the runway that had been used to launch the stranglehold on the increasingly isolated Huguette 6. When this attack ran out of steam, Colonel Bréchignac's 2nd BEP, supported by two companies of 6th Colonial Paratroopers and the residue of 1st BEP, scrambled across the runway in the early light to strike the surrounding Vietminh in the rear. Machine-guns and grenades by the dozen, as well as a fierce spirit of camaraderie, drove them through the masses of Vietminh, who at last broke and ran back through gaps in the barbed wire entanglements in the direction of safety to the north-west. Timed to perfection, just at that moment French carrier-based Bearcat fighters swept in with streams of machine-gunfire.

Eight hundred Vietminh bodies littered the ground in a great circle around and on top of the legionnaire position. The French lost 200 men, including four irreplaceable officers.

French numbers declined as counter-attack followed attack in a grisly recreation of the First World War. Paratrooper drops did not fully replace the losses, nor could supply keep up, especially as the reducing area following the abandonment of Huguette 6 meant increasing numbers of supply canisters falling into enemy hands, perhaps fifty percent. Huguette 6, located at the tip of the northern runway, controlled much drop-zone territory. All types of ammunition supplies ran down and the number of large artillery pieces in action halved. Shells were rationed but an additional problem was the shortage of gunners. On the 7th, some troop replacements were parachuted in, including Dr Hantz with his troop of medics, as tracers arched up searching for the plane.

Dominoes, 7 April press conference in Washington

In Washington on 6 April, there was a National Security Council meeting with Eisenhower as well as Nixon attending. Nixon's diary note mentioned that:

> *...the president was in a very serious mood...from the conversation, however, it was quite apparent that the president had backed down considerably from the strong position he had taken on Indochina the latter part of the previous week.*[41]

Nixon suggested that more technicians should be sent and Eisenhower immediately took this up with his aide. However:

...he seemed resigned to doing nothing at all unless we could get the allies and the country to go along with what was suggested and he did not seem inclined to put much pressure on to get them to come along.

The president was perhaps reacting to the result of Giáp's second offensive and the loss of four further strongholds. At a press conference on 7 April following a meeting with congressional leaders, Eisenhower, in response to a reporter's question, which was no doubt planted, said this of Indochina's importance to the US:

...broader considerations that might follow what you would call the 'falling domino' principle. You have a row of dominoes set up, you knock over the first one, and what will happen to the last one is the certainty that it will go over very quickly. So, you could have a beginning of a disintegration that would have the most profound influences.

He was trying to bring popular opinion and the senate behind the idea of intervention, but there was no time for such finessing.

While Eisenhower was preparing public opinion for intervention, which he certainly favoured, there were doubting voices being raised in congress. In a speech to the senate on 6 April, Jack Kennedy poured cold water on optimistic military assessments:

I am frankly of the belief that no amount of American military assistance in Indochina can conquer an enemy which is everywhere and at the same time nowhere, 'an enemy of the people' which has the sympathy and covert support of the people.

Kennedy repeated his criticism, made one year earlier in 1953. It was an analysis of the failure of the French to hand over power despite assurances:

Politically, French control was and is extensive and paramount. There is no popular assembly in Vietnam which represents the will of the people that can ratify the treaty relationship between Vietnam and the French. Although the associated states are said to be 'independent within the French Union,' the French always have a permanent control in the Assembly of the Union and the Government of France guides its actions. Under Article 62 of the French Constitution, the French Government 'co-ordinates' all of the resources of the members of the union placed in common to guarantee its defence, under policies directed and prepared by the French Government.

He should also have mentioned that Article 61 still referred specifically to the associated states as part of the French Union.

It was a speech powerful in analysis. It was also an 'I told you so' moment. While French troops were dying in the mud defending American interests in Indochina, his speech amounted to no more than egotistical grandstanding. Lacking a solution or policy himself Kennedy, like other democrats, groped with the difficulty for a way out of this contradictory stance by reluctantly supporting united action. He would approve intervention if Churchill supported it and joined in, even though that would obviously be a token. Although intervention was being cast in terms of air power, there was general agreement with Senator Russell's observation. 'Once you commit the flag, you've committed the country. There's no turning back.'[42]

Kennedy carried on the hypocrisy by saying on television that Indochina was 'a lost cause'. In just under ten years, Kennedy as president would be committing ground troops. JFK told an interviewer in 1953 that he believed that in the end China would win because of its proximity and willingness to extend the war.

Crisis diplomacy in Washington, London and Paris

Unfortunately for the French soldier in Dien Bien Phu, fast though Eisenhower and Dulles were trying to move in early April 1954, it was not fast enough.

Political pressures also built up with veterans in France directly and angrily accosting Pleven, the defence minister, at the ceremony of the flame at the Arc de Triomphe. Just as Dulles and Eisenhower were beginning to shape their policy and push for intervention, high level talks with Navarre confirmed that he wanted *Vulture*, a project about which he had initially been sceptical. On 4 April, he communicated his thoughts to Paris. 'The intervention…can have a decisive impact.' In this he was right. Massive B29 strikes while the Vietminh Army was in a parlous condition could well have been decisive.

Frantic discussions flew over the wires between Washington and Paris. By the end of 4 April, Eisenhower agreed to send Dulles to London 'at the earliest convenience.'

Receiving the communication on the 5th at 6 p.m., Churchill replied on the 6th, 'I have received your most important message of the 4 April. We are giving it Cabinet consideration. Winston.'

The end result of Eisenhower's meeting with congressional leaders on 7 April was a qualified yes; a compromise that would undermine the entire effort to save Dien Bien Phu. The congressmen promised support for intervention only if there was international support, if France remained committed, and if France agreed to full independence for Vietnam. 'The French would win in six months if the people were with them,' Eisenhower naïvely told Dulles. Eisenhower wanted a coalition of interested nations, including the UK, Australia, New Zealand, and the Philippines to support US intervention. But in essence that boiled down to the agreement of London, the leader of the Commonwealth. If Churchill supported Dulles, then the deal was done.

Eisenhower's response to the crisis in the Dien Bien Phu valley was weak. There was no constitutional need to give congress the power of veto over the decision. Truman had rushed to support South Korea when invaded without any congressional approval. By this and other precedents, unilateral decision-making would not offend the constitution. Eisenhower certainly put Kennedy and his ilk on the spot by handing the veto to congress. He was playing politics, trying to finesse his political scheme while the people fighting the Cold War were dying and their ally France was in danger of political collapse. On 6 April with the Battle of the Five Hills in the balance, decisive action was needed.

With their backs to the wall there is no doubt that the French government would agree to American terms. Whether those terms could be maintained in the face of collapsing support for the war in France was another matter. As they were speaking, the French government under Premier Laniel was formally requesting *Operation Vulture.* Laying it on thick (and falsely) about the surprising and great extent of direct Chinese involvement at Dien Bien Phu, the French hoped to bounce Eisenhower into action.

Churchill's policy

Eisenhower marshalled logistics and political support not troops in battle and sat on committees to decide strategy. When he came into ultimate power, his fundamental vacuity was to be thoroughly exposed. Even that decisiveness in the most important moment of his life, the decision to launch *Overlord*, had left him in his declining years. A politician to the last he sought out political cover.

Cover came in the shape of congress and the approval of Winston Churchill. Churchill had never visited the Far East. An emotional man, he had no emotions engaged in the region. Unfortunately for Indochina, this region was no longer a vital strategic interest for Britain. Eden and Churchill would not pull French irons out of the fire. Ironically after a lifetime of belligerency, Churchill was styling himself as a peacemaker as he approached his twilight years. His determination to make peace in a great post-war summit was as great as his determination to expose and crush Hitler. Stalin was gone in March 1953. He wished to respond positively to the Soviet initiatives that started after Stalin's death and came to life with the Four Power Conference in Berlin, the purpose of which was to set up the Geneva Conference in Indochina. In his dotage Churchill, like many political leaders, was thinking of his legacy. In consequence, he made mistakes and his preening lapdog Eden was only too happy to star in great diplomatic conferences on the world stage as he cemented his succession credentials. Churchill wanted the word 'peacemaker' chiselled in stone on the epitaph of Churchillian history.

That his faculties were failing is undoubted. Sixty years of excess and alcohol abuse, in legendary proportions, each day and every day a punishing routine of stress and cigars, was bound to take its toll eventually and it is remarkable that he had not already succumbed. According to his biographer Boris Johnson, 'He suffered from atrial spasms; he had skin irritations and eye complaints.'[43] He was also going deaf. A summit. A last chance at glory. World peace. These were the new mantras of a fading old man rushing to write his name in history.

With the Geneva Conference coming up it was surely obvious that the surrender of a major French fortress with over 10,000 prisoners in a battle that had for months been built up as a major media event could only mean Vietminh victory at the peace conference. French public opinion, already wavering, would be crushed. That Churchill and Eden were blind to the significant strategic defeat that would be suffered by the Western Alliance if France surrendered at Dien Bien Phu is astounding given their sure understanding of the threat of Nazism in the 1936–38 period. Where was this the man of Fulton, the man who coined the phrase 'iron curtain'?

Churchill and Eden, the anti-appeasement duo, had been pushing the earlier idea of *détente* with Russia, which the Americans felt was a sort of appeasement. Stalin's death was the catalyst for a change, as was the realisation that arms races were both expensive and unpopular at home. The H-bomb introduced a terrifying new element to warfare. There was also the fear of not being able to keep up with the expenditure and technology required of a great power. Most disturbing for Eden was his analysis that China would not back down. Therefore, intervention in Vietnam risked a Third World War should the US attack China, so triggering the Sino-Soviet friendship treaty. Eden made these points at a cabinet meeting on 7 April. British interests according to Churchill and Eden lay in France's more active participation in European defence and withdrawal from a war that was probably lost. Bao Dai's regime was hopeless. The French were losing. A partition was the best that could be hoped for and this should be the aim at Geneva, with the Indochina settlement part of a global peace solution and an end to the Cold War. Eisenhower's adventurism was not welcome and Dulles' aggressive American tone, coupled with the lack of interest in Geneva, annoyed the British.

Dulles flew to London and arranged a meeting with Eden over dinner at the American embassy on the 11th, just a few hours after Bigeard's dramatic re-capture of Éliane 1 in a ferocious and dramatic counter-offensive.

Hold by the belt

After the failure of the second major offensive to destroy French resistance, Giáp decided to extend the campaign of trench warfare to constrict the Dien Bien Phu garrison even tighter. Every metre was a further twist in the garotte being tightened on France's throat. Trench network tendrils wormed deeper into the French defence zone. Using Gabrielle as a base, the Vietminh dug a trench network to surround Huguette 5 and 4 just to the west of the airstrip and the northernmost strongpoints of the French Army. According to Kim Ne, 308th Division head of propaganda:

Each post was surrounded by several layers of barbed wire and surrounded by large paddy field. It was very difficult to camouflage ourselves. The rainy season had commenced and the trenches were extremely muddy and quickly destroyed by the French.[44]

Following the tactical precept 'steady attack, steady advance', Giáp withdrew his troops to retrain them in siege warfare and attacking fixed positions. He aimed to hold the French by the belt in close proximity trenching and short rushes, a tactic that would reduce the effectiveness of French artillery, unless the French defenders called it down on themselves, which on occasions in desperation they did. Giáp's innovation came out of his shortage of munitions. Burrowing, boring and worming their way forward, the Vietminh soldiery, including many thousands of soldiers and dedicated diggers, created a vast network of trench tendrils around French positions. The 316th Division publication noted that:

They worked without ever complaining. The timetable was unchanging; return to unit area at 7 a.m. or 8 a.m., eat, attend a work review then sleep from 9 a.m. to noon, cut and carry timber from noon until 3 p.m., another meal, then head to the trenches with picks and shovels, and work until long after sunrise.[45]

Genevieve's view

If Vietminh prisoners were wounded, 'once they recovered, they joined the group of prisoners utilised as the work force [PIMs] treated just like the others…' observed Genevieve with her remarkable insight:

We had the feeling that they were living a civil war. Some of them had been trained under Ho Chi Minh thinking that he alone could lead them to their independence. Others suffered from the rigid and terrorist methods of the communists.[46]

Using prisoners in this way was against the Geneva Convention, but the willingness to support the French from amongst the elite troops of the DRV regime is telling. What was surprising, however, was the extraordinary way in which PIMs served, with outstanding courage and sense of duty, whether in delivering provisions or ammunition to the front line or carrying wounded to the medical units.

Casualties were constant, recorded Genevieve: 'The assaults continued less violently than in these of the first days of April. Every day brought new casualties…Colonel Langlais brought cigarettes.' Misery in the hospital, but the trenches were ghastly as the monsoon rains increased, 'with the rain,' wrote Lieutenant Ruiter:

> *…the trenches are filthy mud holes where it is impossible to circulate to get to the medics…the only consolation* [in the hospital], *along with good soups, are the cigarettes, the oranges, and the milk that nurse Genevieve de Galard brings us.*

Bigeard's offensive to re-take Éliane 1, 10 April

Bigeard was tasked with taking back Éliane 1. The hill had been taken in the night of 30 March. Artillery, machine-guns and snipers had been installed by the new defenders. The Vietminh had been making life ever more unpleasant for the tenants of Éliane 2, 3 and 4 and the encampment below. Reinforced by the parachute-drop of the 2nd BEP on 9 April, Bigeard had the reserves to throw at the enemy. Langlais decided to re-take Éliane 1.

Bigeard's French counter-attacks were aided by flame-throwers and tanks. Schoendoerffer's film vividly records the long plumes of flame in the distance when viewed from Éliane 4. The heroics of the legionnaires' counter-attacks against Éliane 1 in the face of overwhelming force is the stuff of legend, as they advanced singing the Foreign Legion song, the *Camerone*.[47] Some of them were wearing the traditional white aprons of the engineering section. Not to be outdone, Vietnamese paratroopers sang the *Marseillaise*.

French casualties were high: 'Serge Genty was wounded by shrapnel and a grenade, that hit him in the belly, the feet and the back.' Corporal Michel Chanteaux, already wounded in previous fighting, got into hand-to-hand combat with the Vietminh and was bayoneted in the stomach. He was saved and fitted with an artificial anus. Another casualty, Sergeant Boulier, was hit in the legs and left hand. He spent the night digging a hole with his right hand before being stretchered off the mountain. Refusing amputation, the doctors saved his legs with some unconventional strapping to hold his shattered legs in place while they mended. Edmond Cheval, a volunteer parachutist, dropped into the battle a few days before, described the chaos and carnage of the battlefield at Éliane 1:

They were inside the furnace, there were Viets who had infiltrated between our positions, so we were fired on from all over the battlefield. Who was enemy, who was friend, we had no idea? So, we fired on anything that moved. We jumped into trenches half collapsed, with bodies, ours, Viets, didn't matter, we got used to it, they were everywhere.[48]

Cheval remembered:

It was night, the artilleries from both camps [including Isabelle] *gave us encouragement with their fire and the troops of the 2nd BEP* [Brigade Etranger Parachutistes] *could do nothing more than sing the* Marseillaise *to give ourselves courage: the Viets launched assault after assault but we continued to hold, stacking bodies to act as a parapet, bullets shredded them. In the night the barrage continued...and then suddenly para [Legion paratrooper] reinforcements arrived.*

Then an exceptional event occurred when:

...at the same time the Viet artillery started up again, shells falling everywhere, with a new fury. All at once it stopped, I raised my head and hearing singing I thought I really was *dreaming...but no it was legionnaire reinforcements singing as they ascended the hill.*

The BEP were singing their legion battle song.

Éliane 1 was now the forward position of the FEC in the five hills sector nearest to the main Vietminh encampment. Exposed, they would now take the fury of Vietminh artillery, who were stung into action by an angry Giáp who dismissed the regimental commander that had failed to re-take the hill.

Schoendoerffer went up to Éliane 1 during the battle:

I then went up Éliane 1 and that, for me, was the worst – Éliane 1 – because it had been taken and re-taken; lost and regained: it was the most blood-soaked. And I felt that disquiet: everywhere around me was the feeling of that dead army. An army of our dead but also of theirs. I thought of all those Vietnamese, probably no more than about 20 years old, whose lives ended there.[49]

Schoendoerffer, the maverick photographer who had volunteered for the military as a photographer, witnessed the hand-to-hand fighting, something he recorded in a film fifty years later. He also recorded in words the scenes of devastation, 'the artillery positions were filled with dead gunners who had been blown apart'. By 16 April, Colonel Langlais was begging Hanoi for more gunners to be parachuted in. With their shirtless torsos glistening in rapid movements, the sweat-drenched West African gunners kept the encampment alive. Without them the place would have been long gone.

The smells were disgusting: decomposing bodies, body parts and excrement. Clouds of flies hung over the battlefield making a loud piercing buzzing cacophony, which was audible above the sounds of war. The association of sound, smell and sight was shocking to the senses and conjured up an idea of horror. Cameraman Schoendoerffer, speaking to Howard Simpson after the war, recounted:

> *It was hot and we were thirsty, a working party of PIMs who had been sent to bring water had been killed by a mortar burst. I saw their bodies when I came down the hill, six mangled corpses killed in the red mud that their blood reddened even more.*[50]

Schoendoerffer, an unemployed, itinerant wanderer and adventurous youth from a middle-class Alsatian family, had drifted out to Indochina with a camera. Upon joining the Army Film Service, he would soon be drafted into action:

> *I was a corporal, and I rubbed shoulders with the top brass. I rubbed shoulders with the rank and file. I was wounded; I was with them, the troops. They had to deal with a formidable adversary.*[51]

Rescue: flight of the condor

On 13 April, Navarre began to plan a rescue mission for the beleaguered garrison at Dien Bien Phu by launching an attack from Lao into the rear of the enemy. He instructed Laotian commander General Boucher de Crevecoeur to plan a break in. A plan developed on the basis of a former larger effort named 'Condor'. The plan involved the commitment of three Laotian and one Meo/Lao tribal battalions with two VNA parachute battalions in reserve. There would be some leavening with a Foreign Legion battalion. Their advance would be shielded by various French-officered partisan groups.

However, it was a hopeless venture from the start because there was not enough air transport to support a column this size let alone drop the VNA paratroopers. In the end this pathetically small force retreated rather than face annihilation.

> *Day by day the area for the parachute-drops diminished and posed problems for the renewal of our supplies of ammunition, foods and medicines…But at the central unit we never ran short of medicine and bandages.*

So recalled Genevieve de Galard. With *Atlante* operations still proceeding along the central coast and with other requirements to supply outposts, the French air transport system was degrading. Even when offered more planes by the US, there were not enough pilots or engineers. Aircraft logistics efforts never overcame the deficiencies identified by US experts several years before.

Eden's diplomatic dance

Eden, who was known as 'draughty mouth' to his political enemies, exchanged views with Dulles over dinner on 11 April. Dulles, who prided himself on his powers of persuasion and analysis held forth on the well played-out domino theory. Eden countered with his analysis and with particular reference to the problem of China. Nothing was concluded in any detail.

Over cigars and brandy Eden was cutting about France. Dulles ruminated with Eden on the decline of France as a power. No doubt this was an indirect bit of flattery as to Britain's status, i.e. Britain *was* a superpower, but France was not. More subtle still, Dulles by implication was posing a quite sinister implied question or suggestion. 'Could Britain really pose as a superpower if it skedaddled away from this fight in Indochina?' Pushing on this sensitivity, the fact of Britain's 'great power status' was becoming objectively less true by the week.

Acerbic about all and sundry, Eden was on that path to arrogance and hubris that would end in his disgrace and fall several years later. On the 14th, a bland and airy communique was issued. Britain and the US were 'in an examination of the possibility of establishing a collective defence,' which committed the UK to nothing. In private Eden was quite undiplomatic in his rejection of American pressure. In parliament he was heavily criticised for his speech by MPs representing a war-weary public, which was increasingly concerned about atomic bombs and the new H-bomb.

On 14 April, Dulles moved onto Paris, where in his youth he had been a student, to try to sew up that end of the proposed conditions for intervention. Here too there were difficulties, because Bidault was also under domestic pressure. From the far left and from Mendes-France's moderate left there was increasing pressure and popularity for the anti-war viewpoint in favour of a negotiated exit. Alternatively, Bidault could not disown the associated states concept because France's continued special interest in Indochina underpinned the rationale for staying involved. Dulles was asking for continued altruistic commitment by France while demanding that they give up their interest in the region. An impossible contradiction. There was already a rising anti-American feeling because it was felt across the spectrum that America was using French lives and treasure for its own foreign policy and economic purposes. Bidault often seemed to be rambling and drunk during the talks. Bibulous by nature, the pressure of events and the nearing catastrophe were forcing him into even more drink and indiscretion than normal.

Navarre had added to the pleas. Bidault and the French position started to move to acceptance of the United Action policy of the US, i.e. the internationalisation of the Indochina conflict involving a coalition of powers. As the day wore on the discussions became more fraught and emotional. The French despair was palpable. Dien Bien Phu was on the brink just as the diplomats ruminated and debated over polished tables surrounded by Louis XIV 'pompadour' décor, as they dined sumptuously off Limoges and drank fine clarets over dinner, vintage cognacs, and cigars to follow. Five star Hotel de La Paix (a UNESCO heritage site founded 1865) was brim full of expense account diplomats.

Bidault understood something that Dulles and the Americans did not, something that he had only recently appreciated. Navarre and the French military elite understood that Dien Bien Phu had been politicised to such an extent that its outcome would determine the future and fate of Indochina. What was clear to Bidault, but only slowly becoming apparent to Dulles, was that defeat at Dien Bien Phu would absolutely and immediately end France's commitment to the war. The French people wanted negotiations and an exit now. Even though the military balance would not be much affected by the battle in terms of numbers or territory, the tipping of the moral and morale scales would be final and absolute. Defeat at Dien Bien Phu meant defeat in Indochina.

But it was not just Giáp who built up the story and importance of Dien Bien Phu, because the French in anticipation of another victory such as General Salan's at Ná Sán had also built-up expectations for another such 'victory'. Navarre and the press had built up the mystique of the impregnable jungle fortress, *le base aero-terrestrial de Dien Bien Phu*, and the magnificent Beatrice fortifications.

On the 15th Eden, the man who had built his political fortunes by opposing appeasement, wrote to Dulles, fundamentally disagreeing with the domino analysis:

> *I am not convinced that no concession could be made to communists in Indochina without inevitably leading to communist domination of the whole of South-East Asia, particularly if we have the proposed security system.*

It was naïve appeasement, but clearly indicated that a deal over Vietnam was being contemplated with the Soviets.

On returning to Washington, Dulles now sought to manoeuvre and box the British into place by the calling of a 'unity' conference in Washington, the idea being to use the interested group of nations to hustle London into agreement on intervention. Without consulting Eden, Dulles invited interested powers, including countries in Britain's Commonwealth sphere of influence. Australia,

New Zealand, the Philippines and Thailand were invited. When informed of Dulles's manoeuvre on the 17th, Eden was incensed, falling out with the UK's Washington ambassador who had airily assumed that the invitation would be accepted. Eden testily refused Britain's participation:

> *I am not aware that the Americans have any cause for complaint. Americans may think the time has passed when they have to consider the feelings and difficulties of their allies…we at least have to bear in mind all our commonwealth partners even if the United States does not like some of them.*

Dulles pointed to written notes that seemed to suggest Eden's agreement to the conference. Eden disagreed with the notes. Eden resented the pressure from the 'crude' Americans, whose aggressive, confrontational and warlike posture he fretted over.

For Eden's part there was another game to play. He had probably reached a tacit agreement with the Soviets to partition Vietnam. There would be a grand peace conference and reconciliation at Geneva that would seal the deal already negotiated. It was also to be the crowning of Churchill's career as well as the harbinger of Eden's accession to the British premiership. With the glow of international success behind him, Eden would become prime minister and could go to the country to secure his mandate.

Huguette 6 final offensive, 17–19 April

Giáp concentrated his attacks in mid-April on Huguette 6. The reason was clear, because the northerly outpost extended considerably the drop-zone for supplies and reinforcements. Already some parachutists had dropped directly into Vietminh territory where they were promptly captured. Meanwhile miss-dropped supplies and ammunition continued to account for as much as ten to fifteen percent of the total.[52] Much of it was useable because the two sides were using the same weapons. Particularly valuable were the 105mm shells. By taking Huguette 6, they could strangle the French garrison even further. But in fact the tendrils of Vietminh trenching had already wrapped around and burrowed into Huguette 1. The key post at Huguette 1, some 350 yards to the south, would become more vulnerable to attack. If Huguette 1 fell, the bastion would be virtually doomed because the drop-zone would become minimal. Momentum was with Giáp and the VPA.

Giáp's long-term game plan of strangling the ability of the French to supply their garrison was beginning to bite. The fewer shells and other ammunitions, the smaller the drop-zone, and then still fewer shells etc., still smaller drop-zone and even fewer shells and so on…it was a logistical death spiral for Dien Bien Phu's garrison because artillery shells were the main defence. Each dropped package had to be fought for by teams of night scavengers, an occupation that became increasingly competitive and dangerous. A mixed-race Vietnamese member of the Foreign Legion noted in his contemporaneous diary:

> *Jean died today. He was trying to retrieve an air-dropped package that fell just beyond our trench. Vietminh riflemen shot him at least a dozen times.*[53]

With the Vietminh trenches wrapped tightly around Huguette 6, the 200-man garrison manned by legionnaires now appeared doomed. The nearest Vietminh trenches were just 30m away. One third of the defenders were already casualties. Bigeard launched a relief attack with legionnaires and paratroopers supported by two tanks. But after several days of fighting they were still 500m short. The momentum of the assault petered out as casualties mounted and exhaustion set in. There was hand-to-hand fighting. One legionnaire remembered that having run out of ammunition, 'we had to use bayonets. For some awful period of time, it was like that. It was a filthy business.'[54]

Another, Felix Guzman, recounted: 'All of a sudden there is a Viet. It's him or me. So you shoot…'[55]

On the 18th, it was decided that the post needed to be abandoned. A breakout attempt was the only way to avoid being overrun.

Given a suicide mission, a wounded legionnaire was given a machine-gun to cover the retreat while the rest armed themselves with grenades and placed half-filled sandbags over their backs and fronts to protect themselves from grenade fragments. It is not recorded whether or not the wounded legionnaire survived, but it is highly unlikely. On Easter Sunday, 19 April, with luck on their side, the great dash for safety began in a thick fog. The exhausted men, galvanised by their last drops of adrenaline, leapt over Vietminh trench after Vietminh trench, tossing grenades as they went.

The Vietminh were taken by surprise, either sleeping or mostly facing the wrong way to ward off the relief effort 300m from their positions as the manic and strangely accoutred legionnaires came bounding out of the fog lit by dozens of flashes from exploding grenades. Figures zig-zagged towards safety followed by hails of automatic fire and more grenades.

One hundred and forty made it to safety but sixty did not. Only five out of sixteen officers survived. It was a success for a mission that could have led to total annihilation.

Churchill says 'No!' The loss of the fortress must be faced

On 18 April, General Ely, chief of the French Army, flew to Washington to plead for immediate action to save Dien Bien Phu, but he was brushed off by Eisenhower and the administration with an evasive reply. With Dulles back in

Paris, Bidault begged for help on the morning of the 22nd. There is a picture of General Ely meeting Eisenhower. Ely looks nervous and has the air of someone timidly about to ask for a big favour. Eisenhower looks down sheepishly with the air of someone who knows what is about to be asked and that he will refuse it.

Meanwhile, the French Army in Dien Bien Phu was being crushed into the mud, blood and slime in a singularly grotesque battleground in the remote valley on the Lao-Vietnam border, just another far-away place for British diplomacy. Aware of the British veto, Bidault argued that London did not matter because the UK contribution, militarily, would be minimal anyway. He missed the point. It was about political perception, smoke and mirrors, and congress's vanity rather than anything tangible. As the atmosphere became more tense, Bidault even took Dulles aside and broached the idea of using the A-bomb.

The French were in a panic at this point. With the situation deteriorating rapidly at Dien Bien Phu, especially as the logistics stranglehold began to bite, France was now willing to offer full independence and to abandon the MRP and Bidault's cherished dream of the associated states. In America, there was added froth whipped into the international mix when Vice-President Nixon made a very hawkish speech advocating armed intervention and an aggressive stance at Geneva. Under the influence, Bidault ranted incoherently that he 'was casting himself to the wolves.'[56] The self-pitying cry of a politician whose world view was collapsing, along with his long life in politics.

As if he had not had enough pressure over intervention Eden, who went to Paris for tri-party talks later on the 23rd, was ambushed at a cocktail reception in the US embassy by Dulles backed by a cohort of senior American officers.

Meanwhile, in the exploding hell of Dien Bien Phu, the soldiers knew that they had been thrown to the wolves, but there was little self-pity amongst the fighting men of the garrison.

Eden flew from Paris and travelled directly to see Churchill at Chequers on the 24th. Much as Churchill regarded the American special relationship as the cornerstone of foreign policy, he did not regard Indochina as the cornerstone of France's international utility for Britain's national interest. The Geneva Conference and the chance of peace and reduction of tension in a nuclear age was the overriding aim. From a realpolitik perspective there was a good line of reasoning indeed to Churchill's thoughts. If France would lose anyway, military intervention was risky, and there were no serious British interests east of Suez. Hong Kong and Malaysia were expendable and, if necessary, even Singapore. And relations with India and Burma, who supported Ho Chi Minh, had to be considered. However, the key driver underpinning his policy was political ego. As were the Czechs to Chamberlain, for Churchill and Eden Indochina was a 'far away country'. Churchill had indeed decided that his life should be crowned in 'peace'. Britain in Churchill's opinion should not go to war 'because of a quarrel in a faraway country between people of whom we know nothing.'[57]

British troops had recently returned from Korea where they had fought magnificently against heavy odds to stop the brutal communist takeover of the country.

Eisenhower fumed, criticising the weak British response. But it was Eisenhower's weakness that had in the first place tied his decision to congress and to London. It was a miscalculation that could not now be undone. On the 24th, Dulles wired to Eisenhower: 'The situation here is tragic. France is almost visibly collapsing before our eyes.'

Dulles signed off on his failure with these notes made on 25 April 1954. It is worth quoting in some detail:

> *Eden made quite clear that the United Kingdom is opposed to air intervention at Dien Bien Phu and also opposed to becoming directly involved in any way with the Indochinese war...I said to Eden I felt the position which his Government had taken would have so little in it in way of comfort to the French that the prospect of the latter standing firm here was very slight. It would be a tragedy not to take steps now which would prevent Indochina from being written off.*

Eisenhower decided to send Admiral Radford to make a last plea to Churchill at Chequers on the 26th. While Churchill sipped cognac and puffed vigorously on one of his huge cigars, the whole domino mantra was deployed. Churchill listened. He agreed that the loss of Dien Bien Phu would be a turning point in history, but he intoned that 'the loss of the fortress must be faced.' Churchill was used to losing fortresses. It was too late to save it. And why, Churchill mused, should Britain fight to save the French empire when she had failed to fight for her own in India.[58]

Information as to these developments was quickly known to the Chinese, as revealed by Zou En Lai's communication to Mao on 28 April:

> *Although the United States fired many blanks on the Indochina issue, they could not scare anyone but themselves...it is now impossible for the United States to stop negotiations on the Indochina issue. Eisenhower's recent words showed his retreat and embarrassed Dulles. Therefore, Dulles decided to run away* [from the conference] *and leave the problems to the under-secretary of state, General Walter Bedell Smith. Eden said that Dulles had already decided to return to the US next week. Molotov responded that 'it will increase the responsibilities of the four'. The current situation shows that Eden will stay, and so will Bidault.*[59]

The close alignment of Eden (Churchill) with the Chinese and Soviets is revealed. Eden and Churchill's policy of *detente* had outflanked Dulles and

Eisenhower. Splitting the US and the UK was a significant diplomatic victory for USSR-China. But only because Eisenhower had self-imposed defeat by tying himself unnecessarily to congress and Churchill.

Fight for Huguette 1, 18–22 April

Behind Huguette 6 was Huguette 1, the next in line for the strangulation-by-trench tactics of the Vietminh. Defended by a company of legion infantry, they needed to be relieved. Captain Chevalier of the 13th Legion Demi Brigade advanced on the night of 18–19 April. They had to fight their way in, trench by trench, because the Vietminh had once again surrounded the bastion with fortifications and machine-gun posts. With artillery and aircraft in support, Chevalier broke in at 10 a.m. with eighty of the 120 men he had started with, having covered 1,000m in fourteen hours. The exiting company suffered heavy losses as well when they retreated to the main encampment.

By the 20th, Captain Chevalier's post at Huguette 1 was under constant heavy attack as Giáp focused his attentions on further reducing the area of the drop-zone. Concentrating on this small patch of chewed up earth, the Vietminh artillery seemed intent on blasting them to oblivion. Dominique 2 looked directly down on Huguette 1, just 1km away so, in addition to 105mm fire, they also suffered direct fire from 75mm cannon and mortars. Vietminh sappers dug hidden saps to within metres of French positions before launching attacks. Metre by metre the defenders were pushed back to the command post bunker and its surrounding trenches. When a human wave attack threatened to overrun his defences, Chevalier called down heavy 120mm mortars onto his own positions. The attackers were decimated. In the morning the enemy dead were tossed out of the French trenches.

Surrounded by four barriers of 5m-deep wire, Huguette was a formidable bastion, but the local Vietminh commander devised a simple but effective strategy by tunnelling under the wire as well as cutting it at night and leaving it in place so that it seemed undamaged. The idea was to pop out within the last perimeter and overwhelm the French defenders. Legionnaire Erwan Bergot described the legionnaires' counter-sapping tactics. They listened and located the direction of approach: 'They killed the first enemy to emerge, filled the hole with explosives, then tamped it with the body'[60] so that the charge would explode inwards to the tunnel wiping out the Vietminh underground.

However, not all of the tunnels were detected. On the 21st, a surprise attack was sprung with legionnaires bewildered by the sudden presence of Vietminh infantry in their midst. The attack had been preceeded by only the briefest shelling, just three 105mm rounds. One problem for the attackers was that three tunnels did not offer a high capacity so, despite getting in amongst the defenders, they could not overwhelm them. Held off for a while, the Vietminh were reinforced by all available troops, including the diggers and the water bailers. Still the enemy came on until Chevalier formed a last stand with the survivors. The radio went dead at 2.30 a.m. on the 23rd as they were overwhelmed. Huguette 1, like the rest of the battlefield, was an obliteration of trenches and craters in a monochrome sea of mud. One soldier escaped and survived the onslaught. It had only taken four more days after the loss of Huguette 6 to capture Huguette 1. Giáp's rapid switching of fronts after the failure of the second general offensive was masterly. In the space of four days he had advanced the front by about 700m, representing an enormous constriction of the drop-zone and leaving over 1,000 uncollected supply drops to be raked in by the VPA. It was the fatal blow. All that remained would be the *coup de grace*. The beleaguered garrison was now in a spiral of declining supplies of men, food and munitions.

Huguette 1 was so vital that de Castries immediately ordered Bigeard to counter-attack to re-take the post. The loss of so much drop-zone territory would be disastrous for the beleaguered encampment's supply position. The post had to be recaptured by 4 p.m. It was a typical pattern: Vietminh attacking at night and the French counter-attacking in the daytime to maximise the precision of their artillery support as well as offering opportunities for close air support.

Bigeard launched the counter-attack using Major Liesenfeldt's recently landed 2nd BEP. Twelve hundred artillery rounds dropped on the Huguette 1 defences. Then B26 bombers pounded the enemy. Smoke shells prevented direct fire from the overlooking Dominique heights. The plan looked to be perfect, and success was expected, but the first problem was that the exhausted Bigeard fell asleep. The BEP were surprised by hidden Vietminh machine-guns allegedly in the nose of a wrecked plane as they advanced across the old air field, which offered no cover at all as it was covered in metal. Zeroed-in on the runway area, the Vietminh artillery appraised of what was afoot simply blasted the area with shrapnel.

When Bigeard was alerted to the problems, he hastened by Jeep to the command bunker and found that Liesenfelt had had no contact with his men and was simply assuming that they had succeeded. Bigeard soon discovered that Liesenfelt's radio was on the wrong frequency, so their desperate pleas for help had gone unanswered. Remaining in his bunker, Liesenfelt had no plain sight of his men, something that Bigeard would never let happen. The gruff colonel always came up to within sight of his troops so as to take command personally. Shocked at Liesenfelt's dereliction of duty, he took personal command. Deciding that the attack had failed, an attack that everyone had advised de Castries against, the order for retreat was covered by artillery fire, the legionnaire paratroopers pulled back but the eighty percent casualty rate was catastrophic for the already weakly manned fortress. Nineteen troops were dead and seventy were wounded. The isolated position at Opera on the corresponding east side of the Pave track would also have to be abandoned. They were unaffordable losses. Another elite unit had been struck from the order of battle and was duly merged. Liesenfelt was left without a command.

Later Bigeard would blame himself for not being on the spot and in personal command. 'In spite of my exhaustion…I have to take personal responsibility for this defeat.' He had been against the counter-attack, believing that the Huguette position was untenable. However, the loss of the post doomed the whole bastion to defeat in short order because AA guns, both 37mm and the lighter 22mm, could be brought even closer to the French central bastion to deter the supply plane runs yet further. Miss-drops increased to about thirty to fifty percent from a drop tonnage that was already in general decline.

Having successfully defended their capture of Huguette 1, the Vietminh, like a rampant cancer, started immediately to burrow their way towards Huguette 4 and 5. At the end of April, a further 300 volunteers were dropped into the valley, but there were no more elite units because command in Hanoi and Saigon refused to deploy the last parachute battalion, the 1st BPC. Nor would they drop other non-paratrooper elite units. Portuguese legionnaire Joachim da Silva volunteered to drop in. He remembered upon landing that 'there were lots of corpses in the barbed wire, a lot of Vietnamese, ours as well…a lot of corpses, a lot of smell.'[61] French high command in Paris had not thought to deploy other units from around the empire or from metropolitan France. Defeat had been accepted. Only large US B29 strikes could now save the day. Without them the FEC could only hope to extend the battle beyond the Geneva talks start date on 8 May and hope for a ceasefire truce.

Scraping the barrel, 20 April

On 20 April, 100 volunteers dropped into the encampment as reinforcements and more over the next few nights. They included ninety-five legionnaires (mostly German), 170 Algerians, European soldiers from various units, four Moroccans, three officers and twenty-seven non-commissioned officers. Scraping the barrel, 100 court-martialled soldiers were offered pardons in return for volunteering.

Langlais also asked Dr Grauwin to see if there were any potential volunteers in the medical and hospital units. When news of the approach leaked out the response was immediate. A horrified Dr Grauwin could only stand by as severely wounded soldiers got up from their fetid beds and hobbled to rejoin their units on the front line:

I saw one-legged men supported by their two-legged comrades; one-armed patients, their chests swathed in bandages. My blind men who claim sight. My patients with punctured lungs and rolling eyes.

Grauwin pleaded with them not to go, but 'Our mates are expecting us,' they replied. 'If we have to die, we want to go with them.'[62] They fully expected to be slaughtered if the bastion fell. They were not wrong, though the manner of the slaughter would be long and agonised.

Washington, 23 April

Eisenhower and Nixon met with congressional leaders. The president vacillated again on the question of intervention and when challenged by Senator Hallek as to the unpopularity of the idea, Eisenhower stepped in saying, 'We had to think of whether it was best to take a strong stand now when we could or wait until later when we could not.'[63] Eisenhower had good reasons to be vacillating and nervous for political reasons. Eighty-five percent of Americans were opposed to the idea of intervention in Indochina, according to a Gallup poll in March 1953.[64] This was reflected in the senate debates in April where democratic senator Edwin C. Johnson said 'he was against sending American GIs into the mud and muck of Indochina on a bloodletting spree to perpetuate colonialism,' 'or hang on to the remnants of empire,' as Jack Kennedy put it when he quoted his own report made in 1951.[65]

Even Eisenhower's Repubican Party had many opponents to aid for France. Senator Barry Goldwater of Arizona was a fierce critic of colonialism. In a senate speech on 1 July, Goldwater attacked Eisenhower's Indochina saying that aid should only be given with a clear promise of independence for Indochina's constituent entities. He presciently attacked the US$400m aid package for France, saying, 'as surely as day follows night, our boys will follow this $400 million.'

New positions and Bidault's desperation

As the big fortified bastions of Dien Bien Phu fell, subsidiary and supporting fortified positions came in to the front line of defences. When Beatrice, Gabrielle, Anne-Marie and the Dominiques fell, then the Huguette positions became the focus for the Vietminh. Other defensive pods, such as Lily 1, 2, 3 and Junon, came into existence, or Éliane 11 and 10, which eventually became the last places of resistance on the right bank of the Nam Youm River. There were Huguettes 1–6. A Dominique 3 appeared to block attacks along the riverbank towards the bridge over the river. Claudine also proliferated. Two of the quad 50s were moved to Epervier to cover infiltrations from the north-west quadrant and suppress the troublesome fire from the commanding heights of Dominque 1 and 2. Located next to the quad position:

> *I was quite used to the sound of the four barrelled machine-guns* [quads] *and the rhythm of their reverberation. It went on day and night. Its four barrels aimed at Dominique from where every sign of life had vanished. But you could just make out mole hills; narrow trenches, camouflaged emplacements.*

It was around these points defended by reduced companies, or even platoons of broken and depleted units, that the battle increasingly swung. The proliferation of bastions had a purpose. Spread out in small pockets, they dispersed enemy artillery fire and offered interlocking fire points for machine-guns. To call them strongpoints or positions is to flatter. They mostly were just holes in a flat landscape, a sea of deep mud with liquifying parapets and collapsing sandbags, one indistinguishable from the next.

On 27/28 April, Zhou En Lai sent Mao a telegram revealing:

> *Bidault and other members of the French delegation have showed a keen interest in contacting members of the Chinese delegation…Therefore, the discussion on the Indochina question could begin ahead of the* [conference's] *schedule.*[66]

Knowing that the American gambit for intervention had failed and that surrender at Dien Bien Phu was only a matter of time, perhaps days, Bidault, desperate to avoid humiliation wanted a ceasefire and a back door negotiation on Indochina's future.

Washington, 29 April

There was more handwringing over Indochina at another NSC meeting. Vice-President Nixon's diary notes an air of pessimism with Eisenhower unsure what to do, but he ruled out unilateral action, which others wanted, because he believed in 'our whole principle of collective defence against communism in all places in the world.' However, the next morning General Cutler met with Eisenhower and Nixon and mentioned that the planning board of the NSC had been discussing the use of the atom bomb. Eisenhower asked Nixon's opinion, who suggested that it should not be mentioned to allies and that conventional strikes should be made first. Eisenhower agreed, and told Cutler:

> *I certainly do not think that the atom bomb can be used by the United States unilaterally and second I agree with Dick that we do not have to mention it to anybody before we get some agreement on united action.*

They were all fiddling while at Dien Bien Phu it rained shells, mortars and Katuysha rockets.

CHAPTER XIX

The Third General Offensive, 30 April

The first of May is a day of celebration in the communist calendar so an offensive to mark the event was most likely. But apart from that, time was running out for Giáp. The whole campaign had been geared to victory by 8 May, which was the date when the Geneva Conference was formally due to start. Hence Giáp's increasingly desperate attacks and cavalier attitude to casualties. The key to winning was to reduce the drop-zone, so reducing the garrison's logistical capacity, before launching his final overwhelming offensive, hoping that the French would simply exhaust their depleted shell stocks and reserves of men. It was brutal attrition but there was no other way. Any cost was worthwhile for the cause, even if it meant stripping the rest of the country of his experienced troops and throwing barely trained youngsters into the maelstrom. Like the French, most of the Vietminh elite troops were already dead, wounded or simply worn out.

At 5 p.m. on 30 April, the full storm of Vietminh firepower landed on three key targets at Dominique 3, Éliane 1 and Huguette 5. Defences and bunkers and men were shattered and buried under the deluge. When it stopped the surviving defenders knew that waves of bo doi would emerge from the saps, some of them hidden and close by. The offensive disrupted the celebration of the *Camerone* by the legion units. Extra supplies of vino-gel had been dropped for the occasion.

As thousands of Vietminh and French were killing each other in bloody close-quarter combat on the night of 30 April/1 May, Sir Anthony Eden and Zhou En Lai were meeting amicably in Geneva.[1] On the 29th, British and Chinese diplomats had been fine-dining together. Zhou En Lai enjoyed Geneva, perhaps because he was a long way from the capricious and sinister Mao. A cultured man known for his love of western dancing, Zhou found time to accept a dinner invitation from Charlie Chaplin, a suspected communist sympathiser, at his luxurious lakeside mansion in Corsier-sur-Vevey.

The bo doi, Moroccans, Algerians, T'ai, Germans and French, who were fighting and dying at Éliane 1, 4, 2 and Huguette, might have been surprised to know that the outcome of their life and death battles would hardly make a jot of difference to the future map of Indochina, which had already been negotiated by Sir Anthony Eden, Molotov and Zou En Lai behind the backs of the Americans, the French and Ho Chin Minh. Churchill would have his triumph.

Attacks on Huguette 5, 30 April–1 May

On 1 May, Vietminh troops from the crack 308th Division closed in on Huguette 5 on the western flank of the shrunken fortress. The renowned 308th, which had taken so many losses, was now relegated to a subsidiary role as the diversionary attacker whilst the final hammer blow was to be delivered against Éliane 2 by the explosion of a huge mine.

Meanwhile, information and rumours circulated amongst the troops as to the points of breakdown and details of fighting. Major Dr Grauwin was unusually well informed because:

> *Stretcher bearers brought news constantly. The Viets had suddenly multiplied by tens and were showing themselves everywhere, they literally rose up out of the mud and water. They were in their element, infiltrating everywhere, into passages, trenches, shell holes, crossing quagmires of mud.*[2]

The French defenders knew they were coming. As they emerged from the sap, the French artillery laid down a barrage in the path of the infantry who were following through the small breach made by the few Bangalore men. 'Section 4 attack,' shouted Tang above the din. 'Suddenly everything went black, I could not see and felt feet treading on my body. I lost consciousness.' The Viets attacked and the French counter-attacked:

> *There too Langlais and Bigeard went with their red forage caps…after their visit the counter-attack took place with grenades and tommy guns; they retook the support post…advancing over the dead bodies of the enemy and those of their own men.*[3]

On the night of the 30th, Huguette 5 would be taken then recaptured by Captain Luciani's legionnaires with two Chaffee tanks in support. Tanks had been instrumental in staving off Vietminh attacks, but five of them were now out of action.

Huguette 5, a few hundred metres to the north of Huguette 4 (Lily 3), on the east side of the perimeter, was just 2km from de Castries' bunker. Shellfire poured in as well as assaults from two entire Vietminh regiments. Defence of Huguette 5 on the night of 1/2 May came down to twenty-six legionnaires, including thrice wounded Second Lieutenant Boisbouvier. Two regiments of the 308th had made the final attack from the north and west while another regiment was held in reserve. The French had held on for one and half hours before being overwhelmed.

Their leader, Captain Stabanrath, was so badly wounded, he was incapable of fighting or walking. A reinforcement counter-attack by fifty legionnaires from Huguette 2 was turned back by heavy shellfire. Dragged back to the central defences, Stabanrath was one of three survivors.

Wounded in the head, by the time Tang recovered consciousness in hospital, his surviving comrades visited and recounted how Huguette 5 had fallen and the battle was over.

Éliane 1, 30–31 May

Éliane 1 was simultaneously attacked by the 312th Division. The position was held by an eighty-man company of the 2nd BPC commanded by Colonel Bréchignac. French artillery was ready for the attack and machine-guns quickly brought into action mowed down the attackers. However, by midnight there were only twelve men left including their officer, whose head wound exposed his brain. Fed into the fight, the reserves were also slaughtered in short order. By 2 p.m. the hill had fallen and the remnants limped back to Éliane 3:

> *They arrived all night, a mixture of French and Vietnamese totally catatonic with shell shock and exhaustion. The Vietminh 105mm shells were falling; a combination of air burst shells, contact fuses, and* [most unnerving of all] *delayed action fuses that buried themselves in the mud* [i.e. secretly] *but were set to explode later…we lived with death. It was a part of life.*

Langlais and Bigeard put in a personal appearance at this critical stage. As ever the mood lifted when they arrived:

> *How many men left in your company?…Oh about 15. The lieutenant was killed right away…if only you had seen it all, Major Langlais and Bigeard came along the trench. I knew it was them with their red forage caps. No helmets! And the stuff was coming down like hell…they said to the remains of the battalion… 'Come on lads. We must put this right. It's the last blow. If we get the hill back we've won. Up the paras.'*
>
> *…galvanised into a mad rush, they swept up to the top of the hill. The Viets were flung down the opposite slope in an inferno of explosions, blood, and smoke, down into the barbed wire holes and trenches.*[4]

Paratrooper Riviere recounted that they succeeded, but then:

> *Hundreds of Viets poured down from Bald hill. I was more or less pushed along by the Viets, with ten lads behind me. I really don't know why we are still alive.*[5]

Éliane 1 fell again, and for the last time.

Vicious fighting swirled around every blockhouse. Dr Grauwin remembered:

> *...a Viet NCO told me how they blew up our blockhouses; a nine foot bamboo with plastic explosives on the end was gradually advanced towards a loophole; suddenly there was a great explosion...strong enough to bring the blockhouse down on its occupants.*[6]

Dominique 3, 2 May

Dominique 3 was a crucial defensive position blocking access to the right bank of the Nam Youm River and the vital bridge linking to the central encampment. At this point in the battle, it was impossible to shield vulnerable units. The last of the Dominiques was defended by amalgamated Algerian and T'ai tribesmen, then stiffened with a half company of Bigeard's 6th BPC. It would face a full-on attack by two regiments of the 316th Division, about 5,000 men against a few hundred defenders. As shells and artillery were short, the focus of French defensive artillery fire was on the support of the Élianes. There was nothing to spare for Dominique 3. So the defence was conducted with machine-guns, submachine-guns, bayonets and grenades. Contrary to some expectations, and perhaps a disappointment to the Vietminh after their efforts at undermining their morale with anti-colonial propaganda broadcast by loudspeaker, the much-maligned Algerians and T'ai fought stubbornly. Only after eleven hours of non-stop bloody fighting did the strongpoint cease to operate when at 4 p.m. the commander radioed back that he had no unwounded men left to fight. The radio went silent.

In Washington, chief of staff Admiral Redford, anticipating defeat, released a statement opposing any idea of a ceasefire that would allow 'the communist Vietminh to build up their strength.' The dispatch rejected any solution except 'outright military defeat of the Vietminh rebels.'[7] It showed the level of fantasy in parts of the administration including the White House, who thought that the war would continue with the French if Dien Bien Phun fell. Having failed to intervene with aerial bombardment, the US was continuing to lose the plot.

Isabelle, 2 May

By noon on 2 May only six out of eleven of Isabelle's 105mm cannon were operational. And it was not just at Isabelle that there was a problem. At last, the consequences of constricted drop-zone and the resulting shortage of shells was beginning to make a decisive impact on the defensive capability of the Dien Bien Phu bastion as the number of operational guns decreased and ammunition was rationed. Flank shellfire from Isabelle had made a crucial difference in the battle, so their fifty-five percent reduction in firepower was a clear sign of a collapsing defence due to damaged or broken guns or a lack of spare parts.[8]

Huguette 4 and Lily, 4 May

At the same time that Huguette 5 came under attack, so too did Huguette 4 and Lily, created after the loss of Huguette 1. Huguette 4 had helped to support Huguette 5.

On 4 May, Giáp changed his axis of attack again and launched a regiment at Huguette 4. Legionnaire Captain Luciani, survivor of Beatrice and the leader of the counter-attacks on Huguette 5, commanded elements of the 1st and 2nd BEP and a Moroccan company of 220 men. Describing the final attack, he recounted laconically that 'there were 3,000 of them against 80 of us.' Proper legionnaire odds in the *Camerone* tradition.

Attacked by a whole Viet regiment just after midnight, the position was snuffed out around 3.35 a.m. An officer's dying scream was heard by de Castries, as he fell at his radio post when the Vietminh troops stormed into his bunker. The Vietminh had suffered massive casualties. Luciani escaped.

Fighting was all around the encampment. 'The shells were falling constantly, the dull explosions from mortars; the crack of the 75s, the deeper impressive sound of the 105s, then our guns started up.'[9]

French casualty lists mounted up. With multiple points of attack, a flood of wounded wormed its way through the trenches and tunnels towards the main medical centre that was already crammed to overflowing. Both Genevieve and Dr Grindrey, without orders, gave up their quarters to the wounded. 'Genevieve had given up her shelter to her friends, the wounded.' She slept on a muddy floor.[10] And 'Grindrey's shelter was crammed. There were Viet soldiers mixed up with legionnaires.'[11] As the wounded came to Dr Grauwin at the triage point, many would say, '*Bitter mein kommandanten nich abschieden?*'[12] or 'Please major no cut please?'[13]

With Huguette 3 gone the fighting moved ever closer to the central area. When Dr Grauwin commented on his colleague Dr Vidal being in a sub-medical operating unit very close to the fighting, Colonel Langlais replied dryly, 'My dear Grauwin, we're all in the front line now.'[14]

Huguette 3

This position renamed Lily 3 also fell on 4 May. Lily 3 was about 250 yards south of Huguette 5, which had been captured in the early morning of the 2nd. What is extraordinary is that three regiments of the 308th took a further three days to capture lightly held Lily 3, which was so close by. One reason was the fierce resistance of the French including badly wounded and incapacitated men who had gone back into the line. When he awoke, a wounded legionnaire told Dr Grauwin and the inspecting general de Castries what had happened:

I was in my shelter with two other blokes and the machine-gun. I was firing through the loophole and saw them fall, five, ten at a time. Suddenly, they got into the shelter and that's all I can remember.[15]

The only rational explanation is that the casualties suffered by the 308th were enormous. From Lily 3, the compact central defences, including Lily 2 and 1, were just 300 yards distant.

'Everything is smashed up,' recounted one legionnaire to Dr Grauwin. 'It was frightful. I was in Russia in 44, but I have never seen anything like this.'[16]

Logistics crisis

The number of serviceable 105mm cannon had dropped from twenty-four to eighteen in the course of the third general offensive and only one of the four deadly 155mm was operational. However, the problem was not so much artillery numbers now but simply the ability to supply them with ammunition, men to man them, and spares to repair them. Ammunition for machine-guns was also running out and they were critically short in the supply of grenades, the most essential weapon of trench warfare. In his bunker de Castries, at dawn on the 5th, transmitted desperate pleas for more supplies and troops:

We are short of all sorts of provisions, stocks of which are at the lowest level. We do not have enough ammunition to fend off enemy assaults in a situation where constant fire is necessary...I do not expect to recover even half of dropped supplies which in any case represent just a small fraction of my requests. It's an untenable situation.

He estimated that less than fifty percent of drops were being collected and the shortage or reluctance of porters and PIMs to undertake the increasingly dangerous task meant that front-line soldiers were taking casualties trying to collect the packages. He made bitter remarks at the lack of round the clock drops, commenting on the double standards applied to the protection of aircrew lives in this desperate situation. Collecting the packages was a deadly business. Each unit was designated to collect the packages at night in their territory:

There had been a special company of coolies for the job but at the end of a week two hundred of them had either been killed or wounded.[17]

Running out of PIMs, soldiers had to be sent. Also, 'a minefield had to be laid at night in front of the Opera position...the Viets were only 50 yards away... suddenly a flare went up and twenty grenades rained down...three dead, six wounded.'[18]

Jumps into hell

Airdrops of supplies were continuing. However, 800 tons were dropped between 1–7 May, which was not nearly enough. But in any case, of that supply, over fifty percent fell directly into the hands of the Vietminh. The balance had to be contested in no man's land between the different strongpoints.

A decision was also taken to drop in the 1st Colonial Parachute Battalion (BPC). On the night of 3–4 May, Captain Jean Pouget, a former aide of Navarre on the general staff, dropped with his 125-man company of parachutists. Pouget had volunteered to leave the staff job because he wanted action. He describes the experience of night-jumping from his Dakota:

> *...the flak opened up, reaching for the sound of the engines, on the predetermined and inexorable flight path...The tracers ascended like wobbling strings of pearls...below, on the ground, shells were bursting in big, ephemeral flashes of dull yellow corollas.*[19]

Within a few hours Pouget's elite troops were in the front line at Éliane 2 (A1), the most important priority of the Vietminh attack. They were on top of one of the largest battlefield mines in history. They knew it was there because digging was heard, and they knew that the explosion was imminent because the digging stopped.

The general's visit to the field hospital

A few days before the end, the newly promoted General de Castries made his first visit to the wounded. Smartly dressed he toured the cramped underground wards listening to the stories of his men with his adjudant beside him taking names and notes as medals were awarded to each man in turn...military medal, *Croix de Guerre*, *Legion d'Honeur*, etc. He triaged medals as Dr Grauwin would drugs. Badly wounded soldiers tried to gather themselves, sit up and salute. A legionnaire who spoke with de Castries recalled that as de Castries was talking to him:

> *The man with the phosphorous burns was groaning in his bunk. He was going to die. The toxic poison had been too severe, the burns too deep...like pieces of anthracite buried in his flesh.*[20]

Halfway through the visit, 'the general had a long look at the scene. He lit another cigarette in his mouth and I think I saw his hand shaking.'[21] 'Soon it will be all over,' de Castries promised his men. It was his first and only meeting with his troops in two months of siege.

At the end of his visit, recounted Dr Grauwin, 'He shook my hand twice … his chin was trembling a little and there was a sudden gleam in his eyes.'[22]

Éliane 2, 5.30 p.m. 5 May

The last great assaults on Éliane 2 began on 6 May. After a two-hour pounding, the assault troops went in on the remaining French positions. The end was near because the artillery at the central zone had only 1,000 rounds for seven remaining 105mm cannon. It was hardly enough to last half a day and no new drops could be expected to make a significant difference. Shell reserves were in terminal decline. It was only artillery fire that had kept the garrison going so long. At Isabelle, which had provided essential artillery crossfire into the approaches to Éliane 2, there was only one more operating cannon left. Officers and commissars of the Vietminh waved on their massed attack with shouts of 'Tin Lien and Mau Len'. Artillery smashed them. Two hundred new bodies surrounded the remaining strongpoint on E2.

The crux of the entire battle, a battle of hundreds of thousands of shells in a small place, would come down to one last big explosion. Vietnamese miners had dug a large tunnel under Éliane 2 over a number of weeks. The sound of mining was nerve-wracking for the French defenders, who heard the scratching beneath their feet. Because it was so deep, counter-mining was not an option, especially as there was not enough manpower to do it. When the mine workings stopped, they knew that the explosives were being packed in and that a big bang was imminent.

The Vietnamese special team in charge of the works was ordered to fill the mine with explosives on 5 May. This was a stressful moment for the Vietnamese as well on two counts. The simple bo doi had an absolute terror of dynamite so just getting the product 2km from the depot to the mine involved sheer terror for the porters who had to carry the 2kg bags into the mine one at a time. Ironically, the sacks of powder were made from French silk parachutes and the powder came from unexploded French bombs.[23]

There was also the fear of what the explosion would do to their own side. Some panicky experts calculated that the troops would have to be 20km away. Eventually this figure was reduced to 1km. In the event, the assault teams were much closer than that.

What was not in doubt was the importance of the attack as the centrepiece of what was hoped to be the last offensive to wipe out the French. Heavy diversionary attacks had already started at Huguette 5. The assault on Éliane following the explosion would be the *coup de grace*. On this Giáp was wrong, because the French could not muster any reserves at all for either flank. Despite the frantic paratrooper drops of untrained men in the last few days, nothing would avail now. So important was the mine that it focused the attention of General Giáp himself, who sent a message of encouragement: 'To comrade engineers at the A1 hill (Éliane 2). I wish you success.' An unusually terse message from the normally verbose general.

As he prepared for battle, Vietminh soldier Tran thought of his family:

> *...my father...was a Mandarin who had been 'sacrificed' for the revolution* [i.e. murdered/liquidated by the communists]. *Of my mother I have no news. I thought if I died in this battle there would be no survivor of my family, because there were no male heirs. As soon as the assault began all these thoughts disappeared.*[24]

The reason for the attention was the tactical importance of Éliane 2. A hill positioned at the southern end of the five hills chain, it enjoyed clear fields of fire and was the least overlooked of the hills. Moreover, E2 directly overlooked the heart of the French defences, including de Castries' command bunker, which was located in the centre of Dien Bien Phu's bastion. If Éliane 2 fell then that really was the end, the 'fortress would be untenable'. The explosion was due to be set off at 8.20 p.m.

Vu Dinh Hoe, the commander of the 249th Battalion of the 174th Regiment of the 316th Division, had to choose his two guinea pigs who would act as suicide detonators in case the explosion failed: Huu and Mau. Their job would be to go in and blow themselves up for the glory of the revolution. Surprisingly, no political commissars volunteered for the job.

Before the great explosion, the Vietminh pounded Éliane 2, 3 and 4 remorselessly. At 6.15 p.m., the Vietminh launched heavy assaults on Éliane 4, reaching Captain Botella's command post before being driven back by mainly French-officered VNA troops. French officer Captain Phan Van Phu's company was reduced to just thirty men.[25] Waves of Vietminh broke against the defences, cut down by machine-gun- and mortar-fire.

It came to close combat. A Vietminh officer leapt into the trench with Sergeant Chabrier and demanded his surrender at the point of a pistol, but was immediately shot dead. Realising that the crisis of the battle was approaching the Élianes, Colonel Langlais sent across the river three tanks to support the defences.

In their saps, Vietminh assault teams of the 316th Regiment waited pensively, fearful and hopeful in equal measure. Fear for the effects of the massive explosion, fear for the withering blizzard of machine-gun bullets and roar of high explosives as the French artillery zeroed-in on them, but hope that the assault would be faced by nothing at all, except a heap of rubble and dead and dazed defenders.

Tran Quay, head of the dynamite group, looked at his comrades as zero hour approached wondering who would be alive by the end of the night. From the hills the Vietminh high command and political commissars trained their ears and peered through the darkness in the direction of Éliane 2 (A1). When the explosion happened at 11 p.m. on 5 May, it was a severe anti-climax. Just a dull and muffled 'crump' was heard. The earth trembled a little. From far away Giáp sent an urgent question: 'Why was the explosion so muffled?'

Nguyễn Phu replied, 'The quieter the noise the greater the capacity for massive destruction.'[26] True in theory. If the mine entrance had been well tamped, then the energy would be trapped inside the hill.

After the explosion blew a giant plume of earth into the air, a huge hole appeared. It is still visible today. One of the first on the scene was the officer commanding one of the first assault teams. Vu The Chau records:

> *On penetrating a bunker I saw that it was divided in two parts, the first part was full of bodies and in the second an electric light was still working and on a table were all the operational maps.*[27]

Other assault teams ran into stiff opposition from the remaining defenders. When the mine went off, Tran was 50m from a French blockhouse at the foot of a broken banian tree. A muffled sound was followed by showers of earth and stones that fell all around.

Taking part in the assault, Tran was in a team of fifteen, each of whom carried a parcel explosive of 15g. They sprinted Indian-file towards the first blockhouse from whence a French machine-gun spat out defiance. Hit in the face by a bullet, he remained conscious and came to rest at the side of the blockhouse:

> *I pushed the detonator and threw the parcel bomb into the bunker...the explosion came six seconds later. I felt my body rise in the air...I felt feet trampling on my body. I was stunned and lost a lot of blood. My comrades thought I was dead and retreated.*[28]

Nguyễn Ngoc Tang was commander of the company that would take the left side sap along the *Champs Elysée* to attack the summit of Éliane 2. The 'avenue' was somewhat of a swamp, which was already sodden by the onset of the monsoon season. 'It had been raining for several days and the trenches were inundated. One waded through the blood of our injured and dead,'[29] remembered Nguyễn Ngnoc Tang. Fifteen soldiers were chosen for the semi-suicide mission, which involved scrambling out of the lead sap and trying to run through the squelching gluey mud to the barbed wire to place the Bangalores. Chances of living through a hail of machine-gunfire, grenades and artillery were minimal.

Sergeant Chabrier and his platoon of machine-gunners mowed down the Viet No. 3 Company of the 98th Regiment, who toppled into the muddy crater. They were hampered, though, by failing ammunition supply and jamming.

Éliane 2 was the crux of the battle, so the desperate French also launched counter-attacks, even though they had so few fit men left. A small contingent of the 1st BCP arranged an ambush of Viets. One paratrooper told Dr Grauwin how they were:

> *...bringing down so many with tommy guns...then suddenly he felt something on his back – a Viet had hurled himself on him not knowing he was a judo expert. In a few moments the Viet had his neck broken but not before he had just time to take the pin out of a grenade.*[30]

After the explosion, which destroyed most of a company of 1st BPC, Captain Jean Pouget, who had only dropped in to Dien Bien Phu on the night of the 3/4 May, forty-eight hours earlier, rallied survivors. Attack was followed by counter-attack. The paratroopers joined the five legionnaires holding out on the top, at first resisting then launching a counter-attack that pushed the Vietminh back to the rim of the crater. Bodies were used to replace sandbags in the defences.

At midnight, the last parachute reinforcement of the 1st Battalion Parachute Chasseurs drop was due to be made, including bottles of whiskey and brandy for de Castries and Langlais. A relief to some, a disappointment to others, it was cancelled just as they flew in because without flares such a gesture would be suicidal.

At dawn, Pouget had thirty men left and requested permission to withdraw if no reinforcements were coming. 'As a para you must fight to the death...' he was told by Bigeard. He was denied his request and the reinforcements. Pouget remembered that at 4.10 a.m. on 7 May, Viet human waves rose up screaming 'di-di, di-di, forwards, forwards.'[31] Overwhelmed, he destroyed his radio set but was immediately knocked unconscious.

Pouget was captured. 'You are a prisoner of the Democratic People's Army of Vietnam. You are wounded. We shall take care of you. Can you walk?'

Last resistance came from two legionnaires firing the heavy machine-gun on a Chaffee tank that had clawed its way to the brow of the hill (where in memoriam it remains to this day).

The brutal civil war aspect of the conflict came into focus when French Army Second Lieutenant Phung died when he called down French mortars on his own position as he was being overrun by Vietminh.

By dawn, Major Thomas at Éliane 2 had twenty men left. However, the central position at Éliane 4 was still held by Colonel Bréchignac and Captain Botella, but they were completely cut off. Vicious fighting was followed by retreat of the remains of the first assault teams. The French hung on, repelling attack after attack on 6 May.

Battalion commander Nguyễn Dung Chi remembered: 'I was in the trench closest to the French. I was always in the front line,' he says:

> *On 30 March we failed to take Éliane. We had made tactical mistakes. On 6 and 7 May we decided to seize the positions on the flanks and at the rear. The assault ended in hand-to-hand fighting...We couldn't see anything any longer, we didn't try to take aim, we just moved forward, jumping from trench to trench, stepping on bodies. When the French command post fell I saw the dead bodies of a white man and an African. In our ranks, people were sometimes dispirited of course, but very little.*[32]

Eventually the defenders were overrun by the sheer number of attackers. There were no reserves left. The radio transmission went silent.

Soldier from 2nd Battalion, 1st BCP:

> *I'm the last man left in my company – the rest are wiped out. When I got away the Viets were yelling around Major Bréchignac's command post. Thousands of them...their dead and injured tip into our trench, falling on our machine-guns and even on our shoulders...it's alright we've got Éliane 2 back. It was marvellous. Blokes from the eighth assault and second Foreign Paras – if only you could have seen them, Major...it was sheer butchery. All the same if that goes on the major will soon be the only man left.*

With conditions intolerable in the main hospital, many of the wounded left of their own accord to go back to their units, ignoring the entreaties of Dr Grauwin. The badly wounded Nicolle told him:

> *There are only 17 of them left* [6th BPC] *and if they are going to be killed I want to be with them...all my persuasions were in vain.*[33]

The surrender of Éliane 2's garrison was taken by Vu Dinh Hoe, commander of the 316th Division, 174th Regiment. The remains of the garrison had taken refuge in an underground command post. Threatened by Vu in French with being blown up by grenades, they came out. Vu demanded to know the rank of the garrison commander. 'What grade are you?' he asked roughly. 'Captain... where are your insignia [of rank]?'

Captain Pouget, still dazed from being knocked out, pulled epaulettes from his pocket. The regimental commander refused to believe that such an important post as A1 could be commanded by a mere captain.[34] For all their efforts and massive casualties, they must surely have captured a general at least. It was testament to the terrible casualties suffered by French officers. The Vietminh were lucky to have found any officer alive at all.

Edmund Cheval recalled his experiences:

> *After several hours* [of bombardment] *the Viets launched their attack. The barbed wire defences no longer existed, so they overran the first trenches. Hand to hand combat broke out everywhere, we grappled face to face, no quarter, no time to take prisoners…they made us suffer but despite that we did not concede anything. It cost them dearly. The resistance was hard, one did not fight any more for victory, there was no longer any doubt as to the result, but to delay the surrender. We were nothing more than a small footnote, but despite that we were willing to be sacrificed. There was no alternative; hold or die, I think we became quite mad.*[35]

Éliane 4

Éliane 4 was at the heart of the five hills position and an essential element in the crossfire support of Éliane 2, the final key to the Dien Bien Phu bastion. Nguyễn Kim Lung was the platoon leader of a group of explosive satchel-throwers in the 318th Division. Reliving his experiences, he recalled:

> *…we succeeded in occupying C2* [Éliane 4] *towards 8 o'clock in the morning of the 7 May. The Company 35 was badly devastated. My company the 38th suffered equivalent heavy losses. The 34th behind us similarly. I had to step over the bodies of my comrades to advance.*[36]

Éliane 4 consisted of the normal medley of defenders, including the detritus of Bigeard's 6th Colonial Paratroopers. That they wiped out huge numbers of the enemy before being overwhelmed or running out of ammunition is clear.

At Éliane 3, Bigeard's 6th BPC repelled attacks.

At 10 a.m. on the 6th, Langlais in the central command bunker still hoped: 'We must hang on for a draw. The enemy is as exhausted as us.' Radio intercepts made it clear that the Vietminh were being regrouped and prepared for a final offensive in the evening.

6 May and Éliane 10

The elite paratrooper battalion, the 1st BEP, repelled attacks at Huguette 2 and 3. At Isabelle, after heavy bombardments, there was only one 105mm gun operating.

Sitting below Éliane 2 on the reverse side was Éliane 10 blocking the way to the Bailey bridge over the Nam Youm River. During the night of 6/7 May, as the fighting raged for E2 (A1) hill itself, Vietminh units circled around the main French defences and started to push against the lesser positions, such as Éliane 10.

This position came under attack at around 10 p.m. on 6 May, from 165 Regiment. Nevertheless, the position was still plentifully provided with machine-guns that chattered unceasingly against the abundant targets offered by the human wave of attackers from 312 Division. It was fiercely defended by the 5th Bawouan, the Vietnamese paratrooper unit led by hardened veteran Captain Botella, along with a motley collection of men from other units and the walking wounded. Assaults were constantly impeded by thick barbed wire defences. Constant attacks failed to dislodge the defenders. 'A whole battalion was decimated,' recorded Tran Quan Lap, political commissar of the 209th Regiment:[37]

> *After four victories for the regiment in its battle honour roll this was the first defeat. On the morning of the 7th there was a party meeting which adjudged that we had been negligent. We had not surveyed the movements of the enemy. We had thought it would be an easy affair.*

Holding Éliane 10 was vital because it both stopped the Vietminh from reaching the bridge and held open the way for reinforcement to reach Éliane 2 and 4. It would also hold the exit open in case they needed to retreat. As defence weakened in the early hours, Langlais stripped two companies of legionnaires from 8 BPC, who were in reserve at Epervier on the opposite side of the river. A further reinforcement of about sixty walking wounded legionnaires arrived. They fended off three furious attacks. Pham was commanding artillery in close support of Vietminh attacks on E2. On visiting the command post, 'we were shocked to find that most of our comrades had been killed or wounded. Our casualties were enormous...we broke down and started weeping.'[38]

Impatient to recover their reputation, the 209th's attack on Éliane 10 was continued at 2 p.m. on 7 May. 'The enemy was panicked...the massive artillery bombardment had slackened,' as the French gunners from the central zone ran out of ammunition or their guns were disabled by Vietminh artillery fire. Éliane 10 was still holding out, however, at 7 a.m.

Éliane 10 was falling and Lieutenant Le Page escaped with a few men.

Adding to the cacophony was the dawn chorus roar of fighter bombers, machine-gunning and dropping bombs.

Assault teams were able to secure an entry into the heart of the French defences but suddenly, in a scene replicated across the battlefield, and as if by sudden weariness and consensus, little white flags began to appear from the remaining bunkers and fox holes at Éliane 10. Botella from Éliane 4 radioed in to Bigeard: 'This time it's finished.' Then the Vietminh came running in, seemingly emerging from the earth in their tens of thousands. They were very close in trenches that had burrowed like a cancer to the core of the encampment.

From Russia with love, 7 May

In the evening at 7.30 p.m. on 6 May, a new fury descended on the exhausted and embattled defenders, as if they had not suffered enough. As the fortress writhed in its death throes, a greeting came from Russia in the shape of the whirring and screaming sound of multiple rockets from lorry-mounted Katyusha launchers (Stalin's organ). Made famous by the Russians in the Second World War, they now rained down on the French Army. They landed in a dizzying cacophony of explosions in the heart of the French defences, blowing great plumes of mud, mire, body parts and debris into the air. Adding to the deadly ensemble of weaponry, 105mm, 155mm, mortar bombs, submachine-guns, bazookas, and grenades, they joined in the grand crashing finale to a symphony of destruction as if to the music of Tchaikovsky. Hearing the noise in the central medical unit, a German legionnaire who had experienced this noise on the Russian Front in the Second World War, joked to Genevieve: 'That is Stalin playing the organ.'[39]

So dazed with fatigue and pain, some prisoners mistook the roar of explosion as a relief column.

When in the morning the first two salvoes of rockets landed, the French artillery fired in return, so four more Katuysha salvoes followed. At 9 p.m., the Vietminh launched a battalion-sized assault on the central command area. Hoang Khoat of the 351st Division described the scene:

> *At 9 a.m. a battalion of French troops rushed across the bailey bridge to reinforce the east bank positions of the Nam Youm. Two more rocket salvos were launched at the bridge and when the smoke cleared no one on the bridge moved. I think the rockets had a terrible morale effect on the defenders.*[40]

Endgame

The end came into sight when Éliane 2 was captured. With the capture of the hills overlooking the central defence area, everyone knew that the battle could not last much longer. Still, they fought on with savage determination. Centrally placed quad AA guns, supplied on the advice of US General Daniels, still spewed out death in all directions, helping to smash Vietminh attacks. But the hug of Vietminh entrenching and sapping grew tighter and tighter. Trenches snaked in all directions around and through the French defences like slowly growing tendrils of a malignant plant wrapping itself round a decaying and dying bough, throttling and squeezing out the last drops of life.

Central zone

In the central zone, the cameramen had been assigned to the bunker with the Meo tribesmen irregulars near the hospital. At this stage in the battle they found themselves on the front line as Vietminh infiltration units attempted to storm the central area. The cameramen had armed themselves and fought alongside their Meo (Hmong) comrades. Schoendoerffer remembered: 'The Meo were good shots and helped break the Vietminh assaults.' He did not recount how many Vietminh he had killed, not surprising because most soldiers do not like to confess let alone remember the guilty details of how they killed fellow human beings. That is normal. What surprised him on reflection about the battle was that 'there were not many screams or cries.'

Another small and specialised detachment in the central area was a troupe of T'ai Royal Ballet dancers located in a bunker at Claudine near the centre. When going out for relief, one of the dancers was hit by a shell: 'We gathered her up with a shovel and a broom. Only a chunk of hair remained intact,' recalled Corporal Blondeau.

The Meo tribesmen who had been fighting alongside Schoendoerffer slipped away to the jungles as did the T'ai, who changed into civilian clothes and passed themselves off as PIMs or locals.

Claudine 5, 6 May 11 p.m.

This position was on what had been one of the less dramatic zones of defence on the south-west of the fortress, just 300m from de Castries' bunker. It came under attack on the night of the 6th from two battalions of 102 Regiment. Although nearby, the attackers did not hear the explosion at E2, which was meant to be the signal for attack. C5 was defended by legionnaires who were forced out.

At Grauwin's main hospital post, six stretchers each with their blood-stained burdens: legionnaires of the 13th Demi Brigade from the Claudine post. The legionnaires told their story to the doctor:

> *There are hundreds and hundreds of them, major...we killed masses and masses of them but always more came, jumping over the bodies of the others. They took the support post but we got it back with the blokes of the 13th, then they came back; there were thousands of them. Now it's all over.*[41]

However, they gathered in reinforcements from the legionnaire survivors of Beatrice in C4 including a platoon of bearded legionnaire pioneers. C5 was re-taken, but the Vietminh came on again around midnight. It was finally captured around 2 a.m.

Éliane 4, 6/7 May

At the side of Éliane 2 was another barbed-wired hill summit defensive position at Éliane 4. Leader of a dynamite team, Nguyễn Kim recorded simply that:

> *We succeeded in occupying C2* [Éliane 4] *towards 8am on the 7 May. The 35th Company was seriously damaged; the unit was virtually annihilated. My 38th Company also suffered heavy losses and the 34th Company coming on behind were similarly handled. In order to advance I had to walk on and over the bodies of my dead comrades.*[42]

Éliane 4 was Bigeard's command.

When the Vietminh were massing for their final attack on Éliane 4, Colonel Valliant only had three 105mm shells left. Towards the end, shortages of ammunition and food became critical after intensive non-stop fighting since 1 May.

7 May

The most vicious to and fro fighting occurred around the Éliane bastions, which overlooked de Castries' central bunker area. Thousands of Vietminh were scythed down. Hundreds hung on the wire defences. As the attacks on the key heights drew in the diminishing French reserves, co-ordinated attacks began against the Huguette and Claudine bastions on the open and flat western side of the battlefield. This squeezed the central zone still more. The French area of control reduced piece by piece. Trenches became clogged with the sick and wounded, increasingly the battlefield became 'Hell in a very small place.'

By dawn the situation was hopeless. Sitting in a bunker, Francois Willer of the 1st Cavalry raised a precious bottle of champagne. Speaking to his captain, the tank commander with two encased arms, he declared, 'My captain, there is no way that the Viets are going to celebrate their victory with our champagne.' They saluted and toasted each other, 'a last gesture of friendship and for many the ultimate goodbye.' Andre Mengelle witnessed the scene and later became a general.

Éliane 4

At 9.30 a.m. on 7 May, Éliane 4, defended by the 2nd BPC and the redoubtable Colonel Bréchignac, was overrun. 'Dede calling Bruno [Bigeard's code name]. It's all over.'[43] His dear friend Bigeard heard his final words on the radio: 'They're arriving *en masse*…I am destroying the radio sets.' And another report of the last radio contact:

Major Bréchignac said goodbye to us on the radio. He was alone with ten of his lads, all men who had been wounded before – amputated in plaster or with only one eye left. He said 'it's all up. The Viets are now level with my command post. In a few seconds the grenades will be there...goodbye Colonel. Goodbye all.'[44]

Bigeard was in tears. But Bréchignac would be captured not killed. After the fall of Éliane 10, its lowland neighbours soon succumbed. Vietminh regiments rolled on to Éliane 11 and 12, the final two posts guarding the Bailey bridge. Soon they would be infiltrating the central encampment.

Finale: the fall of Éliane 11 and 12

De Castries and Langlais followed the last battles on radio sets communicating with the outposts. Positions were lost, re-taken and lost again. Others were overrun. 'The Viets are thirty feet away. Give our love to our families, it is over for us.'[45] Another radio went silent. The French artillery were out of ammunition and had stopped firing. Genevieve heard it all:

6th – 22:15 Vietminh in contact on east face of DBP. 24.00 munitions exhausted 500 rounds left of 120mm mortars/Éliane confused/Éliane 4 contact/Claudine contact/Claudine 5 attacked/Junon attacked: 7th 2.00 a.m. parts of Éliane 2 and 10 holding/hand-to-hand fighting at 2 and 10/attacks on east of central zone 6am; Éliane 2 falls at 4am/no ammunition/dawn 7th: Éliane 2 and Claudine 5 fallen/Éliane 4 re-taken/16.00 Éliane 3 has fallen and hand-to-hand at Éliane 11 and 12/the whole western section being overrun. (S. Cogny's log of communications)

Small units held out at Éliane 3 and Junon on the opposite bank, where T'ai units prevented an attempt by the Vietminh to wade across the river. The collapse of the positions at 11 and 12 precipitated the surrender. For the last days of the battle, the command had shuffled around fragmented remnants of units of legionnaires, T'ai, Moroccans and Algerians, as well as units of walking wounded. At the bridge the E11 and E12 positions collapsed when the Moroccan remnants, out of ammunition and exhausted from days of fighting, started to flee and to wave white flags. Vietnamese units were free to move over the bridge to invade the central command area. Hoang Khoat recalled: 'When we saw the white flags break out in the valley [on the 7th] we jumped for joy and cried out, "bravo for the generalissimo!"'[46]

Afternoon, 7 May

At 1 p.m. in bastion Juno on the south-east of the central encampment, fifty-four legionnaires who had survived savage hand to hand fighting gathered for a breakout. A dud 105mm Viet shell landed at the feet of Sergeant Sammarco, who promised if he got out of this 'we'll get blind drunk for a fortnight,' while his fellow NCO Kubiak filled his water bottle with rum.[47] However, the breakout was cancelled when Langlais thought better of the suicide mission:

> *Heavy fighting still persisted at 3 p.m. on the 7th and the commander of the 312th Division called for a full-scale assault but before the order was given for the assault to commence white flags could be seen flying at all points of the battlefield.*[48]

Then suddenly, 'A calm strange silence settled over the valley,' recounted Genevieve de Galard, 'and we waited.'

No white flags, 7 May 5 p.m.

Last radio chatter between Dien Bien Phu and Hanoi took place at about 5 p.m. on 7 May. De Castries was advised by General Cogny to fight to the end. There should be 'no white flags' because that would spoil the 'magnificent effort', the glorious defeat. Perhaps eighty percent of the French front-line soldiers were either wounded or dead, and even the fit ones were severely exhausted and under-nourished. The remaining effective front-line troops numbered no more than 3,000. They were outnumbered by about twenty to one. Like von Paulus at Stalingrad, de Castries had been promoted during the battle, although his general's bars and the bottle of champagne dropped to him fell into enemy hands. The last radio conversation between Cogny in Hanoi and de Castries varied between the banal, the hopelessly inconsequential, the fanciful, and the melodramatic. 'We are defending every foot of ground, and I consider that the most we can do,' declared de Castries. 'I will try to get as many men out as possible towards the south…yes, General by night of course.'[49]

There followed a rundown of the remaining units: 'Three companies of BT [Moroccan Tabors]…the BT2s have the most men left because they don't fight.' Cogny and de Castries swapped snide comments on their Moroccan colonial troops, most of whose French officers were dead or wounded.[50]

'French honour would be satisfied by dying fighting,' advised Cogny.

'*Bien, mon general*,' said de Castries, who claimed that his main concern was for the safety of the wounded. His last words, '*au revoir*.' '*Au revoir mon vieux*,' replied Cogny. The words, which are recorded, sound clipped and unemotional, but there was emotion. Even when a breakout was being considered he had made clear his determination to stay with the wounded and surrender rather than lead his men in battle.

Dr Grauwin wrote of the end:

> *The wounded are crowded into a long unending column, some sitting, some standing, and the line ends just where contact with the Viet begins. Some are dead already, sinking into the mud. Those wounded coming in from the defensive positions step on them pushing the dead further into the mire.*[51]

In the end the Vietminh raised a white flag and encouraged the French to surrender, something that was informally and spontaneously agreed at a lower level. There was just no ammunition left, no grenades, no artillery and nowhere to retreat. The matter is controversial because there were claims made by the Vietminh that white flags were shown for propaganda purposes, the showing of white flags would add to the humiliation of the French and raise Vietminh prestige.

Similar observations were made by Le Nguyễn, political officer, correspondent of the *Anh Dung* journal, and Tran Quan Lip, political commissar, Regiment 209, Division 312. French sources including Schoendoerffer and Bernhard Fall disagree with the Vietminh claims. They are adamant that there were no white flags. There is plenty of evidence to suggest that there was a plethora of white flags across the battlefield. The logic of the situation, the breakdown in command and communications, and the opening of negotiations with the Vietminh meant that the FEC's soldiery took matters into their own hands and did the existential thing. Why wouldn't they?

Pierre Schoendorffer's film shows no white flags. Schoendoerffer was a veteran of the battle, and his film (*Dien Bien Phu*) is probably the only war film in history directed by a participant. It is possible that the Vietnamese testimony given by political officers, who were seeing the battlefield for the first time, confused the plethora of white silk from parachutes for white flags, or perhaps the 'rats of the Nam Yam' displayed flags. However, it seems unlikely that no soldiers used the time-honoured method of trying to avoid being killed upon general surrender. 'When the firing stopped, I saw French soldiers here and there waving scraps of white fabric,' remembers veteran Nguyễn Dung Chi.

With French and enemy units entangled in the spiders' webs of trenching within feet of each other, the battle had taken on a deadly intimacy. But suddenly, as if by silent mutual agreement, the battle ended. French soldiers smashed their weapons, stove in their kepis or buried their red para berets. Suddenly, thousands upon thousands of enemy tommy gunners swarmed from the shattered earth. Enemy soldiers sporting the distinctive pith helmets and clad in green or khaki fatigues with tennis shoes, teemed over the central zone like an army of termites on a dead animal. Red flags with bright gold stars fluttered in the breeze. French soldiers emerged dazed from their shelter. Chi encountered Geneviève de Galard-Teraube, the *Angel of Dien Bien Phu*. 'I walked towards her,' Chi recalls:

> *She raised her arms and said: 'Don't shoot!' I asked her where the headquarters was. She made a sign with her hand: 'Over there.' I went to see but it was empty. On the general's table I found an atlas open at the page for the USSR, a Parker pen and a paratrooper's knife.*[52]

As 20-year-old Hoang Duang Vinh approached the command bunker:

> *The sky was filled with tall columns of black smoke from burning vehicles. The fields were covered with dead soldiers and destroyed military equipment.*

Vinh advanced into the bunker where he found de Castries with his staff officers who had their hands up, unlike their commander. De Castries simply said 'Don't shoot, I surrender.' 'I was so tense,' recalled Vinh, 'that I pushed my rifle against de Castries' abdomen…thus forcing him to put his hands up.'[53]

De Castries was silent and deathly pale from time spent in the bunker. He emerged immaculately uniformed. Cooped up in the dark bunker for weeks, he came out blinking into the daylight, wearing bright red Saphi cavalry breeches and sporting an array of medals.

Bigeard sported his paratrooper beret defiantly (other paratroopers had buried theirs). He half expected to be shot out of hand, such was the enmity felt towards these fighters by whose hands many atrocities had been committed and so many Vietminh comrades killed. After shouts in Vietnamese outside the command bunker, Bigeard exclaimed: 'I am not raising my hands.'

Schoendoerffer, with time now to reflect on what had happened, 'felt rage and bitterness at being abandoned.' A Vietminh soldier:

> *…began to shout into my face in Vietnamese. His face was angry…then he thrust out his arm; his hand held a half-smoked cigarette. Indicating that I should smoke I did whereupon he and his comrades burst out laughing…the Vietnamese were tense and very young.*

Interviewed by Jean Luc Cotard some decades later, Schoendoerffer recounted:

> *And then I was taken prisoner, so I touched the depths of human misery, because almost three-quarters of my comrades were dead.*[54]

Giacomo Signoroni:

> *It was the end. The Viet were coming from everywhere. We were surrounded, ready for the supreme sacrifice. Piccinini and Guenzi burned the company's pennant. Order was given to surrender. Humiliation.*[55]

Overlooking the scene, Pham felt:

> *Contempt for my fellow Vietnamese who fought on the French side…to the west the sun slowly disappeared behind the Laotian mountains. As the enemy*

surrenders, the Dakotas continue to parachute in supplies...I can hear mines exploding somewhere in the distance. A translucent fog floats down over the fields and the valley, fires burn...fragments of parachutes, twisted iron, and wood torn from the shelters and trenches are lifted up with flames and smoke... the French arms depot is burning. Once in a while, brilliant fireballs explode and dazzle the horizon.[56]

At the national assembly in Paris, Joseph Laniel in a strained and emotional voice paid tribute to the garrison's courage. The whole assembly rose to their feet, except the communist deputies. Newspapers rushed out news of the surrender with banner headlines. France was in shock. Reverberations through the colonial liberation movements of the world brought sudden hope that western colonialism was finished for good, but the Algerian insurgency was soon to start and the horrors of war in Portugal's empire was yet to come. Radio Peking (Beijing) broadcast Giáp's victory message to the world and other liberation movements with a rallying cry: 'The struggle of free peoples against slavery does not end today. The fight continues.'

Isabelle and breakout

A breakout attempt was defeated but there were individual efforts at escape. Seventy-three soldiers did eventually find a way out to join Hmong partisans in Lao. A similar breakout proposal called 'Xenophon' had been considered and rejected by de Castries for the main garrison, because he believed that his men would only be wiped out in the jungles and were not in any fit condition to try.

CHAPTER XX

Prisoners

There were 1,460 FEC troops wounded at Dien Bien Phu, spread out with 1,000 in the battalion infirmaries, 390 in the various medical units, including de Galard's central unit under Dr Grauwin. After the severely wounded were evacuated by the Red Cross, some 9,500 troops were led away into captivity along a 600km trek through the mountains. (Figures for total captured vary from 9,000 to 13,000.) They were separated by rank and by race and subjected to targeted propaganda. Already severely weakened, many died. The prisoners-of-war camps were no better. The excellent Vietminh logistics system seemed not to function on behalf of the prisoners, because only 3,000 of the 9,500 taken into captivity returned four months later.[1] Some may have defected, but it seems that a fifty to sixty percent death rate was the norm with the lower ranks. The International Control Commission responsible for monitoring the armistice reported that only forty-three percent of prisoners were returned.[2]

Captain Pouget survived. Only dropped into the drop-zone on 3 May. He was much stronger than others. He described Camp No. 1:

> *Brainwashing is every day, sneaky, nagging, about everything. Weakened bodies and minds offer less resistance. The perfidious Vietminh methods which skilfully balance moral tortures, hopes, disappointments, and all kinds of bullying shatter the strongest who sometimes surrender, resigned. It is then despair. The healthy will become ill, the sick bedridden and the bedridden will die.*[3]

Schoendoerffer the photographer, like many of the veterans, lived the rest of his life in the shadow of those soul-searing experiences at Dien Bien Phu. He dedicated his life to portraying in film his comrades' suffering, life and death. Unlike Captain Pouget, he had a humanist, romantic and internationalist outlook on the experience of the camps, seeing hope and even joy in little snapshots of common humanity:

> *Even when I was a prisoner, I was able to be happy. In the morning, when I woke up, I was alive – and there were still things I could do. A day had passed, and I was going to live some more.* [He breathed deeply.] *Sometimes, in a way, those Vietminh helped me there. There were guards who, all of a sudden, did something that made them seem more human. Peasants would leave a little bit of tobacco on a tree branch when you went to get the rice.*[4]

Ho's communist discipline prevented massacre at the end of the battle, and for the cameras there was a great show of communist munificence to the defeated. But the Janus head of Ho was revealed in his treatment of the prisoners and the slow death of the majority of the captives on the long march north and in the camps. It was an event to rival the death marches of Soviet prisoners by the Nazis in the Second World War. It was a war crime.

De Gaulle's aborted coup, 7–8 May 1954

Upon hearing the news. de Gaulle immediately realised that the fall of Dien Bien Phu would provoke a major political crisis in France. He started planning a *coup d'état* that was to be triggered by a mass movement and mass gathering at the Arc de Triomphe where de Gaulle planned a visit. He expected a turnout of such enormity that he would be swept to power on a wave of patriotism and an army takeover.

On the day news of the disaster broke in Paris, de Gaulle, the originator of the imperialist fiasco in Indochina, told his aide Terrenoire excitedly, 'I will come back to power...if there is a ministerial crisis I will intervene.' General Ely, presumably at de Gaulle's request, called on him. Ely recorded that de Gaulle had expressed disappointment that the army had abandoned him, 'but in the end only the army could save the situation.' He denied that he was asking for backing for a *coup d'état* but then added archly 'the leaders of the army had to **move in his direction** and all would be fine.' (Author's emphasis.) De Gaulle put it about that he would visit the Arc de Triomphe at 4 p.m. on 8 March 1954 – information that spurred the government to post extra police. The timing of the visit was carefully chosen because he expected to follow a spontaneous mass rally with a call for the army to take power in the night. De Gaulle duly visited, but instead of hundreds of thousands or more hailing the 'saviour', a mere 15,000 appeared. It was not the popular endorsement he expected. The preliminary detonation to set off the coup had fizzled out. Arriving as the returning saviour and strong man of France, he left after fifteen minutes as a sad and deluded chancer. Like Churchill, he would make a late and unexpected political comeback. Like Churchill, instead of becoming a clown of history he became a hero.

New horizons and improving consumer conditions captured the imagination of the French people, who had lost interest in him and in the far-off colonial war. The true saviour would be Pierre Mendes-France, who would become prime minister in July 1954. He showed great dynamism and skill in negotiating an agreement, which even de Gaulle applauded.[5]

Geneva Conference and after

On the day of the surrender, the Geneva Conference opened. Hundreds of diplomats, sundry officials and technical experts were in attendance. Giáp had timed his victory to perfection. That Vietnam was to be partitioned between north and south was a bitter disappointment for Ho. The Soviets, Chinese and the British had fixed up a deal prior to the conference. Under the terms of the agreements reached, a referendum would follow for the whole of Vietnam to determine a final solution. It never happened.

Within two years, the predominant French influence in the south was replaced by the Americans, and Bao Dai was deposed. One million North Vietnamese, of those allowed the choice, chose to leave their homes and go south to escape communism. Giac Duc was typical of many of these:

> *My family had a long tradition of anti-French politics. My father one of Ho Chi Minh's nationalist opponents, had been killed by the Vietminh. so I was afraid... we thought that communists would make life difficult for Buddhists...there were already indications of that in areas that had been communist strongholds.*[6]

At Evian, Bao Dai hung around waiting on events as his kingdom was carved up. Sometimes he travelled from the tranquil gentility of Evian into Geneva in his specially converted Ferrari silver-blue 375 MM Spyder Roadster. His demand of western delegates was that Vietnam should not be split up. It was the same refrain that he had made to Nixon in 1953 when he presciently informed the vice-president that:

> *...there is no point trying to negotiate with them* [communists]. *At the least we would end up with a conference which would divide my country between us and them. And if Vietnam is split, we will eventually lose it all.*[7]

While his patrimony and peoples were being parcelled up by middle-aged white men over mahogany tables between bouts of fine dining, Boa Dai occupied his time by investigating the purchase of the most rare and precious watch in the world. His purchase was recently auctioned at Philips in London. The marketing puff states:

> *A man emerges from the Hotel de Bergues. He decides to take a stroll but his footsteps take him only across the street to Chronomètrie Philippe Beguin, a famed Rolex retailer. The emperor's request to the staff is a simple one. He wants the rarest and most precious Rolex ever made.*

He bought the Rolex Reference 6062 in yellow gold, with a black dial and diamond indexes.

A timepiece that will forever be associated with the last emperor of Vietnam, even taking his name: 'Bao Dai'. A glitzy new watch but time had almost run out for him. Indochina's time of horrors was only just beginning. The Geneva Conference merely reset the clock for the next set of wars and murderous socialist revolutions, including Pol Pot's holocaust in Cambodia.

Following the general liberalisation and softening of ideological rhetoric after Stalin's death and Khrushchev's speech admitting excesses in Stalin's purges, at the 20th Party Congress, the whole communist world took stock and the moderate party factions were strengthened. For a while, Ho and Giáp were able to rein-in the extremists. At the 10th Plenum of the Communist Party, 27–29 October 1956, Giáp stood in front of the assembled delegates and said:

> *...we indiscriminately attacked all families owning land. Many thousands were executed. We saw enemies everywhere and resorted to widespread violence and terror, we resorted to disciplinary punishment, to expulsion, to execution... We also failed to respect the customs of Montagnard tribes, and attacked their leaders...There were grave errors.*

But the party did not change. Leftist pro-Chinese ideologue was ousted but dour Stalinist le Duan took over: he would force his people into an even greater bloodbath.

Giáp's admission, if it had been possible to have an international court, would, using the legal doctrine of 'common enterprise', have led to the conviction of the entire party leadership of the Politburo and the central committee for war crimes, breach of the Geneva Convention and crimes against humanity. Needless to say, some French commanders might also have been complicit in war crimes, although proof for that would have been more difficult because the policy basis and the vital evidential linkages were less obvious except, perhaps, for the attacks on Haiphong and Hanoi. If General Valluy, Colonel Debes and Admiral d'Argenlieu had been secretly encouraged in making such attacks by de Gaulle, as seems likely, that would have made him complicit in war crimes as well under 'the common enterprise' doctrine.

Genevieve de Galard was repatriated under truce. She had, on 29 April, been awarded the *Legion d'Honneur* and a *Croix de Guerre* and was made a Legionnaire 1st class by Colonel Bigeard. In the following year, she would be lionised in the United States with a ticker tape parade in New York and a reception in City Hall. President Eisenhower presented her with the Medal of Freedom in the Rose Garden. Cited by the French military:

> *...with unmatched professional competence and undefeatable morale, she has been a precious auxiliary to surgeons and contributed to saving many human lives.*[8]

She married a colonel – Jean de Heaulme de Boutsocq. Photos show her leaving the church in an exquisite dress and being led on the arm of her uniformed and medal-bedecked beau through an arch of cavalry sabres.

The Vietminh had fought with a passion for the independence of Vietnam, but what were the French troops fighting for? Colonel Pierre Langlais reflected on it:

> *We were not fighting to defend our homes, we were not fighting to chase a foreigner from our land, we were not even fighting to keep Indochina for France. Then why? The honor of the profession of arms, and that is all.*

Battalion commander Nguyễn Dung Chi remembered:

> *Silence had fallen on Dien Bien Phu. It stank. The smell of death but also rotting flesh with all the wounded French soldiers lying there.*[9]

Appendix I

Casualties

Vietminh casualty estimates are 14,000 and French sources indicate 23,000. Academic estimates revolve around these two figures. French casualties are estimated at 7,000 or forty-seven percent of the total forces.[1] About 2,400 PIMs were captured, half of whom were wounded. Martin Woodruff estimates Vietminh casualties at around 25,000, some 2,000 higher than French estimates.

Attritional battles and storming assaults with waves of infantry on powerful fixed positions by troops lacking in tactical finesse, are bound to lead to heavy casualties. If you visit the cemetery at Gabrielle and actually count the number of graves, there are approximately 2,560 Vietnamese dead, from the 308th Division and one regiment of the 312th. The graves of the 312th are the only ones that carry a divisional number and sometimes a name, whereas the graves of the 308th are unidentified.

As one can project at least a one to three or four ratio for KIA to wounded and MIA, a conservative estimate of total Vietminh casualties for Gabrielle alone is 7,000–10,000. Casualties at Beatrice had also been high. If we estimate that Beatrice must have cost Giáp at least 5,000 casualties, then a total of 12,000–15,000 casualties is a reasonable estimate for the first two days of battle.[2] However, the replacement of the 9,000 used up reserves by a new 25,000 reserve perhaps indicates that casualties from the first offensive may have been much higher. Yet we are expected to believe the estimates of most historians for the entire fifty-six-day battle at around 20,000–25,000 casualties. Losses as a percentage of troops deployed reached twenty-eight percent at the battles of Vin Yen, and twenty-six percent at Nghia Lo. Artillery fire accounted for sixty-three percent of wounds at Vinh Yen, seventy-seven percent at Nghia Lo, and ninety percent at Tu Vu during the Hoa Binh battle.[3]

Given the 100,000 heavy shell expenditure by the French out of a total of 238,000 shells, three times higher than the Vietminh, it seems reasonable to believe that Vietminh casualties were much higher than advertised, especially as projectiles such as airburst shells were even more lethal than normal shrapnel or high explosive rounds. Even discounting the 155mm battery, it would be fair to assume that the French caused three times more casualties than the Vietminh caused to them. This implies about 35,000 casualties, plus many thousands of others caused by machine-guns, grenades, etc. If one studies analogies to the First World War, a figure of 40,000 with 15,000 dead would not be unrealistic and may be conservative.[4]

Appendix II

Military Assessment of the French Indochina War

> *It is a singular feature of small wars that from the point of view of strategy the regular forces are upon the whole at a distinct disadvantage compared to their antagonists...the bonds which fetter a modern army to its starting point result... from the necessity to replenish ammunition and military stores, and partly from the obligation of sending the sick and wounded to the rear. They enforce the establishment of a line of communication and its maintenance and defence.*

As for irregular forces:

> *They are operating in their own country. Their food requirements are small – what they need they carry with them...Warriors, such as form the enemy in small wars, simply disperse when they are worsted...so that victory cannot be followed up.*[1]

These excerpts, from the classic book *Small Wars: a Tactical Textbook for Imperial Soldiers* by Major C.E. Callwell of the British Army, were published in 1896 but became the bedrock of staff college and officer teaching in respect to the imperial irregular wars fought in the nineteenth and twentieth centuries. It was also extensively used by the French Army. Giáp may not have seen this classic and thorough work, but he had read, pored over and digested the works of T.E. Lawrence's *Seven Pillars of Wisdom*, which gives the same irregular war instructions and theory through the personal history of Lawrence's desert campaign in Arabia and Mesopotamia during the First World War. Callwell's book sums up the problems, advantages and disadvantages of the French regular army in Indochina.

But the world changes. There were four important matters that were not relevant to imperial war, as covered by Callwell, present in French Indochina in 1945.

Firstly, the idea of imperialism was already dying before the Second World War. Increasingly, it was regarded as an immoral and anachronistic system.

Secondly, mass communications and international media, rapidly projecting news through radio, print and television, put a spotlight on the activities of armies in faraway, underdeveloped societies.

Thirdly, the Russian Revolution, Soviet propaganda, and organised parties had spurred worldwide proselytisation of the communist creed in tandem with an anti-colonial liberation ideology that communists co-opted and developed.

Fourthly, this development led to victory for the Chinese Red Army, which provided for the communist-led Vietminh bases on the Chinese border. This delivered, by degrees, to the Vietminh both the strategic advantages of being a mobile irregular army as well as the tactical advantages of being a regular army so that the French Army found itself increasingly at a disadvantage in both aspects of war. In the new information space of war, the French were also disadvantaged politically by the communist Fifth Column on the home front. Support for the war in France had collapsed even before the Chinese Red Army arrived at the northern border at the end of 1949.

To cap it all, the Vietminh could attack French base areas but the French could not touch the base areas in Red China after 1950 without starting a major war and the world had seen the military disaster that had happened in Korea when the US-led UN forces approached the Yalu River. This development of a hybrid irregular-regular army and the backing of China-USSR and the widespread support of the Vietnamese people in the north made the war difficult if not impossible to win.

Given France's post-war poverty and lack of resources, the French Army's performance was extraordinary and the courage and fighting spirit of its French and African colonial was excellent. However, overuse and retirement of core Second World War veterans would lower quality and morale. Ultimately, effectiveness depended on the quality of French officers. On occasions, its inexperienced Indochinese troops performed well when led by good French officers and NCOs. After all, this was a civil war as well as a colonial and revolutionary war. Hampered by its polyglot makeup and the paucity of its logistics trail, which was heavily understaffed, including, for example, air force mechanics, the French war infrastructure was frail. The air force was underpowered for the tasks required and, overall, French command often made battle plans that stretched available logistic and military capacity too far. As a Western-style road-bound army with a vulnerable road-bound logistics trail in a mostly mountainous and forested country, the French were unable to counter the asymmetric warfare strategy of the Vietminh, especially in Tonkin, the centre, and the north, where Giáp held the strategic initiative.

French high command was structurally weak and lacking in Asian experience and this problem was exacerbated by having the headquarters in Saigon, which was far from being the main battlefront and enjoyed an important degree of pacification. French command was split between Saigon and Hanoi, the latter hosting the deputy commander's headquarters. This split only exacerbated highly strung military egos so that the geographical pairing almost always developed fractiousness on policy and personality. The exception was the de Lattre-Salan pairing and Salan generally. Map-based generalship rather than topographical knowledge, high turnover of appointments, and overreach were the main faults that plagued the French high command.

Surprisingly, the fractiousness of the Fourth Republic hid a remarkable consistency in France's overall colonial, military and geopolitical strategy, although it was gradually undermined by popular disapproval. Approval was less than twenty percent by 1953.

When the Chinese came to the border at the end of 1949, the large Vietminh numbers could now be equipped with modern weapons and almost limitless munitions and ancillary equipment and, in time, AA, heavy mortars, machine-guns, 75mm recoilless rifles, and 105mm heavy artillery. France was also the beneficiary of large US arms deliveries and cash from mid-1950, but this could only mitigate the Vietminh advantages.

Ho Chi Minh's deified status and communist organisation at the grassroots of the peasantry meant that France had little hope of countering this political aspect of the war on which victory eventually hung. Their chosen vehicle was Bao Dai, whose political potential was exceptionally degraded. His political image was mostly negative rather than positive. Although there were some capable politicians in the south, they would never have a strong grip on rural areas where anti-communist village heads and notables had been wiped out by assassination or forced to flee.

The de Lattre lines consisting of hundreds of heavily armed concrete and barbed wire bastions protected Hanoi and the crowded Red River delta, which in turn protected the precious rice crop and aimed to restrict Vietminh access to this vital victual as well as keep the delta clear of Vietminh. This defensive policy largely failed, although it required strenuous Vietminh efforts to keep the rice supply flowing and shortages did hamper operations on occasion. Pushed onto the strategic defence, the main criticism of France's static defence policy was that it held down most of the 500,000 troops available to the French by 1954 and meant that forces available for offensive or emergency actions were limited to only 20,000–30,000.

As the Vietminh started to be armed and trained by the Chinese from a secure base, the strategy and tactics of the VPA started to evolve into a hybrid army that could move from asymmetric guerilla warfare to modern warfare. This process reached its apogee at Dien Bien Phu. However, in moving too quickly from one to the other after the victory on the RC4, Giáp suffered three major and costly defeats in 1951 and again at Ná Sán in November–December

1952. When the VPA came out of the hills onto the flat lands of the delta and the jungle they became easy. The extended Hoa Binh battle 1951–2 fought in topography favourable to the VPA was a draw, but it showed an improved French capability in the *guerre sans front*. However, the VPA was also learning and the defeat at Ná Sán in 1953 in the T'ai Highlands west of Hanoi propelled the Vietminh into a huge logistical and political overhaul, including the land reform programme, which aimed at total war mobilisation of the nation. Giáp's ability to learn from failures and develop his forces from the level of peasant guerrillas to tactically competent regulars was a major achievement on the path to victory.

The VPA's defeats in battles from 1951–1953 were necessarily brought on by the overriding imperative of defeating the French before expected US intervention, both indirect and direct, which had been very effective in Korea. This imperative was informed by the Chinese desire for a buffer state to keep the US-backed French away from their border. The newly trained army had to be 'bloodied in modern warfare'. The most important command decision to switch to an 'indirect strategy' major (as would have been favoured by renowned strategist Basil Lydell-Hart), by advancing west to France's allied tribal areas and Lao, would stretch French resources. It would force the French to defend important political assets, so weakening them by dispersal and stretching both logistical resources (including air transport) and elite paratrooper formations. Indirect strategy also pushed France to operate on the Vietminh's favoured terrain (except on the Plain of Jars) in jungle and mountains where tanks, artillery and aeroplanes counted for much less.

Giáp showed great ability and skill in both strategy and tactics, but his greatest contribution to victory was the construction of a superb logistics system as well as a very effective intelligence network. In all this, Chinese help through CMAG was very important. But the expansive claims by Chinese historians and generals for their role are overdone. Tellingly, they only claim the victories and disassociate themselves from the defeats. Both Ho and Giáp were intelligent and capable war leaders who worked well in tandem. Military clichés handed down from the great helmsman are also given due attention by the communist claque. But they were somewhat off the mark because the VPA were facing modern French and French-trained soldiery, not the Kuomintang Army.

Even if American B52 intervention had won the Battle of Dien Bien Phu for the French, it is still likely that the Vietminh would have won the war because the Chinese were on the border and the peasanty, despite very significant disillusion with the populace, was still broadly supportive of Ho and the DRV. The communists were also the only outfit with an effective grassroots rural organisation. Moreover the French, thanks to media coverage, had already lost the political battle on its home front.

The French Army could be ruthless but the determination to win was pitched against a people and a political party willing and driven to win at any cost. Before the war started, Ho told Saintenay that the Vietminh were willing to fight and 'you will kill ten of us; we will kill one of you but in the end, we will win.' That ruthless purity in utilising the limitless and pitiless horror of war was the theme of the film *Apocalypse Now* and Conrad's novel *The Heart of Darkness*. Learning from the Indochina War, France's veterans in Algeria would adopt an even more pitiless approach to the fighting there. They achieved considerable success against an enemy who did not have a strong base just over the border. But on the cusp of victory in Algeria, the political ground shifted beneath their feet and the Fourth Republic collapsed.

In the film *Apocalypse Now*, Kurtz decried the decadent and half-hearted war being waged by America:

> *As long as cold beer, hot food, rock 'n' roll, and all the other amenities remain the expected norm, our conduct of the war will only gain impotence. And we must kill them. We must incinerate them. Pig after pig. Cow after cow. Village after village. Army after army.*

In essence he was saying the same thing about a French Army tied, as it was, to its road-bound communications trail, bases and air logistics as well as its wine, *baguettes*, and mobile brothels. Ho's army was much more pitiless, and willing to make and impose huge, even limitless, sacrifices on the Vietnamese people.

Abbreviations and Basic explanations, Including Ideological Terms

AGITPROP: Abbreviation for Soviet Agitation and Propaganda

Annam: The traditional name for Vietnam. For a long time a nation subject to Chinese pressure, the country has a significant north-south (Tonkin-Cochin) divide along some cultural and religious lines though the race, geography and language is the same apart from regional dialect. From the nineteenth century Annam was the name given to the middle region of the country. Annam hosted the ancient capital of Hue, the seat of the emperor. In the hills and mountains there are myriad tribes of ancient Han or Austronesian extraction, such as the Jarai.

BEP: Foreign Legion Parachute Battalion, made up of European nationals, mostly German with some East Europeans but also a high percentage of Vietnamese who wore white berets rather than white kepi.

BMEO: Brigade Marine d'Extreme-Orient

BPC: Colonial Parachute Battalion

BPVN: Vietnamese Parachute Battalion

Cambodia: Known as 'Cambodge' by the French, the Cambodian people are known as Khmer and they speak Khmer language. The country is also known as Kampuchea. Buddhism is the very dominant religion. A homogeneous nation, about five percent of the population are Moslem Chams from an ancient seafaring race. Unlike Vietnam, Christianity had made no significant inroads except with Vietnamese immigrants. There was a small but long established Chinese minority.

CFDT: Socialist-controlled trade union

CGT: Communist-controlled trade union

CMAG: Chinese Military Advisory Group sent by Mao to advise and control the Vietminh. There is some controversy about how important they were. Chinese historians say that they were very important and they downplay the role of Ho and Giáp. China was essential for supplies of military equipment and munitions and the CMAG played an important role but the Chinese for obvious reasons overestimate their contribution in terms of strategy and tactics, although basic training was an essential building block, as was training in the use of artillery.

CNIP: French political party in the Fourth Republic, National Centre of Independents and Peasants. It moved into prominence after amnesties for Petainists/Vichyites 1951–53. Antoine Pinay became premier in 1952 as the political system lurched to the right.

Comintern: This was the international body for the Communist Party and, theoretically, the body charged with spreading world revolution and form, co-ordinating and controlling the policies and actions of communist regimes around the world. Highly centralised and disciplined, Ho Chin Minh followed its dictates even where Vietnam's interests were compromised or threatened. In practice the comintern operated solely for the benefit of the USSR. Many members of the comintern were purged in the 1930s when the CPSU was purged. Ho was under investigation for right nationalist deviationism and as a suspect informer was lucky to escape. Abolished in 1943, its functions were taken over by a similar organisation called 'Cominform', and 'Comecon' for economic co-ordination was soon added.

Democratic centralism: This concept is linked to the Dictatorship of the Proletariat concept. Only internal discussion is allowed within the party and such discussion/debate must not leak outside to the wider public when the leadership has decided, then the party line is rigidly enforced.

DGER: The direction générale des études et recherches (English: General Directorate for Studies and Research), was a division of the Bureau Central de Renseignements et d'Action (BCRA), the intelligence agency of the Free French Forces, Charles de Gaulle's French government-in-exile in London. It was created in 1944, and Jacques Soustelle was the first director, from 6 November 1944 to 18 April 1945. In April 1946, DGER became the service de documentation extérieure et de contre-espionnage (SDECE), also referred to as M.5. Jean Sainteny, son-in-law of former premier Saurrat, became the head of station in Kunming (Yunan) where he co-operated with the OSS to start clandestine military operations against the Japanese in Indochina.

Dictatorship of the Proletariat: A key concept in Marxist Leninism that is related to the highly disciplined cell structure of communist parties, and the belief that only a small and highly disciplined party could successfully carry out a revolution and, even more importantly, defend it against counter-revolutionaries. They would do this on behalf of the Proletariat and ascribe to them the right rule over the Proletariat, i.e. 'Dictatorship of the Proletariat', with an absolute monopoly of power in all realms of civic society.

DRV: Democratic Republic of Vietnam (communist)

DZ: Drop zone was the ever-contracting territory into which French supplies were parachuted. The smaller the DZ became, the higher the number of mis-drops into Vietminh hands. This was especially problematic as the standard 105mm artillery shell was used in the same gun operated by both sides.

EDF: European Defence Force was the idea of the US/UK for burden-sharing of defence in Europe in the face of the Soviet threat. It failed over French fears of German re-armament.

FEC: French Expeditionary Force. It was not the only armed forces command by the French because similar numbers were nominally raised and commanded by the three associate states of Vietnam, Lao and Cambodia.

GM: Groupes Mobiles – elite mixed-arms self-contained mobile strike forces similar to the German Kampf Gruppen at the end of the Second World War. With tanks, armoured cars, transport, artillery, logistics, engineering and medical capability they were rapidly deployed from their Hanoi base on special missions to any threatened area around the de Lattre's lines around the Red River Delta and Hanoi. They were renowned for elan and esprit de corps. De Castries was a GM commander.

GMCA: Groupement de Commandos Mixtes Aeroportes. French raised and officered composed mainly of T'ai and Meo tribesmen they numbered 20,000–30,000 and held down large numbers of Vietminh troops and scored notable successes. However the operation inspired by Colonel Trinquier was started too late in the war to have a chance of any substantial impact.

GMI: The name for GMCA – see below – which was adopted from May 1953

Hmong: (also known as Meo) Indigenous tribe, semi-nomadic hilltop-dwellers in Tonkin and Lao whose primary economic activity was the cultivation of opium for export to the huge domestic and Chinese markets.

ICL: International communist league, revolutionary socialists and deadly enemies of the communists since Trotsky's ousting by his rival Stalin in 1927. They were part of Leon Trotsky's 4th International. With propaganda broadcast by their leading paper La Lutte (the Struggle), they worked with the ICP during the war and became more powerful and popular in Saigon than Ho's communists. On taking power, Ho turned against their leader Tạ Thu Thâu, who was captured and assassinated under Ho's orders in September 1945, as were several thousand other Trotskyists. Ho told a French journalist, apparently with unfeigned emotion, that Thâu was 'a great patriot'. The differences between the two were minor but revolved around personality and obtuse ideological differences.

ICP: The Indochina Communist Party was set up to cover all of French Indochina's five constituent parts which were Cochin, Tonkin and Annam, plus Cambodia and Lao. Given that Lao and Cambodia (the people known as Khmer) were so backward, it was believed that the Vietnamese should play a leading role – a corollary to the Dictatorship of the Proletariat concept. The comintern ordered this reconstruction with the idea of creating a system analogous to the USSR in Indochina. Where Russians led in the USSR, so the Vietnamese would lead in Indochina. The ICP replaced the split Communist Party movement in 1930. Not surprisingly the split was essentially between Tonkin (north) and Cochin (south) power centres, though a third split arose in Annam (middle).

KDDH: "New learning group", one of the many nationalist political groups formed in the early 20th Century.

Khmer: Refer above to Cambodia

Lao: The smallest in population of the components of French Indochina, its population, economy and government were entirely dominated by the Lao-Thai along the Mekong valley lowlands. Lao's mountainous uplands are tribal regions where the government still has minimal impact. One of the largest tribes was the opium growing Hmong (Meo) and there are many others including the Leu in the Nam Ou valley.

MAAG: US – Military Assistance Advisory Group – responsible for co-ordinating and advising on US military equipment supplies and training for the French and Associated States' armies.

MRP: French political party of the Fourth Republic, Movement Républicain Populaire, centre-left Catholic party, favouring empire, a key tripartite party that participated in all governments 1945–54, nominated a number of premiers and was predominant in foreign and colonial policy. (Party of Georges Bidault and Robert Schuman.)

NCO: Non-commissioned officer

NKVD: The People's Commissariat for Internal affairs, Russian Secret police and spy organisation run by Lavrenti Beria, the successor of the Cheka, set up by Lenin and run by Felix Derzhinsky. The KGB and recently the FSB are the modern successors.

OSS: American Office of Strategic Services – including espionage, subversion, propaganda, covert activities and support for insurgency groups.

Party secretariat: This is the ultimate source of all power in communist systems because it controls the administrative, disciplinary and personnel functions of the party, the source of all power. At the apex is the general secretary who commands huge powers of patronage in selection of regional party secretaries who form the bulk of the central committee. Most communist leaders rise to power in the secretariat, as Stalin did in his tussle with the Trotskyists. Ho was an exception because he had overarching personal prestige. However, he had to work within the system and was constrained by other views, especially those emanating from the pro-Chinese leftist faction of Truong Chinh, who also controlled the secretariat as general secretary. Only Ho's prestige could keep him at bay. The unpopularity and failure of land reform led to sharp criticism in 1956 when Khruschev's speech at the Moscow 20th congress of the CPSU (Communist Party of the Soviet Union) enabled an alliance of Ho, Giáp and Le Duan to sideline him. Troung also made the mistake of aligning with the much hated traditional enemy, the Chinese.

PCF: French Political Party, French Communist Party, Parti communiste Française, ultra-orthodox and under general secretary Thorez followed all commands from Moscow. In coalition governments until 1947.

PIM: Prisoniers Internes Militaire, who were several thousand-strong plus civilian *suppletifs*. These were drawn respectively from pools of prisoners-of-war and civilian porters who supported the French war effort in the construction of roads, bridges, blockhouses and the supply and logistics train. In the Second World War, the Germans would know them as Hiwis (ex-Russian soldiers) or the British as SEP (surrendered enemy personnel).

Politburo: This is the name for the decision-making body of communist parties that normally consists of no more than about ten people including so called non-voting candidate members. In Vietnam it was known as the Standing Bureau of the Central Committee[1]. The Soviet Party (the communist party for the Soviet Union) renamed it the Praesidium (of the People). The central committee from which the Politburo is dedicated as a leadership body is bigger, perhaps consisting of some hundreds of mainly regional party secretaries. The wider membership was called into congress every four years but was really a laudatory rubber stamp body. Democratic centralism and the closed nature of politicking means that party infighting between factions was particularly vicious in communist systems and struggles within the system, and would often be deadly for the losers. In the 1930s, all the old leaders of the party were killed, including Buhharin, Kamenev, Zinoviev, Trotsky, Radek, etc, and many others. Such deadly outcomes mainly ended with the execution of Lavrenti Beria in 1953. However, in the People's Republic of China, death for the loser continued, for example Li Shaoqui and Lin Piao. In other communist systems, gun fights in Politburo meetings has been known, for example in Yemen and Albania. Imre Nagy was executed when he tried to break Hungary away from the so-called Soviet Bloc or Warsaw Pact bloc, which was the mirror to NATO.

RGR: French political party of the Fourth Republic, Rassemblement de Gauches Republicain – Rally of French left Republicans – essentially the recreated Radical Party of the Third Republic centre-left bloc – party of Mendes France.

RI: French political party of the Fourth Republic, Republicaine Independents. Right-wing Petainist successor party. CNIP and RI started to emerge from 1952 as the Gaullists started to decline and de Gaulle left politics.

RPF: French political party of the Fourth Republic, Rassemblement du Peuple Français – de Gaulle's right-wing nationalist party – anti Fourth Republic democracy, conservative with falangist elements.

SFIO: French political party of the Fourth Republic, Section Francais de L'Internationale Ouvière. The French Socialist Party, part of Tripartite government 1945-48. Party of Pierre Laval, Guy Mollet, Leon Blum. In the book we simply refer to the Socialist Party.

Soviet: A shorthand word used to reference the USSR and peoples collectively. The USSR was made up of many races, only about fifty percent of whom were Russian by the end of the regime.

Thermidorian reaction and Bonapartism: These were fears held by communists and referenced in the French revolution for counter-revolution and takeover by military strong men. Being a suspect nationalist was a serious political allegation that was used against Ho, and Giáp became a natural target for fears of Bonapartism.

Titoism: This is the name given to nationalist deviation tendencies exhibited by the Yugoslav Communist Party under the leadership of Joseph Broz – 'Tito' (*nom de guerre* by which he is best known). Tito's partisans largely liberated themselves under his leadership, holding down some seventeen German divisions in the Second World War and not liberated by Soviet forces. Tito's communist partisans were provided considerable assistance by Churchill, including money and arms and British officers parachuted in or sent in by boat. In consequence, Tito developed his own independent policies and refused to take orders from Moscow. Ho was always under some suspicion for being a nationalistic, rightist deviationist. Expelled from Cominform in 1948, ironically Tito's deviancy came from leftist deviation before switching to rightist deviation after expulsion. The main issue was Tito's refusal to follow Moscow's party line.

UDF: French political party of the Fourth Republic, Union pour la Démocratie. Traditional conservative party encompassing former Petainists and Vichyites.

UDSR: French political party of the Fourth Republic, Union Democratique de la Resistance – party of Francois Mitterrand.

USSR: Union of Soviet Socialist Republics – the successor of the Russian empire – was a federal system that masked a centralised communist dictatorship based in Moscow. The federalist concept was based on the ideological work done by Joseph Stalin under Lenin's direction.

VNA: Vietnam's national army was the army of Bao Dai's national government, but only nominally under their control. As with similar Lao and Kampuchean units (Cambodia), they were under French command in practice.

VNQDD: The Việt Nam Quốc Dân Đảng was a nationalist political organisation founded in the 1920s that became the main rival to the communists.

VOC: Dutch East India company, founded 1602

VPA: Vietnamese People's Army. The Chinese-trained regular army of the Vietminh's crypto communist regime.

Notes

Chapter I

1. Lo van Son, Platoon Leader, 910 Battalion, 148 Regiment, *Dien Bien Phu vu d'en face Paroles de Bo doi*, DBV World Editions, February 2014, p.63
2. *Ibid* p.64
3. *Ibid* p.65
4. Phung Quang Truy, head of a reconnaissance unit of the 148th Regiment, *Dien Bien Phu vu d'en face Paroles de Bo doi*, World Editions, February 2014, p.65–66
5. Martin Windrow, *The Last Valley*, Cassell, 2004, p.198–199
6. Raphael Delpard, *Les Rizieres de la Souffra, Cobatants Francais en Indochine 1945–54*
7. Zoltan Harangi-Toth, *Hungarians Fighting for France in Indochina*, AARMS, Vol 17, No. 3, 2018, p.67–69
8. E. le Breton, *Fuseliers maritime en Indochine, La Revue Martime*, October 1948, p.1,304
9. US Marine Corps, *Dinassaut Operations in Indochina: 1946–47*, USAMC, 1991, p.3–4
10. The author John Pike's recollections of driving on dirt track byways the length and breadth of Lao, Cambodia, Burma, 2009–2020
11. *General Raoul Salan Memoires, Fin de L'Empire*, Presse de la cite, 1971, p.299
12. Dominique de la Motte, *a l'autre cote de l'eau*, Texto, 2009, p.83
13. Captain X, General Ely, *The Lessons of War in Indochina, May 1951*, 31 May 1955, Rand Corporation, 1967, p.157
14. Julia Lovell, *Maoism*, Vintage, 2019, p.229

Chapter II

1. Thomas Ennis, *French Indochina French Policy and Developments in Indo-China*, pp. ix, 230, Chicago: University of Chicago Press, 1936, p.25
2. *Ibid* p.36
3. *Ibid* p.96
4. Haydoin Cherry, *Down and Out in Saigon*, Yale 2019, p. 103
5. Bernhard Fall, *Street Without Joy, The French Debacle in Indochina*, Stackpole Books, 2018, p.293
6. Author's memories, 2009–15
7. Jean-Marie de Beaucorps, *Soldat de Jade, edition Kergours*, 3 March 1998, p.292
8. Marguerite Duras, *The Lovers*, First 1984, Flamingo-Random House, 1985, p.22–23
9. *Ibid* p.74
10. de la Motte, *De l'autre cote de l'eau*, Texto, 2009, p.75
11. Norman Lewis, *A Dragon Apparent*, 1951, p.85
12. Geoffrey C. Ward and Ken Burns, *The Vietnam War: An Intimate History*, 2010, Chapter 1
13. Pierre Brocheux and Daniel Hemery, *Indochina: An Ambiguous Colonization*, University of California Press, 2009, p.52
14. Pierre Mataignon, p.124
15. Pierre Brocheux and Daniel Hemery, *Indochina: An Ambiguous Colonization*, University of California Press, 2009, p.57

16. Thomas Ennis, Russell and Russell New York, 1936, reprinted 1973, p.78
17. *Ibid* p.101
18. Pierre Brocheux and Daniel Hemery, *Indochina: An Ambiguous Colonization*, University of California Press, 2009, p.70
19. *Ibid* p.107
20. *Ibid* p.111
21. Charles A. Fisher, *A Social Economic and Political Geography of South-East Asia*, Methuen, 1967, p.533
22. Pierre Brocheux and Daniel Hermery, *Indochina 1858-1954*, University of California Press, p.185
23. *La Patrie Annamite, Gosha Going Indochinese*, p.58
24. *Federalism Indochinois et Nationalism Annamite*, 28 November 1930
25. The author, who worked in agricultural development in the Mekong delta region, can confirm that the farm sizes remain small, even smaller in fact than in 1954, but intensive farming has been combined with modern technology to develop a major food export industry
26. Charles A. Fisher, *A Social Economic and Political Geography of South-East Asia*, Methuen, 1967, p.542
27. *Ibid* p.540
28. *Ibid* p.547
29. Admiral Jean Decoux, *a la Barre de l'Indochine*, Soukha editions, 2013, p.386
30. Charles A. Fisher, p.549
31. Captain Lucien de Reinach, *Laos*, posthumous, Chemin Duponte, 1911
32. *Ibid* p.368
33. Charles A. Fisher, *A Social Economic and Political Geography of South-East Asia*, Methuen, 1967, p.550
34. *Ibid* p.552
35. Pierre Brocheux and Daniel Hémery, *Indochina: An Ambiguous Colonization*, University of California Press, 2011, p.222
36. *Ibid* p.126–127
37. Balthasar Gibiat, *La Seve Amere de L'Hevea*, p.66–67
38. *Ibid* p.93–94
39. Eric Panthou, *Plantation Michelin Vietnam*, Edition Galipote, 2013
40. Pierre Brocheux and Daniel Hémery, *Indochina: An Ambiguous Colonization*, University of California Press, 2011, p82
41. Denis Cogneau, Yannick Dupraz and Sandrine Mesplé-Somps, Working Paper No. 2018–27, *Fiscal Capacity and Dualism in Colonial States: The French Empire 1830–1962*, p.9
42. Pierre Brocheux and Daniel Hémery, *Indochina: An Ambiguous Colonization*, University of California Press, 2011, p.149
43. Ennis, *French Indochina French Policy and Developments in Indo-China*, pp. ix, 230. Chicago: University of Chicago Press, 1936
44. Rosa Luxemburg, *The Accumulation of Capital*, 1913
45. Final Report of the National Assembly's Commission to Investigate the Traffic in Indochinese Piastre, 17 June 1954 (hereafter Final Report), reprinted in Despuech (1974), 203-208. Johnathan Marshal, *Dirty Wars: French and American Piastre Profiteering in Indochina*, 9 August 2014, Asia Pacific Journal, Vol 12, Issue 32, No, 2
46. Mai Elliott, *The Sacred Willow: Four Generations in the Life of a Vietnamese Family*, Oxford University Press, 1999

Chapter III

1. Sophie Quinn-Judge, *Ho Chi Minh: The Missing Years*, University of California Press, 1999

2. Geoffrey Ward and Ken Burns, *The Vietnam War*, p.9
3. Tim Harper, *Underground Asia*, Allen Lane, 2020, p.368
4. Julia Lovell, *Maoism, A Global History*, Bodley Head, 2019, p.228
5. Michael Kort, *The Vietnam War Reexamined*, Cambridge, 2018, p.87
6. Sophie Quinn-Judge, *Ho Chi Minh: The Missing Years*, University of California Press, 1999, p.203
7. Christopher Goscha, *The Road to Dien Bien Phu*, Princeton 2022, p.52
8. Lacouture interview *Historia Spécial*, no 28, p.124
9. Daniel Guerin, *Aux Services des Colonises, 1930-1953*, Editions Minuit, Paris, 1954 p.22
10. William J Duiker, Introduction, *US Containment policy*, 1st Edition, 1994
11. *Ibid*
12. Max Hastings, *Vietnam: An Epic Tragedy, 1945–1975*, Harper, 2018
13. Ronald Spector, *Advice and Support, the early years, 1941–60*, US Army, 1983, p.59
14. David G. Marr, *Vietnam 1945*, UCP, 1995, p.371
15. Christopher Goscha, *The Road to Dien Bien Phu*, Princeton, 2022, p.21
16. Ronald Spector, *Advice and Support, the early years, 1941-60*, US Army, 1983, p.61
17. *Ibid* p.64
18. Giáp, *Unforgettable Days*, Gioi Hanoi, 2015, p.7
19. Truong Nhu Tang, ex-minister of justice
20. Giáp, *Unforgettable Days*, Gioi Hanoi, 2015, p.8
21. Eric Hobsbawm, *The Age of Empire*, Michael Josephs, 1978, p.217
22. E.H. Carr, *Socialism in One Country*, Vol II, Macmillan 1964, p.617
23. *Ibid* p.612
24. *Ibid* 23 April 1923, p. 612
25. *Ibid* p.619
26. *Ibid* p. 618
27. *Ibid* p. 629
28. *Ibid* p.630
29. Giáp, *Unforgettable Days*, Gioi Hanoi, 2015, p.55
30. Ed. Michael Hunt, *A Vietnam War Reader*, Penguin, 2010, p.12
31. David G. Marr, *Vietnam 1945*, UCP 1995, p.371
32. Christopher E. Goscha
33. Biu Dien, *The Jaws of War*, Indiana University Press, 1999 (first edition 1987), p.19
34. *Ibid* p.19
35. *Ibid* p.19
36. *Ibid* p.103
37. Professor Richard Cobb, *French and Germans, Germans and French*, Penguin, 1983
38. David G. Marr, *Vietnam 1945*, UCP 1995, New York Times, 15 March 1945, p.327
39. David Marr, *Vietnam 1945*, University of California Press, 1995, p.330–332
40. *Ibid* p.325
41. Pierre Mataignon, *L'Indochine francaise 1858–1954*, Texto, 2019, p.264
42. Arthur J. Dommen, *Conflict in Laos*, Preager 1964, 1971, p.71
43. US Department of State, *The Situation in Laos*, Washington, September 1959, p.2–3
44. Michael Kort, *The Vietnam War Reexamined*, Cambridge, 2018, p.87
45. Fritz Langer and J.J. Zasloff, *Revolution in Laos*, North Vietnam and the Pathet Lao, Rand Corporation, 1969, p.68, VWP party document, Issued Bac Can, 1952, Vietminh Central Information Centre
46. Souphanouvong, quoted in *A Chronicle of Principal Events Relating to the Indo-China Questions*, Peking, World Culture Publishing House, 1954, p.35
47. Joseph Stalin, First formal publishing of *Marxism and the National and Colonial question*, Joseph Stalin, Moscow and Leningrad, co-operative publishing society of Foreign workers in the USSR, 1935

48. Christopher E. Goscha, *Going Indochinese*, Nias Classics, 2012, p.143
49. Vo Nguyễn Giáp, *Memoirs 1946-1954*, Phebus, 200, p.144
50. Bui Dien and David Chanoff, *The Jaws of War*, 1999
51. Giáp, *Unforgettable Days*, Gioi Hanoi, 2015, p.229

Chapter IV

1. Frederic Angleviel, *Poulu Condore, un bagne francais en Indochine*, Vendemiare, 2020, p.26
2. Lorraine Pattersen, *Ethnoscapes of Exile: Political Prisoners from Indochina in a Colonial Asian World*, Cambridge, 2018
3. Frederic Angleviel, *Poulu Condore, un bagne francais en Indochine*, Vendemiare, 2020, p.138
4. *Ibid* p.44
5. *Ibid* p.139
6. David Chanoff and Doan Van Toai, *Vietnam, a portrait of its people at war*, TPP, 2009 p.24
7. Frederic Angleviel, *Poulu Condore, un bagne francais en Indochine*, Vendemiare, 2020, p.141

Chapter V

1. Decoux, *Admiral Jean Decoux a la Barre de l'Indochine*, Soukha Editions, 2013, p.64–65
2. *Ibid* p.99
3. Jean Lacouture, *de Gaulle*, Collins, 1991, p.85–6
4. David Marr, *Vietnam 1945*, UCP 1995, p.326–327
5. Ronald Spector, *In the Ruins of Empire*, Random House, 2008 p.102
6. Decoux, *Admiral Jean Decoux a la Barre de l'Indochine*, Soukha editions, 2013, p.286
7. Ronald Spector, *In the Ruins of Empire*, Random House, 2008, p.88
8. David G. Marr, *Vietnam 1945*, University of California Press 1995, p.232–237
9. *Ibid* p.239
10. Giáp, *Unforgettable Days*, Gioi, Hanoi, p.9
11. *Ibid*
12. Jean-Marie de Beaucorps, *Soldat de Jade*, edition Kergours 3rd March 1998
13. *Ibid* p.282
14. Giáp, *Unforgettable Days*, Gioi, Hanoi p.12
15. *Ibid* p.13
16. *Ibid* p.19
17. Decoux, *Admiral Jean Decoux a la Barre de l'Indochine*, Soukha editions, 2013, p.287
18. David G. Marr, *Vietnam 1945*, University of California Press, 1995, Chapter 4
19. Decoux, *Admiral Jean Decoux a la Barre de l'Indochine*, Soukha editions, 2013, p.21
20. Ronald Spector, *Advice and support, the early years, 1941-60*, US Army 1983, p.108
21. Giáp, *Unforgettable Days*, Gioi, Hanoi,p.23
22. Mai Elliott, *The Sacred Willow: Four Generations in the Life of a Vietnamese Family*, Oxford University Press, 1999, p.108
23. *Ibid*
24. David Chanoff and Doan Van Toai, *Vietnam, A Portrait of its People and War*, TPP, 2009
25. Jean Lacouture, *de Gaulle*, Collins, 1991, p.87
26. *Ibid*
27. *Ibid*
28. Douglas Pike, based on Rand Corporation, *200 interviews Vietcong: Organisation and Techniques of the National Liberation of South Vietnam*, MIT Press, Cambridge Massachusetts and London, 1966, preface
29. Admiral Decoux, *A La Barre de L'Indochine-memoirs*, Souka editions, March 2013, first published Libraire Plon, 1949, p.382
30. *Ibid* p.391

31. Christopher Bayly and Tim Harper, *Forgotten Wars*, Penguin, 2008, p.147
32. Ronald Spector, *In the Ruins of Empire*, p.99
33. Germaine Krull, *Diary of Saigon*
34. J.P. Cross, *First in Last out, a British Officer in Indochina*, Greenhill, p.39
35. *Ibid* p.29–30
36. *Ibid* p.29
37. Christopher Bayly and Tim Harper, *Forgotten Wars*, Penguin, 2008, p.148
38. *Ibid* p.151
39. Gibert Bodinier, Ed., *le retour en Indochine 1945–46*, Vincennes 1987, doc 3
40. Germaine Krull, *Saigon Diaries, Forgotten Wars*, Christopher Bayly and Tim Harper, Penguin, 2008 p.147
41. Major Philip Malin, private memoir as part of a Burma Society project
42. Michael Kort, *The Vietnam War Reexamined*, Cambridge, 2018, p.80
43. J.P. Cross, *First in Last out, a British Officer in Indochina*, Greenhill, p.41
44. Major Philip Malin, private memoir as part of a Burma Society project
45. *Ibid*
46. *Ibid*
47. *Ibid*
48. J.P. Cross, *First in Last out, a British Officer in Indochina*, Greenhill
49. *Ibid*
50. Martin Stuart-Fox, *A History of Lao*, Cambridge, 1997, p.61-66
51. T.O. Smith, *Britain and the Origins of the Vietnam War: UK Policy in Indo-China, 1943-50*, Palgrave, 2007, p54-58
52. Ronald Spector, *Advice and Support*, p.68
53. *Commander-in-chief French forces in Indochina, Lessons of the Indochina War*, translated by V.J. Croziat, 1955, p.348
54. Margaret Duras, First 1984, Random House, 1985, p.14 & p.25
55. Major Paul Kennedy, *Dinassaut Operations in Indochina 1946-54*, quoting Koburger, p.15
56. Vietminh. Xuan Vu, David Chanoff and Doan Van Toai, *Vietnam, A Portrait of its People*, p.5
57. Lucien Bodard, p.17
58. Klaus-Heinrich Krause, *Barfuss im Reisfeld*, Epee, 2001, p.123
59. Jonathan Marshall, *Dirty Wars: French and American Piastre Profiteering in Indochina 1945–75*, Asia Pacific Journal 2014, Vol 12, Issue 32, No. 2
60. Ronald Spector, *In the Ruins of Empire*, Random House, 2008, p.94
61. *Ibid* p.332
62. *Ibid* p.229
63. Jean-Marie de Beaucorps, *Soldat de Jade*, edition Kergours, 3 March 1998, p.292
64. Giáp, *Unforgettable Days*, Gioi, Hanoi, 2015, p.111
65. *Ibid* p.165
66. Jean-Marie de Beaucorps, *Soldat de Jade*, edition Kergours, 3 March 1998, p.337
67. General Raoul Salan, *Memoires, Fin de L'Empire*, Presse de la cite, 1971, p.148
68. Pierre Brocheaux, *Ho Chi Minh: a biography*, p.115
69. Paul Mus, *Viêt-Nam: Sociologie d'une Guerre*, Éditions du Seuil, 1952
70. Mai Elliott, *The Sacred Willow: Four Generations in the Life of a Vietnamese Family*, Oxford University Press, 1999, p.118
71. *Ibid* p.120
72. Burns, p.30
73. *Ibid* p.27
74. Gibert Bodinier, Ed., *le retour en Indochine 1945–46*, Vincennes 1987, doc 97
75. General Raoul Salan, *Memoires, Fin de L'Empire*, Presse de la cite, 1971, p.48
76. *Ibid* p.48

Chapter VI

1. Giáp, *Unforgettable Days*, Gioi Hanoi 2015, p.179
2. Michael Kort, *The Vietnam War Reexamined*, Cambridge, 2018, p.87
3. *Ibid* p.207
4. *Ibid* p.227
5. Ronald Spector, *In the Ruins of Empire*, Random House, 2008, p.235
6. Martin-Stuart Fox, *A History of Laos*, Cambridge, 1997, p.65
7. Wilfred Burchett, *Mekong Upstream*, Hanoi: Red River Publishing House, 1957, p.264
8. Authur J. Dommen, *Conflict in Lao*, Praeger, 1974, p. 29
9. Giáp, *Unforgettable Days*, Gioi Hanoi, 2015, p.321
10. Pierre Mataignon, *L'Indochine Francais 1858-1954*, Texto, 2004, p.281
11. Anne Appelaum, *Iron Curtain: The Crushing of Eastern Europe 1944–56*, published in 2012 by Doubleday in the US and Allen Lane in the UK
12. Frederic Longeval, *Embers of War: The Fall of an Empire and the Making of America's Vietnam*, Random House, 2012, p.124
13. Philippe Devillers, *L'histoire de Vietnam*, Parsi, 1952 p.328-329
14. Jean Lacoutre, *de Gaulle*, p.87
15. General Vo Nguyễn, Giáp, *Unforgettable Days*, Gioi, Hanoi, 2015, p.332
16. *Ibid* p.341
17. Gibert Bodinier, Ed., *le retour en Indochine 1945-46*, Vincennes 1987, doc 78 and 83
18. *Ibid* doc 79, and 86
19. Pentagon papers
20. Ronald Spector, *In the Ruins of Empire*, Random House, 2008, p.257
21. Pierre Mataignon, *l'Indochine Francais*, Texto, 2019
22. Ronald Spector, p.260
23. Paul Mus, *Temoignage Chretien*, 10 February 1950
24. Pentagon Papers
25. Bodiner, *le retour en Indochine 1945–46*, VinCennes 1987, p.375
26. Mai Elliott, *The Sacred Willow: Four Generations in the Life of a Vietnamese Family*, Oxford University Press, 1999, p.161
27. General Raoul Salan, *Memoires, Fin de L'Empire*, Presses de la cite, 1979, p.94
28. Christopher E. Goscha, *The Road to Dien Bien Phu*, Princeton, 2022, p.65
29. Frederik Longeval, *Embers of War*, Yale, 2012, p.170
30. Mai Elliott, *The Sacred Willow: Four Generations in the Life of a Vietnamese Family*, Oxford University Press, 1999
31. MISSING?
32. Gilbert Bodinier, Ed., *le retour de la France en Indochine*, Vol 1, Vincennes 1987
33. Jean *Jacques Bonnaud, Prisonniers du Mikado, Temporis*, 2022
34. *Ibid* p.272-277
35. Mai Elliott, *The Sacred Willow: Four Generations in the Life of a Vietnamese Family*, Oxford University Press, 1999, p.148–152
36. *Ibid* p.151
37. *Ibid* p.151
38. Christopher E. Goscha, *The Road to Dien Bien Phu*, Princeton 2022, p.65
39. Dr Grauwin, *A Doctor at Dien Bien Phu*, Hutchinson, 1955, p.35
40. *Ibid* p.41
41. Joseph Dal Magro, documentary by Fabienne Servan-Schrieber, Lucie Pastor, France TV and Cinetv Todjo, 2014
42. Rene Mary, documentary by Fabienne Servan-Schrieber, Lucie Pastor, France TV and Cinetv Todjo, 2014
43. Martin Woodruff, *The Last Valley*, Cassel, 2004, p.178–181
44. Dr Grauwin, *A Doctor at Dien Bien Phu*, Hutchinson, 1955, p.41

45. *The Kingdom of Funan*, Angkor Borei, circa 500 BC
46. Lucien Bodard, *The Quicksand War: Prelude to Vietnam*, Atlanta, 1967, p.37
47. *Ibid* p.39
48. George Robert Elford, *Devil's Guard*, Dell, 1971, p.254
49. Lucien Bodard, *The Quicksand War: Prelude to Vietnam*, Atlanta, 1967, p.39
50. *Ibid* 1967
51. *Ibid* p.81
52. *Ibid* p.83
53. Bernhard Fall, *Street Without Joy*, Stackpole Books, 2018, p.271
54. Pierre Mataignon, *L'Indochine Francais 1858-1954*, Texto, 2004, p.306
55. Frederik Longeval, *Embers of War*, Random House, 2012, p.185
56. John Howard, *Brigadier USAA*, History Net, January 2020
57. General Ely, *Lessons from the Indochina War, 31 May 1955*, Saigon, Rand Corporation, 1967, Vol II, p.385
58. General Massu, *Seven years with Leclerc*, p.256
59. Hele de St Marc, *Memoires*, p.102–6
60. General Raoul Salan, *Memoires, Fin de l'Empire Vol II*, Presses de cite, 1971, p.87
61. Lieutenant Victor Croizat, *St Cyr*, USAG
62. General Raoul Salan, *Memoires, Fin de L'Empire*, Presse de la cite, 1979, p.103
63. Mai Elliott, *The Sacred Willow: Four Generations in the Life of a Vietnamese Family*, Oxford University Press, 1999, p.153
64. Weddell, p.128
65. Grahame Greene, *Ways of Escape*, Penguin, 1982
66. Alfred McCoy, *Politics of Heroin*
67. Shawn McHale, *Ethnicity, Violence, and Khmer-Vietnamese Relations: The Significance of the Lower Mekong Delta, 1757-1954, The Journal of Asian Studies*, vol 72, 2 May 2013, p.367-390
68. French security services report for the High Command, December 1952, Commissioner, BOX 65493, GGI, ANOM
69. *Khmer-Vietnamese Relations From 1930-1954 in the Mekong Delta*, Yan Ba Vu, Columbia, 10 April 10 2019

Chapter VII

1. Norman Lewis, *A Dragon Apparent*, Eland London 2003, first published 1951, p.35
2. *Ibid* p.180
3. *Ibid* p.173
4. Lucien Bodard, *The Quicksand War: Prelude to Vietnam*, Atlanta, 1967
5. Dominique de La motte, *de L'autre cote de L'eau*, Indochine, 1950-52, Texto 2009, p.107
6. George Robert Elford, *Devil's Guard*, Dell, 1971, p.76
7. A. Liddell Hart, *Strange Company*, 1953
8. Lucien Bodard, *The Quicksand War: Prelude to Vietnam*, Atlanta, 1967, p.62
9. *Ibid* p.101-103
10. Dommen, Arthur J., *The Indochinese Experience of the French and the Americans*, Indiana University Press, 2001, p.252. Quoted by Yves Gras
11. Valentino Benjamin, *Final Solutions: Mass Killing and Genocide in the 20th Century*, Cornell University Press, 2005, p.83
12. Arthur J. Dommen, *The Indochinese Experience of the French and the Americans*, Indiana University Press, 2001, p.252
13. Norman Lewis, *Napoli*, p.44
14. Mai Elliott, *The Sacred Willow: Four Generations in the Life of a Vietnamese Family*, Oxford University Press, p.135
15. Paul Grace, *Vietnamese Women in Society and Revolution*, vol 1,1974, "Introduction"

16. David Chanoff and Doan Van Toai, *Vietnam, a Portrait of its People at War*, p.28
17. George Robert Elford, *Devil's Guard*, Dell, p.177
18. Mai Elliott, *The Sacred Willow: Four Generations in the Life of a Vietnamese Family*, Oxford University Press, 1999, p.129
19. General Ely, *Lessons from the Indochina War*, 31 May 1955, Saigon, Rand Corporation, 1967, vol II
20. Lucien Bodard, *The Quicksand War: Prelude to Vietnam*, Atlanta, 1967, p.60
21. Norman Lewis quoting US Journalist Bob Miller, p.182
22. Norman Lewis, *A Dragon Apparent*, Eland, London, 2003, first published 1951, p.185
23. Mai Elliott, *The Sacred Willow: Four Generations in the Life of a Vietnamese Family*, Oxford University Press, 1999, p.136–137
24. Paul Martelli, *On the Devil's Tail*, Helion 2015, p.278
25. George Robert Elford, *Devil's Guard*, Dell 1971, p.254–255
26. Dominique de La Motte, *A l'autre Cote de L'eau*, Texto, 2009, p.72
27. Paul Martelli, *On the Devil's Tail*, Helion, 2015, p.265
28. Michel Bodin, *Les Africains dans La guerre d'Indochine 1947-1954*, p.179
29. Karl-Heinz Krause, *Barfuss im Reisfeld – Karl-Heinz Krause, Indochina Kreig 1949-1953*, Epee, 2012, p.127
30. Paul Martelli, *On the Devil's Tail*, Helion, 2015?
31. George Robert Elford, *Devil's Guard*, Dell, 1971, p.255
32. Adrian Liddell Hart, *Life* magazine, 15 December 1952
33. David Chanoff and Doan Van Toai, *Vietnam, a Portrait of its People at War*, p.7
34. Karl-Heinz Krause, *Barfuss im Reisfeld – Karl-Heinz Krause, Indochina Kreig 1949–1953*, Epee, 2012
35. Paul Martelli, *On the Devil's Tail*, Helion, 2015, p.257
36. *Ibid* p.292
37. *Ibid* p.293
38. *Ibid* p.297
39. *Ibid* p.298
40. *Ibid* p.299
41. Philip Short, *Pol Pot, History of a Nightmare*, Hodder 2005; Henri Locard, Pol Pot's *Little Red Book*, Silkworm: Ben Kiernan, *The Pol Pot Regime,* Yale, 2008
42. David Chandler, *A History of Cambodia*, Westvie, 1983, p.183
43. *Ibid* p.181
44. Martin Fox Stuart and *Darwinist Natural Selection*, Jules Harmand, 1880, p.47
45. Confidential observations of an NCO heath care consultant to the Lao government and the author's personal observations
46. Captain Lucien de Reinach, *Laos*, posthumous, Chemin Duponte, c 1911
47. *Ibid* p.385, chapter XII
48. Charles A. Fisher, *A Social Economic and Political Geography of South-East Asia*, Methuen, 1967, p.544
49. Tim Harper, *Underground Asia*, Allen Lane 2020, p.484
50. *Ibid* p.163
51. Prince Phetsarath, interview with France-Indochine-Goscha, Imagining Indochina
52. Shawn McHale, *Ethnicity, Violence, and Khmer-Vietnamese Relations: The Significance of the Lower Mekong Delta, 1757–1954, The Journal of Asian Studies*, vol 72, 2 May 2013, p. 367–390
53. Fritz Langer and J.J. Zasloff, *Revolution in Laos, North Vietnam and the Pathet Lao*, Rand Corporation, 1964/71, p.28
54. General Raoul Salan, *Memoires, Fin de L'Empire*, Presse de la cite, 1971, p.328
55. Authur J. Dommen, Conflict in Lao, Praeger, 1974, p.24

56. Fritz Langer and J.J. Zasloff, *Revolution in Laos, North Vietnam and the Pathet Lao*, Rand Corporation, 1964/71, p.35–40
57. Authur J. Dommen, Conflict in Lao, Praeger, 1964/1971, p.20
58. Fritz Langer and J.J. Zasloff, *Revolution in Laos, North Vietnam and the Pathet Lao*, Rand Corporation, 1964/71, p.72
59. Authur J. Dommen, *Conflict in Lao*, Praeger, 1974, p.23
60. *Ibid* 1964/1971, p.69
61. Wilfred Burchett, *Mekong Upstream*, Hanoi: Red River Publishing House, 1957, p.267
62. Authur J. Dommen, *Conflict in Lao*, Praeger, 1964/1971, p.78
63. *Ibid* p.80–81
64. Lao Presse bulletin, Vientiane, 26 Nov 1955
65. Joshua Kurlantzik, *A Great Place to Have a War: America in Laos*, Simon and Schuster, 2018, p.67–68
66. Vincent Borel, *Geohistory, L'Indochine*, Avril-Mai 2014, p.52
67. *Ibid* p.52
68. Siddarth Chandra, *Economic Histories of the Opium Trade*, Siddharth Chandra, University of Pittsburgh
69. General Raoul Salan, *Memoires, Fin de L'Empire*, Presse de la cite, 1971, p.385
70. *Ibid* p.385
71. Graham Greene, *Ways of Escape*, Penguin, 1982 p.131

Chapter VIII

1. Donald M. Blackmer and Sidney Tarrow, *Communism in Italy and France*, Princeton University Press, 1975, p.435
2. Philip Williams, *Politics in Post-War France*, Longmans, 1954, p.296
3. McMillan, Guardian Article
4. Rebert Schuermans, Legionnaire
5. Adrian Liddell-Hart, Article, *Life* magazine, 15 December 1952
6. Dorothy Pickles, *The Government and Politics of France*, Methuen, p.223
7. Hackett, *Economic Planning in France*, 1952, p.22
8. *Ibid*
9. Alexander Werth, *de Gaulle*, p.205
10. MISSING?
11. Norman Lewis, *Dragon Apparent*, Johnathan Cape, 2011, first published 1951, p.168
12. Eric Gibbs, *Battle of Indochina, Arms and the Bishop, Time* magazine, 8 January 1951, p.2
13. Ronald Spector, p.103
14. Francois Joyaux, *Chine et le the Reglement du premier conflit d'Indochine*, Geneve, Sorbonne, p.252
15. Qiang zai, *China and Vietnam Wars 1950–75*, University of north Carolina 2000

Chapter IX

1. Translation of the Kommunist article published in EastEurope, June, 1958, p.43–55
2. Michel Kort, *The Vietnam War Reexamined*, Cambridge, 2018, p.68
3. Milovan Diljas, 'Conversations with Stalin', 1961, Wilson Archive; and Wartime, Harcourt-Jovanovich, 1977, p.386–7
4. Khrushchev Memoires, p.481
5. *Ibid* p.481
6. Odd Arne Westad, AVPRFf 059a op.5a.11d 3.0, p.76, *The Cold War a World History*, Penguin, 2018, p.167
7. Xiaobing Li, *Building Ho's Army*, University of Kentuky (UOK), 2010, p.5, *Military History Research Division*, PLA Academy of Military Science (AMS), Military Science Press, 1990; and Mao's Military Manuscripts Since 1949, 1:181–82

8. Xiaobing Li, *Building Ho's Army*, University of Kentuky (UOK), 2010, p. 41–45
9. John Foster Dulles, *War and Peace*, 1951
10. Henry Kissinger, *On China*, p.124
11. *Ibid* p.128
12. Odd Arne Westad, *The Cold War*, Penguin, 2018, p.167
13. Henry Kissinger, *On China*, p.130
14. *Ibid*
15. *Ibid* p.135
16. Oleg, Khkevniuk, *Stalin*, Yale, 2015, p.296; Ledovskii, *Stalin Mao Tzedkun Koreiskaia*, Voina, p.106
17. Philip Short, BBC China correspondent, *Mao a Life*, Holder and Stoughton, 1999. p.432
18. Zhihua Shen and Yafeng Xia, *Mao and the Sino Soviet Partnership 1945–59*, Lexington 2015, p.84
19. R M
20. Adrian Liddell Hart, *Life* magazine, 15 December 1952
21. Norman Lewis, *Dragon Apparent*, Eland, 1982, Cape, 1951, p.180
22. David Chanoff and Doan Van Toai, *Vietnam, a Portrait of its People at War*
23. General Raoul Salan, *Memoires, Fin de L'Empire*, Presses de la cite, 1979, p.94
24. Lieutenant X, General Ely, *Lessons from the War in Indochina*, 31 May 1955, Rand Corporation, p.58
25. Martin Windrow, *French Legionnaire versus Vietminh insurgent*, Osprey, 2018, p.31
26. Lucien Bodard, *The Quicksand War: Prelude to Vietnam*, Atlanta, 1967
27. *Ibid* p.164
28. *Ibid* p.153
29. *Ibid The Quicksand War: Prelude to Vietnam*, Atlanta ,1967, p.167
30. *Ibid* p.168
31. Xiaobin Li, *Building Ho's Army*, University of Kentucky, 2019, p. 69
32. John Gittings, *The Role of the Chinese Army*, OUP 1967, p.100-101
33. Authur J. Dommen, *Conflict in Laos*, Praeger, 1964, 1971, p.48
34. Ezra Vogel, *Deng Xiaoping*, Harvard, 2011, p.271; M.E. Sharpe, *Warfighting the PLA Experience Since 1949*, Armonk, 2003, p.218
35. Yang Kuisong, *Mao Zedong and the Indochina Wars*, p.58
36. Authur J. Dommen, *Conflict in Laos*, Praeger, 1964, 1971, p.45
37. Trung Nguyễn, PHD paper, University Vancouver
38. Xiaobin Li, *Building Ho's Army*, UOK, 2019, p.126; Author's Interview with Truong 2006; Truong, *No Final Victory, No Family Life*, in *Voices from the Vietnam War*, p.55–64
39. *Ibid* p.68
40. Christopher E. Goscha, *Historical Dictionary of the Indochina War 1945–54*, p.101–2
41. Melvin Gurtov, *Indochina in North Vietnamese Strategy 1971*, Rand Corporation, p.1; Ellen Hammer, *The Struggle for Indochina*, Stamford, 1954, p.262
42. Karl Heinz Krause, *Barfuss im Reisfeld*, Epee, 2012, p.93
43. *Ibid* p.93
44. *Ibid* p.104
45. *Ibid* p.135
46. *Ibid* p.135
47. Lucien Bodard, *The Quicksand War: Prelude to Vietnam*, Atlanta 1967, p.240
48. Andre Thevenet, TV documentary Fabienne Servan-Schrieber, *Cao Bang, Les Soldats Sacrificies d'Indochina*, 2014
49. Sergeant Bouchard, Lucien Bodard, *The Quicksand War: Prelude to Vietnam*, Atlanta, 1967 p.55
50. Colonel Bigeard TV interview
51. Lucien Bodard, *The Quicksand War: Prelude to Vietnam*, Atlanta, 1967

53. Shawn McHale, *Caught Between Propaganda and History*, Wilson Centre Public Policy and History, October 2014
54. Lucien Bodard, *The Quicksand War: Prelude to Vietnam*, Atlanta, 1967, p.273
55. Tran Trong Trung, *General Giáp*, Gioi 2014, p.362
56. C. Currey, *Victory At Any Cost*, Vo Nguyễn Giáp, Mass Market, p.162
57. *Ibid*
58. Dominique de la motte, *a l'autre cote de l'eau*, Texto, 2009
59. *Ibid* p.133–4
60. *Ibid* p.101
61. *Ibid* p.137
62. *Ibid* p.138
63. *Ibid* p.141

Chapter X

1. Chen Geng Zhuan, Official Biography, p.385–6
2. Ivan Cadeau, *Cao Bang*, Perrin 2022, p.149
3. Lucien Bodard, *The Quicksand War: Prelude to Vietnam*, Atlanta 1967, p.278
4. Xiaobing Li, *Building Ho's Army*, University of Kentucky 2019, p.76
5. Xiaobing Li, *Building Ho's Army*, University of Kentucky 2019, p.81; *Mao's Military Manuscript Since 1949*, p.1:233–34
6. Lucien Bodard, p.208
7. Rene Mary, TV documentary Fabienne Servan-Schrieber, *Cao Bang, Les Soldats Sacrificies d'Indochina*, 2014
8. *Ibid* 2014
9. Pierre Brocheux, *Daniel Hémery, Indochina; An Ambiguous Colonization*, University of California Press, 2011, p.176
10. Charles-Henri, *Arnoux de Pirey*, TV documentary Fabienne Servan-Schrieber. *Cao Bang, Les Soldats Sacrificies d'Indochina*
11. Mai Elliot, p.166–7
12. Tran Trong Chun, *General Giáp*, Gioi, 2014, p.374
13. Frederik Longeval, *Embers of War*, Yale, 2012, p.248
14. Charles-Henri, Arnoux de Pirey, TV documentary Fabienne Servan-Schrieber, *Cao Bang, Les Soldats Sacrificies d'Indochina*, 2014
15. Charles-Henri, Arnoux de Pirey, TV documentary Fabienne Servan-Schrieber, *Cao Bang, Les Soldats Sacrificies d'Indochina*, 2014
16. Frederik Longeval, *Embers of War*, Yale, 2012
17. *Ibid* p.248–9
18. Andre Tevenet, documentary by Fabienne Servan-Schrieber, *Lucie Pastor*, France TV and Cinitv Todjo
19. Lucien Bodard, *The Quicksand War: Prelude to Vietnam*, Atlanta, 1967, p.307
20. *Ibid* p.307
21. Andre Thevenet, *Regis Lebouef*, documentary by Fabienne Servan-Schrieber, Lucie Pastor, France TV and Cinitv Todjo, 2014
22. A US army issue semi-automatic without bolt action, gas driven reloading, which meant high rate of fire
23. Mai, Elliott, *The Sacred Willow: Four Generations in the Life of a Vietnamese Family*, Oxford University Press, 1999, p.167
24. Xiaobing Li, *Building Ho's Army*, University of Kentucky 2019, p.83
25. Edward Rice-Maximin, *Accommodation and Resistance, The French Left. Indochina and the Cold War, 1945–54*, p.135
26. Lucien Bodard, *The Quicksand War: Prelude to Vietnam*, Atlanta, 1967, p.321
27. *Ibid* p.322

28. *Ibid* p.132
29. *Ibid* p.325
30. A. Werth, *France*, p.553
31. Piketty, Guillaume, *Pierre de Chevigne*, Tallandier, 2022, p.311
32. *Ibid* p.248
33. Ngo Van Chieu, *Journal d'un combatant Viet-Minh*, p.132
34. Julia Lovell, *Maoism*, Vintage, 2019, p.229
35. Xiaobing Li, *Building Ho's Army*, University of Kentucky 2019, p.90
36. Michel Bodin, *Les Africains dans la guerre d'Indochine 1947–1954*, p.91–135
37. Paul Martelli, *On the Devil's Tail*, Helion, 2018, p.250–251
38. Michel Bodin, *Les Marocains dans la guerre d'Indochine, Guerres mondiales et conflits contemporains*, No. 259, L'armée d'Afrique (Juillet-Septembre 2015), Univdersitaires de France, p.57–76
39. *Ibid* p.63
40. *Ibid* p.63
41. Jules Roy, *Dien Bien Phu*, Jon Lewis, ed., *The Vietnam War*, Robinson, p.13
42. Michel Bodin, *Les Africains dans la guerre d'Indochine 1947–1954*, p.171
43. *Ibid* p.186
44. Paul Martelli, *On the Devil's Tail*, Helion, 2018, p.258
45. Norman Lewis, *Napoli*, p.44
46. Lucien Bodard, *The Quicksand War: Prelude to Vietnam*, Atlanta, 1967, p.60
47. Michel Bodin, *Les Africains dans la guerre d'Indochine 1947–1954*, p.13
48. *Ibid* p.324
49. *Ibid* p.165
50. Paul Martelli, *On the Devil's Tail*, Helion, 2018, p.287

Chapter XI

1. Lucien Bodard, *La guerre d'Indochine*, Grasset, 1997, p.663
2. *Ibid* p.664
3. *Ibid* p.713
4. General Salan, *Memoires*, Vol II
5. Pinay was a lightweight prime minister who was backed by a breakaway faction of de Gaulle's RPF
6. de Gaulle, *Memoires*
7. Xiaobing Li, *Building Ho's Army*, University of Kentucky, 2019, p.87–90
8. *Ibid* p.96
9. Lucien Bodard, *La Guerre d'Indochine*, Grasset, 1997
10. Michel Bodin, *Les Africans dans la guerre d'Indochine 1947-1954*, l'Harmattan, 2000, p.155
11. Paul Martelli, *On the Devil's Tail*, Helion 2018, p.308
12. Foreign Relations of the United States Asia and Pacific, Vol pt1 vol VI; de Lattre making a presentation to US officials and generals. General Ridgeway latterly commander-in-chief Korea was present and Ambassador Heath
13. General Ely, Major Y in a secret report from General Ely, *The Lessons of War in Indochina*, 31 May 1955, Rand Corporation, 1967
14. C. Currey, *Victory at any Cost*, Vo Nguyễn Giáp, Mass Market, p.160
15. General Raoul Salan, *Memoires, Fin de l'Empire* Vol II, Presses de cite, 1971, p.197
16. *Ibid* p.202
17. Lucien Bodard, *La guerre d'Indochine*, Gasset, 1997, p.816
18. Lucien Bodard, *La guerre d'Indochine*, Gasset, 1997, p.831
19. Michael Burleigh, *Small Wars in Faraway Places*, Global Insurrection, Penguin, 2014
20. Tim Hieu Lich Su, quoted in a Vietnamese journal, *Bài viết mới*, 3 May 2021

21. Bernhard Fall, *Street Without Joy*, Pen and Sword 2009, p.39, Goscha, dictionary, p.305
22. Lucien Bodard, *La guerre d'Indochine*, Gasset, 1997, p.823
23. General Yves Gras, *History of the Indochina War*, Denoël, 1992, Max Sp.82
24. Lucien Bodard, *La guerre d'Indochine*, Gasset, 1997, p.840
25. General Yves Gras, *History of the Indochina War*, Denoël, 1992, Max Sp.84
26. General Raoul Salan, *Memoires, Fin de l'Empire* Vol II, Presses de cite, 1971, p.220
27. *Ibid* p.221
28. *Ibid*
29. Lucien Bodard, *La guerre d'Indochine*, Gasset, 1997, p.1130
30. Bernhard Fall, *Street Without Joy*, Stackpole, 2018, (first in 1961), p.42–43
31. Raoul Salan, *Memoires* Vol II, Presse de la cite de Paris, 1971, p.221
32. *Ibid* p.222
33. Eric Gibbs, *Battle of Indochina, Arms and the Bishop, Time* magazine, 8 January 1951, p.1–3
34. General Raoul Salan, *Memoires, Fin de l'Empire* Vol II, Presses de cite, 1971, p.233
35. Xiaobing Li, *Building Ho's Army*, University of Kentucky, 2019, p.106, *Qian The Secret War in Vietnam*, p.177
36. *Ibid* p.107
37. General Raoul Salan, *Memoires, Fin de L'Empire*, Presses de la cite, 1971, p.235
38. *Ibid* p.261
39. *Ibid* p.236
40. David Chanoff & Doan van Toai, *A Portrait of its People at War*, p.38
41. *Ibid* p.48
42. *Ibid* p.39
43. Dikötter, Frank, *The Tragedy of Liberation 1945–57*, Bloomsbury, 2017
44. Max Schiavon, *Salan, Defenseur de L'empire*, ETAIT, 2014, p.8
45. Frederic Longeval, *JFK* Vol I, Viking, 2020, p.494

Chapter XII

1. Christopher Goscha, *The Road to Dien Bien Phu*, Princeton 2022, p.77
2. David Chanoff & Doan Van Toai, *Vietnam, a Portrait of its People at War*, p.7
3. Karl-Heinz Krause, *Barfuss im Reisfeld Karl-Heinz Krause*, Indochina, Kreig 1949–1953, Epee, 2012
4. Dr Grauwin, *A Doctor at Dien Bien Phu*, Anchor Press, 1955, p.257
5. Paul Martelli, *On the Devil's Tail*, Helion, 2018, p.264
6. *Ibid* p.292
7. *Ibid* p.293
8. *Ibid* p.297
9. *Ibid* p.298
10. *Ibid* p.299
11. Graham Greene, *Ways of Escape*, Penguin, 1982, p.123
12. General Raoul Salan, *Memoires, Fin de L'Empire*, Presse de la cite, 1971, p.262
13. Admiral of FMEO, General Ely, *Lessons of War in Indochina*, 31 May 1955, Rand Corporation, 1967, p.174
14. C. Currey, *Victory at Any Cost: The Genius of Viet Nam's Gen, Vo Nguyễn Giáp (The Warriors)*, Mass Market Paperback, 2005, p.175
15. General Raoul Salan *Memoires, Fin de L'Empire*, Presse de la cite, 1971, p.264–5
16. *Ibid* p.272
17. Xiaobing Li, *Building Ho's Army*, University of Kentucky, 2019, p.253, CMAG History Compilation Team, Historical Facts of the CMAG), p.31
18. Karl Heinz Krause, *Barfuss im Reisfeld*, Epee, 2012, p.221
19. *Ibid* p.211
20. Christopher Goscha, UQÀM resource material

21. General Raoul Salan, *Memoires, Fin de L'Empire*, Presse de la cite, 1971, p.289
22. *Ibid* p.274
23. Bernhard Fall, *Street Without Joy*, p.56
24. General Raoul Salan, *Memoires, Fin de L'Empire*, Presse de la cite, 1971, p.279
25. Klaus Heinz Klause, *Barfuss im Reisfeld*, Epee, 2012, p.226
26. *Ibid* p.226
27. Pham Thanh Tâm, *War Diary of a Young Viet-Minh in Diên Biên Phu*, 2011
28. General Raoul Salan, *Memoires, Fin de L'Empire*, Presse de la cite, 1979, p.279
29. *Ibid* p.279–80
30. *Ibid* p.287
31. Karl Heinz Krause, *Barfuss im Reisfeld*, Epee, 2012, p.233
32. *Ibid* p.238
33. *Ibid* p.241
34. Henri Navarre, *le Temp de Verites*, Paris Plan 1979, p.247
35. General Raoul Salan, *Memoires, Fin de L'Empire*, Presse de la cite, 1979, p.288
36. *Ibid* p.304
37. *Ibid* p.304
38. Xiaobing Li, *Building Ho's Army*, University of Kentucky, 2019, p.126–7
39. Piketty, Guillaume, *Pierre de Chevigne*, Tallandier, 2022, p.319
40. *Ibid* p.322
41. Xiaobing Li, *Building Ho's Army*, University of Kentucky, 2019, p.121
42. Boot, Max, *The Consummate Warrior Marcel Bigeard, 1916–2010, Evening Standard*, 25 October 2016
43. George Robert Elford, *Devil's Guard*, Dell, 1971, p.206
44. Xiaobing Li, *Building Ho's Army*, University of Kentucky, 2019, p.122
45. Dr Grauwin, *Doctor at Dien Bien Phu*, 1955, p.39
46. Paul Martelli, *On the Devil's Tail*, Helion, 2018, p.314
47. Bernhard Fall, *Street Without Joy*, p.78
48. Jean Guetre, *Un Temoin de son temps, armee de de Lattre Indochine*, Oudin 2011
49. Pierre Brocheux, Daniel Hémery, *Indochina; An Ambiguous Colonization*, University of California Press, 2011, p.367
50. Frederic Longeval, *Embers of War: The Fall of an Empire and the Making of America's Vietnam*, Random House, New York, 2012, p.373
51. A.Werth, *France 1940–55*, p.458
52. The Vichy background to the E, was a concept analysed by political scientist professor Dr Gerd Langguth (d), director of the Konrad Adenauer Stiftung, secretary of state, Merkel biographer and adviser to various CDU leaders
53. General Raoul Salan, *Memoires, Fin de L'Empire*, Presse de la cite, 1971, p.337
54. *Ibid* p.367
55. *Ibid* p.368
56. *The Manifesto and Platform of the Viet-Nam Lao Dong Party, Supplement to People's China*, Vol. III, No. 9, May 1st 1951
57. Diktter, *Liberation*, Chapter 10, p.206
58. Hoàng Văn Chí, *From Colonialism to Communism: A Case History of North Vietnam*, London, Pall Mall, 1964
59. *Ibid* p.162
60. Julia Lovell, *Maoism*, Vintage, 2019, p.231
61. *Ibid* p.233
62. Xiaobing Li, *Building Ho's Army*, University of Kentucky, 2019, p.131; Giáp, *People's War, People's Army*, p.27
63. *Ibid* p.134

64. François Guillemot, *Journal of Vietnamese Studies* Vol. 4, No. 3 (Fall 2009), p.17–60 (44 pages), University of California Press
65. Nguyễn Ti Hue, *Forgotten Women Soldiers of the Vietnam War*, 2003
66. Mai Elliott, *The Sacred Willow: Four Generations in the Life of a Vietnamese Family*, Oxford University Press, 1999, p.161
67. Nguyễn Ngoc-Luu. *Peasants, Party and Revolution the Politics of Agrarian Transformation in Northern Vietnam 1930-1975*, p.284
68. Mai Elliot, *The Sacred Willow: Four Generations in the Life of a Vietnamese Family*, Oxford University Press, 1999, p.207
69. *Ibid* p.208
70. *Ibid* p.208–9
71. Michael Hunt, ed., *A Vietnam War Reader*, Penguin, 2010 p.15
72. *Ibid* p.306
73. Ho Chi Minh, 'Report to the National Assembly of the Democratic Republic of Vietnam, December 1953' in Bernard Fall, Ed., *Ho Chi Minh On Revolution: Selected Writings, 1920–1966*, New York, Frederick. A.Praeger Publishers, 1967
74. Philip Short, *Mao*, Holt, 1999
75. David Chanoff & Doan van Toai, *A Portrait of its People at War*
76. PB 156
77. *The History of the Vietnamese Economy, Vol. 2*, Edited by Dang Phong of the Institute of Economy, Vietnamese Institute of Social Sciences, 2005
79. MISSING?
79. William Duiker, *Ho Chi Minh: a Life 2000*, p. 478

Chapter XIII

1. Marguerite Duras, *The Lovers*, Flamingo-Random House, 1984, p.51
2. Norman Lewis, *Dragon Apparent*, Eland, 1982, p.23
3. Richard Nixon, *Memoirs*, Grosset & Dunlap, 1978, p.123
4. Bernhard Fall, *Street Without Joy*, p.253.
5. General Raoul Salan, *Memoires, Fin de L'Empire*, Presse de la cite, 1979, p.355
6. Xiaobing Li, *Building Ho's Army*, University of Kentucky ,2019, p.123; Quian, The *Secret War of Vietnam*, p.193–4
7. General Raoul Salan, *Memoires, Fin de L'Empire*, Presse de la cite, 1971, p.357
8. Genevieve de Galard-Terraube, *The Angel of Dien Bien Phu, loc 813*
9. Richard R. Schrader, *War and Logistics, Parachutes and Porters 1945–54*, University of Kentucky, 2015
10. John Walker, *History Today, The Battle of Nά Sán*, 19 June 2021
11. Ronald Spector, *Advice and Support, The Early Years, 1941–60*, US Army, 1983, p.161
12. Richard Leighton, *Historical Office of the Secretary of State*, Vol III, p.512–526
13. *Ibid* p.523
14. Guillaume Piketty, *Francais Libre, Pierre de Chevigne*, Tallendier, 2022, p.322
15. Major Callwell, *Small Wars*, Greenhill 1990, p.95

Chapter XIV

1. Joshua Kurlantzik, *A Great Place to Have a War: America in Laos*, Simon and Schuster, 2018, p.60
2. Bernhard Fall, p.122
3. Martin Stuart-Fox, *A History of Lao*, Cambridge, 1997, p.82
4. General Raoul Salan, *Memoires, Fin de L'Empire*, Presse de la cite, 1971, p.405
5. Genevieve de Galard-Terraube, *The Angel of Dien Bien Phu*, Press, ISBN 978-1-61251-386-7

6. Frederick Longeval, *Embers of War: The Fall of an Empire and the Making of America's Vietnam*, Random House, New York, 2012 p.327
7. Martin Stuart-Fox, *A History of Lao*, Cambridge, 1997, p.84
8. Hansard
9. Nikita Khrushchev, *Khrushchev Remembers*, Andre Duetch, 1971, p.323
10. Lord Moran, *Churchill, the struggle for survival 1945-60,* Carrol and Graf 2006, p.261
11. *Ibid* p.211
12. *Ibid* p.227
13. A. Werth, *France* 1944–55, p.609
14. A.Werth, *France*, Le monde, p.611, 6 June 1953
15. Frederick Longeval, *Embers of War: The Fall of an Empire and the Making of America's Vietnam*, Random House, New York, 2012, p.354
16. General Raoul Salan, *Memoires, Fin de L'Empire*, Presse de la cite, 1979, p.408
17. Richard R. Schrader, *War and Logistics, Parachutes and Porters 1945–54*, University of Kentucky, 2015
18. Bruce H. Hupe, *The Generalship of General Henri E.Navarre During the Battle of Dien Bien Phu*, Paperback, 3 June 1994, loc 392
19. Frederick Longeval, *Embers of War: The Fall of an Empire and the Making of America's Vietnam*, Random House, New York, 2012, p.362
20. Xiaobing Li, *Building Ho's Army*, University of Kentucky, 2019, p.137
21. Nixon, *Memoirs*, Grosset and Dunlap, 1978, p.123–5
22. Frederick Longeval, *Embers of War: The Fall of an Empire and the Making of America's Vietnam*, Random House, New York, 2012, p.370
23. Goscha Dictionary, p.132
24. Bernhard Fall
25. Vo Nguyễn Giáp, *Autobiography*, 1994, p.88–9
26. Frederick Longeval, *Embers of War: The Fall of an Empire and the Making of America's Vietnam*, Random House, New York, 2012, p.355
27. Guillaume Piketty, *Francais Libre, Pierre de Chevigne*, Tallendier, 2022, p.323–4
28. Graham Greene, *Ways of Escape*, Penguin 1982
29. Boyan and Oliver, p.269

Chapter XV

1. Dang Quan Thuy, *Department of Operations, Officer*, p98–99
2. Pentagon Papers Gravel Edition, Volume 1, Chapter 4, "U.S. and France in Indochina, 1950–56" (Boston, Beacon Press, 1971) Section 1, p.179–214
3. Frederick Logeval, *Embers of War*, Yale, 2012, p.286
4. Richard Leighton, *Strategy, Money, and the New Look, 1953–56*, Historical Office of the Secretary of Defence, Vol III, 2001, p.23–26
5. John F. Dulles, *War or Peace*, Harrap, 1950 p.13
6. *Ibid* p.6
7. Philip Short, *Mitterrand, a Study in Ambiguity*, Bodley Head, 2013, p.166
8. Martin Gilbert, *Churchill*, Chapter 39, p,1,056
9. *Ibid* p.1,057
10. *Ibid* p.1,062
11. *Ibid*
12. Dr Moran, *Churchill based on Dr Moran's diaries*, Carrol and Graf 2000
13. A. Werth, *France* p. 642
14. Dr Moran, *Churchill*, Carrol and Graf, 2006, p.229

Chapter XVI

1. Vo Nguyễn Giáp, *Autobiography*, 1994
2. *Ibid* p.13
3. Vo Nguyễn Giáp, *Dien Bien Phu*, 1994, p.15
4. Xiaobing Li, *Building Ho's Army*, University of Kentucky, 2019, p.145
5. Pham, *Vietnam*, The Art of War Website
6. Dan Chandoff & Tran, *Vietnam, A Portrait of its People at War*, p.10
7. Pham, *Vietnam*, The Art of War Website
8. Pham, Carnet loc 599
9. *Ibid* loc 606–607
10. Pham Thanh Tam, *Drawing Under Fire*, Asia link 2005, p.47
11. Giáp, *Mémoirs of War, Dien Bien Phu – History, Impressions, Memoirs*, 1994, p.53
12. *Ibid* p.54
13. Pham, Carnet loc 646
14. *Ibid* loc 657
15. Pham Than Tam, *Carnet de guerre d'un jeune Viet-minh a Dien Bien Phu Armand*, Colin, 2011, loc
16. Graham Greene papers, box 1, Georgetown University Library, 16 November 1951, diary entry 13 November 1951
17. Pham Than Tam, *Carnet de guerre d'un jeune Viet-minh a Dien Bien Phu Armand*, Colin, 2011, loc 685
18. Joshua Kurlantzik, *A Great Place to Have a War: America in Laos*, Simon and Schuster, 2018, p.68
19. Howard Simpson, *Dien Bien Phu*, p.33, Martin Woodrow, *The Last Valley*, Hachette UK, 2004, p.261
20. Pham Than Tam, *Carnet de guerre d'un jeune Viet-minh a Dien Bien Phu Armand*, Colin, 2011, loc 702
21. *Ibid* loc 717
22. *Ibid* loc 725
23. George Robert Elford, *The Devil's Guard*, Dell, 1971, p.289
24. Tran Do, *Récits sur Dien Bien Phu, 1962*, p.30
25. Giáp, *Autobiography*, p.69
26. *Ibid* p.100
27. Martin Windrow, *The Last Valley*, Hachette, 2004, p.277
28. Pham Quang Vinh, *Dien Bien Phu vu d'en face Paroles de Bo Doi*, DBV World Editions, February 2014, p.72
29. Vu the Chau, *Dien Bien Phu vu d'en face Paroles de Bo Doi*, DBV World Editions, February 2014, p.76
30. *Dien Bien Phu vu d'en face Paroles de Bo Doi*, DBV World Editions, February 2014, p.72
31. *Ibid* p.76
32. Nguyễn Viet, *Major General Intelligence, Dien Bien Phu vu d'en face Paroles de Bo Doi*, DBV World Editions, February 2014, p78–79
33. Frederik Longeval, *Embers of War: The Fall of an Empire and the Making of America's Vietnam*, Random House, New York, 2012, p.575
34. Richard Nixon, *Memoirs*, Grosset and Dunlap, 1978, p.150
35. US Congress, Committee of Foreign Affairs, General James Gavin, Supplement on Foreign Assistance 1966, p.232–233
36. Frederick Longeval, *Embers of War: The Fall of an Empire and the Making of America's Vietnam*, Random House, New York, 2012 p.434
37. Guillaume Piketty, *Francais Libre, Pierre de Chevigne*, Tallendier, 2022, p.322 p.330
38. Currey, *Victory at Any Cost: The Genius of Viet Nam's Gen*, Vo Nguyễn Giáp, Mass Market Paperback, 2005, p.189

39. PRC Foreign Ministry Position Paper, 6 March 1954, Wilson Centre Archive
40. *Dien Bien Phu vu d'en face Paroles de Bo Doi*, DBV World Editions, February 2014, p.82
41. Le Hai, *Dien Bien Phu vu d'en face Paroles de Bo Doi*, DBV World Editions, February 2014, p.83–84
42. Giáp, *Autobiography*, p.89
43. Ung Rang Battalion Commander, Division 351, *Dien Bien Phu vu d'en face Paroles de Bo Doi*, DBV World Editions, February 2014, p.91
44. Giáp, *The Hardest Decision*, Gioi Publications, 2014 p.90
45. Ung Rang, *Dien Bien Phu vu d'en face Paroles de Bo Doi*, DBV World Editions, February 2014, p.91
46. *Dien Bien Phu vu d'en face Paroles de Bo Doi*, DBV World Editions, February 2014, p.97–98
47. Giáp, *The Hardest Decision*, Gioi Publications, 2014
48. Vo Nguyễn Giáp, *Dien Bien Phu*, Gioi 2008, p.147
49. *Dien Bien Phu vu d'en face Paroles de Bo Doi*, DBV World Editions, February 2014, p.105
50. *Ibid* p.109
51. Hoang Minh Phuong, Chinese interpreter to Giáp, *Dien Bien Phu vu d'en face Paroles de Bo Doi*, DBV World Editions, February 2014, p.112
52. Le Liem, *Dien Bien Phu vu d'en face Paroles de Bo Doi*, DBV World Editions, February 2014, p.112
53. Giáp, *The Hardest Decision*, Gioi Publications, 2014
54. Dang Kim Giang, *Dien Bien Phu vu d'en face Paroles de Bo Doi*, DBV World Editions, February 2014, p.113
55. Giáp, *The Hardest Decision*, Gioi Publications,1994
56. Major-General of AA Artillery, Division 351, *Dien Bien Phu vu d'en face Paroles de Bo Doi*, DBV World Editions, February 2014, p.116
57. Giáp, *The Hardest Decision*, Gioi Publications, 1994, p.31
58. Nguyễn Quang Thuan, *Dien Bien Phu vu d'en face Paroles de Bo Doi*, DBV World Editions, February 2014, p.116
59. The Third Indochinese War involved Vietnam defending an invasion by China, 1970 –71
60. Vo Nguyễn Giáp, *Dien Bien Phu*, Gioi 2008
61. Captain Luciani, Dien Bien Phu veteran YouTube interview
62. Vo Nguyễn Giáp, *The Hardest Decision*, Gioi 2014, p.37
63. Vo Nguyễn Giáp, *The Hardest Decision*, Gioi Publications, 1994, p.34
64. *Ibid*
65. Dang Quan Thuy, Department of Operation, Officer, *Dien Bien Phu vu d'en face Paroles de Bo Doi*, DBV World Editions, February 2014, p.98–99
66. Schrader, *War of Logistics: Parachutes and Porters 1945–54*, University of Kentucky, 2015
67. Michel Bodin, *Les Africains dans La Guerre d'Indochine 1947–1954*, p.194
68. Adrian Liddell-Hart, *Life* magazine Article, 15 December 1952
69. Foreign Legion Information Website, http://foreignlegion.info
70. Mai Elliott, *The Sacred Willow: Four Generations in the Life of a Vietnamese Family*, Oxford University Press, 1999, p.213
71. Pham Than Tam, *Carnet de guerre d'un jeune Viet-minh a Dien Bien Phu Armand*, Colin 2011
72. *Ibid* loc 785
73. *Ibid* loc 838
74. *Ibid* loc 845
75. *Ibid*
76. Tran Do, *Récits sur Dien Bien Phu*, Editions en langues étrangères Hanoi broché, 1962 p.27
77. *Ibid*

78. Ado Sam, 351 Division, *Dien Bien Phu vu d'en face Paroles de Bo doi*, DBV World Editions, February 2014, p.94
79. Christopher Goscha, *The Road to Dien Bien Phu*, 2022, p.425
80. Pham Than Tam, *Carnet de guerre d'un jeune Viet-minh a Dien Bien Phu Armand*, Colin, 2011, loc 821
81. *Ibid* loc 828
82. Pham Thanh Tam, *Drawing Under Fire*, Asia link 2005, p.66
83. Hupe, *The Generalship of Henri Navarre*, loc 605
84. Christopher Goscha, *The Road to Dien Bien Phu*, Princeton 2022, p.47
85. *Auteur de L'armée rouge à nos portes, 1968; ou encore de Le drame de l'armée d'armistice*, 1946
86. Do Sam, *Dien Bien Phu vu d'en face Paroles de Bo doi*, DBV World Editions, February 2014, p.94
87. Ung Rang, Battalion Commander Division 351, *Dien Bien Phu vu d'en face Paroles de Bo doi*, DBV World Editions, February 2014
88. Henri Navarre, loc 621
89. Dr Grauwin, *A Doctor at Dien Bien Phu*, 1955, p.85
90. Pham Than Tam, *Carnet de guerre d'un jeune Viet-minh a Dien Bien Phu Armand*, Colin, 2011, loc 1,151
91. Récits sur Dien Bien Phu, 1962 Editions en langues étrangères Hanoï broché, Nguyễn Phom Nam
92. *Ibid* p.140
93. *Ibid*
94. Giáp, *Dien Bien Phu – History, Impressions, Memoirs of War*, 2004, p.47
95. Andre Galabru, 2004
96. Jules Roy, *The Battle of Dien Bien Phu*
97. General Ely, *The Lessons of War in Indochina*, 31 May 1951, Rand Corporation, p.157
98. John Howard, *Brigadier USAA*, History Net, January 2020
99. Philippe Pottier, GMCA/GMI: *A French Experience in Counter Insurgency During the French Indochina War, Small Wars & Insurgencies in South-East Asia*, London 2009, 257
100. Pham Than Tam, *Carnet de guerre d'un jeune Viet-minh a Dien Bien Phu Armand*, Colin, 2011, loc 983
101. *Ibid* loc 1,005
102. *Ibid* loc 999
103. A sap is a trench dug forward of the main line to act as a jumping off point or a trench dug towards the enemy. a tunnel or trench to conceal an assailant's approach to a fortified place. "In the British army, a standard cry was 'follow the sapper', the term for those who, under engineer officers, dug the saps or shelter trenches used in the attack on fortresses."
104. Howard Simpson, Captain Nicholas, 3rd Legion Battalion, *Dien Bien Phu: the Battle America Forgot*, Potomac, 2011, loc 1,146
105. Pham Than Tam, *Carnet de guerre d'un jeune Viet-minh a Dien Bien Phu Armand*, Colin, 2011, loc 1,959
106. Pham Van Pham, *Dien Bien Phu vu d'en face Paroles de Bo doi*, DBV World Editions, February 2014, p.147
107. Pham Than Tam, *Carnet de guerre d'un jeune Viet-minh a Dien Bien Phu Armand*, Colin, 2011, loc 1,013
108. Tong Tu, *Dien Bien Phu vu d'en face Paroles de Bo doi*, DBV World Editions, February 2014
109. Pham Than Tam, *Carnet de guerre d'un jeune Viet-minh a Dien Bien Phu Armand*, Colin, 2011, loc 1,022
110. Xiaobing Li, *Building Ho's Army*, University of Kentucky, 2019, p.144; Quoted in Quian, *The Secret War in Vietnam*, p.376–77

Chapter XVII

1. Pham Than Tam, *Carnet de guerre d'un jeune Viet-minh a Dien Bien Phu Armand*, Colin, 2011, loc 1,030
2. *Ibid* loc 1,040
3. Hugo Genin, *La memoire des parachutists a Dien Bien Phu*, La Vauzelle, 2004. p.91
4. Howard Simpson, *Captain Nicholas, 3rd Legion Battalion, Dien Bien Phu: The Battle America Forgot*, Potomac, 2011, loc 1,146–1,153
5. Luu Trong Lan, *Dien Bien Phu vu d'en face Paroles de Bo doi*, DBV World Editions, Feb 2014
6. Dr Grauwin, *A Doctor at Dien Bien Phu*, Hutchinson, 1955, p.92
7. Pham, *Carnet*, loc 1,022
8. Yfan Song, *Diaries from Dien Bien Phu*, 2 May 2017
9. Pham Van Nam, *Dien Bien Phu vu d'en face Paroles de Bo doi*, DBV World Editions, February 2014, p.150
10. Pham Than Tam, *Carnet de guerre d'un jeune Viet-minh a Dien Bien Phu Armand*, Colin, 2011 February 2014
11. *Ibid*
12. Captain Nicholas, 3rd Legion Battalion, *Dien Bien Phu: The Battle America Forgot*, Potomac, 2011
13. Howard Simpson, *Dien Bien Phu; the battle that America forgot*, Potomac, 2005, loc 1,172
14. Martin Woodrow, *The Last Valley*, Hachette, Cassell, 2004 p.374
15. Howard Simpson, *Dien Bien Phu: The Battle that America Forgot*, Potomac, 2005 loc 1,169
16. Pham Thanh Tam, *Drawing Under Fire*, Asia link 2005, p.84
17. Pham Than Tam, *Carnet de guerre d'un jeune Viet-minh a Dien Bien Phu Armand*, Colin, 2011, loc 1,129
18. *Ibid*
19. *Ibid*
20. *Ibid* loc 1,301
21. Dr Grauwin, *Doctor at Dien Bien Phu*, Hutchinson 1955 and *J'étais Médecin à Dien-Bien-Phu*, France-Empire, 1974
22. Nguyễn Manh Quan, *Dien Bien Phu vu d'en face Paroles de Bo doi*, DBV World Editions, February 2014
23. Dan Hung Mun, Dien Bien Phu vu d'en face Paroles d Bo doi, DBV World Editions, February 2014
24. *Ibid* p.152
25. Nguyễn Manh Quan, 1935 Company Leader in the 308th, *Dien Bien Phu vu d'en face Paroles de Bo doi*, DBV World Editions, February 2014, p.151
26. Pham Than Tam, *Carnet de guerre d'un jeune Viet-minh a Dien Bien Phu*, loc 1,330
27. Ven Dinh Van, *Dien Bien Phu vu d'en face Paroles de Bo doi*, DBV World Editions, February 2014, p.152
28. Le Pham Pong, *Dien Bien Phu vu d'en face Paroles de Bo doi*, DBV World Editions, February 2014, p.153
29. *Ibid* loc 1,337
30. *Ibid*
31. Howard Simpson, *Dien Bien Phu*, p.155
32. Dan Quang Thuy, *Dien Bien Phu vu d'en face Paroles de Bo doi*, DBV World Editions, February 2014
33. Martin Windrow, *The Last Valley*, Hachette, Cassell, p.410
34. *Ibid* p.426
35. Pierre Langlais, D*ien Bien Phu*, 1963, p.29
36. Kevin Boylan and Luc Olivier, *Valley of the Shadow*, Osprey, 2018.p.262–270
37. *Ibid* p.268

38. Robert Weldon Whalen, *Bitter Wounds*, Cornell, 1984
39. Bernhard Fall, *Hell in a Small Place*
40. Dang Hung Manh, 308 Division, *Dien Bien Phu vu d'en face Paroles de Bo doi*, DBV World Editions, February 2014
41. Hugo Genin, *La memoire des parachutists a Dien Bien Phu*, La Vauzelle, 2004, p.72
42. Tran Quoc Chan, 308 Division, *Dien Bien Phu vu d'en face Paroles de Bo doi*, DBV World Editions, February 2014
43. Kevin Boylan & Luc Olivier, V*alley of the Shadow, The Siege of Dien Bien Phu*, Osprey, 2018, p.123
44. *Ibid* p.279
45. Hugo Genin, *La memoire des parachutists a Dien Bien Phu*, La Vauzelle, 2004, p.72
46. Hugo Genin, *La memoire des parachutists a Dien Bien Phu*, La Vauzelle, 2004, p.72
47. Giang Van Tue, *Dien Bien Phu vu d'en face Paroles de Bo doi*, DBV World Editions, February 2014, p.196
48. Kevin Boylan & Luc Olivier, *Valley of the Shadow, The Siege of Dien Bien Phu*, Osprey, 2018
49. Pham Thanh Tam, *Drawing under fire*, Asia link 2005, p.126
50. Navarre, *Dien Bien Phu*, loc 2,004
51. Martin W?
52. Pham Thanh Tam, *Drawing Under Fire*, Asia link 2005, p.133-136
53. *Ibid* p.111
54. Pham Thanh Tam, *Drawing Under Fire*, Asia link 2005, p.97
55. Duong Van Liam, *Dien Bien Phu vu d'en face Paroles de Bo doi*, DBV World Editions, February 2014
56. Genevieve de Galard-Terraube, The *Angel of Dien Bien Phu*
57. *Ibid* loc 1,169
58. *Ibid* loc 1,195
59. Frederik Longeval, *Embers of War*, Presidio Press, 2014, p.458
60. Frederick Longeval, *Embers of War: The Fall of an Empire and the Making of America's Vietnam*, Random House, New York, 2012, p.468
61. General Ely, Commander-in-Chief *The Lessons of War in Indochina*, May 31st 1951, Rand Corp 1967, p.40-42
62. Karl-Heinz Klause, *Barfuss im Reisfeld*, Indochina Krieg 1949-1953, p.108

Chapter XVIII

1. General Giáp, *Memoires, Dien Bien Phu vu d'en face Paroles de Bo doi*, DBV World Editions, February 2014, p.166
2. Arthur J. Dommen, *Conflict in Laos*, Praeger 1964, 71, p.47
3. Genevieve de Galard-Teraube, *Angel of Dien Bien Phu*, loc 1,254
4. Dang Duc Song, *Dien Bien Phu vu d'en face Paroles de Bo doi*, DBV World Editions, February 2014
5. Nguyễn Huu Chap, *Dien Bien Phu vu d'en face Paroles de Bo doi*, DBV World Editions, February 2014, p.183
6. *Dien Bien Phu vu d'en face Paroles de Bo doi*, DBV World Editions, February 2014, p.184
7. Nguyễn Sy Trinh, *Dien Bien Phu vu d'en face Paroles de Bo doi*, DBV World Editions, February 2014
8. Van Dinh Hoe, *Dien Bien Phu vu d'en face Paroles de Bo doi*, DBV World Editions, February 2014, p178
9. Phan Than Tung, *Dien Bien Phu vu d'en face Paroles de Bo doi*, DBV World Editions, February 2014, p.179
10. Nguyễn Nu Tien, *Dien Bien Phu vu d'en face Paroles de Bo doi*, DBV World Editions, February 2014, p.179
11. Hugo Genin, *La memoire des parachutists a Dien Bien Phu*, La Vauzelle, 2004. p.91

12. Dr Gindrey, *Memoires*
13. Dr Grindrey remembers his friend, *Memoires*
14. Kevin Boylan and Luc Olivier, *Valley of the Shadow, The Siege of Dien Bien Phu*, Osprey, 2018, p.171–172
15. Dr Grauwin, *A Doctor at Dien Bien Phu*, Hutchinson, p.240
16. Dr Grindrey, Memoire for his friend
17. Genevieve de Galard, *Angel of Dien Bien Phu*, loc 1,262
18. Dr Grauwin, *A Doctor at Dien Bien Phu*, Hutchinson, 1955, p.185
19. *Ibid* p.156
20. *Ibid* p.168
21. Genevieve de Galard, *Angel of Dien Bien Phu*
22. Dr Grauwin, *A Doctor at Dien Bien Phu*, Hutchinson, 1955, p.169
23. *Ibid* p.179
24. *Ibid* p.81
25. *Ibid* p.239
26. *Ibid* p.168
27. *Ibid*
28. Giáp, *Memoires*, Gioi, p.155
29. *Ibid* p.151
30. General Ely, Commander-in-Chief, *The Lessons of the War in Indochina*, 31 May 1955, Rand Corporation, 1967, p.385
31. Richard Nixon, *Memoirs*, Grosset and Dunlap, 1978, p.152
32. Dr Grauwin, *A Doctor at Dien Bien Phu*, Hutchinson, 1955, p.183
33. Khrushchev Remembers, *Memoires*
34. Martin Gilbert WC, vol VIII
35. Zou En Li, Letter to Mao, 23 April 1954, Wilson Centre Digital Archive
36. Jian Chen, *China and the First IndoChina War, The China Quarterly* No. 133, March 1993, p.85–110
37. Zou En Lai, Communication to Mao, 26 April 1954, Wilson Centre Archive
38. Hugo Genin, *La memoire des parachutists a Dien Bien Phu*, La Vauzelle, 2004, p.77
39. *Ibid* p.71
40. *Ibid* p.76
41. Richard Nixon, *Memoirs*, Grosset and Dunlap, 1978, p.151
42. Frederik Longeval, *Embers of War*, Viking, 2020, p.577
43. Boris Johnson, *The Churchill Factor, How One Man Made History*, Hodder and Stoughton, 2014, p.290
44. Khim Ne, *Dien Bien Phu vu d'en face Paroles de Bo doi*, DBV World Editions, February 2014, p.189
45. 312 division publication p. 426.
46. Genevieve de Galard, *Angel of Dien Bien Phu: The Lone French Woman at the Decisive Battle for Vietnam*, Naval Institute Press, Chapter 6
47. It is the song to commemorate their last stand in Mexico during the defeat of Napoleon III's ill-judged attempt to foist a French-backed monarchy on the country
48. Ethe song to Edmond Cheval, 2003, p.15
49. Jean-Luc Cotard, 'Being 'a little candle marvelling at life' avec Pierre Schoendoerffer, Interview Inflexions 2011/3, No. 18
50. Howard Simpson, *Dien Bien Phu; the Battle that America Forgot*, Potomac Books, 2005 loc 2,093
51. Jean-Luc Cotard, 'Being 'a little candle marvelling at life' avec Pierre Schoendoerffer, Interview Inflexions 2011/3, No. 18
52. Boylan & Olivier, *Valley of the Shadow*, Osprey, 2018
53. Yifan Song, *Diaries from Dien Bien Phu*, 2 May 2017
54. ESCAP docu-2nd BEP
55. *Ibid*

56. Frederik Longeval, *Embers of War*, p.297
57. The words of Neville Chamberlain about Czechoslovakia
58. Dr Moran
59. Zou En Lai to Mao, 28 April 28, Wilson Centre Archive
60. Erwan Bergot, *Les Jours de Dien Bien Phu*, p.170
61. ESCAP documentary, 2nd BEP
62. Dr Grauwin, *A Doctor at Dien Bien Phu*, Hutchinson, 1955
63. Richard Nixon, *Memoirs*, Grosset & Dunlap, 1978, p.153
64. US News and World Reports, 7 May 1954, p.25–26
65. *New York Times*, 19 & 6 April 1954, p.5,281 and 4,672–81 respectively
66. Zhou En lai, Telegram to Mao, 28 April 1954, Wilson Centre Archive

Chapter XVIX

1. Zou En Lai, Communication to Mao, 30 April 1954, Wilson Centre Archive
2. Dr Grauwin, *A Doctor at Dien Bien Phu*, Hutchinson, 1955, p.257
3. *Ibid*
4. *Ibid* p.274
5. *Ibid* p.276
6. *Ibid* p.257
7. Arthur J. Dommen, *Conflict in Laos*, Praeger, 1964/71, p.47
8. Erwan Bergot, *les 170 Jours de Dien Bien Phu*, Presses Pocket, 1992, p.272
9. Dr Grauwin, *A Doctor at Dien Bien Phu*, Hutchinson, 1955, p.241
10. *Ibid* p.245
11. *Ibid* p.245
12. *Ibid* p.245
13. *Ibid* p.247
14. *Ibid* p.273
15. *Ibid* p.259
16. *Ibid* p.275
17. *Ibid* p.181
18. *Ibid* p.247
19. Jean Pouget, *Nous Etions a Dien Bien Phu*, Presse de las Cite, Paris, 1964, p.326
20. *Ibid* p.264
21. *Ibid* p.263
22. *Ibid* p.270
23. Nguyễn Phu Xuyen Khung, To Quang Khoan, *Dien Bien Phu vu d'en face Paroles de Bo doi*, DBV World Editions, February 2014; Head of Special Team, the Administrative Head of the Company 671 in 316th Regiment, p218
24. Vin Din Hoe, *Dien Bien Phu vu d'en face Paroles de Bo doi*, DBV World Editions, February 2014, p.220
25. Jules Roy, *Dien Bien Phu*, Jon Lewis Ed., *The Vietnam War*, Robinson p.5
26. Nguyễn Phu, *Dien Bien Phu vu d'en face Paroles de Bo doi*, DBV World Editions, February 2014, p.221
27. Vu Chau, *Dien Bien Phu vu d'en face Paroles de Bo doi*, DBV World Editions, February 2014, p.222
28. Tran, *Dien Bien Phu vu d'en face Paroles de Bo doi*, DBV World Editions, February 2014
29. Nguyễn Ngoc Tang, *Dien Bien Phu vu d'en face Paroles de Bo doi*, DBV World Editions, February 2014, p.217
30. Dr Grauwin, *A Doctor at Dien Bien Phu*, Hutchinson, 1955, p.274
31. Jules Roy, *Dien Bien Phu*, Jon Lewis, Ed., *The Vietnam War*, Robinson, p.7
32. *The Guardian*, 7 January 2004
33. Dr Grauwin, *A Doctor at Dien Bien Phu*, Hutchinson, 1955, p.240
34. Vu Dinh Hoe, *Dien Bien Phu vu d'en face Paroles de Bo doi*, DBV World Editions, February 2014, p.226

35. Edmond Cheval, 2004, p.17
36. Nguyễn Kim Lung
37. Tran Quan Lap, *Dien Bien Phu vu d'en face Paroles de Bo doi*, DBV World Editions, February 2014, p.225
38. Pham Thanh Tam, *Drawing Under Fire*, Asia link 2005, p.142
39. Genevieve de Galard, *Angel of Dien Bien Phu*, p.70
40. Hoang Khoat, *Dien Bien Phu vu d'en face Paroles de Bo doi*, DBV World Editions, February 2014
41. Dr Grauwin, *A Doctor at Dien Bien Phu*, Hutchinson, 1955, p.274
42. Nguyễn Kim, *Dien Bien Phu, vu d'en face Paroles de Bo doi*, DBV World Editions, February 2014
43. Jules Roy, *Dien Bien Phu*, Jon Lewis, Ed., *The Vietnam War*, Robinson, p.11
44. Dr Grauwin, *A Doctor at Dien Bien Phu*, 1961, p.277
45. Genevieve de Galard
46. Hoang Khoat, *Dien Bien Phu vu d'en face Paroles de Bo doi*, DBV World Editions, February 2014
47. Jules Roy, *Dien Bien Phu*, Jon Lewis, Ed., *The Vietnam War*, Robinson, p.17
48. Le Nguyễn, *Dien Bien Phu vu d'en face Paroles de Bo doi*, DBV World Editions, February 2014, Le Nguyễn political commissar editor of the communist journal 'Bravery', 312th Division
49. Jules Roy, Dien Bien Phu, Jon Lewis, *The Vietnam War*, Robinson, p.14
50. *Ibid* p.13
51. Dr Grauwin, *A Doctor at Dien Bien Phu*
52. *The Guardian*, 1 July 2014
53. Hoang Dung Vinh, *Al Jazeera*, May 2016; and *Straits Times*, 4 May 2014
54. Jean Luc Cotard interview 2011–2013 with Pierre Schoendoerffer
55. Souvenir, Francais Haute, Seine delegation, *Memories of Indochina*, 11 January 2011
56. Pham Thanh Tam, *Drawing Under Fire*, Asia link 2005, p.147

Chapter XX

1. Frederick Longeval, *Embers of War: The Fall of an Empire and the Making of America's Vietnam*, Random House, New York, 2013
2. Martin Woodruff, *The Last Valley*, Hachette Cassell, 204, p.655
3. Jean Pouget, *Le Manifeste du Camp No 1*
4. Jean Luc Cotard interview 2011–2013 with Pierre Schoendoerffer
5. Jean Lacouture, *de Gaulle*, Collins Harvill, p.157
6. David Chanoff & Doan Van Toai, *Vietnam: a Portrait of its People at War*, 2009, p.39
7. Richard Nixon, *Memoirs*, Grosset and Dunlap 1978, p.123
8. Dr Grauwin, *Doctor at Dien Bien Phu*, Hutchinson, 1955, p.67
9. *The Guardian*, 1 July 2017

Appendix I

1. Martin Windrow, *The Last Valley*, Cassel, 2004, p.624
2. Foreign Legion source and average of various historians as well as grave counting by the author at Dien Bien Phu
3. UQÀM resource material, Christopher Goscha
4. Christopher Goscha, *The Road to Dien Bien Phu*, Princeton 2022

Appendix II

1. Colonel Callwell, *Small Wars*, Greenhill Books 1990 p.85–87

Bibliography

Admiral of FMEO, *General Ely, Lessons of War in Indochina, 31 May 1955*, Rand Corporation 1967

America Forgot, Potomac, 2011

Angkor, Borei, *The Kingdom of Funan*, circa 500 BC

Angleviel, Frederic and Condore, Poulu, *un bagne francais en Indochine*, Vendemiare 2020

Appelaum, Anne, *Iron Curtain: The Crushing of Eastern Europe 1944–56*, published in 2012 by Doubleday in the US and Allen Lane in the UK

Asia Pacific Journal, Vol 12, Issue 32, No, 2

Battle for Vietnam, Naval Institute Press 2010

Bayly, Christopher and Harper, Tim, *Forgotten Wars*, Penguin 2008

Bergot, Erwan, *Convoi 42 France loisirs*, Presse de La cite 1986

Bergot, Erwan, les 170 Jours de Dien Bien Phu, Presses Pocket 1992

Bien Phu, Paperback 3 June 1994

Blackmer, Donald M. and Tarrow, Sidney, *Communism in Italy and France*, Princeton University Press 1975

Bodard, Lucien, *La guerre d'Indochine*, Gasset 1997

Bodard, Lucien, *The Quicksand War: Prelude to Vietnam*, Atlanta 1967

Bodin, Michel, *les Africans dans la guerre d'Indochine 1947-1954*, l'Harmattan 2000

Bodin, Michel, *Les Marocains dans la guerre d'Indochine, Guerres mondiales et conflits contemporains, No. 259, L'armée d'Afrique (Juillet-Septembre 2015)*, Univdersitaires de France

Bodinier, Bernhard, *Le retour de La France en Indochine*, Vincennes 1987

Bonnaud, Jean Jacques, *Prisonniers du Mikado,* Temporis 2022

Borel, Vincent, *Geohistory, L'Indochine*, Avril-Mai 2014

Boylan, Kevin and Olivier, Luc, *Valley of the Shadow, The Siege of Dien Bien Phu*, Osprey 2018

Brocheux, Pierre and Hemery, Daniel, *Indochina: An Ambiguous Colonization*, 1858-1954, University of California Press 2009

Brocheux, Pierre, *Ho Chi Minh*, Cambridge 2007

Brogan, D.W., *The Development of Modern France 1870-1939*, Hamish Hamilton 1963

Bruge, Roger, *Les Hommes de Dien Bien Phu*, Tempus 2003

Burchett, Wilfred, *Mekong Upstream*, Hanoi: Red River Publishing House 1957

Burleigh, Michael, *Small Wars in Faraway Places*, Global Insurrection, Penguin 2014

Cadeau, Ivan, *Cao Bang 1950*, Perrin 2022

Callwell, C.E. Colonel, *Small Wars*, Greenhill Books 1990

Carr, E.H., *History of the Soviet Union, Socialism in one country 1924-28 vol III*, Macmillan 1961

Chandler, David, *A History of Cambodia*, Westview 1983

Chanoff, David and Toai, Doan van, *Vietnam, a portrait of its people at war*, TPP 2009

Chen Geng Zhuan, *Official Biography: Beijing : Dang dai Zhongguo chu ban she*, 2003 Chicago: University of Chicago Press, 1936

Chen, Jian, *China and the First IndoChina War, The China Quarterly* No. 133, March 1993

Cobb, Richard Professor, *French and Germans, Germans and French*, Penguin 1983

Cogneau, Dennis, Dupraz, Yannick and Mesple-Somps, Sandrine, *Fiscal Capacity and Dualism in Colonial States: The French Empire 1830–1962*, Working Paper No. 2018–27, Columbia, 10 April 2019

Commander-in-Chief French Forces in Indochina, Lessons of the Indochina War, translated by V.J. Croziat, 1955

Commissioner French Security Services, *French security services report for the High Command, BOX 65493, GGI, ANOM*, December 1952

Cotard, Jean-Luc, 'Being 'a little candle marvelling at life' avec Pierre Schoendoerffer, Interview Inflexions 2011/3, No. 18

Cross, J.P., *First in Last out, a British Officer in Indochina*, Greenhill Books

Currey, C., *Victory at Any Cost: The Genius of Viet Nam's Gen. Vo Nguyễn Giáp*, Mass Market Paperback 2005

Dang Phong, *The History of the Vietnamese Economy, Vol. 2*, Edited by the Institute of Economy, Vietnamese Institute of Social Sciences, 2005

de Beaucorps, Jean-Marie, *Soldat de Jade*, edition Kergours 3 March 1998

de Galard, Genevieve, *Angel of Dien Bien Phu: The Lone French Woman at the Decisive Battle for Vietnam*, Naval Institute Press

de Gaulle, Charles, *Memoirs of Hope*, Weidenfeld 1971

de Jomini, Antoine Henri, *The Art of War*, Greenhill Books 1992

de la Motte, Dominique, *a l'autre cote de l'eau*, Texto, 2009,

de La motte, Dominique, *de L'autre cote de L'eau, Indochine, 1950-52*, Texto 2009

Decoux, Admiral, *A La Barre de L'Indochine-memoirs*, Souka Editions, March 2013

Delpard, Raphael, *Les Rizieres de la Souffra, Cobatants Francais en Indochine 1945 – 54*

Devillers, Philippe, *L'histoire de Vietnam*, Parsi 1952

Dien Bien Phu vu d'en face Paroles de Bo doi, DBV World Editions, February 2014

Dien, Biu, *The Jaws of War*, Indiana University Press 1999 (first edition 1987)

Dikötter, Frank, The Tragedy of Liberation 1945 – 57, Bloomsbury 2017

Diljas, Milovan , 'Conversations with Stalin', 1961, Wilson Archive; and Wartime, Harcourt-Jovanovich 1977

Dinh Hoa, Nguyễn, *From the City Inside the Red River*, McFarland 1999

Dommen, Arthur J., *Conflict in Laos*, Preager 1964, 1971

Dommen, Arthur J., *The Indochinese Experience of the French and the Americans*, Indiana University Press 2001

Duiker, William J., US Containment Policy, 1st Edition, 1994

Dulles, John F., *War or Peace*, Harrap 1950

Dung Vinh, Hoang, *Al Jazeera*, May 2016

Dung Vinh, Hoang, *Straits Times*, 4 May 2014

Duras, Marguerite, *First 1984*, Random House 1985

Duras, Marguerite, *The Lovers, First 1984*, Flamingo-Random House 1985

Eden, Sir Anthony, *Full Circle*, Houghton 1960

Eisen, Arleen, *Women and Revolution in Vietnam*, Zed books 1984

Elford, George Robert, *The Devil's Guard*, Dell 1971

Elliot, Mai, *The Sacred Willow: Four Generations in the Life of a Vietnamese Family*, Oxford University Press 1999

Ely, General, Commander-in-Chief French Forces in Indochina, *Lessons of the Indochina War*, translated Croziat, V.J. 1955

Ely, General, *Lessons from the Indochina War, 31 May 1955*, Saigon, Rand Corporation 1967

Ennis, Thomas, *French Indochina French Policy and Developments in Indo-China*, University of Chicago Press 1936

Fall, Bernard, Ed., 'Report to the National Assembly of the Democratic Republic of Vietnam, December 1953', in *Ho Chi Minh On Revolution: Selected Writings, 1920–1966*, New York, Frederick A. Praeger Publishers 1967

Fall, Bernhard, *Hell in a Small Place*

Fall, Bernhard, *Street Without Joy*, Pen and Sword 2009

Fall, Bernhard, *Street Without Joy, The French Debacle in Indochina*, Stackpole Books 2018

Fisher, Charles A., *A Social Economic and Political Geography of South-East Asia*, Methuen 1967
Fisher, Martin, *A social Economic and Political Geography South East Asia*, Methuen 1967
Foreign workers in the USSR 1935
Francais Haute Souvenir, *Seine delegation, Memories of Indochina*, 11 January 2011
French Indochina War, Small Wars & Insurgencies in South-East Asia, London 2009
Genin, Hugo, *La Memoire Des Parachutistes A dien bien Phu*, Lavauzelle 2004
Genty, Robert, *Ultimes Secours Pour Dien Bien Phu 1953-1954*, L'Harmattan 1994
Geohistory L'Indochine, Geohistory Avril-Mai 2014
Gettleman, Marvin, Ed., *Vietnam A Fawcett Premier 1966*
Gettleman, Marvin, *Vietnam Documents*, Fawcett 1965
Giáp, *Memoirs of War, Dien Bien Phu – History, Impressions, Memoirs*, Gioi 1994
Giáp, *Unforgettable Days*, Gioi Hanoi 2015
Giáp, Vo Nguyễn, *Autobiography*, Gioi 1994
Giáp, Vo Nguyễn, *Dien Bien Phu – History, Impressions, Memoirs of War*, 2004
Giáp, Vo Nguyễn, *Dien Bien Phu*, 1994
Giáp, Vo Nguyễn, *Dien Bien Phu*, Gioi 2008
Giáp, Vo Nguyễn, *Memoirs 1946-1954*, Phebus
Giáp, Vo Nguyễn, *The Hardest Decision*, Gioi Publications 1994
Gibbs, Eric, *Battle of Indochina, Arms and the Bishop*, Time Magazine, 8 January 1951
Gibiat, Balthasar, *La Seve Amere de L'Hevea*
Gilbert, Martin, *Churchill Vol III Never Despair*, Heinemann 1988
Gilbert, Martin, *Winston Churchill*, Vol VIII, Heinemann 1988
Giles, Frank, *The Locust Years: The Story of the Fourth Republic 1946-58*, Carol and Graf 1992
Gittings, John, *The Role of the Chinese Army*, Oxford 1967
Goscha, Christopher E., *Going Indochinese*, Nias Classics 2012
Goscha, Christopher E., *Historical Dictionary of the Indochina War 1945–54*
Goscha, Christopher, *The Penguin History of Modern Vietnam*, Pengiun 2017
Goscha, Christopher, *The Road to Dien Bien Phu*, Princeton 2022
Goscha, Christopher, UQAM resource material
Gosha La Patrie Annamite, Going Indochinese Federalism Indochinois et Nationalism Annamite, 28 November 1930
Grace, Paul, *Vietnamese Women in Society and Revolution*, Vol 1,1974
Gras, Yves, General, *History of the Indochina War*, Denoel 1992
Grauwin, Dr, *A doctor at Dien Bien Phu*, Anchor Press 1955
Grauwin, Major, *Doctor at Dien Bien Phu*, Hutchinson 1955
Greene, Graham, Papers, box 1, Georgetown University Library, 16 November 1951
Greene, Graham, *The Quiet American*, Vintage 1955
Greene, Graham, *Ways of Escape*, Penguin 1982
Grindrey, Dr, *Dr Grindrey Remembers His Friend, Memoires*
Griottteray, *Dien Bien Phu, Pourquoi?*
Guerin, Daniel, *Aux Services des Colonises, 1930-1953*, Editions Minuit, Paris 1954
Guetre, Jean, *Un Temoin de son temps, armee de de Lattre Indochine*, Oudin 2011
Guillaume, Piketty Francais Libre, *Chevigne de Pierre*, Tallandier 2022
Guillemot, Francois, *Journal of Vietnamese Studies* Vol. 4, No. 3 (Fall 2009), p.17–60 University California Press 2009
Guillemot, François, *Journal of Vietnamese Studies* Vol. 4, No. 3 (Fall 2009), University of California Press
Gunn, Geoffry, *Asia Pacific Journal*, vol 14, issue 1 2016
Gurtov, Melvin, *Indochina in North Vietnamese Strategy 1971*, Stamford 1954
Gurtov, Melvin, *Indochina in North Vietnamese Strategy*; Rand Corporation 1971
Hackett, *Economic Planning in France*, 1952
Hammer, Ellen, *The Struggle for Indochina*, Stamford University Press 1954

Harper, Tim, *Underground Asia*, Allen Lane 2020
Hastings, Max , *Vietnam: An Epic Tragedy, 1945 – 1975*, Harper 2018
Haydoin, Cherry, *Down and Out in Saigon*, Yale 2019
Hele de St Marc Memoires
Historical Office, the Secretary of Defence Vol III 2001
Ho Chi Minh, *The Vietnam People's Armed Forces*, Gioi 2012
Hobsbawm, Eric, *The Age of Empire*, Michael Josephs 1978
Howard, John, Brigadier, *USAA*, History Net, January 2020
Hunt, Michael, Ed., *A Vietnam War Reader*, Penguin 2010
Hupe, Bruce H., *The Generalship of General Henri E. Navarre During the Battle of Dien Bien Phu*, Paperback, 3 June 1994
Jackson, Julian, *De Gaulle,* Belnap Harvard 2020
Jackson, Julian, *De Gaulle,* Harvard 2018
Jackson, Julian, *France on Trial: The Case of Marshal Petain*, Allen Lane 2023
Jennings, Eric T., *Imperial Heights, Dalat and the Making and undoing of French Indochina* ,UOC 2011
Johnson, Boris, *The Churchill Factor, How One Man Made History*, Hodder and Stoughton 2014
Joyaux, Francois, *Chine et le the Reglement du premier conflit d'Indochine*, Geneve, Sorbonne
Katcher, Philip, Armies of Vietnam Osprey 1980
Kennedy, Paul Major, *Dinassaut Operations in Indochina 1946-54*
Khrushchev, Nikita, *Khrushchev Remembers*, Andre Deutsch, 1971
Kiernen, Ben, *The Pol Pot Regime*, Yale 2008
Kissinger, Henry, *On China*, Penguin NY 2011
Kort, Michael, *The Vietnam War Re-examined*, Cambridge 2018
Krause, Karl-Heinz, *Barfuss im Reisfeld – Indochina Kreig 1949-1953*, Epee 2012
Krull, Germaine, *Diary of Saigon*
Krull, Germaine, *Saigon Diaries*
Krull, Germaine, *Saigon Diaries, Forgotten Wars*
Kuisong, Yang, *Mao Zedong and the Indochina Wars*
Kurlantzick, Joshua, *A Great Place to Have a War: America in Laos*, Simon and Schuster 2016
Kurlantzik, Joshua, *A Great Place to Have a War: America in Laos*, Simon and Schuster 2018
La Patrie, Annamite, *Gosha Going Indochinese*
Lacouture, Jean, *de Gaulle The Ruler 1945-1970*, Collins Harvill 1991
Lacouture, Jean, *de Gaulle The Rebel 1890-1994*, W.W. Norton 1990
Langer, Fritz and Zasloff, J.J., *Revolution in Laos, North Vietnam and the Pathet Lao*, Rand Corporation 1969
Langlais, Pierre, *Dien Bien Phu*, 1963
Lawrence, T.E., *The Seven Pillars of Wisdom*, 1926
le Breton, E., *Fuseliers maritime en Indochine, La Revue Martime*, October 1948
Leighton, Richard, *Strategy, Money, and the New Look, 1953 – 56*, Historical Office of the Secretary of Defence
Lewis, Jon, Ed., *The Vietnam War*, Mammoth 2015
Lewis, Norman, *Dragon Apparent*, Eland, 1982 ??
Lewis, Norman, *Napoli,* Cape, 1951 ??
Liddell Hart, A., *Strange Company*, 1953
Locard, Henri, *Pol Pot's Little Red Book, Silkworm: Ben Kiernan, The Pol Pot Regime*, Yale 2008
Longeval, Frederic, *Embers of War*, Presidio Press 2014
Longeval, Frederic, *Embers of War*, Viking 2020
Longeval, Frederic, *Embers of War*, Yale
Longeval, Frederic, *Embers of War: The Fall of an Empire and the Making of America's Vietnam*, Random House 2012
Longeval, Frederic, *JFK Vol I*, Viking 2020

Lord Moran, *Churchill, The Struggle for Survival 1945-60*, Carrol and Graf 2006
Lovell, Julia, *Maoism, A Global History*, Bodley Head 2019
Lovell, Julia, *Maoism*, Vintage 2019
Luciani, Captain, *Dien Bien Phu Veteran*, YouTube interview
Luxemburg, Rosa, *The Accumulation of Capital*, 1913
Macmillan, Margaret, *Versailles 1919*, John Murray 2019
Mahan, Alfred Admiral, *Naval Warfare*, Dover 1st 1911
Marr, David, *Vietnam 1945, UCP 1995 Biu Dien, The Jaws of War*, Indiana University Press 1999 (first edition 1987)
Marshall, Jonathan, *Dirty Wars: French and American Piastre Profiteering in Indochina 1945 – 75, Asia Pacific Journal* 2014, Vol 12, Issue 32, No. 2
Martelli, Paul, *On the Devil's Tail*, Helion 2014
Massu, General, *Seven years with Leclerc*
Mataignon, Pierre, *L'Indochine Francais 1858-1954*, Texto 2004
Maynard, William Philip and Harrison, Martin, *Politics and Society in de Gaulle's Republic*
Maynard, William Philip, *Crisis and Compromise: Politics in the Fourth Republic*, Longmans 1964
Maynard, William Philip, *Politics in Post War France*, Longman Green 1954
Maynard, William Philip, *War, Politics and Scandals in Post War France*, Cambridge 2010
McCoy, Alfred, *Politics of Heroin*
McHale, Shawn, *Caught Between Propaganda and History*, Wilson Centre Public Policy and History, October 2014
McHale, Shawn, *Ethnicity, Violence, and Khmer-Vietnamese Relations: The Significance of the Lower Mekong Delta, 1757-1954*, The Journal of Asian Studies
McHale, Shawn, *The First Vietnam War*, Cambridge 2021
McMillan, James, *Dreyfus to de Gaulle*, Arnold 1985
McMillan, James, *France; Politics and Society 1898-1991*, Arnold 1992
McMillan, James, *Modern French History*, Hodder Arnold 1992
Mirmont, Franck, *Les Chemins de Dien Bien Phu*, Nimrod 2015
Moran, Lord, Churchill, *The Struggle for Survival 1945-60*, Carrol and Graf 2006
Murret, Malcom, *Cold War Southeast Asia*, Marshal Cavendish 2012
Mus, Paul, *Temoignage Chretien*, 10 February 1950
Mus, Paul, *Viêt-Nam: Sociologie d'une Guerre*, Éditions du Seuil 1952
Navarre, Henri, *Dien Bien Phu*
Navarre, Henri, *le Temp de Verites*, Paris Plan 1979
Ngoc-Luu, Nguyễn, *Peasants, Party and Revolution the Politics of Agrarian Transformation in Northern Vietnam 1930-1975*,
Nicholas, Captain, 3rd Legion Battalion, *Dien Bien Phu: The Battle America Forgot*, Potomac 2011
Nixon, Richard, *Memoirs*, Grosset & Dunlap 1978
O'Neill, General, Giáp, Cassell Australia 1969
Odd, Arne Westad, *The Cold War*, Penguin 2018
Oleg, Khkevniuk, *Stalin*, Yale 2015
Osborne, Milton, *The French Presence in Cochinchina and Cambodia*, White Lotus 1997
Panthou, Eric, *Plantation Michelin Vietnam*, Edition Galipote, 2013
Paroles de Bo Doi Dien Bien Phu vu d'en face, Nouveaux Monde 2014
Pattersen, Lorraine, *Ethnoscapes of Exile: Political Prisoners from Indochina in a Colonial Asian World*, Cambridge 2018
Paxton, Robert, *Vichy France*, Barrie and Jenkins 1972
Pentagon Papers Gravel Edition, Volume 1, Chapter 4, "U.S. and France in Indochina, 1950 – 56" (Boston, Beacon Press, 1971)
Philippe, Pottier, *GMCA/GMI: A French Experience in Counter Insurgency During the*

Pickles, Dorothy, *The Fourth Republic*, Methuen 1955
Pickles, Dorothy, *The Government and Politics of France*, Methuen 1972
Pike, Douglas, Based on Rand Corporation, 200 interviews Vietcong: Organisation and Techniques of the National Liberation of South Vietnam,
Piketty, Guillaume, *Francais Libre*, Pierre de Chevigne Tallandier 2022
Pottier, Philippe, *GMCA/GMI: A French Experience in Counter Insurgency During the French Indochina War, Small Wars & Insurgencies in South-East Asia*, London 2009
Pouget, Jean, *Le Manifeste du Camp No 1*
Pouget, Jean, *Nous Etions a Dien Bien Phu*, Presse de las Cite, Paris 1964
Questions, Peking, World Culture Publishing House
Quiang Zhai, *China and the Vietnam Wars 1950-1975*, Chapel Hill 2000
Quinn-Judge, Sophie, *Ho Chi Minh The Missing Years,* Horizon 2003
Quinn-Judge, Sophie, *Ho Chi Minh: The Missing Years*, University of California Press 1999
Reinach, Lucien, de Laos Librairie Orientale & Americaine C1900
Rice-Maximin, Edward, *Accommodation and Resistance: The French left. Indochina and the Cold War 1944-1954*, Greenwood 1986
Roy, Jules, *Dien Bien Phu*, Jon Lewis, Ed., *The Vietnam War*, Robinson
Roy, Jules, *Dien Bien Phu*, Jon Lewis, Ed., *The Vietnam War*, Robinson
Roy, Jules, *The Battle of Dien Bien Phu*
Sacrificies d'Indochina, 2014
Salan, Raoul General, *Memoires, Fin de L'Empire*, Presse de la cite 1971
Salan, Raoul, *Memoires Vol II*, Presse de la cite de Paris 1971
Salan, Raoul, *Memoires-Fin d'un empire vol II,* Press de La cite 1971
Schiavon, Max, *Salan, Defenseur de L'empire*, ETAIT 2014
Scholl-Latour, Peter, *Death in the Rice Fields*, Orbis 1981
Schrader, Richard R., *War and Logistics, Parachutes and Porters 1945 – 54*, University of Kentucky 2015
Schuermans, Robert, *Legionnaire*
Sharpe, M.E., *Warfighting the PLA Experience Since 1949*, Armonk 2003
Shen, Zhihua and Xia, Yafueng, *Mao and the Sino-Soviet Partnership 1945-1959*, Lexington 2015
Short, Philip, *Mao a Life*, Hodder and Stoughton 1999
Short, Philip, *Mitterrand, a Study in Ambiguity*, Bodley Head 2013
Short, Philip, *Pol Pot, History of a Nightmare*, Hodder 2005
Siddarth, Chandra, *Economic Histories of the Opium Trade*, University of Pittsburgh
Simpson, Howard, *Dien Bien Phu: The Battle that America Forgot*, Potomac 2005
Smith, T.O., *Britain and the Origins of the Vietnam War: UK Policy in Indo-China, 1943-50*, Palgrave 2007
Song, Yfan, *Diaries from Dien Bien Phu*, 2 May 2017
Souvenir, Francais Haute, *Seine delegation, Memories of Indochina*, 11 January 2011
Spector, Ronald, *Advice and Support, the Early Years, 1941 – 60*, US Army 1983
Spector, Ronald, *In the Ruins of Empire*, Random House 2008
Stalin, Joseph, First formal publishing of *Marxism and the National and Colonial Question*, Moscow and Leningrad
Stone, David, *Dien Bien Phu, battles in focus*
Stuart-Fox, Martin, *A History of Lao*, Cambridge 1997
Stuart-Fox, Martin, *Darwinist Natural Selection*, Jules Harmand 1880
Suisse France and Vietnam Inistute franco Suisse d'etudes colonial
Texts 1945-1946 Le Retour de La France en Inochine-Textes Documents Service historique Vinncennes
Than Tam, Pham, *Carnet de guerre d'un jeune Viet-minh a Dien Bien Phu,* Armand Colin 2011
Than Tam, Pham, *Vietnam*, The Art of War Website

Thanh Tam, Pham, *Drawing under Fire*, Asia Link 2005
Thanh Tam, Pham, *War Diary of a Young Viet-Minh in Dien Bien Phu*, Armand Colin 2011
The History of the Vietnamese Economy, Vol. 2, Edited by Dang Phong of the Institute of Economy, Vietnamese Institute of Social Sciences, 2005
Ti Hue, Nguyễn, *Forgotten Women Soldiers of the Vietnam War*, 2003
Tran Do, *Récits sur Dien Bien Phu, Editions en langues étrangères Hanoi broché*, 1962
Tran Trong Trung, *General Giáp*, Gioi 2014
Truman, Harry, *Years of Trial and Hope 1946-52* Vol II, Doubleday 1956
Truong, *No Final Victory, No Family Life*, in *Voices from the Vietnam War*
Tucker-Jones, Anthony, *Dien Bien Phu, First Indochina War*, Battles in Focus, Pen and Sword 2017
Tuong Vu, *Vietnam's Communist Revolution*, Cambridge 2017
US Marine Corps Dinassaut Operations in Indochina: 1946–47, USAMC 1991
Valentino, Benjamin, *Final Solutions: Mass Killing and Genocide in the 20th Century*, Cornell University Press 2005
Văn Chi, Hoang, *From Colonialism to Communism: A Case History of North Vietnam*, Pall Mall 1964
van Chieu, Ngo, *Journal d'un combatant Viet-Minh*, Du Seuil 1955
Vogel, Ezra, *Deng Xiaoping* , Harvard 2011
Vu, Xuan, Chanoff, David and van Toai, Doan, *Vietminh. Vietnam, A Portrait of its People*, TPP 1987
Vu, Yan Ba, *Khmer-Vietnamese Relations From 1930-1954 in the Mekong Delta*
Walker, John, *The Battle ofNá Sán*, *History Today* 19 June 2021
Ward, Geoffrey C. and Burns, Ken, *The Vietnam War: An Intimate History*, 2010
Weber, Eugen, *The Hollow Years; France in the 1930s*, Sinclair Stevenson 1996
Weldon Whalen, Robert, *Bitter Wounds*, Cornell 1984
Werth, Alexander, *de Gaulle*
Werth, Alexander, *France 1940-1955* Readers Union, Robert Hale 1957
Williams, Philip, *Politics in Post-War France*, Longmans 1954
Windrow, Martin, *French Legionnaire versus Vietminh Insurgent*, Osprey 2018
Windrow, Martin, *The Last Valley*, Hachette Cassell 2004
Woodrow, Martin, *Dien Bien Phu*, Osprey 2021
Woodrow, Martin, *Foreign Legion Paratroops*, Osprey 1985
Woodrow, Martin, *French Foreign Legion Since 1945*, Osprey 1996
Woodrow, Martin, *French Foreign Legion Versus Viet Minh Insurgent*, Osprey 2018
Woodrow, Martin, *French Indochina War 1846-54*, Osprey 1998
X, Captain, *General Ely, The Lessons of War in Indochina, May 1951, 31 May 1955*, Rand Corporation 1967
X, Lieutenant, *General Ely, Lessons from the War in Indochina, 31 May 1955*, Rand Corporation
Xiaobing Li, *Building Ho's Army*, University of Kentucky 2019
Yves Gras, General, *History of the Indochina War*, Denoël 1992
Zeldin, Theodore, *France 1848-1945* Vol II, Oxford 1988
Zoltan, Harangi-Toth, *Hungarians Fighting for France in Indochina*, AARMS